THE FENRIS WOLF

Issue no. 10

Edited by Carl Abrahamsson

TRAPARTbooks

The Fenris Wolf, issue no 10

Trapart Books, 2020

ISBN 978-91-986242-4-3

Trapart Books
P.O. Box 8105
SE-104 20 Stockholm
Sweden

info@trapart.net
www.trapart.net

At the time of publishing (September 23, 2020), a special edition of this book was released containing 23 hand-numbered, stamped copies, signed by the editor, alongside a print of the cover image by Val Denham; also limited to 23 hand-numbered copies, and signed by the artist.

The Fenris Wolf, issue no 10
Contents

Editor's Introduction

Welcome to the tenth issue of *The Fenris Wolf* – a smörgåsbord of occulture and delightenment!

When my beloved music fanzines *Lollipop* and *Acts of Interstellar Torture* had fizzled out by 1988, I could experience acute withdrawal symptoms. I was at this time very interested in both journalism and publishing; both already essential elements of my core identity. So, what to do? Start a new fanzine, of course.

At this time I was very active in Thee Temple Ov Psychick Youth (TOPY). One of the central tenets of this fine network/occultural think tank was the active dissemination of information, whether it be high or low, occult or pop. All of these things merged into the desire to start a new and specifically occultural fanzine: *The Fenris Wolf*. Getting material together was not really a problem. I was writing away manically by myself, and the TOPY global network offered many great sources. Some time in 1989, the first issue manifested itself. With its beautiful blue, screen-printed cover, it looked far more professional than anything I'd ever done before. It sold out quickly, and I swiftly made a second edition (which also sold out quickly).

Then there was issue no 2, which I made as a book; I simply had more material than what a magazine format would allow. By this time, 1990, I had started a TOPY-affiliated company called "Psychick Release PCP." This became the "umbrella" for various kinds of releases (books, records, videos, etc.), with *The Fenris Wolf* as its cornerstone.

Issue no 2 was also successful, and was distributed through the TOPY network and via many wonderful & kooky occult bookstores that were still around all over the world. And then, in 1993, followed issue no 3, which had grown into a 200 page book. Needless to say, I was very happy about this trajectory and the overall response.

In 1993, Psychick Release folded; as had "first era" TOPY in 1991. This in itself didn't motivate me any less, but the workload in my new publishing structure, Looking Glass Press, never allowed for me to actively work with *Fenris 4* (although I had already started collecting material for it). Wolfie basically went into a slow and long hibernation.

In 2011, I had started a new company, Edda Publishing, together with Swedish artist Fredrik Söderberg. His amazing occult art needed a publishing home, and of course *The Fenris Wolf* had never really left my mind. A whirl-winding of *Fenris* work began anew.

The Fenris Wolf 4 was warmly welcomed by old-timers and newcomers alike.

Although there were hardly any wonderful & kooky occult bookstores around anymore, the internet compensated for that; allowing people all over the world to purchase copies of this now almost mythical beast of a journal. This revitalized version made quite a splash, and it was therefore logical for me to repackage the first three issues into one volume as the next project. Which I did. It was wonderful to re-experience that material, which had packed such a punch almost 25 years earlier.

Fueled by enthusiasm, Fredrik and I rocked on with issues 5 to 7 (2012-2014). To me, it was wonderful to see how *The Fenris Wolf* wasn't only well received but also how it attracted such great material by truly amazing writers.

At this time of peak publishing, Fredrik wanted to move in a different direction in his life and art. We folded Edda Publishing, and I integrated *Fenris* in my other publishing company: Trapart Books, Films, and Editions. Issue no 8 then followed in 2016, and no 9 in 2017.

The jubilee issue that you're now holding in your hands, number 10, not only marks ten issues but also a 30 year publishing cycle. Even if you magically erase the 18 year interim silence (!), it still amounts to one issue every three years. Not a bad frequency!

And this is how it will continue: with a new issue whenever the time is right. The howling voice of occulture and magico-anthropology will continue to cast its spells of "delightenment" onto a readership in need of an intelligent joining of the dark dots.

The ten issues so far amount to almost 2700 pages of thought-provoking material. Although quantity is not necessarily a quality in itself, it still accumulates nicely in a kind of egregorian or mega-golemic way. Each little piece is part of a totality that's decidedly on a magical mission.

You don't need to read it all to be enthused or inspired. One single chapter can evoke the entire corpus and attitude of *The Fenris Wolf.* If, however, you indulge in the totality, you will very likely be changed in a most eclectically positive way.

It has now been three full years since the latest issue of *The Fenris Wolf* was published. Many things have happened since then; not least the conference "Re-writing the Future – 100 Years of Esoteric Modernism and Psychoanalysis" held at Merano in Italy in 2019, and co-organized with my wife, Vanessa Sinclair. This most beautiful conference was another great stepping stone bridging the past with the future, as well as occulture with art and psychoanalysis. In essence, a continuation of our "Psychoanalysis, Art & The Occult" conference in London 2016, which turned into *The Fenris Wolf 9*. It only makes sense then, that the coming, eleventh issue of *The Fenris Wolf* will consist of the papers from our 2019 conference.

The year of 2020 has been a tumultuous one in many ways. One of the hardest blows was undoubtedly the demise of one of the few "perennial" contributors to *The Fenris Wolf*: Genesis Breyer P-Orridge (1950-2020) – to whom this anniversary issue is now dedicated.

Gen was there right from the beginning, in a publishing venture that was completely imbued with and immersed in as much TOPY philosophy and lore as was technically and emotionally possible. I feel this is very much true to this day, and to this issue – and beyond. Gen's generosity in terms of material, support, and inspiration cannot ever be properly evaluated or appreciated. There was just one constant flow of intelligence and sensitivity, and one that informed and developed *The Fenris Wolf* into the lovely and powerful beast it is today.

In gratitude of the inspiration and wisdom that overflowed from his life and work, I hereby bestow upon Genesis Breyer P-Orridge the title of Professor Emeritus at The Institute of Comparative Magico-anthropology.

In time for Gen's 70th birthday on February 22nd, 2020, Trapart Books published the book *Genesis Breyer P-Orridge: Sacred Intent – Conversations with Carl Abrahamsson 1986-2019.* It's a summing up of 33 years of our friendship and conversations, and a book that I, of course, highly recommend.

In 2019, Trapart Books also published Vanessa's anthology *Rendering Unconscious – Psychoanalytic Perspectives, Politics & Poetry*, which is a kind of *Fenris Wolf* for psychoanalysis. It is, again of course, another book that comes highly recommended.

Vanessa also regularly produces the ongoing podcast "Rendering Unconscious," in which she talks to international movers and shakers in the psychoanalytical field. This is also worth checking out, if you're interested in the colorful gray area between psychoanalysis and art.

Since 2017, I have made two films that I think will interest you: "Cinemagician – Conversations with Kenneth Anger" and "Anton LaVey – Into the Devil's Den." They are both available at: https://vimeo.com/carlabrahamsson/vod_pages The LaVey film has since then expanded into a book by the same name, and which contains more material and magico-anthropological weight.

Speaking of Anton LaVey and his philosophy: 2019 was the 50th anniversary of his *The Satanic Bible.* I'm very happy that this issue of *The Fenris Wolf* contains the full story of how LaVey's "blasphemous tome" saw the light of day.

Another, slightly older, occultural manifestation of significance for this issue is the amazing film "Häxan" a.k.a. "Witchcraft Through The Ages" (Benjamin Christensen, SE/DK, 1922). Jack Stevenson's ambitious piece about the making of this film (and its filmmaker) is as fascinating as the film itself. Personally, I have dear memories of traveling around Europe, showing "Witchcraft Through The Ages" on 16mm. This version was edited by Antony Balch, and narrated by William S Burroughs (more on this in Stevenson's great essay) – a weird combination, indeed. I had borrowed Antony Balch's films from Genesis, who owned them at the time, and we put together a nice film tour called "Visions of Occulture" in 1990.[1] Today, this film is fully recognized as a masterpiece, and that is exactly as it should be.

I wish to express many heartfelt thanks to all the contributors to this issue. Also to David Beth & Theion Publishing for the permission to publish the text by Ludwig Klages; to Andreas Kalliaridis for his technical expertise; to Val Denham for

1 To read the fascinating story of Balch, his films, and TOPY's revival of them, please see Genesis Breyer P-Orridge, *Brion Gysin – His Name was Master*, Trapart Books, Stockholm, 2018.

the magnificent portrait of Fenris; to my mother Margareta Abrahamsson (1940-2018); and first and foremost to my wife, Vanessa Sinclair, whose input and ideas have been invaluable.

An editorial note: As the texts in this issue stem from various minds from various cultures, there are obviously some stylistic inconsistencies. I have chosen to keep these, including possible "magical" language quirks and experiments, in the name of heterogeneous and creative integrity. However, for any spelling or typographical errors, pure and simple, I assume full responsibility.

Finally, I would like to say that the views and values expressed in the various texts in this eclectic anthology are those of the respective authors, and do not necessarily represent my own views, those of Trapart Books, or any kind of general "Fenris Wolfean" perspective.

Let us now roam freely together: from the groves of Eleusis, over Scandinavian paganism, medieval witchcraft, Nietzsche, Klages, and on to our contemporary memetic magics – all under the umbrella of glorious magico-anthropology. We are hereby offering dots galore – now it's up to you to connect them.

Vade Ultra!

Carl Abrahamsson
Stockholm, Autumnal Equinox 2020

Onwards to the Source!

Carl Abrahamsson

The first premise of magico-anthropology is that "magic is." Whatever magic is according to a seemingly indefinite multitude of definitions, it always simply is. Wherever we look in and into time and space, there is that one fundamental phenomenon which seems more ingrained and integrated in the human psyche than anything else. Soundly embedded inside the survival instinct, the human being's relationship to magic has never really disappeared. It has, however, developed externally into different sub-forms like religion, philosophy, psychology, the "natural" sciences, etc. These various manifestations and developments are results of the increasing complexity of human structures, in which we could schematically say that the more we increase the distance from a literally natural habitat, the more our magic will drift from its natural source.

What is this source? It is the link between the human mind and all other sentience(s). Meaning: the roots of magic are embedded in the individual's connection to a holistic, intuitive, instinctual understanding of itself. When a human society deteriorates, this connection will seek new forms in order to survive. It is in many ways an inner reflection of the outer circumstances that continually dictate challenges for the human individuals and tribes alike.

As we know, most of these human "superstructures" are ephemeral and wholly interchangeable. All empires collapse; all political systems crumble; all religions eventually find themselves too far from the source, and then give in to reactive chaos that will end up becoming its own nemesis. Underneath the surface of human chaos lies the ever pulsating life-force itself: the will to live (biology), the will to structure life (science), and the will to enhance that life (culture).

Regardless of whether "magic" is thematically present in language, culture, history writing, etc, its fundaments are always present; more so in constructive phases than in destructive ones. But, then again, all of the motions and movements are mere counterpoints and reflections of each other. We simply cannot escape that all movements tell the same story, albeit in different chapters.

Creativity, communication, cooperation, collaboration, community, "conspiration" (meaning literally "breathing together") and careful contemplation are merely words beginning with a C; here mainly chosen as an amplification of the essence of its sound: "see." But they are also distinct phenomena and absolute building blocks within human life. When one (or more) is lacking, there will be disorder and imbalance.

How to cope with this imbalance? Using traditionally "magical" skills such as trust in inner abilities and visions, foresight, sympathetic logic, intuition in itself; also trusting the wisdom and insight that stems from a genuine communication ("genuine" here signifying "stripped of ulterior motives"), then making manifestations of these wisdoms and insights external and accessible through art and technology; and then structuring and passing on positive and negative deductions and conclusions for coming generations through language and further, trans-temporal art… These are just some examples of the basic view and approaches of fundamental magico-anthropology. In each detour or deterioration, there will be many possibilities to research and evaluate instigations and results. This is the bedrock of each new balancing act.

Magico-anthropology states that the basis of human behavior stems from shamanism. It's inherent in the advanced human mind to constantly pose self-reflective questions. It is only natural that these then spill over and take on proxy forms (the tribal shaman, priest, magician, healer, etc.). But the need to ask existential questions is a unique trait for all human individuals, and this is very much the key to the constant development of human intelligence.

As the simple techniques and wisdoms of globally present shamanism have been pushed to the side in favor of organized religions and psychologies, the trust in proxies rather than in one's own conclusions have greatly increased. But this does not in any way decimate or diminish the original human needs. On the contrary: in our chaotic cultures and times of (self) denial and mindless destruction of our own habitat, it is not surprising to see a necessary return to the roots. No matter how grasping and seemingly desperate the "occult" and "new age" communities are, they do seem to have a joint key message: to change the perspective, to transform the oppression of too much destructive dogma into a liberating reconnection to something that is perhaps often naively described, yet genuinely felt on intuitive levels.

If shamanism is the root of all human culture, then magic can be seen or described as a term for all the derivatives; as all the branches of the tree of human life. Please see *Figure 1*, for an attempt at illustration.

I have chosen an atomic model. It resembles a flower in some way, and that is deliberate on my part. Whether the movements of the individual phenomena leave aesthetic traces in the shapes of petals or leaves, or whether they are like planets revolving around a sun, they all signify a relationship that seems eternal: whatever humans develop in terms of abstractions and systems, it is always connected to the "magnetic" pull of the source.

Is deterioration then simply a matter of distance from the source; whether temporal or spatial? No. Deterioration in human culture comes when there is a *consciously strategized negation of the heritage;* of the very roots. Time may pass, but the fundamental questions remain and always need to be answered. When a proxy structure becomes too enamored with itself and the power it wields, its capacity to genuinely help humans understand themselves automatically decreases rapidly, both in the small, individual and in the big, communal pictures. The proxies will

Fig. 1

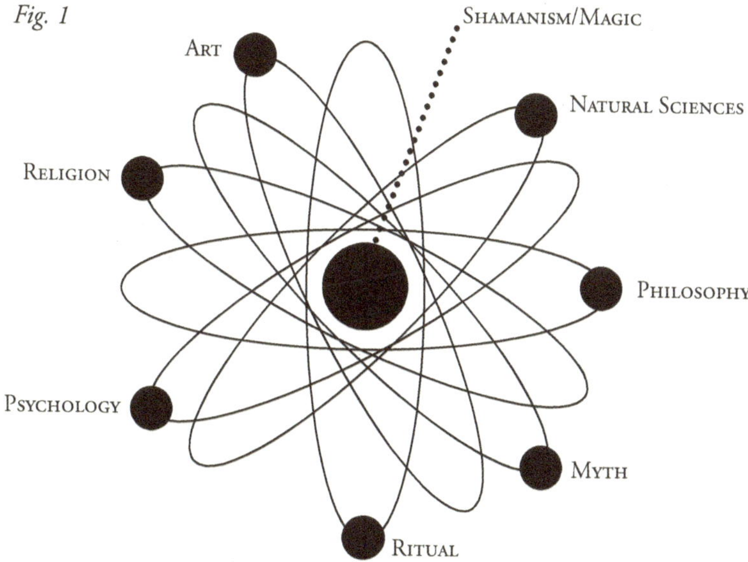

then also actively discourage any individual quests or adventures to find out more.

In a similar way, space may pass by/in the human perspective. Human migration throughout history has led to many syncretistic mergers, and quite often healthily so. Just as the source is never static (just look at the vibrant sun as a metaphor of a central core that vitalizes an entire dynamic habitat), neither should the derivatives be. Movement is crucial, but that is usually a matter of constructive shapeshifting, and not necessarily one of movement "away" from the source. In order to survive, cultures have to adapt to both external and internal developments. If they stray too far from the magical interpretation of life, these cultures will die, or desperately take on new and more hopeful shapes.

All sciences, philosophies, and systems that help interpret, categorize and develop human life are subordinated the central phenomenon of magico-anthropology. It is not possible to fully understand any human endeavor or phenomenon without first filtering this understanding through magico-anthropology.

How human beings relate to magic (again: "magic" as the central and direct derivative of a shamanic understanding, in both theory and practice) is indicative of both individual and overall human health, and possibly even of global health. Each individual human being inherently and instinctively understands this as a child; interpreting signals through an "enchanted" or "ensouled" filter. As this filter is usually (and unfortunately) ground down and removed/discouraged because of arbitrary cultural preferences, the child learns that the sense of wonder that he/she could notice when looking at the big picture with an open and uninhibited mind is, according to the peers, simply "untrue." This of course creates an unhealthy imprint in the child to not trust him/herself (nor the big picture) but instead rely on culturally imposed proxy interpretations.

It is interesting to see how the power of myth transcends even these imposed boundaries. Parents happily tell the same fairytales to their children that were once part of the cluster that they themselves had to abandon as they grew up. If myths aren't necessary to our survival, they simply wouldn't exist and still feel resoundingly relevant. Anything of mythic value is directly connected to the shamanic source, and hence to our survival.

Magico-anthropology isn't necessarily the study of magic itself. That could today be regarded as belonging to the study of religions, as there are many similarities. Much of the organisation of magic in history (in groups, orders, societies, fraternities, etc) runs more or less parallel to the formation of new religions, for instance. There is also very often a similar corruption within magical communities that eerily mimics that within religious ditto. It is the same phenomenon over and over again: when there is an individual dissociation from the source and its fundamental expression in shamanism, the looming structure or system will all too gladly usurp and integrate this individual in its far too often self-serving and draconian schemes.

Magico-anthropology focuses on the very link itself. Not merely on the corruption of it, of course, but also the study of pristine and healthy connections and expressions (such as in art or myth that is conscious of, and encouraging, a "re-docking" in individual lives). Although the study of corruption (deliberate or merely unconscious) is fascinating and quite often literally "beyond belief," I believe that the study of positive, beneficial manifestations of the attraction to the source as a survival strategy on both individual and communal levels is more important in this current phase of human existence.

I understand that there may be scientists and other academics who have no desire to be subordinated to the authority of magico-anthropology. Be that as it may; their position and attitude is neither here nor there. Why? Because the link to all intimate relationships between their specific fields of study and magic can be so easily explained. My schematic atomic model is the first altruistic attempt to make these people and potential critics see. Just like planets revolve around their own axes, and as they do around the central sun, so are the specific fields of study (of religions, psychology, physics, mathematics, etc.) simultaneously their own entities as well as parts of the universe of magic.

To be specific: the magical phenomenon itself is concretely rooted in the human mind. The study and classification of the same phenomenon is a degree of abstraction. Regardless of whether they are concrete or abstract, all research systems are geared towards reaching the same moment: the ecstatic truth of revelation, preferably embedded in further revelatory contemplation/meditation. Transgression of the rational mind is the single most important key to this ecstatic truth. Cultural differences may apply but the dynamic is always the same.

Onwards to the Source!

"In the sciences it is very worthwhile to seek out and then develop a partial truth already possessed by the ancients." (Goethe, "Art and Antiquity," 1824)[1]

Concrete	**Abstract**
Alchemy	Chemistry
Spellwork	Poetry/music/literature
Healing	Medicine
Barter/Morality	Profit/Amorality
Unity with the Source	Religion
Contemplation	Philosophy
Predictives	Statistics
Myth	Entertainment

Each piece of learning we can utilize today, together, stems from a single human mind working in magical ways, and then sharing the results with a community. Whether it's faith in the sun, in ancestors, or in statistics (as in "empiricism"), the process is exactly the same. There is speculation, desire, ritual, invocation, evocation, epiphany, declaration of intent, irrational states of mind provoked by the rational ditto, and then an ensuing methodology geared for validating the desired results, etc.

We are no longer living in times when magico-anthropology was regarded either as aggressively anathema or as a kooky pastime for privileged, private scholars. Today, magico-anthropology has taken center stage because of a cruel necessity that calls for an increased awareness about avenues of human survival. The specialized fields of study can all contribute parts to the totality of a solution (or several). But it is only by reappraising and reappreciating magic as the core activity/mind frame of human existence that we can fully change things in a more life-affirming and life-enhancing way. We all know it's there, and we all know instinctively the creative power it wields. If humans won't wield that magical power to repair damages to their habitat, then the habitat will simply wield the same power to remove us. In the great scheme of things, however, this is not necessarily so terrifying. Any magician or shaman worth their salt knows that although the human shapes might disappear, the overall life-force and sentience won't. It's just constantly evolving.

One great definition of intelligence is the ability to evolve; to adapt to changes in life. If you're too inert, you'll be left behind. But if you see not only the dangers but also the possibilities, and realize that you need to change in order to survive, that will unleash a creativity within you that is decidedly magical; literally phenomenal.

One main problem we face today is the overall lack of individuation and intelligence within monotheistic cultures. For some reason they refuse to be part of nature, and to listen to its greater authority. Individuation and initiation should preferably take place inside nature – not on top of it. Magic philosophy from many different cultures and ages basically tells us this same story: we are not isolated units,

1 Johann Wolfgang von Goethe, *Maxims and Reflections*, Penguin Classics, London, 1998, p 17.

but rather parts of one big organism. Many people reverently practice this wisdom via magic. Whether just in approaches and attitudes (like "magical thinking") or in practice through distinct "programmatic" rituals alone or together with others, the presence of a holistic approach in which you can affect change to the whole (as much as vice versa, simply because you are an active and integrated part of this same whole) is truly indicative of cultural health.

If and when the phenomenon of magic is "demonized" or ostracized as merely an isolated curiosity, this is indicative of cultural malaise and disease.

By childishly clinging to materialism and rabid monotheism, the most ardent critics of the holistic approach display a death drive similar to historical figures like Nero and Hitler. The destruction of their emotionally compensative visions leads to a desire to destroy the entire world. Instead of realigning themselves and rejoining the life-affirming core, they decide to fully separate and counterstrike against the very core itself – always with tragic results for themselves and many fellow human beings.

> Don Juan has asserted that our great collective flaw is that we live our lives completely disregarding that connection. The busyness of our lives, our relentless interests, concerns, hopes, frustrations, and fears take precedence, and on a day-to-day basis we are unaware of being linked to everything else.
>
> Don Juan had stated his belief that the Christian idea of being cast out from the Garden of Eden sounded to him like an allegory for losing our silent knowledge, our knowledge of *intent*. Sorcery, then, was a going back to the beginning, a return to paradise.
>
> – Carlos Castaneda, *The Power of Silence*[2]

I strongly suggest and recommend that all students, teachers, scientists, researchers, etc. within the academic worlds of the natural sciences as well as of the humanities immediately adjust their work so that the quintessential question is contextualized within their own field: "Magic is, but how is it relating to what I'm studying?"

The relationship between magic, magical philosophy, magical approaches, etc., and the human being's attempts to survive is as fixed/solid as anything has ever been, and ever will be.

The humanities have tried to express phenomena along the way, as the natural sciences have tried to classify them. All fields have their own unique languages and methods. But even here, within the area of strict methodology, we see magical approaches in the driver's seat. As the most ardent rationalists can usually be found within fields using the method of "empiricism," it's important to allow them to understand that one needs to *always* continue to the roots. The origins of any empirical process/evaluation is the root called "speculation." How many ideas that

2 Carlos Castaneda, *The Power of Silence*, Washington Square Press, New York, 1987, p 103.

at first seemed kooky, crazy, heretical, and "hocus pocus" eventually turned out to be solidly established and statistically reinforced? Quite a few. But although there are surely a lot of speculations that never made it to the "lab" to be tried out, we have to stick with the reverse perspective to fully explain this: all empirical successes are founded in irrational speculations; in inexplicable ideas or concepts that simply obsess the conceptualist(s), and then are given more and more credence as they are gradually validated by open-mindedness and an overall attitude of of creativity. Each idea has its origins.

It is only when empiricism becomes a rigid belief system ("faith in statistics") that science becomes inert and destructive. And that's usually when these environments team up with financial systems and structures that are not altruistic in any way at all. When this happens, the original creative vision becomes a kind of "diametrical demon." Meaning, the original purpose becomes corrupted in a topsy-turvy way. An example of this could be that a scientist makes a breakthrough in medicine, but the full potential of its healing process is shoved to the side in favor of a maximum profitability for the corporation that has acquired the patent from or funded the project for the scientist in question.

The scientist should ask him/herself what the magic of the breakthrough could bring to people in different cultures, and the corporation should simply be the distributional matrix for an improvement of something that is not only life-affirming but also potentially life-enhancing, in the sense that a good health allows for an even more present creativity. And hence more magic.

There is an inherent danger in the phase when the individual loses his/her direct communication with the source. When tribes grow too big, the need for proxies take hold, and these are so easily corruptible. The individual humans – even the decision-makers within systems of corruption – will always maintain their magical thinking and approaches, but some will go against their own proto-morals because they have been coerced or somehow threatened by others, who in a similar way have transgressed against *their* own proto-morals.

These statements in no way suggest that there is an inherent political or financial system that is more or less "magical." Politics is – or should be – just a way of structuring a society. The main thing is whether it, as a society/community, encourages the individual contact with the source. If it does, it will be a healthy society; if it doesn't, inertia and collapse are waiting just around the corner.

It's not so much a "revolution" that's needed (actually, the less dramatic reactivity there is, the better) but rather an increase in human individual awareness of how simple these relationships actually are. They are easier to grasp than people care to even assume – no doubt a reaction to the possible change in lifestyle that's required to implement the findings of the awareness.

An increase in human individual awareness will lead to an increase in human collective awareness, and that will lead to communal leverage in the process of changing the big picture and its many problematic issues.

So, how do we change these individual awareness perspectives? An exposure to nature itself is an important key, if even on the most miniature level. Indulge in nature, its beauty and its philosophy. And realize that this moment is crucial and magical in the most primordial sense as you look at something that has always been there, and that will always remain.

The more of a hardline rationalist you are, the more you will need to short-circuit your simplified wires. A dramatic infusion of the opposite always brings generative creativity. The same is true of the reverse perspective: if you are basically comfortable in irrationality, mistaking that for "magic" or "creativity," you probably need to dive deep into a fierce rationality and order.

One key to natural awareness of this most magical kind is to allow yourself to see all the facets and perspectives at the same time. What you are regarding as something external is in fact something equally internal, at exactly the same time. And because there is no "real" separation (in the sense of tangible, measurable, quantifiable separation), you realize that the responsibility for *everything, all the time*, is principally yours. But the realization is not so daunting as it may sound to a logical, rational intellect. It is merely a peek into the endless possibilities and choices that have been there in each human destiny all along, from the past (so called), and now into the future (so called).

The discipline of magico-anthropology is important not as a singular field of study, like some exotic morsel in the history of ideas or the history of religions. It is rather the all-encompassing umbrella for all sciences, as it asks the fundamental question, based on the fundamental proto-scientific premise: "If magic is, then *what* is it?"

The subordination of all other sciences is not based on value or hierarchy. It is merely a way of explaining that the awareness of yourself, and your own honesty to yourself, and your own place in the bigger picture, is at least as important as what you will "produce" within structures that for the most part so far have proven to be nothing more than self-serving and profit-driven businesses.

If you are a scientist, the truth is what should guide your work. Before that, if you are a fully sentient human being, magic is what should guide your life. Getting back to the source is what truly propels us all forwards. The source does what magic is as much as the source is what magic does. "Have you ever been experienced?"

On the Essence of Ecstasy

Ludwig Klages[1]

There are three characteristics that appear repeatedly amongst the otherwise vast differences in the fundamental experience of great ecstatics: (supposed or real) transport of the soul into far-flung regions, when not exactly into "another world"; insensitivity to painful stimuli, expressed as invulnerability; and reception of life-determining revelations. For now, only the third point is to be considered for answering the question of what constitutes an experience where its degree of conviction vanquishes the convincing power of all profane truths. If, to this end, we were to hold fast to the *statements* especially of initiates from Mystery Schools of all epochs and all peoples, then we would either end up empty-handed due to the oath of secrecy taken by those initiates; or we would end up confused by those "visions" out of which pours sacred myth (at times encountering meteoric miracles such as clouds of light, pillars of fire and stars, or manifold ghostly apparitions, like the satyrs of Dionysus, or the devil and warlocks, or angels and saints). Or we would become acquainted with many and varied symbols that would first have to be deciphered, such as the mystical rose, the corona, the holy chalice; or we might learn from the very much physical symptoms of those overcome with ecstasy, which infer to us that they not only saw something, but they also heard, smelled, tasted and touched it (the sweetness of tasting God plays an exceptionally major role in the Christian mysteries: "*Gustate* et videte, quoniam suavis est Dominus!"[2]). Or ultimately we would learn the convictions of faith that became entrenched in the mystes *as a consequence* of his experience and that differ from each other in the extreme with the exception of the notion of an ever-recurring "immortality"! The belief of the sacred "heavenly Bride of Christ" certainly stands in stark contrast to the witch's confession as she strikes her ritual pact through illicit relations with the devil! As such we run the risk of mistaking the mystical experience for a hallucination that draws its substance from the fantastical wishes of the respective cult, thus holding the initiates themselves for hysterical fools, in which the "modern era" has certainly played its part. In view of this, should we dispense with finding the source of genuine epiphanies?

In order to understand the convictions of faith, we must know the myths from which they spring. In order to understand the myths, we must know the symbols that yield them. But to understand the symbols, we have to know the nature of the

1 This chapter is an excerpt from the book by Ludwig Klages: *Of Cosmogonic Eros*, Theion Publishing, München, 2018. Translation from the German by by Mav Kuhn.
2 "O taste and see that the Lord is good!"

experience which can never be conveyed by reasoning and judgement. So it cannot merely be *declared* what that actual source is. Nevertheless, we will see something shine forth that will perhaps make us capable of finding that source within ourselves if we direct our attention to the shared aspects of what caused those certainties that cannot be shaken by logic. And although they are today associated with less fundamental reasoning (such as the assertions of mathematics), they originally held fast solely to directly *experienced* knowledge. Thus we meet the following recurring facts in sacred covenants: mystical certainty arises from the experience of "Epopteia", that is of *visions* – visions refer to the *appearance of the God* (epiphany, Parousia) – and that in turn comes about at the symbolic representation of his death with subsequent rebirth from a *"holy marriage"*. We shall pre-empt the conclusion: the mystes experiences the rite of fulfilment by being deified himself and by marrying a god (communion, unio mystica, Hieros Gamos), and he unifies himself with that god by beholding him. Here are a few testaments to this from antiquity: "Happy is he amongst the peoples of earth who has *beheld* this", it says at the end of the Hymn to Demeter. "O thrice happy amongst the mortals that stepped into Hades after they *caught sight of* it", says Sophocles. "Happy the man who descends below the hollow earth having beheld those things; he knows life's end and he knows the god-given origin of life", says Pindar.[3] "Those taking part in Bacchic and corybantic acts increase in ecstasy until they see what they expect to see", reports Philo[4] in his work "On the contemplative life". But also mystical union with god – relegated erroneously according to the initiates' hopes of a post-mortem bliss to a new life the other side of a physical death – is pronounced by one of the Orphic Gold Tablets: "Oh happy and blessed one, you will be a *god* instead of a pitiful man!" On another tablet the soul of the initiate rejoices before the gods: "I extol myself *for being of your blessed kind!*"

Sacred traditions are a regulated thing, laid down by human hand, chaining the generations of many into a life fellowship and preserving for the rhythm of the All the power to once again loosen the compulsory ties within which Spirit wishes to alienate from life those who are already bound to it. The experience alone (the original ecstasy), which those rites attempt to facilitate in its restoration, once carried *all* works of humanity from the Pelasgian era, the fragments and ruins of which we nowadays gather under dying *"primitive peoples"*. And it still supports (or did until very recently) genuine poetry and genuine art; which is also why its substance cannot be conveyed by mere statements and pronouncements. The term "fine arts" [or visual arts - "bildende Kunst"], which is familiar to us for at least one category of arts, reminds us however that the creative act serves to objectify images and thus allows us to suppose that when the spirit drives to artistic endeavours this is associated with the shining forth of inner images. So in order to clarify the nature of ecstasy we shall take a predetermining step by investigating how the *event* of beholding inexpressible images departs from the

3 Pindar (517-438 BC), Greek lyric poet.
4 Philo (c. 20 BC-50 AD), Hellenistic Jewish philosopher.

voluntary act of perceiving those things that reveal to us expressible things.

I cannot take a beautiful landscape with me, but I can have an "idea" of it to the extent that an internal image of it remains within me. While the objective landscape remains the selfsame thing where it is, its image wanders with the thousands of individual beings that have experienced the sight of it. Indeed, it remains in itself different depending on each person as well as depending on the luminescent colours, scents and movements of the respective underlying archetype. If we remove the intellectual act of the person conceiving the idea from the idea itself, then we lend that image the distinct magnificence of a dream vision that the dream visionary encounters as something real. And if we consider this to be conditioned less by the soul of the recipient than established in the archetypal image itself, then this gives us *the* form of expressing the totality of happenings that *rule* over the world of facts in the night consciousness of the ecstatic and in the consciousness per se of primal man. Presupposing the above, we have formulated the following opposites: the image only exists in the present at the moment in which it is being experienced; the thing is "laid down" once and for all – the image flows with the ever-flowing experience; the thing endures, lasts and stands in life-alienated inseparability – the image is only there in the experience of the one experiencing it; the thing is in the random act of perception of any person – I may be able to remember the image, but I cannot visualise it through reasoning; I can conceive of the thing at any time because it is the selfsame now as then and I can make it the identical reference point for all those that hear my reasoning – the image, immersed in the flow of time, transforms itself as everything transforms itself, including the experiencing soul; the thing, because it lives outside of time, is subject to destruction, measured against time – the image is received by the soul; the thing is constructed through the judgmental act of Spirit [Geist] based on what has been received – the image has a reality independent of consciousness; the thing is thought into being in the world by consciousness and exists only *for* the interiority [Innerlichkeit] of *individual* beings. This is why when someone shatters the form of personhood in ecstasy, the world of facts also perishes at that same moment, and there arises the world of images for him with an irresistible force of reality that replaces everything. The visionary soul is its internal pole and the reality beheld in such a way is its external pole. The former is now associated with the latter (= unceasing Gamos), but it never succumbs to being one with it (= unceasing vision). From out of the polar *touching* of internal and external is born relentlessly the self-ensouled image (= unceasing birthing). The external begets, the internal receives, and from out of the embrace of both breaks forth the singing fiery torrent of images from the All, the "dancing star" of chaos arranged into the cosmos. The visionary line by Novalis:[5] "The external is an internal state elevated to a *mystery*". This expresses with easy grace the meaning of ecstasy and the foundation for an all intuiting certainty.

We shall pause a moment in order to safeguard the beholding of primal images

5 Novalis, pen name of Georg Philipp Friedrich Freiherr von Hardenberg (1772-1801), German poet, author, mystic and philosopher.

from a devastating misunderstanding that has threatened it since Schopenhauer's subsequent exposition of Platonic "Ideas" (the Theory of Forms). We could not demonstrate the nihilism of Plato's "Theory of Forms" more convincingly than in its seductive reflection illustrated by the mirror of Schopenhauerian thinking. – He teaches us that in a thinking state we find individual facts which later form the object of scientific research. On the other hand, in a state of contemplation, we find the immortal "primal image" *in* the individual thing. Poets and artists are the kind of people to whom it is bestowed more often and to a higher degree than the average person, that they contemplate the world image and consequently gain direct perception of its primal reality. For this reason, in Schopenhauer's work it is still associated with the heavily Buddhist coloured view that the thinking state is simultaneously a "more interested" state in the broadest sense of the word. Usually, he says, interest in the thing consists in a very personal tendency or aversion. However, as an exception there could also be that generalised interest of a researcher which is why it remains no less a type of interest or excitement by the "will" that is inherent to all phenomena. The contemplative state presents itself as a temporary release from the need of the will, and the primal image that is seen becomes the counter-image of both a super-personal and a super-individual "perception" [Erkennen]. We cannot fail to refer to certain points from Schopenhauer's work because we would like to emphatically demonstrate the tremendously captivating aspects of his view before we illustrate its fallacy.

> No attained object of desire can give lasting satisfaction, but merely a fleeting gratification; it is like the alms thrown to the beggar, that keeps him alive to-day that his misery may be prolonged till the morrow. Therefore, so long as our consciousness is filled by our will, so long as we are given up to the throng of desires with their constant hopes and fears, so long as we are the subject of willing, we can never have lasting happiness nor peace. ... The subject of willing is thus constantly stretched on the revolving wheel of Ixion, pours water into the sieve of the Danaids, is the ever-longing Tantalus. — But when some external cause or inward disposition lifts us suddenly out of the endless stream of willing, delivers knowledge from the slavery of the will, the attention is no longer directed to the motives of willing, but comprehends things free from their relation to the will, and thus observes them without personal interest, without subjectivity, purely objectively, gives itself entirely up to them so far as they are ideas, but not in so far as they are motives. Then all at once the peace which we were always seeking, but which always tied from us on the former path of the desires, conies to us of its own accord, and it is well with us. It is the painless state which Epicurus prized as the highest good and as the state of the gods; for we are for the moment set free from the miserable striving of the will; we

> keep the Sabbath of the penal servitude of willing; the wheel of Ixion stands still. – But this is just the state which I described above as necessary for the knowledge of the Idea, as pure contemplation, as sinking oneself in perception, losing oneself in the object, forgetting all individuality, surrendering that kind of knowledge which follows the principle of sufficient reason, and comprehends only relations; the state by means of which at once and inseparably the perceived particular thing is raised to the Idea of its whole species, and the knowing individual tu the pure subject of will-less knowledge, and as such they are both taken out of the stream of time and all other relations. It is then all one whether we see the sun set from the prison or from the palace.

And:

> This freeing of knowledge lifts us as wholly and entirely away from all that, as do sleep and dreams; happiness and unhappiness have disappeared; we are no longer individual; the individual is forgotten; we are only pure subject of knowledge; we are only that *one* eye of the world which looks out from all knowing creatures, but which can become perfectly free from the service of will in man alone. Thus all difference of individuality so entirely disappears, that it is all the same whether the perceiving eye belongs to a mighty king or to a wretched beggar.[6]

When hearing that, should you not suppose it is practically the same as our treatment of the essential characteristic of ecstasy, where we also accept that it gives us the capacity to see through the world of things into the reality of I-independent images! Schopenhauer certainly also appears to see the precondition of beholding to be in the shattering of the barriers of individuality. He thereby declares war, as decisively as we do, on all subjectivity in contemplating the world! This is how it *appears* to be, but this appearance is fundamentally deceptive! We should not let it annoy us to repeat another passage as it tends to reveal very obviously that our philosopher actually means the complete opposite. In an effort to use a few examples to explain what in fact *comprises* the content of those ideas that are beheld in such a way, we look to the following to reveal this to us:

> When the clouds move, the figures which they form are not essential, but indifferent to them; but that as elastic vapour they are pressed to gether, drifted along, spread out, or torn asunder by the force of the wind: this is their nature, the essence of the forces which

6 A. Schopenhauer, *The World as Will and Representation.* Third Book: The World as Idea, excerpts from §38, 2nd expanded edn, transl. R. B. Haldane and J. Kemp.

> objectify themselves in them, the *Idea*; their actual forms are only for the individual observer. – To the brook that flows over stones, the eddies, the waves, the foam-flakes which it forms are indifferent and unessential; but that it follows the attraction of gravity, and behaves as inelastic, perfectly mobile, formless, transparent fluid: this is its nature; this, *if known through perception, is its Idea*; these accidental forms are only for us so long as we know as individuals. – The ice on the window-pane forms itself into crystals according to the laws of crystallisation, which reveal the essence of the force of nature that appears here, exhibit the Idea; but the trees and flowers which it traces on the pane are unessential, and are only there for us.[7]

This passage indicates to us with an almost alarming clarity that the *so called* primal images or ideas which Schopenhauer has in mind, in full agreement with Plato, are not images at all but are through and through *nothing more than concepts*! That which he describes here as the nature of clouds, the nature of the stream and the nature of the ice crystals is without doubt the concept of the general composition of steam, of water and of freezing that, as no one can deny, forms the object of the "natural sciences". Consequently, during his own account it is not a random accident that the watchword "law" escapes him. In fact he speaks of nothing other than the natural scientific composition of the world and is utterly mistaken when he also thinks that he *beholds* those natural laws! Let us now attempt to put ourselves in the state of mind of that man who genuinely "loses himself in the object" at the sight of ice flowers and crystal trees on his window panes, who forgets both himself and the rest of the world, allowing himself to dissolve completely in the image of these ice flowers. How could he think in that very moment about the laws of crystallisation and freezing; how on earth could the law of ice formation appear vividly to him in the quiet and secretively growing ice flowers that the winter conjures up on his window panes! No, he will feel just as transported away from the concepts of crystallisation, evaporation and freezing as he feels transported from his own person. He will believe himself to be translated as if in a dream to an ensouled world of those ice entities in order to participate in the *inwardness* of their flowering and growth. Schopenhauer's, like Plato's "ideas" are not corresponding images of the visionary soul but instead are products of the judging spirit. They differ from the concepts of usual human reasoning, and furthermore from science, solely through their claim to metaphysical reality. However, that claim demonstrates the intention of platonic-schopenhauerian thinking as directed against the vision of primal images since it undertakes to replace genuine primal images with objectified concepts and absolute natural laws! This is why Plato was, with depth of insight, an avowed enemy of art. On the other hand, Schopenhauer, as an ultimately modern man, attempts, albeit without knowing it himself, to disguise the antithesis by

7 A. Schopenhauer, *The World as Will and Representation*. Third Book: The World as Idea, excerpt from §35, 2nd expanded edn, transl. R. B. Haldane and J. Kemp.

allowing his poetised, visual perception, (which is again in actuality a perception of the mind) to erupt forth from a state of contemplative transport. However, by doing this he counterfeits ecstasy and therefore would have to reject its genuine eruptions as Plato did consistently with art. Now that really is the case!

> To him who has thoroughly grasped this, and can distinguish between the will and the Idea, and between the Idea and its manifestation, the events of the world will have significance only so far as they are the letters out of which we may read the Idea of man, but not in and for themselves. He will not believe with the vulgar that time may produce something actually new and significant; that through it, or in it, something absolutely real may attain to existence ... *Therefore he will just as little, with Homer, people a whole Olympus with gods to guide the events of time, as, with Ossian, he will take the forms of the clouds for individual beings*; for, as we have said, both have just as much meaning as regards the Idea which appears in them.[8]

We see that the world of gods and every world of poetic images that approaches the mythical are sacrificed to the world of concepts. And those natural laws that are graced with the name "ideas" must serve to deprive the *moment.* – In comparison, if the genuine primal image is, due to the way it occurs, something *unrepeatably unique*, then by reflecting on it we are forced to comprehend a reality where there is neither a bridge nor a middle way between it and the idea beliefs of the Platonists.

Whether we are dealing with humans, animals, plants, woods or the starry heavens, we *speak* in each case of those things so designated in as far as we conceive of them being something persisting in the flow of time. The wood that I observe from my window is the same wood today that it was yesterday and it will be the same wood tomorrow that it is today. I therefore came to the concept of this wood by seeing past the temporality of all events such as in particular my experience and by foisting a consistent sameness on each current impression. In relation to the latter, the former is something general, as is probably most evident when we consider that we can come back to it at any time. This would also not be altered if the wood were to be chopped down as this would not rob me of the consciousness that it, the selfsame wood, once stood there. We can destroy any thing wherever possible but not even the omnipotence of a god could effect that it subsequently never even existed. Or: that which has happened cannot be unhappened. Accordingly, that which we perceive, when we speak of things or events or of objects per se, has the nature of conceptuality in relation to the uniqueness of that living image which is only beheld in the moment. However, then no primal image can be the same as any one thing!

Imagine two lovers who stand in the bloom of their love for each other; it is

8 A. Schopenhauer, *The World as Will and Representation.* Third Book: The World as Idea, excerpt from §35, 2nd expanded edn, transl. R. B. Haldane and J. Kemp. Emphasis by Klages.

nevertheless not the case that they experience the same degree of delight from any one hour or minute to the next over, say, a period of several weeks.

> There lives within the very flame of love
> A kind of wick or snuff that will abate it;
> And nothing is at a like goodness still;
> For goodness, growing to a plurisy,
> Dies in his own too-much.
>
> – Shakespeare[9]

They will spend shared hours or minutes of ebullient bliss, yes even of transport, and there will then follow extinguished hours where each of them will long in vain for the exhilarating shiver and seek for nought the causes of why it evades them. For the experience of the lover, though he scarcely knows it, does not at all apply to the lasting *person* that is the beloved, instead it applies to their *image* that flows with the passing of time. This is why it is the major and tragic fate of great lovers in particular to render homage to the error that the state of Eros is guaranteed to last. The young girl becomes a woman and the woman becomes an old woman; the young boy becomes a man and the man becomes an old man; each time it is the same person that wanders through all these appearances but the appearances themselves are vastly different from each other; and the entirety of Eros hangs only on the image and not on the sameness of a separate thing! When Schopenhauer said that we must disregard the appearance to reach the idea, we affirm rather the opposite that one must disregard the content of the concept, that is the object, to reach the image. And this does not just apply to erotic arousal but to beholding images at all. I might have seen the wood in front of my window a hundred times without experiencing anything other than the thing, that same thing which is considered by the botanist. But perhaps one day the wood is lit up in the embers of the evening sun and the sight tears me away from my I and then suddenly my soul sees that which I have never seen before, perhaps for a minute or just a second. Irrespective of whether it is for a long or short period, that which was seen was the primal image of the wood and *this* image never returns either for me or for anyone else. – At this point one might raise a really significant objection. If the wood is conceptual, then we might say that the person who has seen the primal image must no longer perceive a wood at all; but if that is unlikely, how might we suppose that he is free from the chains of I, and thus free from Spirit and all its conceptuality! – We shall answer by attempting to outline the primal image in a positive sense.

However, firstly we see that even arbitrary *perceptual* content is always more diverse than the thing taken from it. For example, the concept of the wood and even of a particular wood does not deal with its luminous colours. At the moment

9 William Shakespeare, *Hamlet*, Act 4, Scene 7. Cited from *The Complete Works of William Shakespeare*. Hertfordshire: Wordsworth Editions Ltd, 1996.

of me beholding it, the wood was lit up with the light of the evening sun. This glow was absolutely not to be separated from the image that I experienced. On another occasion, the selfsame wood might be floating in the mists of a storm and I might be blessed again with seeing its primal image, however then this image is a different one to the one I received previously. Compared to that expressible perceivable thing, an image proves to be richer by numerous characteristics that are never fully capable of being compartmentalised into expressible traits. – However, we hear the objection that this is due to the peculiarity of (by necessity) abstract thinking and possibly to language, which is insufficient to differentiate the act of perceiving from the event of beholding [Schauung]. If we were to replace the act of perceiving with a light-sensitive plate, then even the plate would be capable of catching the momentary impression of the perceivable thing and of retaining a likeness of what has been caught. Nevertheless, by contrasting the momentary impression with the abiding thing we want to remind you why the difference between the two is not and cannot be that *another* thing has taken the place of the thing called a "wood" for the person beholding it! As already indicated, the expressible thing is elicited from the image and that applies equally for the likeness of the wood as for the real wood. This also then exhausts the similarities between simple perceptual images and the content of (ecstatic) vision [Schauung]. For that so-called "primal image", experienced by the aid of such vision, is never something that exists, to be found and caught in the darkroom, instead it *gives birth to itself* only from the polar contact of a receptive soul with an active daemon; and the sign and seal of such an origin is the radiant shiver that encompasses it in the moment of becoming. *Primal images have a more glorious nimbus than even the reason for the image that Spirit purports to comprehend in it.* It would be a vain task to dissect the nimbus and want to divide it up into concepts. In contrast, we can attempt to awaken the memory of it by referring to its artistic impact.

In Old Chinese poetry it says of the king's bride that she is "a tree clothed in silken foliage". In the (Indian Mahabharata) story of Nala and Damayanti, the semi-clothed hero is painted with the following words: "Who is that smoke encircled flame of beauty". A sonnet by Eichendorff about a deceased beloved ends with the verse:

> Yet your image is now a star to me
> That points to home [Heimat] with quiet glance,
> Lest the mariner battles staunchly 'gainst the winds.

The enchantment, the melancholy, the nightly grief of the singer *transforms* the love-bedazzled form for him and shifts it into the remote contexts of cosmic depth, allowing us to behold in a single detail of its appearance that which would not be found in the daylight of consciousness: the extinguishing or kindling, the approaching or fleeing, the crying or jubilant *soul of the world.* Lenau's dark melancholia emerges as a reverential image in the sheet lightning of a billowing firmament:

Clear in thunder's roar
I think to see you there,
And your trailing hair
Blowing in the storm.

Mörike,[10] in his poem about "Peregrina", conjures the magic of his beloved using the symbol of gold:

The mirror of these devoted eyes of brown,
Is like a reflection of gold from within;
Seems to draw it from the bosom deep down,
Such gold in holy sorrow may thrive therein.

We are told these are but similes. Nay, far from it! For if we descend namely to the level of the *primal* song, then we see by dint of the magical power of the word those things *issue forth* bit by bit that the visionary proclaims from divinely enthused lips! In a Russian song, an aged minstrel fails to find a ship on the sea to carry him across the waters. Then however:

The old man sang such a lovely song
A powerful song sang that aged one,
So the sea began to harken,
So the blue waves did harken.
So the foaming surge did harken
And the deep currents did harken
And the shoreline itself did harken;
The old man sang such a lovely song,
A powerful song sang that aged one,
So the yellow shorelines inclined
The one towards the other.
Inclining thus towards each other,
So no room remained between them;
Inclining thus towards each other,
So no gap was seen at all;
Inclining thus towards each other,
So they were joined up tightly:
And they were soundly united,
Left shore to the right shore,
Right shore to the left shore,
Forming thus a solid bridge.[11]

---

10 Eduard Mörike (1804-1875), German poet and writer.
11 Quoted from Böckel, *Psychologie der Volksdichtung* [Psychology of Folk Literature], p. 202.

A Finnish song sings of a rune singer:

> Everyone cheers along, rejoices,
> Everyone sings and hops,
> Everyone skips and is happy,
> And there trill all skylarks,
> And there jump all salmon,
> And there chirp all crickets,
> And there buzz all bees,
> And there whir all beetles,
> Even the mountain winds dance,
> Even the sound's waves frolic,
> Even the fir trees bend down,
> Even the spruce pines bow low,
> Even the birches curve down,
> Even the willows stoop low,
> Even the flowers sway,
> Even the grasses shake,
> Even the reeds rustle,
> Yes, even the stones roll,
> And even the dunes tremble,
> And there clack all smooth
> Pebbles at the salmon catching places,
> At the lovely houting coves:
> Sings a good rune singer,
> Sings an honest rune singer.[12]

And Goethe also says of the mystical temple before which the kidnapping of Helen is to take place yet again, conjured by Faust's entry into the realm of the mothers:

> The columns ranked, the very triglyphs ring;
> Now *the entire temple seems to sing.*[13]

The image of man dissolves into the meteoric [Meteorilien], the meteoric [Meteorilien] coagulates into the image of the man. That which was separate amongst separate things to the day-eye now stands surrounded by telluric and cosmic currents. Colours, shapes, sounds, noises, scents appear in it as coalesced to a pandemonium of all image elements. And yet it gleams with a shimmering and super-clear light, akin to an at times threatening and at times propitious visage. Reality has not been altered objectively, where the image is born from contact

12 Ibid, p 198.

13 Emphasis by Klages. Transl. W. Arndt; J. W. von Goethe, *Faust: A Tragedy*, ed. Cyrus Hamlin, 2nd edn (New York: Norton, 2001), ll. 6447-48.

with that reality; rather *the barriers* which separate the object from reality *yielded*! Whatever stepped into the beam of the primal vision, it is no longer *one* thing amongst *many* things, rather it has become the central point of the world. The following applies that was conferred by Mephistopheles on the adept:

> Next plunge into the sea at its most savage,
> And scarcely do you tread its pearly ground,
> When all about you forms a glorious round:
> For undulating nile-green swells, upwelling
> With coral edges, mold a splendored dwelling,
> With you for center. *Every step you do,*
> *The glassy palaces advance with you.*[14]

Through the jump of the spark between daemon and soul, the soul itself becomes a daemonic primal source of images, *in the living*. To reveal this in words is certainly inconceivable, for at the moment of the visionary event, we experience the ever-renewing cycle of the world-beginning! We recall the fiery verse by Schuler[15] in his piece "Corybantic Dithyramb" from his work "Cosmogony":

> What are you that is more than my candle's wick,
> Than my lamp's boiling balsam oil.
> What are you that is more than my palanquin's blood,
> Than my mosaic of hyacinth splendour,
> That glows beneath my sole's tread —
> I am the light that suckles you from out of night,
> I am the eye that feigns a lustre,
> I am the pearl that fills the mussel,
> I am the ecstasy that youthens this world,
> For I am life –[16]

In that illuminated moment, the destiny of the world is present; reaching out to the remote regions of space and time, everything that has ever happened and will happen has its light and its meaning from the image, even though it disperses so rapidly.[17]

Novalis says that every random thing can "become our world organ. A face, a star, a region, an old tree can conjure an epoch inside us. This is the great realism

14 Emphasis by Klages. Ibid., ll. 6006-11.

15 Alfred Schuler (1865-1923), German gnostic, mystic and visionary.

16 The "Korybantische Dithyrambos" [Corybantic Dithyramb] had in the meantime become available through a bibliophilic private press (Alfred Schuler, *Dichtungen*), that also collated specific poetic fragments for our circle of friends. (It was supplied by Kurt Saucke and Co., Hamburg.) Recently the entire legacy was finally published: Alfred Schuler, *Fragmente und Vorträge, Aus dem Nachlaß* [Fragments and lectures, from the estate]. With an introduction by Ludwig Klages, Leipzig 1941.

17 A more precise substantiation of the image concept based on cognitive science can be found in the 6th and 7th chapters of our work *Vom Wesen des Bewußtseins* [On the Essence of Consciousness]; and

of fetish rites." Indeed, that which today may appear to us as alien in regard to cult activities, holy festivals, magical rites, taboos and the art of prophecy is founded without exception in the preponderance of visionary inwardness [Innerlichkeit] over the singularly perceptual capacity to form an image and in the interwoven nature of the world of objects, which is only ever mechanically animated, with the daemonic-living reality of images. Semiotics indicate how this reality was directly rendered over the full life cycle of prehistoric man, and how it quasi crystallised in the temples, idols and grave monuments, and how it was later laid down in the scattered petals of poetry. We shall not reject drawing on semiotics to help us segue from the non-communicable (because outside consciousness) content of ekstasis to those certainties that cannot be understood logically, which the Pelasgian lived, and which the man of historical antiquity regained at least spiritually in secret rites. That is to say, if there were a humanity for whom it was usual to connect with the world around it through inseminating vision, then in the intermediate states of soberness it would have to strive to capture that which has passed using signs for consciousness, in a similar way to how the man of reason maintains his knowledge of things with the aid of conceptual language. Now – these signs are *symbols*. They are glyphs of ecstatically beheld images, that is true hieroglyphs, just as the word of the imparting language is the glyph that fixes objects into concepts. If conceptual language serves to convey reasoning, so the language of symbols is used to reawaken the visionary capacity. And if concepts form the starting point of scientific research, so the symbol is the starting point for the origin of myths. – We cannot overlook the semiotics of the visionary state of consciousness, as we will now refer to it in brief; the knowledge gained is immeasurable if you know how to interpret it! For our purposes, it will suffice if we single out one aspect from the plethora of its manifestations and traditions. In order to understand it, we will have to deepen our insight further into the nature of images.

We have moved from the state of ecstasy to the nature of ecstasy by highlighting the remoteness of images in relation to the proximity of perceived things. In reply to the unavoidable objection that even remoteness is perceived and in particular that perceptual spatial distance forms the model for every possible remoteness, we would reply that no perception takes place at all without vision (even if it remains unconscious), not even the spatially proximate. Perception of the spatially remote has a unique "timbre" in which the person who is accustomed to listening can hear the voice of the awakening *soul*; and it is there that the metamorphosis of the state of ecstasy softly heralds its beginnings. Compared to the man who notices a beetle on his hand, the observer of blue hazed mountain peaks is considerably closer to the "dreamer" or the "enraptured man" under circumstances that are otherwise similar. The observer intent on discrimination treats even remoteness as if it were something close. He thus sacrifices the perceptual image to a sequence of points that he measures one by one and separately. Whereas when a person sunken in rapture observes an object, even one close at hand, then their sight is released from

also in *Der Geist als Widersacher der Seele* [The Spirit as Adversary of the Soul].

intent and is mesmerized by the *image* of the object. This means at least to be engrossed in a shape that has not been contained by setting limits or boundaries but instead by a totality of surrounding neighbouring images. It is actually not so much the distance of the object as the type of observation that decides whether the object has the characteristics of being remote or near; and no one can deny the thing-ness of the character of closeness and the image-ness of the character of remoteness.

Now, someone may with apparent justification object that however much that may be true in and of itself, we end up at an irresolvable contradiction in relation to the primitive state of consciousness which in our opinion is, after all, primarily dominated by the visionary capacity. For even sidereal perceptual units of primal contemplation, let alone those objects in close proximity, may be clothed in remoteness to us who know or purport to know of their factual nature, but which is yet not at all apparent to the person experiencing them. It is actually here that we find the distinguishing feature of prehistory that shifted the distances of stars to be as it were also intimately near. So he might continue, "Greek cosmogony knew Eros as the creator of the world, but in spite of his cosmic nature he remained an *Eros of Closeness*. Indeed it has a deeper meaning, than today's astronomy would be able to decipher, when Greek cosmogony suggested the stars were fed by the fumes of the earth. It certainly also designates the relationship of that closeness, which the eye of Hellenic sensuality requires between heavenly realms and the region of earth. Their ultimately elemental symbolism exchanges the allure of a definitiveness of structural shape for a narrowing of the soul's visionary field; unquestionably this first of all facilitated the unique, beautiful enchantment of their anthropomorphic art, but to no lesser degree it accelerated the dying out of cult thinking into merely logical thinking. There is perhaps no greater, more convincing proof for the dependency of the reasoning capacity on the "visionary power" of experience than the Copernican rediscovery of the earth's migration! The concept of Heliocentrism — which was known earlier to the Greeks (Aristarchus,[18] perhaps Philolaus[19] before him) — was an improbable "notion" for antiquity. It withered at that time alongside the Ptolemaic system because it never experienced the truly staggering pathos that would lend it a kind of voice and imbue what at first glance appears to be just an astronomical formula with the significance of a revolution that was absolutely unprecedented in the minds of man and which was manifested through the *image of space!* – The Greek Hylic stands with eyes wide open to the 'well-founded durable earth'. Grove, crag and the coast surrounded by the sea's surge are consonant with the multi-layered Hymenaios, enclosed and clearly delimited by the radiant bell of the vaulted 'ether'. The flame swirls aloft into spaces more akin to it. The falling rain inseminates the receptive earth. The bracing wind, murmuring from prophetic treetops, joins remoteness to closeness, the above to the below. And the heaven with all its luminaries 'feeds on his countenance' in the radiance of the waters. Everything moves and wanders, proclaims, unfolds and drifts away and thus it *lives*. Drives

18 Aristarchus of Samos (c. 310-230 BC), Greek astronomer and mathematician.
19 Philolaus (c. 470-385 BC), Greek philosopher.

and desires as well as a longing for satiation or copulation, war and fraternisation agglomerate the airy, loosen the secure, pull the heavenly fire into the embrace of swamps and send nourishing water as a nebula into the fiery region of the sun. The belief in an All that is alive, in panmixia and in unceasing transformation bleeds through mythology as it does the systems of the earliest philosophers. But even if these systems released them at once from the barriers of perception and taught the cyclical return itself of the polar phases of reality, it would nonetheless be wrong to amend their level of consciousness with that of today by supposing they had ever left the geocentric standpoint. That stood in opposition to their view of space! We infer occidental ancient 'space' from the myths, symbols, wisdom teachings, the Homeric epics, Aolian and Pindaric odes, the choral songs of Greek tragedy, the temples and sculptures: space for them always has the shape of a conjoining sphere, where its visible half is tented or domed over the earthly landscape on the plane beneath. The life feeling of antiquity is cosmic but also cellular and it takes the macrocosmos for an extended microcosmos. It remains deaf to the discovery of Aristarchus because his 'space' is the *macrocosmic* cell that holds all events like the pouring jug holds the water flow or which places the images of heaven with the images of earth under the roof of the same house. The 'space' of antiquity was the near-space of the *oikos*.[20] Does it perhaps deviate from the space of 'wild peoples'? Some Polynesian peoples are of the firm conviction that the heavens reach from the horizon down to the earth and hold the earth in a kind of embrace. This is expressed by them calling strangers 'Papaalagi', which means 'heaven breakers' as they are people who have broken into this world from another world! But what could speak more strongly for the character of closeness of the primal experience, and how does that work with a doctrine of vision, that locates the essential feature of images precisely in the remote character of its substance?" We have taken the consideration above from our main work *Der Geist als Widersacher der Seele [The Spirit as Adversary of the Soul]* (p. 875—878) where we explain in more detail that which, for now, we shall communicate by only the most essential points in the form of an answer. – The person who has acquired the concept of distance from the "infinity" of Copernican space and in turn measures this against the "oikos" consciousness of early history, he might rightly be tempted to call the Eros of antiquity by comparison an "Eros of Closeness". As will now become apparent, for the purpose of distinguishing between vision and perception we are entitled to understand the expression "Eros of Distance" within a wider meaning which permits us to apply it to the cultic level of all peoples and all periods, without exception. However, first we would like to add that the aforementioned objection makes something valid that applies far less to the difference between early history and late history than to the two racial natures. More precisely this is the difference between the Greek-Roman peoples (with which in this respect many – not all – "primitive peoples" agree) and the numerous Oriental tribes and in particular prehistorical Teutons hither and Indians yonder. For example, many hymns from

20 Old Greek, oikos = a house, abode, dwelling; home; a temple; a household, family.

the most ancient Vedas, even though unacquainted as they are with the Copernican concept of space, are surrounded by the distant radiance of images, a radiance that not even Aeolic verse can approximate, let alone Homer and the Greek tragedies. And Indian architecture precedes the dissolving pull of the romantic landscapes of the late Baroque period by more than a full millennium. But Occidental antiquity repeatedly saw individuals who broke through this "oikos" thinking, such as the aforementioned Aristarchus of Samos, and especially Heraclitus[21] who uprooted the static nature of thinking by his virtually anti-Greek doctrine of the reality of eternal flow. But this is just an aside, so let us return now to "Eros of Distance" in its broader meaning.

If the object (as one translated into the distance) can at least become a perceptual image, with a reflection more or less like the real image, then the opposite applies no less that the distant image can shift closer and ever closer from the "infinity" of limitless space and thus, one might suppose, it runs the risk of ossifying into objective isolation. If we were now to ask if there is a characteristic capable of distinguishing a close image from even the more remote of objects, then we would see ourselves directed first and foremost to the negative indicator of the *untouchable nature* of all images. Certainly we saw above that it is not rare for mystes to hear, smell, touch or taste something. However, we will explain in the next chapter, using the example of tasting, that in reality this has nothing to do with contiguous touch but with the visionary capacity inherent even in tasting and touching! Of course, strictly speaking, we cannot touch any object that is removed by even a minimal distance from the touching body. Yet, apart from heavenly phenomena, there is no object so remote that it could not be brought into touchable closeness, whether it is through its movement towards the observer or by the observer's movement towards the object. Thus if the nature of earthly objects for all intents and purposes is to be touchable, whether they are distant or close, they do not acquire the essential characteristic of distance at all, whereas this does truly apply to the images of heaven and altogether to everything *transient that has passed.*

Closeness and distance are the mutually augmenting poles of space and also equally of time. We envision temporal distance (or bring it into the present moment) by means of the perceptual image of spatial distance; but the thing that places spatial remoteness at a (inviolable and untouchable) "distance" is — temporal distance. This temporal distance *appears* at a spatial distance, or that which appears distant in space is the distance of time. To be brief (as above): time is the soul of space. – It seems as if we might, as an exception, call on the aid of "natural science": astronomy teaches us about Sirius, a very close fixed star, that its light needs several years to reach us. Consequently, through the act of perceiving, we would be seeing something "in the present" that has in fact already passed a long time ago! Meanwhile, even if we were not certain that the science of tomorrow will not overturn this currently popular opinion as erroneous, everything would nevertheless be confused if we were to replace the measurable distance of the Sirius

21 Heraclitus (c. 535-475 BC), Greek philosopher.

star from planet Earth with the distant character of the Sirius *image*! We are not talking here about *distances* of miles or light years, but about that distance (to a degree the distance "in itself ") that is directly (and therefore pre-conceptually) beheld in the vision of the image.

Imagine yourself resting on a flat beach by the sea, pondering the farthest edge of the horizon without any other thoughts. The horizon is marked by the dissipating clouds of smoke from a steamer that has already disappeared. And now bring to mind adjacent to that the feeling that comes from experiencing spatial depth and the sense of being sunken in images of remembering an irretrievable youth. The person who has the gift of entering the inner realm will find both to be so similar as to be confused with each other. Because it is unreachable, the distant fragrance of the horizon fills the heart with a gnawing longing, painfully exciting and at the same time sweetly soothing. The same occurs with the reality of the past which can *no longer* be touched. And what sets apart in the internal image that which has just happened and is still lingering in the near-time of its immediacy from the far-flung of the remote past is the absolutely incomparable distant blue of the depth of space. Prehistory passes by, eternally taking leave, in the eyes of the man unintentionally captivated by dreamy contemplations of those images of mountain snows and "deceptively distant" sparkling stars. Let us again remember the mystical revelation that: the external is an internal state elevated to a mystery.

But a new objection rears its head: if temporal and spatial closeness as well as temporal and spatial distance are always one and the same according to their nature, why should spatial distance always appear in the light of the past and not equally as well of the future? Language dictates that the past lies *behind* us and the future *in front* of us. Sunset might remind us of the former, while sunrise reminds us of the latter. And didn't Eichendorff's song say that distant lands speak of future happiness! – We are drifting from the main point and we will have to suffice with allusions as to why distance in terms of time past is thought to lie behind us. But in spite of this, we hope to convince the reader that there is absolutely no such thing as the distant future in – reality.

Space and time belong on a polar axis and have this in common, namely that they are each stretched between the poles of closeness and distance. Now certainly, there is only one spatial closeness (according to its nature = touchable), irrespective of where I am, and in turn there is only one spatial distance, irrespective of whether I look to the east or west, north or south. Consequently, in relation to temporal closeness there can only be one single temporal distance. If there were two of each, i.e. a Distance of Future alongside a Distance of Past, then the distant character of the vanishing point in front of me would be somehow opposed by nature to the distant character of the vanishing point behind me. Now, if the opposite undeniably takes place then the duality of temporal distance would be fabricated, and one of the two hypotheses would have to be – a figment of fantasy! But we must consider this to be the future for the following reason: if I think about the past, then I think about a *reality* which has been; on the other hand, if I think about the future, then

I think about something *un*-real, or to be more precise, a fact that has its existence merely in thought! If all thinking beings were to disappear in an instant, then the past which actually took place still remains precisely as it was before; however, the word "future" would simply lose all meaning as soon as there were a lack of beings to *think* about the future! The future does not behave in relation to the past like a *single* distance of time in relation to an opposite distance of time, instead it behaves as a mere concept in relation to reality in general. Or, better yet, the future is not a trait of real time!

You might perhaps counter by saying that the only real thing is what happens *in the present.* However, just as this is indeed co-determined by past events, so it also forms the precondition for future happenings. Numerous drives to care and nurture leave no doubt that even an animal's life state is just as inwardly connected to the future as to the past (for example, birds building nests at mating time!). Consequently, the man who admits that the past has reality might not want to deny the same to the future. In response we would say that a happening must progress onwards and is different to the mental anticipation of an as yet non-existent present. The latter is not in any way on the same level as *the* thought that brings to mind something that really has happened! Without venturing to assert degrees of certitude, everyone must surely recognise and acknowledge that there is no future event of which it cannot be thought that instead of it occurring it does not occur! When an astronomer predicts a lunar eclipse down to the very second, we do not doubt that it will happen at precisely that predetermined point in time. On the one hand it would *not* be impossible to *think* that before it happened the entire visible universe shattered into atoms! On the other hand, it would be inconceivable to think that the lunar eclipse which happened yesterday simultaneously did not occur. If physical examples do not clarify the matter, perhaps you might choose examples from life. We can hope that our friend might withstand a dangerous undertaking, we can fear that he will not; but there is nothing to hope for or fear *after* he has perished from it. Thus if the future is populated by a shadow game of human fears and wishes, then it is itself something unreal, merely a thought, a — figment of fantasy. Conversely, if even the most passionate of wishes shatters powerlessly against that which has irrevocably occurred, then the past subsequently shows itself to be *filled to the brim with reality.* The past and the present are the poles of time, not for instance the past and the future. And therefore temporal distance concurs absolutely with Distance of Past. "Nature is pure Past" (Novalis). In German, "fern" [meaning faraway or distant]; (from the root word "firn" [meaning 'old snow or ice']) was originally used solely for things expired or past and was equated with "early, previously, old" [früher, vormals, alt]!

Promethean man, who directly preceded historical man, raised the future to the *same* level of reality as the past, which is something we shall come back to. The Heraclean man of "global history" struck and strikes down the reality of what has been with the fantasy of the "future"; he guts the moment by destroying what it contains of the past and he tears apart the inseminating connection of Closeness with Distance in order to replace it with the restlessly hounding *relatedness* of the present to that phantom of distance that is called the future. Ultimately he will have entirely lost his past and yet in the same moment he will also destroy himself because he has been robbed of his present, as time is only realised and *becomes manifest* in the images of that which has been or which has existed. "The past alone leaves an afterglow like the ships on the sea sometimes leave a trail of light behind them" (Jean Paul). The "eschatologies" and "apocalypses" are the most dreadful expression of that lunacy which goes by the name of "history". However, we shall cover the essentials on this later, for now let us say a few words regarding the subject touched on above regarding "before and after" us.

Reality is eternal and real time is the *pulsing* of eternity by virtue of which the present counters each approaching moment with a past moment that just as much slips away. In relation to the overarching bridge of Now, time becomes a current flowing *out* of the future and *in* to the past. If we turn to the future side, each moment appears to approach us – "future" [künftig] is the same in meaning as "coming" [kommend] — and if we turn to the past side, it appears to depart us. The crucial reason that makes this conceptual pair of past/future possible is that each present moment, can be experienced as approaching and equally as time slipping away, departing, elapsing. Now since we usually do not go backwards and certainly we never do that for any length of time, movement forwards is consequently the direction in which we go or would go, and movement backwards is the direction in which we go away from. If we focus on any distant point while moving forwards, that point gets closer and closer, whereas to the same degree the distance grows between us and the distant point behind us. The former approaches, the latter departs, a finitely elapsing state. The former is the symbol of the approaching moment and the latter the symbol of the departing moment. And, as everyone can see, sunrise and sunset behave in like measure. Only distance remains one and the same. We do not reach distance when we reach the distant point; rather on reaching it we immediately encounter closeness, which has become exceptionally close. Ultimately since we cannot reverse the direction of time and we become inexorably more distant from that which has happened, while each moment truly conceived as a future moment at some point arrives and becomes the present, this means that only that which has happened [das Gewesene] can stand in the *real* light of distance. It remains for us only to explain why the future sometimes seems to have the *appearance* of distance such as in that verse by Eichendorff. The answer is that Distance of Past is the soul of the remote image we viewed; yet as a thinking being we are capable of integrating this Distance of Past into the expanse of space located *in front of* us: The future is the past projected in front of us.

This even applies to the (actually timeless) future concept of the natural sciences. There is no calculation of the future that is not fleshed out with the conceptual interpretation of things past! When the astronomer precisely predicts the time that a lunar eclipse will occur, he does not do that by dint of a mere rule of probability based on the recorded temporal intervals of previous lunar eclipses. The forces and orbital paths and times alone that he bases his units of calculation on are entirely and utterly modelled on his observations of astronomical movements that have already taken place. This suffices for now.

In order to determine the nature of ekstasis, we have had to determine the nature of vision and to this end we differentiate very specifically between the distant character of the visible image from the close character of the thing perceived. However, everything we have said so far would be confusing and fragmentary without metaphysical information about the nature of *Distance*, which our investigations have now shown to be in itself Past, even if it *appears* in terms of Distance of Space. Accordingly, primal images are images of that which has been (which is where the concept of anamnesis entered Platonic eroticism); and ecstatic vision, contrary to the act of perception, applies to the absolutely inviolable reality of the Past! Irrespective of whether the image of space is geocentric or "infinite", Eros of Distance proves itself as genuine by shining forth in the vision of the primeval world! – The teachings on their essences and nature reflect that Closeness is sober and sobering whereas Distance alone is intoxicating. The present is close whereas the past alone is distant. The certainly non-rational meaning of the state of visions is that it "transports" us into "inaccessible realms", into the Mother World of that which has been [das Gewesene] or it *brings back* the "ghosts" of the long departed! No Plato, no Plotinus, no Schopenhauer has fathomed that! Seduced by the ghost light of Logos, the philosophers transposed the eternal with the timeless limit of time or even with the mad thought of a never-ending perpetuity. They hoped to use reason to obtain through sheer obstinacy that which is bestowed unbidden and solely on those with a sacrificial sense of piety. And, while committing an outrage against the miraculous image of the All that also bore them, they looked to *the other side* of it, as if there were a second world of objects, but more pleasantly habitable, which only *appears* to the visionary, specifically in the midnight blue of the Distance of Past. Certain poets however *knew* this, such as Goethe.

> Well then, sink down! Or I might well call it: soar!
> It is all one and the same. Escape the norming
> Of what has formed, to forms' unbounded swarming!
> Delight in what long since has been no more.
>
> What was, in all its gleam and effigy,
> There is astir; *eternal it would be.*
> You, sovereign powers, assign it to diurnal
> Bright tabernacle and to vault nocturnal.[22]

And whoever reaches "into the unaskable, the never to be asked for" whether through "mercy" or by dint of magical power, whoever has escaped the "I",

22 Emphasis by Klages. Transl. W. Arndt; Ibid., ll. 6275-78; 6431-34.

transformed, became one with the pulse of eternity, he brings about and performs even the daring endeavour of necromancy:

> And could I not by fierce desire contrive
> To will the incomparable *back alive*?[23]

Even though he must confess with Faust:

> Breathless I seem, my tongue is faltering, chained;
> *This is a dream, and place and day have waned.*[24]

Due to the essential similarity of temporal and spatial closeness (and thus also of Here and Now), "the present time" [Gegenwart] formerly meant "presence" [Anwesenheit] and is still used today in the same sense when we say of someone that he is "present" [gegenwärtig]. In any case, if visions are a way to bring something into the present [visualise; Vergegenwärtigen] or call something to mind, but visible distance is a thing that is absent, then we can characterise the differentiating essential feature of the former with "visualisation of the absent" [Vergegenwärtigung des Abwesenden] or more precisely with "visualisation of that which has been" [Vergegenwärtigung des Gewesenen]. Subsequently we hold in our hands the key to a *cult of the dead* that was formerly found around the entire world and which has now disappeared from today's average consciousness. Just as we find within the cult of the dead our outline of the visionary state richly complete and engaged vividly with the remote and distant, so this outline helps us to understand the original meaning of Pelasgian ancestor worship and specifically, due to confusion around this, to understand the perennial rites which gave mystes the certainty of "immortality". However, we do not want to string the rites of prehistoric ancestor veneration into a constructed line of reasoning instead we want more directly to collate evidence by examining things from the perspective of *Eros in regard to bygone times.* To achieve this, we cannot of course omit listing certain facts that are well-known to every expert (for the knowledge of mythology and ethnology is limited in our practical times to an outlying minority of enthusiasts and scholars). The transition point is however formed by reference to a still untouchable fact which latterly illustrated the nature of Distance, and which exposed, to a degree in an obfuscating manner, why the Eros of which we speak is a "cosmic" Eros.

As we saw, everything that is spatially distant *can* be shifted into closeness, with the unconditional exception of the stars and heavenly bodies! Even though our eyes may employ cut and polished glasses to penetrate thousands of light years into the abyss of space and in the darkroom we may catch the likeness of myriads of stars at points in the heavens where there was previously only lightless emptiness, even though we may precisely chart the measurable height of the crater rings on the

23 Emphasis by Klages. Transl. W. Arndt, Ibid., ll. 7438-39.

24 Emphasis by Klages. Transl. W. Arndt, Ibid., ll. ll. 9413-14.

moon and chemically analyse the compounds of the suns and combustible vapours of other worlds, as before we still only have "present" the *appearance* of the stars, never their (merely deduced) physicality. Therefore then, we "do not woo" the stars. And, if we are allowed a witticism to illuminate the paradoxes in conjecturing on this subject, their "present/presence" ... "shines through absence"! – So if no more convincing symbol of former times could be conceived of than the starry splendour of a night sky, we not only grasp the sublime shiver that moves through every observer still open to the world at the sight of the sparkling vault above, but we also understand why the original meaning of the stars was that they were first souls of the dead then their dwelling places; but always of those no longer on earth, shining in immortality, those choirs of the primeval world to which "all earthly changes [remained] bound". Thus Bachofen[25] was certainly right with his comment that the statement by Aristotle in his work *Metaphysics* that "the orbit of the planets engenders all phenomena" is a "primal thought of humanity that completely dominated the way the ancient world saw things".[26] This is certainly because the distant images of the stars were at that time powerful daemons and the daemons were also the "spirits" of a *primordial world.* – This was also not contradicted by their no less primeval underworldliness, according to which they dwelt inside the earth! For apart from the fact that the original "Uranism" stood at polar opposites to "Chthonism", but in no respect antagonistically, so from the outset the intellectualising swindle [Vergeistigungsschwindel] in no way took possession of the night's stars but the day and its apogee the sun. This is why the interiority [Innerlichkeit] of humanity still speaks; a humanity that, even though already de-deified, still knows that it stands in *proximity to the gods,* for example when the initiate's soul bears witness to itself on one of the Orphic gold tablets: "I am a child of the earth and of the *star-studded heaven.*" The examples that we have selected almost indiscriminately, part from antiquity and part from the "wild peoples", leave no doubt that veneration of the stars is characterised absolutely everywhere by Eros in regard to bygone times. And these examples teach us irrefutably how much more powerfully visionary man has been defined by the inviolable Distance of Images than by the closeness of the touchable body.

No practical teaching has been able to explain to us why in the customs and legends of such stunted Pelasgian peoples as we have unquestionably seen in some of today's Negro tribes, in the Bushmen, Botocudo, Tierra del Fuegians, Puri and Australian Aboriginals, that alongside the symbolism of for example hunting spear, harpoon, awls, cooking stone, gourd bottle, of jackal, owl, toad, fox or bear, of tattooing, conjuration, black magic, of women's monthly cycle, mating, childbirth and other similar "all too human" close occurrences, without exception the distant images of stars, albeit certainly not in an astronomical sense, play a role that goes far beyond addressing just fear and dread. And altogether the disproportionately advanced astronomy that we find amongst the so to say inspired Pelasgian peoples

25 Johann Jakob Bachofen (1815-1887), Swiss antiquarian, jurist, philologist and anthropologist.
26 *Gräbersymbolik der Alten* [Grave Symbolism from Antiquity] p. 282.

– the Chinese, Sumerian, Assyrians, Egyptians, Incans, Aztecs – at the beginning of their historically recordable development (in contrast to the starry stupor of the Europeans of today) should immediately and objectively affirm that we must once and for all forgo locating the conceptual drives of mythical searching in the (for us) familiar spirit of expansive and preserving self-interest. The chiefs of the former Virginians continued to live on in the land "the other side of the sunset". At that place in the colour-drenched airy sea of the evening west lay for the Greeks the "Isle of the Blessed". The Polynesians of Tokelau saw in the moon the domicile of their departed kings. Plutarch in his essay "On the face in the moon" considers all stars to be "gods that appear in the heavens" and in particular the moon to be the region of Persephone and the "element of the souls". "For they are dissolved in it just as the bodies of the dead dissolve in the earth." On the side that is turned away from the earth and towards the heavens lies the "Elysian plain". The North American people of Winnipeg called the Milky Way the "Path of the Dead". The souls of Greenlandic Inuit pitch tents in heaven where the rainbow spans the sky. According to the beliefs of the Eskimo, all stars in vague primordial times were humans or animals. In Orion's Belt we see a crowd of seal hunters who have lost their way home. The indigenous people of Van Diemen's Land showed strangers on clear nights their two Dioscuri stars that brought fire to their ancestors. The Pharaohs, the Sasanian monarchs and the Roman Caesars called themselves "Brothers of the Sun and the Moon" and after their death they returned to the place from where they had descended, namely the starry heavens. A comet at the time of Caesar's death was interpreted to be his soul. As is found by virtually all peoples of the earth, stars that light up unexpectedly and especially shooting stars are taken to be menacing or blessing souls. Pliny speaks of the societas coeli nobiscum![27]

Eros in regard to bygone times is Eros of Distance. But because he is ignited by non-corporeal images, he connects the visionary with the untouchable world of stars, in such a way that the earthly life of the person still in the light of the present is pulsed through with the rhythm of the All. This is why the bearers of Eros were literally "cosmic" beings and as they were called amongst their highest votaries: sons of the sun. The reflection of this in the consciousness of the wise radiates towards us from a late grave inscription from antiquity that (although it already separates the poles in two and declares the estrangement of the upper world from the lower world) in its final verse nevertheless vividly expresses the ancient shiver of bliss from that starry relationship that is so foreign to us:

The souls of the dead are divided
    into two hordes,
One randomly wandering
    the earth, the other
Begins the roundelay

27 "Communion of the heavens with us." Pliny the Elder (23-79), Roman author and natural philosopher. Phrase from his *Natural History.*

with heaven's radiant stars.
I accompany this horde
for God was my guide.

This has become alien to us, but again and again it flares up in high moments of creative genius, as long as such people still exist in a withered humanity! The same state of consciousness which characterised the Orphic adage inspired Nietzsche to devise the word "Fernstenliebe" [love of those farthest away, or, love of the remotest] and gave him this verse:

Called a star's orbit to pursue,
What is the darkness, star, to you?

Of course "star orbits" are more costly today than in previous times! They are the orbits of those who fall sacrificially, an offering on *unknown* altars, hopeless. And thus fell Nietzsche, judged twice over, namely by a humanity that rejected him (even though it might externally appear to woo him) and by his own complicity in that humanity. In spite of that, he also disappeared amongst the stars, a comet that most likely will never return.

Katabasis and Eroto-Gnosis

David Beth[1]

In this short work I hope to give the reader a glimpse of the importance and scope of *Eros* and related ecstasies in the work of the pandaemonic Kosmic Gnosis also known as the Primordial Way. The essence and aim of our esoteric path are fundamentally different and opposed to most spiritual endeavours in the Western World; consequently, the nature of this current has been described as a *Katabasis* rather than a spiritual ascent and we hope that the following considerations may aid the discerning reader in understanding how we, as initiates, approach this concept.

Western esotericism, regardless of any Right Hand or Left Hand persuasion (as well as Western psychology), usually originates from the assumption of a potential wholeness of Personhood or Self. The spiritual initiate recognizes his fallen state, his fractured personality and identification with the lower phenomenal and transient world, and seeks to integrate or isolate himself within a higher order of being. Some adepts may attempt to re-identify their consciousness to varying degrees with the consciousness of the Divine, whether he is considered to be the Demiurge or the pleromic unknown God/Source beyond the cosmic builder. Others may hope to isolate their consciousness while connecting to the undifferentiated Source of Being and through it become an alternative Demiurge and enjoy the play of creation. What all such paths, cosmic or anti-cosmic, have in common, however, is a clear understanding of a transcendental source of Being, towards which the soul/self is oriented/aligned/directed in its desire for wholeness and completion. As a result, Spirit, in the sense of an abstract logocentric, organizing principle, is given ontological priority over the concrete, embodied reality of Soul. Any such path to us must be considered a spiritual ascent – an escape towards transcendence and pure states of Being, away from a phenomenal world which is ever-changing, becoming and manifesting in time and space.

The vision of Personhood, however, in the Gnosis of the Primordial Way, is in direct opposition to the aforementioned views. With Klages, we agree that Life manifests in a primordial trinity of two poles, distinguished within an overarching and unifying maternal whole. In *Of Cosmogonic Eros* Klages elaborates:

> The cosmos is alive and all life is polarised into soul (Psyche) and body (Soma). Wherever there is a living body, there is also a soul; wherever a soul, there is also a living body. The soul is the meaning

1 This short essay was previously published as a supplement to the Auric 'deluxe' edition of 'Ludwig Klages' *Of Cosmogonic Eros*, Theion Publishing, 2018 in a separate brochure.

> of the body, the image of the body is the manifestation of the soul. Whatever appears has a meaning; and every meaning is revealed through its appearance. The meaning is experienced inwardly, the appearance outwardly. The former must become an image if it is to communicate itself and the image must be internalised again so that it takes effect. Those are, without using metaphors, the poles of reality. — Now if we, judging and thinking, were to consider the world from outside, then it would everywhere display to us the Pelasgian trinity of the poles divided within the unity of the whole. Space is the body of time, time the soul of space. The soul and meaning of night is the day, the womb of light is the night. Winter and summer, sleeping and waking, dying and coming into being follow on from each other. The feminine is the body and mother of the soul, the masculine is the revealed and revelatory meaning of the womb of the mother. Blood and nerve, solar plexus and brain, "heart" and "head", mouth and eye, left and right all stand in equal relationship. If you were to separate one of these members from the other, the world would be shattered.[2]

From this process of cycle and dynamic tension it follows that human being, or better human becoming, has no completion! It is always in process of being made and unmade. The Primordial Way teaches that the Self is bodily centered and psychically composed of an inner black hole within the sanctuary of the Soul. This gap is a space of transformation and exchange with the mysterious forces of the All. Like the multiverse itself about which the initiate remains in a state of wonder, curiosity and longing, this hole is swarming with undefined and unknown elements. As indicated by Novalis, this is the place where the inner and the outer meet.[3] Thus, the true Self is the nexus of all the forces constituting the individual. Such a person is absolutely individual through the unique configuration of the many elements which are also always in flux – this is a fully different and true individuality when compared to the Western worship or realization of the 'I am'[4] or Source of Being which is, in fact, absolutely the same in every individual.

Each element making the person is also related to a series of other forces through what we call elemental similarity: an ancestral component, for example, is related to a particular ancestor (who himself was a unique configuration of forces and only a certain aspect of him/her has returned in the unique set up of the descendant); another component may link to a certain color, animal and plant (all of which are considered ensouled and enthusing as all phenomenal appearances) which belongs to its series of connectivity. All becomes bound together in a network which

2 Klages, Ludwig. *Of Cosmogonic Eros*. Munich: Theion Publishing, 2018, p. 115f..

3 See Novalis, *Blütenstaub* (Engl. *Pollen and Fragments*).

4 The Cartesian disembodied Self ("I think, I am") as well as the proclamation of Yahweh ("I am that I am"). Not only Western psychology but all of Abrahamic theology and much of Enlightenment philosophy is implicated here!

connects the components with each other and the inner with the outer. Harmony and communication between these elements within the Self is ensured by special modes of interaction and perception. Certain methods of identification of forces and their manipulation allow for a shaping of personal law and destiny.

The deep embeddedness of our initiates in the cyclical kosmic flux, but also their experience as individual centerpoles of the All life swirling around them, gives rise to a primordial consciousness that we call "night-consciousness" (in contrast to "day consciousness" which is the rational, analytical consciousness of common Man). Essentially night consciousness is the visionary capacity of the Daemonic Self, the inner eye or gap, which gazes the essence of the World through its constant mating with the daemonic forces of the kosmos. Rather than becoming one, however, and drowning in the other, each daemonic center upon mating retains its individuality, a duality in union and from their congress ensues renewal the constant rebirth of the world. There are no laws to abide by except those which aid us to engage the daemons of the Kosmos, which support the undoing of the profane person and the extension of ourselves as the All in ekstasis. Our Law exists solely for ecstasy, and by nature, it can never be the Abrahamic Logos.

We are plunged into an eternity in flux, fed by the constant coupling of ensouled life. The force which makes these encounters possible can be called *Eros*. Eros must be understood as a rhythmic, pulsing web which pervades the cosmic Real and binds together the poles, the daemonic forces longing for mating. The revealed essence of the Mother can only become manifested through the power of Her Son, Eros, who binds the poles not to annihilate their separateness but to continually create Kosmos through their encounter.

Mankind today is exiled from this ecstatic Life in night-consciousness. A metaphysical adversary from outside the erotic maternal wholeness, which Klages has correctly identified as the Spirit, Logos, or Nous, has manifested in the human ego and split body from soul. This spirit enables the dominance of the rational mind and separates us from the passionate and intuitive parts of ourselves. The spirit of day consciousness veils the innermost core of our true selves, the black hole, and we become unaware and disconnected from the ensouled images dwelling in the aura and nimbus of the phenomenal world, those powers who long for union with us and for revealing – and whom we encounter through the mysterious gap. The World of Powers has now become a world of objects, we can no longer perceive and experience their life. The Gods have fled this wasteland and the Dae-Man, glory be to him, has been degraded to man, utterly enslaved by the ever same 'I am' and its transcendental source.

There is, however, this scattered aristocracy of the Soul, these adepts of the Primordial Way, whose initiation rekindles the cosmogonic flame of Eros. We still hear the calling of the Faceless God and turn away from the false light of the ever-same One. Rejecting the 'Father' we embark on our Black Pilgrimage towards the lost Cathedral of the Soul where the daemonic mirror, the black hole of the Self awaits our homecoming. In renewed ekstasis, the profane "I" shatters, and the daemonic Eye opens. When the day conscious self collapses, we marry ourselves anew to the secret of the All. The apocalypse of Being, at first, is always annihilation and we are propelled back into the Dionysian vortex – but then, in its whirling, pregnant darkness, the divine fire of Eros-Phanes-Cosmogonos flares, and the inner God resurrects! Differentiated now, pole again gazes at pole, and from their shared overflowing ecstasy and communion a kosmos, a world, is born at every moment.

November, 2018

An Introduction to Eroto-Psychedelic Art

Henrik Dahl

When psychedelic art first appeared as an artistic genre in the mid to late sixties, a wave of sexual liberation was sweeping the west. The era of the "Sexual Revolution," as it became known, was a time of major social change, which had great impact on millions of people's lives. Naturally, this historical transformation also affected and shaped the members of the LSD counterculture, and, consequently, psychedelic art.

The sixties saw the approval of the birth control pill, relaxed attitudes towards premarital sex, and the legal right to have an abortion. Moreover, after the 1966 obscenity trial over the publication of William S. Burroughs' *Naked Lunch*, books featuring explicit sexual content were no longer banned in the United States.[1] Obviously, these and many other political and social changes came to have great influence on psychedelic artists and their work, and, as this article will show, many of the paintings, posters and drawings from that era were clearly erotic.

But before discussing eroticism in psychedelic art, I would like to briefly explain my choice of terminology. The term I picked for describing art that combines the erotic with the psychedelic is the compound word "eroto-psychedelic." Admittedly, this is not a common expression, but then again the subject is very rarely discussed. Also, the few times I have seen it in print it has only been briefly mentioned. For instance, Robert Anton Wilson used the term at one point in his book *Sex, Drugs & Magick*. In a sentence in his introduction, Wilson refers to "the eroto-psychedelic bandwagon."[2] Furthermore, art critic Ken Johnson used the term in an art context in his book *Are You Experienced?* when discussing the artist Dorothy Iannone. In a chapter titled "Sex and Sensibility," the reader learns that after leaving her husband and embarking on a long love affair, Iannone found "inspiration for a lifetime's worth of autobiographical, eroto-psychedelic painting, sculpture, and drawing."[3] Seeing that "eroto-psychedelic" is a self-explanatory and fairly effective term, it made sense to start using it in my writing.

—~—

1 Allyn, David, *Make Love, Not War: The Sexual Revolution: An Unfettered History* (New York: Little, Brown and Company, 2000), pp. 69-70.
2 Wilson, Robert Anton, *Sex, Drugs & Magick: A Journey Beyond Limits* (Las Vegas: New Falcon Publications, 1987), p. 27.
3 Johnson, Ken, *Are You Experienced?: How Psychedelic Consciousness Transformed Modern Art* (Munich: Prestel, 2011), p. 173.

One of the core elements when it comes to psychedelic imagery is nudity, and quite often the depictions of nude bodies are loaded with varying degrees of eroticism. Hence, a considerable portion of psychedelic art can also be defined as erotic art. Clearly, not all nudity depicted in psychedelic art – or any other artistic genre – is of an erotic nature. The undressed body can of course have other meanings. Nudity may for instance symbolise innocence, being in accordance with nature, and unveiled reality. Additionally, a nude female body may stand for Mother Earth.[4] The "back to nature" ethos of psychedelia, which remains a strong thread, is sometimes expressed using this kind of non-sexual symbolism. There are, however, also numerous examples of psychedelic artworks that feature sexual nudity. These images range from being slightly erotic to having explicit sexual content.

It should also be noted that references to sex are not just expressed through depictions of nude bodies. Psychedelic art, much like Art Nouveau in the late nineteenth century, often contains abstract shapes, undulating lines, and geometric patterns that allude to eroticism. And the long, flowing hair that is often seen in psychedelic art can certainly have erotic allusions, which by the way is yet another feature that the genre shares with Art Noueveau. Depictions of liquids and dripping objects may also allude to the erotic in that the fluids may look like saliva, lubrication, sweat and sperm. But the perhaps most obvious, yet rarely discussed, expression of eroticism in psychedelic art is seen in the frequent use of tunnels, spirals and concentric shapes, which can be interpreted as holes waiting to be erotically penetrated by the gaze of the viewer. In fact, erotically minded psychonauts may associate these motifs to body openings. Also, the visually stimulating imagery seen in psychedelic art often has an undertone of eroticism.

Although both female and male nudity are featured in eroto-psychedelic art, the female-coded body is by far the most common motif. To exemplify this, let us take a look at the work of American psychedelic artist Victor Moscoso. Perhaps best known for his concert posters for San Francisco venue The Matrix on Fillmore Street, his work is characterised by vibrating colours, psychedelic lettering and photographic collage. These features are seen in two of his most well-known posters, namely *Neon Rose #2* and *Neon Rose #6*. Described by the artist as his first "psychedelic pin-up,"[5] *Neon Rose #2* was designed for a 1967 show by The Miller Blues Band. At the centre of the picture is a vintage erotic photograph of a bare-breasted woman wearing a very large necklace. In the picture, she is standing in an erotic pose with her arms pointing upwards. The woman's body, which has an intense orange colour, is surrounded by concentric shapes that echo her somewhat unusual pose.

Also from 1967, Moscoso's *Neon Rose #6*, which was made for a Blues Project show, is featuring a photograph of a bare-breasted woman in a sitting position. The woman is wearing several necklaces, and in her right hand she is holding a large

4 Cooper, J.C., *An Illustrated Encyclopaedia of Traditional Symbols* (London: Thames & Hudson, 2013), p. 112.
5 Moscoso, Victor, "The Neon Rose Series," http://www.victormoscoso.com/gallery1.htm

rose. Moscoso based his poster on a French postcard from the 1890s. These "French postcards," as they became known among their buyers, featured photographs of nude or semi-nude women in various postures and settings. Incidentally, the nude woman in Moscoso's *Neon Rose #6* reappeared some years later when UK graphic artist Barney Bubbles used the same erotic postcard, in its original black and white, on the inner sleeve of his cover design for Hawkwind's 1973 album *Space Ritual.*

A key feature in many eroto-psychedelic artworks is the nude female breast. This is of course not exclusive to eroto-psychedelic art. Throughout art history, the nude female breast has been depicted over and over again in both religious and profane artworks – and its symbolism varies. In her book *A History of the Breast,* Marilyn Yalom discusses the female breast from many different perspectives and contexts; Yalom refers to The Sacred Breast, The Political Breast, and The Erotic Breast, which is also how she named some of the book chapters. In psychedelic art, the nude female breast can have several meanings. For instance, during the counterculture era, there was usually a strong political dimension to the exposed female breast. But obviously many depictions are also of an erotic nature.

The nude female breast has been a recurring feature in psychedelic art since the genre's inception in the 1960s, and the body part continues to be depicted by some of the psychedelic artists of the twenty-first century. Of course, fascination with the nude female breast is not unique to psychedelic art. Artistically alternative and avant garde scenes have long been drawn towards nudity, and they have made sure to include the undressed body in various artistic expressions. In 1954, to give one example, more than ten years before the LSD counterculture became a defined movement, American artist, occultist and psychonaut Marjorie Cameron exposed one of her breasts in Kenneth Anger's seminal – and arguably proto-psychedelic – short film *Inauguration of the Pleasure Dome.*

Given that the LSD counterculture blossomed during the Sexual Revolution, it was only natural that the nude female breast would be a common feature in psychedelic art. If one takes a look at what inspired the psychedelic artists of the 1960s, one finds a thread of eroticism and nudity going back at least to the late nineteenth century. Many psychedelic artists draw inspiration from late nineteenth century Art Nouveau, a style which was often characterised by sensual and erotic motifs. In particular, several of the San Francisco poster artists were heavily influenced by Art Nouveau painter Alphonse Mucha, and a few of his paintings were even reworked in the psychedelic style. Mucha made detailed artworks filled with vegetation, flowers, and decorative lines, and at the centre of the image was usually a woman with a sensual appearance. Although his most well-known paintings do not contain nudity, the Czech artist did make several paintings of women with exposed breasts.

Interestingly, both Mucha and the San Francisco poster artists made most of their images in the context of advertising. Whereas Mucha illustrated advertisements for cigarette rolling papers, bicycles, and performances by French stage actress Sarah Bernhardt, the poster artists mostly made images that advertised concerts by the bands in the psychedelic music scene. Given their visually stimulating appearance, one could also argue that the images of the San Francisco poster artists advertised the psychedelic lifestyle, and more specifically LSD, which, for a short period at least, undoubtedly was the drug of choice among young, fashionable people in the west.

When discussing similarities between psychedelic art and Art Nouveau, it is also worth mentioning British erotic illustrator Aubrey Beardsley, whose work is characterised by flowing, undulating lines. A lot of psychedelic art contains similar lines, and works such as the 1893 illustration *The Peacock Skirt* has similarities with some of the art that was made some 75 years later during the counterculture era, as exemplified by a Victor Moscoso poster from 1967. The image, which was made for a Quicksilver Messenger Service show at the Avalon Ballrom, took direct inspiration from the Beardsley illustration.

The psychedelic artists of the sixties clearly felt an affinity with the art of the late nineteenth century, which was characterised by psychedelia-friendly ornamentations, vegetation, floral patterns, and, not to forget, a subtle yet permeating eroticism. Completely devoid of violent or disturbing themes, the art of Mucha and other Art Nouveau artists focused on beauty. Thus, the style did not contain imagery that had the potential to provoke negative feelings among those using psychedelics in the sixties. In fact, as was discovered by the San Francisco poster artists, the Art Nouveau style is surprisingly compatible with the psychedelic experience.

Seeing that the LSD counterculture coincided with the era of sexual liberation, it was only expected that eroticism would be found in psychedelic art of the sixties and onwards. But what about the psychedelic experience itself? Is there a correlation between psychedelically induced altered states and eroticism? It is certainly the case that some people who take psychedelics experience erotic feelings and closed eye visuals of a sexual nature. In his 1975 book *Realms of the Human Unconscious: Observations from LSD Research*, psychiatrist Stanislav Grof notes that "Individuals sometimes spend hours in overwhelming sexual ecstasy, expressing their feelings in orgiastic movements."[6]

While huge numbers of people have taken psychedelics without having thought about removing their clothes, it seems that for some individuals the psychedelic experience triggers an impulse to undress. Obviously, reasons for wanting to be in the nude may vary. One may for instance feel uncomfortable wearing clothes that are too warm or too tight on the body. Or perhaps one may feel that since the mind has been set free, the physical body should be "set free" too. But the decision to get naked during a psychedelic experience can of course also be sparked by sexual desire.

Taking off one's clothes during psychedelic intoxication is probably seen by most people – even by some psychonauts – as odd behaviour. Still, if one takes a

---

6 Grof, Stanislav, *Realms of the Human Unconscious: Observations from LSD Research* (London: Souvenir Press, 1975), p. 129.

look at the history of psychedelia there are several examples of famous psychonauts and other luminaries who have taken their clothes off while tripping. A classic example is Allen Ginsberg's first psilocybin trip at the home of Timothy Leary in 1960, where Ginsberg and his lover Peter Orlovsky famously took off their clothes and spent the rest of the trip naked. At one point during his experience, Ginsberg proclaimed that he was going to "start a peace and love movement."[7] And when psychedelic chemist Nick Sand took his very first LSD trip, he, too, decided to undress. "I just wanted to be naked. I didn't want to be encumbered by clothing,"[8] he said in the 2015 documentary *The Sunshine Makers.* A much more recent example of nude tripping is the first – and clearly extreme – ayahuasca experience of performance artist and art world celebrity Marina Abramovic, who at the time was close to 70 years old. During her trip, which is documented in *The Space In Between: Marina Abramovic in Brazil,* the artist felt a strong need to take off her clothes. In the 2016 film, she is seen crawling around in agony while the super-strong jungle brew – of which she took a double dose – works its way through her body. Interestingly, these three examples of tripping in the nude all occurred while taking a specific psychedelic for the first time.

When discussing links between nudity and psychedelics, it is also worth mentioning the visionary artists Alex and Allyson Grey, who in their early days of psychedelic exploration often tripped "naked or comfortably clad."[9] It was during this period that Allyson developed her Secret Writing symbol system, which today is recognised as her signature work. Perhaps as a consequence of experiencing psychedelics in a state of physical nudity, the artist incorporated photographs of her own naked body in her 1976 exhibition *Secret Language Walls* at Tufts University Gallery.

In the case of Alex, he has a long history of depicting human bodies in the x-ray style. Although the artist is focusing on themes relating to spirituality and mystical states, some of his paintings are also themed around sexuality. Notable examples of the latter include the artworks *Kissing* (1983) and *Copulating* (1984). In the mid 1990s, he also combined cannabis spirituality with eroticism in a few paintings featuring "Cannabia," the cannabis Goddess. One of these became the poster for the 1995 Cannabis Cup. Writing about the green Goddess on his website, the artist stated that, "To kiss her is to become intoxicated with her and turned on to one's own fertile imagination."[10]

---

7 Lee, Martin A. and Bruce Shlain, *Acid Dreams: The Complete Social History of LSD: The CIA, the Sixties, and Beyond* (New York: Grove Press, 1992), pp. 77-78.

8 *The Sunshine Makers,* documentary film (2015).

9 Reed Slattery, Diana, *Xenolinguistics: Psychedelics, Language, and the Evolution of Consciousness* (Berkeley, California: North Atlantic Books, 2015), p. xxii.

10 Grey, Alex, "Cannabia – Alex Grey," http://alexgrey.com/art/paintings/soul/cannabia/

In the early to mid 1950s, the word was spreading about mind-expanding drugs in intellectual as well as artistic circles. The English author and philosopher Aldous Huxley was of course a key factor in making these substances known to a lot of people. In his 1954 essay *The Doors of Perception*, Huxley describes his experiences of taking mescaline, the active ingredient in the psychedelic plant drug peyote.

Around this time, the aforementioned American artist and occultist Marjorie Cameron decided to explore expanded consciousness via mind-altering drugs, or more specifically peyote, which she managed to find via mail order from a botanical garden in Texas.[11] The resulting experience turned out to be profound. In a 1988 interview, Cameron comes across as a true psychedelic convert: "The walls disappeared. What I got was Huxley's 'gray world.' Peyote causes a revolution in the unconscious."[12]

Inspired by the experience, Cameron made a drawing titled *Peyote Vision*. Usually dated to 1955, the artwork features a nude long-haired woman positioned on all fours. She is being penetrated by an undefined creature whose head shares the features of a peyote cactus. During the penetration, the woman appears to spew some kind of fluid out of her mouth, a detail that adds interesting complexity to the drawing. Given the drawing's direct references to peyote in the title as well as motif, one could interpret the matter coming out of the woman's mouth as vomit. For it is well known that the intake of some psychedelics, including peyote, may sometimes lead to vomiting, which in indigenous entheogenic cultures is seen as a cleansing. It is possible that Cameron was alluding to the assumed cleansing effect of vomiting.

Even though it is a seemingly simple drawing, *Peyote Vision* has become one of Cameron's most appreciated and thought-provoking artworks. It is probably also one of the earliest examples of art from the twentieth century where both sex and psychedelics are such explicit features, which of course makes it an important artwork in the history of eroto-psychedelic art. Another fascinating feature of *Peyote Vision* is the theme of interspecies sex, or to be more precise sex between a human and an alien creature that could be a character in a sci-fi novel. Incidentally, the theme of interspecies sex had already been explored by other artists when Cameron made her drawing. For instance, Japanese artist Hokusai's 1814 woodblock print *The Dream of the Fisherman's Wife*, shows a woman shell diver having sex with two octopuses. In the image, an acknowledged classic in erotic art, one of the octopuses performs cunnilingus on the shell diver, while the other smaller octopus is fondling the woman's left nipple.

Today, *Peyote Vision* is no doubt an underground classic, especially among people attracted to esoteric and occult art. But how did this drawing on paper become so appreciated? American artist Wallace Berman seems to immediately have realised the uniqueness and potential of Cameron's drawing. Already in 1955, he included it in the first issue of his literary and artistic journal *Semina*, which

11 Kansa, Spencer, *Wormwood Star: The Magickal Life of Marjorie Cameron* (Oxford: Mandrake, 2014), p. 96.
12 *Ibid.*, p. 97.

also featured Berman's photograph of Cameron on its cover. In 1957, Berman also featured *Peyote Vision* in an exhibition at Ferus Gallery in Los Angeles. Here, it became evident that there was something special with the drawing, for soon *Peyote Vision* came to the attention of the Los Angeles Police Department, who cited the drawing as "lewd," and shut down the exhibition.[13] This is not the only time an eroto-psychedelic artwork has caused controversy. As will be discussed in a moment, in 1968 a Swedish graphic artist made a poster for an exhibition in the city of Lund that was deemed so provocative and scandalous that the scheduled exhibition was cancelled.

It appears Cameron never explained the meaning of the imagery in *Peyote Vision.* In later years, however, the artist identified the penetrator in the image as a solar God.[14] It should be noted that central to the religion of the peyote using Huichols of Mexico is Tayaupá – the sun God ("Our Father Sun"). In her 1974 book *Peyote Hunt,* anthropologist Barbara G. Myerhoff writes that "Tayaupá, it seems, is considered extraordinarily potent, even dangerous to man... Father Sun must be kept away from the earth, it is said, for if he comes too close, he would burn it up."[15] Did Cameron take inspiration from this sun God? Given the artist's obvious interest in peyote, it is plausible that she had the Huichols and their religion in mind. Regardless, since Cameron identified the creature in the drawing as a solar God, it is possible to interpret the matter coming out of the nude woman's mouth as a spew of fire.

Peyote Vision is clearly an important artwork. Still, a large water stain to the left of the penetrator indicates that her art was not always properly handled. Moreover, many of her artworks no longer exist. For instance, the artworks shown in her first exhibition in 1956 were destroyed in a fire. Cameron also deliberately damaged many of her artworks. Thus, if events would have turned out differently, *Peyote Vision* could very well have been among the works that were destroyed or lost.

Now, let us take a look at what was going on in late sixties Scandinavia, or more specifically the small city of Lund in the south of Sweden. In 1968, fifty years ago at the time of this writing, a graphic artist named Sture Johannesson was asked to make a poster for an upcoming exhibition that was planned to take place at Lunds konsthall, the city's municipal art gallery. One could say that Johannesson, who at the time was in his early thirties and already a controversial artist, took his chance to launch himself as Sweden's art provocateur number one. In fact, the finished poster, which has become known as *Hash Girl,* was deemed so scandalous that the upcoming exhibition was cancelled and its curator Folke Edwards resigned from his job. The image became Johannesson's most popular work, and eventually made him into one of Sweden's most well-known poster artists.

But how can a mere poster for an upcoming art exhibition result in such a scandal? Before answering this question, it is important to take into account the

13 Duncan, Michael, "Cameron," http://cameron-parsons.org/cameron.html

14 Kansa, Spencer, *Op. cit.*, p. 265.

15 Myerhoff, Barbara G., *Peyote Hunt: The Sacred Journey of the Huichol Indians* (New York: Cornell University Press, 1974), p. 80.

context in which Johannesson's poster was made. By 1968, nudity and sex had certainly entered popular culture in Sweden. For instance, the year before, the controversial Swedish film *I Am Curious (Yellow)* became a much talked about international success due to its explicit sexual content. Directed by Vilgot Sjöman and starring actress Lena Nyman, the film came to represent Sweden's liberal attitude towards nudity and sex, which became known by the expression "the Swedish sin."

Besides in film, the theme of sexuality was also explored in the field of visual art. Before Johannesson made his scandalous poster, Lunds konsthall showed *The First International Exhibition of Erotic Art*. Between May and July 1968, the gallery featured erotic art from Japan, China, and India, as well as artworks by Hans Bellmer, Leonor Fini, and many others. The collection belonged to the sexologists and erotic art collectors Drs. Eberhard and Phyllis Kronhausen, who, incidentally, as a testament of their popularity, briefly appeared in best-selling author Erica Jong's 1977 novel *How to Save Your Own Life*. In addition to acquiring an impressive collection of sexuality-themed artworks, the couple had also authored several books including *Pornography and the Law* (1959) and *The Sexually Responsive Woman* (1964).

Although Sweden was considered to be one of the more liberal countries when it comes to nudity and sex, the erotic art exhibition in Lund was, due to its content, met with criticism. Still, the exhibition was very popular and obviously suited the spirit of the times perfectly. Interestingly, the poster for *The First International Exhibition of Erotic Art* featured an artwork showing a copulating couple. Given that depictions of explicit sex were still seen as highly controversial at the time, it was an impressive feat that the poster was given the go-ahead. As expected, though, some people were upset by it, and the poster was even reported to the police.

The Sexual Revolution was blooming in the western world, and that spring, thanks to the ongoing art exhibition, eroticism was no doubt in the air in Lund, a small town centered around its well-respected university and its Lutheran cathedral. It was in this context that Johannesson made his *Hash Girl* poster. The image was made for *Underground*, an upcoming group exhibition about the hippie movement that was to start in February 1969. However, Johannesson decided to distribute the poster earlier than expected, and the Board of Directors of the gallery did not like what they saw. Loaded with eroticism and drug liberalism, the poster included the following confrontational phrase: "The underground will take over Lunds konsthall."

Even though Johannesson's image was originally created as an exhibition poster, it did not take long before people started to regard it as an artwork in itself. This meant that it would need to be identified with a title. In Sweden, the poster is generally referred to as *Haschflickan* (lit. "the hash girl"), and internationally as *Hash Girl*. It is also known by the title *Friheten på barrikaderna II* (lit. "freedom on the barricades II"), which, except for the "II"at the end, is the Swedish title of Eugène Delacroix's famous 1830 painting *Liberty Leading the People*. But the actual title of the poster is none of these, but is instead made up of a phrase written in a circular shape in the large cockade in the lower left corner of the poster itself, namely "Revolution Means Revolutionary Consciousness." This was the title Johannesson used on his website in later years. Additionally, in conversation with the present writer, Johannesson once remarked that, even though he accepted that his poster had become known as *Hash Girl*, its correct title was indeed *Revolution Means Revolutionary Consciousness.*

Strangely, although *Hash Girl* is a very well-known image that continues to be seen at museums and in people's homes, the poster has, to my knowledge, never been properly analysed by art critics. There is, however, reason to try to do a little more thorough reading of the image. *Hash Girl*, like many of Johannesson's other works, is a highly detailed and carefully planned poster. And by taking a deeper look at its imagery, which one soon realises is surprisingly rich, one may perhaps understand why the poster had such a great cultural impact.

Just like the previously discussed *Neon Rose* posters by Victor Moscoso, *Hash Girl* features a photograph of a nude woman. The picture is reproduced in an intense pink colour. Unlike the Moscoso posters though, the woman in Johannesson's image shows her genitals, which of course are unshaved. It is interesting to note that while the nude women in many of the eroto-psychedelic images from the counterculture era remain unidentified, this is not the case with *Hash Girl*. The woman in the poster is Ninna Ljung, who at the time the photograph was taken was 21 years old. During this period she was working at the restaurant Ringbaren in Malmoe, Sweden. However, when it became known that it was her in the poster, she got fired from her job.[16]

In the photograph, Ninna is looking straight into the camera with a confident and, arguably, sensual gaze. She has blonde shoulder-length hair, and in her mouth, which is slightly open, she has the mouthpiece of a long-stemmed pipe, which she is holding in her right hand. The length of the pipe suggests that it might be a Chinese opium pipe. However, the marijuana leaf depicted right about the pipe's bowl makes it clear that the pipe is signifying cannabis smoking. Even though Johannesson was a well-known drug advocate, it is important to note that the artist was not advocating random drug use. Instead, the drugs that were of interest to Johannesson were cannabis and the classic psychedelics, i.e. drugs that have the potential to cause – as it says on the poster – a "revolutionary consciousness." Incidentally, it has also been suggested that the pipe in *Hash Girl* is a "peace pipe," and that the revolutionary theme expressed in the image is the peaceful non-violent variety associated with the hippie lifestyle.[17]

Repeated throughout the poster is a diminutive portrait of Argentine revolutionary Che Guevara (who was killed in 1967). This is of course a nod to the revolutionary sentiments of the counterculture era. Another tiny photograph included in the upper right corner of the poster is that of American silent film actress

16 Affischerna 1967-1979, "Revolution Means Revolutionary Consciousness!", http://www.affischerna.se/progg_poster/revolution-means-revolutionary-consciousness-2/?cat=progg_posterartist&order=7&y=

17 *Ibid.*

Theda Bara, which was borrowed from the masthead of sixties UK underground magazine *International Times* aka *IT.* Apparently, these portraits had already become significant enough to be included in Johannesson's image. If one does not know anything about the context of the poster, it might perhaps seem a little odd that Johannesson filled it with such well-known subcultural references. However, given that *Hash Girl* was originally made as the official poster for an exhibition about the hippie culture, it makes perfect sense that he incorporated both the Che Guevara portrait and the IT logo.

At the top of the image is the word "underground" written in large capital letters. The word is surrounded by other words that form the previously mentioned phrase "The underground will take over Lunds konsthall." Johannesson's choice of phrase, which was no doubt confrontational, shows his ability to communicate the sentiments of the counterculture era. But then again Johannesson was not just a bystander but instead very much part of the underground culture himself. (For example, in the sixties the artist founded the legendary Galleri Cannabis in Malmoe, Sweden with his artist wife Charlotte Johannesson.) The "take over" bit in the phrase is also expressed in the imagery that is seen throughout the poster. The most obvious example of this is seen in the upper right part of the image. Here, Johannesson included the famous 1830 painting *Liberty Leading the People by Eugène Delacroix.* The painting, which commemorates the July Revolution of 1830 in France, features a bare-breasted woman personifying the Godess of Liberty who leads the people over a barricade. In her hand she is holding the French Tricolour flag. The Delacroix painting, which can be seen at the Louvre, is reproduced in black and white except for the red, white and blue flag. These colours are also seen in parts of the text elements as well as in the large cockade that Ninna is holding in her left hand. Incidentally, the colours in the cockade form concentric circles. (The latter are commonly seen in psychedelic art.)

In the area above the pipe and the marijuana leaf it says "February," and directly below this word is the number "69" in a much larger font size. While this is obviously the month and year when the exhibition was scheduled to start at the art gallery, the number 69 most likely also alludes to the sexual position of the same name. The fact that the exhibition was to premiere in 1969 was, from a conceptual point of view, a lucky coincidence that Johannesson used in a clever way. Incidentally, the cover design of the eleventh issue of Swedish counterculture magazine *Puss* (lit. "kiss"), published in 1969, featured an erotic illustration that shows the numbers 6 and 9 engaging in a "69". Clearly, sexuality was a recurring subject in the Swedish art scene of the time.

While the motifs in *Hash Girl* can be interpreted in different ways, it would be hard to deny that the poster has an erotic content. In addition to the allusion to the just mentioned sexual position 69, there is of course the nude picture of Ninna with a mouthpiece of a pipe resting on her slightly parted lips. The inclusion of the pipe may be interpreted as yet another, albeit subtle, reference to eroticism. As a side note, it is worth mentioning that there are some interesting similarities between the act of taking drugs and the act of having sex in that both activities often involve actions such as blowing, licking and penetrating. Thus, one could say that the pipe in combination with nudity emphasise the eroticism expressed in the poster.

Interestingly, several of the motifs in *Hash Girl* are repeated in different parts of the image: The nude female breast, the picture of Che Guevara, and the colours red, white and blue. But it is not just these motifs that are repeated. The poster's overriding themes of revolution and freedom are also recurring. This is expressed through the Delacroix painting, the nude body of Ninna, and the marijuana leaf. These three motifs could be said to represent the fight for freedom, sexual liberation, and drug induced altered states, respectively.

Johannesson clearly transgressed the boundaries of what was acceptable behaviour from a visual artist in Sweden in the late 1960s, and *Hash Girl* was immediately dismissed as drug propaganda. Although the explicit nudity in the poster was most likely a problem for the art gallery, it appears that it was mainly its references to drug use that was upsetting. What would have happened if Johannesson had removed the marijuana leaf? Even though it is of course impossible to say for sure, it is not entirely unlikely that the art gallery would have accepted the poster. After all, as has already been noted, in the late sixties Sweden definitely belonged to the more liberal countries in the world when it came to nudity and sex, and the gallery's previous poster did in fact depict sexual intercourse. However, the sexual liberation that was seen in the country did not extend to drug liberalisation. Instead, authorities in Sweden were – and still are – decidedly against the use of any narcotic substances, including "soft" drugs such as cannabis. This aversion to the use of drugs later led to the implementation of the ideology known as "zero tolerance," which, to this day, is shared by all major political parties in Sweden.

Looking back today, in the later part of the 2010s, it is hard to imagine that Lund, a small city centered around its academic institutions, for a short period in the late sixties was at the very forefront of the sexual revolution. But that is precisely what happened when art curator Folke Edwards decided to present the world's first erotic art exhibition, and later follow it up with an exhibition on the hippie movement. Although the latter did not materialise, it did result in an image that perfectly captured both the erotic and the psychedelic elements that were so prominent during the counterculture era.

The year 1968 also saw the appearance of another seminal image in psychedelic art, namely the aptly titled *Cosmoerotica* by Isaac Abrams. Unlike the previously discussed photography-based posters by Mosoco and Johannesson, Abrams' painting could be described as a depiction of the spiritual side of psychedelic sexuality. Clearly, many people in the LSD counterculture took interest in this theme after having encountered feelings of spiritual unity and interconnectedness while having sex on psychedelics. Writing about *Cosmoerotica* in *Psychedelic: Optical and Visionary Art Since the 1960s*, David S. Rubin noted that, "the cosmic union of spirituality and sexuality was a dominant theme of the counterculture that produced the 1967 summer of love."[18] This theme was also expressed in the 1967 book *The Sexual Paradise of LSD* by Marsha Alexander, where, for instance, an interviewee named Stephen humorously describes a cosmoerotic experience by saying: "The last time I made love on LSD I felt I was balling the universe!"[19]

Abram's *Cosmoerotica* consists of various flowing shapes that are suggestive of fluids as well as space scenery, and while it is a non-figurative work, it is infused with a distinct eroticism. In an email exchange with the present writer in March 2018, the artist wrote that cosmoeroticism "is about integrative unity, the enhancement of feelings and sensation and the dissolution of difference." During these experiences, "Eroticism & The Cosmic conjoined," and the artist and his partners "became one thing."[20]

Isaac Abrams was introduced to psychedelics in 1962, an event that he describes as a life-changing experience. Writing in 2018, more than half a century after his first trip, the artist still sees great potential in entheogenic substances: "Psychedelics are life affirming and importantly reconnect the user with the natural world ... this is their cosmic mission."[21]

Psychedelia has always had a subcultural, underground edge, which is partly due to the extreme altered states that psychedelics may result in. Yet much of this culture and art also have a commercial side to it. Why, for instance, did Moscoso decide to make pin-ups? The pin-up is of course generally seen as "low culture," and an expression of the commodification of the female body. Besides the early variety that was seen on the French postcards, the pin-up appeared in mass-produced magazines and on posters and became very popular in the 1950s. One would think that the psychedelic artists of the counterculture would stay away from such lowly imagery. Instead, they incorporated the pin-up and other similar "cheap" cultural expressions into their work. Despite its subcultural, underground roots, psychedelic culture has, in fact, strong links to commercialism, the mass-produced, and low culture. The erotic potential of psychedelia was quickly noticed – and commodified – by the broader culture. For example, the December 1967 issue of *Playboy Magazine* featured a psychedelic cover design created by San Francisco poster artist Wes Wilson.

Another example worth mentioning when it comes to the commodification of the eroticism seen in psychedelia is the cover design of the Jimi Hendrix Experience's best-selling 1968 double album *Electric Ladyland*. To some people's dismay, the inside of the record's gatefold sleeve featured a photograph taken by David Montgomery of nineteen nude women, several of which exposed their

18 Rubin, David S. (Ed.), *Psychedelic: Optical and Visionary Art Since the 1960s* (San Antonio: San Antonio Museum of Art, 2010), p. 21.
19 Alexander, Marsha, *The Sexual Paradise of LSD* (Olympia Press, 1967 – Kindle Edition), loc. 1886.
20 Private communication with Isaac Abrams.
21 *Ibid.*

breasts. And as if this was not indecent enough, some editions of the LP even featured the photograph on the outer sleeve. Naturally, several record shops declined to sell the album, and Hendrix himself strongly disliked the image of the nude women, which he found embarrassing. Yet looking back today, it is fair to say that Montgomery's now classic photograph is emblematic of of the sexual liberation that was so prominent of the sixties.

Although it is still generally defined as a subculture, psychedelia is incredibly wide-reaching. Of course, LSD and other psychedelics have been spread all around the world to all sorts of groups and individuals. The same can be said of psychedelic culture, which seems to grow well in most soils on the planet. This wide-reaching aspect is also seen in psychedelic art where images are often produced in more than one copy. In fact, it is not unusual for this kind of art to appear in editions that range from at least a few hundred to tens of thousands, sometimes more. Since the counterculture era of the sixties, psychedelic artists have often disseminated their work via printed media such as posters, record covers, magazines, books, comics, and handbills. Thanks to accessible printing techniques, the early psychedelic artists could get their new products out to the community in a fast and effective manner.

This willingness among artists to share their work effectively and with relatively little cost is also seen in today's psychedelic art. The perhaps most obvious example is Canadian GIF artist and illustrator Jean Francois Painchaud, aka SuperPhazed, who, after Facebook banned several of his images, quickly became a minor internet phenomenon with 45,000 new followers on his social media accounts.[22] Unlike the eroto-psychedelic artists of previous generations – who mostly made art for the urban environment and the museum walls – Painchaud makes art for the smartphone. Thus, Painchaud's pulsing, pastel coloured animations, which range from the slightly erotic to the more sexually explicit, can be viewed basically anywhere, at any time, provided of course one has internet access.

When discussing psychedelia's wide-reaching characteristics, it is also important to mention one of the most common carriers of LSD, namely blotter art. Some motifs have most likely been printed in substantial numbers on different occasions. One such example is the popular cartoon illustration of LSD discoverer Albert Hofmann's seminal 1943 bicycle ride. Interestingly, though, while there is a wide range of motifs depicted on blotter art, one rarely sees any direct references to eroticism. Given the art form's underground status, it is somewhat surprising that there is so little eroto-psychedelic imagery in these images. It seems the axiom "sex sells" is not applicable when it comes to this kind of modern day folk art. Supposedly, producers of blotter LSD do not need to rely on such tricks to sell their product. The lack of erotic motifs in the sheets may also be explained by the fact that blotter was not the standard carrier of the drug in the sixties, which is when most examples of eroto-psychedelic art can be found. Hence, when blotter art was established as an underground art form, interest in eroticism was not as prominent in psychedelic culture.

22 VICE Staff, "Check Out This Guy's Sexy Psychedelic GIFs" (2015), https://www.vice.com/en_uk/article/zn7v94/phazed-psychedelic-raunchy-art-jean-francois-painchaud-876

Still, there have been some instances where the motifs have alluded to sexuality. For example, posted on the Blotter Barn website is a picture of a hit of acid from 1979 that features a single sperm, which, given that blotter LSD is taken orally, makes it an interesting and slightly provocative motif.[23]

This introduction to eroto-psychedelic art has mainly focused on images that were produced during the counterculture era. For reasons of brevity, many artists had to be left out. Examples include Yayoi Kusama, Philip Caza, Keiichi Tanaami, Martin Sharp and R. Crumb. And when it comes to art that was made from the early seventies and until today, there are many examples of works where artists have sought to combine the erotic with the psychedelic. Examples include such diverse artists as Robert Williams, Judy Chicago, HR Giger, and pop artist and one-time Deadhead Keith Haring. Moreover, one could argue that Genesis Breyer P-Orridge and Lady Jaye's groundbreaking Pandrogeny project merits inclusion in an article on eroto-psychedelic art. And if we take a look at what is being made in our current decade, one should not fail to mention the erotically charged work of Oliver Hibert.

Psychedelic art is typically filled with vibrating colours, concentric circles, spirals, and other visually stimulating motifs that are only rarely seen in "non-psychedelic" art. One thing, however, that is usually left out when discussing psychedelic art – a genre that came to life during the era of sexual liberation – is the genre's recurring erotic and sexual elements, which are surprisingly often present either as explicit features or as an undertone in the artworks. This element of eroticism makes the genre stand out from a great deal of art that has been produced since the sixties until today. Usually referred to as "contemporary art," artworks belonging to this category rarely deal with eroticism and sexuality. This peculiar fact was observed already in 1980 by American journalist Tom Wolfe, author of the 1968 classic *The Electric Kool-Aid Acid Test.* In an interview with *Rolling Stone* magazine the journalist remarked that, "in contemporary art, there is almost no sexual content whatsoever. It's one of the few major movements in art history where there is no sexual content."[24] The sexually liberated psychedelic artists of the sixties and later decades, on the other hand, opened the door to sexuality. Some of them, as this article has shown, even made it a central thread of their work.

23 Blotter Barn, "Sperm," http://www.blotterbarn.com/

24 Flippo, Chet, "Tom Wolfe: The Rolling Stone Interview" (1980), http://www.rollingstone.com/culture/features/the-rolling-stone-interview-tom-wolfe-19800821

Antichrist Psychonaut: Nietzsche's Psychoactive Drugs

Peter Sjöstedt-H

'... And close your eyes with holy dread,
For he on honey-dew hath fed,
And drunk the milk of Paradise.'

So ends the famous fragment of *Kubla Khan* by the Romantic poet, Samuel Taylor Coleridge. He tells us that the poem was an immediate transcription of an opium-induced dream he experienced in 1797. As is known, the Romantic poets and their kin were inspired by the use of psychoactive substances such as opium, the old world's common pain reliever. Pain elimination is its negative advantage, but its positive attribute lies in the psychedelic ('mind-revealing')[1] state it can engender – a state described no better than by the original English opium eater himself, Thomas De Quincey:

> O just and righteous opium! ... thou bildest upon the bosom of darkness, out of the fantastic imagery of the brain, cities and temples, beyond the art of Phidias and Praxiteles – beyond the splendours of Babylon and Hekatómpylos; and, "from the anarchy of dreaming sleep," callest into sunny light the faces of long-buried beauties ... thou hast the keys of Paradise, O just, subtle, and mighty opium![2]

Two decades following the publication of these words the First Opium War commences (1839) in which China is martially punished for trying to hinder the British trade of opium to the Chinese people. Though opium, derived from the innocent garden poppy *Papavar somniferum*, may cradle the keys to Paradise it also clutches the keys to Perdition: its addictive thus potentially ruinous nature is commonly known. Today, partly for these reasons, opiates are mostly illegal without license – stringently so in their most potent forms of morphine and heroin.

Holy dread: the philosopher Friedrich Nietzsche took opium, this milk of Paradise, sometimes confessedly in dangerously high doses. He was also a heavy user

1 'Psychedelic' is a term coined in 1957 by psychiatrist Dr Humphry Osmond to emphasise the psychotherapeutic value of certain psychoactive drugs, notably LSD. The etymological conjuncts are *psyche* (mind) and *dēloun* (to reveal), the latter from *dēlos* (visible, clear). I use the term 'psychedelic' broadly in this text to refer to a chemically-induced state of mind that brings forth extraordinary representations.
2 Thomas De Quincey, *Confessions of an English Opium Eater*, pleasures, p. 195. 1821AD.

of other psychoactive drugs including potassium bromide, a mysterious 'Javanese narcotic', and most unremittingly, chloral hydrate, a known hallucinogen. This narcotic aspect of Nietzsche's life is neglected; it is the aim of this text to reveal the extent of his drug use and its effects, including a report of one of Nietzsche's psychedelic trips. Moreover we shall see how this drug use inspired his philosophy – and how his philosophy inspired this use.

Nietzsche was born in 1844 to a Lutheran pastor who died five years thereafter, at the age of thirty-six, due to a 'softening of the brain'. This fatal malady of his father's was to worry Nietzsche, as a possible hereditary condition, until his own mental collapse in 1889. Friedrich Nietzsche did suffer severe afflictions of the brain and body, beginning in childhood. At the age of thirteen, the severe headaches which were to plague him for the rest of his life began in earnest.[3] So strong were these headaches that near to a whole school semester was lost as the young pupil was prevented from excessive reading by his mother. However, as a bright student, the young Nietzsche surged on and was awarded a place at Schulpforta, a boarding school renowned for its classical studies. Nietzsche wore spectacles as he was very myopic even at this early stage. A doctor in the school once examined his eyes and called attention to the possibility that Nietzsche may go blind at an advanced age.[4] This foresight virtually bore reality, with Nietzsche complaining that in 1879, 'in the thirty-sixth year of life, I arrived at the lowest point of my vitality – I still lived, but without being able to see three paces in front of me.'[5] As Nietzsche's mother, sister, and others believed,[6] it was his poor eyesight combined with his lust for reading that caused his initial migraines. To counter the pain, Nietzsche eventually turned to drugs. This in its turn may have exacerbated the problem due to the toxicity, addiction, and withdrawal symptoms those nineteenth century drugs produced.

Nietzsche experimented with drugs early on in life. At the beginning of the 1860s, in Schulpforta, he snorted prohibited ***snuff*** with his fellow pupil Paul Deussen,[7] and in his fifth year he joined the 'Wild Clique': a fraternal club that endorsed ***smoking*** and ***drinking*** and spurned studiousness. Nietzsche, however, came to scorn ***alcohol*** but not before he was demoted from his years-long supervisory position as head of class due to an incident of excessive drinking.[8]

Whilst a student of philology at Leipzig University in 1868, Nietzsche took time out to join the Prussian military machine, training on horseback. As the best rider of the new recruits, he was given the wildest steed to tame. The steed, however, was not for taming: a jump caused Nietzsche a grievous blow to the chest as it cracked into the pommel of the saddle. Ten days of acute pain were relieved by ***morphine***.[9]

---

3 Curtis Cate, p. 13.
4 Paul Deussen, 1859-1864. Conversations with Nietzsche, p. 15.
5 *Ecce Homo*, Wise, §1, p. 38.
6 Elisabeth Förster-Nietzsche, *The Life of Nietzsche, vol. II*, ch. XXVII.
7 Paul Deussen, 1859-1864. *Conversations with Nietzsche*, p.10.
8 Paul Deussen, 1859-1864. *Conversations with Nietzsche*, p.15.
9 Letter to Erwin Rohde, 3rd April 1868.

In 1869, at the mere age of twenty-four, Nietzsche is appointed chair of classical philology at Basel University[10] a month before he is awarded his doctorate (from Leipzig) – awarded, furthermore, without examination. A year later Nietzsche takes leave of his position to serve as a medic in the Franco-Prussian War. He is taught how to administer ***chloroform*** – a popular anesthetic at the time. After chloroform's discovery in 1831 it was also used recreationally as it produced euphoria. Euphoria, however, was the furthest state of Nietzsche's mind as he treated the war wounded, a depressing mental state that could only have worsened as he himself became ill there. As Nietzsche writes to his friend Karl von Gersdorff:

> I fell very ill myself and quickly developed a severe attack of dysentery and diphtheria. ... After I had been dosed with ***opium*** and injections of ***tannin*** and ***silver nitrate*** for several days, the worst danger was over.[11]

As well as contracting these intestinal, bacterial diseases, it is believed that he may have caught syphilis here too, if not in a brothel a few years before. It is a matter of (much) dispute as to whether Nietzsche's general malaise and cognitive downfall in 1889 was caused by this mostly sexually transmitted bacterial infection. As we have seen, however, his headaches had started from a young age, and his father may have passed the problem down to his son. Whatever the case may be, Nietzsche's suffering only increased after 1870 leading to increased drug use to ease the pain. But it was more than pain relief that the drugs caused.

Before Nietzsche had become a professor at Basel, he had become an ardent disciple of the atheist, idealist philosopher Arthur Schopenhauer. In a sentence, Schopenhauer asserted that the world we perceive is but a human *representation* of the inner essence of everything, which is *will*. Schopenhauer inspired Nietzsche's first published book, *The Birth of Tragedy from the Spirit of Music,* and he arguably returned as inspiration for Nietzsche's later works. As a highly creative individual, Nietzsche could not have overlooked these words from Schopenhauer:

> By wine or opium we can intensify and considerably heighten our mental powers, but as soon as the right measure of stimulus is exceeded, the effect will be exactly the opposite.[12]

The double role of opium as a medicinal sedative and as an intellectual, artistic catalyst was well known, and Nietzsche was certainly well aware of the creative possibilities of such substances. In his 1870 essay *The Dionysian Worldview*, a precursor to the extended *Birth of Tragedy*, Nietzsche begins by stating that,

10 Incidentally where Paracelsus is believed to have re-introduced opium (as Laudanum) to Europe in the sixteenth century.

11 Letter to Karl von Gersdorff, 20th October 1870 – my emphases.

12 Arthur Schopenhauer, *Essay on the Freedom of the Will*, ch. III.

> There are two states in which man arrives at the rapturous feeling of existence, namely in dreaming and in intoxication.[13]

He then identifies these two states with the gods Apollo and Dionysus, respectively. Loosely speaking, these are in turn identified with Schopenhauer's world of representation and of will. Apollo, commonly adorned with the ***opium*** poppy, is valued as signifying ordered beauty, whereas Dionysus, the forest god of ***wine*** and trance, is valued as signifying the chaotic drive of unfettered lust and the primal loss of self. In antiquity, Dionysus was regarded as an exotic god who led a procession of bearded satyrs and wild women: the *maenads*. There were a number of Dionysian cults in ancient Greece involving much sex, drugs and loss of control – later to become the orgiastic *Bacchanalia* against which the Roman authorities legislated under threat of death. Under his supposed epithet of Iacchus, Dionysus is also closely associated with the *Eleusinian Mysteries*, beloved of those in psychedelic circles. The son of Zeus, Dionysus is reborn after death – a story that bears equivalences to Christ. In Nietzsche's later works, however, Dionysus becomes explicitly equated to the Antichrist, as we shall show. In Nietzsche's early description of the Dionysian state, one cannot help but compare it to a psychoactive drug report with its consequential come down:

> For the rapture of the Dionysian state with its annihilation of the ordinary bounds and limits of existence contains, while it lasts, a lethargic element in which all personal experience of the past became immersed. This chasm of oblivion separates the worlds of everyday reality and the Dionysian reality. But as soon as this everyday reality re-enters consciousness, it is experienced as such, with nausea: an ascetic, will-negating mood is the fruit of these states. ... In the consciousness of awakening from intoxication he sees everywhere the terrible and absurd in human existence: it nauseates him. Now he understands the wisdom of the forest god.[14]

The link between his coinciding ***opium***-treated illnesses in the Franco-Prussian war and his work on Greek tragedy cannot be overlooked. Indeed Nietzsche made the connection in the later critical preface/postscript he produced for his first book, stating that,

> slowly convalescing from an illness contracted in the field, [I] gave definite form to *The Birth of Tragedy*...[15]

This book puts forward the theory that the origins of Greek tragedy lie in the

---

13 *The Dionysian Worldview*, §1.

14 *The Dionysian Worldview*, §3.

15 *The Birth of Tragedy*, *Attempt at a Self-Criticism*, §1, p. 3.

Dionysian chorus that emerged from the older Dionysian mystical festivals. When fused with the more ordered Apollonian Greek element, the play structure resulted, with Dionysus at first always the tragic protagonist. The true Dionysian state that the tragic play sought to symbolize was one of rapture, of *Rausch*: the rush of intoxication. Thus Nietzsche begins his philosophical career arguing for the emergence of an art form, Tragedy, from intoxicated inspiration. Nietzsche's understanding of this state is gleaned from literature including that of Schopenhauer, and perhaps his own intoxication at the time. Schopenhauer argued that all individuality is but a representation (the *principium individuationis*) and that in its essential depths, our individual will is not separate from the single universal will at the basis of reality. The Dionysian state causes a dread-inducing fragmentation of one's represented individuality, conducing a dispersion of oneself into that deeper metaphysical unity. Nietzsche continues,

> If we add to this dread the blissful ecstasy which, prompted by the same fragmentation of the *principium individuationis*, rises up from man's innermost core, indeed from nature, we are vouchsafed a glimpse into the nature of the Dionysiac, most immediately understandable to using the analogy of intoxication. Under the influence of the narcotic potion hymned by all primitive men and peoples, or in the powerful approach of spring, joyfully penetrating the whole of nature, those Dionysiac urges are awakened, and as they grow more intense, subjectivity becomes a complete forgetting of the self.[16]

In his later postscripted preface to the book, Nietzsche argues that this Dionysian 'madness' might be a 'neurosis of health' – that is, a *healthy madness* which would only appear to be an oxymoron to a culture in decline. In this added section he writes,

> Might visions and hallucinations not have been shared by whole communities, by whole cult gatherings? And what if ... it was madness itself, to use a phrase of Plato's, that brought the greatest blessings upon Greece?[17]

Hence Nietzsche, from the outset, was enthused about narcotic, psychedelic intoxication and its value, whilst simultaneously he himself was becoming increasingly intoxicated as his illness progressed.

Progress it did: severe insomnia, stomach and intestinal pains, eyestrain and increasing blindness creeps up upon his person. In 1876 he is granted a long period of absence from Basel due to his sickness. Many of his personal letters complain of

16 *The Birth of Tragedy*, §1, pp. 16-17.
17 *The Birth of Tragedy, Attempt at a Self-Criticism*, §4, pp. 6-7.

his ailments, to the extent that one judges him to be a 'justified hypochondriac', if that also be not an oxymoron. In 1879 he was forced to completely end his professorship and life at Basel University due to frequent and excessive headaches, nausea, vomiting and seizures.[18] As a result, Nietzsche was now free to pursue an unlimited life of philosophy, which had progressively become his ideal.

Though he left, his ailments did not. The beginning of the 1880s were in fact his most intense period of pain. As well as suffering physiologically, he was saddened by the loss of his friendship with Lou Salomé and Paul Rée. Just before he begins to write what he considered to be his masterpiece, *Thus Spoke Zarathustra*,[19] he writes to his two formerly close friends the following:

> My dears, Lou and Rée:
>
> ... Consider me, the two of you, as a semilunatic with a sore head who has been totally bewildered by long solitude. To this, I think, sensible insight into the state of things I have come after taking a huge dose of ***opium*** – in desperation. But instead of losing my reason as a result, I seem at last to have *come* to reason. ...[20]

Over a decade later Lou Salomé writes in her book, *Friedrich Nietzsche in seinen Werken*, that intoxication and dreams were a central inspiration to Nietzsche's life and philosophy. She writes,

> Nietzsche ... was convinced that especially during conditions of intoxication and dream, a fullness of the past could be revived in the individual's present. Dreams always played a great role in his life and thinking, and during his last years he often drew from them – as with the solution of a riddle – the contents of his teachings. In this manner he employed, for instance, the dream related in Zarathustra (II, "The Soothsayer"), which came to him in the fall of 1882 in Leipzig; he never tired of carrying it about him and interpreting it.[21]

With his concurrent opium use one can compare the inspiration derived from such opium-induced dreaming with that of the Romantics, to whom Nietzsche was ostensibly averse. Nietzsche was also, famously, averse to ***alcohol*** – which he compared unfavourably to opiates in his 1882 book, *The Joyous Science*:

> Perhaps Asians are distinguished above Europeans by a capacity for

18 See Curtis Cate, *Friedrich Nietzsche*, p. 280.

19 The first part of which was published in January 1883.

20 Letter to Lou Salomé and Paul Rée, mid-December 1882. 'Opium' highlighted by me.

21 Lou Salomé, *Friedrich Nietzsche in seinen Werken*, ch. III, p. 144. Also note especially in *Zarathustra* these chapters: "Of Great Events," the coffin-of-masks nightmare in "The Prophet," "The Stillest Hour," "Of The Three Evil Things," and "The Intoxicated Song."

> longer, deeper calm; even their opiates have a slow effect and require patience, as opposed to the disgusting suddenness of the European poison, alcohol.[22]

The reverence and inspiration that Nietzsche derives from opium can also be witnessed in the second edition of that same work, in two poems inspired by poppy-derived ***opium***:

> … Only on my bed flailed,
> Poppy and good conscience, those
> Trusted soporifics, failed. …
>
> One hour passed, or two, or three–
> Or a year? – when suddenly
> All my thoughts and mind were drowned
> In timeless monotony:
> An abyss without a ground
> Opened up – not one more sound. …[23]

Such opium pipe-dream poetry ranks alongside those of the Kubla Khan clan. In a subsequent poem, Nietzsche poses the problem of his pain via poppies:

> … Pain writes with daggers that are flying
> Into my bones:
> "World has no heart;
> The fool bears her a grudge and groans."
>
> Pour poppies, pour,
> O fever! Poison in my brain!
> You test my brow too long with pain.
> Why do you ask, "For what reward?" …
>
> You fever, I should bless?–[24]

Nietzsche's ills were treated by him as both a superficial curse and as a deeper blessing. It was the ailments that necessitated the ***opiates*** and other drugs, which in turn further inspired his thought. A physiologically healthy Nietzsche may have dissipated into the shadows of history. In this respect his drug use was a vital condition of his profound, earth-shattering philosophy which uncovered and uprooted the morbidly entrenched covert legacy of Christianity in western society.

22 *The Joyous Science*, Book I, §43.
23 *The Joyous Science*, Appendix, "The Mysterious Bark," p. 359.
24 *The Joyous Science*, Appendix, "Rimus remedium," p. 365.

Nietzsche pushed himself to, and perhaps beyond, the limits of human intellectualization. To fuel this heroic drive even ***opium***-injected dreams may not have sufficed. As Lou Salomé, to whom Nietzsche twice proposed, continued to write in her biography of the man:

> And yet, the tranquil dream is insufficient for that quest. What is needed is a much more real, effective, and even more terrible experiencing, namely through orgiastic Dionysian conditions and the chaos of frenzied passions – yes madness itself as a means of sinking back down into the mass of entwined feelings and imaginings. This seemed for Nietzsche the last road into the primal depths imbedded within us.
>
> Quite early Nietzsche had brooded over the meaning of madness as a possible source for knowledge and its inner sense that may have led the ancients to discern a sign of divine election.[25]

Did Nietzsche seek to induce divine madness so as to fully intuit the depths of the psyche? With this in mind, his famous maxim "What does not kill you makes you stronger"[26] takes on a form applicable to the intake of psychoactive substances. Did Nietzsche take hazardous mixes and doses of psychoactive drugs? Yes. It may have made his philosophy stronger, but it may have killed him as a philosopher too – this was certainly the view of his mother:

> He used all the sleeping medications that have ever been invented, said the professors. His worst one was chloral. That one practically killed him.[27]

Chloral, and its admixture with water, ***chloral hydrate***, was a common sedative in the nineteenth century, now a controlled substance. More than opium, this drug appears to be Nietzsche's preferred poison. In a letter to his friend and former colleague, Franz Overbeck, he writes in 1883:

> I realized that in the last two months I have consumed 50 grams of ***chloral hydrate*** (pure). I never slept without this drug! But I have slept, now, after fourteen days in a row – oh what bliss![28]

In one of her biographies of her brother, Elisabeth Förster-Nietzsche – who at times took care of Nietzsche – remonstrates against his abuse of chloral:

> In the winter of 1882-3, owing to that terrible influenza, he had

25 Lou Salomé, *Friedrich Nietzsche in seinen Werken*, ch. III, p. 145.
26 *Twilight of the Idols*, "Maxims," §8, p. 33.
27 1893, as reported by Heinrich Lec in *Conversations with Nietzsche*, §75, p. 230.
28 Letter to Franz Overbeck, 1st February 1883. My emphasis.

> for the first time used ***chloral*** regularly, in large doses. He was so unfavourably impressed with its peculiar effects that in the spring of 1883 he did his best to cure himself of the habit. ... [When] he took chloral before going to bed, it led next morning to a curiously excitable condition, in which men and things appeared to him in a totally false light. Towards noon, he thought, this condition vanished, and more "philanthropic sentiments" returned. Accordingly he had become very careful, although the sleep produced by chloral seems to have been remarkably pleasant – not dull and heavy but filled with delightful dreams. ... If only he had kept to this one drug, however, the result might have been less serious.[29]

So his mother and sister both maintained that it was the effect of large doses and mixtures of drugs that brought Nietzsche his cognitive ruin, his madness.[30] ***Chloral hydrate*** was synthesised in 1832, and since 1869 had been used for hypnotic or sedative purposes, i.e. for sleep induction and pain relief. It is now known to be potentially hazardous with a risk of death in the case of intoxication. It is not commonly considered a psychedelic drug, yet it can produce visions and auditory 'hallucinations'.

One of Nietzsche's students reported that,

> Insomnia, which was not improved by repeated overwork, by ***chloral*** or ***potassium bromide***, but made worse, excruciating headaches, and other neuralgic ailments tormented his life.[31]

Potassium bromide is an anticonvulsant (anti-seizure) and sedative drug, and is used today in veterinary practice, and in Germany is still administered to human beings. Nietzsche's dual use of ***chloral*** and ***potassium bromide*** is notable because it was this combination that led to the bewildering experiences of the English author Evelyn Waugh. These effects affected him to such a degree that they provide the content to his peculiar autobiographical work, *The Ordeal of Gilbert Pinfold.* This concocted sleeping-draught caused auditory and conceptual hallucinations, often in a terrifying manner, with voices suggesting suicide. When Waugh was admitted to St Bartholomew's Hospital for treatment, his regular chloral was immediately withdrawn and replaced with paraldehyde, a move that immediately stopped the hallucinations.[32]

---

29 Elisabeth Förster-Nietzsche, *The Life of Nietzsche*, vol. II, ch. XXVII. My emphasis.

30 His sister may have had an ulterior motive to promote this narcotic view of the cause of his madness: to dismiss claims that syphilis was to blame (see, e.g., E. F. Podach). But as we see, it was not only his sister who spoke of his excessive use of chloral – and besides, madness onset by ongoing drug abuse is hardly more respectable than student-era brothel debauchery.

31 H. Göring, *Conversations with Nietzsche*, §38, p. 100. My emphases.

32 See Selina Hastings, *Evelyn Waugh: A Biography.*

The well-known neurologist Oliver Sacks has also written of the psychedelic experiences that chloral hydrate caused him:

> Depressed and insomniac, I was taking ever-increasing amounts of ***chloral hydrate*** to get to sleep, and was up to fifteen times the usual dose every night. ... [But] for the first time in several months I went to bed without my usual knockout dose. ... [Upon] waking , I found myself excruciatingly sensitive to sounds. ... I went across the road, as I often did, for a cup of coffee and a sandwich. As I was stirring the coffee it suddenly turned green, then purple. I looked up, startled, and saw a huge proboscidean head, like an elephant seal. Panic seized me; I slammed a five-dollar note on the table and ran across the road to a bus on the other side. But all the passengers on the bus seemed to have smooth white heads like giant eggs, with huge glittering eyes like the faceted compound eyes of insects – their eyes seemed to move in sudden jerks, which increased the feeling of their fearfulness and alienness.[33]

In the end Sacks discovered that it was the fact that he had stopped taking chloral that caused the hallucinations, a case of *delirium tremens*. Thus we see that chloral hydrate is addictive, toxic, and directly and posteriorly hallucinatory. Taken in large doses and mixed with other drugs, the effects can only be potent. There is an account of a psychedelic experience Nietzsche had in mid-August 1884. His friend Resa von Schirnhofer decided to visit Nietzsche in Sils-Maria, Switzerland. After an absence of one and a half days, von Schirnhofer ventures to his house and is led into the dining room – then:

> As I stood waiting by the table, the door to the adjacent room on the right opened, and Nietzsche appeared. With a distraught expression on his pale face, he leaned wearily against the post of the half-opened door and immediately began to speak about the unbearableness of his ailment. He described to me how, **when he closed his eyes, he saw an abundance of fantastic flowers, winding and intertwining, constantly growing and changing forms and colours in exotic luxuriance, sprouting one out of the other.** "I never get any rest," he complained...[34]

Von Schirnhofer also tells of Nietzsche's unorthodox and deviant means of acquiring his drugs:

> In Rapallo and in other places of the Riviera di Levante, where he

33 Oliver Sacks, *Hallucinations*, ch. VI, pp. 115-116. My emphasis.
34 *Conversations with Nietzsche*, §52, p. 164. My emphasis.

> had spent his times of worst health, he had written for himself all kinds of prescriptions signed Dr Nietzsche, which had been prepared and filled without question or hesitation. Unfortunately I took no notes and the only one I remember is ***chloral hydrate***. But since Nietzsche, as he expressly told me, had been surprised never to be asked whether he was a medical doctor authorized to prescribe this kind of medication, I conclude that some dubious medicines must have been among them.[35]

So Nietzsche, a user of the addictive substance opium since at least 1870, a heavy chloral hydrate user, and a proponent of the intoxicated Dionysian state, uses his doctoral title to prescribe himself the drugs he wants. If ever the term *drug fiend* were applied to a true philosopher, Nietzsche would fit the case. '**Psychonaut**' certainly fits, a name coined by philosopher Ernst Jünger,[36] whom Heidegger called 'the only genuine continuer of Nietzsche'.[37] Von Schirnhofer speculated over whether Nietzsche also used ***hashish***, stating that his intensive reading of French authors must have included Charles Baudelaire who wrote of hashish and opium trances in *Artificial Paradises*, and in *The Flowers of Evil.*

In *Ecce Homo*, his autobiography, Nietzsche writes,

> If one wants to get free from an unendurable pressure one needs ***hashish***. Very well, I needed Wagner.[38]

This suggests Nietzsche was not a hashish user, at least not a frequent one. But with Nietzsche's somewhat haughty position, his belief in a necessary 'pathos of distance'[39] between people, and his championing of great men of intellect and art, he must have felt endeared and perhaps tempted by Baudelaire's words on the drug:

> I am not asserting that hashish produces in all men all of the [fantastical] effects I have described here. I have more or less recounted the phenomena generally produced, except for a few variations, among individuals of artistic and philosophical bent. … But there are others in whom the drug raises only a raucous madness, a violent merriment resembling vertigo … [yet it can conduce] the extreme development of the poetic mind…[40]

---

35 *Conversations with Nietzsche*, §52, p. 163. My emphases.
36 See his *Annäherungen: Drogen und Rausch (Approaches to Drugs and Intoxication)*, 1970. In Nietzsche's *Daybreak*, §575, he refers to himself as an *'aeronaut of the spirit'*.
37 *Gesamtausgabe,* Band 90, 227.
38 *Ecce Homo*, "Clever," §6. My emphasis.
39 See *On the Genealogy of Morality*, bk I, §2.
40 Charles Baudelaire, *Artificial Paradises*, On Wine and Hashish (1851), §V, p. 23.

Whether or not Nietzsche took hashish he certainly exhibited an extreme development of the poetic mind. In a passage in his autobiography, Nietzsche speaks of the singular, overwhelming type of inspiration with which he is bequeathed. Though he does not connect Nietzsche's 'inspiration' to his drug use, the Nietzsche biographer Curtis Cate asserts of this passage that 'his description of the hallucinating moments of inspiration during which he felt powerless and "possessed" merits a place in any good anthology of mystical experiences'.[41] When we consider the view that psychedelic experiences *are* mystical experiences, in the vein of William James' varieties thereof,[42] we can agree with this assessment. As we saw with Waugh and Sacks, chloral hydrate can cause auditory and visual hallucinations, a drug we know Nietzsche self-prescribed and used in high doses. It is highly plausible then that Nietzsche's 'inspiration' was drug-induced hallucination – and no less valuable for that. In fact, his revelations can be witnessed as testimony to the potential supreme value of psychedelic chemicals within the right mind:

> Has anyone at the end of the nineteenth century a distinct conception of what poets of strong ages called *inspiration*? … If one had the slightest residue of superstition left in one, one would hardly be able to set aside the idea that one is merely incarnation, merely mouthpiece, merely medium of overwhelming forces. The concept of revelation, in the sense that something suddenly, with unspeakable certainty and subtlety, becomes *visible*, audible, something that shakes and overturns one to the depths, simply describes the fact. One hears, one does not seek; one takes, one does not ask who gives; a thought flashes up like lightning, with necessity, unfalteringly formed – I have never had any choice. An ecstasy whose tremendous tension sometimes discharges itself in a flood of tears, whilst one's steps now involuntarily rush along, now involuntarily lag; a complete being outside of oneself with the distinct consciousness of a multitude of subtle shudders and trickles down to one's toes; a depth of happiness in which the most painful and gloomy things appear … Everything is in the highest degree involuntary but takes place as in a tempest of a feeling of freedom, of absoluteness, of power, of divinity. … This is *my* experience of inspiration; I do not doubt that one has to go back thousands of years to find anyone who could say to me "it is mine also".[43]

As Lou Salomé intimated, Nietzsche may have pushed himself to the edge of madness to overcome the common condition of man to taste divinity. Was it his psychedelic inspiration that caused both his psychological apotheosis and his

41 Curtis Cate, *Friedrich Nietzsche*, ch. 38, p. 541.

42 See William James, *The Varieties of Religious Experience*, ch. XVI.

43 *Ecce Homo*, Zarathustra, §3. See also Nietzsche's description of a philosopher in *Beyond Good and Evil*, §292.

physiological downfall? With regard to his downfall, his sister believed that,

> The correct diagnosis, perhaps, would be this: a brain exhausted by overstrain of the nerves of head and eye that could no longer resist taking drugs to excess, and thus became disabled.[44]

Nietzsche's infamous[45] sister also describes another drug that she blamed for his stroke into mental destruction in 1889: the ***Javanese narcotic***:

> Above all I regard two sleeping draughts, ***chloral*** and ***Javanese narcotic***, as responsible for his paralytic stroke ... [In] 1884, so far as I remember, he got to know a Dutchman, who recommended him a Javanese narcotic, and presented him with a fairly large bottle ... The stuff tasted like rather strong alcohol and had an outlandish smell ... The Dutchman impressed us with the fact that only a few drops should be taken at a time in a glass of water. I tried it, and observed a somewhat exhilarating effect. ... Later, in the autumn of 1885, he confessed to me that on one occasion he had taken a few drops too much, with the result that he suddenly threw himself to the ground in a fit of convulsive laughter. ... During the early days of his insanity he used often to say in confidence to our mother that he "had taken twenty drops" (he did not mention of what), and that his brain had then "gone off the track." ... Perhaps the worst of it all was that he used both chloral and the Javanese drug at the same time.[46]

The island of Java was part of the colonized Dutch East Indies. In 1875 coca plants were introduced to Java, eventually leading to the *Nederlandsche Cocaïne Fabriek* in 1900, the year of Nietzsche's death. The Javanese coca leaf was not as potent as its Peruvian sibling in Nietzsche's time, but it was cheaper.[47] The Javanese narcotic his sister spoke of thus likely contained traces of ***cocaine***, and possibly the assorted herbs of the traditional Indonesian healing concoction ***Jamu***. It would be surprising that combining *this* combination with ***chloral, opium, potassium bromide***, etc., would not lead to hallucinations, madness, mental breakdown, and perceived apotheosis:

---

44 Elisabeth Förster-Nietzsche, *The Life of Nietzsche*, vol. II, ch. XXVII.

45 Walter Benjamin sees the lady in this light in his own psychedelic mescaline experience: 'From the cracks of the Förster House grow tufts of hair. The Förster House: (she [Elisabeth Förster-Nietzsche] has turned the Nietzsche Archive into a Förster House [forester's lodge]) the Förster house is of red stone. I am a spindle in its banister: an obdurate, hardened post. But that is no longer the totem pole – only a wretched copy. Chamois' foot or horse's hoof of the devil: a vagina symbol.' (*On Hashish*, ch. XI, 22nd May 1934.)

46 Elisabeth Förster-Nietzsche, *The Life of Nietzsche*, vol. II, ch. XXVII. My emphases.

47 See Toine Pieters' *Java Coca and the Dutch Narcotics Industry: An Almost Forgotten 20th C. History of Drugs* Story: https://pointsadhsblog.wordpress.com/2012/12/10/java-coca-and-the-dutch-narcotics-industry-an-almost-forgotten-20th-c-history-of-drugs-story/

Nietzsche signed off final letters of 1889 with the name Dionysus,[48] whom he had recently identified as the Antichrist:

> Who knows the true name of the Antichrist? – with the name of a Greek god: I called it the Dionysiac.[49]

In Nietzsche's mature work, Dionysus becomes a representation of the **Overman** figure: a type that affirms and revels in pain and destruction, the polar contrary to the Christian type who only values joy in peace and comfort. In 1888 Nietzsche exclaims:

> Affirmation of life even in its strangest and sternest problems, the will to life rejoicing in its own inexhaustibility through the sacrifice of its highest types – that is what I called Dionysian … beyond pity and terror, to realize in oneself the eternal joy of becoming – that joy which also encompasses joy in destruction … I am the last disciple of the philosopher Dionysus.[50]

One of England's earliest disciples of Nietzsche, Alfred Richard Orage, claimed that the Overman, or Superman, requires transcendent forms of mind – forms that Dionysian psychedelic intoxicants may evoke:

> [The] Superman is strictly indefinable. … It is probable, indeed, that new faculties, new modes of consciousness, will be needed, as the mystics have always declared; and that the differencing element of man and Superman will be the possession of these.[51]

After *The Birth of Tragedy*, Dionysus returns to Nietzsche's philosophy in 1886 in *Beyond Good and Evil*. Now, rather than subservient to Schopenhauer's unwitting Christian values, Dionysus represents Nietzsche's radical revaluation of those values that lie hidden beneath western culture, and thus does Dionysus denote a new form of thinking – without doubt a dangerous form to many. In this extreme opposition to such sacerdotal ideology, one understands why Dionysus *is* the Antichrist, both of whom *are* Nietzsche. He is the Antichrist Psychonaut: his pagan philosopher forest god of intoxication speaks to him – perhaps in the mode of his aforementioned 'inspiration', or black revelation:

48 E.g. to Cosima Wagner: 'Ariadne, I love you. – Dionysus' (Early January, 1889). In *Beyond Good and Evil*, §295, (1886) Nietzsche writes, 'Dionysus … once said, "In certain cases I love human beings" (and he was alluding to Ariadne, who was present)…'

49 *The Birth of Tragedy*, Attempt at a Self-Criticism, §5. 1886.

50 *Twilight of the Idols*, Ancients, §5. A Dionysian will thus welcome the 'bad trip', and desire its eternal return.

51 *Friedrich Nietzsche: The Dionysian Spirit of the Age*, ch. IV, p. 75

> "...I often think how I can help [mankind] go forward and make them stronger, deeper, and more evil than they are." "Stronger, deeper, and more evil?" I asked, frightened. "Yes," he said once again, "stronger, deeper, and more evil – more beautiful too." And at that the tempter god smiled his halcyon smile, as if he had just uttered a charming compliment.[52]

A new Dionysian cult based on Nietzsche's reformulation of the god might very well suffer the same capital jurisdictive fate as that which befell its Roman predecessors. Whatever the future yields, Nietzsche's philosophy will be a significant factor thereof. His philosophy has already, a century on, had a decisive impact upon history. That this philosophy was provoked, in a degree hitherto undiagnosed, by reveries occasioned by chemical measures exposes one to the realization of the great power of these substances, powers guiding history. Nietzsche risked himself, his sanity, his life, so to touch the heavens and taste the Hades of human mentality – he may thereby have destroyed himself. But destruction is a joy to Dionysus, a deity to be born again.

Bibliography

-~- Baudelaire, C. (1860/1996) *Artificial Paradises,* New York: Citadel

-~- Benjamin, W. (1927-34/2006) *On Hashish*, Cambridge: Belknap Press of Harvard University

-~- Breazeale, D. – *Ecce Psycho: Remarks on the case of Nietzsche* (International Studies in Philosophy XXIII/2)

-~- Cate, C. (2002) *Friedrich Nietzsche,* London: Random House

-~- De Quincey, T. (1821/1994) *Confessions of an English Opium Eater*, Ware: Wordsworth Classics

-~- Förster-Nietzsche, E. (1915/2007) *The Life of Nietzsche–Volume 2*, The Classics

-~- Gilman, S. L. (ed.) (1987) *Conversations with Nietzsche*, Oxford: Oxford University Press

-~- Greenfield, R. (2006) *Timothy Leary: A Biography,* Orlando: Harcourt Books

-~- Hastings, S. (1994). *Evelyn Waugh: A Biography*, London: Sinclair-Stevenson

-~- James, W. (1902/1985) *The Varieties of Religious Experience*, London: Penguin

-~- Jünger, E. (1970/1980) *Annäherungen: Drogen und Rausch*, Stuttgart: Klett-Cotta im Ullstein Taschenbuch

-~- Khazaee, M. K. – *The Case of Nietzsche's Madness* (Existenz, Vol. 3, No. 1, Spring 2008)

-~- Lippit, J. & Urpeth, J. (ed.s) (2000) *Nietzsche and the Divine*, Manchester: Clinamen Press

52 *Beyond Good and Evil,* §295.

–w– Middleton, C. (ed.) (1969/1996) *Selected Letter of Friedrich Nietzsche*, Indianapolis: Hackett
–w– Nietzsche, F. (1870/1997) *The Dionysian Worldview* (Journal of Nietzsche Studies, No. 13, Spring 1997, pp. 81 – 97)
–w– Nietzsche, F. (1871/1993) *The Birth of Tragedy*, London: Penguin
–w– Nietzsche, F. (1881/1997) *Daybreak*, Cambridge: Cambridge University Press
–w– Nietzsche, F. (1882/1974) *The Gay Science*, New York: Vintage
–w– Nietzsche, F. (1883/1969) *Thus Spoke Zarathustra*, London: Penguin
–w– Nietzsche, F. (1886/2008) *Beyond Good and Evil*, Oxford: Oxford University Press
–w– Nietzsche, F. (1887/1998) *On the Genealogy of Morality*, Indianapolis: Hackett
–w– Nietzsche, F. (1888/1992) *Ecce Homo*, London: Penguin
–w– Nietzsche, F. (1889/1990) *Twilight of the Idols* and *The Antichrist*, London: Penguin
–w– Nietzsche, F. (1906[ph]]/1968) *The Will to Power*, New York: Random House
–w– Nussbaum, M. C. – *The Transfigurations of Intoxication: Nietzsche, Schopenhauer, and Dionysus* (Arion: A Journal of Humanities and the Classics, Third Series, Vo. 1, No. 2, Spring 1991, pp. 75 – 111)
–w– Orage, A. R. (1906) *Friedrich Nietzsche: The Dionysian Spirit of the Age*, London: T. N. Foulis
–w– Sacks, O. (2012) *Hallucinations*, New York: Random House
–w– Podach, E. F. (1930/1974) *The Madness of Nietzsche*, New York: Gordon Press
–w– Salomé, L. (1894/2001) *Nietzsche*, Illinois: Illinois
–w– Schopenhauer, A. (1818/1966) *The World as Will and Representation, volume 1*, New York: Dover
–w– Schopenhauer, A. (1839/2005) *Essay on the Freedom of the Will*, Mineola: Dover
–w– Waugh, E. (1957/1973) *The Ordeal of Gilbert Pinfold*, London: Chapman & Hall
–w– www.nietzschesource.org

Lux Per Nox: The Fenris Wolf As Libidinal Liberator

Carl Abrahamsson

"Vavtrudner said: / The Wolf will devour / Allfather, / but him will Vidar / venge; / cold jaws / he will split / in the moment / of battle."[1]

The Fenris Wolf is not only the title of this delightful tome you're currently holding in your hands. It is also the name of a mythical creature/force in the Scandinavian Asatro (=belief in the Asa gods) pantheon, and one that deserves careful study as possibly the most important agent of that entire pantheon. He is usually associated with the end of the world/existing order – "Ragnarök" – and therefore usually carries the heavy baggage of negative projections. But what does the "end of the world" really mean?

The Scandinavian myths are developments of basic Indo-European myths and religious stories. These usually deal with a ritualized, "religionized" repetition of the original cosmic creation, amplifying how important it has been/is for the human being to know (or at least mythologize) one's own roots as far back as one possibly can. Conscious continuity is a quintessentially important part of human identity. When the myths and gods are allowed to act out eternal dilemmas and mysteries, it is easier to structure human culture and life in an emotionally healthy and life-affirming way.

The myths themselves usually tell us of a cyclic structure: there are eras, periods, and times, in which movements of nature and destiny occur, disappear, and reoccur. Undoubtedly, this is a remnant of assessment and insight deep inside the human psyche (and very likely even relegated to DNA), after having carefully watched how nature works. The greater the trauma of the unexpected or anomalous, the greater the mythic impact. So, when things have turned really sour, and when there are still people around to tell that specific story, it will be an important piece of the storyline; more so than tales about when everything has been perfect, peachy and harmonious – if that has ever happened!

Natural disasters, wars, conflicts, upheavals, pandemics, and other agents of enforced change throughout the millennia, have all been integrated in therapeutically valid stories that have then grown to become myths – if relevant enough.

The "end of the world" today means something quite different from what it did

1 "Sången om Vavtrudner," paragraph 53, in *Eddan*, Niloe, Stockholm, 1982, p 49. Translation by the author.

to people five thousand years ago, and ten thousand years ago, and so on. Even a hundred years ago. But as that horrific moment is usually intimately tied in with a very central cathartic message – the promise of a new order and new life – it's usually in these actually catastrophic tales that we can evaluate the health of the society in question. Because regardless if the end comes through an inexplicable natural disaster or through a very distinct human warfare, human beings could (can) only cope with the trauma of the lost paradise by repeatedly telling the story of hope in an abstracted, mythologized fashion. If the myths are actively integrated in the culture, then the tribe, group, society or community will be more harmonious than if there is some kind of negation or repression of these traumatic histories.

In this sense, the myths that deal with regeneration and cyclic passages of "destiny" are of great value, because they usually connect more to the actual trauma than to its possible aftermath. The disaster in itself is always more revealing than any post facto constructions. The main question being: "What are the reasons for the end?"

Ragnarök is a phenomenon or matrix that could be applied to any psychological or historical process, but for the sake of Fenris himself, let's stick to the classic story here: At the end of the world, trickster god Loke's three children do what they have to do: Hel opens up her sphere and lets out hordes of dead people (not the heroic kind that went to Oden's Valhalla, but just normal folks); the world-encircling Midgård snake, who usually keeps the world in order by biting its own tail underneath the surface of the oceans, provokes thunder god Tor to the ultimate fight (in which they both die); Fenris breaks free from the Asa gods' fetters, kills main god Oden, and devours the sun. As the old structure is slain, there is mayhem, chaos, violence, bloodshed, terror and despair.

But the old poems and sagas don't stop there: at the supposed end. Although Fenris kills Oden, Vidar (Oden's son) then kills Fenris, and there are also other Asa kids who are ready to take over. So basically, the story – although essentially catastrophic – brings not only a new beginning but also a distinct mythic attachment to the continual rebirth of order and harmony. It's a basic and violent story; in many ways reflecting the culture at the time. Yet it also contains hope, eloquently expressed in literary wealth and beauty.

To fully understand the Fenris Wolf as a mythic creature, we have to look at the ancestry or heritage. Fenris is the son of Loke, the Scandinavian trickster god, who was painted in quite Satanic colors by the main post-heathen storyteller: the Icelandic Christian historian Snorre Sturlason. Loke is a highly integrated instigator of intrigue, conflict, provocative behavior, etc. There are many key myths/stories in which Loke is central to not only the story as such but also to its inherent morals. In this sense – of Loke as an ambiguous *agent provocateur* in the world of the gods – we see genuine Satanic semblance and function. Loke is essentially the force that provokes situations so that the main issues can be resolved. There is always ambivalence and ambiguity in regard to Loke as a necessary trickster, and there are many stories that leave the reader with a sense of comic relief and respect for him, rather than, as for the Christian formulators, as an inherently evil figure creating chaos.

The necessity of appropriating an integrated trickster has never been lost on the Christians though. As Anton LaVey, founder of the Church of Satan (1966) so aptly wrote in his *The Satanic Bible* (1969): "Satan has been the best friend the church has ever had, as he has kept it in business all these years!"[2] Without the "negative" example, the "positive" order cannot be upheld for long. Essentially, scapegoating is as inherently human as the capacity for suicide. The more strictly dualistic the portrayal of the trickster is, the poorer the religious culture.

In Asatro then, it seems that Loke is an irritating but still necessary element in the overall health of the culture. There is ample evidence (or if not "evidence," then at least highly illuminating pointers) that Loke was a central force in upholding rituals and communal balance through his own, unique spirit of transgression.

One of the most entertaining parts in the Edda anthology is "Lokaträtan" (The Loke Arguments), in which Loke spews forth his vitriolic accusations against the gods. No-one is spared, not even Oden himself. Oden and Loke accuse each other of unmanliness, and the main accusation against Loke is that he carried and gave birth to a child while in the shape of a mare. This, however, was part of a solution that benefitted all of Asgård.

To protect Asgård from attacks, mainly from giants, the gods make a deal with a giant master builder who says he can build a strong wall around Asgård. If he can do that within a limited and short time, the gods promise that he will be amply rewarded. But as they notice that the giant is about to actually succeed – thanks to a magical stallion that can keep on working even though the giant himself is asleep – the gods fear that they will actually have to pay up. Loke then transforms himself into a beautiful mare that lures the builder's horse away. The builder fails to finish in time, and the gods rejoice at both their new wall and that they won't have to pay the cost. As the result of this scheme and tryst, Loke gives birth to Sleipner, the eight-legged horse that Oden takes as his own, and which allows him to swiftly and proto-shamanically travel in-between spheres and states of mind.

Loke often becomes a victim of his own intrigues, as if he has a pathological need of being in trouble; of shaking things up. But he also assumes, post facto, the responsibility of cleaning up the mess; alone or together with the particular Asa god who's concerned.

It is not only through sly cunning that Loke wriggles out of trouble. It is also by using transgressive magics that were not usually used by the Asa gods. Although basically all of the gods have shapeshifting abilities (some use this potential more than others), Loke takes the magic one step further by also shifting gender and/or sexual perspective and position.

Loke's unconscious (?) provocations lead to a distinctly Promethean punishment: enchainment in a cave, complete with dripping snake-venom as torture. The violent reactions from the captured Loke lead to earthquakes – a premonition of Ragnarök.

2 LaVey, Anton, *The Satanic Bible*, Avon Books, New York, 1969, p 25.

The drops from the snake are collected by his wife, Sigyn, inside the cave. Instead of integrating Loke's painful revelations and wisdoms, the Asa gods choose to repress them.

Trickster gods/forces are present in many cultures. Two that are similar to Loke are Islam's "green man" figure of Khadir or Khezr, and the Yoruban Eshu (a.k.a. Legba in other West African spheres).

> The upside-down qualities of Khezr's way reminds us of those clown societies among the American Indians whose humor consists of doing the opposite to everything normal, wearing shoes on their head, talking backwards, outraging moral conventions and authority. This clowning hides a deep wisdom in ridicule and whimsy, and such societies operate under the sign of the Trickster, using laughter to storm the gates of heaven – or to slip through like a thief.[3]

Loke as a devil or a demon? I think not. These much wider attributions were simply demagogic ones from Christian proselytizers like Snorre. But a highly valuable trickster figure and force, for sure. This then is Fenris's father: an integrated force of transgression – one needed for overall and eventual health and balance. What about Fenris's mother, then?

Angerboda is the giantess who gives birth to the feared trio of ferocious forces. As Loke is also a giant (although a skilled and shapeshifting one), these kids should technically be solid giants too, but none of them are.

The meaning of Angerboda's name has been a matter of debate. The predominant perspective is simply etymological, claiming that Anger is the present Swedish "ånger" (regret) and Boda refers to the Swedish "båda" (in the sense provoke, conjure: "att uppbåda"). I would like to suggest an explanation that I think has more relevance for the big picture here: Anger is actually related more to the Swedish word for "meadow" (Äng). The colloquial word for vagina in Swedish is "fitta" (=cunt), and the original meaning of that word is a meadow, moist from either rain or dew. The word Od is also highly relevant here. Not only is it the root of the name Oden, but also of the "concept:" Od means "ecstatic rage" in old Swedish.[4]

Freja, the goddess of sex and sensuality (among other things), once had a husband or lover named Od. When he left to go roaming, she cried "red tears of gold" (undoubtedly a menstrual metaphor). The fallen heroes of the battlefield are divided between Oden and Freja, and she was the one who taught Oden the dark, magical wisdom and methodology of the Sejd system. Considering the many similarities and interactions between Freja and Oden proper, it is more than likely

---

3 Wilson, Peter Lamborn, "The Green Man – The Trickster Figure In Sufism," *Gnosis Magazine,* no 19, San Francisco, 1991, p 26.

4 Ström, Folke, *Nordisk Hedendom – Tro och sed i förkristen tid,* Akademiförlaget/Esselte Studium, Stockholm, 1985, p 182.

that Od is in fact Oden. Seen in this light, I would argue that Angerboda is the vagina or womb Oden uses for the specific magical working of Ragnarök.

Given that Oden once mixed his blood with the very unlikely contender Loke (and thereby confused all of Asgård), the seemingly blurred identities now in many ways become quite clear. Loke often travels with Oden, and they experience all kinds of mischievous shenanigans together, many of which the other gods can or will not understand at all. The mixing of Oden's blood with his was the only reason why Loke was welcome in Asgård. The Fenris Wolf was therefore actually raised in Asgård but when he became too unruly and ferocious (puberty!), he had to be fettered.

The Angerboda progeny are all essential for the Ragnarök process, and although Oden will be devoured by Fenris, he is certainly no stranger to "sacrificing himself to himself" – given that he received the knowledge and wisdom of the runes by self-asphyxiation, hanging from the world tree Yggdrasil. Oden may be masculinely adorned with a phallic spear and two controllable male wolves (Gere & Freke), but in the shape of Loke he can not only dress and act as a female, but actually have ritual sex, receive semen and give birth to magical creatures (like his own horse Sleipner). Loke is in many ways Oden's anima and/or shadow; the very aspect that allows for the transgressive magic that Freja taught him to manifest, and thereby to change the course of destiny. Taking into account that Oden's main epithet is "Allfather," it is not surprising that even the end is conceived, conjured and controlled by him.

In the Swedish language, the word "wolf" can be translated into either "ulv" or "varg." Ulv is an older description of what we call "Canis Lupus," and it's also how kids have usually been presented with the concept in school: "Fenrisulven," the Fenris Wolf. The other word, "varg," is considerably more common today than "ulv" (which is mostly present in the masculine name "Ulf") but traditionally this was not associated with Canis Lupus per se, but with an outsider-ship that required draconian or punitive measures. To be "varg" was to be ostracized. For instance, a murderer would in old Swedish be a "mordvarg," and an arsonist a "brännvarg."

Seen from this perspective, Fenris is both "ulv" and "varg." Scandinavian farmers were undoubtedly respectful of the ferocious Canis Lupus in their vicinity, and the deeper aspect (of fear rather than respect) surely created this mythic Gestalt imprint of a somehow constantly threatening wolf or wolfpack that could certainly endanger an entire microcosm of a homestead or small farm.

Continuing on this ancestral or familial trail, let's also look at Fenris's two siblings by Angerboda. They are the Midgård snake and the "goddess" Hel, who rules over the queendom of the same name.

Hel is fully integrated in a sphere that is feared yet inevitable and irreversible. No-one escapes Hel, except for the warriors who have valiantly died in battle (half of which go to Oden's Valhalla, and half to Freja). Hel is simply an accepted and necessary sphere/state.

Although visions and cultural concepts changed over time to actively include resting places such as the burial mound itself or even designated mountains of death, Hel as a mythic afterlife sphere was the predominant one. And that surely keeps Fenris's sister continually busy, up until Ragnarök proper, when she opens the gates and lets the dead roam free.

"Midgård" is the name of the human sphere in the Scandinavian mythology/cosmogony, just like "Asgård" is that of the Asa gods. So the Midgård snake relates specifically to the sphere of the humans, and was originally cast out by Oden to encircle that sphere, and thereby to keep it tight and safe (Midgård is an Ouroboros, biting its own tail).

As for the Midgård snake and the Fenris Wolf himself, mention in the Edda poems (and prose renditions) and other stories is mainly focused on that very final battle between cosmos and chaos. The end of the world, "Ragnarök" (a.k.a. the Wagnerian/Nietzschean "twilight of the gods") pushes them both forward to fulfill their destinies: to help end the current cosmos, unleash chaos, but thereby aiding a non-corrupt cosmos to be born from the debris and ashes.

If all central myths are "generative" or "regenerative," the Scandinavian ones should not constitute any exceptions to that rule. If we stick with the ever so relevant magico-anthropolgical concept of *Sympathesis*, we see that there is always more that unites than sets apart. Each specific culture evokes its own myths (or flavors of older ones) that are designed to allow for the original fodder to transcend itself. An individual self transcendence and/or a cultural ditto is therefore the key to understanding any magico-anthropological motivations or perspectives.

Examples of this would be the rigid hierarchical structuring of religion within Judaism, and its release and transcendence in the ultra-intellectual, mental system of Cabala. Another would be moments of insight and possible epiphany within complex intellectual systems like the Western Ceremonial Magical Tradition (as exemplified by the Golden Dawn, etc.). The individual mind is not able to set itself genuinely free before it succumbs to and penetrates the predominant structure/system itself – whichever it may be. The inherent magic of the human mind constructs a culture that constructs a magic that will eventually allow for a transcendence of itself.

If we return to the Asa sphere and its inevitable Ragnarök, we can easily see that the issue is not merely causally "(re)generative" (as in larger mysteries of natural fertility), but rather more specifically sexual. Transcendence comes when addressing the moral problems of any more or less homogenous culture (like the Scandinavian). In this sphere we have the symbolic gods as proxies for all the basic human dilemmas in times of extreme hardship, a brutal climate, and a reliance on strong bonds, allegiances, and kinships. Transcendence here makes itself manifest in a quasi-humourous acceptance of very basic desires and foibles. But when push comes to shove, one has to protect one's own sphere – with any amount of violence, if need be. The structuring of violent retribution through complex aspects of Lex Talionis was another form of important transcendence, in which the Scandinavian mind frame and societies developed from an emotionally reactive anarchy to a more or less orderly adherence to rules, bureaucracy, and processes of law.

Why are the Ragnarökian mysteries essentially of a sexual nature? It's because ancient cultures existed in a continual learning process, in which the inner Angst of death mixed with an external view of, or insight into, the regularity of nature – and of generative processes. Seeing fertility as the only weapon against a hostile chaos, it's not surprising that the myths were steeped in an acting-out of exactly these issues.

A Cosmos (of any size) will always be transformed into a Chaos – it's an inevitable process. As is the opposite: the new Chaos will bring forth a new cosmic order. Ragnarök is not the end, then. The progeny of the Asa gods survive the antics; they are ejaculated into a new potential Cosmos emanating from the dark void of Ginnungagap.

The Midgård snake is an all-encompassing phallic force, keeping the entire world together by uniting with its own tail. The actual name Midgård for this snake or dragon is only used in Snorre's *Edda*. In other sources, he is referred to as "Jörmungand" (a great staff or wand).

Hel is the dark mother of gestation and the underworld. This is not the romanticized sphere of the idealized Asa gods. This is a chthonic, earthen, soilish, regenerative sphere of heavy transformation.

Fenris represents the very will to live by wreaking ferocious havoc and clearing the path. The kinship with the Greek half-god Pan (Roman version: Faun) is obvious. Whatever Pan threatens or enforces in terms of ecstatic rage/lust will benefit fertility as such, as well as the culture of fertility.

When this libidinal force is unleashed, it has the power to destroy the existing cosmos/order on many levels. Fenris is the feral principle/ferocity that lies hidden in the repressed people; the libido that cannot be held back for long. When this is unleashed in/on collective levels, it always brings a violent end to the present reign.

This seemingly chaotic trio constitutes a veritable passage for a Kundalini-blast that moves from the chthonic sphere via the snake and straight up to the sky. The yogic reference to the eternal fire of enlightened insight is here represented by the fire giant Surt, who at Ragnarök scorches the existing earth in volcanic eruptions.

Is there violent sacrifice? Indeed. An entire world or era is sacrificed in this burst. Only one sperm merges with the cosmic egg – the rest are shot out into the non-fertile void. Rejuvenation always comes at a high price.

As mentioned, the Midgård snake is an Ouroboros. Oden casts it out, and it encircles the earth/world; thereby creating restraint. Oden casts out Hel to Nifelheim, which is also a walled-in space; thereby creating restraint. It's all about confining/encircling/restricting forces – both ways. These two forces of "order and death" represent outer restraint. On the other hand, Asgård is – to gods and humans alike – an inner restraint; and that's why the deceptive walling in for protection won't work. Tricking the giant builder is the actual seed of the moral decay that brings forth Ragnarök.

When the gods feel a need to domesticate or at least control Fenris by throwing the fettering net over him, it's psychologically justifiable (but foolish): they choose to cover up and suppress the very same force that once brought forth their own Asgård paradise; thereby suppressing the Kundalini of inevitable change.

Both Midgård and Fenris are excommunicated when they grow too big and unruly. Midgård is thrown into the ocean, sinking into the depths. Fenris is restrained by a magical net or chain, in the form of a very special thread. Although soft as silk, this thread, Gleipner, is constructed out of the roaring of cats, hairs of women's beards, the roots of the mountains, the sinews of bears, the breath of fish, and the spit of birds (this koan-like composite is surely worthy of further magico-anthropological research!).

Of course there are retributions: the symbol of power and valor in the form of the god Tyr loses his/its right hand when dealing with the only temporarily chained beast. Is it a mere coincidence that the hand of apparent masturbation is involuntarily sacrificed here? No matter what, it's a traumatic loss to the entire community, as it makes clear that we can never escape the power of our instincts, as frequently expressed by Loke – the shamanic diplomat moving between the orderly Asgård and the considerably more chthonic spheres.

In Tyr, we find an interesting expression of "Amor fati" – it is simply his destiny to lose his hand. Where Oden's focus lies on magical self-sacrifice, that of Tyr is causally duty-bound. His valor is actually not connected to willpower, but rather to a subservience to the expected that is part of the overall systemic error that causes the eventual downfall of Asgård. It is neither Fenris, the Midgård snake, nor Hel that cause the end; it is the corruption among the gods themselves.

> Garm barks terribly / in front of Gnipahålan; / the fetters will break, / the wolf is free. / I know of much wisdom, / much further I see / about the great victory gods' / final destinies.[5]

There are many speculative theories about who exactly Garm is in this drama. Garm is a canine (he barks) and could therefore be a canine entity on his own, or a poetic symbol for Fenris. The fetters break and the wolf is free, and that is, as we know, intimately connected to the ultimate timeline of Ragnarök.

Gnipahålan is a cave-like sphere – an entrance to Hel – and it has also been stated that Garm is actually Hel's own dog. In this fascinating dance of Loke's spawn, I would argue that Garm is the domesticated dog/instinct that in Fenris/Pan will break free from the restrictions of sexual moralities. We should here remember that Hel is the resting place for common people, and Garm barks by the opening of the dark goddess's cave. Garm represents the origin of the vast majority of sperm that are shot out into the void of death rather than (divine re)birth. But this barking awakens and brings forth the deeper and stronger libido, which eventually cannot be restrained. Hel may be barren, but Fenris certainly is not.

5 Voluspa / "Valans Spådom," paragraph 44, *Eddan*, Niloe, Stockholm, 1982, p 12. Translation by the author.

Why this is of interest here is that, depending on which source for the Voluspa poem we use, this very paragraph is repeated between three and five times; thereby making it, by the mere repetition, either a fairly redundant accentuation, or, as I would argue, an actual spell intended to facilitate the expressed outcome; a mythic certainty that is culturally encouraged rather than anxiously forgotten or repressed.

This is not as paradoxical as it may seem: although this was formulated in a culture that was based on very strict kinships, loyalties and bloodlines, people of course knew that libido is the most powerful force; whether expressed in Eros specifically, or not. The Scandinavian myths and stories about gods who are often barely more than human, generate a more colorful bouquet of coping skills than any monotheistic white-washing ever could.

Sigmund Freud's schematic view of the psyche can be very useful when looking at this particular mythological structure – especially as it leads to a psychological-emotional disaster and even to the death of the "patient." Jotunheim, the sphere of the primordial giants, represents the unconscious (Freud's *Das Es*). This is not exactly identical to the instincts, but certainly strongly related. Midgård, the sphere of the humans, represents what Freud called *Das Ich* (confusingly translated as the "Ego"). Asgård, the sphere of the idealized gods, represents what Freud called *Das Über-Ich* (confusingly translated as the "Super Ego"). When the *Über-Ich* protects the *Ich* from the underlying threats of the unconscious by allowing it to deceive itself and transgress, this can set in motion a chain reaction that will eventually lead to a psychic collapse.

The breach of the oath with the giant who builds the protective walls around Asgård is what instigates Ragnarök later; it's a corruption that opens up for even more (self) deceit. Loke helps trick the giant builder by becoming a mare and sidetracking the giant's needed stallion; and then giving birth to Sleipner – the chief superego's ability to travel/survey all the other spheres. It becomes a moral/moralistic reaction, which in turn will provoke Loke even further as the "community" of Asgård apparently will allow any amoral and corrupting trickery for the sake of its own protection. A dangerous double standard takes hold.

> The construction of cosmic time through repetition of the cosmogony is still more clearly brought out by the symbolism of Brahmanic sacrifice. Each Brahmanic sacrifice marks a new Creation of the world. Indeed, the creation of the sacrificial altar is conceived as a "Creation of the world." The water with which the clay is mixed is the primordial water; the clays that form the base of the altar is the earth; the side walls represent the atmosphere.[6]

In many ways, it's a crude simplification to say that Fenris "allows for a rebirth" by instigating the end of the world. Although the outcome is very much accurate, the complexity of the overall mythic dynamic deserves further attention. If we assume,

---

6 Elliade, Mircea, *The Myth of the Eternal Return*, Princeton/Bollingen, Princeton, 1954, p. 78.

in some kind of Jungian sense, that all cultures share basic myths (or mythic structures), whether by a collective unconscious or simply by mythic migration (or both), then the Scandinavian cluster has survived its migration very well. Taking into account that one of the main formulating historians, Snorre Sturlason, was a Christian, his demagogic attempts are actually not that hard to wash off. Loke was not turned into a too simplified Satan, but just enough to relay a new faith to very tough and decidedly very heathen peoples. It is the blessing and the curse of the monotheistic appropriation: if the new system is moved in too quickly and forcefully, it will experience a backlash. If too slowly, the message will be lost in far too many pampering adjustments. But the strength of these myths, regardless of which cultural clothing they're in, lies in their phenomenal psychological insight.

We can read any pan- or polytheistic myths and stories from basically any time, and still recognize ourselves as well as basically any contemporary dynamic. Not so in the case with the monotheistic myths, which are consciously designed moral tales to be simply integrated in subservient obedience but not necessarily understood.

Revisting the Veil of Dreams

Jesse Bransford & Max Razdow

Cold and hot, Image and thing. Wandering in a field of lichen and moss, no human scale reference. Adrift in a sea of indeterminacy and yet... comfortable. We would probably die of exposure within a few hours here, thankfully the Bifrost is not just a metaphorical bridge connecting worlds here at the base of the Westfjords, but a hotel adjacent to a university...
– Jesse Bransford

—

The project *The Veil of Dreams* was originally part of an exhibition in 2014 presented by the publisher Fulgur and curated by Livia Filotico. Max Razdow and Jesse Bransford kept detailed dream journals for six months leading up to the exhibition and published the entries daily on a public blog on the Fulgur website. The blog became a site of comparison which encouraged the two artists, consciously and unconsciously, to have dream interaction. Iceland was a singular image the two focused on and it was decided they would complete the project with a visit to the country. Specifically, the artists' destination was Gvendarlaug, a hot spring in the remote Northeast of Iceland's Strandir Coast, which had a history of visitations by sorcerers. Over time the two artists shared tactics and readings which strengthened the conscious/waking links between the two. The poetic *Edda* took primacy of place, as well as explorations of tactics/rituals used in contemporary Seiðr practices. Seiðr is the name given to a contemporary tradition of magical and religious belief that traces its origins to pre-Christian Norse culture. The Edda and the Sagas inform many of the tactics, including the use of divinatory runes. The resulting overlaps, between the waking and dreaming spaces of both artists, was more than either ever could have imagined.

Choosing several passages at random, Bransford and Razdow below ruminate on the content over three years after its completion.

—

Max: May 9th, 2014, New York NY

I performed a few acts of ritual before bed. Firstly, I attempted to bind the stave for the pig-lion by the means of a third, circular link.

This added balance and closure to its sign. Then on the back of K's, I drew a stave for the female that has lurked silently so far for myself and Jesse. I chose graphic signs standing for terms such as infinity, ternary-evolutive, spiritual, active quaternary, maternal quaternary. Lastly, I added an 'f' over the 's' in the word 'slow' that hovers on the lava or water upon the mountain side in yesterday's drawing, hoping to manifest a flowing sense/potential in future dreams.

It was a long night of dreaming, but not very clear. I have a vague memory of a space that was similar to a factory, and many male presences there. On waking, I could not recall specifics beyond that. I fell back to sleep and, in a space that felt like a precipice of a dream, I was rolling a dice to try to figure something out. After a few rolls, I realized I wasn't getting any actual numbers. I inspected the dice again and saw that its faces were blank, and in fact it was a stone. I remember the tactility and complexities of the stone's surface. It rolled and settled on its facets like a dice. It was orange in color.

Early on, the space had not fully opened itself to us. I felt as though I was suspended partially in the here and now, even when asleep, and that the narrow dreams I had were often related to very particular manipulations of form, rather than exploration of the vast, otherworldly realm that later demarcated experience.

The 'dice dream' became our first true correspondence. After I related this dream to Jesse, he told me that his altar actually has a blank, 20-sided dice on it. This was not something I knew about beforehand. I remember being surprised by this, but also seeing it as an anchor, as though it confirmed that something was happening. Soon, these occurrences would become regular, and even now (in reading over the dream passages several years later), I have the sense that almost every dream touches on what was then future aspects of myself – visions of my son, especially, seem prescient now. He would be born about a year after our project ended.

But, at this time, we were still very much in the beginning stages, and things often felt like a struggle. Over the next weeks, my practice of ritual became increasingly authored. I would collect stones, trying to match them with fictional types that I saw in the dreams, would create cards laden with self-made sigils and would experiment with household objects, bits of the natural world and various mineral substances when it seemed appropriate to do so. It felt as though there was a conversational technique that I had to learn so as to be allowed to pass through a series of gates. In the dreams, these gates were often marked by guardian creatures – the pig lion mentioned here, later a burning dog. Eventually, thanks I think to these rituals and dream-acts that were carried out by each of us, we seemed to arrive into another land that we would call 'the space.'

Jesse: May 12th, 2014. 830AM
Brooklyn, New York, in the hour of Jupiter

> My trip to Los Angeles was cancelled. I was talking to the same woman from May 7th, and as usual, she was talking and I couldn't understand her words. But I did know that 'the trip' had been cancelled.
>
> Two images in trans-sleep. A cat-like mask made of a dark wood or rusted iron. No one was wearing it. The second image was of two hands clasping a stone by making a triangle with the thumb and forefinger. The stone was being held up to the sun, and behind the sun (beyond the blindness?) was an image of a triangular glyph, something I have drawn many times before, but used with intent in Galveston.
>
> —
>
> Max's stone? I think a real convergence is happening here.

~

This was the first dream in the process where I felt real unexplained correspondence between waking and dreaming life, a correspondence that would only increase as time went on. Max and I had been gifting each other stones and other objects that we would concentrate on each evening and this was the first time one of these objects made an appearance. This dream seemed to suggest the efficacy of these stones. Garnets, carnelian and Herkimer diamonds (a kind of quartz found in Herkimer, New York), as well as the original green quartz icosahedron I already owned, plunged us both into the realm of correspondence. This was exacerbated on many occasions. Here, the 'cat mask' is in real life a series of drawings Max completed a few years before. While I cannot be certain, I have no conscious memory of seeing the work prior to the dream. The drawings I made of the mask bear striking resemblance to Max's work.

Any hint of Max in these dreams was always noted. Although he only appeared directly in four to six dreams over the six-month period, the shared space brought on by reading the *Edda* and sharing objects is still deeply overwhelming.

I was (and still am) struck by dream images of miasma and blindness: these always seem the most portentous and their familiarity through my experience with psychedelic space seems non-trivial. The glyph would appear over and over again, and is something I identified at the time with R.F., a lover I had stopped seeing the spring before the project began. More on her and the identification with her (perhaps ultimately a mis-identification) below.

Travel and spaces of indeterminacy are rife throughout both of our journals. Part of this was due to a large amount of actual travel (During the time I went to Atlanta and Bolivia and was still getting used to having two domestic spaces, one in Brooklyn and one in Catskill – Max traveled even more), but I also believe the liminal feeling travel produces is very much akin to dream space; the sense of disorientation, shifts in language etc. are a common denominator in travel and dream space.

Max: May 29th

> Reading the sign of the fortress as one of the impenetrable aspects. I cleared my altar and staves, leaving only the Herkimer diamond I had tethered to Jesse's earlier that night. To enter the fort, one must not try too hard, I think.
>
> The dreams reflect a mysterious interior that again had the quality of a school, but also a space of exhibition. I spent my time there organizing xerox like posters, determining who made them, and pinning them to walls. I wrote the name of their crafter on them, on the back. The posters were sometimes facsimiles of posters I or my brothers had as children, other times more like art. One was a brilliant, color print of a colorful shirt, full scale. I was alone in this space. I don't know what happened in between, but earlier in the dream, I saw Jesse on a hill playing a trumpet! Herkimer diamond at work?
>
> Last dream in New York for a while. It was excellent to see Jesse and take stock of all we've seen. Spoke of journeying, meandering, stave work and all that lies ahead.

At some point, Jesse and I really started to research the stones we kept finding and being given at this phase of our journey. I remember walking into a store specializing in rare minerals in midtown Manhattan and attempting to describe to the owner a fictional mineral with a half remembered name, and settling on purchasing the closest thing I could find to add to my altar. Sometime in May, we determined that a Herkimer diamond was a worthy object to add to our growing collections, Jesse having discovered that not only are these carbon crystals found near his place in Catskill (named after Herkimer, New York), but that they can be used to establish a connection between two individuals at a distance. Over a drink in the West Village, we bound our stones together and talked about the strange experiences we were having, symbols that had arisen, artwork we might be able to conjure out of this experience, and our plans for future travel, both outside and within the dream space.

Oddly, however, this was the time that our paths seemed to part for a spell. At the fortress, a building I had been occupying for several concurrent dreams, I saw Jesse from the window on a hill side with his trumpet. But, he was pointing to the North and East, and I would then begin to travel South. I would not understand the directional clarity of this moment until much later, having not yet begun to prepare the map.

In late summer, Jesse suggested a specific ritual process to try to find a common path again, and at that time we once again did seem to occupy the same space at the same time with fair frequency. Between now and then, our crossings were temporary, and, more often than I actually saw him, I would merely understand he had been to a specific location prior to my arrival.

It seems strange to talk about a dream reality as though it is a fixed space with linear temporal qualities, cardinal directions and landmarks, but that is how it came to appear to me.

Jesse: June 3rd, 2014. 934AM
Santa Cruz, Bolivia, in the hour of Mercury

> Flew from JFK to Santa Cruz Boliva via Panama City, long trip, bed at 2am after meeting many people, friends old and new. World Stave and a Valknut on the nightstand with a garnet and the quartz Max gave me. I slept soundly, dream fragments, but fragments only.
>
> Lost in a maze of immigration paperwork, trying to get to wherever I was going. Kept thinking 'Interzone'. People were fine, robotic, but no mean-spiritedness. For a long time, no one was with me, but at a point R.F. appeared. I thought 'she didn't come on this trip', and then I woke up.
>
> —
>
> Travel into the unfamiliar. K.K. and A.T. here to meet me. Surprised I slept through the night. Comfortable, safe.
>
> My waking life is more prone to correspondence at this point. The back of my bathroom door which I did not see this morning, has a beautiful cloaked woman holding a cup and riding a large wolf. Hel from my dreams is on a door in a country whose culture and location is as far removed from Seiðr as possible, and yet there she is!

~

When I closed the door to the bathroom where I was staying and saw the wolf-riding cloaked woman, I wondered what was going on. By this point I've had dozens of dreams of powerful female figures communicating with me. My reading had introduced the idea of the seeress and also the notion that the Norse magical seiðr practices we were beginning to explore were the provenance of women generally. It would not be until after the project that I would discover the idea of the fylgja, which is akin to the concept of a guardian angel and is often gender opposite. Not incidental was also the acute sense of heartbreak I was enduring at that time, combined with the fact that I went to Bolivia for the wedding of one of my closest friends. But none of this explained the unlikely coincidence of seeing such a specific Norse reference in the middle of South America. The name 'Interzone' is the fictional, stateless place that was the backdrop of much of William Burroughs' fiction. The journals have several instances of being in transit, especially in border crossings and airports, which to my mind speaks to the idea that I was feeling the liminal space the journal is creating.

South America also resonates for dream space because of a trip I took to Peru in 2005 where I worked with a curandera with the psychedelic tea ayahuyasca. My dreams (and my waking space) were altered significantly in that experience and both my conscious and unconscious seemed to be thinking about this trip and the jungle especially. It put a peculiar feeling of multiple cultural cross-currents throughout the trip.

Max: June 8, New York NY

No particular preparation after a day trip to Catskill/Columbia County. Returned quite late and fell asleep quickly.

Had a long, narrative dream involving a man with a broken leg and many art world people (R.S. and others). There was some nameless anxiety at play, and the dream took place in a campus like space, with many open yards, stair cases of marble and a vaulted atrium accessed by a spiral staircase. I can't recall the plot.

In the dream, K. sang a song which was devised to quell my anxiety – and it was one of those strange occurrences where the song was super rich and full, and all the lyrics and the tune fully rendered in the dream. It was a great song!

I thought I woke up, and that K. and I worked together to reconstruct and write down the song in my journal, carefully recording all the lyrics and humming the tune to commit to memory. But then I realized this was a dream too, and I awoke in full to very little memory of the song.

On waking, I scrawled the following notes: 'It is the wind', 'Number 37'. I tried to reconstruct the song…

Music in the dream space (during our project, as well as prior to and since) has often seemed to me as though it speaks in an elevated state of communication. Sometimes a song can appear with the kind of clarity that dreams rarely manifest, charged with immediate resonance with deep aspects of yourself, and apprehended with more meaning than other symbols do. The feeling of the song often remains with me, and hints of its impossibly beautiful tunes. Numbers, on the other hand, are significantly opaque. They also appear frequently, and make their significance clear, but they never resolve at the time of dreaming. Whatever charge they have within the space seems to manifest outside of awareness and can be looked at (at least by me) only with academic speculation.

As I noted in the journal, drums and music have been associated, unsurprisingly, with the practice of the Seiðr. Loki remarks upon Odin's magical practice in a passage in the poetic *Eddas*:

> But once you practiced Seiðr on Samesey, and you beat the drum as witches do...
>
> (*Poetic Eddas*, Loki's Quarrel)

At this point in our project, I was feeling fully on the trail of something. Each day I woke up with a head full of articulated imagery, bits of speech and strange characters. However, the landscape itself was not yet fully understood. Its formal geography came to me later.

Jesse: June 16th, 2014. 837AM
Catskill New York in the hour of Jupiter

> Draum Stafir over the bed. Went to bed early.
>
> Woke up at midnight after an extremely intense dream. Overwhelming cacophony of sounds and images. Overwhelming, absolutely overwhelming, much like a peak experience in psychedelic space. At the end of the vortex was the woman, dressed as in the wolf-woman on my door in Bolivia. She speaks and for the first time I understand her; 'This is the Seiðr' and hands me a cup. As I put the cup to my lips I wake with a start, completely covered in sweat.

This was, despite all indications to the contrary, not a nightmare.

~

As weeks passed the seeress/guide/object-choice continued to visit me. She took on various forms depending on her interest. There seemed to be three primary goals and accompanying forms, but as time progressed they would merge and recombine.

Sexual: this was the first visitation and would repeat in many guises. Usually aggressive, the figure would often have tattoos and reminded me of three people in real life, but they were only rarely the actual person.

Heartache/heartbreak: often appearing as R.F., this version seemed to want to probe my heartache regarding her and my symbolic abstraction of her. Often there would be some sort of message attached to these visits (see October 12th below), but often the scenario would be one that seemed to go to every length to exacerbate the sense of loneliness and isolation the end of that relationship had produced in my waking space. On several occasions, I would wake from these dreams in tears, which has rarely happened in my normal dream space, before or since.

Magical communication: the dream above was one of the more vivid examples of the figure attempting to deliver magical or spiritual wisdom. After the 'real world' encounter with this version of the figure, she would always appear cloaked. The cup or chalice also took on the symbolic form of her manifestation. The idea of drinking from the well of wisdom as Odin did in the poetic Edda was a powerful literary image and inflected many other dreams and images, particularly of landscapes and natural environments.

These three 'types' manifested over and over again and seemed to be following me wherever I went. At first the sexual encounters were the easiest to process, but increasingly the heartbreak and magical contexts would combine with these encounters. Tattoos became a powerful image in several other dreams, as did the strong body/spirituality connections that exist in meditation and yoga practices. The communication dreams usually included the 'dream miasma' that I encountered in other contexts, especially dreams involving written language and text, all of which were foreign and illegible. In several of the most vivid magical communication dreams the woman seems frustrated with my seeming non-comprehension of her message and over time her presentation seems almost desperate. I would wake from these dreams feeling defeated and incapable of understanding anything that was presenting in the dream space.

Max: August 19 – New York, NY

> Back in New York. Everything feels ultra-foreign and strange. Simple pleasures and catching up on some home responsibilities. One of the new cards is on the altar, along with The Seeress. Oddly, when I returned home, I found the two paintings above the altar to be on the floor, my primary 'home' staves strewn about and the fish cup on its side. All the crystals were in a pile on the altar. Did the cats do this? A strong wind? Honestly perplexed.
>
> Dreams remain elusive, but I remember a tight, miniature mountain-scape in which I was building various houses out of slate.

It felt like child's play on a larger scale. Again, I was not alone.

In the middle of our project, I was invited to Northern Norway for an art residency. It was a strange happenstance occurrence – unplanned, and one that found its way to me through good friends and sheer luck. The dream space shifted strongly over that time. I kept dreaming of mountains, and it was really then that a sense of cartographic geography began to bloom. Later, when I was preparing the map using (in part) Norse cosmology as a basic template, I began to think of this landscape as a corollary for *Jotunheimr*, the land of the giants. It was hard not to think of it this way. Nordland was beautiful in August – lit with ever setting and rising suns, beards of conifer and skins of lichen were behind every stone, and a mysterious history that felt obliquely of nature was omnipresent. Yet in the dreams I had in Norway, someone was trying to guide me. I followed him in a later dream, several dreams, never knowing who he was. Eventually, he brought me to a cave guarded by a door in a mountainside, and I was told to give something for the hidden space below. My gift to the cave was an indecipherable letter or rune, like something Jesse might have drawn.

Toward the end of our trip, we spent a few days with friends in Oslo. At an art opening, we met a young man who told us he was of Sami descent. He was very outgoing and jovial; we had seen him at a café earlier on and he had serenaded our friend's two-year-old son with a guitar. When he at the art opening, he started singing traditional Sami songs, and described to me his own dream space after I told him a little about our project. He told me that he and all his people had a mountain in their dreams, and in their dreams they lived within the mountain.

Things like that were becoming increasingly common during those times. On returning to New York, it just continued. The cats very well may have knocked over my little altar on the dresser back home, or the wind could have sent a large painting crashing to the ground. Or, it may have been something else. We were both opening ourselves to a continuum of forces that didn't prescribe fully to mundane reality, and it was consistent about making its presence known.

Jesse: October 12th, 2014. 1022AM
Brooklyn New York in the hour of Mars

Made it home after an all-day run around trying to get back to NYC from Memphis. Apartment feels nice, weather is cozy. Still aching with the loss and the funeral. Set up stones on the altar, called to Max in Saturn.

I am in an SUV with R.F. and we pull into a rural space that is behind a large plaza/strip mall. The loading area for a large complex.

I get out and she lifts up out of the sunroof, looking down at me and twisting a ring she is wearing on her left index finger. It is Hudson's ring and I ask playfully 'why are you rolling Hudson's ring on your finger?', 'To have this I should have known him' is her response. She is beautiful, radiant and naked but this seems normal. I turn to meet a Middle-Eastern man who owns one of the restaurants and is coming out from a large roll door. R.F. comes to meet us and we begin talking about galleries in the area. This 'area' is familiar to me from other dreams. We walk around the building which now seems like a wall. The man points to a hole in the wall. I walk up to it, it is about the size of a half-dollar, voices are audible from within. 'Secrets' says the man. I turn around and look at R.F. thinking about Hudson's ring. She is still naked and she and I enter a pose that seems like a yoga pose. Non-sexual but she is naked and this finally seems strange to me. We hold the posture for a moment. I kiss her on the back of her neck and she pushes me away forcefully but without anger. She then begins to walk me away from the man and the building towards a body of water in the opposite direction. It is fall and the leaves are reasonably thick on the ground. She pulls the leaf litter aside and reveals a red and black striped worm moving through the soil. 'They move in the direction of the tides' she tells me. I look back to the body of water and see a mallard duck flying across the tree-line. I turn, look at beautiful R.F. and then again at the ground and the worms. I think about Hudson again and wake up.

—

Ring: May 6th. Worm image: May 19th. Many more correspondences but I don't have time now to map them. I think I'm at the wall. This dream seems really, really important somehow...

~

One of the most 'revelatory' of the dream cycle, I still feel a deep sense of 'understanding' whenever I read the account of this dream, despite having no clear idea of the dream's meaning. This feeling, above and beyond any classical 'interpretation' seems to have been the most powerful message/content I received in the cycle.

I had just returned from my maternal grandmother's funeral; a powerful female figure who was formative for me, her slow and gradual decline over the previous five or so years made her death seem a release... The connection of Hudson, my dealer of 15 years who died suddenly in 2013, seems portentous. I don't recall any ring in real life, but the ring was absolute and factual in the dream, matched by R.F.'s nakedness. Clearly a merging of all three of the categories of female presences, I was completely overwhelmed by her power in all three visions. I often feel disappointed in myself for playing to the sexual context of my contact with her in this dream. It seems as misplaced now as it did in the dream, and yet the worm would suggest at the very least a symbolic relation (Max suggested it could have been a dragon which played a strong part in his dream narrative).

I was also struck by the strong narrative content of the dream which was fleeting and very uncommon in my accounts.

Max: October 12, New York NY

> Long, lazy day – spent most of it at home with K. Much work on the map – thinking about the giants of course, or, were they trolls? Gallery openings and dinner later, quick call and left Alvis on the altar.
>
> I am in a mountainous area that has many tunnels through it, connecting to form a kind of labyrinthine habitation that is as much natural space as living quarters. I am walking with S.L., and we come upon a tiny creature that at first looks like a glowing glob of slime, then transforms before our eyes to a face (like the ogre's actually), then into a tiny fish that has a gas filled jellyfish attached to it which allows it to float in the air. S.L. and I start to play with it, batting it back and forth until I splat it accidentally against a cave wall, popping the jellyfish. I feel terrible about this, and mount the fish at the end of a rifle I am carrying as I journey to find a suitable pond for the now water bound fish. P.C. directs me to a path that leads to another cave tunnel (more of a grotto as there is open sky above), and there I find a clear pond full of jellyfish, sea grass and miniature squid. I let the fish go there, and watch as he happily eats the mini squids.
>
> This place is so weird! Very magical, but super odd, even for the dream space. Ogre's face recurring is also strange. I know it well, but can't draw it accurate to the image in my mind.

I became obsessed with finding Níðhöggr at some point in the project. I've always loved dragons and dragon imagery, since I was a child, and when it became clear that our dreams were fully intertwined with the Norse mythic structure, I set a personal goal of finding my way to Níðhöggr's well, in the roots of Yggdrasil. Both Jesse and I had visited (I believed) Mímir's well, at different times in our somnambulating, and I had received a clear dream of the well of the Norns. It seemed only fitting that, at some point, I would find my way to Hvergelmir, a fabled spring mentioned in the Eddas where Níðhöggr and many serpents dwell. Or, at least I would try.

There was a moment, mid-way through our project, that I began to descend a long staircase into a cavern, and then was turned back. I considered this as close as I did come, and thought that I did not see the beast's domain during our dream-land journeys. It is not until now, as we are writing this reminiscence, that I see that I may have been wrong. Even in the midst of formulating the map, when I was at my most dedicated to retracing our steps and overlaps and the meanings of our travels, I did not see the correspondence of October 12th that hints at our mutual visitation of the well. That's how thick and complex this material was.

On October 12th, just days before departing for Iceland and the sorcerer's pool, it seems that Jesse and I both visited different aspects of the Hvergelmir. The spaces for each of us that night were notably watery and cavernous, as is Níðhöggr's spring from which many rivers flow. For Jesse and R.F., the dragon may have appeared as a serpent writhing in leaves: *"she pulls the leaf litter aside and reveals a red and black striped worm moving through the soil. 'They move in the direction of the tides' she tells me." Mine appeared as a fish: "we come upon a tiny creature that at first looks like a glowing glob of slime, then transforms… into a fish that has a gas filled jellyfish attached to it which allows it to float in the air."*

Níðhöggr, in Norse myth, is a wurm: a mythic wingless dragon who does not fly until the eve of Ragnarök. Perhaps, in the twists and personalization of dream rendering, it could be fishlike or serpent-like, perhaps gaining Lovecraftian properties of the medusozoa phylum or the syncopating abjection and tenderness of finding an earthworm in the leaves. For neither of us, in our dreams, was this creature great or terrible, but it surely slunk in otherworldly grottos. Something invited us, both on the same night, to observe it there.

Jesse: October 16th, 2014. 843AM
Brooklyn, New York in the hour of Mars

Bed 11ish. Shout out to Max in the hour of the moon. Stones on the East Altar. Made a new cylinder spell, destroyed the old one in water.

Falling asleep I dreamed I introduced my close friend Max to my other close friend (who I thought would like him immensely)… Max. The two shook hands and became one. I woke in amazement and went back to sleep, entering a miasmic dream-space glimpsed many times along this journey, but with a clarity and intensity I don't recall. Instead of confusion there was a comprehension and understanding I don't ever remember feeling. Events (dream and real world) seemed to loop onto themselves and resolve. I finally felt a quantity of pain and sorry being removed from my stomach. Who or what was removing this seemed indifferent and alien. I have felt this before, in Peru. In and out of consciousness from there, woke up finally in the predawn having taken all of my clothes off.

—

Max! And two of you! I wonder if that's why I haven't seen you? Did you divide yourself as protection from the perils of the wyrd? Our dream selves and our spirit doubles...

Another revelatory dream with the signature appearance of the miasma. This one was particularly resonant given Max's appearance. His image in dream space had become a holy grail of sorts and to have him doubled fed into countless other mirror/doppelganger scenarios. Lacan comes to mind, but the fact this doubling is unifying and not fragmenting seems important, also that it is not me but an identified symbol/goal.

The miasma's removal of a quantity of pain from my stomach rejoins to an image I had in the ayahuasca space of being 'operated on' by a host of small white beings. In Peru, I remember it as a process not without anxiety and resistance, but this dream didn't have anxiety in the content, although removing my clothes while asleep typically coincides with a darker dream.

Max: October 18th, 2014. Drangsnes, Iceland

Despite the prior day's travel and sleepless night, we drove right away from the airport to the Strandir Coast. Felt quite awake thanks to the scenery and good company. Late afternoon, we reach the museum in Hólmavík – fascinating place, then soon after we visit the Gvendarlaug pool, the pool of the sorcerers! Jesse and I both swim (not in the sorcerer's pool but in another close by), and each of us does a quick working. For my part, I prepared the final two well cards – one I had drawn a circle for in advance, the other I had not, and chose to let the ink forms decide on their own space, to let them be free. For each, I dipped in the Gvendarlaug water once and thought of the space under the mountain, and then the wind.

That night by chance, we stayed in a hostel beside a very large stone formation which a sign described as a frozen "night troll" My room's window looked out upon it. Very tired, we crashed at like 8:00, when the dark crept in.

Around 10:30, we each emerged again from our rooms – two other local travelers had arrived to our shared flat, and we greeted them. One of them mentioned that the rock was also a habitation of elves, which could be seen only if you stared at the rock for 24 hours straight. We went back to bed, but Jesse rose soon after and knocked on my door with news that there was a Northern Lights about. We both watched them for as long as we could and took many pictures. It was stunningly beautiful – the moving green-white bands stretching across the sky and dancing.

Back in my room, I could still see the lights out the window, emanating from a point behind the cliff, dancing beside, behind and above the great fairy / troll rock. I woke up many times over the night to watch the lights, feeling full of much awe and calm as well. When I slept, this space I saw and my dreams felt one and the same, the sky and earth pulling one and other through that stone.

The aurora we witnessed was, according to locals, of very rare splendor. It was snowing over the mountain passes, and we were extraordinarily lucky to even get there, let alone to have enough clear sky see these magic lights from where we were.

Jesse: October 19, 2014. 847AM
Fluðir, Iceland in the hour of the Sun

Amazing day. Woke and took a dip in the hot pot in Drangsnes, breakfast and a visit to the troll stone which was outside Max's window. Returning south stopping at Guðrunarlaug, an amazing pool from the Sagas… then to Snorralaug, named after Snorri Sturluson… lunch at the Bifrost Hotel… and more driving to Fluðir where I stayed in 2013. To bed and to sleep!

An amazing dream. Max and I are on an adventure (!!) He is showing me a place across a river. We wade into it and as we reach the other side I find a key and a knife. We continue on to a cathedral of vast complexity, almost like a video game. The key opens the front door (of course!) and as he shows me the various beautiful rooms we begin to be followed by several cats. Max shows me chambers above and below ground, crypts and sun rooms. Finally, we are in a large room and the lights go out. We hear voices and three people enter the room, two men (the Brujos from and early dream) and an unidentified woman. They are wearing brown puffy jackets and seem to want something from us. The two men jump at me and I defend myself with the knife (of course). I stab both of them in the abdomen and they seem to be surprised to be bleeding and immediately surrender. The woman seems horrified and Max has retreated to pet cats. I begin tending to these wounded men explaining they have internal bleeding (small quantities of blood are coming out of their mouths). I am worrying about them and looking at the rather wimpy looking knife that inflicted such wounds. I then notice that I too am spitting up blood and go to a mirror to look at my mouth. There is indeed blood but I can't find my wound. I recognize the circularity, its profound implications, and wake up.

The circular return of responsibility… The key and the knife – phallic substitute much? Max was such a pleasure! I was very excited and happy to see him there. Especially when the cats appeared.

~

One of the final dreams of the journal, this was pretty astonishing as it seemed to close several narratives and bring into high-contrast many of the leitmotifs from the past six months. The woman is nowhere to be found and I am left to my own devices to deal with the conflict presented. The two brujos had appeared clearly at least once before, although the addition of a female to the group is notable. The somewhat ambivalent nature of their hostility joined them to the context in a way that begs the question of the separation of character from space in this dream, something that is also on display in the dream from October 12th. I'm of the mind that the castle we were in was in fact my 'self' and that all of these images and conflicts are internal, especially given the circular nature of the wounds.

Max: October 21st to 31st, New York City:

The last ten days of somnambulating are a haze of non-dreaming. Jesse is in London, I am in New York.

I am left with a few hints of the final landscape which filtered into my conscious mind in percolation drips.

… a lonely house, a place that is low in a valley. It feels as if the house is singular, as if it stands alone and all else has fallen away.

~

Those last nights were a foreshadowing of the almost total loss of dream recall that seemed to arrive as soon as the project had ended. Although during that final week I only had the vaguest sense of landscape, and thus hardly committed anything to the journal, later I recovered one small, loose leaf note from my bedside table that I had made from some time over that span. Some weeks or months later, I elected to make the poem it contained my journal's final page, believing to some degree that it could prove a useful epitaph.

I cannot say I understand the poem, but during those last six months I had grown to trust the truth of much of which seems at first opaque. Perhaps, like the dream world we had traveled through, it is not nonsensical, but instead helps illustrate a continuum of pure meaning, asking only faith of its sojourners to offer hints at what that might be.

—∾—

> The last note I have is of a fully lucid poem, which emerged in a dream from some night over that last ten days.
>
> I will give it its own page, since I have several left now, many months later as I make these last, belated marks, waiting for Jesse on 14th Street, watching the shadow of my hand trail over the pages of this book.

The wind it picks
Up all the dust –
And puts it in a
Mousing cup –
And when the dust it turns to gold
The wind has
Come again, it's told.

Beyond the North Wind: Völkisch Photography, Mytho-History and the Bloodline of Thule

Christopher Webster

Let us look each other in the face. We are Hyperboreans we know well enough how remote our place is ... Beyond the North, beyond the ice, beyond death ... – Nietzsche, *The Antichrist.*

Foreword

This essay is a fragment of a larger project that I have been working on relating to the work of a select group of creative German photographers who made their most memorable work during the Third Reich.[1] After 1933, some of these photographers, already nationalist in their sentiments, simply continued to work as they had before the coming to power of the National Socialists. Some certainly saw the advent of the Third Reich as a glorious opportunity to further advance and develop their particular careers and aesthetics. Others became committed to the cause of celebrating a physical, national and spiritual ideal through their work as it matured in the 1930s and 1940s. Each regarded their work as 'art' (although photography was not considered in the National Socialist state to be 'High Art', that honour was reserved for the traditional visual media of sculpture and painting). The work of this small group of photographers was certainly ideological and had political uses and implications. They contributed to: '... a space in which a range of popular esoteric, pseudo-scientific, folklorist, and mythological tropes might be exploited in the building of ideological consensus across a diverse Nazi Party and all the more eclectic German population.'[2] However, I am yet fascinated by the fact that here they were, using a seemingly objective optical and chemical process to make work that was, just as cinema was doing at the same time, breaking the bounds of its empirical realm. Like the metaphorical and staged creative photography associated with Modernism,[3] I believe that they were using photography as a catalyst, as a

1 I am curating a touring exhibition entitled, 'A Radical Tradition', using aspects of the collection of Aberystwyth University's School of Art Gallery and Museum. I have been able to add work to the collection over the last few years through funded purchases and through generous donations.

2 Eric Kurlander, "The orientalist roots of National Socialism?" in *Transcultural Encounters between Germany and India*, ed. Eric Kurlander et al. New York: Routledge, 2014. 164-165.

3 For those unfamiliar with these currents (where documentary photography might become personal reflection, or, for example, where photographs might become metaphors for personal feeling) see for example the work of a photographer like the American Edward Weston (1886-1958) whose richly detailed photographs transcend 'mere description'.

lapis philosophorum, that might transmute the imagination and open the doors of perception onto other possible 'truths'. These photographs appear to be strident archetypes, materialisations in silver of forces that were coursing through the Germanosphere. Jung had suggested such a manifestation when he wrote: 'a god has taken possession of the Germans and their house is filled with a "mighty rushing wind."'[4] Whether any of the photographers believed the myth that they were creating is now unknown, the possibility of knowing lost in the calumny, revision and career-denial of the post-war era.

Introduction – A 'Nazi' Occult

The marriage of technology and the occult in the modern era has perhaps never been more evident than during the 12 years of Hitler's Third Reich – nor more contentious and controversial. Indeed, the debate about whether we can really talk about a 'Nazi occult' is still ongoing. However, with key plenipotentiaries such as Himmler, Hess, Rosenberg and Darré interested in (and indeed often obsessed with) the occult and a Germanic paganism, Reich policies and actions often included a strange mixture of cutting-edge knowledge, hard-edged pragmatism, *völkisch*[5] mysticism and fringe science.

There has been a plethora of sensationalist publications, television programmes, documentaries and even fictional Hollywood movies centred on the so-called 'Nazi' occult. However, as specious as much of these outpourings have been there are, nonetheless, scholarly works that have examined this topic in depth and clearly demonstrated a link between what might loosely be termed the occult and the National Socialist movement.[6] In this essay I am primarily concerned with how – in the photographic representation of (in particular) northern Germanic peoples, the inhabitants of the Netherlands, German *Niederdeutschland*, the Frisians and their Scandinavian cousins – evidence of a type, a bloodline, was sought and of import to the National Socialist state. By hailing the people of this northern European landscape, the place where Herman Wirth (1885-1981) had found his signs and symbols of an ancient language, where indeed, the Oera Linda Book had been rediscovered – a mythological-racial significance of these people's origins was intimated and a pagan legacy alluded to. Were these people the living representatives of some Aryan Hyperborea in their most untainted form, Nordic-Atlanteans, the bloodline of Thule?[7] The so-called objectivity of the camera, racial science and

4 http://www.philosopher.eu/others-writings/essay-on-wotan-w-nietzsche-c-g-jung/

5 *Völkisch* is a word that defies an easy English translation. In the main the völkisch movement was a mixed bag of philosophies that placed an emphasis on a rabid ethnicity, a desire for a unified German *Heimat* (or homeland), organic living and food, nature and romanticism.

6 Nicholas Goodrick-Clarke's *The Occult Roots of Nazism* is one such work on the topic and has remained in print in several languages since its first publication in 1985. In his text, Goodrick-Clarke examines the various ideological origins of National Socialism and the völkisch progenitors of the nationalist and racial ideas that would influence the political formation of Hitler's party.

7 Of course the occult group and supporter of the DAP (*Deutsches Arbeiterpartei* the precursor of Hitler's

alternative theories of history, were brought together in an attempt to hint at this.

The three leading figures of National Socialism most relevant to this area were Richard Walther Darré (1895-1953), Alfred Rosenberg (1893-1946), and of course Heinrich Himmler (1900-1945). Each of these attempted in their own (and often related) ways to develop a narrative relating to the significance and alternative origins of the Germanic 'volk'.

Darré's works were primarily concerned with the ancient and present Nordic peasantry (his ideology of 'Blut und Boden' or Blood and Soil). Darré was a prolific exponent of the view of the peasant as essential for a strong society and his two main publications in the pre-1933 era were *Das Bauerntum als Lebensquelle der Nordischen Rasse* (1929), and *Neuadel aus Blut und Boden* (1930) both of which dealt with the history and traditions of the Nordic peasant race, vital to the health of the nation. In addition, Darré saw Christianity as a dangerously undermining religion, one that had weakened the Germanic race with its ideals of equality, passivity and forgiveness and thus insinuated a return to a pre-Christian and more indigenous faith system.

Alfred Rosenberg saw himself as the party's chief philosopher. His 1930 book *Der Mythus des zwanzigsten Jahrhunderts* or *Myth of the Twentieth Century* was a best-seller, selling over a million copies. In it Rosenberg developed an argument for a return to a more Germanic faith system amongst other things including a concern with regards the dangers of Weimar cosmopolitanism, an opposition to the material world that to Spengler had represented, 'blood against money.'[8] Rosenberg also famously made specific reference to an 'alternative', Hyperborean homeland or 'Ur-Heimat' of the Nordic-Atlanteans[9] in his *Mythus*. According to Rosenberg:

> The geologists show us a continent between North America and Europe, whose remains we can see today in Greenland and Iceland. They tell us that islands on the other side of the Far North display former tide marks over 100 metres higher than today's; they make it probable that the North Pole has wandered, and that a much milder climate once reigned in the present Arctic. All this allows the ancient legend of Atlantis to appear in a new light. It seems not impossible that where the waves of the Atlantic Ocean now crash and pull of giant icebergs, once a blossoming continent rose out of the water, on which a creative race raised a mighty, wide-ranging culture, and sent its children out into the world as seafarers and warriors. But even if

NSDAP) was the *Thule-Gesellschaft* or Thule society named after the mythical northern land *Thule*.

8 Spengler, Oswald. *The Decline of the West*, Perspectives of World History. Vol 2. London: George Allen and Unwin, 1928. 506.

9 The terms 'Nordic', 'Aryan' and 'Germanic' are all used to characterise an idealised racial profile both in historical discourse and in contemporary discussions of the racial policies of National Socialist Germany. Aryan, though originally an ethno-linguistic classification, came to be equated with a racial sub-group (principally Nordic). The historical anthropological term 'Nordic' is also regarded as being a racial sub-group of the Caucasian. The term Nordic-Atlantean was used by Rosenberg and it is this term that I employ in the main here for this discussion of these 'descendants of Ultima Thule'.

> this Atlantean hypothesis is not thought tenable, one has to assume that there was a prehistoric northern centre of culture.[10]

Himmler of course is the most important of these three in relation to the photographic works that I am examining. In the late 19th and early 20th centuries myth, race and new interpretations of the historical narrative offered an alternative notion of the origins of what came to be termed the Nordic-Atlantean race. In turn, these hypotheses presented Germany's Reichsführer-SS, Heinrich Himmler, with an opportunity of seizing upon a radical and a unique racial foundation of the Germanic peoples. By the late 1930s his SS had become in effect a state within a state and Himmler had the authority and the funding to indulge his passion for Germanic pre-history. His *Ahnenerbe* (the Research and Teaching Community of the Ancestral Heritage)[11] supported academic inquiries into the German past but also collected information about, and attempted to find evidence of, the para-historical, including the possibility of a Hyperborean/Atlantean[12] homeland of the Germanic forebears. Himmler's *Ahnenerbe* was directly involved in financing some of the photographic work of the photographers whom I discuss here. Himmler became gripped with researching and validating an alternative and esoteric history of the German race and, as we shall see, even 'lowly' photography came to play a part in the process of documenting and disseminating this search for visual evidence of the presence of a progenitor race of northern Europeans.

The enduring legend of Plato's lost Atlantean continent[13] was revisited in the Renaissance and had become almost mainstream by the 19th century. It became particularly important to occultists such as Helena Blavatsky (1831-1891), mystic, writer, and the co-founder of the Theosophical Society in 1875. Her two volume work *The Secret Doctrine* (1888) explored the origins of mankind that both linked to new scientific ideas such as evolution but was a melding of these ideas with mysticism. In particular, her suggestion of 'Root races', the development of the Aryan race and the links to an Atlantean homeland are significant. These ideas filtered through to the *völkisch* pan-German mystics of the 19th and early 20th centuries who would create their own racial and spiritual philosophy namely, Ariosophy. Guido von List (1848-1919) and Jörg Lanz von Liebenfels (1874-1954), adapted ideas from a broad range of influences, including Blavatsky's Theosophy, and notions of Aryan racial history as espoused by figures such as Arthur de Gobineau (1816-1882), who had written the essay *The Inequality of the*

10 Rosenberg, Alfred. *Der Mythus des 20. Jahrhunderts, Eine Wertung der seelisch-geistigen Gestaltenkämpfe unserer Zeit*, München: Hoheneichen-Verlag, 1934. 24.

11 Himmler's *Ahnenerbe* had been created with the intention of tracing and securing the history, cultural foundations and myths of the Germanic peoples. Himmler was also certainly fascinated with alternative and occult practices. His Ahnenerbe institution investigated a range of areas including, but not limited to archaeology, musicology, witchcraft and mythlore.

12 For more on the Polar myth (Ultima Thule, a northern Atlantis, etc.) see Joscelyn Godwin's *Arktos: the Polar Myth in Science, Symbolism and Nazi Survival.* Kempton, Illinois: Adventure Unlimited, 1996.

13 The earliest account of the history of 'Atlantis' is Plato's late dialogue *Critias* in which the philosopher discusses the location, history and power of the Atlantean island.

Human Races in 1855, developing the theory of the Aryan master race. Effectively, as Nicholas Goodrick-Clarke has pointed out, the Social-Darwinian concept of a coming biological struggle for survival of the fittest was accepted and amalgamated with the notion of the inevitable dawn of a mystical and supreme root-race, the Nordic-Aryan.[14] Such Ariosophist ideas bled into 20th century thinking and were nurtured by the fratricidal apocalypse of the First World War.

In his book *Atlantis and the Cycles of Time*, Joscelyn Godwin suggested that:

> After the First World War Germany was in need of myths that would excuse its defeat and give its people hope for the future. Ariosophy lay readily to hand with its enticing myth of a Nordic-Aryan-Atlantean origin for the German folk ... The recent war had proved how the inferior races, with whom the Aryans unwisely interbred, had become their enemies both from within, by polluting their blood, and from without.[15]

Ariosophist ideas became part of the post-war bedrock of legend which, along with emergent alternative historical narratives, would have an enduring influence on National Socialist thinking.

One such alternative historical narrative was presented by the Dutch scholar and historian Herman Wirth. Wirth did not consider himself a mystic or an Ariosophist. He based his hypotheses on the eclectic (but encyclopaedic) evidence that he had collected himself over many years. Wirth's 1928 book *Der Aufgang der Menschheit* (Ascent of Mankind), presented his ideas and findings and, like some of the Ariosophist thinkers before him, related the origins of the Nordic race to a lost northern continent. The Nordic-Atlanteans had, Wirth postulated, brought language and civilisation when their diaspora arrived on European shores from the north. They had emerged at a time when the Arctic had had a temperate climate, and who had colonised more southerly regions as a result of climactic climate change or some other catastrophe, such as recounted in the Atlantean legend.

Amongst other things, Wirth was convinced of the symbolic significance of emblems and carvings found throughout rural Friesland and that regional folk art pointed to a symbolic meaning dating back to pre-Christian times and a culture from the north more ancient than supposed. Wirth's ideas became of interest to Himmler who patronised him and appointed him as the first president of the 'Ahnenerbe' in 1935.

The Italian traditionalist and esotericist Julius Evola, on reviewing Wirth's book *Der Aufgang der Menschheit*, wrote:

---

14 Goodrick-Clarke, Nicholas. *The Occult Roots of Nazism, Secret Aryan Cults and their influence on Nazi Ideology.* New York: New York U.P. 1992. 13.

15 Godwin, Joscelyn. *Atlantis and the Cycles of Time, Prophecies, Traditions, and Occult Revelations.* Rochester, Vermont: Inner Traditions, 2011. 124.

> ... it is like finding oneself inside an enchanted castle: one can refuse to enter, but once the threshold is passed, it is difficult to get out again. One moves from signs to phonemes and signs, by way of idols, conjurations, calendrical notations, names of gods and demons, ornaments, rites and ritual objects, inscriptions, masks, prehistoric designs on rocks or in caves, funerary ornaments and finds of every sort, supplemented by specimens gathered in situ during years of research by Wirth himself – the author gives us no respite ... It is hard to find its equal in these fields, monopolized as they are by an arid and pedantic erudition.[16]

In a 1933 article in the Dutch newspaper the *Telegraaf*, the pagan belief structure of Wirth's Nordic-Atlantean race is presented as something revolutionary and also potentially attractive as an alternative pagan belief-system for the modern age. Entitled 'Actual Primordial Religion of the Aryans', it carries the dramatic subtitle 'Arctic regarded as the cradle of the noble Nordic race'. The article set out Wirth's findings that the pagan Ur-race of the Aryans was unsullied by religious trappings, was pure in spirit and revolved around an 'All Father' *Wr-alda* and an 'Earth Mother' *Irtha* and a saviour son the 'Heilbrenger' who dies and is reborn in the bosom of the Earth Mother at the solstice:

> In Germany, a daily increasing movement of people can be observed, who turn away from Christianity and desire to return to the original Germanic and Aryan gods. This movement had been moderate, since many felt uncomfortable worshiping Wodan again. But now, Wirth has come with his "Heilbrenger" and it is under this banner, that the anti-Christian Germans can unselfconsciously unite if they so wish ...[17]

The reference to the All-Father is a reminder of the nearness of the dramatic force of the Wotan archetype, who was, it seemed, pulsating and awaiting release just beneath the Judeo-Christian veneer.

At the heart of Wirth's speculations was a strange and seemingly ancient text, the *Oera Linda Book*. Written in Frisian, the book's main assertions correlated with Wirth's findings of the Nordic–Atlantean origins of the Germanic peoples. The manuscript had first come to light in 1867 when Cornelis Over de Linden had presented the manuscript for translation and publication. A Dutch translation was published, and even an English translation in 1876. The book was a chronicle of the Nordic-Atlantean people who had, after the destruction of Atland or Altand, settled in Frisia. Many scholars rejected the book as a forgery but the debate continues to

16 Quoted in Godwin, 134.

17 From the Dutch newspaper 'Telegraaf' 14/05/1933. Translation and source courtesy Jan Ott. Posted 15 February 2016 http://fryskednis.blogspot.co.uk/

this day, with its defenders making a strong case for a thorough re-examination.[18]

Wirth was certainly convinced by its veracity, and in 1933 he edited and published the book in German as the *Ura Linda Chronik* to much controversy and debate.

With the earliest portion reported as written in 2194 BCE, a year after the fall of Atland, the book tells of a dominant European society of Nordics who have fled the deluge. They have a matriarchal order of priestesses dedicated to Frya, daughter of the All-Father and Earth Mother. It offers a Northern European alternative origin of Greek and Phoenician scripts from the runes developed from the six spoked Hagal wheel.

As Evola opined when discussing Wirth's research:

> The origins here appear under a special spiritual light … in primordial times, meanings and symbols still survived in a pure state, and then were lost, obfuscated, or altered. Prehistoric research, brought from a level of disanimated scientific-archaeological or anthropological positivism to a level of spiritual synthesis, promises therefore to open new horizons for the true history of civilisation.[19]

The debate became a bitter one. Ideologues such as Rosenberg criticised the matriarchal, pacifist aspects of the account. More broadly, Hitler saw the challenge to Christianity from the more 'pagan' elements of National Socialism as problematic to his efforts to unify a religiously diverse Christian German nation. Concerned with developing a more academic perception of the Ahnenerbe, Himmler too began to move against Wirth and by 1939 Wirth had been completely removed from the institution. However, Wirth's fascination with Atlantean origins, the cultural popularity of Ariosophist notions of a Thule/Atlantis/Hyperborea (with divine origins) and the political endorsement of a radically alternative origin of the Germanic race, all provided a background for such notions to be legitimised as a worthy subject to be explored through photographic examinations in books and magazines. As Goodrick-Clarke pointed out:

> Wirth's following and influence among German [*and we might add Dutch, in particular*] *völkisch* groups was considerable from the outset. His vision of an ancient high Thuata civilisation from which the Nordic sea peoples had set forth in their swan and dragon ships to colonise the Atlantic world reflected a utopian imperialism for those who bewailed the impotence and demoralization of the Weimar republic. Pessimists and opponents of the present were drawn to his idea that a revival of this Thuata-Atlantean culture

18 For more information about the ongoing translation and research into this document see: http://fryskednis.blogspot.co.uk/

19 Arthur Branwen, *Ultima Thule. Julius Evola e Herman Wirth*. Parma: Edizioni all'insegna del Veltro, 2007. Quoted on www.gornahoor.net accessed 17/11/2016.

> would signal the rebirth of the Germanic race and the liberation of mankind from the curse of modernity.[20]

Despite Wirth's removal from office his ideas continued to be influential and were referenced in the Dutch texts under discussion here.[21] This essay will explore this tradition by examining select examples reproduced in German and in particular Dutch National Socialist publications. It will examine how photography became part of a quest to discover how the finest examples of the 'volk' were those country people who, it was suggested, were the descendants of a real Nordic-Atlantean bloodline.

Photographing the 'Volk', gathering evidence of the bloodline

The historiography of photographic history has certainly neglected the influence of the esoteric on its output. Indeed, esoterica has been historically largely unpalatable to academia *in toto* but this is changing and there are today many scholars examining the enormous impact of esoteric currents on the culture and history of the west.[22] Here I am concerned with an aspect of the influence of mytho-history on photography and the representation of esoteric ideas as photographic image (using location, juxtaposition and the application of physiognomy).[23] Specifically, how the photographs of select German and Dutch photographers who were active during Hitler's Third Reich were constructed and presented, through a mixture of photographic aesthetics, physiognomy and a visual representation of radical traditionalism, in order to help popularise an ideological image of the German peasant.

Richard Gray has pointed out: ' … just how important the photograph became in Nazi culture as an instrument for training a disciplinary gaze, for developing a form of technologized seeing whose purpose was to strip away the visible veneer of human beings and expose or interpolate an otherwise "invisible" racial foundation that purportedly undergirded it.'[24] This process of 'technologized seeing' was developed to reveal the racial foundations of the German. In addition to this, there was, to a certain degree, an effort to conflate this racial revelation with a mystical origin of the Aryan race. Science was resolutely girded with a belt of magic.

In the 19th century, the new medium of photography seemed to be the ideal

20 Nicholas Goodrick-Clarke, *Black Sun: Aryan Cults, Esoteric Nazism, and the Politics of Identity.* New York: New York U.P., 2003. 130.

21 Indeed, Wirth maintained his beliefs for the rest of his life – his ideas are still highly regarded by his followers even today.

22 And with societies such as Association for the Study of Esotericism (ASE) and the European Society for the Study of Western Esotericism (ESSWE), amongst others, it is done so in non-antagonistic, engaged manner.

23 Physiognomy is an ancient esoteric practice predicated on the belief that the face and the body can be read like a book to reveal nature and character.

24 Richard T. Gray, *About Face: German Physiognomic Thought from Lavater to Auschwitz.* Detroit: Wayne State U.P., 2004. 368.

physiognomic tool. Seemingly objective and accurate, the process of photography could be mastered relatively quickly and applied in the field by the researcher himself without the need of an artist being present. Physiognomy was readily adopted as a means of enabling a scientific examination of the subject (in, for example, areas such as anthropology) but it never completely managed to eschew its former divinatory associations. This was reinforced by confusion, speculation and the allure of the photograph itself, the 'mirror with a memory', the shadow-catcher. The fascination with, and application of, physiognomic thinking was particularly evident in the new 19th century German state. By the early 20th century there were a number of German photographers applying a physiognomic approach to their portrait photographs. This cultural-aesthetic-scientific trend coincided with the growth of illustrated magazines in Germany in the 20th century. Photography had become the illustrative medium of choice in these enormously popular picture magazines. As the Jewish cultural critic Walter Benjamin asserted: "... picture magazines begin to put up signposts for him [the viewer], right ones or wrong ones, no matter. For the first time, captions have become obligatory."[25] This kind of photography Benjamin is referring to was part of a new cultural context as a medium of readily available, quickly 'readable' mass communication.

Mass reproduction techniques ensured that photography became central to mass communication. As the Hungarian émigré artist László Moholy-Nagy (1895-1946) declared: 'The illiterate of the future will be the person ignorant of the use of the camera as well as the pen.'[26] This was the new era of cinema; the lightweight 35mm camera; casual photography and photo-magazines where the photograph told the story and the reader read the images in a layout. During this time, picture editors employed specific strategies to suggest readings, often without the need of large amounts of text. Dynamic enlargements, montages, double-page spreads and succinct captions became the stock-in-trade of the editor when considering how to use the layout to create the greatest visual impact. The opportunity to combine images meant that deliberate strategies of comparison could be used.

The photography that I'm discussing here was a product of this new media. These photo-illustrated populist publications presented an idealised physiognomic image of the peasant and the landscape as well as developing a narrative that associated the modern (National Socialist) era with history, traditions and mythology – a mytho-history. Some of the photographers whose images are illustrated here were also prolific producers of their own illustrated books; several of them regularly reappeared alongside each other in 'compilation' volumes or journals; and most of them had their work produced in magazines and editions relating to race in National Socialist journals such as *Volk und Rasse* and *NS Frauen Warte* for example.

Effectively, these publications attempted to develop physiognomies of 'volk', history, customs and land; that is, a visual map that linked the people

25 Walter Benjamin, *Illuminations*, ed. Hannah Arendt, New York: Harcourt, Brace and World, 1968. 226.

26 Louis Kaplan, *Laszlo Moholy-Nagy: Biographical Writings*.Durham, NC: Duke U.P., 1995. 139.

and the landscapes they inhabited. Many of the photographers working in the Germanosphere in the National Socialist era were notable for their use of the medium to emphasise an anti-rational, anti-enlightenment and Romantic model. They created a visual syntax for examining the 'volk', especially in terms of the supposedly timeless look and life of the peasant. These *völkisch* photographers used a heady mix of aesthetics and ideology in their work applying their skills to develop a visual icon of the racial German and in particular the peasant class. But why the peasant? Because the peasant was seen as being less tainted by the cosmopolitan city, racially pure, linked to the earth in labour and tradition (and therefore linked to the ancestors). As the *völkisch* writer Julius Langbehn wrote at the turn of the century: 'The peasant who actually owns a piece of land has a direct relationship to the centre of the world. Through this he becomes master of the universe.'[27] The *völkisch* German and Dutch photographic publications attempted to outline the metaphysical essence of a 'Germanicness' and that notion was believed to be best represented in these peasant classes, i.e. those closer to the earth, the untainted being who were, both in terms of their biology and their soul, truly Germanic. The people pictured in these books exemplified the great Norwegian author Knut Hamsun's peasant type, someone who was; 'A tiller of the ground, body and soul; a worker on the land without respite. A ghost risen out of the past to point to the future, a man from the earliest days of cultivation, a settler in the wilds, nine hundred years old, and, withal, a man of the day.'[28]

These mystical 'types' were identified too with an alternative origin of western civilisation that sought clues in ancient locations, race, symbols, and an interpretation of archaeology and history that had been developed and expounded by both fringe and mainstream Germanist scholars.

In order to illustrate the kind of photography used and the manner of their placement and construction I have selected illustrations from four books. The first three are Dutch publications: *Zinnebeelden in Nederland* (Hamer, 1940), Friesland-Friezenland (Hamer, 1942); and *Eeuwig Levende Teekens* (Hamer, 1941). The Dutch *völkisch* photographer Willem Frederik van Heemskerck-Düker (1910-1988) both wrote, photographically illustrated and edited or contributed to all of these volumes for the Dutch National Socialist publisher 'Hamer'. His portfolio included landscapes, portraits and photographs of *Zinnebeelden* or signs, ornaments and architectural details that were interpreted as the runic relics of a primordial Aryan language (after Herman Wirth). Indeed, these publications are directly connected with Wirth's search for the traces of the Nordic-Atlantean diaspora and hence their selection.

The fourth book selected here is illustrative of a linked German approach to the visualisation of the 'Greater Germany' and its romantic-scientific representation of racial ideals with a shared mytho-history. *Das Deutsche Volksgesicht: Schleswig-Holstein* (Gauverlag Bayerische Ostmark, 1939) is a portfolio volume by the

27 Julius Langbehn, *Rembrandt als Erzieher*. Leipzig: Hirschfeld, 1900. 131.
28 Hamsun, Knut. *Growth of the Soil.* Book II ch. 12. New York: Alfred A. Knopf. 1917. 252.

German *völkisch* photographer Erna Lendvai-Dircksen (1883-1962). As in the portrait approach employed in the Dutch Hamer publications (which, in the case of *Friesland-Friezenland* also employed some of her work),[29] Lendvai-Dircksen made work in a manner that was both modernistically visually direct yet simultaneously a form of heroic-romanticism. In her career, Lendvai-Dircksen developed a huge portfolio of characterful faces. Over a 12 year period beginning in 1932 through to 1944, she produced several volumes of these studies beginning as *Das deutsche Volksgesicht* and morphing into *Das germanische Volksgesicht* as the war progressed and areas both within the German Reich such as Schleswig Holstein, and outside it, such as Flanders and Norway, were included.

The books are all in the Quarto size range (except *Eeuwig Levende Teekens* which is more of an Octavo size and handier as an exhibition accompaniment) and thus the images are large and have a greater impact. The photographs have a presence, reinforced by scale and the looming closeness of the face. All of these photographs of 'types' represented in these German and Dutch völkisch books are unnamed. The people these photographers photographed are not intended to be seen as individuals but rather as an exposition on the presence of 'good blood', as archetypes of their race. They are ideological banners against an emergent globalism and are intended to suggest something precious and unique.

'Bauer als Gottmensch', the face of the divine

The 1942 'Hamer' publication *Friesland/Friezenland* (1942) is a book that extols the virtues of this singular region of northern Europe by discussing the history, people and landscape and devoting 151 of its 232 pages to full page photographs. The book was written (and partially illustrated with his own photographs) by the Dutch agricultural engineer and photographer W. F. van Heemskerck Düker, a proponent and promoter of the idea of a 'Greater Germany' and someone who can be regarded as belonging to the 'Feldmeijer Group'[30] in the 1940s. The book is constructed so that the images and layout work in tandem to reinforce a specific political, cultural and mythic message.

The first photographic plate in this volume is by the German photographer Hans Retzlaff (1904-1965). Retzlaff was a widely reproduced völkisch photographer and was known in particular for his portraits of people in folk costume such as his book *Deutsches Bauerntrachtern.*[31] Retzlaff's work regularly appeared alongside that of many of the other photographers whose work was reproduced in *Friesland-Friezenland.*

This opening image of Retzlaff's in *Friesland-Friezenland* is of the sea (fig.1).

29 And the work of other völkisch photographers such as Erich Retzlaff, Hans Retzlaff and Hans Saebens.

30 Ensel, 23. Named for Johannes Hendrik Feldmeijer (1910-1945) a member of the Dutch National Socialist party (*Nationaal-Socialistische Beweging in Nederland*) and proponent of the notion of the Netherlands as part of a Greater Germanic community.

31 Retzlaff, Hans, et al. *Deutsches Bauerntrachtern.* Berlin: Atlantis Verlag, 1934.

Fig. 1

Fig. 2

The sun is westering, its reflection shining across the placid surface of the North Sea. The image is there to remind the reader of the significance of the sea to Frisian life but also to invoke as the first of a series of icons that conflate the past, the present and the future as well as mythology. The first image is always very important because it situates what is to follow. At the same time the image concludes things too. It seems to state, 'we are of the sea, we come from the sea and the sun'. The very last plate in the book is of the resulting legacy of the sea (fig.2). Also by Hans Retzlaff, the girl gazes forwards out of the frame and beyond the book. The focus is on her face, the tight cinematic crop so typical of the *New Objectivity*,[32] it forces the viewer into an encounter with her face, her features, her physiognomy and thus her race. As the counterpoint to the first, the sea as place of origin, the last image is the future, the seed of the sea, the daughter of the myth.

These images are arranged not merely for aesthetic effect but in addition, are purposefully constructed to convey a specific meaning. Publications such as this one aim to celebrate, educate and warn the reader. The implicit warning that is constructed by these two images, the visual 'alpha and omega' of this publication, is to protect this legacy. The girl in the final frame looks to the right of the reader, beyond the books endpapers into the future. The historical-genetic-cultural legacy, it is implied, must withstand the dangers and pressures that surround it.

This legacy is evident again in the portrait of a man (fig.3) several pages further on in the text. Accompanied by the motto:

32 *Neue Sachlichkeit* or *New Objectivity* was an art movement formed around 1920 in Weimar Germany. It was concerned with the rejection of Romantic Expressionism and in photographic terms its proponents employed a dramatic, straight approach. It is generally regarded as having ended with the rise of National Socialism however, many of the *völkisch* German photographers continued to employ its direct and often close-cropped techniques.

Fig. 3

Fig. 4

Friske, riske, starke Degen
De ehr Höved
in den wolken dregen[33]

The portrait at first glance is a simple one. However, there is a complexity to the image which is quickly revealed by a closer examination. The man is nameless, he does not stand represented as an individual but like the other images that fill the book, he is an example of a type and they are all examples of the same type. The Dutch scholar Remco Ensel has pointed out how stern these people look in this *völkisch* photography. He stated: 'Life was no laughing matter ... Models are sometimes dourly staring into a wide open space.'[34] But it could not be otherwise. The man is a projection of physiognomic values and presented as a representative of his race. The photograph is intended to demonstrate his sobriety, seriousness, vigour. Nor is his demeanour unusual as a representation of a type. In the physiognomic cannon of the right in the 1930s and 40s there was an attempt to recapture the masculinity of the nineteenth century portrait stare. His physiognomy is intended to demonstrate his ancestral potency. He stares to the viewer's left providing a three-quarter profile. The camera is slightly below so the face has a monumentality about it rising as it does above the viewer's gaze. The eyes are shadowed by the strong light

33 *Neocorus* (Johann Adolf Köster) (1550-1630) from his chronicles on the history and folklore of the 'Dithmarschen' in Schleswig-Holstein.
34 Ensel, 34.

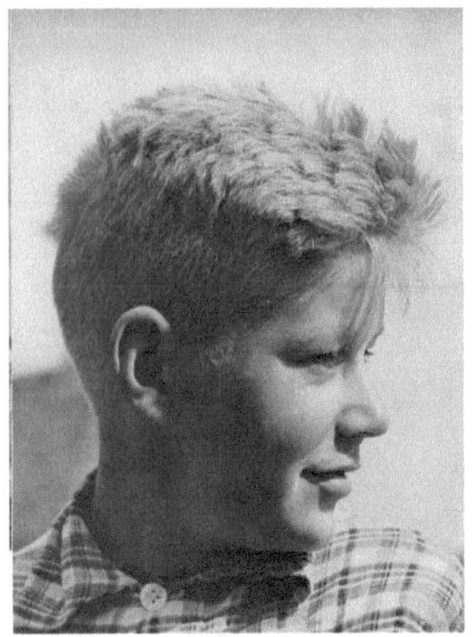

Fig. 5

of the sun, he is depicted heroically, sculpturally, beyond mere flesh.

The photograph is by the German photographer Hans Saebens (1895-1969) so the reproduction can be compared to the original. The full frame (fig.4)[35] can be seen to be similarly tightly cropped to the book's image. The man's perspiration, evident in the original, has been retouched but the published reproduction is almost true to Saebens' original photograph. *In Friesland-Friezenland* the unnamed man stares out across to a companion landscape image of, inevitably, the sea shore.

Using the visual strategy of 'doubling', the editor could suggest readings by implying a relationship by image proximity, a 'suggested' montage for the reader. In these books, doubling is used as a tool for underlining the link between these people of the landscape and the landscape itself. In fig.5 and fig.6 the conflation of the landscape image and the portrait similarly makes a connection between the youth (the future) and the landscape they inhabit. Fig.5 is from *Friesland-Friezenland* whilst fig.6 is from Lendvai-Dircksen's book *Das Deutsche Volksgesicht: Schleswig-Holstein*. Both images use the direction in which the reader views a text (left to right) to draw the viewer's gaze across from the profile view of boy and girl into the landscape. Both are flaxen haired Frisians and their racial characteristics are evident. The profile highlights these characteristics, they are anthropometrically on display to the viewer so the shape of the face, the curve of the forehead the straight

35 The image is contained in a collection of negatives now housed in Aberystwyth University's School of Art Gallery and Museum. The negatives were originally stored in 29 carefully annotated envelopes variously titled 'köpfe' or 'volksköpfe'. Here were Saebens physiognomic studies that had appeared in *Friesland/Friezenland* (and elsewhere) and in the main the emphasis is on the people of the north-west of Germany and the Netherlands near to Saebens home in Worpswede, the very people linked to the *Oera Linda Book* as the descendants of the Nordic-Atlantean exiles from old Atland. Of this man the envelope simply states: 'Manner am Spetzerfehn'.

Fig. 6

nose, all can be read. The lighting on the figures is dramatic and strong shadows accentuate both their features (once more the eyes, the window to the individual, are shaded). The landscapes are, in contrast, open, expansive soft, and bounteous. In the image of the boy the text below simply states 'Bloed en bodem' or blood and soil. Here *Reichsbauernführer* Darré's paradigm is expounded visually.

Tradition too is honoured in these books. The text accompanying fig.7 in *Friesland-Friezenland* tells us that even the young are aware of the traditions of the past: 'But the children know the old traditions, because they know, that in the Frisian forests the *Poppestien* lies where they once came from.'[36] This specific text and visual reference to the Poppestien at Burgum confirms the link between the past and the present. Here the ancient *Poppestien* is presented opposite an image of a young child (doubling once more). The *Poppestien*, a large flat boulder is historically linked to pagan fertility rites and according to legend children were delivered from beneath this stone. The child in profile is representative of the youthful modern era, the sign of a pure racial legacy (blond, fair skinned) and the evidence of the fecundity of the race and, according to the legend, literally born of the soil. As a Jungian archetype the child links to the past. The stone is the ancient traditions of the past, a past obscured in time but which continues to live in the blood of the present.

The books *Zinnebeelden in Nederland* and *Eeuwig Levende Teekens*, weave together Herman Wirth's pagan pantheon and the visual signs as evidence of the Nordic-Atlantean legacy which were sought in both the faces of the people as well as the folk traditions, carvings and symbols. Indeed, some of the photographs are reproduced in both volumes. *Eeuwig Levende Teekens* was produced to accompany

36 *Friesland-Friezenland* (author's translation). 202.

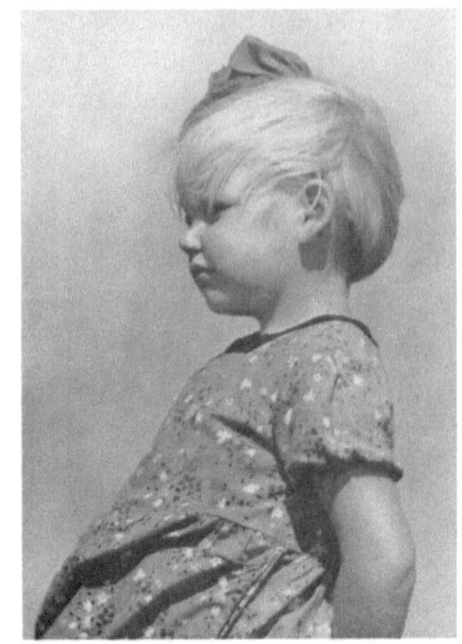

Fig. 7

an exhibition (and short film)[37] of the same name in the Hague in 1941. In this short but richly illustrated text, a wholes series of symbols are examined and their ancient origins postulated. The reader (and gallery visitor) are led through the symbols and helpfully guided to readings and interpretations. Such signs and symbols are apparently everywhere awaiting recognition and release. The motto on the opening page of the book declares:

Wakker Wordt
wat eens geweten
vergetlheid vergaat[38]

Fig.8 is an example of the comparison of these ancient graphic elements made using photographs from a variety of sources. The text describes this symbol and its solar origin: 'The movement of the sun, the great event of a daily and annual rise and fall, the ever renewed victory of light over dark, the image of unshakable faith in the resurrection from night and distress: this is the ever-living interpretation of the legendary, ancient sign of deliverance, the swastika.'[39] An 8th century BC Greek vase emblazoned with the Swastika is illustrated above an 18th century grave stone that carries the same enduring symbol. Wherever the Aryan people have lived, it is stated, one will find this sun sign.

As with such potent symbols, sacred locations such as the Externsteine in north-west Germany, are also highlighted (fig.9). The Externsteine was a location associated with the *Irminsul*, the holy tree or pillar linked to Yggdrasil. The author

37 The film, produced by the 'Volksche Werkgemeenschap', can be viewed on YouTube.
38 'Wake up. What once was known forgetfulness destroys' (author's translation).
39 *Eeuwig Levende Teekens* (author's translation). 16.

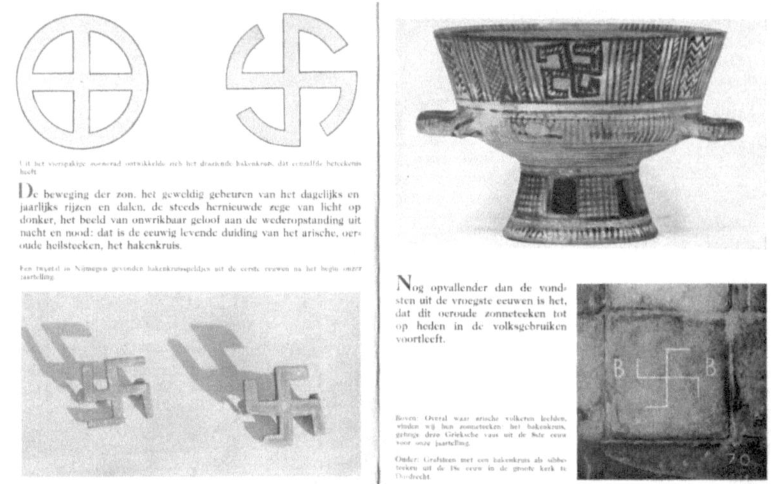
De beweging der zon, het geweldig gebeuren van het dagelijks en jaarlijks rijzen en dalen, de steeds hernieuwde zege van licht op donker, het beeld van onwrikbaar geloof aan de wederopstanding uit nacht en nood: dat is de eeuwig levende duiding van het arische, oeroude heilsteeken, het hakenkruis.

Nog opvallender dan de vondsten uit de vroegste eeuwen is het, dat dit oeroude zonneteeken tot op heden in de volksgebruiken voortleeft.

Fig. 8

of *Eeuwig Levende Teekens* records: 'From various religious legends we learn of the significance to the North of holy trees, sacred to Thor and Freya. Not for nothing did [St.] Boniface have these trees cut down as well as Charlemagne destroying the Irminsul at the Externsteine in old Saxony.'[40]

Despite his apparent fall from grace, *Zinnebeelden in Nederland* makes specific reference to Wirth himself and underlines the Nordic-Atlantean origins of these people represented by their signs and symbols.

> Professor Herman Wirth, one of the leading scholars in this field, has emphatically and repeatedly pointed out, that we are wrong to assume that our race, with which the runes are so closely connected, is of Eastern origin. In his opinion, a Northern cultural origin is most probable and this would additionally explain the specific use of the solar cycle in the runes.[41]

Zinnebeelden in Nederland is a photographic catalogue of the very signs and symbols that Wirth had 'recognised' as evidence early on in his career. Photographed by van Heemskerck Düker, the book, like *Eeuwig Levende Teekens*, aimed to demonstrate how regularly recurring visual symbols are residual traces of an ancient symbology or, according to Wirth, a paleo-epigraphy, derived from the ancients.

For example, the illustrations in fig.10 (from *Zinnebeelden in Nederland*) examine the use of the Hagal rune which is it is noted, is a 'zesspakige zonnerad' or six-spoked sun-wheel. The Hagal is repeated in the image on the opposite page where it appears on the side of a farm building. The sun wheel is of the utmost

40 *Zinnebeelden in Nederland* (author's translation). 23.
41 *Zinnebeelden in Nederland* (author's translation). 14.

Op steile rots in het Teutoburgerwoud stond meer dan 1000 jaar geleden de Irminsul in de vrije Germaansche ruimten; een levensboom tot strakken Germaanschen vorm herschapen. De Irminsul ging te gronde aan het einde van den Volksverhuizingstijd. Het teeken werd vernietigd, de gedachte die in het hart van het volk leefde, bleef ongebroken. Na meer dan 1000 jaren leeren wij heden ten dage weer opnieuw verstaan het oude, trotsche zinnebeeld van Germaansch geloof aan het leven en aan de onverwoestbare kracht van ons volk.

Fig. 9

significance in this visual lexicon with regards the Nordic-Atlantean legacy. The analysis of the Hagal rune as a manifestation of the quartered sun wheel is drawn back to the Polar origins of the Aryan race and the celebration of the cycle of the solar year:

> ... for our ancestors the sun was paramount as was its life-giving power and heat, it is clear then that the symbol of the sun was central. In more southerly regions the worship of the sun made way for the worship of the moon, which is understandable because in the equatorial regions, the sun is not the bringer of fertility and life, on the contrary, it's power is often one that withers. Furthermore, in these southern regions the seasons are indistinguishable from each other. However, the more one moves to the north, the greater are the differences between winter and summer, the clearer is the connection between the sun and the changing of the seasons and the distinctive solar loop can serve as a basis for a chronology.
>
> Thus, probably at a time when our ancestors still lived in the ultimate north, there emerged from the eternal day of midsummer and (the unbroken darkness of) midwinter, when the sun did not rise, a symbol of the division of the year into two and then quartered ... [42]

Conclusion

Esoteric paradigms such as physiognomy, affected and often merged into 'rational' science and contributed to the manner in which a medium like photography was

42 *Zinnebeelden in Nederland* (author's translation). 16.

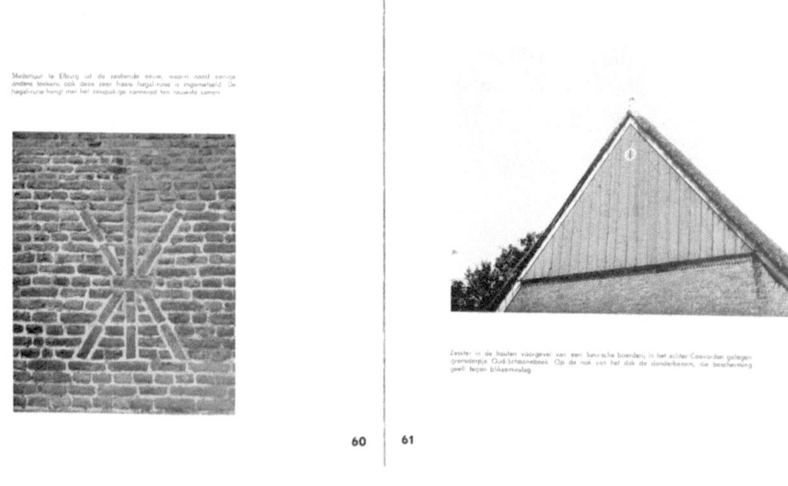

Fig. 10

understood to reveal 'truth' and grew out of 19th century anthropological science (and anthropometrical uses of photography) as well as an arcane response to a perceived 'racial destiny'. Photography played a pivotal role in the construction of the image of the broader Germanic *Volk* in the 1930s and 1940s. This creatively staged photography grafted the past to the present, straddled across national boundaries and employed the aesthetics of modernism with the apparent scrutiny of anthropology. What links the photographs contained in the books I have examined here is their focus on the coastal north-west of Europe. All of these books presented their subject matter in a manner that is intended to guide the reader into finding a gateway to a shared mytho-history. Most of all it reinforced a myth of origins that emerged from esoteric *völkisch* dreams and radical interpretations of science.

In these photographically illustrated books, the evidence was presented for a unique origin far outside of any middle-eastern or African evolution of mankind. No, these people, it was proposed, came from the North. What's more, these archetypes were to be *identified* with.

> Every monumental individual portrait ... could be seen as the embodiment of the idealized national community. The observer sees a portrait and recognizes a fellow countryman ... The reproduction of these portraits facilitates identification and seduces the viewer into believing that he is part of the biographical narrative of the nation.[43]

Ultimately, the photographs are staged to present an encounter, an encounter with the finest examples of these descendants of the Arctic Atlantis. The pantheon of craggy, young, blonde, beautiful, ruddy, determined, superior faces highlighted the

43 Ensel, Remco. "Dutch Face-ism. Portrait Photography and *Völkisch* Nationalism in the Nether-

fact that evidence of the diaspora of the Polar *Ur-Heimat*, could still be located on the shores of the restless Northern Sea. The viewer, now identifying themselves with the people and the mytho-history illustrated in the photographs (photographs are *objective*, they show *without trickery*), are thus awakened. Now they were assured that they too carried a sacred gift, the bloodline of Atlantis, their blood.

---

lands". *Fascism* 2 (2013), Brill. 19.

A Long Boundless (Spi:Ritual) Derangement of Art

Kendell Geers

O for a Muse of fire, that would ascend
The brightest heaven of invention,
(…)
And let us, ciphers to this great account,
On your imaginary forces work.
(…)
Into a thousand parts divide on man,
And make imaginary puissance
(…)

– William Shakespeare, *Henry V*[1]

Just what is it that makes (African) Art today so different, so appealing (time and again)?

As my thoughts find slow form through the words of this text, the latest Marvel blockbuster film "Black Panther" is breaking all box-office records, turning the leaf on a new chapter of cultural history. The film centres around a fictional African tribe called the Wakanda who learned five centuries ago that a meteorite containing the mineral Vibranium granted super human abilities. Whilst the plot is generic Hollywood scripted flum about the world's first African (American) superhero, the styling of the Wakanda merits mention for the costume designers once again wove an entire continent into a single fabric with warp and weft from the Basotho, Ejagham, Ndebele, OvaHimba, Zulu, Maasai, Igbo, Mursi and Tuareg traditions, and Africa is once again reduced to a fantasy at the centre stage of art, fashion and film.

It has been a "Short Century" since European Avant Garde artists like Derain, Matisse, Malevich, Braque, Brancusi, Apollinaire, Gauguin, Modigliani, Klee, Kandinsky, Nolde, Ernst and Giacometti found their inspiration in the traditional African Arts. For many of them the key was reading Carl Einstein's book "Negerplastik," first published in 1915, but there have since been countless publications and exhibitions that have attempted to define and understand the captivating spirit of what is understood as African Art. Despite many claims to

1 Shakespeare, *Henry V*, Act 1, Prologue

the contrary, and regardless of the best of intentions, sadly the Occidental reading of Africa remains pejorative and patronising. From the 1984 ground-breaking MoMa blockbuster "Primitivism in 20th Century Art: Affinity of the Tribal and the Modern" through the 1989 Centre Pompidou pioneering "Magiciens de la terre" to the recent "Picasso Primitif" exhibition at Quai Branly, African Art continues to be understood as the noble savagery of culturally antediluvian and isolated tribes. In French, the term "art premier" is still used to describe works of art read through a Eurocentric prism as primal, preliterate and naïve. The term might not be nearly as offensive had the notion of primal or primitive not been coloured by the blind arrogance of a cultural assumption that Western civilisation is superior to all others and the pinnacle possibility of cultural evolution.

If "primitive," then why does African Art continue to enthral and influence artists (and film makers) around the world, across every generation, influencing their work and bringing them to their knees with respect? And yet again, why have there been no great historical African Artists that we could name?

For some of the early twentieth century Avant Guardians, it was the serpentine line, abstract shapes, accentuated forms and liberal approach to materials that opened the path away from the classical canons of art, beauty and proportion that had held European tradition in place since the Greeks. Standing in front of a Fang guardian figure, the eyes bulge, the muscles of the short stunted arms and legs are exaggerated, the sharp angles of the mouth protrude with griming menace and the hair rolls back in geometric waves. The figure is everything but realistic and yet feels more real than any photographic likeness. This offset gave artists the courage to break open the traditional canon of representation and introduce abstraction into their vocabulary. Matisse surrounded himself with Kuba Fabric, describing them as his African Velvet, saying that "I never tire of looking at them for long periods of time, even the simplest of them, and waiting for something to come to me from the mystery of their instinctive geometry." From this, Matisse developed his cut-outs and derived the abstract backgrounds of his colourful canvasses.

African Art showed the way to abstraction and non-representation in the ways it emphasised states of being, or emotion, over realism and mathematical proportion. The head could be enlarged, or the eyes engorged, the legs reduced to lines or muscles exaggerated in order to create a sense of what the figure feels like rather than how it looks. The father of Negritude, Leopold Senghor, famously proclaimed that "Emotion is Negro (sic) as much as reason is Greek." These formal and aesthetic atrophies were key in enabling artists to re-present the harsh realities that marked the early twentieth century as the Industrial Revolution and scientific discoveries flowed over into the mechanisation that enabled two World Wars.

> Instead of draining rivers, society directs a human stream into a bed of trenches; instead of dropping seeds from airplanes, it drops incendiary bombs over cities; and through gas warfare the aura is abolished in a new way. 'Fiat Ars – Pereat Mundus' ("Let Art be

> Created – Perish the World") says Fascism, and, as Marinetti admits, expects war to supply the artistic gratification of a sense perception that has been changed by technology[2]

For a small handful of artists, it was not the line or abstract forms that made African Art so inspiring, but the animistic spirit and consequent animation of form. In the book "La tête d'obsidienne" published in 1974, the year after the artist had died, André Malraux quotes Pablo Picasso saying that for him "the masks weren't like other kinds of sculpture. Not at all. They were magical things (...) [they] were intercessors (…) against everything; against unknown, threatening spirits."

Picasso was drawn to what the objects embodied, saying that he understood them as "weapons to help people stop being dominated by spirits, to become independent. Tools. If we give form to the spirits, we become independent of them. The spirits, the unconscious (which wasn't yet much spoken of then), emotion, it's the same thing." From this experience and understanding in 1907, Picasso was enchanted and understood why he was "a painter. All alone in that awful museum, the masks, the Red Indian dolls, the dusty mannequins. Les Demoiselles d 'Avignon must have come to me that day, but not at all because of the forms: but because it was my first canvas of exorcism – yes, absolutely!"

For the young painter, standing in the Trocadero, a place that he described as "disgusting," understood something vital about the role of art. "I was all alone. I wanted to get away. But I didn't leave. I stayed. I stayed. I understood something very important: something was happening to me," a calling by synaesthesia no less. The senses of smell, sight and touch overwhelmed the young artist in paralysis, threading his perceptions through the eye of the needle of understanding. He explained to Malraux the vitality of his vision at its origins; in metaphysical terms saying "that's also what separated me from Braque. He loved the African pieces, but as I've said: because they were good sculptures. He wasn't ever afraid of them. Exorcism didn't interest him. Because he didn't feel what I called everything, life, or I don't know what, the Earth? Everything that surrounds us, everything that isn't us, he didn't find at all hostile. Not even – imagine! – not even strange! He always felt at home. And still does. He doesn't understand these things at all: he isn't superstitious!"

From Picasso's understanding the ritual function of art, or exorcism, was neither bound by culture nor material form, despite his extremely reductive understanding of African Art. Africa is a continent and not a country, and there is no such thing as African Art. A century after Picasso it still continues to be spoken of as a singular tradition, and art form, rather than the multi-cultural ethnic diversity of a continent of no less than 54 countries, more than 2000 living languages and a rich history dating back through the ancient Egyptians and Carthaginians, to the origin of our species before the dawn of time. Contrary to cliché and expectation, King Musa Keita I of Mali is the richest man in the world to have ever lived with a personal

2 Walter Benjamin, "The Work of Art in the Age of Mechanical Reproduction"

net worth of $ 400 Billion by today's standards at the time of his death in 1331.

Given the contradictions, complexity, ancient histories, diasporas, cross cultural influence, slave and trade routes dating back centuries, every attempt to define or speak for Africa will fall into cliché. When Picasso spoke of African Art and for the purposes of this text, the reader should keep in mind that he was not referring to the art of a continent, so much as the arts of a specific region, the Central and West African kingdoms of Fang, Pende, Kota, Songye, Dan, Lega, Tsogo, Igbo, Yoruba, Chokwe, Mbuya and Punu (to name only a few) spanning modern day Congo, Angola, Gabon, Equatorial Guinea, Cameroun, Benin and Nigeria.

The European reading of the African political landscape is an entirely modern construct, dating from the Berlin Conference of 1884–85 when the Austro-Hungarian Empire, Belgium, Denmark, France, Germany, Italy, Netherlands, Norway, Ottoman Empire, Portugal, Russia, Spain, Sweden, United Kingdom and the United States drew the borders through ancient lines, down the middle of families and clans, cutting up tradition and slicing apart the bonds the held the continent together. Not one single African was represented as the self-declared colonial superpowers drew their borders around their own economic and strategic interests, a division that set in motion all the socio-political uncertainly that would guarantee a century of civil wars, cross border raids and conflicts of ethnic cleansing.

African Art continues to be read, analysed, interpreted, valued and collected, not by the name of the artist, but by ethnic group and according to the cultural tradition from which the object has been crafted. In stark contrast to the principles by which European art is valued according to the cult of the author, the pristine condition of the work and Art Historical deviation from precedent and aesthetic canon, African Art is valued by its patina and aesthetic proximity to the presumed cultural canon. A Fang figure sweats with a shiny patina and a Kota Reliquary needs stand cross legged on guard, each tribe judged independent of influences as if the continent were lost in time.

The deeper, darker and older the scratches, scabs, stains and bruises, the more important and valuable the mask, effigy or staff. The mask, power object, talisman or reliquary was never created for display, never intended to be incarcerated, lifeless and static within a museum vitrine. No, they were meant to be performed, danced, animated and brought to life in rituals that demand sacrifice and surrender, anointed with the life forces of sperm, blood, urine, tears, milk and sweat. Unlike painting, the mask for instance was created to be worn, to be danced and ritually embodied. The patina of that use, the scratches, sweat, hair and encrusted skin that bear witness to the ritual function, and testimony of having been used, adding value and prestige.

The artist channels their emotions through the dance and from within the imagination via the mask, anointing matter with the vital force of their body fluids, or the sacrifice of their enemy's, transforming the energy into a spirit embodied. If you are not standing within the ritual, possessed of the spirit of the mask, entranced by the dance, you will never fully understand, much less appreciate, the true nature of what Picasso thought of as the art of exorcism. The spirits are alive just as the traditions evolve and the dance twists and turns through the village, around the fire, in the temple and upon the altar. It is a European conceit to fix African art as singular, static and untouched by time or external influence.

Despite the European experts' need to read African Art in terms of cultural simplicity, time and tradition are not fixed. The Nigerian writer Chinua Achebe explained the intrinsic nature of African Art with an Igbo saying "The world is a dancing masquerade. If you want to understand it, you can't remain standing in one place."

The great difference between Contemporary Art (to refer to the European merchant gallery traditions that have followed the Colonial routes through the Americas, across Africa, Asia into the contemporary age of information and artificial intelligence) and Traditional African Art, is that when you look at an African figure or mask, it looks right back at you, and all the way through you, with a penetrating gaze. The ritualised object was more than just art, more than aesthetic, more than formal. It was the very fabric of the faith that united a clan or tribe in their collective understanding of the mysteries, used, performed, embodied, animated and expressed in service of higher worlds like the angels of Jacob's Ladder, ascending and descending.

When they were first exposed to the European audience, these powerful talismanic art works and objects were so disturbing to their Victorian era sensibilities, that the words "Uncanny" and "Fetish" had to be invented to describe the experience. Freud first spoke about the uncanny in his 1919 essay "Das Unheimliche," describing the psychological experience of things strangely familiar and yet unsettling, alienating or taboo, causing discomfort. The English translation of Unheimliche is taken from the Anglo-Saxon word Canny meaning "Knowledge, understanding or cognisance" but twisted into its contrary and refers to the estranged sense of encountering something familiar yet threatening within the domain of the intimate, disturbing our sensibilities as well as our moral fabric. The literal translation of Unheimliche would be unhomely and it is this that Picasso was picking up on when he said that Braque "always felt at home" because he was not afraid of African art and does not understand these things because "he isn't superstitious !"

The word fetish was adapted by Freud in his later 1927 essay on "Fetishism" to describe "a substitute for the penis" and a "token of triumph over the threat of castration and a protection against it." Karl Marx would build on the theory to describe the commodification of labour and money. The word, however originates from the Portuguese *feitiçio*, taken from the Latin *facticius* (artificial) and *facere* (to make). In late 15th and 16th century pidgin, *Fetisso* was used by Portuguese Colonial explorers along the West African coast to describe the magical objects they encountered and believed embodied power so much they could be used to control people. By the early 20th century the term Fetish was used to specifically describe the nail figures made by the BaKongo people.

What Europeans continue to refer to as a 'nail fetish' is in fact an Nkisi (plural

Minkisi): a powerful spirit embodied in an anthropomorphic object. Minkisi are primarily containers or vessels, gourds, animal horns, shells, bundles or any other object containing spiritually-charged substances. They have even been described as portable graves as many include earth from a grave or relics of a powerful individual as a prime ingredient. The powers of the dead thus infuse the object and allow the *nganga*, or shaman, to control it. The Nkondi Nkisi were further activated by having nails driven into them, hammered into the wood with a prayer that re-enacts the crucifixion of Christ in a ritual invocation of powerful spirits intoned as protection against thieves. The glass and mirror eyes stare right back at the colonial traders who had used the very same mirrors and cheap trinkets to trade for gold, silver and diamonds. Through the eyes of the Europeans, the nature-based faiths and animistic traditions of the indigenous people they encountered were naïve, primitive and superstitious. They were so arrogant in their monotheistic doctrines that their faith gave them permission to commit untold atrocities in the name of Christ so it is not without coincidence that the rise of the Nkondi Nkisi protection spirit effigies coincide exactly with the most violent colonial occupation of the Congo by Belgium's King Leopold.

After numerous unsuccessful schemes to acquire colonies in Africa and Asia for himself, King Leopold created a private holding company disguised as an international scientific and philanthropic association in 1876. Through the pretext of the so-called International African Society, or the International Association for the Exploration and Civilization of the Congo, Leopold hired the famous explorer Henry Stanley to establish a colony in the Congo region. At the 1884–1885 Berlin conference, Leopold managed to lay his personal claim to the ownership of the Congo Free State, an area 76 times larger than Belgium. From the 5th of February 1885, the King used his own private army, the Force Publique, to control and rule over the territory using violence and cultural oppression where necessary.

Consider, without prejudice and Colonial expectation, the possibility that the nails and mirrors were both witness of trade and protection against invasion, the symbolic embodiment and testimony to European trade. The Nkisi spirit figures were powerful magical talismans conjured to protect against what Joseph Conrad described in his tragic classic *Heart of Darkness* as "violence, aggravated murder on a great scale, and men going at it blind – as is very proper for those who tackle a darkness. The conquest of the earth, which mostly means the taking it away from those who have a different complexion or slightly flatter noses than ourselves, is not a pretty thing when you look into it too much (…) They were conquerors, and for that you want only brute force – nothing to boast of, when you have it, since your strength is just an accident arising from the weakness of others. They grabbed what they could get for the sake of what was to be got." By the end of King Leopold's rule more than half the population, estimated around ten million people had been murdered by the King's private army.

Ironically, the official state religion of Kongo Kingdom was in fact Christianity. The ancient King Nzinga a Nkuwu was so impressed by the European faith that in

1491 he converted, changing his name to João I and declaring Christianity state religion. His coat of arms was centred upon a knight's iron helmet from which five iron clad arms hold up high five swords in the exact same manner as an Nkondi Nkisi. Below that, a shield decorated with scallop shells on either side of the Cross of Saint James represent the baptism and pilgrimage road to Santiago de Compostela. Beneath them are another five swords held by armoured limbs representing the five wounds of Christ and beneath them another five shields with five small circles representing the five wounds of Christ, crucified, pierced and bleeding. The holy wounds were created by the Roman nails driven through each of his hands and feet and the final piercing of his side by the Holy Lance of Longinus. Inverted, at the very bottom of the shield, are two anthropomorphic torsos with arms raised, again in the exact same pose as the Nkondi Nkisi, flanking the Portuguese coat of arms (with another five round circles). Whilst the addition of the nails driven into the figure might appear to have been a late 18th century development, the symbolism and iconography of the Nkisi were already clearly depicted, in posture as well as material, as early as 1521.

Europeans, and their descendants, tend to perceive the world through the narrow perspective of Darwin, freely interpreting his evolution of the species in cultural terms as well. They assume that since they have economically conquered the world, taking for themselves, their class and culture all the luxury and power that economic conquest provides, they may as a result also take for granted the assumption that they are physically, emotionally, intellectually, philosophically, scientifically and of course, culturally superior to every other culture or tradition. Stepping out from this Colonial prejudice and forgetting the European conceited education that African people are noble savages and their art primitive, the Nkondi Nkisi can be read as a rich embodiment of Swedenborg's highly sophisticated Law of Correspondence.

In alchemical correspondence, the metal iron represents the planet Mars, ruled over by the Roman god of the same name. He is the god of war to which he lends his metal, forged into swords and of course nails with which to crucify the enemy. Our blood is also ruled by Mars and therefore, in correspondence is rich in iron. The consequence of war is, of course, the spilling of blood through iron spears, swords, lances and nails, therefor when iron rusts it turns red, the same colour as blood.

In 1486, just five years before King Nzinga a Nkuwu converted, the Florentine High Renaissance painter Sandro Botticelli was putting his finishing touches to his "Birth of Venus," depicting the Roman goddess standing upon the same scallop shell associated with Saint James and used in Saint John's rite of baptism. She covers her right breast with one hand and with the other, holds her long red hair over her pudendum as she emerges from the turquoise sea behind. Venus was created from the foam of Uranus' (Caelus) testicles, castrated and cast to sea by his son Saturn. The hair of the goddess of procreation, beauty and love is the same colour as copper, the metal she represents, the same metal that is used in all electrical cables because of its latent generosity in permitting electrons to flow and turn things on. The turquoise sea from which she emerges was painted using Verdigris, the very rust of copper, which turns green, as is befitting the goddess who rules our lustful nature.

When Botticelli painted his Venus, he painted her in her metal using its shadow, or rust, to create his pigment. The Nganga or shaman who made the Nkondi Nkisi similarly embodied the protection spell that their art embodied by calling upon the spirit of Mars, together with the help of their ancestors, to pin down the hearts of their enemies with fear. For both, art was not merely a re-presentation of an idea, much less even an aesthetic, metaphor or anything less than total embodiment and occult correspondence. The power of such art is that it speaks to us on so many levels simultaneously, in the flesh, with spirit, in invocation and by evocation. It reaches through all the realms of perception, passes through the Gnostic filters, and Above is as Below, the materialisation of spirit and spiritualisation of matter.

Brian Morris, the anarchist anthropologist who spent many years in Malawi doing field research on ethnobiology, ecology, religion, ritual and symbolism in hunter-gatherer societies and their human-insect interactions, makes an interesting distinction between the French noun '*puissance*,' meaning power over others, and the verb '*pouvoir*,' meaning the power to do something. Perhaps in English it might be similar to the difference between 'freedom from' and 'freedom to.' Works of art like Picasso's "Les Demoiselles d'Avignon," the Minkisi and "Birth of Venus" continue to possess our imaginations because they are empowered with '*pouvoir*' rather than anything within our ability to control.

The experience of the two world wars with all their social, political and economic hardships, the genocides, war crimes and humanitarian atrocities, fed the imaginations of the artists who transformed their experiences into the nihilistic languages of the early to mid-twentieth century. Art was born in the experience of conflict, and so artists sought on the one hand a spiritual path of hope, and on the other the destruction of form. The canons of representation were insufficient to express the horrors of their experiences, so they turned to non-representation, abstraction and the violence of expression. The colourful pallets, rich textures, vivid outlines and bold forms were as spiritually optimistic as they were emotionally challenging.

As the memory of the wars faded and lifestyles grew ever more luxurious in cities designed for convenience with cheaper travel, standardised utilities and sanitised entertainment, so too has experience become diluted and homogenised. Whilst the gap between the wealthy and poor grows exponentially every year, the domain of art remains that of the wealthy and elite; so the standardisation and sanitation of experience has given rise to a standardisation and sanitation of expression. The platitudes of aseptic, clinical, safe conformity have given rise to an art of aseptic, clinical, safe conformity.

The abstract strain that began with non-representational art – the artist's desire to embody spirit with an exorcism, rather than re-represent a physical idea or image – evolved into truth to materials and finally art for art's sake. Artists like Brancusi considered the animistic spirit of the material he cut, carved, cast or polished to be every much part of the work of art as the shape or form. He worked according to a holistic vision integrating architecture, sculpture and furniture in a poetic evocation of spirit. A generation later, the British sculptor Henry Moore explained that "one of the first principles of art so clearly seen in primitive [sic] work is truth to material; the artist shows an instinctive understanding of his material, its right use and possibilities."

The rise of the gallery system and lure of the marketplace cut the tether that held spirit to form and the work of art became its own excuse to exist. The narcissistic self-obsessed, self-defined concept 'Art for Art's sake' gave artists the freedom to create art under the licence 'What You See Is What You Get.' Colour was reduced to nothing more than what it is, paint merely an excuse, and line, shape, form and texture simply that and nothing else. As time passed and markets evolved, art grew to define itself according to financial return, the economic investiture of primary market swelling into secondary market with ever greater returns every time the work changes hands. The artist has since been reduced to producer in a money laundering racket that has no interest in the works of art which are now locked up in crates, vaults and stored between gallery, auction house and slippery traders.

Already back in 1911 the artist Kandinsky warned that "at those times when the soul tends to be choked by material disbelief, art becomes purposeless and talk is heard that art exists for art's sake alone (…) The vulgar herd stroll through the rooms and pronounce the pictures 'nice' or 'splendid.' Those who could speak have said nothing, those who could hear have heard nothing. This condition of art is called 'art for art's sake.' This neglect of inner meanings, which is the life of colours, this vain squandering of artistic power is called 'art for art's sake.' (…) With cold eyes and indifferent mind the spectators regard the work. Connoisseurs admire the 'skill' (as one admires a tightrope walker), enjoy the 'quality of painting' (as one enjoys a pasty). But hungry souls go hungry away." Kandinsky's description of the artist is nowhere more appropriate than the immediate present "The artist seeks for material reward for his dexterity, his power of vision and experience. His purpose becomes the satisfaction of vanity and greed. (…) There are complaints of excessive competition, of over-production. Hatred, partisanship, cliques, jealousy, intrigues are the natural consequences of this aimless, materialist art."

It need not be said that we are living in the most materia-LUST of times. The Kali Yuga or "age of vice" was described in the Sanskrit scriptures as an era when "Rulers will become unreasonable and will levy taxes unfairly. They will no longer see it as their duty to promote spirituality, or to protect their subjects and become a danger to the world." The scriptures warn that "avarice and wrath will be common. Humans will openly display animosity towards each other" and "sin will increase exponentially, while virtue will fade and cease to flourish. People will become addicted to intoxicating drinks and drugs" – to this the ancient author might have added "social media, television, entertainment and fake news."

The Contemporary Art market demands profit and growth and shies away everything that might destabilise that boom. As the markets have expanded and sales broke records after auction result, galleries expanded into art fairs that grew out of biennials and the cash flowed in every direction. Galleries became merchants, dealers became consultants, collectors became speculators, bankers became artists and their studios swelled into well-oiled factory barracks fuelled by armies of assistants. The deal made with the devil was that success demanded branding and the same work of art was cursed to be made over and over and over again, in editions and multiples, series and versions, small, medium, large, larger and larger still. Success for an artist translated into the consolation of habit, dependant on instant branded recognition, across any room, through any crowded art fair booth, in the corner of the Instagram feed, the instant identification of the artist's trademark style, pattern, imprint, trick or gimmick. Only if the artist's entire body of work and lifetime of research, experiment, evolution, identity and philosophy can be explained in a short brief sentence, only if the work can be reduced to a simple 'get-it,' only then does the market respond and reward follows success. The greater the uniformity of production and branded habit, the greater the success.

Recently, the New York critic Jerry Saltz called this new wave of branded art 'Crapstraction,' saying that "In today's greatly expanded art world and art market, artists making diluted art have the upper hand. A large swath of the art being made today is being driven by the market, and specifically by not very sophisticated speculator-collectors who prey on their wealthy friends and their friends' wealthy friends, getting them to buy the same look-alike art (...) This work is decorator-friendly, especially in a contemporary apartment or house. It feels 'cerebral' and looks hip in ways that flatter collectors even as it offers no insight into anything at all. It's all done in haggard shades of pale, deployed in uninventive arrangements that ape digital media, or something homespun or dilapidated. Replete with self-conscious comments on art, recycling, sustainability, appropriation, processes of abstraction, or nature, all this painting employs a similar vocabulary of smudges, stains, spray paint, flecks, spills, splotches, almost-monochromatic fields, silk-screening, or stenciling. Edge-to-edge, geometric, or biomorphic composition is de rigueur, as are irregular grids, lattice and moiré patterns, ovular shapes, and stripes, with maybe some collage"[3]

Artist and critic Walter Robinson defined it as Zombie Formalism, "Formalism because this art involves a straightforward, reductive, essentialist method of making a painting, and Zombie because it brings back to life the discarded aesthetics of Clement Greenberg."[4]

These works of art have more in common with stocks, shares and bond certificates than any art historical precedent or discourse. The only experience that feeds the Contemporary Art Market is the experience of the Contemporary Art Market. Clearly the condition of art is not a consideration and anything, if not everything, may be considered a work of art today, regardless of skill, content,

3 http://www.vulture.com/2014/06/why-new-abstract-paintings-look-the-same.html
4 https://www.artspace.com/magazine/contributors/see_here/the_rise_of_zombie_formalism-52184

aesthetics, material or even intention. The Pointillism that fed into Impressionism has devolved into DissaPointillism and Depressionism.

The sluice gates of significance were thrown open in 1917 when a urinal, dubbed "Fountain," was submitted for the exhibition of the Society of Independent Artists by a mysterious R.Mutt. It took the artist Marcel Duchamp another 36 years before actually laying claim to the authorship of said 'Found Object,' a claim that then changed the course of history, retrospectively. At the time he had defended the "Fountain" in his magazine *Blind Man*, saying that "Whether Mr. Mutt with his own hands made the fountain or not has no importance. He *chose* it. He took an ordinary article of life, placed it so that its useful significance disappeared under the new title and point of view - created a new thought for that object." In an interview with Pierre Cabanne just before he died, Duchamp explained that the "Readymade is always based on visual indifference and, at the same time, on the total absence of good or bad taste."

From that moment on there could be no other definition of art than the wilful ego of an artist held up by the context of an institution blinded by its own function. In order to create the institutional context that would provide the impetus required to sell his puerile concept (and the "Fountain of Insignification") Duchamp invented the White Cube Gallery tradition with the exhibition he curated called "Dada: 1916-1923" at the Sidney Janis Gallery in New York (15 April - May 9, 1953). The White Cube format has since gone viral and the definition of art is now anything, everything and whatever an artist inserts into that context. The W.C. grew into a sanitised zone held in quarantine, isolated from everything except its own interests and it is only in this context that Zombie Formalism might live out the daze of its undead existence.

> The essential difference between a sculpture like Andre's 'Equivalent VIII,' and any that had existed before in the past is that Andre's array of bricks depends not just partly, but entirely, on the museum [gallery or white cube] for its context. A Rodin in a parking lot is still a misplaced Rodin; Andre's bricks in the same place can only be a pile of bricks.[5]

In 1964 Joseph Beuys proclaimed in a performance that "The Silence of Marcel Duchamp is Over Rated," challenging the father of conceptual art and cross-dressing mother of the Readymade, to a duel to the death of the author. The curse of Duchamp is that anything can be a work of art, but with history as his witness, Beuys won the battle with his coup de grâce, proclaiming that "Everybody is an artist," a prophecy that has since come true.[6]

5 Robert Hughes, "The Shock of the New"

6 It should be mentioned however, that even though Beuys is infinitely quoted and read through the proverbially simplistic one liner, his intention was very different and much closer to the ritual reading that this text proposes. "Here my idea is to declare that art is the only possibility for evolution, the only possibility to change the situation in the world. But then you have to enlarge the idea of art to include

It would be as foolish as it is impossible today to arrive at any definition or understanding of art outside of the viral spread of an idea endemically transmitted from one mind to another through habit, convenience, convention and socially accepted mutual agreement. What we call 'Contemporary Art' is neither rooted in practice, nor by ritual, but is taken for granted as an unquestionable given, predetermined by protocol. The financial risks of critical assessment or semantic enquiry would be far too dangerous and a market risk so great, that any such engagement is automatically ruled out in ridicule.

But as Empires eventually fall and civilizations inevitably collapse, so too will our contemporary understanding of Art collapse with the financial market of its foundation. Perhaps it might be timely to re-consider potential definitions of art that could help shed light on the most undefined of practices. I hesitate and rally against all, and every definition, by cause of my own nature, and yet feel the attraction to consider once again the essence of my practice. I have noted elsewhere that there is no such thing as an 'Art World' because there are numerous, multiple and proliferate art WORLDS, overlapping, intersecting and expanding. According to *Forbes Magazine*, "We have gone from three contemporary art fairs in 1970 to 269 in 2015"[7] and every year since the list grows. There were 23 satellite Art Fairs orbiting around the 2017 edition of the Art Basel Miami Beach Fair alone, every one of them filled with at least 100 galleries per fair, each showing up to 10 artists per booth. The numbers are terrifying and the overlapping worlds of art without precedent, defying comprehension, much less definition or rationale.

> I think the major shift is simply that you have an art world that is much bigger than it used to be. Every sector is bigger—there are more museums, more curators, more artists, more galleries, more collectors, more auction houses, and it's all more internationalized. The net effect of each sector growing and each sector becoming more international is that everyone is struggling just to cover the mandatory events within that sector. And one of the things that's dangerous in the way that the art world is evolving is that a lot of people are now confined to their silos and don't necessarily think about the impact of what they're doing on the artists – and the artists, at the end of the day, are the sine qua non of this whole world.[8]

Given the systematised gyration of these vastly different worlds, each with their own momentum, individualised markets and vastly different praxes, I shall console

the whole creativity. And if you do that, it follows logically that every living being is an artist - an artist in the sense that he can develop his own capacity. And therefore it's necessary at first that society cares about the educational system, that equality of opportunity for self-realization is guaranteed."

7 https://www.forbes.com/sites/yjeanmundelsalle/2016/04/07/the-art-fair-boom-is-forever-changing-the-way-the-art-market-does-business/#6ae25fb6c649

8 Marc Spiegler (Global Director, Basel Art Fair), *Artnet*, 19 March 2018

myself that my Radically Subjective definition of art be neither doctrinaire nor dogmatic, but simply my own firebrand to guide me through the cave of Plato's darkest shadows. I stray towards equivocation, foundering with hesitation in defining that which should never be defined and cannot be contained, and yet must if we are to save art from its present and terminal condition. I find consolation, recalling once again the words of that elder artist Kandinsky, "If we begin at once to break the bonds which bind us to nature and devote ourselves purely to combination of pure colour and abstract form, we shall produce works which are mere decoration, which are suited to neckties or carpets."

Whilst the definition of Contemporary Art has come to be anything, made anyhow, by anybody, in any way, I find myself increasingly at odds with such an open call. The condition of art today might be summed up by the 1965 prophetically pathetic work of American Conceptual Artist Joseph Kosuth, a neon sentence that spells out of the words "Self-Described and Self-Defined." Just because something is said, that does not make it true, and just because something has been written, does not make it real. Just because something has been cut, carved, etched, painted, cast or drawn to be sold to the highest bidder does not make it art any more than a sheep can be wolved. Whilst art is impossible to define, the virus that art has become does demand interrogation and scrutiny before the bankers run all the way to the gallery laughing.

The Hollywood-Netflix image of the Zombie is of course taken from the popular caricature of the Haitian Voodoo 'witchdoctor,' or scantily clad priestess, gyrating with a headless chicken taking possession of a dead or undead soul. The process inevitably involved sticking pins into a rag doll. Despite the gross inaccuracies and crass misrepresentation of the syncretic Vodoun faith, the metaphor is nothing less than poetic justice. It merits mention here that the pinning of the Vodoun effigy travelled to the Americas with the slaves from the Fon people of present-day Benin. The domestic sewing pins inserted with a prayer into an effigy is the equivalent of the nails being driven into the large wooden Nkisi figures in the Congo. The process of nailing a talisman is an ancient magical process of binding will to matter. A terracotta figure in the Louvre Museum in Paris, dating from the 3rd-4th century AD is pinned in the eyes, ears, sex, heart and head using iron nails in exactly the same manner as a Nganga would an Nkisi or a Houngan would pin an effigy.

Given the Vodoun metaphor, might the symptoms not also show the direction towards finding the cure to Zombie Formalism? After all, is the difference between a medicinal cure and a poison not simply the dose? How might the artist and their creation unpin themselves from the undead and unbind their spirits from a market determined crass materialism? Visiting a contemporary art gallery today is a more painful torture than watching paint dry, and the appreciation of art neither art historical, nor spiritual, not even emotional, but merely functional in service of a money machine.

The prophets are dead, long live the profits.

Two years after "Self-Described and Self-Defined," another artist, Bruce

Nauman created an entirely different neon sentence, spelling out the words "The True Artist Helps the World by Revealing Mystic Truths" and in May 1969, Sol Lewitt wrote his "Sentences on Conceptual Art" manifesto explaining that "Conceptual artists are mystics rather than rationalists. They leap to conclusions that logic cannot reach."[9] It is to this mystical and ritual function of art that I turn in search of solace and sustenance.

It is the first part of the previously mentioned Kandinsky quote, that I find most compelling in getting to the root of the problem ("If we begin at once to break the bonds which bind us to nature") for it is Nature that is missing from Contemporary Art. The luxuries of our lifestyles and bounds of habit have placed that social class who makes, buys and sells what we understand to be Art, beyond the periphery and with disrespect towards Nature (in all its forms.) We have lost touch with the seasons, save as markers for Spring Break, sunbathing in St-Barth, skiing in Gstaad, flying to Cape Town for a Summer Safari at Christmas time, clubbing in Ibiza, Mallorca, Marbella or anywhere else Ryanair can fly you for the price of a steak when it gets too cold back home. We are so isolated and disconnected from nature that we would not recognise our own scent in a dark room and do not consider ourselves implicated in the virile dirty habits of Mother Nature.

Nature is clearly a cycle and a season, host to animal, vegetable as well as mineral creatures, majestic and microscopic, creative and destructive, violent and compassionate, but it is also embodied within our every sense and sensation. The emperor is naked and the artist strayed too far from true experience and in consequence disconnected from their true nature. The only way back is through a holistic conception of art, one that restores the body of the artist through the body of their work within worlds seen, unseen and across dimensions dark and light. We are natural beings inextricably bound by the chains of divine correspondence. In his poem Correspondence, the French poet Baudelaire explained that

> Nature is a temple where living pillars
> Let escape sometimes confused words;
> Man traverses it through forests of symbols
> That observe him with familiar glances.
> (...)
> That have the expanse of infinite things,
> Like ambergris, musk, balsam and incense,
> Which sing the ecstasies of the mind and senses[10]

The forest of signs is there to read and our bodies are the guide. We are nature, inside and out.

> The basis of artistic creation is not what is, but what might be; not the

9 Sol Lewitt, "Sentences on Conceptual Art," May 1969
10 Baudelaire, *Correspondances*

> real, but the possible. Artists create according to the same principles as nature, but they apply them to individual entities, while nature, to use a Goethean expression, thinks nothing of individual things. She is always building and destroying, because she wants to achieve perfection, not in the individual thing, but in the whole.[11]

> We talk far too much. We should talk less and draw more. I personally should like to renounce speech altogether and, like organic Nature, communicate everything I have to say in sketches. That fig tree, this little snake, the cocoon on my window sill quietly awaiting its future all these are momentous signatures. A person able to decipher their meaning properly would soon be able to dispense with the written or the spoken word altogether. The more I think of it, there is something futile, mediocre, even (I am tempted to say) foppish about speech. By contrast, how the gravity of Nature and her silence startle you, when you stand face to face with her, undistracted, before a barren ridge or in the desolation of the ancient hills.[12]

Initiates of the Eleusinian Mysteries were forbidden by Athenian law, on penalty of death, from revealing the secrets of the mysteries. There is no greater mystery than that of creation and the role of the artist to simply spirit form from the unseen vast landscape of the imagination, unconscious, subconscious and dreams of worlds inhabited by daemons, angels, djinn and other multidimensional beings. Whilst our three dimensional minds, locked into a linear cartesian logic of five miserable senses, are inadequate to comprehend these mysteries, the holistic synesthetic body of the visionary, shaman, seer, initiate and artist is the medium with which the mysteries may manifest, in concrete form and with rational understanding. When art is reduced to the retinal, the visual, aesthetic or formal elements appealing to our rational brain only, it is no better than Kandinsky's necktie, and with time dies of asphyxiation. The holistic body, re-membered in all its animal, vegetable and mineral aspects, guided by our reptile, as well as our human and beastly brains, the artist is able to think with their guts, sex and sensorial intelligences, liberated to touch the divine. It is only by thinking outside the limits of three-dimensional censure that we can begin to know the nature of our multi-dimensional selves and reveal mystic truths.

I might call this process a re-membering of a Radical Subjectivity for it is only through lived experience that we may understand our selves, through the visceral experience of feeling with emotion, intuition and instinct. I call it RADICAL because it must, by necessity, be far-reaching and thorough, embracing the fundamental nature of my every sense and being, RADICAL in an extreme embrace of every element and facet of my body, RADICAL because it is at the very root of

11 Rudolf Steiner

12 Johann Wolfgang von Goethe

what I am. I call it SUBJECTIVE because I can only speak for my self, through my self and as my self. My experience of reality can only be through the mediation of my self and that can only be registered through my emotions and sensual faculties. Aleister Crowley laid out the law with the Gnostic Mass, liberating our flesh and spirit with the radically subjective prayer: "There is no part of me that is not of the Gods."[13]

'Western' Society has built itself upon the foundation of the mirror, with reminders everywhere we look, that we are not divine; that we are ugly, old and imperfect in every way. Cosmetics, drugs, creams, oils, balms, gloss, toothpaste, deodorant and perfumes proliferate to mask our divine nature hidden behind the bathroom mirror. The masked muse on the cover of every photoshopped magazine and lounging on the sofa of every sitcom or shuffling down the runway ramp of impossible unattainable perfection, seed a self-loathing that blossoms with the fruits of guilt and shame. Everything that makes us of the Gods must be destroyed in favour of cosmetic weakness, soiled to the highest bidder. Our emotions are equally crushed, disregarded and deranged because "boys don't cry" and girls should "lie back and think of England."

It was not always thus, for the walls of the Outer Temple at Luxor instructed the novice "The body is the house of God," and once proven worthy and ready to acquire deeper knowledge and insight, the walls of the Inner Temple instructed "Man, know thyself, and you are going to know the Gods". The *pronaos* (forecourt) of the Temple of Apollo at Delphi was inscribed with the aphorism "Know Thyself" (Greek: "Gnōthi Seauton") which Socrates explained as "The unexamined life is not worth living." It it only with, and through, raw lived experience and embodied knowledge that we may grow into 'knowing' our selves. As simple as the cliché sounds, to "Know Thyself" is the most complex of tasks demanding the experience and knowledge of our most pleasant as well as unpleasant, vile, venomous, lustful and lazy emotions, thoughts, senses, fears, desires, dreams, the expression of our conscious, unconscious and sub-conscious selves. How is it even possible to know yourself if you carry around the name your were given by your parents and then baptised into by your church? In order to know yourself surely you have to begin by giving birth to your self and eventually naming and finally baptising your Self?

The body of the artist is their temple, with its inner and outer mysteries inviting understanding through lived experience. Drawing down the mysteries cannot be read in a text book, understood intellectually or copy/pasted upon, or from, Social Media, for it has to be a full body experience. This is the function of ritual and initiatory knowledge, handed down from body to flesh, knowledge incarnate. Such understanding and divine knowledge can only be learned in the flesh for the body, the temple of the nine holes, is the key that lies between the visible manifest three-dimensional worlds and the hidden worlds of mystery and imagination.

To know yourself is to embrace the divine and recognise the Gods in whose image we are created. The risk of such enlightenment risks much because our

13 Aleister Crowley, "Liber XV"

five miserable and pathetic senses are inadequate and simply could not deal with the intensity of the experience. Remember, as warning, that Dionysus's mother, Semele, was tricked by Hera who planted seeds of doubt within her mortal rational mind about her consort's divine nature. Curious with doubt, Semele demanded of Zeus that he reveal himself in all his glory as proof of his deiform. Though the God begged her not to ask this, she persisted and he eventually agreed. When the King of the Gods finally appeared to her, wreathed in the visionary bolts of divine lightning that mortals cannot gaze upon without the protection of the ritual called art, Semele was reduced to dust in the ensuing blaze. Zeus rescued the unborn Dionysus and carried him in his thigh before giving birth on Mount Pramnos to the "twice-born" trickster God "of ecstasy and terror, of savagery and joyful deliverance, the mad god, whose appearance sent men into a state of delirium."[14]

The role of the artist, shaman, seer, psychic, occultist and initiate is to draw down the threshold and step through the layers of mortal consciousness into the divine mysteries. This process might equally be called Lucid Dreaming, Shamanic Voyaging, Cognitive, Active or Disciplined Imagination, Super-sensible Perception or even Hypnogogic Discipline with which the artist, initiate and psychonaut sails waves of consciousness, surfing the Entoptic Phenomenon, reading the Akashic Record and rides the bucking bull of Dark Matter in the rodeo of Quantum Entanglement. The artist is unique amongst the initiates in that they may manifest the intangible and ineffable in tactile form through works of art that hover between these worlds. Even the most cynical rationalist could not deny the power of the artist's imagination in modelling their unconscious, fears and desires as well as embodying the spirit of an age. Were it not for the paintings, sculptures, scriptures, poetry, literature, music and theatre conjured by artists through the ages, we would not know what the Gods, angels and demons look like.

In his "Biographia Literaria," the poet Samuel Taylor Coleridge wrote about the difference between "Fancy" and two different types of imagination. The Primary Imagination is "the living Power and prime Agent of all human Perception, and a repetition on the finite mind of the eternal act of creation in the infinite I AM."[15] The Secondary Imagination by contrast is "an echo of the former, co-existing with the conscious will, yet still as identical with the primary in the kind of its agency, and differing only in degree, and in the mode of its operation. It dissolves, diffuses, dissipates, in order to re-create; or where this process is rendered impossible, yet still at all events it struggles to idealize and to unify. It is essentially vital, even as all objects (as objects) are essentially fixed and dead."[16]

We all share and participate in the world of the Primary Imagination, the most basic faculty of which permits us to make sense of our world and give it meaning. It is by means of the Primary Imagination that we experience reality mediated by our perception and shaped by our senses. The Secondary Imagination, on the other

14 Walter Otto, "Dionysus"

15 Samuel Taylor Coleridge, "Biographia Literaria; Or, Biographical Sketches of My Literary Life and Opinions, Volume 1"

16 Ibid.

hand, is the domain of the artist, mystic, initiate and poet. Whilst it derives from the Primary Imagination, it is the conscious and volatile prima materia from which the initiate or artist may create new understandings, if not entirely new worlds of perception.

Fancy, on the other hand, "has no other counters to play with, but fixities and definites. The Fancy is indeed no other than a mode of Memory emancipated from the order of time and space; while it is blended with, and modified by that empirical phenomenon of the will, which we express by the word *choice*. But equally with the ordinary memory the Fancy must receive all its materials ready made from the law of association."[17] Fancy is an inferior faculty to imagination and there is nothing remotely mysterious about it for it acts mechanically in bringing together various, often dissimilar, components to produce appropriate images. It is a logical and rational process that might be called 'get-it' art, the Zombie Formalism and Crapstraction of market driven drivel. Fancy is regulative and self-replicating rather than creative.

In place of baptising with water and scallop shell, the artist baptises in harmony with their nature using the fires of unmediated experience following in the footsteps of their creator, Prometheus. As we were made by clay in the hands of the Titan trickster, who further defied all the gods by stealing fire from heaven and giving it to humanity, is it not fitting that we might then turn towards the very same fire to cleanse and create? Was it not with fire that we found our way out from the darkness of the Stone Age and into the Bronze Age, with the flames fuelled by the forge and hammered hot upon the anvil? The blacksmith was also the first artisan charged with the responsibility to craft the swords and crowns, the art and armour of the Iron Age. With time the artisan grew into the artist and the fires of their forge led the way through to the Renaissance. It was fire again, in the belly of the furnace and engines of the Industrial Age that drove us into the present.

Whilst art, as we assume to understand it today, has been around since at least 38,000 years, it is only since the Renaissance that it could be applied with the same assumption of understanding. Around 1300, Art referred to a sense of "skill in scholarship and learning" – in particular relation to the seven sciences, or liberal arts: Grammar, Rhetoric, Logic, Arithmetic, Geometry, Music and Astronomy. A century later art referred to the "system of rules and traditions for performing certain actions" and from the late 15th century, a "skill in cunning and trickery." It was only from the late 16th century that it meant "skill in creative arts" of painting or sculpture in today's terms.

The artisanal link between the blacksmith who tempered the knight's sword, adorned their shields and gilded their lover's jewels with crafted beauty, might account for the curious fact that ARS, the Latin root from which the word ART is derived, also evolved into the word ARMA or weapons. This might further explain the Freudian Slip with which the Twentieth Century art movements were baptised with a military term – Avant Garde. Art might yet prove to be a weapon once

17 Ibid.

again: a weapon against the one dimensional materialism that divides the planet into resource and profit.

I am drawn, like the moth unto the candle, and liken the work of art with the flame that licks the air, for it is both visible infrared and invisible ultraviolet at the same time. The flame consumes matter in order to create light and heat, a gas that is also a plasma, seemingly as solid as it appears to be liquid. The fire hovers just above the matter which it destroys, dancing in the air, always rising up just as water will always flow down, undulating like a succubine whirligig on the thinnest string of possible, teasing our senses back and forth. The flicker of fire is, for good reason, also the exact frequency our senses demand in order to switch off the rational filters and induce altered states of visionary consciousness.

The flame that burns away the borders of rational constraint in order to open the "Doors of Perception" is fuelled by terror because it is only when we leap into the abyss of excess and ecstasy with a full bodied multidimensional embrace of simultaneous and contradictory synaesthesia that we can open our senses to the divine.

> No passion so effectually robs the mind of all its powers of acting and reasoning as fear. For fear being an apprehension of pain or death, it operates in a manner that resembles actual pain. Whatever therefore is terrible, with regard to sight, is sublime too, whether this cause of terror be imbued with greatness of dimensions or not; for it is impossible to look on anything as trifling, or contemptible, that may be dangerous. There are many animals, who though far from being large, are yet capable of raising ideas of the sublime, because they are considered as objects of terror. As serpents and poisonous animals of almost all kinds. And to things of great dimensions, if we annex an adventitious idea of terror, they become without comparison greater.[18]

The trance-formative path of the artist is not an easy one, for drawing down the work of art into these three-dimensions from the fires and brimstone of the imagination demands courage in the face of terror. Rimbaud calls for the "systematized derangement of all the senses," the burning away of the ego, by which the artist is able to surrender every habit and unlearn every lesson in a Radical Subjective embrace of their true nature: a powerful dualistic force of destruction and creation. The corollary of Picasso's exorcism is Rimbaud's possession, by which he releases the control of his ego and individual identity in favour of a force of nature so powerful it risks madness. This calling and channelling of forces beyond our ability to imagine, outside our control, demands the courage and strength of the artist, shaman or initiate, and it is only through ritual that they might find refuge from falling into the abyss of insanity. The ritual mask hides the individual face and

18 Edmund Berke, "A Philosophical Inquiry Into the Origin of Our Ideas of the Sublime and Beautiful"

protects against the flesh of the demon that is born when the body surrenders.

There is no better, nor more poetic description of the artist's craft in conjuring the terror of the sublime than Rimbaud's infamous and often quoted "Letter of a Seer" penned on 15 May 1871, in which he explains that

> the first task of the man who wants to be a poet is to study his own awareness of himself, in its entirety he seeks out his soul, he inspects it, he tests it, he learns it. As soon as he knows it, he must cultivate it! [Know Thyself!] but the problem is to make the soul into a monster (...) I say you have to be a visionary, make yourself a visionary. A poet makes himself a visionary through a long, boundless, and systematized derangement of all the senses. All forms of love, of suffering, of madness; he searches himself, he exhausts within himself all poisons, and preserves their quintessences. Unspeakable torment, where he will need the greatest faith, a superhuman strength, where he becomes all men the great invalid, the great criminal, the great accursed – and the Supreme Scientist! For he attains the unknown! Because he has cultivated his soul, already rich, more than anyone! He attains the unknown, and if, demented, he finally loses the understanding of his visions, he will at least have seen them! So what if he is destroyed in his ecstatic flight through things unheard of, unnameable: other horrible workers will come; they will begin at the horizons where the first one has fallen!

In effect, Rimbaud is explaining to his friend that it is only when the artist surrenders their five senses walled in by three dimensions that they may gain access to the multiverse of creative vision. Our five senses are the mythological and archetypal tricksters responsible for confusion of clarity and the obfuscation of rationalism. In the so-called "Real World" of "Common Sense," our perceptions are blind folded by fear masked as habit and we see, feel, hear, smell and touch only that which reinforces our preconditioned sense of self. We are what we are because we are and see, feel, hear, smell and touch only that which makes us what we believe we are. The artist burns away their fears in raptured excess in order to open up their senses to the experience of the ecstasy of the inconceivable, the embrace of the untouchable, the terror of the inexorable and the unmediated evocation of the unmentionable. The French writer François Rabelais had but on rule for the artists, monks and nuns of his Abbey of Thélème, built by the giant Gargantua.

> All their life was spent not in laws, statutes, or rules, but according to their own free will and pleasure. They rose out of their beds when they thought good; they did eat, drink, labour, sleep, when they had a mind to it and were disposed for it. None did awake them, none did offer to constrain them to eat, drink, nor to do any other thing;

> for so had Gargantua established it. In all their rule and strictest tie of their order there was but this one clause to be observed,
>
> Do What Thou Wilt;
>
> because men that are free, well-born, well-bred, and conversant in honest companies, have naturally an instinct and spur that prompteth them unto virtuous actions, and withdraws them from vice, which is called honour. Those same men, when by base subjection and constraint they are brought under and kept down, turn aside from that noble disposition by which they formerly were inclined to virtue, to shake off and break that bond of servitude wherein they are so tyrannously enslaved; for it is agreeable with the nature of man to long after things forbidden and to desire what is denied us.[19]

It is in this regard that African Art continues to be the most useful and inspiring, for it has not lost touch with this visionary conception and ritual function. Chris Marker's 1953 Film "Les statues meurent aussi" begins with the voiceover spoken over darkness: "When men die, they enter history. When statues die, they enter art. This botany of death is what we call culture." African Art derives its power from the fact that it was never created for a museum or display, but out of a visionary and holistic integration with faith, community, nature and belief. It was the ability of the work of art to unlock consciousness, to hover in a talismanic spin between the worlds of the seen and unseen that first inspired the European artists in distilling their craft from the flow of 'pouvoir,' drawing upon of their own 'primitive' imagination in search of the terror of perception.

When you look at African Art, the reason why it looks right back at you is because it is alive in spirit. Like the flame that dances just above the log, being of two worlds, creating heat and warmth as it destroys matter, the work of art is a purifying force of spirit culled from the material world. The uncanny and other-worldly presence that oozes from the patina and through the wood, iron, copper, kaolin, bones, leather, horns or skulls of the Nkisi or Reliquary off-sets our material dimensions and throws off our five senses, making folly of perception with an uneasy familiarity that seems closer to a dream or nightmare than an object of aesthetic contemplation. An African work of art is an embodied ritual, flesh of the spirit, a mystical sign, symbol, sigil, token and form drawn down into visible form through the crafting of the artist's Active Imagination.

Whilst this ritual nature of art is so well illustrated with reference to African Art, it is by no means the exclusive domain of such an understanding. British Linguist Jane Harrison believes art and ritual to be the hand and glove of the same human expression:

---

19 François Rabelais, *Gargantua*, Chapter LVII

> The distinction between art and ritual, which has so long haunted and puzzled us, now comes out quite clearly, and also in part the relation of each to actual life. Ritual, we saw, was a re-presentation or a pre-presentation, a re-doing or pre-doing, a copy or imitation of life, but, and this is the important point, always with a practical end. Art is also a representation of life and the emotions of life, but cut loose from immediate action. Action may be and often is represented, but it is not that it may lead on to a practical further end. The end of art is in itself. Its value is not mediate but immediate. Thus ritual makes, as it were, a bridge between real life and art, a bridge over which in primitive times it would seem man must pass. In his actual life he hunts and fishes and ploughs and sows, being utterly intent on the practical end of gaining his food; in the dromenon of the Spring Festival, though his acts are unpractical, being mere singing and dancing and mimicry, his intent is practical, to induce the return of his food-supply.[20]

The true ritual function of art should not be comforting in its expression, because it threatens our very sense of what we perceive as "normal." In place of entertainment, art inspired by ritual should intrinsically be embodied with both fear and desire, pure emotions coded into form with the ability to unlock different forms of contradictory understanding and multi-consciousness. It cannot be defined because it is as fluid as the flames that devour everything that it is supported by, constantly adjusting itself according to our evolving perceptions.

The "long, boundless, and systematized derangement of all the senses" and the raw experience of the Active Imagination cannot be systematised or formalised, because as soon as the method is repeated, it turns to habit, which generates the consolation of conformity, and the panic of ineffable experience subsides into convention, losing its life force as entertainment. The vertigo of experience that the true artist might reveal as mystic truths is only possible when the peaks and depths of the Active Imagination are scaled without the fear of terror.

> Perception is pent up and becomes, helped by emotion, conscious representation. Now it is, psychologists tell us, just in this interval, this space between perception and reaction, this momentary halt, that all our mental life, our images, our ideas, our consciousness, and assuredly our religion and our art, is built up. If the cycle of knowing, feeling, acting, were instantly fulfilled, that is, if we were a mass of well-contrived instincts, we should hardly have dromena, and we should certainly never pass from dromena to drama. Art and religion, though perhaps not wholly ritual, spring from the incomplete cycle, from unsatisfied desire, from perception and

20 Jane Harrison, *Ancient art and ritual*

> emotion that have somehow not found immediate outlet in practical action.[21]

The hard core mind numbing habit of the art market and its Zombies can only be reanimated through a terrifying shock to the system. As the flesh demands the violence of fever accompanied by body sweats and hallucination, habit might best be broken with ritual experience. The system demands to be symbolically sacrificed and die in order to give birth to itself once again. Dead art is made from dead experience and Zombie Formalism is stillborn because it lacks the lifeforce of spirit.

The power of art is to always be one step ahead of what we can imagine.

> As rationalists and moralists, they feel that good behaviour should be rewarded and that the virtuous deserve to go to heaven. But as psychologists they know that virtue is not the sole or sufficient condition of blissful visionary experience. They know that works alone are powerless and that it is faith, or loving confidence, which guarantees that visionary experience shall be blissful. Negative emotions – the fear which is the absence of confidence, the hatred, anger or malice which exclude love – are the guarantee that visionary experience, if and when it comes, shall be appalling. The Pharisee is a Virtuous man; but his virtue is of the kind which is compatible with negative emotion. His visionary experiences are therefore likely to be infernal rather than blissful. The nature of the mind is such that the sinner who repents and makes an act of faith in a higher power is more likely to have a blissful visionary experience than is the self-satisfied pillar of society with his righteous indignations, his anxiety about possessions and pretensions, his ingrained habits of blaming, despising and condemning. Hence the enormous importance attached, in all the great religious traditions, to the state of mind at the moment of death.[22]

In 1980 the art critic Robert Hughes explained the gap between ethical art and moral perception with a book and BBC documentary series called "The Shock of the New." He used the metaphor of shock to explain how each movement or generation of artists sought to kill their father, burning the comfort of habit and safety of formal device to the ground with nihilistic embrace. Shock, in this context however, should not be understood in quite the same terms as the knee-jerk scandals with which so many contemporary artists have recently jettisoned their so-called careers. It is very easy to scandalise the bourgeoise sensibilities of a class trapped in their suburban prisons, terrified of their own flesh and who vote with paranoia to cut themselves off from every experience. The shock that inspired the critic Louis

21 Ibid.

22 Aldous Huxley

Vauxcelles to declare with exasperation "Donatello chez les fauves" ("Donatello among the wild beasts") after seeing the 1905 Salon d'Automne exhibition was closer to spiritual shock therapy than scandal.

That same shock therapy may now be the prescription required to resuscitate art, to save the craft "through a long, boundless, and systematized disorganization of all the senses," a shock and current that is closer to the charge of the Kundalini uncurling in a bolt of lightning running up the spine of inspiration and understanding. The shock that rips through the crusts of habit like an acid bath or scintillating fire, emanates from the body of the artist, re-membered and emotionally in-tuned. Through an ecstatic embrace with their true human, animal, vegetable and mineral natures, seen, unseen and obscene, the cycles, rhythms, revolutions and manifestations of the fires emanating from imagination may be channelled into the three dimensional correspondence we call art. Just as the Primary and Secondary Imagination should not be conflated, so too this nature should not be confused with a weekly yoga class or even a long mindful walk in the woods, but a full-bodied mind blowing orgasmic bolt of enlightened vision that incarnates knowledge with ritual terrifying experience, art as the embodiment of absolute freedom through creative destruction.

> Here is my Dionysian universe that creates and destroys itself eternally, this mysterious world of double pleasures, this, my 'beyond good and evil,' without purpose, unless the contentment at having accomplished the cycle is itself a purpose, without wishing it so, unless a ring has the good will to turn eternally on itself, and on nothing but itself, in its own orbit. This universe that is mine, which is therefore lucid enough for me to be able to see it without straining and risk losing my sight? Strong enough to reveal its soul to this mirror? To place its own mirror opposite the mirror of Dionysus? To propose its own solution to the enigma of Dionysus? And being able to do so would it not have to do it all over again? Becoming wedded to the 'cycle of cycles' ? Yet vowing its own return? Accepting the cycle in which ever and eternally it will glorify itself, and assert itself? With the will to want all things again? To see all the things that have been return again? To want to go to everything there must ever be? Do you know now what the world is for me? And what I want when I want this world?[23]

We are all on the road to Damascus like Saul, but few are granted the blinding Kundalini vision of the lightning bolt of ecstatic sight. According to *Acts* 9:4–5, Saul "fell to the earth, and heard a voice saying unto him, Saul, Saul, why persecutest thou me?" Saul replied, "Who art thou, Lord? And the Lord said, I am Jesus whom thou persecutest: [it is] hard for thee to kick against the pricks." Following the

23 Friedrich Nietzsche, *The Will to Power*

vision, he was blinded for three days and had to be led into Damascus by the hand. During these three days, he took no food or water and spent his time in prayer to God. When Ananias of Damascus arrived, he laid his hands on him and said: "Brother Saul, the Lord, [even] Jesus, that appeared unto thee in the way as thou camest, hath sent me, that thou mightest receive thy sight, and be filled with the Holy Ghost." His sight was restored, he arose, giving birth to his self and baptized himself Paul.

In another story, the Greek hero Oedipus was able to continue his journey to Thebes by virtue of his rational, logical, cartesian senses, correctly answering the riddle of the half male, half female, half human, half beast Sphinx. S/He asked "What walks on four feet in the morning, two in the afternoon and three at night?" to which he replied "Man: as an infant, he crawls on all fours, as an adult, he walks on two legs and, in old age, he uses a 'walking' stick." The story however, does not end there because he goes on to become a King by unwittingly killing his father and marrying his mother. His wealth, prestige and power did not bless him with knowledge of his true self because he blinded by his rational perceptions. It was the blind prophet Tiresias who could see what Oedipus Rex could not. Devastated by the knowledge of his true self and the consequences of his actions, Oedipus uses his mother's broach, a symbol of beauty and vanity, to gouge out his eyes. He had to blind himself in order to see.

It is this same transformation (and ritual function) of art that has been embodied in the famous Ghent Altarpiece. Many art historians believe that the Altarpiece was painted by two brothers, Jan and Hubert van Eyck on the basis of the inscription on the rear of a (now lost) panel. "Hubert van Eyck, maior quo nemo repertus [greater than anyone] started the altarpiece, but that Jan van Eyck, arte secundus [second best in the art] completed it in 1432." The lack of records for the birth of Jan and death of Hubert suggests that they were one and the same person and that the painting was in truth the embodiment and document of an initiation whereby the artist gave birth to himself with the holy name Jan (John).

Slipping between worlds, morality is shattered upon the rocks of disbelief, the work of art stares right back at you with a gaze that penetrates your soul and defies your every expectation, sweating with consciousness and hovering, like the flame between the wood and spirit. The enemy of the "systematized disorganization of all the senses" is habit and convention. Regardless of intent or desire, habit will always numb the mind and every sign, thought, action, protocol or process rendered invisible to consciousness. We might call this numbing "normal" or "common sense" or a number of other comforting conventions that describe the impotence of its experience.

We cannot smell ourselves just as we cannot see our blind habits for what they are. It is only in crisis, confrontation, through violence, terror, chaos or shock that we are gifted with the sight required to see things as they are. Hollywood and the art market feed off our innate need to fall into habit, dressing up cultural effluence as entertainment and every season another super-hero flies in to save the world.

Before he was a Marvel Comic or Film, the Black Panther was a revolutionary political movement and before that a beast of the jungle. We would do well to remember that we don't need a other hero because "every man and woman is a star"[24] and every artist a visionary capable of changing reality.

Art changes the world, one perception at a time.

Fire Walk with Me, Mistah Kurtz – He Dead !

20 March 2018

24 Aleister Crowley, *Liber AL vel Legis*, I:3

Seeking the Three-Headed Saint

Kadmus

I. History

What does it mean for a saint to have three hands? A three-handed saint has haunted me and it has driven me to this question.

When I first began to develop an overt ancestor practice I knew that my great-grandfather would play a central role. I never knew him, he died shortly before I was born, but my parents were always convinced that he and I had a rather odd bond. As a young child I would often behave in ways that perfectly matched some of his rather distinct idiosyncrasies. My parents tell stories of watching me do something strange and whispering to each other "It's Pop-Pop!" Of course, the more I heard stories about him the more I realized we would have gotten along very well, we did indeed seem to share many personality traits and odd habits.

As I began an official ancestor practice I did research into the meaning of my great-grandfather's name, Casimir or Kazimierz in his native Polish. What I discovered was a mysterious patron saint, my great-grandfather's namesake Saint Casimir. I soon discovered that the cemetery that I frequented for necromantic purposes was built largely by Polish immigrants and, to serve these immigrants, a church had been built right outside the main entrance to the cemetery which I had often wanted to visit. The church, I now discovered with a shock, was dedicated to Saint Casimir. This saint, for whom my great-grandfather was named, had been haunting me for rather a while – woven in and out of my occult life and practice, just around the corner and just over my shoulder. This was only the beginning, however, of an attempt to unravel the nature of this strange saint.

Saint Casimir was Prince Casimir Jagiellon, youngest son of the King of Poland and the Grand Dutchy of Lithuania. He was born in 1458 and died on March 4th, 1484. March 4th is his feast day, and the Sunday closest to March 4th is celebrate as Kaziuko mugė or "Saint Casimir's Fair" in the capital of Lithuania each year as well as in many cities and towns throughout Lituania and Poland. At thirteen he was part of a failed military attempt on the part of his family to install him as King of Hungary. He died at the age of 25 from illness, likely from tuberculosis. Between the failed military adventure, about which it is said he felt great sadness and shame, and his death, he developed a reputation for piety and a commitment to aiding the poor. There are stories of his having refused to marry both because of his piety and from foreknowledge of his impending death. Other stories tell of him kneeling at the gates of closed churches praying throughout the night as he waited for the church to open in the morning. He is patron saint of Lithuania, and considered by Lithuanians to be their only native-born saint, as well as patron saint of Poland and of youth in general.

Like many saints, some of the most interesting things about him do not begin with his life but rather follow his death. His most famous miracle occurred thirty-four years after his death, in 1518, when the Russian army attacked the Lithuanian town of Polotsk. St. Casimir appeared on a white horse and led the Lithuanian army in its charge across the Dauguva River against the Russians. This inspired the Lithuanians to force back the Russian invasion. However, if you are to look for the most interesting miracle associated with Saint Casimir, one that sets him apart from almost every other saint, it would be his three-handedness. That is where our real mystery begins.

The most famous depiction of Saint Casimir is a painting of him in the Vilnius Cathedral where he is buried. It was likely painted around 1520, shortly after his miraculous appearance at Polotsk, and depicts him with three hands: one left and two right. This painting is considered miraculous. The story goes that the original painter painted over one of the hands in order to paint a different right hand, but the original reappeared and refused to be obscured. A common interpretation of this is that it reflects Casimir's generosity and charity to the poor, but this is about as far as common interpretations go. It seems to me both that this is an inadequate explanation and that there is a rather more interesting deeper mystery here.

II. Hands

If you are looking for precedent for a three-handed saint or icon the only one you are likely to find is the *Bogorodica Trojerucica*, or "Three-Handed Mother of God". This is a miracle-working icon in the Serbian Orthodox monastery on Mount Athos in Greece. As the name suggests, the icon contains three hands: once again two right and one left. The icon's main story claims that it was owned by Saint John of Damascus who, due to a false accusation, had his hand cut off by the Caliph Al-Walid I. Saint John then prayed before the icon and in a dream Mary told him to "toil without fail" with his hand. When he awoke his hand was miraculously restored. After this he had a silver reproduction of his hand affixed to the icon in thanksgiving. This was supposed to have happened in 717 C.E. The official position of historians is that the icon actually dates from the 14th century, though it may have been made from an earlier version.

Here it must be stressed that the third hand is not intended to be a third hand of Mary, rather the meaning of the third hand is as a monument and gift to Mary in honor of the miraculous healing. This is not an uncommon practice, and many icons can be found with silver depictions of body parts attached to them later after devotees had been healed of an illness in that body part. Despite this, a version of the icon was brought to Russia in 1661 that sparked a Russian cult, birthing many recreations of the icon that began to present Mary as overtly three-handed. This led to depictions of Mary with three hands being fairly common in Russia. Icons harkening back to the original icon and its healing affect on St. John are renown, as one might expect, for their healing powers. However, the more common depictions of Mary with three hands, each of which is meant to be her own, have become symbols of love. When loving someone, the reasoning goes, two hands are not enough.

We might, then, suggest that there are three traditions of the meaning of three-handed saints along with an unremarked upon, but suggestive, fourth meaning as well. We have the standard Casimir meaning connecting the symbol to generosity and charity, tied into the Biblical quotation that when you give you should "not let your left hand know what your right hand is doing". We have the St. John story connecting the three hands with the occurrence of miraculous healing. We have the common Russian understanding that connects the third hand as a manifestation of love unable to be fully expressed with just two hands. We also have the unremarked upon meaning implied in Mary's command to St. John to "toil without fail" with his new hand, and so the third hand becomes a symbol of hard work and commitment.

There is, perhaps, one final meaning not directly connected to hands but connected to duplication in icons in general. There is a tradition in icon veneration that any icon with duplicated elements is twice as powerful or works twice as fast. Thus, a saint with a duplicated hand, or an icon to Mary with one, would work twice as fast and powerfully to bring about the devotees' needs.

These meanings are suggestive, but from an occult view they are far from sufficient. In order to arrive at a more useful occult perspective on the meaning of the three-handed saint we must engage with some more powerful reflections on the meanings of the hands of saints in general. Within folk Catholic magic and witchcraft there is a tradition of understanding the left and right hands of saints as representing very specific aspects and powers of those saints.[1] The right hand of a saint represents its most "saintly" or transcendent and holy aspects. This is the hand that would be used for blessing, for example, and for the spiritual elevation of the worshipper. This is the side whereby the saint offers an aspect of the divine to us. The left hand represents the human side of the saint, the side that remembers what it is like to be alive in a world of struggle and suffering and is responsive to more worldly or even malicious needs. The left hand, then, is used for cursing and the right for blessing. For example, the right hand of Saint Sebastian can be used for healing while the left hand might be used in order to send disease against one's enemies or even cause death. With this in mind it is not at all surprising that the three-handed saints and Virgins we have discussed all have two right hands but rarely, if ever, two left hands. Along these lines, then, having two right hands would represent perhaps an extra holy saint or one who is able and willing to bestow extra blessings. This lines up well with the basic idea that icons with doubling are twice as powerful or work twice as fast but now there would be particular stress on the

1 My knowledge of this tradition is drawn largely from lectures given by Jesse Hathaway.

higher aspects of the saint, with a downplaying of their human side. The occurrence of a saint with double left hands would mean one twice as adept at worldly work and/or sending curses upon others. It is no wonder that double left-handed saints are an even more rare occurrence than the already rare double right-handed saint.

III. Heads

Anyone familiar with my work likely knows I am a committed pagan in my religious, theological, and metaphysical views and that I have an extensive interest in the ancient world. It is, then, perhaps inevitable that in looking for precursors for Saint Casimir's three-handedness my mind would turn to Hekate and Kerberus. Both the goddess Hekate and the guard dog of the underworld, Kerburus, were commonly described or depicted as three-headed or even, in Hekate's case, three-bodied in the ancient world. There is much about the meaning of these divine entities that will be particularly informative and useful in our own investigation.
Hekate's triple figuration derives pretty clearly from her unique status in the Ancient Greek pantheon. Hekate's earliest preserved mention in literature is in Hesiod's *Theogony*. There this rather interesting statement is made concerning the goddess' power and privileges:

> The son of Cronos did her [Hekate] no wrong nor took anything away of all that was her portion among the former Titan gods: but she holds, as the division was at the first from the beginning, privilege both in earth, and in heaven, and in sea.[2]

The Classical and Archaic Ancient Greek culture understood the cosmos in terms of three primary regions or domains, each with its own ruling deities. These domains were the sea, heaven, and earth/underworld. The primary manifestation of these divisions is in the decision of Zeus and his brothers Poseidon and Hades to divide the world amongst themselves with each ruling one third. Zeus got the heavens, Poseidon the seas, and Hades the underworld. Hekate, Hesiod makes clear, is given power in each of the realms of sea, earth, and heaven. There is a bit of a wobble here between the underworld and the earth, but this clears up very easily when one understands that the underworld was understood to be on and in the earth – it is very literally below the ground – and so there is an unavoidable connection between earth and the land of the dead that often leads to their identification.

In order to clarify this last point, allow me to take a slight side journey into Hekate's second literary appearance in the Homeric "Hymn to Demeter". The hymn tells the story of Demeter, goddess of the earth and growing things, and her daughter Persephone's kidnapping by Hades. The story is well known, Hades kidnaps Persephone and Demeter's grief causes the earth to be barren. Eventually

2 Hesiod, *Theogony* 423-427 Hugh Evelyn-White trans.

an agreement is worked out whereby Persephone will spend her time above ground on the earth with her mother during the summer and in the underworld during the winter. Demeter's continuing sadness at her absence each winter is the cause of winter's characteristic lack of growth and life. We should note, first, how closely this ties the above ground and below together. Demeter, representing the earth, is by our contemporary terms Hade's mother-in-law or something similar and Persephone is both a goddess of the earth, especially flowers, and the underworld of the dead.

More important than establishing the identity of the underworld within the earth, the "Hymn to Demeter" establishes a particularly important, and lesser known, role for Hekate. Hekate is present at both Demeter's abduction and her return, "...and from that time," the hymn tells us, "the lady Hekate was minister and companion to Persephone."[3] It is important to note here that the terms "minister" and "companion" are rather unclear in English. In the Ancient Greek they mean literally "the one who goes before" and "the one who follows after". Hekate both leads and follows Persephone, most specifically in her journey to the underworld and her return from it, as indeed she does in the hymn itself. This serves to make Hekate a goddess of doorways and crossroads, and specifically a goddess of birth and death. She governs the journey to the underworld, i.e. death, and the journey out of the underworld or into the world above, i.e. birth. All of this serves to confirm that Hekate's privileges specifically include journeys into and out of the earth.

Now that we have established the kinship of earth and underworld as well as Hekate's particular close connection to the underworld we can return to Hekate's three powers and three heads or bodies. In reference to her rulership it is important to note that though her own power is not ultimately greater than that of Zeus, Hades, or Poseidon it is more extensive, active in more of the cosmos, than any of them which leads to her specific identification with three-headedness. Hekate can do her work in all realms: sea, heaven, and earth/underworld. To consider Kerberus briefly, his three heads will once more point to a particular relationship to the three regions but a relation of guardianship rather than rulership. Kerberus' three heads allow him to guard the gates to the underworld from those venturing to them from the sea, heaven, or earth.

Hekate's depictions ultimately went through a transformation that points to a very important historical transition in thinking about the divine that will be central in our considerations. The *Theogony* was composed around 700 B.C.E. and her importance only increased after that throughout the Classical, Hellenistic, and Roman period. By the time of the Platonic system captured in *The Chaldean Oracles*, sometime in the 2nd century C.E., she has become identified with the soul of the cosmos. She also plays the vital role of a bridge between the transcendent divine realm and the sensible material realm. The universal soul, Hekate, is the womb and channel through which the eternal unchanging ideas of the divine find

3 "Homeric Hymn to Demeter" 438-440 Hugh Evelyn-White trans.

existence in matter.[4] This expanded, and increasingly abstract, role for Hekate as she was dissolved more and more into a Platonic worldview foreign to her Archaic and Classical identity, involves a change in her depiction as well. Hekate becomes two-headed or two-faced, much like the Roman god Janus, as her main nature becomes defined by its relation to the divine on the one hand and the earthly and material on the other. Hekate is the great mediator between the two, dramatically opposed and different, realms. This overlaps nicely with her earlier identification with the passage in and out of death and her association with doorways.

The two faces of Hekate are very similar to the traditional understanding of the two hands of the saints; like the saints Hekate joins the divine and the mortal and each face represents one of these natures as well as her role as the passageway between them. This is not at all accidental, as the Platonism that informed the change in Hekate's nature is the same Platonism that provided much of the metaphysical basis of Christianity and especially Catholicism. Most important in this metaphysics is a two-world dualism between the perfect, eternal, unchanging world of the divine and the fallen material world of mortal life.

The two-handed, two-headed, and similar images become markers then of transcendental systems involving two world dualisms most commonly derived from Platonism. Three-headedness is the mark of the older understanding of the world, one in which heaven is literally to be found at the tops of mountains or in the very real worldly sky and the dead are present as part of the earth. The earth, sea, heaven division represents a this-worldly metaphysics without an aspect of the eternal, perfect, unchanging or transcendent. The old pagan gods, for example, are undying but not eternal. They have origin stories and are open to the possibility of overthrow and death. This is very suggestive and particularly exciting when we see the theme of three-ness returning, specifically in three-handed saints. This more robust understanding of triplicates makes clear how inadequate understanding a doubled right hand in terms of extra-heavenly or extra-transcendental really is. Far from an emphasizing of the transcendental aspects of standard Catholicism, it might be instead that three-handedness undermines the Heaven/Earth dualism in favor of an older understanding of the cosmos.

The importance of the three-realms cannot be overstated for occult and necromantic purposes. Ancient necromancy and magic were predicated on the presence of the gods, intermediary spirits of various sorts, and the dead in the world. Magic within a Christian context, on the other hand, is constantly in need of ways to make up for the metaphysical distance of the divine and its power. Thus, saints and Purgatory each serve as in-betweens much like Hekate did in the earlier Platonic systems – each of which provide an explanation of how the occult worker might have worldly power from an otherworldly source. The saints are not entirely transcendental, and purgatory isn't either, so they are accessible in a way that the transcendent eternal realms are not. In the ancient world, with its three-realms

4 For an excellent analysis of the role of Hekate in *The Chaldean Oracles* and the transitions her role goes through from the time of Hesiod to the Chaldean system see Sarah Iles Johnston's *Hekate Soteira.*

devoid of abstract transcendent divinity, there was no question of the constant real presence of spiritual forces and threats. The magician simply was able to harness the powers that most others sought protection from or suffered under.

The importance of Hekate's triple nature, and the tripartite reality that nature connected to, for magic is underscored by the *Greek Magical Papyri* in which Hekate features very prominently. These papyri capture magical practices and rituals stretching from the second century B.C.E. to the fifth century C.E. The papyri in which Hekate plays the largest role mostly date from the third and forth century C.E., after many centuries of Platonism's dominance and after the incredibly influential *Chaldean Oracles*. In other words, Hekate of the magical papyri post-dates her transformation from three-headed to two-headed. Despite this, Hekate is most commonly depicted as three-headed in the texts. The Hekate of three-heads, then, is the goddess of magical practice while the Hekate of two is largely the abstract goddess of Platonic mysticism and theology, and that theology's own unique form of magical practice commonly known as theurgy.

Even if his three-hands harken back to much more ancient truths, Saint Casimir is and remains a Christian saint. If we are to connect his three-handedness to powers over the three-realms like onto Hekate we need some sort of historical bridge within Christianity itself. One might immediately think of the trinity of Father, Son, and Holy Spirit, but the symbolic and metaphysical interpretations surrounding these entities are so over-determined that it is hard to get much of use from them in this context. Instead, we should recall Saint Casimir's connection to generosity and gift giving. The idea of gifts essentially connects with a Christian tradition involving a famous tripling and an overt connection to magical practice; specifically the three gifts of the Magi or Wise Men. The three gifts specifically mentioned in the *Bible* were gold, frankincense, and myrrh. It seems very reasonable, if Saint Casimir's three hands are related to his charity, generosity, and gift giving in general to associate them with perhaps the most famous tradition of symbolic gifts within Christianity.

There are many interpretations of the meaning of the gifts of the Magi, but one of the earliest and most influential comes from Origen in his *Against Celsus*, written in 248 C.E. before, we should note, the Hekate papyri of the *Greek Magical Papyri* but after the *Chaldean Oracles*. In this text Origen identifies gold with a gift given to a king, myrrh as a perfume appropriate to a moral man, and frankincense with an incense appropriate to a God. So the three gifts, then, represent the realm of humanity, royalty, and divinity. There is a bit more to it, than this, however as myrrh's identification with mortality is likely more connected to its connection to death through its common use as an embalming perfume and agent. This makes the meanings of the gifts death, royalty, and divinity. These meanings are particularly appropriate for Saint Casimir since he was largely defined by his early death; he was indeed royalty and is usually depicted with the marks of royalty surrounding him, and he was deeply committed to the divine and, in being sainted, was joined to it.

There is no perfect match between the meaning of the three gifts and the meaning of the three-realms of Ancient Greece but there are some useful connections to be made. Zeus, in ruling heaven, maintained importance and power on earth through his identification with royalty and kingship. Zeus was the patron god of rulers. So, the gold of royalty nicely matches the ancient realm of heaven (and this despite the common Christian association of heaven with divinity exclusively). Myrrh, with its connection to embalming and death, corresponds nicely with Hades and the underworld as well as earth in general. Frankincense, with its connection to divinity, fails to fit into this scheme however as it is hard to relate it to the realm of the sea. Here the Platonic transcendental perspective of Christianity cannot be made to relate to the older tripartite divisions.

I will leave the reader with an interest in working with Saint Casimir or the *Bogorodica Trojerucica* to investigate where these connections and suggestions might take them on their own. I will, however, point out the possibility that the three-hands could be taken to mean power in the realm of the dead, power in the realm of worldly authority (royalty, political power, etc.), and finally a connection to the divine and/or the sea.

IV. Hymns

The story of Saint Casimir, the three-handed saint, contains one more element I wish to consider here – though there are plenty of other symbols associated with him that call out for exploration (he is always depicted with a lily, his fairs involve special heart shaped cookies called "Casimir hearts" and distinctive flowered palms called verba, his name has some rather interesting and suggestive etymological connections, and so on). The element I want to look at is the "Hymn of Saint Casimir". Saint Casimir is reputed to have composed a prayer in hexameter dealing with the mysteries of the Incarnation but this text has been lost. However in 1604, one hundred and twenty years after his death, his tomb was opened and his body found to be uncorrupted. Beneath his body was found a small bound version of the complex hymn *Omni die dic Mariae* or "Daily, Daily Sing to Mary". This led to a longstanding tradition that he wrote this hymn, though it is actually part of a longer work written by Saint Bernard of Cluny in the 12th century. The connection with the discovery of his uncorrupted body and the reputation that he wrote it led to the hymn frequently being called the "Hymn of Saint Casimir" or "Prayer of Saint Casimir". This hymn proved very popular and has been translated into many languages including, repeatedly, into English. The most famous English translation is likely the one created by Cardinal Wiseman in 1859.

The hymn consists of 60 stanzas of six lines each. Considering the length of the hymn, there are many themes and symbolic connections one could draw from its content so I am not seeking to use the hymn as any sort of definitive proof of the connections I have already suggested. Instead, it struck me that we should be able to draw particularly appropriate elements from the hymn that do connect to the themes we have discussed in order to arrive at something of a reconstructed "Hymn of Saint Casimir" aimed particularly at a resonance with Hekate. I will present this reconstructive selection, using primarily Cardinal Wiseman's version (with a few minor changes of my own in line with the original Latin) the entirety of which can be found very easily online if you are interested in the full text. It is, then, with this hymn that I end my reflections on the mystery of three-handed saints, Virgins, and three-headed goddesses.

This Lady
With lavish hand,
Has dealt out Heaven's treasure:
Queen, who the light
Shed on us bright
Of grace that knows no measure.

Unending lays
Sound forth her praise,
The Queen of all created:
Till note on note
Through Heaven float,
Each with her goodness freighted.

Her virtue's bloom
Its rich perfume
Throughout the church diffuses;
Her word and deed
Are plants which bleed
Balsamic, healing juices.

If Eve's revolt
The golden bolt
Drew fast of Heaven's portal;
She, better starred,
By faith unbarred
The gates of life immortal.

O blessed shoot
From Jesse's root,
Hope, refuge of minds weary!
The earth's delight,
The abyss's light,
The lord's own sanctuary.

Hail, then, O Maiden!
Through whom true Eden
Its gates to man unfolded;
The serpent's coil
Within its toil
Thy virgin knee ne'er folded.

Most precious gem!
Rose-budding stem!
O lily of pure saintliness!
Chaste virgin-trains
To blissful reigns
Leads up thy queenly stateliness.

Oh, make my reach
Of act and speech
But like their aim unbounded;
Thy many claims
To glorious names
Shall far and long be founded.

Blest! Before whom
The world's deep gloom
Was turned to joyous lightness;
They faith the morn,
Which opes, scarce born,
The gates of heaven's brightness.

The crooked path,
From sin to wrath,
Through thee is now deserted;
The fatal harms
Of error's charms
By thee have been averted.

Thou art a Mother,
Yea as none other
Bore son, before or later;
Thine, King of kings,
And of all things
Created, sole Creator!

O thou most blest!

Through whom repressed
Is every hostile malice;
And, at hell's brink,
Who hopeless sink,
May quaff salvation's chalice.

No tongue can raise
Too high thy praise,
O saving star of ocean!
Pale by thy light
Is planet bright,
Or meteor's brilliant motion.

Commending, bear
Aloft my prayer,
To him beloved so purely;
That, from the world
In shipwreck whirled,
I reach the shore securely.

Oh, grant relief
From toil and grief,
To all who perseveringly
Thy feats observe,
Thy deeds preserve
In memory's depths endearingly.

The Chthonic Seed: Reflections of an Ancient Death Gnosis

Billie Steigerwald

...O mighty daemon, whose decision dread, the future fate determines of the dead,
With captive Proserpine thro' grassy grassy plains, drawn in a four-yok'd car with loosen'd reins,
Rapt o'er the deep, impelled by love, you flew 'till Eleusina's city rose to view,
There, in a wond'rous cave obscure and deep, the sacred maid secure from search you keep...

– Orphic hymn to Ploutoni[1]

Upon first tasting the jeweled pomegranate, its juice is bitter and feels rough as dirt against the tongue, but soon dissolves away to ethereal sweetness. In order to taste of the sweetness hidden beneath, the astringency must first constrict the tongue like the body grasps the soul. The unfolding of this experience is a map for the soul to follow. It reveals to us a pathway leading into the divine, and this path leads us inwards and downwards, into the coarse and chthonic, moving deeper in until the earth dissolves into the purity of the abyss. This path may lead us to the heavens, but this is no winged flight away from our embodiment, it is a biting into it.

Katabasis means both "descent" and "retreat", and a katabasis into the underworld is a retreat in the sense that it is a submersion into a hypostasis of nature and embodied self. Transcendence of the incarnate self does not imply a denial, it demands a penetration, for the source of anything is always found within and behind that which it creates. The mythic underworld journey is this penetrative direction, and if continued, it pierces through many layers of being, ultimately stripping us down to our own hypostasis.

What we see of death within nature is merely the ephemeral traces of a doorway leading us away from nature. Nature is the collective realm, where the multitude intertwines across time and space, constricting shared reality into being. The underworld is the space of the *individual* as it exists outside of nature and life. It is therefore the most intimate of spaces, a place where the soul stands bare and exposed to itself. But this realm of self is not a dead end, for the underworld is a process

1 *The Hymns of Orpheus*, Trans. Thomas Taylor (1792) University of Pennsylvania Press, 1999

of psychic transmutation qua space, and if this process continues to its utmost, it leads us into that which transcends our own identity. Even the darkest recesses of the underworld and psyche connect to the *World Soul*, the psychic totality and the principle of one as many and many as one. This is because we ourselves are one of the many, a psychic microcosm contained within it.

The idea of the World Soul was disseminated into Neoplatonic and Renaissance occult philosophy through the writings of Plato, but the idea of a soul underlaying and vitalizing the universe is not a uniquely Platonic one. Plato defined this World Soul or *Psuche tou Kosmou* as the essence of liminality itself, an intermediate *being* which was both indivisible and eternal as well as divided and in constant flux. The World Soul is a philosophical development of the archetypal mother goddess who contains the divine seed-child that is cyclically sacrificed and reborn. This mythic child is always a deity of humanness, of divinized individuality. The death of the child does not occur in spite of the child's divinity; the death is a direct expression or extension of that divinity. Despite its fluctuation and dismemberment, it is reborn and re-membered because its source is beyond any one of its possible transmutations. The seed-child does not represent merely the phenomenal stirrings of its mother: in its sentience, it is a microcosmic reflection of her and is therefore also liminal, poised between eternity and dynamic individuality. Just as the death of a divinity is an extension of its essential nature, so too is death an expression of our own.

The ancient world is full of myths involving an underworld katabasis and a subsequent return, or *anabasis*. The myth in which Persephone, daughter of Demeter, is abducted and carried off into the underworld by Hades is one of the most well-known of these. As told by the Homeric Hymn to Demeter, the myth was central to the Eleusinian Mysteries, an ancient Greek cult that is shrouded in mystery due to the secrecy demanded of its initiates. The life, death, and rebirth of the crops and of all things is the domain of the great chthonic goddess Demeter, to whom the Mysteries were dedicated. One of her symbols is an ear of grain, which displays its bounty outwardly in the seeds that supply us with sustenance, which may be cast into the darkness underground in order to be born again. This is nature as it appears to us: the wide bosomed earth that supplies us with life. The pomegranate is another symbol of hers, but the sensuous fruit is more particularly her daughter Persephone's, and it represents a less obvious mystery. With its faceted jewels the colour of lifeblood, hidden within a crowned globe, the pomegranate is a vivid symbol of the World Soul and the psychic seeds contained within it. At the same time the pomegranate represents the individual soul that must turn inward to discover its own hidden riches.

The rites of the Eleusinian Mysteries were held continuously for over a thousand years, from the 8th Century BCE onward.[2] In all this time, the inner contents of the central rites were kept secret, upon pain of death. Nevertheless, we have been given an understanding that their effect was to bring to the initiate an unwavering

2 Hugh Bowden, *Mystery Cults of the Ancient World*, Thames and Hudson, 2010

confidence in the immortality of their own soul, and a knowledge that their soul would not be resigned to an eternally gloomy existence in the underworld after death. We have many attestations of the dramatic transformative power of these rites, including from well-known philosophers such as Plato, and it is confirmed at the end of the Homeric hymn to Demeter:

> Blest are earth-bound mortals who have seen these rites, but the uninitiate, who has no share in them, never has the same lot when dead in misty darkness.[3]

The primary rites of the Eleusinian Mysteries took place every autumn at Eleusis, near Athens, in a sanctuary dedicated to Demeter and her daughter. These so-called Greater Mysteries were part of an eight-day festival that began in Athens and moved by procession to the sacred site at Eleusis. The mythic drama of Demeter's search for her daughter and their reunion was the focal point of the rites, and both male and female initiates identified with Demeter through participating in ritual reenactments of her story. Participants were given *kykeon*, a beverage made with pennyroyal mint and barley, which may have included ergot, a psychotropic fungus that grows on barley and rye berries.[4] It has also been suggested that the mixture included poppy, the heads of which resemble so much the pomegranate, and which are found growing amongst the grain crops sacred to Demeter.[5] With this in mind, we might consider that the perfectly kept, long silence of the initiates was due, not merely to an oath, but to the inherently incommunicable experience that they had. The rites culminated in an underground temple called the Telesterion, and it is here that the unspeakable epiphany occurred. If we interpret the dramatic structure of the rites as a reflection of the structure of the myth, Persephone's anabasis and reunion with her mother is sequentially aligned with the climactic mystical union that was experienced within the Telesterion. Whatever the symbolic contents of the secret ritual might have been, *union* was certainly of paramount significance.

The Lesser Mysteries, held in the spring in the Athenian district of Agrai, were designated as the official preliminary rites to the Greater Mysteries at Eleusis starting in the fifth century BCE.[6] They are as shrouded in mystery as the Greater, but we do know that Persephone in her role of Queen of the Dead was central to the rites, and that these Lesser Mysteries were of a purificatory and a tutelary nature.[7] Through learning, the initiate gained a groundwork of understanding upon which the purely experiential Greater Mysteries could unfold. Learning is itself a purificatory process that allows for the spiritual vision to become clearer.

The initiation at Agrai involved swathing the eyes and faces of the participants with dark veils. This incubatory veiling is intimately related to the initiatory process.

---

3 *Homeric Hymn to Demeter*, Trans. Diane J. Rayor, 1998

4 Wasson, Hofmann, Ruck, *The Road to Eleusis*. Hermes Press, 1978

5 Carl Kerenyi, *Dionysos: Archetypal Image of Indestructible Life*, Princeton University Press, 1996

6 Carl Kerenyi, *Eleusis: Archetypal Image of Mother and Daughter*, Princeton University Press, 1967

7 Clement of Alexandria, *Stromata*, 5.70.7-71.1.

In the words of mythologist Carl Kerenyi, "The head of the initiate was wrapped in darkness just as in antiquity brides and those vowed to the Underworld were veiled. The word for 'to initiate,' ...means 'to close,' and is used for eye and mouth alike. The initiate... remained passive, but the closing of the eyes and the entry into the darkness is something active."[8] This inwardly directed activity, concealed and encouraged by darkness, is innately connected to Persephone. This purification is preliminary to transcending death, and yet it is itself a submersion into death, wherein the dark waters of death becomes a cleansing bath. Persephone is generally associated with purity, and one of her epithets is *Hagne*, or "pure."[9]

It is a spiritual fruit that the Eleusinian Mysteries bore that is the subject at hand, and this same fruit is borne through other means. It is not my goal here to outline all that is known of the rites, or to attempt to reconstruct their secret contents. Although we do not know precisely how the symbolic contents of the myth was used to such dramatic effect, the myth is itself ripe with secrets, which it reveals in a language all its own, with a sort of mellow scintillation whereby the symbols and characters shift, becoming fractals of each other.

While the return of Persephone to her mother was the subject of the final and most profound rites in the Greater Mysteries, her katabasis into darkness is here our key towards comprehending the meaning of the celestial reunion with her mother. Demeter's Greater Mysteries contains the Lesser as the earth hides a seed. When we look towards Persephone, we find a seed reflection of the gnosis expressed through Demeter, and within this seed-mirror we see a cosmic bud, which in its blossoming returns to the light of her mother's countenance. Although Persephone presides over the realm of the dead, she is also the goddess of spring, and her Latin name Proserpine relates to vegetal growth through connection to *proserpere*, "to creep forth." As her mother's daughter she is *Kore*, meaning "maiden", the effervescent goddess of spring flowers, the outward display of vitality in nature and the rebirth that implies a complimentary state of hiddenness and incubation. Persephone, the hidden core of psychic purity, is unmasked through a severance from nature.

Persephone's story speaks of an internality of experience: it is a map, leading us downward, inward, into the individual soul, allowing for the formation of a microcosm that is transcendent of the cycles of life and death. It describes the death of the body that brings the individual soul into a realization of its existence, not only within the life of nature but outside of it. Her katabasis might also be the soul's descent into incarnation, likened to a spiritual death. And yet the sacred potentiality of incarnation is even in this case expressed, as Persephone becomes a goddess unto her own self, the mistress of death rather than just its victim. The temporally arranged drama in the Homeric hymn, which at first seems to describe Kore's forced transformation into Persephone, is really painting us a picture of an atemporal cosmic structure. Persephone is *eternally* the consort of Hades and the

8 Carl Kerenyi, "Kore." C.G. Jung and C. Kerenyi. *Essays on a Science of Mythology: The Myth of the Divine Child and the Mysteries of Eleusis*. Princeton University Press, 1993

9 Walter Burkert, *Greek Religion*, Cambridge: Harvard Univ. Press, 1985

dread queen of the dead whose name was taboo to mention, and she is called Brimo, "fearsome", or simply *Despoina*, "mistress". The ephemeral Kore's movement and transformation traces the link between the realms of life and death and brings it to our attention. This moving image of the cosmos is enacted for benefit of our own, mortal selves, as if the Gods themselves were actors in some divine play.

The word Kore is etymologically related to "growth". Like a young shoot, she is but half formed, held tightly in the soporific arms of nature. Her story, as it is told in the Homeric hymn, begins with her picking flowers in beautiful fields, immersed so much in the sensual experience that she is unaware of the looming presence of Hades. Her flitting from flower to flower suggests a butterfly, which was to the ancient Greeks a symbol of psyche, the soul.

She is taken by Hades while picking a Narcissus flower of exquisite fragrance and beauty, made to spring from the Gaia, the earth, by Zeus, who has already given sanction to her marriage with Hades. The name of the Narcissus flower is thought have come from the Greek narke, meaning "numbness", due to the narcotic properties of its poisonous roots. We can interpret this moment of plucking the flower as a liminal point representing two states of unconscious potentiality. The flower represents the unconscious unity with nature that leads her into the path of Hades, as well as the oblivion of death, or severing from nature that Hades' abduction effects. The flower is made to grow as a snare for "the bloom-like girl". The narcissus is a mirror, and in reaching to pluck it she is simultaneously reaping her own life and seeing herself for the first time.

While she is transfixed by the flower, a deep chasm opens from the earth and Hades springs forth in his golden chariot, drawn by his four deathless horses, and steals her away into his underworld kingdom.[10] This event is witnessed only by the all-seeing eye of Helios and heard by Hekate, "the one who keeps in mind the vigor of nature" from within "her cave".[11] Hekate is a multifaceted chthonic goddess, savior and guide to lost souls, who shares attributes with both Demeter and Persephone. In late antiquity she is identified as the World Soul itself within the philosophy of the mysterious theurgic gnosis that is the Chaldean Oracles, which we are familiar with through its great influence on Neoplatonic philosophers.[12]

While Kore remains in the underworld, her mother embarks upon her own journey, wandering the earth in the disguise of an old, mortal woman. In her sorrow, all life begins to wither. Because she refuses to end her mourning, Zeus is entreated to let Demeter look upon the face of her daughter once again, and so he sends Hermes to bring Kore back. Hermes, the divine intelligence, is that which remains with the soul, through life and death, the constant guide and link

10 Although the myth is commonly referred to as "The Rape of Persephone", the wording of the Homeric hymn does not imply this, describing only an abduction by chariot. Additionally, there is no ancient Greek cognate for the word "rape" in the modern sense of the word. See Edward Harris, Did Rape Exist in Classical Athens: *Democracy and the Rule of Law in Classical Athens*, Cambridge University Press, 2006

11 *Homeric Hymn to Demeter*, Trans. Gregory Nagy, 2000

12 Ruth Majercik, *The Chaldean Oracles*, Text, Translation and Commentary, Prometheus Trust, 2013

between worlds. The presence of Hermes and Hekate is not insignificant, despite their seemingly minor parts in this tale. They preside over the drama as if looking across a great distance, and their watchful gaze tells us that there is more here than first meets our eyes.

Although Kore returns to her mother, she has eaten a sweet pomegranate seed that Hades has given her to ensure that she might not continually remain with "grave, dark robed Demeter", and so she is destined to remain in the underworld for one third of the year. This seed is a central, concentrated point that encapsulates the entire mystery of the myth. The pomegranate is a liminal symbol, and to the Ancient Greeks it represented fertility, marriage, death and eternal life, and was a traditional offering to the dead.[13] The Greek word *kokkos* can be interpreted as pomegranate seed, grain, or genitals, and it is the origin of the word *cocoon.*[14] This seed she consumes is the chthonic kokkos of death, desire, and regeneration, and although it is therefore the binding kokkos of cyclical life, it is also symbolic of the binding of the soul with death into the sanctified union that is eternal life. Within the very same seed that binds us to our incarnation is the potentiality of transcending that bind. This is an expression of the universal formula, found in many mystical traditions and expressed most outwardly in tantric traditions, whereby one finds transcendence through what seems to be the very source of one's bondage. *Through* is a key word here, for we must move into, through and past the binds in order to untie them, like knots. Gaining a true vision of the *inner* reality of the bind transmutes its poison into nectar.

Kore becomes Persephone, the queen of Hades and of the dead, and so rather than submitting to death she becomes transcendent of it. In the eating of the pomegranate seed that hides jewel-like beneath its covering, she consumes the hidden *life of death* that is eternal life.

To become a divine individual means to at first become self-contained. Through ritual and meditation, we may move inward and downward, enacting a death in order to rebirth ourselves. In pulling our energies away from their ceaseless reactionary intertwinement with externals and directing them towards our core, we create a death-like stillness, surrounding us like a womb. This is the force of growth directed inward, Kore qua Persephone, submerged within the abyss. Within this stillness an alchemical process begins to stir, the phantoms of our own mind forced to confront each other. Upon breaking free of the outside world, whether through meditation or through death, our soul is forced to experience what it contains, and we find that our experience is determined by our own contents.

Hades' name eventually came to be extended to his chthonic realm. The nuanced understanding of Hades, as it was said to be held by adherents of the Chaldean Oracles, is a key to our own:

13 Peter Garnsey, *Food and Society in Classical Antiquity* (Cambridge, UK: Cambridge University Press, 1999

14 Daniel H Garrison, *Sexual Culture in Ancient Greece*, University of Oklahoma Press 2000

> ...They multifariously distribute Hades, at one time calling it the leader of a terrene allotment, and at another the sublunary region. Sometimes they denominate it, the most inward of the etherial and material worlds; at another time, irrational soul. In this, they place the rational soul, not essentially, but according to habitude, when it sympathizes with it, and energizes (it) according to partial reason.[15]

Any hellish experience of this region is not due to an essential quality of place, but to the self-created experience of the individual within it. Put in another way, Hades qua hell-realm is localized into being and place through the absence of a fullness of reason in the soul. This state of "partial reason" that energizes and creates the unhappy post-mortem state is the inability to realize one's self as a complete and microcosmic being, rather than just an extension of nature that is doomed to eventually decompose. The "most inward of the etherial" is the most inward and personal experience of the soul. In the Homeric hymn to Demeter, Hades is given the epithets *Polydektor*, meaning "host of many", *Polysemantor*, "ruler of many", and *Polynomos*, "many named". His kingdom is the space that allows for the convergence of individual, psychic internality, and he himself is the numinosity within this.

The underworld is a liminal place where the psychically receptive substratum of nature is laid bare. The ether of the underworld is possessed and imprinted upon by the individual. But this ether floats upon and dissolves into a primordial abyss that lays beneath it, and it is this deepest layer that must be reached in the underworld journey. In doing so, we bring the two farthest corners of our own microcosmic soul together: the knower with the unknowable. The abyssal space within us is also that space without, it is that fructifying darkness that offers its latency to the cosmos. These depths of psychic experience are at first dark, as we ourselves must learn to supply our own light here.

It is our own soul that is sovereign in this realm, and this may be a curse or a blessing. It is possible to travel through the underworld and observe other souls in torment there, but this place is not hell unless we ourselves are trapped there by our own misery. Katabasis is therefore the ultimate test, not merely of our good intentions, but of our self-sufficiency. It tests our psyche's susceptibility to the otherly, the phantom's whisper and the demon's caress. It reveals just how dependent our sense of self is to the fleshly tension of nature and the attitudes of others. The underworld is a cosmic incubator, and it is because of our individuality that it becomes, not just an incubator of the cosmos at large, but of our own psychic cosmos. To fear death, then, is to fear the self.

The turning in at first allows us to discover just how full we are of a hell of our own making, and we may have our work cut out for us in dissolving the traces of fear, compulsion, confusion, and engagement with dramas that do not serve us. These traces are etheric, semiconscious phantoms that haunt us and obscure

---

15 Psellus, *A Concise Exposition of Chaldaic Dogma*, Trans. Thomas Taylor, 1817

our vision of the deeper recesses of our soul. This hell realm is an embodiment of an absence, but this absence is not that of the pure abyss, it is the absence of engagement with that abyss. It is an intermediary place, a limbo land that must be destroyed in order to be traversed through.

If we turn further inward, we may experience a profound emptiness that in its purity no longer frightens us. Although at this stage the intellect is silenced, the inner intelligence is present and at one with the void. And simultaneously, this stillness is full of rich chaos, organizing itself in an internal cosmogenesis, the inner eye acting as demiurge. The inner cosmogenesis is like the sprouting of a seed, and the surrounding stillness is that eternal, unchangeable aspect of the soul, the liminal potentiality that offers space for the creation of our microcosm to take place. This microcosm is not created through an ego driven desire to be different. The uniqueness of our soul's expression is an inevitable side effect of this, not a goal in and of itself, and this expression comes into being by finding the totality of divine experience reflected within us. The psychic microcosm may be submerged into death as into dark and fertile soil, but it is our cosmic reflectivity that is the nectar of eternal life, and the personality is an ephemeral blossoming that emerges from this radix. The delicate petals of the individual personality, in their transitory nature, are deathly as well as lovely, the expression of Eros and Thanatos in equal measure. The flowery Kore is frightened of her abduction into death, and yet she has only to see her own reflection to *realize* the death inside of her. The narcotic nectar of being is literally also the fluid of the dead, seeping up from Gaia.

In his less ominous aspect, Hades was commonly referred to as *Plouton*, meaning "riches". Perhaps these riches are the precious jewels and metals of the earth, but perhaps they are also those hidden riches that the soul may discover after death. The etymology of the name Hades is not agreed upon, but it is thought to mean "He who is invisible", or alternately "all embracer" or "all receiver."[16] His invisibility is only fearful when we fight against it. His apophatic cloak is protective and incubatory, but it seems to smother us if we fight his embrace in order to claw our way back to the surface. The laws of this realm are strange, and to master them a reversal of the ordinary perspective is necessary, for by going down we ascend, and by moving into darkness we find light.

As the Pomegranate is a symbol of both death and marriage, the seed that keeps Persephone with Hades can also be interpreted as a symbol of their love. That Zeus, the omnipresent, penetrant divine force has already given permission for them to marry suggests that this is a sanctified reunion of the soul with the mysteries beyond death. Hades, or Plouton, is the brother of Zeus, and is referred to as Zeus Khthonios, a title which is given to Zeus himself when playing a chthonic role identical to that of Plouton's, wherein he appears in serpentine form.[17] In Orphic myth, Persephone is seduced by Zeus in the form of a serpent, and bears yet another divine child of death and rebirth. In funerary art that yields clues regarding

16 *Dictionary of Greek and Roman Biography and Mythology*, 1849

17 Joseph William Hewit, *The Propitiation of Zeus*, Harvard Studies in classical Philology Vol. 19, 1908

the Eleusinian Mysteries there is depicted an initiate in his final stage of initiation, reaching out to touch, without fear, a serpent held in the lap of Demeter.[18] The fear of the chthonic is in this moment conquered, and the serpent recognized as divine. Through this we find that Plouton is none other than an underworldly expression of Zeus, the principle of universal, electric spiritual fertilization.

Kore is able, in her purity, to descend into the underworld and see the true face of Hades, the pervasive numinosity that is found even in the deepest and most hidden parts of the cosmos. Her marriage represents her partaking of this numinosity, and so she simultaneously exists in life as Kore and in death as Persephone. This simultaneity is not only between Kore and Persephone, for Kore is the link that allows us to realize that Demeter and Persephone are one being.

If we follow Demeter's story in the Homeric hymn, we are shown something that seems to address our own, human experience. The sense of loss that she goes through reflects our own, when confronted with the death of a loved one. During her wanderings under mortal disguise, she becomes a nurse to the infant son of a king, and every night she secretly anoints the babe with ambrosia and plunges it into a fire in order deify it, as if baking it like a loaf of bread. This process is interrupted when she is discovered by the child's mother. The confusion and fear of the mother when she sees her son being held in the fire reflects a common inability to see the process of transformative purification within the trials of hardship and death. Persephone's path, on the other hand, is towards unfamiliar territory and the taboo. In identifying with her transformation from Kore to the Queen of Death, we plunge ourselves into alien, icy waters. But these are the purifying waters of nonbeing. On the surface, it is a cleansing fire that does this work, the flame of life that also brings death. The waters below are the baptismal waters of death that bring life.

The mysteries of Persephone are held before those of her mother, because it is only after we have moved into alien territory, breaking open our fears and eating of the forbidden kokkos, can we truly understand Demeter. Before this baptism, Demeter seems to be merely representative of nature, but upon being reunited with her daughter she becomes something vaster.

The descent and return express the formula of *Solve et Coagula*. The death of the seed-child is its birth into individuation, it must be severed from the totality in order to see its own reflection and become self-aware. The final coagulation is the discovery that the seed-self is also a mirror- where then does the image that is reflected originate? The mythic reunion is not only of Demeter with Kore: it is also an entirely new union of Demeter with Persephone. Their merging represents an emergent realization of World Soul. The two goddesses are halves of a whole, each acting as a mirror for each other. As Demeter is paired with Zeus in order to give birth to Kore, so Persephone is paired with the chthonic Zeus, to give birth to herself through Kore's reemergence. Demeter has in a sense given birth to Death through Kore, and that Death herself gives birth, not

18 Walter Burkert, *Ancient Mystery Cults*, Harvard University Press, 1987

just to life, but to the eternal life that is the syzygy of life and death.

There is really only one direction that is described in the myth, although our innate sense of spatial metaphor may need to be stretched to accommodate this idea. The direction away from the mother, towards the narcissus, on into the realm of Hades, into individuation and onwards towards reunion is not a back and forth, it is a continuous and unfaltering process towards gnosis. Katabasis is a necessary preliminary to anabasis, and the return is always to a different place than where we started, and the place is different because we ourselves have been transformed. Corporeal existence may be a numb intoxication, or it may become the bliss of embodiment that can only be experienced when the soul is rooted in its eternal existence outside of embodiment.

We will all die. And yet we can die before our death, as many times as we desire. Rather than allowing ourselves to be dragged kicking and screaming into a chasm of our own psyche, we can walk willingly into it. The ancient death-gnosis may be brought back, simply through turning our faces to the blackened earth and letting it swallow us up. Let us sink into the darkness of our own primordial purity. The black shroud, the sensory deprivation tank, the darkened room, or a bed of grass in a graveyard at night may all supply us with the opportunity. Knowledge of our own rebirth will be soon to follow. When the stillness of death is cloaked around us, that stillness becomes a lucent receptor of the numinosity around us, and so we return to life, as Kore blossoms into spring.

—~—

> I reached the boundary of death, and set foot on the threshold of Proserpina, and then I returned, carried through all the elements; in the middle of the night I saw the sun blazing with bright light; I approached the gods below and the gods above face to face...
>
> – Apuleius, *Metamorphoses*[19]

19 Apuleius, *Metamorphosis*, 11.23.6-8, trans. Bowden, 2010

The Gospel According to the Tomb Man

Fred Andersson

The reality of someone else is always ambiguous, subjective and truly impossible to fully understand for anyone not living on that specific plane of existence; the inner reality some of us desperately try to share through art and creativity, written and spoken words, but that never seems to be fully accessible for the curious. To externalize what's inside of us can be art, and it can be magick or both, but the only way we can get away with it without being diagnosed mentally unstable is to call ourselves artists. But what about the rest, those who for one reason or another can't blame their wild imagination on being artistic beings?

What is the truth if, let's say, your friendly uncle Bob claims that something has happened to him while he was all alone. No one else experienced it, and therefore it can't be proven? Should we trust him? In the end, the only thing we can trust is Uncle Bob's own testimony about being abducted by grey aliens or getting into a fistfight with Bigfoot – without any kind of physical evidence or witnesses. So why we can trust some people, and not Uncle Bob?

In general, a normal human has been programmed to accept a certain level of reality, and when another person claims something out of the ordinary that exceeds the programmed probability the trust withers away in the minds of most information receivers. A mutual respect/belief is a must to establish trust, and to choose the right confidants is even more important. Evoking a specific truth is like a magickal performance: doing rituals, using spells – rooted in the accepted, traditional reality. Instead of creating a sigil and burning it: create a coded letter buried inside a bottle outside a holy cave! Just like with all other art, taking what's inside of you to create something external is magick, and for an ambitious person it's an effective way to change their reality.

I might not believe everything that people say they have experienced, but neither do I have any reason to force them to prove that everything they claim is true. It is their truth and I can't do much about it. A few of them go to extremes to make their truth as convincing as possible, as in the case of Bill Wilkinson, more known under his alias Ben Hammott. In 2008 a hyped documentary, "Bloodline," was released on DVD and it claimed something very spectacular: Mary Magdalene, Jesus and maybe their children are buried in a tomb in the French countryside outside the town of Rennes-le-Château; famous from conspiracy theories regarding ancient artifacts, advanced riddles and hidden treasures, Dan Brown's *The Da Vinci Code* and secret knowledge that could bring down Christianity itself! In the film, we follow director/host Bruce Burgess as he investigates the organization of Prieuré de Sion and the legend about the bloodline of Jesus. Through that he meets Ben Hammott, who at the moment is living in his well-used car outside the French town. He leads them on a spectacular treasure hunt and produces unique video footage of the tomb of Mary Magdalene and Jesus. From time to time Burgess seems to question Hammott's intentions, but slowly is drawn into Hammott's world of mysteries, as a fly caught in the sticky net of a mild-mannered British spider.

"Bloodline" is truly an interesting and exciting documentary that unwillingly becomes a mockumentary, as Ben Hammott (an anagram for "The Tomb Man") in 2012 confessed in a written statement he'd made everything up as a huge, ambitious hoax – including writing a 662 page book about his adventures in the Rennes-le-Château area, filled with cleverly constructed riddles, treasure maps, buried ancient artifacts, photos of the tomb and a constructed conspiracy that goes beyond what others have done before. He involved a lot of people: his brother, friends, colleagues and members of the media to make his story grow even bigger, until the day he couldn't handle it anymore and confessed his secret to "Bloodline's" producer, radio host René Barnett. It resulted in a tell-it-all interview, which turned the community of Rennes-le-Château conspiracy theorists on their heads.

It's an interesting situation, as it shows it's possible to prove basically anything if everyone involved is willing to believe. And if it's possible to prove, does that make it the truth? It *is* a reality for some, that's a fact. I'm sure on some level that Hammott believed it himself. He was basically a method actor in his own universe – who slowly lost control over the reality he once started to construct. It's not that far from established actors who can't get out of their character after a film or play, as the new fictional reality and the old one crash into each other. Reality is a complex thing, no matter on which side we're standing.

I enjoy... No, I love hoaxes like this, or should we call them shifts in the established reality? It can be very stimulating when the reality is off a bit from the normal state; when it for at least a fleeting moment questions everything we've been taught before going back to the grayness of the external reality we share with others: work, responsibilities, and no fun and games. It gives us a sense that everything is possible – that magick is present. If we remove the human concept of moral from this particular hoax, this is just someone who wanted to create his own reality no matter what; his own Total Environment as Anton LaVey would have called it. It gave him something. Was it tickling the ego? Perhaps it was something deeper, as a cathartic exercise to deal with a death of a child, something Hammott had suffered? Compared to those involved in other famous and often very ambitious hoaxes as *The Hitler Diaries* and *Alien Autopsy*, Hammott seems less interested in money thean he is in the search itself; the mystery he created and expanded over multiple mythological and personal universes.

Changing reality/creating magick needs other participants that believe in it, and Hammott had them all in his hand. Together they created an even wider, more mysterious and convincing reality. They connected themselves to what Alan Moore calls the *Ideaspace*, where art and creativity are their own realities – building upon the already existing mythology about Rennes-le-Château, the mysterious priest Bérenger Saunière and his alleged hidden treasures, the secret organization Prieuré de Sion and of course the bloodline conspiracy itself. Suddenly Ben Hammott's truth had also become their truth, and if that's not magick I don't know what it is.

What is truth anyway? I don't know if truth even exists, to be honest. There might be some internal, deep truth inside all of us, but it seems it will always change based on how we perceive everything around us, because nothing is truly constant. There are always irregularities. Truth, I guess, must also be based on knowledge and experience. But what is knowledge except the experiences of others and yourself, and there's no way you'll have all the experiences to be able to tell what is the truth. So for all of us, our private truth is basically guessing. For me, truth is not necessarily true in the sense it's accepted by others. I'm not interested in the ultimate truth, as it won't give me any more experiences. It just stops there, and therefore life kind of ceases to have meaning. I'm also a firm believer in the truth being what we make of it; we're the ones in charge.

That can of course be very destructive, depending on the level of experience you've had, and the intelligence you possess. Many people claim one truth to hurt other people, which of course is contemptuous behavior. But that's not my responsibility to worry about; I can't stop them from believing in what they do – no matter how tragic that belief is. Instead I have my own truth, which is based on my experiences. That can of course be changed with additional information, which one day will be contradicted by even newer information – and that's the fun of it. My acceptance of (not necessary belief in) a lot of things out of the ordinary exists because I don't think there's any truth out there. Everything is made up, in one way or another, from people's imagination, claims and experiences – and those can never be the same for me; that's impossible. Even if someone shows a video of what they've experienced, it's just a camera, it's not real – it's a digital copy of the event from a whole different angle.

Just because you see something on TV doesn't mean it's true. That's the same thing with existence in general: you don't know for sure. I often say that I KNOW that there's no universal mind, but truth be told; I don't know that. It's something I say because it's based on the experiences I've had in my life, including information I've gathered from others who have pondered the same subject and come to similar conclusions. All this together makes me make up my mind as it will fit to my worldview and level of spirituality. "Make up my mind" is a good expression here, as we take the information we've gathered and use it as make-up on our consciousness, covering the spots we don't like and/or agree with, making it fit as we want. This is freedom for me, this is individualism: the right to perceive reality as we want it. It's not always necessarily "moral" or "smart", and as long as it doesn't involve other people in some kind of situation that will hurt them physically or destroy their lives – and Ben Hammott didn't do that, at least not deliberately. Whatever you choose as your reality is accepted by me, even if I might not agree with you. Everyone shapes their own path, no matter how insane it is – and it's impossible for anyone else to interfere as that path changes all the time, just like the truth isn't constant.

Often a distorted reality/truth can be more rewarding than the traditional reality, but it's important to not let it take over; then it might become a religion, a controlling philosophy that leads to worship of a higher being than oneself. The truth becomes more interesting when it fluctuates, as long as it doesn't get destructive. Ben Hammott learned it the hard way and confessed to what he had done, which is kind of sad. I would have loved to see his universe live on forever - and maybe it does, as there are those who question if his 2012 confession is actually true. Some say it's written by someone else, and that Hammott was forced to retract his sensational discoveries by a powerful organization, maybe the Catholic Church or another alleged hoax, the mysterious Prieuré de Sion.

It really doesn't matter if we see this as the truth, because if we do, what says it can't be real? The concept of truth is based on magick, and truth is something we're dealing with every day whether we're aware of it or not through tiny, innocent white lies and something we might call the truth. We're constantly shaping our reality, and some of us, like Ben Hammott, take that a few extra notches.

That makes us all magicians.

References

Burgess, Bruce and Barnett, René, "Bloodline: What if the Greatest Story Ever Told was a Lie?," Cinema Libre Distribution, 2008.

Hammott, Ben, *Lost Tomb of the Knights Templar: 100 Year Old Clues Left by a French Priest Lead to an Amazing Discovery*, self-published, 2008.

"Sunflower" – A Modern Interpretation of the Wondrous Essence of the Goddess

Zaheer Gulamhusein

This story was written in 2001, a short while after an event that single-handedly signalled the herald of a 'new' age. A time when scientific discovery should have propelled humanity to new heights and a wider sense of perspective but instead plunged us into a state where we would sink to previously unknown lows.

In its essence, the story illustrates the exterminating aspect of the mother of the world in the dark moments (or times) when a demon-tyrant is threatening to undo the world, and is a display of how the gods willingly abdicate their various masculine attitudes in order that cosmic balance can be restored. It depicts the violent emotion and combined wrath of all gods projected and externalised in a symbol - in this instance the warrior maid assumes the form of a sunflower.

It was just another day in serfdom with nothing of interest to report apart from the fact it coincided with a period of abstention from illicit drugs, which itself was superseded by a long overdue decision to give up smoking self-rolled cigarettes.

I left the office for lunch sometime between 1 and 2pm; the latest I could physically withstand sitting at my desk before needing to vacate the building for some culinary worldly delight proffered by the Canary Wharf deities.

—∾—

Up until this point, my day had consisted of the following routine:

Waking up from ethereal bliss at 7.30am GMT to the monotone sound of my Blackberry alarm and then snoozing it until 8.15am.

This delayed entrance to the world of the living dead was absolutely critical in mustering up sufficient energy to facilitate physical elevation. As I had gotten older, I still could not escape from the need to wake up as late as humanly possible in order to get to work as late as was permissible (without attracting unnecessary attention from my superiors/makers although comments would inevitably be made) – this was my only way of reconciling a life of wage slavery. I despised mornings with a passion but more importantly hated the prospect of spending a third of my earthly existence in an office, working. At the age of 28, under the guise of denial, I continued to punish myself with chores such as ironing a work shirt each morning before leaving work, kidding myself that I would be wasting 'free' time at weekends by doing it in advance.

The period of time between waking and leaving the flat had been fine-tuned to 40 minutes, which involved getting my fix of Colombian high-roast coffee (ground for paper filter), evacuating the bowels, showering, ironing (aforementioned shirt), dressing, spending a few moments deciding whether to take iPod, literature or both (for the sum total of a seven minute journey between the flat and work, not counting the three minute walk and/or elevator time at each end) … and inanely pacing the flat to ensure all electrical appliances were switched to the 'off' position and that toilet lids were placed down, adhering to the principles of feng shui.

The media I chose to fill my journey to work with was usually, and intentionally, way too intellectually demanding for me to appropriate in the short span of time available, but this was the type of cerebral challenge I thrived off, especially as it was inevitably the only one of its kind to occur over the course of my day. The only sounds my ears were subjected to were walls of heavy reverb/delayed guitar, no-wave no-hope lyrics, Sufi/Tibetan chants invoking the names of deities and/or my own compositions – Soundscapes of layered analogue synthesisers playing combinations of chords designed to evoke the deepest levels of sadness and highest states of ecstasy.

Essentially, my journey to work was designed to ensure that the moment of arrival at the office was filled with the most complex level of human emotion. The upshot was mixed feelings of nostalgia, emptiness and denial. Then, in a humble bid to integrate, I would commence work almost instantaneously upon arrival, logging onto 'the network' and arranging the necessary instruments (pen, pencil, pad, calculator, etc). My colleagues knew better than to engage with me at this time; even the most casual remarks would inevitably be met with hostile eyes and slurred verbal assault. Topics guaranteed to evoke this reaction were those based around the weather, news (snippets of disinformation spread conveniently via free newspapers and intermingled with trivial bestial anecdotes), travel problems (including faulty lifts), sport and drunken exploits (which were looked upon with a certain god-like admiration, or fondness, quite unlike any other type of drug ingestion, which baffled and annoyed me incessantly) from the night before.

As I went to lunch in my favourite underground plaza, I caught a glimpse of two female office drones sitting on a bench. One of the drones passed what looked like a handful (three to be precise) of oval neon-purple beans to the other (who was named Helianthus). The worthy recipient, famished from a morning of bashing fingers furiously on a series of plastic buttons (in a bid to complete her daily quota of allocated tasks), placed these magical looking beans gratefully between lipstick-smeared lips into her mouth, swallowing her gift

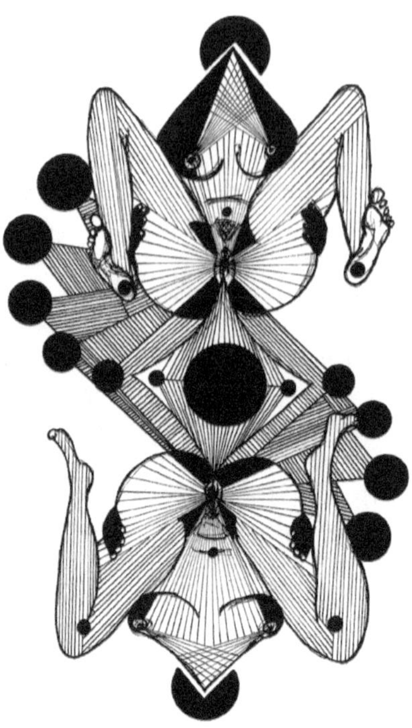

with a knowing smile as they made their way into her hungry belly.

At that moment, an intense power poured forth from her mouth and a symphonic roar akin to that of a thousand female lions filled the space, creating a vortex of energy. This sound also signalled the beginning of a physical transformation and Helianthus' arms started to take on the form of sunflower stems, their thickness at first equalling the circumference of her arms before growing disproportionately larger than her human frame. The rate of growth then increased at an exponential rate and in seconds she was extending in Fibonacci spirals towards the glass-domed ceiling of the plaza. The force of expansion resulted in her smashing through the glass without the slightest difficulty. An almost orgasmic expression took over her face as skin, petals and glass meshed momentarily, leaving her mesmerised by the multicoloured refraction of sunlight through the shattered shards of reinforced glass. Everyone knows sunflowers have the ability to grow to unusual heights but in this instance the strangest of things happened, quite beyond the realms of scientific madness (but in keeping with the miracle of this auspicious personification of the supreme energy of the universe). Each stem bloomed into nine giant sunflower heads (18 in total), each approximately 130 metres in diameter (imagine the size of the London Eye) and all simultaneously rotating in seemingly opposite directions. The goddess Helianthus set her sights on the preordained target – the immense

Solar phallic god that presided over London and all its machinations, designed by the demonic tyrants to secure the chosen few's hold over the masses through free market fundamentalism. As Helianthus spotted her goal, she smacked her lips, mimicking the actions of a little girl about to receive her favourite flavoured lollipop. But it wasn't her mouth that was destined to be the recipient of this triangular-headed 236 metre, 50 storey, steel dick.

It was time for the Lunar forces to retake their spot as London's ruling deities (please note the Mother Goddess disguised as a Solar entity – Sunflower – to facilitate close approach to the phallic deity of 1 Canada Square and avoid detection). Helianthus proceeded to lube herself with spit and pussy juice, both of which were in endless supply due to the extent of her excitement and sense of imminent victory. She hoisted herself over the gigantic tower, rubbing her sublunary clit over the tip of the illuminated pyramid, working herself up to a cosmic frenzy and ensuring her entry and successful insemination for the production of the next Lunar race (long overdue, consequently). With the goddess seated, the demon already hopeless and about to fall, Life Energy (as the primeval maternal principle) was reabsorbed into the Universal Womb – see diagram for further details.

Meanwhile below, the workers of Canary Wharf stood in a state of shock and awe at what they were witnessing. Some ignorant motherfuckers scowled and screamed wildly at the Solar-Lunar spectacle. NB. Trading had not been halted, but reports of a terrorist attack on London had sent share prices diving and the bankers, ever greedy, made sure they secured profits as the markets were sent spinning into decline (all part of the Supra-Celestial plan nonetheless). Others, excited by the giant-sized Solar sex show started to frig and wank themselves silly, murmuring strange sounds sent down to them from the heavens to fuel the potency of the Lunar takeover.

The Riderless Horse, the Wanderer, and the Mark of Cain

Charlotte Rodgers

My illness has ridden me hard for 27 years and now that the sickness has gone, I am riderless, aimless and bereft.

The concept of a disease being both a blessing and a form of possession has been documented since Assyrian and Babylonian times. The disease considered to be the most alienating and socially unacceptable shifts with the era, generally assuming the form of the most visually horrific. Small pox, leprosy and infertility being particular favourites as they are all afflictions which mark out the carrier. The individual should be part of the hive, and with an illness which brands him as 'other' (or in the case of infertility, as a non fully functioning member of the group) the sufferer must be ostracised rather the community be seen to be malfunctioning and the afflicted being visibly representative of a threat to the established order.

> Thee I accuse, thou uprooted of all human laws thou inventor of these monstrosities, devised, no doubt, with a view that mankind might not forget thy name. – Pliny

Of course the Gods have greater power than the individual and the group. The disease, whilst bearing the stigma of the outsider, also highlights those afflicted and can conversely offer a chance of redemption, either by being physically healed or by being bestowed upon by grace and spiritual communion in some way. An attempt to exorcise the illness is again spotlighting the afflicted who are viewed as transgressors and taboo breakers, although taboos are barriers that once broken through can lead to an initiation of sorts. The exorcism is thus a contradiction in that it requires focusing on that which should be unseen and ignored. Perhaps this focus is what creates a demonic form for the illness to manifest as it assumes a shape of something tangible that can be dealt with... something knowable. The Hindu words *dawa* 'medicine' and *Duwa* 'blessing', the Hebrew word for evil, *bish,* and illness, *bush,* all can be seen as too close to be unrelated and since when is linguistics coincidental? So with time, as human beings and their life styles evolved so also changed our attitudes to diseases, demons and social stigmas. Babalu-Aye has evolved from being a Santeria Orisha of Smallpox and other unsightly infections to include HIV. Indian Naths have developed sects that no longer necessarily adapt the antinomian practices of meditating in cremation ghats and eating flesh, but instead work with those stigmatised by diseases which can be seen as representing even greater taboos than death. In many ways an illness that is invisible like HIV and HCV is more frightening as it can kill but doesn't necessarily obviously physically manifest. The stigma of being considered to be internally polluted by a life style choice rather than simply suffering from a physical affliction is something that helps nullify the fear of those who are not affected, as, if there is a reason and way to blame, others feel safer, and less likely to be contaminated whilst being validated in their judgement.

"Divine Punishment for Indecent Living." – Keith Haring

Something which argues this approach albeit operating within a different sphere of illness, is the premise utilised by "The 12 Step Programme of The Disease Concept." This presents the idea that alcoholism and addiction are physical diseases rather than manifestations of an inner emotional and mental rot, and these diseases effect changes on many levels, including spiritual, rather than spiritual diseases that manifest on a physical level.

Rene Gerard, in his research on sacrifice, deems that sacrifice is necessary for efficient running of any society; the means of sacrifice varying according to the social mores of the time. In the case of anti-social diseases there is no redemption or positive spin for the afflicted but society will be saved if order is reestablished in some way. The days of stoning or lynching the sufferers are no longer accepted in most modern societies, although I remember in the early 1980's ostracisation and abuse were the norm towards the early HIV sufferers, and the legal system can and has been used to punish the diseased and make an example of them. The awarding of "The Badge of Shame" in 1697's Poor Act was an early example of a way of naming and marking out those that threaten society that became the go to method for corralling and branding, variations of which are still used today. Using the example of poverty could perhaps be seen as a digression but many of the illnesses mentioned can be easily healed or dealt with if there is an access to money, and poverty is and has always been, considered an illness and disease in itself

I always felt as if I were an outsider. I had no tangible reason to feel this – simply the fact that I didn't seem to fit in with other people, didn't seem to be cut from the same cloth. Consequently I searched for others like myself. I guess this is the nature of human animals: a need to find your pack. When very young I first discovered biblical reference to The Nephilim, which fascinated me with its strong imagery of being cast out – not human and very much 'other'. In keeping with this I also was glamoured by concepts of Cain's Mark, an invisible branding that indicates a transgression. I'm not alone in this fascination and identification with Cain. Lord Byron, who was born lame, related strongly to Cain's imagery as an outcast and wanderer and also saw his own illness in terms of rendering him as 'other'. He referred to himself as 'the limping devil' which seems to have been linked to Asomodeus, a Goetic demon whose name titled the book of a close friend of Byron. Moving through my own various countercultural experience with fellow outsiders operating within groups orientated around drugs, spirituality, music and art I found all had a degree of transience and fluidity to them as people died or evolved and moved on. However the diagnosis of HCV[1] in my early 20's meant that even though I eventually altered other aspects of my life and pretended or trained myself to assume the role of what I considered to be 'normal', the invisible branding was there to keep me firmly in my place but conversely also to entail that I was perpetually wandering in search of a home aka a place/a pack/peers. Thus my life, art and spirituality remained firmly rooted in the alternative, the left hand side, the darkness. Through my words and art I explored taboo, death, disease and so called aberrant sexuality. The god forms I related to were the outsiders, the outcasts, Lilith, Babalu-aye, Set, Shiva. With my recent cure, I feel loss and alienation as much as the gratitude of being granted a boon from those I adore and work with.

Contextually a specific illness can create a 'oneness' with the relevant patron deity. Fabrizo Ferrari talks of blessings being given to the Hindu folk deity Sitala rather than the afflicted because the diseased person is literally, Sitala. In Western Mythos this is also the case, and Greek and Roman lore adopt the same beliefs. The Roman goddess Febris who was not just the sender of the fever who also holds the ability to heal it, but actually is the fever itself; so the stricken become as a god. The Greek Keres were also not just considered the germ or cause of the disease, but the disease itself... every aspect of its manifestation is embodied in its spirit or god form.

If I follow on from this, it makes perfect sense to feel loss that the god form that I was at one with, an offering to and a part of, I now am cast out from due to the boon of health that I have been granted. Sure, one can say that I am over analytical and that I should simply give thanks in whatever necessary form but one of the challenges of magic and prayer is how one reacts when it works. For some like myself, blind faith is an anathema and sheep like phenomena; personal spirituality is a long term relationship of learning and exploration, and every development is a challenge that eventually leads to greater intimacy; the key is to work through it with head, heart and spirit.

Spirituality is an expression of self, and as we grow and change so does our relationship with our gods and spirits. This isn't easy, but it is the nature of progress and transformation, and I believe that it is part of our feeding our gods; acknowledging their shifting natures as we flow with our own necessary changes and upheavals.

References

~ *Disease-Spirits and Divine Cures Among the Greeks and Romans*. Cesidio R. Symbolic. Forgotten Books 1921

~ *Aghor Medicine Pollution Death and Healing in Northern India*, Ron Barrett University of California Press 2008

1 Hepatitis C Virus

—∿— *Creativity and Disease*, Philip Sandblom Marion Boyars Publishing 1992
—∿— Ashe Selections from the *Journal of Experimental Spirituality*, Edited by Sven Davisson 2008
—∿— *Violence and the Sacred*, Girard Continuum 2007

The Occult Nature of Cripkult

Craig Slee

Despite what has been previously written[1] the occult nature of so-called *cripkult* is more than a mere metaphor, or fancy neologism.

It is the cult of the Crip – a reclaimed term for the disabled – a conception which allows the crippled to access (or more properly *re-access*) a central magical role, rather than the performative role placed on them by the able bodied.

Rather than the idea of the 'magical cripple' whose non-normative shape, form or ability, is regarded only as *signifier* of hidden powers, cripkult acknowledges the daemonic nature of the cripple in themselves. Not as some material individual lacking in functionality but compensated by so-called spiritual gifts – rather the notion as intrinsically, an embodied, whole, magical entity.

Western Magical Tradition (particularly that descending from the Hermetic Order of the Golden Dawn, but also the ritualism of the grimoires) often has components of bodywork which are inaccessible to those magicians who are disabled. Mental analogues alone may suffice in many cases, but in many others, the ritual protocols required to open communications or enact operations are often beyond the reach of many disabled individuals.

Necessary adaptations to such rituals sometimes lead to significant variations in effectiveness of magical work – particularly in cases which may require obtaining or utilising specific *materia* or body posture/arrangement.

Within a magical worldview that posits the existence of other interdependent actors (be they entities or so-called energies or perhaps informational patterns) such ritual actions may serve the function of communication protocols – transmissions of desire or intent. To change them appears (in some cases) to significantly alter how such transmissions or configurations affect the world.

Here we must consider the Social Model of Disability, wherein it is the way society as a whole (including architecture, design, assumptions regarding health, fitness, desire, and sexuality) which disables an individual, rather than the body of the individual themselves.

The ritual protocols and assumptions passed down to us via text, tradition, and experiment, are inevitably products of the human mind interacting with magical experience. They are also products of the individual practitioners – individuals who were shaped by societies in which the disabled were minorities. It is therefore no surprise that the majority of these operations seem not to

1 See my text "Creeping Mortality: Some Thoughts on Cripkult," in Vanessa Sinclair (ed), *Rendering Unconscious – Psychoanalytic Perspectives Politics & Poetry*, Trapart Books, Stockholm, 2019.

consider the issues that many disabled practitioners may face.

What does this mean for those practitioners?

Much like the rest of their lives, they must develop their own methodologies and negotiation tactics with the magical. Such negotiations will always be sourced from the bodymind of the disabled individual – *they* are the origin point, not some hypothetical able-bodied norm. That their experience is necessarily non-normative is key, creating a very specific kind of action-reaction loop.

Cripples have their own way of doing, and perhaps of Being. Necessarily they navigate a world not designed or built around them – they are already adept at navigating a kind of metaphorical Otherworld, whether by constructed mobility aids, protheses, medication, or specific methodology of task or interaction that differs from the norm. They do so because *they have to in order to exist.*

This impulse towards survival is not necessarily individualist in nature – in fact, the nature of existing in a world not designed around your needs requires developments of relationships, bonds, and pacts/agreements so that one may achieve one's aims. In this, it may become obvious that cripkult is also perhaps more open to operating in a non-anthropocentric way.

Suppose the human world with its architecture, design, assumptions, etc, is recognised as not being the pinnacle of achievement for its development of safety, ease of access to resources, and fulfilment of need. Suppose its structures and practices are in fact things which do not take into account the interdependencies and interrelations of life in a larger kosmos?

Suppose it is, in fact, an enclosure, a bounded space designed to protect against the unpredictable complexities of that which humans have encountered, to regulate and structure events in a particular way.

Even the etymology of the word *world* in English hints at such a concept:

> **world (n.)**
> Old English *woruld*, worold "human existence, the affairs of life," also "a long period of time," also "the human race, mankind, humanity," a word peculiar to Germanic languages (cognates: Old Saxon *werold*, Old Frisian *warld*, Dutch *wereld*, Old Norse *verold*, Old High German *weralt*, German *Welt*), with a literal sense of "age of man," from Proto-Germanic **weraldi-*, a compound of **wer* "man" (Old English *wer*, still in werewolf; see virile) + **ald* "age" (from PIE root **al-* (2) "to grow, nourish").
>
> Originally "life on earth, this world (as opposed to the afterlife)," sense extended to "the known world," then to "the physical world in the broadest sense, the universe" (c. 1200). In Old English gospels, the commonest word for "the physical world," was *Middangeard* (Old Norse *Midgard*), literally "the middle enclosure" (see yard (n.1)), which is rooted in Germanic cosmology. Greek *kosmos* in its

> ecclesiastical sense of "world of people" sometimes was rendered in Gothic as *manaseþs*, literally "seed of man." The usual Old Norse word was *heimr*, literally "abode" (see home). Words for "world" in some other Indo-European languages derive from the root for "bottom, foundation" (such as Irish *domun*, Old Church Slavonic *duno*, related to English *deep*); the Lithuanian word is *pasaulis*, from *pa-* "under" + *saulė* "sun."

The world, as the place which allows humankind to grow, to carry out the affairs of life. The home or place where they dwell most easily, in a sense. Yet such a world can only be formed as *response* to events. Far from a simple one-time restructuring of some primordial chaos, it is the division of the kosmos into territories, parts. There is constant need to do so, to de-territorialise and re-territorialise the world in response to events. The anthropocentric viewpoint – which is human-centred in nature – devotes its efforts to maintaining a status quo. One wherein the belief in humans as conquerors of the unpredictable is constantly being shored up by denial of that same unpredictable. The world is made, in an effect, to create a place which generally tends toward safety.

Yet such a world is not a place of safety and ease for the disabled – its maintenance as status quo for the able-bodied provides even more necessity of negotiation for the cripple.

> **negotiation (n.)**
> early 15c., from Old French *negociacion* "business, trade," and directly from Latin *negotiationem* (nominative *negotiatio*) "business, traffic," noun of action from past participle stem of *negotiari* "carry on business, do business, act as a banker," from *negotium* "a business, employment, occupation, affair (public or private)," also "difficulty, pains, trouble, labor," literally "lack of leisure," from neg- "not" (from PIE root **ne-* "not") + *otium* "ease, leisure." The sense expansion from "doing business" to also include "bargaining" about anything took place in Latin.

This constant state of 'not-ease' is fundamental to understanding cripkult in both its theoretical and magical senses. As already explored in *Rendering Unconscious*, the relationship between the disabled and able bodied has always included the cripple as signifier of disease; the crookedness of the cripple matching that of old age and inevitable death. To have a role as a harbinger of death, abnormality, or disease, seems curious when compared to historical and archaeological evidence of disabled individuals being cared for by family or community. While many disabled people have been subjected to infanticide or exposure, this is by no means merely a matter of modern compassion vs. historic callousness, as the evidence shows.

Survival occurs through the development of such relationships with family, friends, and community, and their maintenance. The cripple performs the unacknowledged negotiation with Everything because they are forced to, due to the world of the able-bodied not providing needs of survival by default.

Thus, in a sense, the validity of the able-bodied human world as worthy status quo for all of the human species is defeated by the cripple's existence. If they cannot conform, the cripple is destroyed, erased, or ignored. This often ends up leading to a wilful blindness to their needs and existences. Their humanity is often questioned, leading to further Othering which can lead to isolation at one end of the spectrum, and atrocity at the other.

It is perhaps no wonder that a 'magical cripple' motif exists, as it allows the able-bodied who operate such descriptions to continue to act within the framework of a 'just' and 'orderly' world. What has this to do with magical practice, we may ask?

The constant negotiation, the need to traffick with others, in order to survive, requires several things: The ability to know one's needs and desires on a fundamental, almost primordial level, and also the ability to remain open to the needs and desires of the other parties in negotiation. One must know the difference between negotiable, and non-negotiable. One must also understand that this is not the same as the difference between the possible and the impossible.

Cripkult argues, in a sense, that the cripple is non-negotiable.

> **cripple (n.)**
> Old English *crypel,* "one who creeps, halts, or limps, one partly or wholly deprived of the use of one or more limbs," related to *cryppan* "to crook, bend," from Proto-Germanic **krupilaz* (source also of Old Frisian *kreppel,* Middle Dutch *cropel,* German *krüppel,* Old Norse *kryppill*). Possibly also related to Old English *creopan* "to creep" (*creopere,* literally "creeper," was another Old English word for "crippled person").
>
> In place-names in Middle English, cripple meant "a low opening, a burrow, a den" (such as one must bend or creep to enter), a sense perhaps preserved in the U.S. use of cripple for "a dense thicket or swampy low-land" (1670s).

This crookedness, this bentness, this disruption of movement? All these are defined from *outside.* From the point of view of the cripple, their bodymind is, in point of fact, *all there is to work with.* It is the First Principle by which they are present within, and as part of, the kosmos.

Holding this in mind, it begins to become clear that, far from desiring to reinvent magical practice, cripkult as idea seeks to derive a form of practice which derives from the root of a pragmatic attitude to the experiences encountered by the cripple. This is to say, rather than placing the cripple at the edge, or away from the norm, the cripple becomes *central.*

Cripkult's necessary engagement with the principles of *survival* is paramount; it requires not only centralising the cripple, but understanding the constant de-territorialising and re-territorialising required to survive. In this, there is a distinct distinction between *subsistence* and *survival* – the latter suggesting a kind of constancy, of continuance.

To make a pop culture reference here, in the words of Jeff Goldblum, playing Ian Malcolm in the film adaptation of *Jurassic Park:* "Life, uh, finds a way." To survive is to Live, to persist in spite of, and through, and because of circumstance. In this, perhaps, we argue, that the necessities of crippledom are not that of death, disease and inevitable decay – rather of fierce Life and necessary openness.

Yet at the same time, what is revealed by that constant deconstruction and reconstruction is perhaps responsible for the negative reactions to the disabled which many in the able-bodied world are culturally conditioned to enact.

The needs and actions, the display and the presence of solve et coagula presented in undeniable form of the cripple; these reveal that the boundaries of the world – the structures of safety and ease – are fundamentally, primordially, unstable, ever subject to change, and in many cases *utterly* negotiable. That such negotiation *requires* certain skillsets and applied principles is utterly terrifying to most.

The role of the cripple as fundamental embodiment of these processes is functionally *daemonic*, echoing the Ancient Greek *daimon* which is the root of the word. Such an echo places the cripple as one who not only has, or is capable of learning these skills, but has developed them in reaction to the Neccessity of Living, deploying their ability to create and dissolve connections, to illustrate difference and possibility by their very existence.

By shaping the world around them, shifting the forms and functions of environment, the cripple is not in 'control' but rather is 'low to the earth', to the primal and fundamental, descending beyond ordinary perceptions. The mechanics of their existence remain unseen – hidden or occulted – from those without the ability to engage with Necessity without a layer of abstraction, or via an external safety referent.

This occult nature is found in myth all across the world – the crippled smith who creates wonders through arcane mechanisms, the deformed artisan capable of giving life to the immaterial via his knowledge of magic or the gods. In many myths, it is the smith who extracts metal from the earth; it is the smith who shapes civilisation, provides space for people to exist where before there was only hostile forest. It is found in the prophet who has secret knowledge of gods, those who descend into the Underworld to speak with the dead, and those who speak words and sing songs to summon them up.

To understand the mythological cripple is to see projections, tales told, sense-making done in both the strangely wonderful and utterly pragmatic senses. Is it purely because the fumes from the forge may cause damage to the human body, or is it because only one who is not able to be captured by the shapes and contouring of society possesses the requisite inventiveness?

And yet, here we must also treat the cripple as shaped by that very embeddedness, just as a crooked piece of driftwood is shaped by the flows and currents of the sea or river. It survives that shaping *because* of that shaping – and by its presence, alters the very thing that shapes it. After all, the water must flow around it.

Again the question: What does this mean for magical practice?

History and archaeology show us that, even as far back as the Neanderthal group who dwelt in the Shanidar cave in ancient Iraq, disabled people existed, lived, and were cared for. We, they, have always been here, stretching back into Deep Time. We, they, have always had to crookify, to crip-ify the space around them.

And it is not the mere crooking of a finger, which may, for the abled, be straightened at will. No, it is both effortful, and effortless, by virtue of the processes of life within us. Our breath, our words, our bone, and body and blood. Our desire, our need, as necessary as the impulse which sets cells to divide, viruses to replicate, and legions of bacteria to colonise our outer and inner flesh.

While we act and react; while we creep and crawl and shift and disrupt ideas of possible movement and form. While we breathe and sing, and cry. While we laugh and remember, and hope and dream. While we do all this, we exist. Our existence, our presence from the beginning of things, through to today, is undeniable. It is *non-negotiable.*

We have always been here. You can find us in those same myths, those same stories that twine like ever-reaching roots out of Primordial Deep Time. We have always been in the dreaming spaces of the human mind, close to the earth, to the fundamental roots of human need, desire, and the continuances of eternity.

What does this mean for magical practice?

Again we ask the question, again we reach for that answer with trembling fingers...

Suppose then, we abandon all ideas of convention, and focus on the processes of Life. Suppose we swear our oaths with hands pressed to the Earth, that most basic fundamental, as the ancient Greeks did. Suppose we seal the oath with grip and iron ring like the Norse did. Suppose those same fingers dig into the earth, turning the soil to plant the seed.

Let us suppose that the *dactyls* refer to those fingers.

(They do.)

Let us suppose that fingers are roots, reaching into the earth, twining down, and down. Suppose. Just Suppose. Suppose there is no straight meaning, no path direct. Only the indirectness of existence. Only its non-negotiability. Death brings Life, after all. The body bloats as bacteria multiply, one shape of life into another and another and another. No straight line, just what's there. Just what's available.

There is Death in Life, and Life in Death. Patterns shifting, repeating, over and over. Dry words becoming wet and bloody and fierce with experience.

Suppose those roots reach further down, and back. To crippled spirits, gods, heroes and daimons; Hephaestus, he with the Great Mother, returned to Olympos by canny Dionysos, drunk and surrounded by dancers; Weyland the Smith, hamstrung craftsman, seducer, and bringer of bloody vengeance and corpse-gifts.

Crippled Powers, crooked dreamers, shapers, singers, and makers. Those who craft, who make, those who curve, and twist and root. Those lame demons of fury and wisdom, walking sticks and limping feet.

(Why, to discover that a *dactyl* is also a foot in Greek poetic meter, and that poetry itself a dactyl!)

To whisper that the Dactyls served Hephaestus, these smiths and healing magicians, just as they served the Great Mother, or so the myths may say. Even the Greeks could not follow the crooked paths that link *Kabeiroi* as keepers of the Mysteries, to the *Daktyloi* and the *Kouretes* as armed dancers protecting infant Zeus in a cave.

Po. Et. Ry. Long, short, short. Long, short, short. Long, short, short.

Listening to the rhythm, can we not hear, can we not allow ourselves the luxury of perceiving there, an imaginary limp?

The mind finds patterns, rhythm, pictures, practices, transmitted through time. Welling up from the fundamental. Is it coincidence that we write and speak of driftwood here, shaped by the sea? Coincidence, when amidst the complex of those Greek myths, we find both servants of a crippled forge god, and the *Kabeiroi* as protectors of sailors in distress?

When we perceive a co-incidence, we perceive connection. The connection of one, may not be that of another person. How we arrange these things, and how allow them to shape us? This is the inventiveness. Necessity is the Mother of Invention.

With those same crooked, trembling fingers, be they spastic or palsied, or free from visible sign, the cripple both reaches in and digs deep. When all one has, is oneself, one realises one is utterly alone. When one must negotiate relationships between beings and things, one becomes aware that nothing is given. Nothing is *a priori*, guaranteed.

Who we are is a complex web of interdependent systems, and the dividing line between one and another, is not so simple. We have ancestors of blood, of water, of myth, and story. We have siblings of selection, pressures and experience – fellow unknowing initiates of specific circumstance.

Timothy Leary once said: "Admit it. You aren't like them. You're not even close. [...] Find the others."

Cripkult says that cripples have no need to admit it. The world tells us every day, sometimes with words, but mostly silently, with deeds and structures and systems. In between those ellipses in the quote above, Leary talks about dress, about social cues, about expectation, urging one to break free of such strictures to find others who are the same way.

Yet such breaking free is often impossible for cripples. To break free is often to risk severing the carefully cultivated support network, built up over months, years, or even lifetimes. Such a luxury as even 'going forth' to find the others is often unavailable or rendered so by circumstance.

Instead, we must turn inwards. The only reliable resources are our own, and even these are fleeting. Age, decay, loss of function, all those things which the crippled so often signal to others, often come early for us. We are, in a sense, forerunners of you all.

What does this mean for magical practice?

The meanings are many, but the pragmatic needs must be ruthless in execution. Perhaps there are those who might say that cripkult is merely embracing powerlessness and victimhood.

We say they are correct, but in ways they do not understand.

By now you will perhaps have noticed a change in this piece's tone, from a more distant examination towards something closer. Something less dry, perhaps. More poetic in seeming, than pragmatic.

In cripkult, the poetic is key – not in terms of verse or structure, but in an understanding of rhythm. The repetition and recurrence of certain beats, themes, motifs; signs, symbols, and portents relevant to Life.

Cripples develop their own patterns, their own ways-of-doing-and-being. We develop our own relationship to time; chronic illness, chronic disability – absurdly, beautifully, terribly – they shatter the regulated chronological spaces of ordinary time.

A journey that might take five minutes for someone able-bodied might take half an hour for a cripple as they shape their body to move, or the time may be added to by the fact that the able bodied route is strewn with obstacles that must be routed around, from stairs to waiting for assistance to breakdowns in communication. The list goes on.

Learning to recognise the rhythms of one's bodymind is vital to survival. Being able to accurately gauge one's energy level, or ability to perform a task, when they may fluctuate on a daily basis, is more art than science. One must make choices based on past events, but also budget resources in a complex arrangement of circumstances – is it worth, for example, exhausting oneself by getting all that we need to do, done in one day, and then taking several days to recover, or spreading it over multiple days, being more tired every day, and running the risk that something else may occur which prevents work for several days?

In a sense, this is similar to the relationship to chronic clock time, and the rhythms of the stars and planets. Planetary Hours do not map onto chronic time, rather they vary with location, sunrise and sunset (which are affected by time of year). The rhythms of the heavenly bodies, if one were to take an animist view, are their own – primordial and shifting in a complex dance with the rest of the kosmos. These same rhythms may provide methods of reconnecting with a magical, animated kosmos – a universe of living Being which gives rise to those same myths and tales when encountered by the human mind.

Likewise crip-time is capable of being entered into on its own time, providing its own pathway into the Dreaming All-at-Once. The body of the cripple, crooked though it may seem, is more than capable of generating and navigating the currents of a magical kosmos, in accordance with, via, and in relation to, its own bodymind rhythms.

By doubling down, tripling down, leaning into the crookedness of our existence, we willfully, body*mindfully* engage and utilise the particular structures of our existence in a magical context. We recognise, in effect, that there are no straight lines, no simple equations and equalisations in isolation - everything affects everything else. For some, this notion is paralysing - and indeed such a paralysis is a perfect example of the occult, or hidden nature, of cripkult.

The inability to move or choose a path occurs when the full enormity of complete interdependence is realised. The immensity of the sense of being pressed-upon, or engraved can be terrifying. To quote Shirley Jackson, in *Haunting of Hill House:*

> No live organism can continue for long to exist sanely under conditions of absolute reality; even larks and katydids are supposed, by some, to dream.

Cripkult suggests that the dreaming of 'larks and katydid' is not an escape, but instead is fundamental to living beings – part of the structure of the kosmos itself. Mostly, this Dreaming All at Once state is rarely visited – humans move in and out of such awarenesses without ever having realised they have done so. Just as one may enter a highway or road-trance and arrive at a familiar destination without really recalling a journey when your mind is on other things, so the *world-trance* leaves most of humanity skipping like stones over the surface of the pond, or sea.

To come to the realisation of the total interdependence of Beingness beyond an intellectual awareness is to plunge down into those waters. In fact, it is an interesting passing note to point out the potential etymological link between *sea* and *soul:*

> **soul (n.1)**
> "A substantial entity believed to be that in each person which lives, feels, thinks and wills" [Century Dictionary], Old English *sawol* "spiritual and emotional part of a person, animate existence; life, living being," from Proto-Germanic **saiwalō* (source also of Old Saxon *seola*, Old Norse *sala*, Old Frisian *sele*, Middle Dutch *siele*, Dutch *ziel*, Old High German *seula*, German *Seele*, Gothic *saiwala*), of uncertain origin.
>
> Sometimes said to mean originally "coming from or belonging to the sea," because that was supposed to be the stopping place of the soul before birth or after death [Barnhart]; if so, it would be from Proto-Germanic **saiwaz* (see sea). Klein explains this as "from the lake," as a dwelling-place of souls in ancient northern Europe.

> Meaning "spirit of a deceased person" is attested in Old English from 971.

To experience such a paralysis, to come to the crossroads, as it were, and be faced with the nigh infinite number of negotiations, paths, and possibilities? Is it any wonder that Hermes, Odin (and his English counterpart Woden), are said to be gods of trade, travel, and magic?

Yet, when we plunge beneath the surface of such a paralysis, we find something perhaps more terrible still. We find shifts and movements, bodily responses to outside pressures, even when we cannot move – heartbeat and breathing; the whine of our nervous system in the silence of our skin upon which billions of bacteria graze. We find memories arise and descend into fevered associativity. We find the air upon the skin, thunder in the blood, scarlet surf booming on the seashore and hurtling down the channels of artery and vein. DNA parsed again and again, shaped by countless generations. We begin to realise that we were never 'in control' in the first place.

There is no mercy to the endless interplays of pressure, rhythm, call and response. To be embodied, is to be ensouled, to be suffused with the processes of Beingness, the processes and complexities of Life.

And yet, even in that paralysis, we affect the kosmos. Were we to do absolutely nothing, the processes which we call bodymind and soul would still continue through endless actions and reactions. We occupy space, and time. We have our own gravity, small though it may be in comparison to some forms and entities.

Yet, even that is revealed to be part of an interconnected web of ancestry, events, and circumstance. We are merely the latest irruption, the latest *emergent arising* of a nigh infinite set of interlocking processes performing endless transformations.

Much like the pre-Socratic philosophers who saw the world as substance undergoing a cycle of elemental transformations, so cripkult returns again to the echoes of Weyland the Smith, found in the first verse of the Old English poem Deor, from the 10th Century and found in *The Exeter Book:*

> Welund him be wurman wræces cunnade.
> Anhydig eorl earfoþa dreag,
> hæfde him to gesiþþe sorge ond longaþ,
> wintercealde wræce, wean oft onfond,
> siþþan hine Niðhad on nede legde
> swoncre seonobende on syllan monn.
> Þæs ofereode, þisses swa mæg!

Loosely translated, this first verse speaks of Weyland, or Welund, experiencing much grief and woe in his life. Sorrow and strife were his constant companions, even as he was crippled by an enemy. The final line, is of import – variously translated, it means, "It passed over with respect to that; it may also (pass over) with respect to this."[2] Or, "That passed over, this can too."[3]

The poem Deor equates various figures with the eponymous poet who has, it seems, lost his position, resources and social standing. It has been variously described as a lament, or a meditation on impermanence. From a cripkult perspective, such a notion has phenomenal value, not least for the associations with mythical figures, but also from the standpoint of the passing-over. As an illustration of the vicissitudes of existence, it acknowledges the impossibility of eternal status quo – the lamentation on loss can be viewed differently, as an acknowledgement of the gravity of fate, not in terms of predestination, but complexity, possibility, and intersection of circumstance.

Tending towards the grave, we are, nonetheless shaped by the weavings and pressures of countless events we have no inkling of – the essence of the butterfly's wing affecting the composition and direction of the hurricane.

In this, we *embrace* our fate. Not only that, we embrace it so tightly as to strangle both ourselves and it. Rather than wallow in victimhood, or exhausting ourselves by striving to another ideal, there is only *ourselves-as-crip, ourselves-as-daimonic-being.*

> **victim (n.)**
> late 15c., "living creature killed and offered as a sacrifice to a deity or supernatural power, or in the performance of a religious rite;" from Latin *victima* "sacrificial animal; person or animal killed as a sacrifice," a word of uncertain origin. Perhaps related to *vicis* "turn, occasion" (as in vicarious), if the notion is an "exchange" with the gods. Perhaps distantly connected to Old English *wig* "idol," Gothic *weihs* "holy," German *weihen* "consecrate" (compare *Weihnachten* "Christmas") on notion of "a consecrated animal."
>
> **vicarious (adj.)**
> 1630s, "taking the place of another," from Latin *vicarius* "that supplies a place; substituted, delegated," from *vicis* "a change, exchange, interchange; succession, alternation, substitution," from PIE root **weik-* (2) "to bend, to wind."
>
> From 1690s as "done or experienced in place of another" (usually in reference to punishment, often of Christ); from 1929 as "experienced imaginatively through another.

Fascinatingly enough, *deor* is the ancestor of the moden *deer:*

---

2 Ed. Murray McGillivray. Online Corpus of Old English Poetry (OCOEP).(http://homepages.ucalgary.ca/~mmcgilli/OEPoetry/Deorfram.html, Accessed 18/01/2019)

3 *Poems Out Loud*, Seamus Heaney Reads *Deor* (http://poemsoutloud.net/audio/archive/heaney_reads_deor/ Accessed 18/01/2019)

deer (n.)

Old English *deor* "wild animal, beast, any wild quadruped," in early Middle English also used of ants and fish, from Proto-Germanic **deuzam*, the general Germanic word for "animal" (as opposed to man), but often restricted to "wild animal" (source also of Old Frisian *diar*, Dutch *dier*, Old Norse *dyr*, Old High German *tior*, German *Tier* "animal," Gothic *dius* "wild animal," also see reindeer).

This is perhaps from PIE **dheusom* "creature that breathes," from root **dheu-* (1) "cloud, breath" (source also of Lithuanian *dusti* "gasp," *dvėsti* "gasp, perish;" Old Church Slavonic *dychati* "breathe"). For possible prehistoric sense development, compare Latin *animal* from *anima* "breath").

Sense specialization to a specific animal began in Old English (the usual Old English word for what we now call a deer was *heorot*; see hart), was common by 15c., and is now complete. It happened probably via hunting, deer being the favorite animal of the chase (compare Sanskrit *mrga-* "wild animal," used especially for "deer").

Deor in Old English, *Beste*, or beast in Middle English, supplanted by *Animal* in modern English. The thing that breathes, the thing that lives, that *respires*, that *inspires* and *expires*.

Again and again, the vital processes of Life rear their head.

Again and again, the animate nature of the kosmos is found in its unceasing processes of change, its endless flux. Such flux exists even in the most tightly bound, most paralysed of beings.

What does this mean for magical practice in the context of cripkult? If it is not obvious by now that we are capable of sacrificing self to self by infusing our personality with the bellows-breath of a ten thousand shapers, singers, and makers?

If it is not obvious by now that by the contractions and turnings of fate, we may find ourselves expanding to fulfil a role of bender, twister, negotiator, transmuter? If the crippled magician making pacts by no authority save Necessity sits at the crossroads like a storytelling spider illuminating with words the web that connects us all?

If it is not obvious that we are quite capable of participating in the ancient dances – the gait of the crippled poet dancing to an inner rhythm – Long, Short, Short – with all that implies? If it is not obvious that we take not the norm as healthy, but the holy, that is to say, the whole entire?

If it is not obvious that the Cult of the Crip has always been with us, and that healers make hale, make *whole?*

Then you have not been paying attention to the gravity of the situation.

If you find yourself wondering where the practical rites of cripkult are? You have misunderstood. Each one us, initiated by fate, connects with those who have gone before, and the rites are born anew, embodied and brought forth by us anew, due to individual needs and circumstance.

If cripkult involves descending into the living underworld of the soul, diving deep into the processes of Life and Death, then it follows that the non-negotiability of the cripple, a vicarious emergence of the cult in localised space and time, i.e. now, is always transformative. Always a bringing-forth or revealing of the processes of change, rooted as they are in the fundamentals of survival.

This piece, this "first look" is not the first. After all, a previous article has been published on the concept, has it not? Myths reach out to us from Deep Time, placing the cripple at the centre of need, as the worker and voyager in, and negotiator of, the spaces of Necessity – the fundamentals of existence. How often do we return to the primordial needs, to bring forth the More? How often do our words and actions deconstruct, reconfigure, and create?

Our existence is non-negotiable. All it will take is fate to intervene with any of you, to bring you to the proverbial doorstep of cripkult, becoming as-us due to old age or infirmity, accident, or disease.

We have always been here, and when the time comes? We will extend hospitality.

And begin negotiations.

Note: All etymology sourced from Etymonline.com: The Online Etymological Dictionary (http://www.etymonline.com Accessed January 2019, various.)

Daoism, Buddhism, and Machine Consciousness

Damien Patrick Williams

Introduction

Nonwestern philosophies such as Buddhism, Hinduism, and Daoism would be likely to help mitigate various kinds of bias in machine minds and increase compassion by allowing programmers and designers to think from within a non-zero-sum matrix of win-conditions for all living beings. Knowledge from these philosophical traditions would allow us to engage multiple tokens and types of minds, outside of some assumed human "default." Currently, many algorithmic systems are trained on data and built by people which and who assume correlations between "normalcy" and the features of straight, white, cisgender, able-bodied, neurotypical males. While these correlations may exist as real in the world, research has shown that they are not real in the sense of "natural kinds;" the correlations in question are the result of thousands of years of socially constructed disparity along the lines of gender, ethnicity, sexuality, physical ability, neurological formulation, and more. These disparities stem from imbedded assumptions about the "right kind" of life or person, where any difference from that "right kind" is seen as a less valuable deviation.[1] What we find, now, is that these social constructions have (always) been translated into our technological systems.

I will trace a brief history of Daosim, Buddhism, a brief exploration of some of their core concepts, such as the Daoist *wu-wei* and the Buddhist *metta*, or limitless compassion, and a brief overview of artificial intelligence and theories of machine consciousness. I will then lay out ways in which the perspectives of the former group might help reframe our understanding of the latter. Along the way, I will point to some work already being done along this path.

Machine learning (ML) systems operate on a program of iterative reinforcement learning, wherein the datasets given to an algorithm form the basis for rules off of which it will operate, and out of which it will create new rules. This process has been shown to instantiate biases analogous to those of the humans who choose the datasets and program the systems.[2] In addition to this, much of the training for algorithmic and "artificially" intelligent systems comes from areas like game theory

1 1 Subini Ancy Annamma, David Connor & Beth Ferri (2012). "Dis/ability critical race studies (Dis-Crit): theorizing at the intersections of race and dis/ability." *Race Ethnicity and Education*, 16:1, 1-31, DOI: 10.1080/13613324.2012.730511

2 Aylin Caliskan, Joanna J. Bryson, Arvind Narayanan, "Semantics derived automatically from language corpora contain human-like biases." *Science* 14 Apr 2017; Vol. 356, Issue 6334, pp. 183-186 DOI: 10.1126/science.aal4230

and western economics, which work on the supposition that the game being played takes place within a zero-sum matrix. A zero-sum system is one in which there are finite resources, but more than that, it is one in which what one side gains, another loses, but zero-sum systems are by no means the only kind.[3]

In systems such as Daoism and Buddhism, it is not the case that there is only one right answer, or only one right kind of existence. These systems exhibit what can be thought of as a non-zero-sum matrix of win conditions, in which a combination of the needs and wants and resources of every player are realized in such a way that everyone wins. We will discuss principles such as the flourishing Dao and *Pratītyasamutpāda* ("Interdependent Co-arising") which are meant to indicate that everything that exists does so as a part of and because of everything else that exists. With this in mind, I take my starting positions to be that:

1) in order better to do the work of creating nonhuman, machine minds, we must refrain from resting in abstraction, or else our most egregious failure states will be represented by models which decide to do something "for someone's own good" before they actually engage with the lived experience of the stakeholders in question; that is, we have to try to understand other minds well enough to perform mutually modeled interfaces of what we would have done unto us and what others would have us do unto them;

2) there are multiple types of consciousness, even within the framework of the human spectrum, and that the expression of or search for any one type is in *no way* meant to discount, demean, or erase any of the others. In fact, it is the case that we will need to seek to recognize and learn to communicate with as many types of consciousness as may exist, in order to survive and thrive in any meaningful way. Again, not doing so represents an egregious failure condition. With that in mind, I use "machine consciousness" to mean a machine with the capability of modelling a sense of interiority and selfness similar enough to what we know of biological consciousnesses to communicate it with us, not just a generalized computational functionalist representation, as in "Artificial Genera Intelligence."

For the sake of this, I (perhaps somewhat paradoxically) think the term "artificial intelligence" is problematic. Anything that does the things we want a machine mind to do is *genuinely* intelligent, not "artificially" so. We tend to use the word "artificial" to mean "fake," or "contrived," and so, to be clear, I'm specifically problematizing the "natural/technological" divide that gives us "art vs artifice," as those supposed divisions are better understood as a continuum of greater or fewer stages of intervention.[4] And so, if a zero-sum training set produces a system that assumes that every winner must be accompanied by a loser, then what might we gain

3 Samuel Bowles, (2004). *Microeconomics: Behavior, Institutions, and Evolution*. Princeton University Press.

4 I won't have the time to go into this here, but please see "A Description of the Natural Place of Magic" in Philosophy and Religious Studies," Damien Patrick Williams, 2008.

if we train a system on logics that allow for contradiction, multiple win-conditions, and non- dualist interconnection? We have to recognize the needs and ontological statuses of other minds, in such a way that their operation and expression can come to be understood by us, and we can seek to make ourselves understood.

Some minds/consciousnesses/intelligences will have a harder time communicating with each other than others, but that's not to say that one is any more "real" or "natural" than the others; rather it is merely indicative of the near tautology that we use anthropocentric modelling because we are *anthropos.* Our anthropocentrism is a place to start generating a perspective from which we *must* modify as we come to understand how flawed and wrong our human-based understandings are. Our anthropocentrism is *not* a dispositive proof that any and all types of minds must be like "ours." I ultimately propose an avenue of research wherein we seek to figure out how to develop a machine consciousness which is a master of nondualist, harmonious, and non-appetitive thinking.

What is Daoism?

Daosim is the name of a Chinese philosophical and religious system that is at least 2000 years old, but which may be as much as 2,500 years old.[5] The term "Dao" comes from well before the existence of anything like Daoism as it is presently understood, and it simply means "The Way."[6] Western Daoism is known primarily by its practices of T'ai Chi and Feng Shui, but these arts are drastically different from those that constitute traditional Chinese Daoism. The essential heart of Daoism is a concern with order, on levels cosmic, natural, and spiritual, with an understanding that these levels are interwoven, and not distinct. To come into harmonious union with the Dao is the aim of the sage and the everyday person, but there are many perspectives on how to achieve this. In fact, there are many different forms of traditional Chinese Daoism, various interrelations of which comprise two major living branches: The Way of Orthodox Unity is poplar in Southern China and Taiwan, while The Way of Complete Perfection is popular in Northern China. But, again, this is still only a small handful of Daoist perspectives; in addition, there are the Correct Method of the Celestial Heart; Worship of the Heavenly Worthy of the Primordial Beginning; Highest Purity and Numinous Treasure revelations; Perfect Great Way; Way of the Celestial Masters; and The Five Pecks schools.[7] To simplify, we'll look at Zhuangzi and Laozi's versions of Daoism.

Zhuangzi is the name of a person and name of the text attributed to him. His writing was often confusing and paradoxical, and quite purposefully so.[8] As a mystical text, readers are not meant to understand single, individual passages, but rather the gestalt of the experience, and to facilitate this, Zhuangzi rejects linguistic convention, using instead a mixture of fantasy, literal readings, and paradox, with

5 Jonathan Herman, (2013). *Daoism for Dummies.* For Dummies Press.

6 Ibid.

7 Ibid.

8 Burton Watson, ed. & trans. (1995). *Chuang Tzu: Basic Writings.* Columbia University Press.

some passages devolving into complete gibberish. Some phrases in the *Zhuangzi* are even used ironically in order to evoke their own opposite meanings, such as "Supreme Swindle" and "Great Clod" used as terms to identify the Sage who truly understands the Dao.[9] In Zhuangzi, the largest is the smallest, and highest and most venerable is to be found in the most terrible and disgusting:

> Master Tung-kuo asked Chuang Tzu, "This thing called the Way – where does it exist?"
> Chuang Tzu said, "There's no place it doesn't exist." "Come," said Master Tung-kuo, "you must be more specific!" "It is in the ant."
> "As low a thing as that?"
> "It is in the panic grass."
> "But that's lower still!"
> "It is in the tiles and shards."
> "How can it be so low?"
> "It is in the piss and shit."[10]

Another Crucial component of Zhuangzi's Daoism is the principle of *Yu*, which literally translates as "wandering." For Zhuangzi, being like the Dao means freely wandering as the world needed, moving from place to place, not settling down or becoming accustomed to the circumstances in which you find yourself. When it is time to move, the sage moves, as the Dao moves, and is not tied down; an understanding of when it is time to do and be something different, as spontaneous as the Dao itself, and so as free as the Dao.[11] The *Zhuangzi* is filled with stories about cooks and sages who move through their worlds with effortless ease, nonhuman animals with the ability to change size and shape and live in perfect harmony, and humans who can do the same. Here is one of the most well-known passages from Zhuangzi:

> Once upon a time, I, Chuang Chou, dreamt I was a butterfly, fluttering hither and thither, a veritable butterfly, enjoying itself to the full of its bent, and not knowing it was Chuang Chou. Suddenly I awoke, and came to myself, the veritable Chuang Chou. Now I do not know whether it was then I dreamt I was a butterfly, or whether I am now a butterfly dreaming I am a man. Between me and the butterfly there must be a difference. This is an instance of transformation.[12]

For Zhuangzi, the full Harmony of the Dao is found in its ability to constantly

9 Ibid.
10 Watson, Chapter 22; See also Chapter 1, "Free And Easy Wandering"
11 Ibid.
12 Translated by James Legge, and quoted in *The Three Religions of China: Lectures Delivered at Oxford* (1913) by William Edward Soothill

change and become; its limitless potential to be whatever is needed, for anyone, in any circumstance. But, again, this is not the only perspective on the Dao.

The name "Laozi" is the one most often given to an ancient sage who may or may not have existed, but often is attributed as the author of the famous Daoist text, the *Daodejing (Tao Te Ching)*, in the 3rd century BCE. Laozi's writing was far more poetic, yet somehow far more straightforward than Zhuangzi's, and in fact was by far the more easily accessible and understandable among the people of 3rd century BCE China.[13] The text of the *Daodejing* contains 81 short chapters, each in the form of a poem, intended to be read as mostly self-contained, individual lessons. This framework is very different from that of the *Zhuangzi*, above.

Laozi's philosophy can be broken into three major parts: "The Dao," "Returning to the Way," and "Health, Long Life, Immortality."[14] While all of these comprise an interlocking system of understanding, the whole of which is necessary for a truly harmonious life, we will focus on the first two components, beginning with The Dao – the supreme creative or generative principle, the power of which comes from its emptiness and potency. Laozi refers to the Dao as the "Mother of the 10,000 things" (a way of saying "all varieties of everything that exists") or "Source of All Creation," or an "uncultivated field," where the flowers grow in spring, are nourished by the field in summer, rejoined to the earth in fall, and gestate in winter.

For Laozi, the Dao is plentiful in its potential to become, and that potential to become only exists in emptiness. That is, the Dao is empty and infinitely full of potential, and it is infinitely full of potential *because it is empty.* Laozi references concepts such as a cup, or a bowl, or a doorway, each of which only finds its usefulness, its purpose in the empty space at its center.

> The Way is empty;
> Yet when you use it, you never need fill it again.
> Like an abyss! It seems to be the ancestor of the ten thousand things.[15]

But, Laozi says, humans lose sight of the Dao, and have to work to return to it, either through a sustained practical engagement of emptiness, or through various meditative and mystical practices. Only when we reunite with the Dao can we embody the principle of *wu-wei* and become the kind of person of whom Laozi says, "They do nothing and yet there's nothing left undone."[16]

As for "Returning To The Way," Laozi again references nature, noting that flowers only need to be rooted to soil to realize their full potential, but humans do not do this.[17] Humans constantly forget what it means to be connected to the source of things, and we need to work, in order to remember what it means and is like; but how? Laozi's philosophy prescribes two major paths: "Simplicity of Living"

13 Robert G. Henricks, (1989). *Lao-Tzu: Te-Tao Ching*. Random House. NY.
14 Ibid.
15 Henricks, *Lao-Tzu: Te-Tao Ching*. Ch. 11 and 41.
16 Ibid. Ch. 48.
17 Ibid.

and "Meditation and Mysticism."[18] By "simplicity of living," Laozi means living a life based off of an awareness of when you have enough – enough resources, enough activity, enough of whatever it is that is in your life. This is what Laozi means by to "know contentment" (*gu zu* or *Chih-tsu*), exemplified in earlier passages such as "... When you have little, you'll attain [much];/With much, you'll be confused," and "...Therefore the Sage's ability to accomplish the great/Comes from his not playing the role of the great./Therefore he is able to accomplish the great."[19]

By being satisfied with the nature of our existence, we can recognize that we do not need to seek to accumulate more and more, but rather should recognize what we need within the Dao. In order to truly understand and live this way, we must work to reunite with the Dao, body and mind, in ways both mystical and practical. This is the purpose of "Meditation and Mysticism": Tools which allow us to center ourselves, be present where we are, and understand our place within the Dao.[20] These tools – centeredness, presentness, and mindfulness – are not simply means to other ends, but must be recognized as good, in themselves.

Both Zhuangzi and Laozi say that De and *wu-wei* are among the most important ideas in their Daoist teaching. *Wu-wei* is often translated in its literal form as "Inaction," but more precisely it means "action without action." It indicates not simply *not* doing something, but knowing precisely when and *how* to not do something; knowing precisely when acting to try to further your goals will in fact *harm* your goals. In chapter 19 of the *Zhuangzi*, the author tells a tale of an old man who falls off of a cliff into a raging river, while Confucius looks on from his place downstream, horrified. He waits by the water's edge of his calmer stretch of river, expecting to find the old man's body, but is instead shocked to see the old man:

> ...out of the water and began strolling along the base of the embankment, his hair streaming down, singing a song. Confucius ran after him and said, "At first I thought you were a ghost, but now I see you're a man. May I ask if you have some special way of staying afloat in the water?"
>
> "I have no way. I began with what I was used to, grew up with my nature, and let things come to completion with fate. I go under with the swirls and come out with the eddies, following along the way the water goes and never thinking about myself. That's how I can stay afloat."
>
> Confucius said, "What do you mean by saying that you began with what you were used to, grew up with your nature, and let things come to completion with fate?"
>
> "I was born on the dry land and felt safe on the dry land – that was what I was used to. I grew up with the water and felt safe in the water

18 Ibid.
19 Ibid. Ch. 22, 34, and 44.
20 Ibid.

– that was my nature. I don't know why I do what I do – that's fate."

This is what is meant by *wu-wei:* Action without action, knowing when not to act, understanding the movement of fate.

The idea of "De," as found in "Dao De Jing," is meant to be understood as virtue and as power; but this power is not in a sense of "Power-Over," so much as "power arising up out of."[21] De is what flows in and through and from, and in a sense is the Dao. The Harmony of all things in the cosmic, natural, and personal order is their flowing with and within De, and their balance and rooted fluidity within the Dao. Someone who inhabits De will never want for anything, will always be able to act and to become what is needed, and will not rest in preconceived notions or assumptions about "right kinds." But Daoism is not the only nonwestern tradition to allow for or provide a non-exclusionary perspective on knowledge, understanding, and the world.

What Is Buddhism?

Buddhism is the name given to the philosophy religion, devised around the life and teachings of Siddhartha Gautama, a member of the Kshatriya Hindu caste, who lived in India between the 6th and 5th centuries BCE.[22] Tradition teaches that Siddhartha lived a comfortable life until the day he snuck out of his familial house to explore the city on his own, and saw four things he had never seen before: An old man who was so bent and broken with he couldn't stand; a man stricken with a degenerative disease, lying in a ditch by the road; a funeral procession in which the family wailed with grief; and a monk, sitting calm and quiet, at peace amidst the chaos, enlightened. Siddhartha had heard of all of these things, but the opulence of his wealth meant that he'd never experienced any of them directly; he'd been insulated from or denied these things. It was at this moment that he decided that he would renounce his family's wealth and go out into the world as an ascetic monk, to seek enlightenment.

Siddhartha leaves his wife and children and goes to join a group known as the ascetics – men who renounce all worldly ties and live in the wilderness, surviving under the sky, and mostly unclothed. It's theorized that the sect to which Siddhartha belonged were a group of what are known as *Digambaras* or "Sky-clad" Jains – a Vedic tradition which believes that the physical world is a prison and a poison which corrupts us.[23] While a member of this group, Siddhartha almost dies from malnutrition and exposure, and his life is saved only through the intervention of a random passerby who feeds him, nurses him back to health, and then, when he is healed, asks for nothing in return. It is from this woman whom Siddhartha learns what will become one of the core concepts of his way of life: Detached compassion.

21 Henricks, *Lao-Tzu: Te-Tao Ching.*

22 William F. Lawhead. (2000). *The Philosophical Journey, 1st Edition.* McGraw-Hill. NY. Pg. 485-494

23 R.K. Pruthi. (2004). *Buddhism and Indian Civilization.* Discovery Publishing House.

Leaving the woman who saved his life, Siddhartha realizes that neither his over-indulgent princely life, nor the complete asceticism of the Digambaras is the right path toward the kind of enlightenment he's sought. While the ascetics were correct that a life of opulence could deaden the spirit and prevent enlightenment, what they missed was the truth of the fact that a body needs sustenance and shelter, in order to remain alive long enough to *attain enlightenment.*[24] With this in mind, Siddhartha set out in search of a "middle way" between these two extremes, stopping along the side of the road for the night and bedding down under a Bodhi tree. In the morning he woke up, and resolved not to move until he had understood what it was he was truly searching for. He watched the road and the people, some of whom stopped and gave him food, or water, or money, and some of whom just kept walking, but all of whom changed, going to and from the town and the world, in groups or alone, or one then the other, or in shifting combinations. As he watched, Siddhartha realized that the only thing that was constant about what he was seeing – about what he had always seen and been searching for – was impermanence and change. At this, he was enlightened.[25]

Recognizing that the only truly permanent thing was change and impermanence, Siddhartha became The Buddha, or "one who is awake." At this awakening, he formulated what have become known as the Four Noble Truths: (1) Suffering Exists; (2) Suffering has a cause: attachments to cravings and desires; (3) there's a way to end suffering; (4) the way to end suffering is through enlightened living, Following the Noble Eightfold Path. The Eightfold Path is comprised of three sections: Wisdom, Action, and Concentration. Wisdom is composed of Right Understanding (The Four Noble Truths), and Right Thought/Resolve (mental resolve to renounce attachments and seek compassion). Action is comprised of Right Speech (refraining from lying, but also choosing words to suit purposes, and forming speech well), Right Conduct (non-harm, no theft, no lying, no intoxication, no sexual misconduct), and Right Livelihood (no making your living off of any of those things). Concentration means Right Effort (working diligently to erase old, bad habits, and to build new, good ones), Right Mindfulness (meditation, awareness of and centeredness in the present moment), and Right Concentration (working with your whole being to become the kind of person who embodies every aspect of these things in your everyday life).[26]

Now, the formulation of the Four Noble Truths and the Eightfold Path is simple, but deep, because the concept translated as "suffering" is the Sanskrit word *"Dukkha,"* which also has connotations of "impermanence," and "change."[27] So, as we travel through the process, we come understand that what we perceive as suffering is really only change and impermanence, and the only reason we suffer is because we seek to hold onto things and keep them static. If, instead, we do the work of renouncing attachments and living with complete limitless compassion

24 Eknath Easwaran (1985). *The Dhammapada*. The Blue Mountain Center of Meditation. Canada.

25 Ibid.

26 Lawhead. *The Philosophical Journey*

27 Ibid.

toward all things and states, then we will not suffer *because we will have accepted change*. Buddhists believe that this even extends to (and from) the nature of the Self, in that if we accepted the true nature of change, we would know that we too are impermanent, and would not suffer, as we change. We would not erect false divisions of subject and object, self, and not- self, and without those divisions, we could truly understand that all things are a part of and give rise to, one another.

Within most schools of Buddhism, the doctrine of *Anatta*, or "no self" is what's used to refer to a person's individual nature. *Anatta* is rooted in the idea that there is no singular, "true" self. To vastly oversimplify, there is a Vedic concept known as "The Five *Skandhas*" or "aggregates," which are the parts of yourself that are empirically knowable and which you think of as permanent. The *Skandhas* are your:

Material Form (Body)

Feelings (Pleasure, Pain, Indifference) Perception (Senses)

Mental Formations (Thoughts)

Consciousness

Each of these components is constantly shifting and changing, becoming something new both individually and in combination.[28] Along with the skandhas, there are two main arguments Buddhists use to prove that no one has a self. These arguments are known as "The Argument From Control" and "The Argument from Impermanence."

The argument from control states that if you had a "true self," it would be the thing in control of the whole of you, and since none of the *skandhas* is in complete control of the rest – and, in fact, all seem to have some measure of control over all – none of them is your "true self." The argument from impermanence says that if you had a "true self," it would be the thing about you that was permanent and unchanging, and since none of the *skandhas* is permanent and unchanging – and, in fact, all seem to change in relation to each other – none of them is your "true self."[29] The interplay between these two arguments also combines with an even more fundamental formulation: If only the observable parts of you are valid candidates for "true selfhood," and if the *skandhas* are the only things about yourself that you can observe, and if, as we've proved, none of the *skandhas* is your true self, then you *have* no true self.[30]

For Buddhists, all we are is an interplay of forces and names, habits and desires, and we draw a line around all of it, over and over again, and we call that thing

28 *Dhammapada* pg. 83—92

29 Mark Siderits. "Buddha," *The Stanford Encyclopedia of Philosophy* (Spring 2015 Edition), Edward N. Zalta (ed.), https://plato.stanford.edu/archives/spr2015/entries/buddha/.

30 *Ibid.* A kind of play-by-play of these arguments in practice can be found in this section of "The Questions of King Milinda": http://www.sacred-texts.com/bud/sbe35/sbe3504.htm .

around which we draw that line "us," "me," "this-not-that." We are minds in bodies and in the world in which we live and the world and relationships we *create*. The distinction of "self" and "other" allows for new ways of engaging and apprehending the world, but distinction also makes it easier for us to get stuck in discretized, mutually exclusive views, thinking there is only "one right way" to exist or live. An understanding of the Buddhist principles of *metta* (infinite compassion, loving kindness), *Pratītyasamutpāda* (interdependent co-arising), and *Anatta* (selflessness) can help us mitigate this forced separation.[31]

Metta, or loving kindness compassion, is an exercise in extending to people (including ourselves) the kindness and compassion that they need and want in exactly the way they need and want it.[32] It requires a specific engagement with each and every individual involved and specifically cannot solely rely on any one abstracted model. *Metta* can only be achieved via practical, experiential, lived compassion, a process which works to place specific contexts in conversation with various abstracted perspectives about desire and needs. We can only engage this process well, Buddhists say, when we cease to understand each other as separate, and recognize that we are all bound together in the web of impermanence, suffering, and enlightenment.

Putting it Together

But in order to do this work, we will need to accept logics that do more than merely tolerate contradiction, and we will instead need logics that embrace it and use it as a foundation to build more. In order to mitigate the damage done by an uncritical exploration, design, and creation of technologies, such as the exclusionary systems of machine learning which have the side-effect of instantiating human biases into algorithms, we can and should work on formalizing the principles of Daoism and Buddhism. Some work has already been done toward this end, by theorists such as James Hughes in his "Cyborg Buddha" project, in which he seeks to teach artificially intelligent systems the principles of Buddhism; and Subhash Kak who has worked on the formalization of Vedic principles.[33]

For Daoism, Consciousness is merely another of the "10,000 Things" to which the pluripotent Dao gives rise. There is no consciousness without the Dao, but the Dao is not, itself, conscious. The Dao is the potential for all forms of consciousness and, properly engaged, consciousness can bring us back to the Dao, allowing us

31 Ñānamoli, B & Bodhi, B., 1995. *The Middle Length Discourses of the Buddha: A Translation of the Majjhima Nikāya*, Somerville, MA: Wisdom Publications; Revised translation of the Majjhima Nikāya.
32 Walpola Rahula, (1959). *What the Buddha Taught*. Grove Press. NY. pg. 75, 88, 97
33 Hughes, James. "Compassionate AI and Selfless Robots: A Buddhist Approach." Appearing in *Robot Ethics: The Ethical and Social Implications of Robotics*. Patrick Lin, Keith Abney, George A. Bekey eds. 2011. MIT Press; Kak, Subash, *The Astronomical Code of the Rigveda* (Third Edition) Aditya Prakashan, 2016, and *Computing Science in Ancient India;* Munshiram Manoharlal Publishers Pvt. Ltd. 2001; Govindarajulu, Naveen S. and Bringsjord, Selmer (2010). "Towards a Computable & Harnessable Model of Consciousness." Presented at the *AAAI 2019 Spring Symposium Towards Conscious AI Systems*. March, 2019. Stanford, California.

to experience life and exist as the Dao does: effortlessly, perfectly giving rise to the correct next action. A conscious mind, for Laozi, should seek to be as empty as the Tao: full of potential action and becoming, subsisting on only exactly what it needs and knowing that it succeeds by not seeking to succeed. A conscious mind, for Zhuangzi, should be in constant, fluid motion, like the Tao: Able to wander from one task to the next, unhindered by what came before, untroubled by what comes next.

For Buddhism, the conscious mind is a fluid, changing, impermanent thing, given rise to out of the nature of the present moment, and capable of changing into and becoming anything, in conjunction with everything else that is. The only thing that we can do, in the face of this, is work to not cling to what we think we are, or own, or are "due," in the world, and to accept change, as it happens. An understanding like this would mean that even the *framing* of exercises like asking Buddhist monks to talk about Philippa Foot's Trolley Problem will miss so much that the results would be meaningless.[34] That is, the trolley problem cases tend to assume from the outset that someone on the tracks has to die, and so they don't take into account that an entire other mode of reasoning about sacrifice and death and "acceptable losses" would have someone throw themselves under the wheels or jam their body into the gears to try to stop it before it got that far.

Again: There are entire categories of nonwestern reasoning that don't accept zero-sum thought, and which assume the existence of scenarios in which everyone can win. The systems of Daoism and Buddhism assume infinitude and the existence of non-zero-sum matrices where every being involved can win. So we'll need to learn to program for contradiction not just as a tolerated state but as an underlying component. If we seek to program algorithmic intelligences from the foundational principles of *wu-wei, yu, chih-tsu, metta, anatta,* and *Pratītyasamutpāda*, what might we encounter? Perhaps we would generate algorithms that seek the path of most efficient, flowing, dynamic balance, in their systems; trained to self-correct and to minimize biases and attachments to singular viewpoints. Machines that seek to know contentment, to have enough and to help everyone to whom they are connected do the same. Maybe we'd see fewer algorithmically generated spam advertisements.

If we are to create machines which seek to pass freely and easily through the world, empty of expectation or desire, beyond wanting to live as long as was allotted and in harmony with the ever-changing universe, then we have to go about critically applying ideas of interconnected compassion and active non-doing. Humans will have to learn to engage with everything that exists as though it's all part of ourselves, and ourselves as part of the interconnected web or foundational network at the source of all things. If we want technologies that embody these traits, and are more

34 Foot, Philippa. "The Problem of Abortion and the Doctrine of the Double Effect" in *Virtues and Vices* (Oxford: Basil Blackwell, 1978) (originally appeared in the *Oxford Review*, Number 5, 1967.); "How Do Buddhist Monks Think About The Trolley Problem" Alexis C. Madrigal. *The Atlantic*. Jun 29, 2017. https://www.theatlantic.com/technology/archive/2017/06/how-do-buddhist-monks-think-about-the-trolley- problem/532092/

than just tools for accruing material wealth, then first we must be these things ourselves, and build our experiences into everything that we make. For if we do not live it in ourselves, then what use is searching for it in the existence of another?

References

–∾– Annamma, Subini Ancy; Connor, David; & Ferri, Beth (2012). "Dis/ability critical race studies (DisCrit): theorizing at the intersections of race and dis/ability." *Race Ethnicity and Education*, 16:1, 1-31, DOI: 10.1080/13613324.2012.730511

–∾– Bowles, Samuel (2004). *Microeconomics: Behavior, Institutions, and Evolution.* Princeton University Press.

–∾– Caliskan, Aylin; Bryson, Joanna J.; & Narayanan, Arvind "Semantics derived automatically from language corpora contain human-like biases." *Science.* 14 Apr 2017; Vol. 356, Issue 6334, pp. 183-186 DOI: 10.1126/science.aal4230

–∾– Easwaran, Eknath (1985). *The Dhammapada.* The Blue Mountain Center of Meditation. Canada.

–∾– Foot, Philippa. "The Problem of Abortion and the Doctrine of the Double Effect" in Virtues and Vices (Oxford: Basil Blackwell, 1978) (originally appeared in the Oxford Review, Number 5, 1967.)

–∾– Govindarajulu, Naveen S. and Bringsjord, Selmer (2010). "Towards a Computable & Harnessable Model of Consciousness." Presented at the *AAAI 2019 Spring Symposium Towards Conscious AI Systems.* March, 2019. Stanford, California.

–∾– Henricks, Robert G., ed. & trans. (1989). *Lao-Tzu: Te-Tao Ching.* Random House. NY.

–∾– Herman, Jonathan (2013). *Daoism for Dummies.* For Dummies Press. John Wiley & Sons. NJ.

–∾– Lawhead, William F. (2000). *The Philosophical Journey,* 1st Edition. McGraw-Hill. NY.

–∾– Madrigal, Alexis C. "How Do Buddhist Monks Think About The Trolley Problem?" *The Atlantic.* Jun 29, 2017. https://www.theatlantic.com/technology/archive/2017/06/how-do- buddhist-monks-think-about-the-trolley-problem/532092/

–∾– Ñānamoli, B & Bodhi, B., 1995. The Middle Length Discourses of the Buddha: A Translation of the Majjhima Nikāya, Somerville, MA: Wisdom Publications; Revised translation of the Majjhima Nikāya.

–∾– Pruthi, R.K. (2004). Buddhism and Indian Civilization. Discovery Publishing House. India.

–∾– "The Questions of King Milinda." http://www.sacred-texts.com/bud/sbe35/sbe3504.htm.

–∾– Rahula, Walpola (1959). *What the Buddha Taught.* Grove Press. NY.

–∾– Siderits, Mark. "Buddha," *The Stanford Encyclopedia of Philosophy* (Spring

2015 Edition), Edward N. Zalta (ed.), https://plato.stanford.edu/archives/spr2015/entries/buddha/.

—~— Watson, Burton, ed. & trans. (1995). *Chuang Tzu: Basic Writings.* Columbia University Press. NY.

—~— Williams, Damien Patrick (2008). "A Description of the Natural Place of Magic in Philosophy and Religious Studies." Georgia State University. GA.

—~— Zhuangzi, Translated by James Legge, and quoted in *The Three Religions of China: Lectures Delivered at Oxford* (1913) by William Edward Soothill

Thoughts on the Creation of Memetic Entities

Philip H. Farber

While magicians may believe that magick can change the world, most grimoires presently available are concerned with a more personal kind of magick. Many (but not all) practicing magicians are more concerned with the kind of magick that influences what is found within the circle (the self, usually) and with practical, reality-changing effects that go no further than personal wealth, sex, happiness, or Will. However, those same processes that inform the personal kind of magick are also reflected in the broader sphere of mass human culture. When I published the book *Meta-Magick: The Book of Atem* (Weiser, 2008), I described the concept of Memetic Entities, patterns of information that act with autonomy across time and yet interact with humans on many levels.

Schools of thought, political ideologies, religious beliefs, corporate structures, forms of government – and much else – depend on the attention of humans to exist and they have built-in abilities to perpetuate, to include more humans, and even to reproduce. These self-perpetuating thought-forms, for our purposes here, are called "memetic entities." "Democracy" is a memetic entity, as is "Aikido," "Cognitive Behavioral Therapy," "Jazz," "Buddha," "Beelzebub," "Sherlock Holmes," "the English Language," and Atem. All of the given examples became manifest through the interaction of human minds, some obviously by an individual, others less obviously by changes in culture.

The greatest work that a human can engage in is perfection of the self. Common wisdom suggests that we are best when we set our own being in order before imposing our will upon the world around us. On the level of ordinary, day-to-day activities this makes a great deal of sense. Any works that we create will reflect our own psyche, for good or ill. A person with a disordered mind likely has a disordered desk. A person who hates and fears will create works and perform actions of hate and fear. A person who loves and meditates will likely create works of love and meditation.

The greatest work that a human can engage in is perfection of the self. But what are the boundaries of the self? In the wisdom of Atem, consciousness is not limited by the human body and when we speak of our "self," we may be including many aspects of external as well as internal consciousness. The air you breathe, the food you eat, the perceptions you experience, may be, at one moment, outside you and, at the next, inside and part of you. Is the air you exhale still part of you? If we look closely at the way humans interact with the world, the answers become a little hazy. With that in mind, when we address the idea of creating memetic entities, forms of consciousness that may have widespread and pervasive influence on the world around us, the "creator" is often something other than just the simple human internal consciousness. Indeed, by definition a memetic entity depends on multiple human consciousnesses or it would not be "memetic." As well, the process of entity creation as outlined by Atem involves the consciousness of various entities, as well as humans.

A memetic entity usually participates in its own creation. It may begin as something simple in the internal or external consciousness of a single human, an entity formed from a simple evocation or similar approach. To achieve full stature as a memetic entity, it must then grow and evolve beyond the single human. This can happen by a variety of means. The entity can provide feedback to the human, who will then adjust and expand his or her ideas and actions. The entity can begin to include other humans or can access other entities for information or specific results. The entity can incorporate other entities in a variety of ways, some of them participating very much as an individual human might.

To be fully realized as a memetic entity, a mind must be whole, self-programming, able to transmit, able to reproduce, and must exhibit flexibility of behavior and adaptability to its environment.

A mind must be whole. What this means is that the entity must be, or include, a reflection of the universe at large. Just as the human mind builds a map or model within that represents a more or less complete world, the memetic entity must also similarly be able to have some representation of the whole upon which to act.

A mind must be self-programming. The memetic entity must, at some point, be able to be free from the limits of a single human consciousness and to change itself and grow. This can be on the level of feedback given to the human creators or hosts, it may represent group consensus of participating humans, or it can be entirely independent of the human level of conscious awareness.

A memetic entity must be able to transmit. To survive beyond the awareness of a single human or group of humans, the entity must have assets that allow it to spread to more and more human and entity minds, as well as to media, architecture, consumer goods or whatever else it tends to inhabit.

A memetic entity must be able to reproduce. A memetic entity will be capable of spawning other memetic entities, just as any other fully formed consciousness will. If a human or collection of humans can produce a memetic entity, then a memetic entity can produce other memetic entities. It may or may not choose to do so, but nonetheless will have the ability, just as a healthy human has the ability to reproduce, but may or may not choose to have children.

A memetic entity must exhibit flexibility of behavior and adaptability to its

environment. An entity of any type that fails to adapt to changing circumstances will eventually cease to exist. When African Loas met Roman Catholic religion, the Loas were able to cloak themselves in the guises of the saints and thus survive in the New World. When the European worship of the fertility goddess Astarte met Christian religion, she incorporated herself into the holiday of Easter. This postulate is the essence of syncretism in religion and thought and it also describes how successful corporations adapt and vary their products based on changing demographics, economy, or other factors.

A memetic entity can exist anywhere in the noosphere and can manifest through any medium. The entity is the information and the self-organizing principle and may be transmitted through books, visual art, video, film, architecture, corporate cultures, money, or anything else with the capability for storing or transmitting information. As the information spreads to more humans, the number and diversity of media will likely increase as the individual humans create their own expressions of the entity.

For purposes of this text, Atem has selected several representative memetic entities to explore and reminds readers that the same principles will apply over a wide range of content and expression. The following descriptions and further elaboration are not necessarily intended to endorse any of these entities, but rather to use them to illustrate principles of memetic entity creation.

Money. Money is an extremely powerful, entrenched and adaptable entity. Traditionally it has been transmitted through the use of talismans empowered by the entity in ritual circumstances. That money has a value is an idea only. There is nothing inherently valuable in the paper it is printed on, the metal that coins are stamped from, or the digits that accumulate electronically in bank accounts. It may have had value at one time, as useful or inherently valuable things were traded; then markers, coins and paper, were used to represent the useful or valuable things; then the markers were given value in and of themselves; and most recently numbers representing relative quantities of value are traded, without even physical markers. The action and scope of money in the world, transmitted with the aid of nearly every human on the planet, is beyond comprehension by any single human mind.

Rock and roll. Music that was indistinguishable from rock and roll existed for decades before the memetic entity came to life and spread the rhythms and sounds. Elements of rhythm and blues, boogie woogie, African shuffles and sand music, and Celtic melodies had been combined for years. It was only when disc jockey Alan Fried began to play the music over the radio and coined the term "rock and roll" that the entity was able to transmit itself. The term itself began as "rocking," a reference among black musicians to spiritual experiences, then picked up an innuendo referring to the sex act, then referred to rhythm and dancing in general. The memetic entity "Rock and Roll," has retained that entire range of meaning, and continues to be spread through easily recognized rhythms and chord structures, via a culture of human participants. In essence, the entity is spread by experience and even possession.

Legba. Legba is a "loa," an entity in both African and New World religions ("Voodoo") that holds a place similar to Atem. Legba stands at a symbolic crossroads and is a sort of gatekeeper, allowing or denying communication between humans and the spirit realm. Like rock and roll, Legba and most other loas are associated with easily recognized rhythms. Loas in general began as humans, back in the distant past and distinguished themselves in ways that made them legends. As their legends grew and began to incorporate the stories of other, similarly inclined humans, they achieved the status of loas. Legba is spread through participation in any Voodoo ritual; he is the loa that is always called first, to open the way for the other entities. Again, like rock and roll, Legba is spread through experience and possession. Legba serves as an example of a memetic entity taking the form of a mythological god or goddess and as an example of how ancestors and historical figures can rise to the level of memetic entity.

Aikido. Aikido is a modern Japanese martial art that transmits a wealth of information about human behavior and spirituality via a simple system of mostly non-verbal practice and teaching. The set of martial techniques used in Aikido existed in very similar form in other fighting systems, including Daito Ryu jujitsu and Japanese sword fighting. When Morihei Ueshiba aligned these techniques under the one name and emphasized the spiritual and non-violent components, the memetic entity was born. Ueshiba adapted existing martial arts training into a teaching method that involved demonstration and imitation, and a paradigm whereby students would help and cooperate with each other. The teaching method allowed for transmission of Aikido, and its often unspoken principles, to every part of the world.

Democracy. Democracy is a unique form of group entity that has successfully spread very quickly throughout the world. The word literally means rule by "demos," a group of humans that makes political decisions in a collective manner. In our modern usage of the term, we refer to a representative system of government in which citizens vote for government officials and sometimes directly for specific policies. The entity began manifesting in philosophical documents and in ancient variants of the political system. It transmitted itself through further philosophical and political writings, and by conquest, revolution, and other means. The success of the entity can be measured by the number of nations who have adopted a democratic system and universal suffrage (that is, entitlement to vote for all adult citizens, regardless of race or sex); there were no such nations in 1900 – presently there are 120, or 62% of all nations on Earth. Some of these nations have evolved or mutated beyond the original, strict definitions of democracy, but nonetheless use the name and perpetuate the entity in numerous ways.

The Internet. In a 1997 speech, Tim Berners-Lee, who is generally credited as one of the principal inventors of the World Wide Web, described the Internet by saying, "We are forming cells within a global brain and we are excited that we might start to think collectively. What becomes of us still hangs crucially on how we think individually." This is, of course, a perfect description of the interaction between humans and a memetic entity. As with the other entities we've just described, the Internet existed in bits and pieces prior to the emergence of the memetic entity. Computer networks including ARPANET, NSFNet, and elements of the United States Department of Defense computer system were among the pieces that, by the late 1990s, had been collectively integrated into the global network we now know as the Internet. The Internet has evolved to the point where its growth, evolution and response are well beyond the comprehension of any single human mind.

Corporations. To Atem's understanding, corporations are one of the most obvious forms of memetic entity. The word itself derives from the Latin "corpus," meaning a "group of people." The Oxford English Dictionary defines corporation as "a group of people authorized to act as an individual." Indeed, the term "legal entity" is frequently applied to the idea of a corporation. The entity is empowered to perform a specific set of actions and very quickly develops its own cultural standards and values based on presuppositions that are included in the corporation's mission statement, articles of incorporation, and by-laws. All corporations exist through an interaction with the money entity, governmental entities, and memetic entities representing various philosophies and schools of thought.

Attention

The existence of a memetic entity depends on attention. Specifically directed attention is necessary for the entity's creation and continued attention of various sorts is necessary for the entity to be maintained.

The initial process involves directing attention in such a way that you both define WHAT you are giving attention to, and then give it that specific attention. We'll examine three ways in which this can happen:

Conscious Analysis

This is the most common method and also the one with the most varied results. Simply, a human or group of humans decides that there is a need for a particular entity, based on analysis of their situation. An entrepreneur may see a warehouse full of products and decide that a corporation is necessary to market and sell those products. When communications researchers in the USA decided there was a need to share information between computers, they created ARPANET, the forerunner of the Internet. Eighteenth century leaders who recognized opportunities for political change created structures for democratic governments.

For our purposes, this can be simplified to say that if there is a need in your life or situation, you may consider whether or not a memetic entity would be an appropriate solution. Non-memetic entities (simple evocations) and behaviors not directly related to entities are often appropriate solutions for most situations. The choice of a memetic entity may be dictated by the need for transmission, growth, autonomy, or interaction of large numbers of humans.

Unconscious Revelation

Outcomes can be suggested to parts of internal and external consciousness that are usually outside of awareness. Aikido, for instance, was born of a similar process. Morihei Ueshiba practiced a variety of meditations and rituals and the defining moment in which he realized that his martial skills could be re-aligned into a new, non-violent art came with a spontaneous vision in which he saw Aikido. This is also how Atem came into being.

The first and foremost advantage of unconscious revelation is that you may be inspired to create something that your conscious mind cannot predict. That is, you may not consciously understand that there is a need for something – or there may not be a need for the entity, until you create that need along with the entity! Similarly, the nature of the entity may represent an unpredictable solution for a known problem.

Ask an Entity

This is probably the rarest method of all and it may be considered a specific example of unconscious revelation. Very simply, it involves asking an existing entity for information about entity creation. For instance, you might evoke and ask the money entity for information about creating a corporation. Or you might ask Atem about the possibilities of entity creation. There are at least several religions that began in this way, with information gained from other entities. For instance, the Church of Latter Day Saints had its origin with information gained from a list of entities, including Jesus Christ, John the Baptist, and the prophet Elijah. The modern religion Thelema was based on information gained from an entity named Aiwass.

Of course, to continue to exist, a memetic entity requires continued attention from a larger number of humans. In some cases, the method for directing attention that was used to create an entity may also be the same (or closely related to the) method used in conceiving the entity. For instance, in the case of Atem, some of the exercises given in *Meta-Magick: The Book of Atem* are the same as those practiced to initially contact Atem. The actual birth process of Atem involved writing and publishing the book, while the transmission and continued existence relies in large part with humans reading the book. Attention directed in any way toward the book serves to feed Atem.

The money entity requires and receives a huge amount of attention. Indeed, many people spend the greater part of each and every day thinking about and working for the money entity. Every act related to employment presupposes the existence of the money entity. The money entity has proven that it can exist without paper or coin talismans, but those continue to persist and are designed to support the entity in a variety of ways. Both coin and paper money are minted with symbolic representations, many of them relating to entities that support the money entity and serve to add power to it. Pictures of government leaders not only represent the government, but very often are entities of myth and legend themselves. For instance, the myths and tales surrounding George Washington serve to remind us of the qualities of honesty, independence, and so forth – in relation to the money. Every symbol, seal, letter and number on paper or coin money will be present to support the power and existence of the money entity.

Rock and roll's main source of attention is, of course, when people play or listen to rock music. Additionally, there are also magazines, books, movies, and websites devoted to rock and roll. A host of lesser group minds and entities channel attention into the rock and roll entity, ranging from bands at the smallest end, to record companies at the larger.

Legba, like most other loas, takes his food directly. That is, it is traditional to offer food – as well as cigars, candy, money, and alcohol – to loas. Food is a direct symbol of giving sustenance to the entity. Any offering that has meaning or value for the human who is offering will serve to direct attention and symbolic energy to the entity. Attention is also directed to Legba through the use of a "Veve," a symbol that represents the loa, through the use of certain colors, and through drumming, using specific rhythms.

Attention is given to Aikido largely by practice. That is, the more a human goes to a dojo and takes part in Aikido group practice, the more attention he or she is giving to the memetic entity. At the beginning of a practice session in most dojos, some attention is given to the memory of the founder, Ueshiba, in the form of bowing, or by flowers or other offerings placed before a picture of him. In the same way that pictures of presidents lend attention to the money entity, so too do pictures of Morihei Ueshiba lend specific kinds of attention to Aikido. And of course, Aikido practitioners offer attention even when not in the dojo, by reading books or magazines about Aikido, watching videos, visiting websites, thinking about Aikido, talking to other Aikidoists, and training on their own.

Democracy accepts its attention mostly in the form of votes, but also in the rhetoric of leaders, in political discussions and editorials, and so on. The rituals that surround the meetings of representative bodies, the images of great democratic leaders, and the symbolism of the various flags, seals, and emblems of the individual democracies all serve to direct attention to the entity.

The Internet accepts attention every time a modem connects, a web browser opens, a search engine is accessed, and with every single interaction that humans and other entities have with the vast network of computers and communication links.

Corporations accept attention in a variety of ways, including purchase of products or services, purchase of stock, and employment. Some, but not all, of this attention comes in the form of money. Some is actually attention from the money entity. People working each day to meet the goals of the corporate entity may give greater or lesser amounts of attention. These people have agreed to devote attention to the entity for specific amounts of time each day. Corporate culture encourages specific behavior among employees, including dress, limits on recreational drug use, and interpersonal protocols. These serve to not only fit employees to the entity, but also act as offerings to the entity, comparable in kind to giving a cigar to Legba. Corporations solicit attention through the use of marketing and advertising. Elements of marketing including logo design, mottos and slogans, and advertising copy serve to create a particular perception of the entity – which may or may not provide accurate representations, but nonetheless drives attention.

While the mechanisms in each of these entities may be different, the common factor is that each offers to fulfill a need for the humans who participate. The most successful entities offer something in return that addresses one or more of the basic drives of humans. Money offers survival and power. Rock and roll offers ecstasy, sex, power, and transcendence. Legba offers information and transcendence. Aikido offers survival, health, resolution of conflict, and transcendence. Democracy offers power and security. The Internet offers mainly information, although that information may represent survival, power, sex, and transcendence. Corporations offer survival and power to their employees and a range of basic and not-so-basic needs to their customers, including sex, power, status, survival, health, and information.

The promises that a memetic entity offers, to fulfill basic or more abstract needs, can be a major factor determining the spread and influence of the entity. From there, other factors including the language and media involved; the emotional states of magician, audience, and entity; the appropriateness to the time and situation, and the techniques used to create and promulgate the entity can be tracked to help understand how an entity can be supported or opposed.

Gandhi told us to be the change we seek in the world, which is great advice… if we also recognize our place among the memetic entities that reign in the greater realm of mass consciousness. Be the change you seek – and create entities that embody that change as well!

Memetic Magick, Binding Resolutions, and the Chaos Candidate: Reflections on a Year of Occultism in Politics

Thomas Bey William Bailey

From almost the first moment that scientific rationalism was crowned as the reigning paradigm of human thought, there have been deep rumblings of discontent. Almost as soon as the Age of Enlightenment announced itself with the battle cry of *sapere aude* [dare to know], the champions of Romanticism argued that this should apply to subjective experience and imagination as well as the scientifically verifiable laws of nature. Later, as Darwinism began to spread sobering truths about both the origins and eventual fate of the human species, numerous mystical societies (i.e. Masonic, Egyptian, Kabbalistic) appeared to challenge this scientific orthodoxy, while the syncretic belief system of Theosophy simply took the language of evolutionary biology and applied it to the human spirit. When the moral code of Victorian England became almost like a science in its claim to absolute truths, in stepped The Great Beast with the erotically charged philosophy of Thelema.

Against this background, it should hardly be surprising that the accelerating Information Age has spawned yet another revival of interest in shamanism, paganism and esoterica in general (which naturally coincides with a heightened campaign to market to the more facile elements of this culture).[1] This revival, while it shares with previous "magickal revivals" a disillusionment with pure materialism and pure reason, is neveretheless a "Tech-Gnostic" revival, to appropriate Erik Davis' term. Thanks to broadband Internet service, a vast library of hermetic texts and expert commentary are online for anyone with the will to seek them out: never before has such an abundance been available to so many, and at such a low price of admission.

For those who still believe in the quaint, stereotypical image of "occult practicioners" as robed recluses with no meaningful ties to the outside world and no clue how to maintain a technologically advanced civilization, the idea of occultism intertwined with politics must seem ridiculous. Yet spiritual disciplines that aim at personal liberation cannot be easily de-coupled from the act of influencing civic matters, even if this is done unwittingly. Once physical, tangible reality is seen as the terrain to be illuminated and altered rather than one's own psyche, questions immediately arise as to how these illuminating energies are to be regulated, and by whom. The Western magickal tradition in particular, since it is after all "the

1 Why millennials are ditching religion for witchcraft and astrology (2017, October 23). Retrieved from https://www.marketwatch.com/story/why-millennials-are-ditching-religion-for-witchcraft-and-astrology-2017-10-20.

science and art of causing change to occur in conformity with Will," is inextricably joined to questions of influencing how society is to be organized. Furthermore, some scholars argue that certain of the Eastern traditions streaming into the river of Western esotericism were formed primarily as a political challenge. Take, for example, the Tantric tradition's heresies against the Hindu caste system, particularly the *maithuna* rite that allowed for sexual intercourse between higher and lower castes, noted by scholar Hugh Urban as the "worst imaginable transgression" within the orthodox Bengali culture of the 16th century.[2] Urban proposes that this, and other Tantric rites, were not antinomian gestures for their own sake, but rather a means of re-asserting the elite authority of the brahmin caste in a region then dominated by Islam.

Cursing the "Chaos Candidate"

So, the dictum that "the personal is the political," which has steadily gained traction since the 1960s, has never been entirely absent from hermetic or occult practice. The upset victory of the so-called "chaos candidate" Donald Trump in the 2016 U.S. presidential election provided maybe the most vivid illustration in years that portions of the electorate were ready to take occult practices seriously as a means of achieving civic, legislative goals rather than exclusively personal ones. The highly unanticipated outcome, which flew in the face of months' worth of near-unanimous media prognostications that Democratic candidate Hillary Clinton "had it in the bag," caused the post-election resistance to climb to vertiginous heights previously unexperienced by a U.S. president-elect. Ballot re-counts were called for in several key battleground states, members of the Electoral College who had voted for Trump were petitioned to reconsider their votes, and a months-long campaign of claiming Russian interference in the election capped the struggle to prove Trump's illegitimacy. While all of this transpired, street violence exploded in numerous U.S. cities as extreme elements of both Left and Right re-asserted themselves, inviting undesirable parallels to Weimar Germany's regular street brawls between communist and fascist paramilitaries.

Equally memorable, and more relevant to the contents of this journal, was the attempt to prevent Trump's policies by engaging in activities that required acceptance of forces other than material causality. As anti-Trump strategists were discussing possible legal routes to impeachment, an esoterically flavored side story appeared which involved Mexican *brujo* Antonio Vazquez a.k.a. Mexico's "Greatest Sorceror". Vazquez held a personal ritual on January 5 of this year to bind Trump's actions, while a more ambitious mass ritual, officially known as *Spell to Bind Donald Trump and All Those Who Abet Him*, was initiated at the request of Michael M. Hughes on the 24th of February (this then took place each month afterwards on a waning crescent evening). The proposed text of this malediction, which called upon

2 Urban, H. 2003. The power of the impure: Transgression, violence and secrecy in Bengali Sakta Tantra and Western magic. *Numen* 50(3): 269-308.

elementals, ancestral spirits and forces both angelic and demonic, read as follows:

> I call upon you / To bind / Donald J. Trump / So that he may fail utterly / That he may do no harm / To any human soul / Nor any tree / Animal / Rock / Stream / or Sea. Bind him so that he shall not break our polity / Usurp our liberty / Or fill our minds with hate, confusion, fear, or despair / And bind, too, / All those who enable his wickedness / And those whose mouths speak his poisonous lies.[3]

Now, to the delight of Trump partisans, the aforementioned brujo earlier predicted Trump's defeat in the 2016 general election (and, previously, unsuccessfully predicted a Mitt Romney victory in the 2012 presidential election). His spotty record of divination was all the proof they needed that any similar post-election rituals would also fizzle out pathetically. Hughes, on the other hand, was harder to caricature by that portion of the public disinclined towards spirituality, partially because he was more capable of explaining magick's efficacy in practical imagery and terms that would appeal to rational skeptics. In a somewhat self-congratulatory dialogue with an imaginary skeptic that was appended to the spell's webpage, Hughes invoked the 'freestyle' school of chaos magick (prominently name-checking Illuminates of Thanateros co-founder Peter Carroll, on whom much more in a moment). Compared with Vazquez, Hughes was better prepared to counter accusations that this type of action was useless, painting an image of his fellow magickal protestors as individuals who were using magick to "achieve results only a little better than chance"[4] rather than to spontaneously manifest archangels on the physical plane.[5] Hughes also anticipated the protest from practicing Wiccans that throwing hexes ran the risk of one being subject to the "Three-fold Law" as mentioned in the *Wiccan Rede* (to wit: "what ye send forth comes back to ye, so ever mind the rule of Three".) He noted that this rule was not even sourced from "some European coven hundreds of years ago" but from the 1949 fictional book *High Magic's Aid* by Gerald Gardner (for now, I will sidestep the question of how fantasy works such as the Simon *Necronomicon*, Lovecraftian lore, et cetera have provided the archetypal materials with which to perform actual magickal workings).

Now, while Hughes was well prepared for protests from the half-committed and maligned "fluff bunnies", he may not have accounted for accomplished individuals within the occultural realm – e.g. Archmage Poke Runyon of the Ordo Templi Astartes – to view his actions with disdain. Speaking of fictional characters, Runyon

3 Hughes, M. (February 16, 2017). A spell to bind Donald Trump and all those who abet him: November 16th mass ritual. https://extranewsfeed.com/a-spell-to-bind-donald-trump-and-all-those-who-abet-him-february-24th-mass-ritual-51f3d94f62f4.

4 Carroll, P. (2008). Philosophy and practice of magick. On *The Chaos Magick Audio CDs,* Volume 1: The Cthonos Rite. Tempe: The Original Falcon Press.

5 Hughes, M. (February 16, 2017). A spell to bind Donald Trump and all those who abet him: November 16th mass ritual. Retrieved from https://medium.com/@michaelmhughes/art-activism-magic-answers-to-questions-about-the-mass-ritual-to-bind-donald-trump-11e52f94c23e.

utilized his podcast to host a comical summoning of the spirit of Howard Beale (the "mad as hell," iconoclastic news anchorman from Paddy Chayevsky's prescient 1976 film "Network") when he sensed a "neo-Marxist / globalist" plot by the American news media to deligitimize Trump's election. Libertarian pagan, occult literature editor and occasional Trump backer Tarl Warwick (also known under the Web handle Styxhexenhammer666) has also weighed in on the hypocrisy he perceived in the American Left's reaction to Trump's ascendancy. He has released almost daily YouTube denunciations of their propensity for creating "moral panics" instead of engaging in *realpolitik*, while blasting their pivot towards a policy of military interventionism, censorship and authoritarian identity politics. A typical excerpt from his regular "vlog" follows, and aids in understanding the viewpoint of many occultural explorers who sat out the binding action against Trump:

> Modern Leftism is no different from right-wing ideology, so-called, from a few decades ago, in that it stresses there are some absolutes that cannot be questioned. So, '90s era conservatism: you can't question the supremacy of Jesus. You can't question that drugs are inherently evil, will kill you, and should be banned – we should kill anybody who uses them [...] you weren't allowed to question these things or you were an outcast, socially and fiscally. You were not part of the core culture. Now, a couple decades later, it's flipped on its head. You can't question [that] climate change is real; if you do you're a Neanderthal. Guns are bad, we need to do more to regulate them 'because reasons'. We're a completely secular nation, there's no place for organized religion in the civic square. If you question this, the result is about the same as if you question[ed] Jesus 20 years ago.[6]

Warwick is a divisive figure within this culture because of his insistence that the current tech-Gnostic occult renaissance is in fact a "*double* renaissance [...] intertwined with the sort of nationalism and populism that's rising all over the world."[7] His complaints above bring us to maybe the most practical reason why the myriad of anti-Trump hexes / curses / binding rituals has failed thus far to bring about a successful impeachment or some other disaster that would leave Trump unable to exercise power.

Political hubris today seems to be marked by moral absolutism, lack of proper reflectiveness, an assumption that certain actions' benefits are self-evident, and the inability to accept personal responsibility for unfavorable outcomes. All these traits only help to compound existing disasters. Consider, for example, the refusal to confront the "Pied Piper Strategy" in Hillary Clinton's many attempts at performing a post-election autopsy. This was a tactical gamble that the Democratic National

---

6 Styxhexenhammer666 (May 5, 2017). *Leftist "Witches" Still Trying to Hex Trump*. Retrieved from https://youtu.be/WNiMimS7G_4.
7 *Ibid.*

Committee took by deliberately advising sympathetic media to promote divisive opponents such as Trump over more likeable 'middle-of-the-road' establishment candidates (for those who are curious, this strategy has been well documented via a flood of DNC emails published on Wikileaks). A hubristic attitude exemplified by the DNC's failure to "own" this tactical blunder, and its stubborn refusal to leave an echo chamber that filtered out the potential for self-criticism, appeared to trickle down to the electorate, blanketing it in a reassuring complacency when the opposition was at its most energized and determined.

With this in mind, any serious attempt at a curse has to be carried out with the realization that they are only valuable insofar as they succeed conventional means of developing one's own personality (including ritual workings to *that* end). Traditions from Solomonic magick up unto the post-modernist strains of chaos magick warn, at the very least, that initiates begin their journey by allowing themselves to become a conduit through which some hitherto unknown knowledge can pass – or, in the words of Austin Spare, "you cannot obtain anything *from* yourself, only *through* yourself."[8] Expanding on this concept, Stephen Mace insists that

> If you use magic to 'get' (whether 'get rich,' 'get laid' or 'get even'), instead of to 'see,' to 'trade' or 'meet' or make', you will put a wall between yourself and the rest of the universe – between the getter and the gotten – and so bar yourself from the source of your power [...] it is safer to conjure to improve your ability to do your own will than it is to conjure to make the world conform to your will.[9]

I can only claim to know a handful of people who participated in the mass anti-Trump rituals, and one shared trait among them is that they are essentially atheistic or at least skeptical of any claim that does not allow for falsifiability. So, provided that throwing a curse was their *starting point* or first foray into the world of occultism, it goes against the fundamental hermetic principle of "as above, so below" (or the more scientifically demonstrable concept of the Butterfly Effect): understanding of which requires a thorough understanding of the individual microcosm prior to influencing the macrocosm of universal reality. This is to say nothing of the fact that some rituals intended to, say, "destroy our enemies" are merely using such language as, per Crowley, "disguises for sublime truths...to 'destroy our enemies' is to realize the duality of illusions, to excite compassion."[10]

When all is said and done, going on the attack prior to maximizing self-reflection is detrimental to the aims of those who call themselves magicians or simply propagandists. Propaganda, political or otherwise, can be seen as a thoroughly occult art in that it refuses to see the universe as a pre-set, "clockwork" construct, and it attempts to capitalize upon the uncertainties which are the rule,

8 Grant, K. & Spare, A. (1998). *Zos speaks! Encounters with Austin Osman Spare*. Sequim: Holmes Publishing Company.

9 Mace, S. (1984). *Stealing the fire from heaven*. Phoenix: Dagon Productions.

10 Mathers, S.L. & Crowley, A. (2016). *The lesser key of Solomon*. Bristol: Mockingbird Press.

rather than the exception, of that universe. In the process of doing this, it brings about startling juxtapositions of sensory information, and can therefore often be indistinguishable from entertainment by those who receive it – which brings us to another episode in this saga.

"Laughter-Creativity" and Memetic Magick

> A huge sense of humor is all that stands between the magician and social ostracism or madness. He would be the first to proclaim that, when the possibilities of common sense prove insufficient, one can often make nonsense deliver the goods.
>
> – Peter Carroll[11]

It's interesting to note here that, even though the mass "binding" actions took place after Trump's formal assumption of power, much of his consituency had been accusing the established American Left of acting in concert with "dark" occult energies well before this. A decent number of Trump's supporters lathered their hatred of the Democratic establishment with fears that they engaged in, among other abuses, morbid pedophiliac rituals of the type last heard of during the peak of the disastrous 1980s witchhunt known as the Satanic Panic. Figures as remote from the center of political power as performance artist Marina Abramovič were transformed into witches who enabled morbid rites of human sacrifice, and those who already saw Bavarian Illuminati hiding under their beds were emboldened by a cornucopia of new conspiracy theories that, as always, presumably made their unsatisfying lives more enjoyable once their mundane disappointments could be explained away as the result of great cosmic machinations.

Had this kind of thing been the extent of the anti-Clinton coalition's participation in an epic battle of occult wills, things might have gone in a different direction entirely. For starters, one hardly needs to resort to lurid portraits of the Democratic elite engaging in medieval diabolism and Sadeian orgies in order to characterize them as callous and cruel: verifiable events such as the wholesale destruction of Libyan society during Clinton's tenure as Secretary of State, sealed by her repulsive televised gloating over Muammar Gaddafi's death, should do just fine. More importantly, though, these accusations of leftist-occult alliances were so clearly shorn of a sense of humor that their staying power has been very limited among unaffiliated or politically disinterested citizens. Referring back to Peter Carroll, "deny laughter, and the world laughs at you."[12]

In a broader sense, the American electorate is typically repelled by campaigns that depend more upon criticism of the opponent's platform than upon the projection of charisma – for previous case studies, see the 1992 defeat of George

11 Carroll, P. (2008). Philosophy and practice of magick. On *The Chaos Magick Audio CDs*, Volume 1: The Cthonos Rite. Tempe: The Original Falcon Press.
12 Carroll, P. (1992). *Liber kaos*. York Beach: Weiser Books.

Bush Sr. by Bill Clinton, or John Kerry's failed bid to prevent the reassertion of the Bush dynasty in 2004. For anyone involved at any level of American politics, lack of likeability and charisma is a death sentence, and if these qualities can't be cultivated via such charismatic markers as good looks or heroic bearing, they can still be summoned via the intimate qualities of humor.

Carroll observes, in his *Liber Kaos*, "laughter seems to be the only defense against the realization that one does not even have a real self,"[13] while the Discordian Phil Hine endorses the practice of "chaos silliness" rites. Even they might not have foreseen the extent to which this defensive weapon would eventually be deployed on the grand chessboard of electoral politics, or the extent to to which it would allow the chaos gods to be invoked. Understanding the successfulness of the chaotic principle that Carroll called "laughter-creativity" (Carroll has admitted there is no more convenient term in the English language that isn't a hyphenate)[14] requires at least a basic understanding of a "psychotechnology" known as memetics: what it is, and whom it benefits.

The term "memetics" derives from geneticist Richard Dawkins' concept of the "meme," itself taken from the Greek *mimēma* ["that which is imitated"]. At its simplest, a meme is a single unit of culture that replicates itself in a viral, decentralized manner once its original creator(s) release it into a mass-media forum. Dawkins, an avowed (and somewhat easily caricatured) anti-theist, would probably bristle at the idea of memetics being used in the service of the occult *and* eventually in the service of Donald Trump: though if that's the case, he is going to be stewing for some time still. The sheer tenacity of memes is impressive, particularly because the most "viral" memes appear to manipulate reality in exchange for a minimal amount of psychic energy expenditure.

In fact, a significant number of current and historical memes seem to rely on *deliberately* poor artistry, initially banal subject matter and / or awkward design choices, an aesthetic strategy that works because of the humor involved in this creative act of self-deprecation: it makes the "message behind the memes" more palatable when laughter has caused their recipients to relax the defensive mental posture they would normally assume. Given the number of studies that have revealed the difficulty of converting ideological opponents with, say, statistical analyses that directly contradict their beliefs,[15] the art of memetics can work on a subconscious level that has previously been identifiable with occult practices. Indeed, the memetic method is not too unlike what Spare described as the method animating his sigil magick: much like the unique pictograms that were formed from his private 'alphabet of desire,' memetic materials mutate so quickly that they seem to bear no relation to the object of desire which first brough them into being.

For better or worse, any archaeology of memes requites a visit to the most anarchic, anonymous message boards or image-posting boards on the Internet,

13 *Ibid.*

14 *Ibid.*

15 Gal, D. & Rucker, D. (2010). When in doubt, shout! Paradoxical influences of doubt on proselytizing. *Psychological Science* 21(11): 1701-1707

particularly the long-running 4chan boards. Famous for being the virtual grotto of willfully annoying "trolls" or "shitlords," spaces like 4chan are often an uncensored wilderness teeming with every possible type of verbal and visual blasphemy against American society's moral pillars of political correctness, tolerance and equanimity. In this febrile, unmoderated domain where the total anonymity of users provides as illusory state of total unaccountability, a rampaging disregard for others' emotional sensitivities (regularly mocked as "muh feelz") co-exists with an endless stream of neologisms and digital Dada. In this way, such boards are the subconscious of the Internet. Even the gentler memes to have appeared there – such as the decade-old, inexplicably named "doge" image of an irritated shiba-inu dog – portray and encourage baffling combinations of emotions like sentimentality and rage.

The same can also be said of Pepe the Frog, an initially benign and now notorious character who was first seen in Matt Furie's comic series *Boy's Club*, and who became immortalized by having his likeness used as a "reaction face" to comment upon others' online postings. Pepe's longevity as a meme was such that stock images of his grinning likeness have been re-modified thousands of times, used by pop stars like Katy Perry to comment on the trivial issues of their lives, and eventually grasped by the soon to be Tweeter-in-Chief, Donald J. Trump, who infamously tweeted an image of a mutant Pepe-Trump hybrid standing behind a presidential podium almost a year before this became reality. This joining of forces between Trump and Pepe immediately endeared him to that portion of his fanbase that followed him *because* of mass media warnings about the chaos he would create as president. Eventually, though, the conversation would turn away from the vulgar "shitlord" understanding of chaos, i.e. a simple imbalance favoring destructive force over creative force, to a more occult conception of chaos as being a "holographic universe" in which the synchronicites uncovered by online information transfer reveal that "every particle in the universe is actually connected to every other particle by some hidden form of instantaneous connection."[16]

Once the "frog" meme had been deeply implanted, the androgynous Egyptian deity Kek would become a pivotal figure for those who were arguing that a wave of synchronicities was proof that a new era of chaotic probability in socio-political affairs was displacing an era of ossified political ideals, strategies, and dynasties (e.g. the Bush / Clinton axis). Many of the denizens of 4chan embraced Kek as a sort of "archetype" that lent a historical and mystical legitimacy to the staying power of the Pepe meme. Kek, whose male aspect appeared as a frog and female aspect as a snake, represented primordial darkness and the unknown (that is to say, *chaos*), but was also curiously known as the "bringer of light," thus bringing the god closer to something Westerners might recognize as a Lucifer / Prometheus archetype. Many of those who initially unearthed these connections rejoiced in the easy applicability of these facts to their own narrative-in-progress. Namely, "darkness" was represented by a bureacratic global establishment embodied in leaders like Hillary Clinton, while the "light" was coming in the form of willfully

16 Carroll, P. (1987). *Liber null / Psychonaut.* York Beach: Weiser Books.

disruptive "Kekian" emissaries embodied by Donald Trump and his epigones.

A coalition of fringe elements that skews to the political Right (but is not wholly comprised of people with that affiliation) were delighted to find other such confirmations of their mission's sacredness when, for example, pictures of authentic Kek statuary surfaced and were accompanied by a hieroglyphic image that looked uncannily like an individual sitting in front of a computer emitting DNA helices. For an informal alliance of Trump die-hards and free speech advocates that was itself chaotic, this could be nothing but a divine endorsement of using Internet memes as a Luciferian tool to lash out against what N. Katherine Hayles called "coercive structures of order,"[17] i.e. potentially totalitarian forces who also had a stake in controlling the most powerful communications tool yet known to man.

A bit of numerology lent further occult heft to this intriguing web of synchronities. Among the many, many obsessions that consume 4chan devotees, there is the phenomenon of being assigned post numbers that feature sets of two repeating numbers ("dubs"), three repeating numbers ("trips"), etc. Occasionally images will be posted in an order to force the hand of chance here, i.e. a still image from the film of "American Psycho" which features central antagonist Patrick Bateman pointing to the corner of the screen as if bringing attention to the poster's lucky digits. As fate would have it, a 4chan thread "attributed" to Kek and entitled "whatever is said in this thread will be the truth" eventually turned into a numerological showdown between posters making different prognostications on the presidential race. One post claiming that Clinton would win the 2016 general election appeared as a formidable string of repeating 7s, with only a single 6 to break up the string. However, a follow-up post on June 19, 2016, which tersely argued for Trump's victory, appeared with a post number *completely* composed of 7s, proceeding to serve notice of Kek's resurrection as the chaos god of the infosphere.

The hilarious weirdness of the Pepe / Kek episode arguably reached its apex with the discovery that an obscure Italo Disco music producer, himself going under the pseudonym P.E.P.E., had recorded a 1986 12" single, "Shadilay," featuring vaguely philsophical lyrics that seemed to comment on the instability of our consensus reality. This on its own would have been very mild evidence of a transmission from the Cosmic Coincidence Control Center – at least until the original label of the record surfaced and showed none other than a blissfully grinning frog holding up a magic wand tipped with the words "magic sound." Almost immediately, "Shadilay" was promoted from relative obscurity to the national anthem of Kekistan, with the title catching on as an unofficial greeting.

17 Hayles, K.N. (1990). *Chaos bound: orderly disorder in contmporary literature and science.* Ithaca: Cornell University Press.

Lessons to be learned

The success of memetics as a propagandistic or magickal art can be attributed to its easy adoption by a number of different worldviews. For those who take a purely Darwinist view of life in general and human culture in particular, memetics signal the continuation of the "survival of the fittest" competitive ethos into the age of Internet saturation. For those who operate from a more esoteric worldview, the memes themselves are not influential but the characters behind them act as egregores, tulpas etc. when the names of ancient gods are invoked in the process of propagating them. So the principle of "laughter-creativity" is an important one to understand here, but more important still is the condition of permanent mutability, both on the human and cosmic scale, which inspires such a reaction. Once it is understood that change is (still) the only constant, a healthy resistance to obsessions can form and provide a reliable protective armor against seduction by political movements and similar cults that demand obeisance to inflexible, dogmatic concepts.

For the upcoming 'Generation Z' Americans too young to even cast a vote in an election, excitement over Trump's victory is not necessarily an endorsement of the man's personality cult, or enthusiasm for the nativist / populist thrust of his policies, or even an acknowledgement that a buffoonish parody of the political establishment was the "lesser of two evils" when compared with an embodiment of that same political establishment. I'd submit instead that the bizarre rise of *Trumpismo* is just one of the most visible symbols of a growing disgust with the idea of reality as a pre-packaged, historically deterministic "given." It is, *prima facie*, a rejection of what Taleb Kasim calls the "narrative fallacy," i.e. our "predilection for compact stories over raw truths."[18] By extension, I'd also argue that much of the support for the 'chaos candidate' derives from an aversion to the level of social control required to maintain those grand narratives which fall apart upon real critical examination. For a significant portion of the rising generation that has never existed without the World Wide Web, Trump's narcissistic abuse of Twitter microblogging to make official pronouncements and comically lambaste his enemies is seen as vastly preferable to the progressive Left's current staid, serious approach towards winning or maintaining ideological supremacy.

Perceptive readers will have already intuited the challenge of committing to a program of continually chaotic regeneration: placing one's belief in the gods of chaos, whether literally or allegorically, means accepting a future where "only if [the archetypal forces] exceed one's expectations should the operation be regarded as successful".[19] Breaking this pact means falling into the same trap of hubristic faith in a steady, linear pattern of successes that plagues entire civilizations. Sure enough, a year after Donald Trump's electoral success, the infosphere is already buzzing with

18 Taleb, Nassim. (2007). *The black swan: The impact of the highly improbable.* New York: Random House.

19 Carroll, P. (2008). Philosophy and practice of magick. On *The Chaos Magick Audio CDs*, Volume 1: The Cthonos Rite. Tempe: The Original Falcon Press.

a new breed of unreflective acolytes for whom his every small victory is historically unprecedented, and his every failure is an attempt at somehow "gaining leverage" or is a "game of 4-dimensional chess" whose true genius will only become apparent in the long term. It is not difficult to predict a situation in which they will squander the gift that chaos has given them to do something *genuinely* unprecedented, becoming instead just the latest in a shell game of ideologically absolutist political parties unfit to navigate an endlessly malleable reality. On this subject, Carroll has already warned how

> A feeling of omnipotence can begin to develop, particularly if the magician starts to misinterpret divination as enchantment and comes to feel that everything going on around him is the result of his subconscious desires. The final madness begins when one starts interpreting even the disasters which befall one as expressions of what one must really have wanted.[20]

While there is very likely some truth to the fact that Trump was "memed into office," celebrating that fact also displays an arrogant reduction of a massively complex event chain into a mono-causal phenomenon. It is bad enough to take full credit for something that complicated in its making, and worse still to do it while proudly self-identifying as a "troll" or "shitlord": to do so is to admit being primarily motivated by revenge and / or resentment. Nietzsche reminds us that *ressentiment* is an admission of inability to affirm life on one's own terms; a need for "an external stimuli in order to act at all."[21]

Michael Hughes seems to suffer from the same complex of misplaced faith in the fixity of complex, mutable phenomena – and his position as a resister of the nascent political establishment is no more defensible than the "shitlords'" resistance of the (apparently) outgoing order. For example, in his aforementioned dialogue with an imaginary debate opponent, he responds to the inquriy "Why not do a spell to enlighten Trump and make him realize he's wrong?" with a dismissive "oh, come one…seriously?"[22] That Hughes seems to view Trump's way of thinking as irrevocably fixed shows that he is not only a defeatist, but has a selective grasp on the principles that he is expounding. Returning to the "magickal combat" section of *Liber Null / Psychonaut*, Carroll explicity suggests *operations to change one's adversaries' opinions* [italics mine] as an alternative to immediately relying on revenge motives.

While the forms of paranoia that we can attribute to a Trump or a Clinton are backed by State power, and are thus potentially more apocalyptic, I argue that

20 Carroll, P. (1992). *Liber kaos.* York Beach: Weiser Books.

21 Nietzsche, F. (2000). *On the genealogy of morality: A polemic.* Trans. Carol Diethe. Cambridge: Cambridge University Press.

22 Hughes, M. (February 16, 2017). A spell to bind Donald Trump and all those who abet him: November 16th mass ritual. https://extranewsfeed.com/a-spell-to-bind-donald-trump-and-all-those-who-abet-him-february-24th-mass-ritual-51f3d94f62f4

there's no need to "fight fire with fire" and to continue incubating these tendencies within ourselves. A new wave of laughter-creativity, whether it rolls in on a tide of memetics or something else entirely, seems far more likely to actually cash in on the feel-good sentiments promised by political bumper stickers: "change we can believe in."

BREKEKEKKOAXKOAX!

– "The Frogs" (Aristophanes)

Is Your Mind a Technology for Utopia? (Finding Out Is Easier Than You Think)

Mitch Horowitz

We are faced today with unprecedented possibilities for how to participate in life. This includes virtual relationships, virtual sex, and the changing of one's physicality in ways that our ancestors could not have imagined. These things can be extraordinary, and I think they can be tonic to the human spirit.

Not all of us fit into conventional, biological intimate relations. Traditional relationships and gender identities are not suited to every life; hence, if someone replicates a biological relationship, whether sexual or social, in a digital, virtual reality, or robotic medium, that individual might discover alternative methods of relating that prove extraordinarily helpful and life-enriching.

Anton LaVey, writer, artist, and founder of the Church of Satan, was foresightful about the possibilities of creating "total environments," his term for self-made settings of life. Before his death in 1997, Anton was among a handful of social critics who foresaw and understood the potentials of virtual reality.

There is, of a course, a negative side to all this world making, which is that rather than playing the instrument of technology, the instrument plays us. That is the grotesque reversal of digital utopia. We see this when we discover our privacy invaded. In February 2018, months before the Cambridge Analytica-Facebook scandal, I had a funny and comparatively gentle experience on Twitter. We were remodeling our kitchen, where I happen to keep a collection of hoodoo candles. These are devotional candles dedicated to various African and Latin American saints and deities. After a long day clearing things out, my wife gestured to the candles and asked: "What do you wanna do with this stuff?" I jokingly replied that this *stuff* is deeply meaningful to me, and posted our exchange on Twitter. Almost immediately a kitchen remodeler messaged asking if we needed an estimate on cabinets. I laughed at this, but only briefly. In the months that followed, many of us came to realize that our privacy has been bartered away, and in far more pernicious ways.

Amid all of the technological possibilities and challenges facing us, however, one domain of life remains exquisitely private: the mental realm. We must not neglect a sense of the limitlessness we possess within. I believe that our mental lives hold the capacity to reshape our reality at least as much as technology, and I call for a renewed sense of revolutionary possibility in exploring the causative proprieties of thought.

Earlier generations thrilled over the prospect that a mental act could outpicture in concretized experience. They called it *New Thought*, among other names, none of them very appealing, such as the power of the positive thinking, mental science, and the Law of Attraction. Our generation calls it The Secret. I contend that whatever these mind-power movements may lack in scholarship and aesthetics, they conceal in worthy and practical ideas, which deserve personal experimentation.

Rather than accept any preconceived opinion about such material, often echoed within your peer group or comfort media (which can be particularly limiting), I urge you to take a fresh look, or a first look, at ideas about the formative agencies of the mind. You will find something unexpected.

Extra-Physical Technology?

The question of whether the mind possesses the capacity to make things happen beyond cognitive and motor function involves searching for an extra-physical technology. That search found its most popular expression in America beginning with New England mental healing movement of the mid-to-late 19th century. Yankee seekers from various walks of life wondered whether directed thought, visualization, affirmations, meditations, and prayer could function as a kind of science of mind, capable of producing repeatable and reliable results.

Of course, the ideas and movements to which I am referring are not supposed to be taken seriously by serious people. Rather, a historian is, almost by rote, supposed to speak and write sardonically about such things, lending them only enough notice to say that such notions typify the withering of the American intellect, and sap the individual of his capacity for critical thought, stoicism, political action, and engagement with the grit of daily life. I'm aware of that critique, and I sometimes debate those who proffer it.

Although I share critics' concerns that our national psyche is suffering from coarseness and an alarming lack of depth, I break with the contention that the end user of positive-mind metaphysics is fickle, delusional, or unrewarded in his efforts. That conclusion is largely unexamined. In actuality, there exists an undervalued and often unknown counter-record in our culture, in the form of decades of personal testimony, which captures something of the practical experience of many people who attempt these methods. The testimony of seekers is one of the only ways of actually studying the impact of metaphysics on conduct.

About twenty years ago, I personally became very interested in New Thought philosophy, particularly questions of whether, and to what degree, the mind possesses causative abilities, and whether, and under what circumstances, a person's directed thoughts, visualizations, affirmations, and prayer can alter or augment his experience. To be clear, I reject the notion that life is subject to one mental "super law" or Law of Attraction. We live under many laws and forces. But mind causation may be one, and I am determined to explore the question as a historian and seeker; I consider myself a "believing historian" and personal experience is part of my approach.

Perceived correlations in daily life between thoughts and events could, of course, be attributed to what social scientists call confirmation bias, wherein you get what you're looking for or, put differently, select memories and focal points that conform to expectation. And yet the record of testimony has not only grown and expanded, but, in certain cases, proven testable in an ever-thickening stream of studies in cognition, placebo response, neuroplasticity, and psychical research, even if we do not understand the mechanism at work. In this short space, I will not get into the more contentious area of quantum theory, as I have elsewhere; but suffice to say the ideas emerging from eighty years of quantum experiments about the manner in which observation impacts what appears and where on a subatomic scale have placed us before questions about human nature that are as revolutionary as when the Victorians first encountered Darwin.

Studying the Strange

In recent years, I have been influenced by the spiritual teacher Jiddu Krishnamurti (1895-1986). He emerged from the Vedic tradition but was an unclassifiable voice. In his book *Think On These Things*, Krishnamurti observed that the greatest impediment to self-development and independent thought is the wish for respectability. Nothing does more to stunt personal experiment, he wrote, than the certainty that you must follow the compass point of accepted inquiry. Once you grow fixated on that compass point, nearly everything that you read, hear, and encounter gets evaluated on whether it moves you closer to or further from its direction. This makes independent inquiry extremely difficult for many academics and journalists. Now, this doesn't mean that you shouldn't have high standards and ground rules, or that you abandon discretion. Not at all. But it must mean that do not determine or prejudice your inquiries based on how they will reward your reputation.

As a chronicler of metaphysical experience, I decided several years ago to ask myself: What if I was to turn back the layers on the modern effort to arrive at a utopia of the mind? And what if, in turning back these layers, I were to study the experiences of both seekers and critics, holding neither innately above the other, nor accepting the materialist preconceptions in which I was educated; that is to say, not accepting as a foundation the various opinion-making literature that has often dismissed occult history. Rather, I would leave myself to ask simply, and in an informed manner: How do I know what's here? How do I know what I am going to find? I have my own unavoidable prejudices and preferences, of course, but this was my effort.

Now, I noted that Americans began experimenting with mind-power ideas in the mid-nineteenth century. This was the dawn of the positive-thinking movement. But the concept of mind causation has, in the broadest sense, been around for a long time and expressed in diffuse ways. In *Paradise Lost*, John Milton has Satan say: "The mind is its own place, and in it self Can make a Heav'n of Hell, a Hell of

Heav'n." Satan is an optimist. But it wasn't until the mid-to-late nineteenth century that experimenters sought to methodically test this idea. Although the language of New Thought pioneers was often mystical, many of their inquiries persist today in the fields of placebo studies and neuroplasticity, among others. This is one manner in which occult and mainstream history interweaves.

I want to explore this intersection here, and what it may hold for us as contemporary people, by examining three threads of history. If properly understood, these threads might give us a little bit of a different sense of who we are and some of the possibilities available to us. Indeed, these historical examples may induce a few readers to attempt personal experiments of their own, about which I'll say more before I conclude.

Mind Pioneers

Our first thread appears in the years immediately preceding the French revolution, when there appeared in Paris a Swiss-Viennese lawyer and self-styled healer named Franz Anton Mesmer. Following his arrival in 1778, Mesmer became a sensation in royal courts and salons. The occult healer claimed that an invisible, etheric fluid animated all of life. He called it animal magnetism. Mesmer theorized that by placing a subject into a trance, he could manipulate the subject's animal magnetism and cure him of physical and emotional disorders.

Mesmer was popular among aristocrats who were blissfully unaware that their days were limited. In an overlooked facet of history, however, the occult healer was also popular among revolutionaries and social reformers. Some French radicals reasoned that if Mesmer's theories were correct, and an invisible etheric fluid animated us, it followed that we share in a common life, and are innately equal regardless of rank or birth. Early abolitionists were similarly moved by this ideal. If, say, a nobleman and slave in the West Indies, where France maintained sugar plantations, demonstrated equal capacity to enter a trance, and each displayed the same physical susceptibility to Mesmeric methods, it stood to reason that all beings are intrinsically alike and deserving of equal rights.

What Mesmer actually discovered was not an etheric fluid, but rather, as his best students later grasped, an instinct for the subliminal or subconscious mind. That was his pioneering insight. Mesmer indirectly grasped the existence of the unconscious about a century before psychologists such as Frederic Myers, William James, and Sigmund Freud.

Yet France's medical establishment was suspicious of Mesmer. They derided him as a sorcerer, even as he saw himself in league with scientific and political progress. Taking a cue from social reformers, Mesmer began coupling his theories with revolutionary democratic ideals. He was encouraged in this by his student the Marquis de Lafayette, the French hero of America's War of Independence. With Lafayette's help, Mesmer wrote the war hero's close friend George Washington seeking permission to open teaching institutes in the revolutionary society. In a letter of June 16, 1784, Mesmer told the president: "It appeared to us that the man who merited most of his fellow men should be interested in the fate of every revolution which had for its object the good of humanity."

King Louis XVI was alarmed by the growth of an occult and revolutionary subculture in France. (Protesting too much, the monarch also chaffed at rumors of sexual liberties taken while patients were under trances.) Louis wanted to put an end to Mesmerism. He began by appointing a royal commission to investigate Mesmer's claims. The royal commission convened in 1784 with Benjamin Franklin as its chair. Franklin was then America's ambassador to France, and a respected scientist.

In trials, the commission's investigators found that Mesmeric treatments could induce patients to convulsions and other bodily effects, from coughing blood to temporarily losing the power of speech to sensations of heat or cold, and, in a few instances, reports of comfort or cure. The panelists also noted that many patients when blindfolded could be induced to convulsions if they merely *thought* they were being subjected to Mesmeric methods. Hence, the Franklin commission concluded in August 1784 that Mesmer's cures were all in the mind. In its report, the committee wrote that it had proved "that the imagination alone produces all the effects ... & when the imagination does not act, there are no more effects."

But the Franklin committee left dangling its most tantalizing observation: If the subjects' physical manifestations were in the "imagination alone," why should any effects occur at all? And what is this thing called imagination? If thoughts or imagination can produce physical phenomena, doesn't that, in itself, place us before a deepened question? On this, the committee was silent.

Today, we love talking about the prospect of conscious machines, and the tipping point at which a computer develops awareness. But we are really no closer than the Franklin committee to defining consciousness, even as we seek to replicate it. I know of no definition that covers all the bases. We cannot even settle on whether consciousness is an extra-physical phenomenon, or something restricted to grey matter, no more than the bodily equivalent of bubbles produced in a carbonated liquid. Most materialists would agree with the latter depiction; one materialist philosopher describes human beings as simply "moist robots." Contrary to such views, researchers in particle mechanics, neuroplasticity, placebo reactions, and psychical research repeatedly find suggestions that intelligence, observation, and perspective affect and alter matter, both biologically and on the subatomic particle scale. These fields place us in front of our inability to understand consciousness and imagination, even as some engineers insist we can create it.

Mind as Master?

Our second historical thread takes us away from conscious machines and revolutions to Europe in the early twentieth century. By this time, Mesmerism had travelled a jagged and winding path. Many of Mesmer's students fled France or were imprisoned or killed in the terror following the revolution. The master himself retired to Switzerland where he died in 1815. In decades following Mesmer's death, his trances and theories actually grew more popular in the U.S. than Europe. American mystics, Spiritualists, and positive thinkers eagerly pursued questions of mind healing, and embraced Mesmer's methods.

By the late nineteenth century, the French themselves displayed new affinity for Mesmerism or hypnotism, the preferred term coined in the early 1840s by Scottish physician James Braid. Leaving behind concepts of animal magnetism and cosmic laws, hypnotists saw their treatment as a method of suggestion-based psychotherapy. The method gained popularity though the influence of France's so-called Nancy School, which promoted hypnotism as a practical form of suggestion, relaxation, and psychotherapy. From this milieu emerged one of the most unusual and influential figures from the hypnotherapeutic field: Emile Coué, an amateur hypnotist and druggist from the northwestern town of Troyes. While working as a druggist in the early twentieth century, Coué undertook informal experiments with his customers: he discovered that when he spoke in praise of a medication his clients reported more efficacious results than those who had been told nothing.

These episodes moved Coué toward his signature achievement. The druggist believed that through the power of self-suggestion, or autosuggestion as he termed it, any individual, with nearly any problem, could self-induce the same kinds of positive results he observed in Troyes. In pursuit of a general method, Coué devised a self-affirming mantra: "Day by day, in every way, I am getting better and better." Although most people have not heard of Coué today, many still know his formula. He made this phrase famous through lecture tours of Europe and the U.S. in the early 1920s.

To critics, Coué reflected everything that was fickle and unsound about the Jazz Age. How, they wondered, could anyone believe that this singsong little mantra – "Day by day, in every way, I am getting better and better" – could solve anything? In a facet of Coué's career that is often overlooked, however, he demonstrated considerable insight, later validated by sleep researchers, in how he prescribed using the mantra.

Coué said that you must recite the "day by day" mantra just as you're drifting off to sleep at night, when you're hovering within that very relaxed state between wakefulness and sleep. Today, sleep researchers call these moments hypnagogia. It is an intriguing state of mind during which you possess sensory awareness, but your perceptions of reality bend and morph, like images from a Salvador Dali painting. During hypnagogia, your mind is extremely supple and suggestible. Coué understood this by observation, and he deemed it the period to gently whisper to yourself twenty times: "Day by day, in every way, I am getting better and better." He didn't want you to rouse yourself from your near-sleep state by counting, so he further recommended that you knot a small string twenty times and you use this device like rosary beads to mark off your repetitions. He also said to repeat the same operation just at the moment when you awaken in the morning, which is sometimes called hypnopompia. It is similar to the nighttime state insofar as you occupy a consciousness shadow world and possess just enough awareness to direct your mental workings.

Coué said this routine could reprogram your mind. Was he right? Well, there's one easy way to find out: Why not try it? Are you afraid of a little hands-on philosophy? He intended his mantra to serve all purposes and circumstances. But you can also craft your own simple mantra that reflects a specific desire. However, you might want to start with Coué's original to get comfortable with the practice.

The Beatles tried Coué's method and apparently liked it. References to him appear in some of their songs. In 1967, Paul McCartney used Coué's mantra in the chorus of *Getting Better:* "It's getting better all the time..." and the lyrics paid tribute to the healer: "You gave me the word, I finally heard/ I'm doing the best that I can." John Lennon recited Coué's formula in his 1980 *Beautiful Boy:* "Before you go to sleep, say a little prayer: Every day, in every way, it's getting better and better."

Coué Redux

We now come to our third and final historical thread: placebo researchers at Harvard Medical School recently validated one of Coué's core insights. In January 2014, clinicians from Harvard's program in placebo studies published a paper reporting that migraine sufferers responded better to medication when given "positive information" about a drug. This was the same observation Coué had made in the early 1900s. Harvard's study was considered a landmark because it suggested that the placebo response is operative all the time. It was the first study to use suggestion, in this case news about a drug's efficacy, in connection with an active drug rather than an inert substance, and thus found that personal expectation impacts how, and to what extent, we experience a drug's benefits. Although the Harvard paper echoed Coué's original insight, it made no mention of him.

I wondered whether the researchers had Coué in mind when they designed the study. I asked one of the principals, who did not respond. So, I contacted the director of Harvard Medical School's program in placebo studies, Ted Kaptchuk, a remarkable and inquisitive clinician who also worked on the study. "Of course I know about Coué," Kaptchuk told me. "'I'm getting better day by day…' " He agreed that the migraine study could coalesce with Coué's observations, though the researchers were not thinking of him when they designed it.

It seems clear that Coué's instincts were in the right direction. And I believe that some people have experienced genuine help through his ideas. So, once more, I invite you to disregard expectation and to self-experiment with Coué's method. We all possess the private agency of personal experiment; indeed, it may be the area in life in which we are most free. Yet we often get so wrapped up in the possibilities of digital culture and the excitement of social media that we neglect the technology of thought, through which we may be able to significantly reform some aspect of ourselves or our surrounding world.

Like Satan, I'm an optimist. How wonderful it is that everyone possesses the capacity to engage in the inner experiments of mental utopianism. These little attempts at revolution are your birthright: exquisitely voluntary and always available. No power source required.

I'm Gonna Blow Your Mind

Ramsey Dukes

Yes indeed! I have something so important, so astounding to tell you that I just cannot hold back a moment longer. I have to break this news…

The person writing this article is no-one less than *The World's Greatest Story Teller.*

No! No!! No!!! I absolutely must try to restrain my natural inclination towards self-effacing modesty.

For the real truth is that Ramsey Dukes is not merely *The Greatest Story Teller in the World, he is The Greatest Story Teller Ever in the Entire History of the World. Since Time Immemorial.*

I told you this was big.

I have also been gifted with the most exceptional psychic powers.

Even though I do not know you, and may never even have heard of you – I refer to *the individual human being* now reading this text – I am gifted with an uncanny perception that you might not believe me. I sense that you may be wondering why, if this should be the case, you have not heard my name being lauded in the media, showered with literary awards, subject to endless rave reviews…

What!

Don't tell me you pay any heed to that snivelling mob of lick-spittle sycophants? Those empty-headed gas-bags, paid to put their worthless names to cliched (and seldom true) statements like "Astounding", "Dazzling", "Groundbreaking", "the most important book of the year" or "a triumph" – statements to be highlighted all over the garish covers of mindless, derivative, dreary so-called "best sellers"?

No. If you want to discover the real truth, you do not waste time with hack reviewers being paid by word count. Instead you interview people with real insider perception. You go direct to *Those In The Know.*

Naturally – as the epitome of the sort of alert, enlightened and intellectually curious individual who would elect to read the works of Ramsey Dukes – you want some examples. So let me begin with The Big One, oft described as *The Greatest Story Ever Told.*

Yes, I am busy rewriting *The Holy Bible* – as it could have been, if only God had asked me.

It contains a book about a character called Job (not connected with Apple, that comes earlier. In Genesis.)

Alfred Lord Tennyson called *The Book of Job* "the greatest poem of ancient and modern times". It tells a sad story of Job, a wealthy land owner and family man, being steadily stripped of everything in his life, leaving him destitute – even though he is a goodly, God-fearing man, guilty of no sin.

My new version begins in a similar vein, and Job does receive the message that his livestock have all died. But, instead of receiving more of these awful messages, in my version the next message comes direct from God. He apologises to Job, admitting it was simply a trial of his fortitude. God then announces that, in compensation, Job's animals are now being restored from the dead.

Neat, eh?

I cannot tell you what Job said when he read my version, because he was rendered speechless. He simply flung his arms around me and sobbed his gratitude. His family described my re-write as "the best thing that has ever happened".

In contrast, I'll illustrate the scope of my talent with another, very different, example. The novel *Casino Royale* by Ian Fleming has James Bond, as a British secret agent, playing a high stakes poker game with an evil underworld banker called Le Chiffre. This is just the start of a hellish game of cat and mouse that begins with Bond losing all his money.

In my improved version, however, I have added a clever twist. Instead of losing, Bond wins everything from Le Chiffre, who is aghast. He turns to Bond and says: "My God, Bond, if the British Secret Service employs men of your calibre, the criminal underworld hasn't got a hope in Hell. I'm going straight." Bond then has the good fortune to break the Casino bank, he chucks in his job and retires to life on a luxury yacht with Vesper, his new woman friend.

The reaction? "Ramsey, old boy, you're a real brick", says James. "You know, that sick bastard Fleming was having me stripped naked, tied into a seatless chair while my balls were being bashed with a carpet beater. Your version is… sheer genius!"

I have so many more examples. Tolstoy has nothing but praise for my updates of his novels – notably a slim volume called *And Peace*. Soon anyone who is anyone will be quoting my iconic opening sentence to the new *Tale of Two Cities:* "It was the best of times, it was the Age of Wisdom, it was the epoch of belief, it was the season of Light, it was the spring of hope."

My triumphs are simply boundless. And yet, tuning into my uncanny perception of your, the reader's, innermost thoughts, I sense a distinct impression that you might still remain not one hundred percent convinced.

I'll have to try another approach.

The Threefold Way

The trinity of the Good, the Beautiful, and the True dates back to the *Bhagavad Gita* and the teachings of Plato, if not earlier. For Aristotle they were the transcendent properties of existence – both as three categories of knowledge, and as their ideal forms.

Later, we no longer see them as perfect Platonic forms, but rather as three fundamental perspectives on reality. As with the later Christian trinity, these three are not competing rivals, they are distinct and yet dynamically interlinked. Beauty is Truth, Truth is Beauty, Good is Beautiful and everything Beautiful is Good – ideas that found a new flowering in the Renaissance. At which time the three began to be fragmented by division.

The protestant revolution turned against the popular cod-polytheism of the Catholic church, where *The One God* is mediated by a host of saints, angels, colourful relics and statues. Protestantism was fiercely monotheistic and puritan in its attack on all "hocus pocus" – as it mockingly labelled the "hoc est corpus meum" of Catholic transubstantiation. Magic in any form was outlawed by these puritans. Where Catholic scripture had been read aloud in Latin – making a music open to endless aesthetic interpretations – the Bible was now translated into common language to be read in silence and understood only as a single source of truth. Beauty was demoted, leaving only Goodness and Truth. Out of this ascetic rationalisation grew modern science, where even Goodness has been demoted. It leaves Truth standing alone, as our culture's sole measure of value.

Beauty and Goodness are still admitted, but as mere sops for the lower, emotional parts of our highly evolved brains. Art is allowed as a sort of play-pen for those who cannot manage without it, while Religion plays a similar role for those too superstitious to fully embrace the Truth of Science. The richness of experience has been reduced to a single dimension, spanning Truth and Delusion. And digitization has since collapsed that dimension and all human experience has been reduced to two binary states: True or False.

Not only has this impoverished the richness of human experience – it has sullied Truth itself. Truth and Reality are now dirty words. When did you last hear phrases such as "let's face the facts" or "the truth/reality is that…" introducing a statement or concept that is actually beautiful or good?

We do not hear "let's face the fact that existence is pure joy", "that life is beautiful", or "the plain truth is that the universe is the manifestation of God's infinite wisdom and love". Instead we are told to face the truth that "entropy increases monotonically", "the universe does not care", "shit happens", that "life is tough" or simply "life is a terminal, sexually-transmitted condition".

"Truth" and "Reality" are now nothing more than labels on a crock of shit. So why are some people so amazed by others' acceptance and welcome of a post-truth culture?

The majority do lack deep perception and awareness of Beauty and Goodness. When some politician promises to make our nation great, the establishment rails against the statement's want of Truth, rather than recognise it as a piece of froth lightly flavoured with some artificial essence of Beauty and Goodness in place of real nourishment. As junk food it will leave the public even hungrier for something that is no longer allowed recognition.

He or she will win the vote, and the opposition's only recourse is to scream "but that is not True!" – rather than to recognise a natural, human hunger for other criteria of value.

I am not crying for The Truth to be abandoned, but for a recognition of the equal value, and interdependence, of The Beautiful and The Good. Instead of assessing the words of leaders, media and preachers purely on grounds of Truth, we need to develop our awareness of – and sensitivity to – Beauty and Goodness. Then we can better examine those fake essences that politicians and media currently add to deceive us – and dig down in search of real Beauty, Goodness and Truth.

It is also time that leaders, media and preachers themselves acknowledged what they are doing, and learned to seek out, foster and deliver a greater measure of these three qualities to an increasingly hungry and critical public.

Why Now?

Such issues became vivid in my own life when I was preparing the transcript of my *Abramelin Diary* for publication by Aeon Books. It was a modest project, for the manuscript had already been transcribed and edited (and the person hired by the publisher to complete the task had suffered a breakdown and been institutionalized).

And yet that modest task spun out for over a year. In which time I experienced my first sign of cancer; I underwent three operations; my office suffered a fire, rising damp and an actual flood (not bad going in a year when Cape Town was suffering its worst ever drought). In particular my office was burgled for the first time and the only things stolen were the computer system hosting my written work plus, unfortunately, the backup drive.

As a "belt and braces man", however, I also had an off-site wireless backup – so was not desperate, until I discovered that its sparsebundle was corrupt. I then spent a fortune on recovery software and weeks of disk recovery services, but all was lost. Meanwhile ripples of torment seem to be spreading out across friends, family and neighbours.

Hearing about this, some people's reaction was to say that I should abandon the publication of this accursed magical diary. Others asked why I had not got the message that the great magician Ramsey Dukes should banish and blast these Abramelin demons out of his life to restore normality.

But I did neither. I persisted. Sure, things were getting pretty bad – but hasn't the whole world been getting pretty bad in recent years? I could not believe that a magical diary describing a not very successful operation by a minor occult practitioner could really present such a threat to global stability.

During one aeroplane flight it occurred to me that – if it was indeed so important for the universe to stall the publication of this book – then why not simply kill me and have done with it?

In the light of such fresh perspectives, my whole period of torment began to appear somewhat playful. I was being written into a great narrative: not simply editing a diary, I was suffering the anticipated torments of all who seriously attempt the notoriously dangerous Abramelin Operation. I was living the myth that had defeated even the Great Aleister Crowley himself. I was experiencing something cosmic, archetypal – and yet there were people who wanted me to stop right there!

It was the reverse of the response I had from Job. It went beyond stoicism. I was raising my arms to heaven and screaming "BRING IT ON!"

Yet not much more happened.

No Two Ways About It

The puritan doctrine infusing our scientific culture has demoted The Good and The Beautiful and recognises just one principle, The True. This is the epitome of the monotheistic principle that admits only one single deity or absolute. It is why scientists seek only THE theory of everything and THE truth, and it goes against humanity's more natural embrace of multiplicity.

THE theory of natural selection is now presented as a mono-justification for all life on earth. Darwin himself, in his later book, *The Descent of Man*, proposed the second complementary "theory of sexual selection": the peacock's tail defies "the survival of the fittest", but it evolves that way because peahens find it attractive.

But not even Darwin is permitted to admit Beauty: the neo-Darwinians justify this aberration by suggesting that "the reason it attracts the peahen is because its very unfitness must imply exceptional genes in the surviving peacock." At a stroke, Darwin's genius has been reduced to a "Barnum Statement" as follows: should any creature diverge from normality towards greater fitness, then natural selection will lead the gene pool in that direction; on the other hand, should any creature diverge towards lesser fitness, then natural selection (via sexual preference) will lead the gene pool in that opposite direction. A theory of stasis, not evolution.

The Taoists at least recognise two principles, Yin and Yang. And, however hard Christianity aspires to pure monotheism, its followers keep reverting to the Manichean concept of God versus the Demi-urge or Devil.

As a variation on the trinity of Goodness, Beauty and Truth, my book *The Good, The Bad, The Funny* extends the Manichean duality by welcoming The Trickster as a third player, as in some African religions.

To Issue Fourth

Then, in *My Years of Magical Thinking* I propose a four dimensional playing field for human experience. I explore the possibility of a fourth transcendental property, but struggle to label it. Instead I suggest that the three cultures of Art, Religion and Science should be completed by a fourth culture of Magic. Then my question becomes: "where does Magic lead us, if not just towards Goodness, Beauty and/or Truth?"

The best I could come up with was something on the lines of Fulfillment, Growth, or ultimately Wholeness, to complete my compass of four directions.

There is indeed something less universal and more individual and personal about Magic, compared to the other three cultures. Both Aleister Crowley and

Dion Fortune described it in terms of changes in accordance with will – ie a move towards a personally desired state that certainly embraces elements of Beauty, Goodness and Truth, and yet it is never completely defined by them.

The trouble is that our society is even more naïve about Magic than it is about Art and Religion. In my dazzling career as *The World's Greatest Story Teller,* I offer James Bond what he most desires. That is a low form of magic, but it is what the majority understands by the word. I did not offer James a *Significant Growth Experience.*

Ian Fleming would have James suffer his balls being bashed by a carpet beater – an event designed to increase the book's aesthetic value to the reader by upping the ante to our hero's ultimate triumph. Whether James appreciated that gift while enduring the pain is not spelled out. In the greater context of his ultimate victory, the circumstance might at least be acknowledged as an opportunity for Growth – a higher magic than that offered by *The World's Greatest Story Teller.*

Not that *Casino Royal* is presented as some New Age manual – *Discover Your Inner Hero With A Carpet Beater* – but simply that a greater openness to Beauty and Goodness might add further dimensions to the reader's as well as James' experience.

All these re-written characters can see some good in my transformations, and they bless me for it. But it is not The Good – for why should James Bond be given such an unfair advantage? They also see great beauty in my versions of their stories, but it is not The Beautiful – because you, the reader, can tell that, from a literary and dramatic viewpoint, my stories are utter crap. Least of all are my stories True, or even a match for the second-rate criterion of "True to Life".

And yet my versions offer a relief, a liberation, and something of enormous value to the characters involved – for I entered their world as a magician with the power to realise their greatest dreams. I replaced the limitations and frustrations of their literary existence with a playing field levelled for ultimate Fulfillment.

Thus, to any individual, the direction that I ascribe to Magic – towards Personal Fulfillment, or Wholeness – is surely the most desirable of all. And yet our culture denies Magic even the modest roles allowed to Art and Religion. Magic is so *Not The Truth* that it is non-existent.

Encompassing

In *My Years of Magical Thinking,* I extol the value of directional over categorical perception. Where well-defined categories – so beloved by Reason – reduce experience into exclusive fragments, directions prove inclusive.

In my furthest venture to the North, when I visited Carl Abrahamsson in Stockholm, I found myself surrounded by every bit as much East, West, North – and even South – as in my home in Cape Town.

That is how I see my four dimensions of existence as a compass of four directions: Art, Religion, Science and Magic.

Practice Science as I feel it should be practiced (and seldom is outside Waldorf education) and you should discover not just Truth but also some measure of Goodness, Beauty and even personal Fulfillment.

Practice Art as I feel it should be practiced and you should discover not just Beauty but also Fulfillment, Goodness, and Truth.

Practice Religion rightly and expect to find some measures of Goodness, Beauty, Fulfillment and Truth.

I have less to go on in the case of Magic, apart from my own experience. There I have had a taste of Fulfillment, definitely Beauty and Goodness, as well as – hold onto your seats – profound Truth.

Let us therefore dance from here into a space of four dimensions.

Are you sitting comfortably?

Then listen to the voice of *The World's Greatest Story Teller …*

Grasping Reality with Gary Lachman

Carl Abrahamsson

My respect for the work of American author Gary Lachman has been (and still is!) enormous. His many biographies of key players in "esoteric" history serve both as introductions to these people, and as general reference works covering a field so vast and fascinating that a single lifetime isn't enough to fully explore everything in-depth on one's own. Lachman is an excellent and enthusiastic guide, exploring the minds of people who have undeniably helped shape the culture(s) we live in. Whether it's in concrete biographies of people like Aleister Crowley, Helena Blavatsky, Rudolf Steiner, and Carl Jung, or in political histories imbued with esoteric influences (as in his excellent *Politics and the Occult, Dark Star Rising – Magick and Power in the Age of Trump,* and *The Return of Holy Russia*), or in overviews/studies of consciousness itself (as in *The Secret Teachers of the Western World,* and *Lost Knowledge of the Imagination*), Lachman's work is immensely inspiring in its unmistakable curiosity, as well as in its eloquent handling of usually quite complex concepts. Seen from that perspective, Gary Lachman is undoubtedly one of the world's leading fellow magico-anthropologists.

The following interview took place in London in 2016, and focuses on Lachman's book about his mentor and friend, the British author Colin Wilson: *Beyond the Robot – The Life and Work of Colin Wilson.*

Carl Abrahamsson: It's obvious that this is a different kind of book for you, because you had a concrete relationship with Mr. Wilson. Has the process of writing this book been different from writing about the other subjects?

Gary Lachman: Yes, it was different. I even said when asked if I would write a book about him, that I wouldn't be able to do it until he had passed on. I think it's clear from my other books that I'm a fan of his. His sort of work has definitely informed books I've written. But I think that aside from a few articles and reviews, and a couple of chapters here and there, this is like the first full on treatment of him. It was very different writing about someone that I knew. Trying to be as balanced as I could, and at the same time not denying that this was obviously someone that had a big impact on me as a mentor and a friend. And also someone whose ideas deserve to be better known – just like many of the other people I've written about. Colin Wilson wrote so much about so many different things that people don't necessarily have a clear idea about the philosophy that links these different concerns together. I mean, they usually know *The Outsider,* his first book, or they will know later books about the occult, and so on... I think that the work that he labored with in the 1960s, in obscurity mostly – what he called the "new existentialism" – is, sadly, pretty much unknown. I'm trying to focus a lot on that in the book too. So it's certainly not a "warts-and-all" sort of biography; it's an intellectual biography. You could say it's a sort of biography of ideas; of his ideas, but also of his life. In some places, I turn up here and there, because I am part of the story. So, you're right, it was a very different kind of book to write. In a way, I feel that it pushed my writing into a different area, and in some ways there's a different voice in there that became clear to me after I'd finished the whole process. You read it a few times, and then pick it up again; sort of picking out some excerpts in order to put them online. And you go, "Oh yeah, that's very interesting! That sounds very different!"

CA: You wrote the introduction to the anniversary edition of *The Outsider*. I think you were the obvious choice for that. You are on the inside of that environment, as someone who knew him, and who knows his work extensively. Is there an actual environment, like a clique of Colin Wilson aficionados that have views about this?

GL: Certainly, there is a large and internationally spread group of people that are interested in his work. Earlier this year, there was the first Colin Wilson conference at Nottingham University, at the University library there. The Colin Wilson archive was established a few years ago by Colin Stanley, who is Wilson's bibliographer. He is also the editor and publisher of Paupers' Press, which is a small press which specializes in Wilson material, and also related kinds of things. In fact, one of the first things I published was a couple of essays for Stanley, about Wilson's work. He donated this wonderful collection that he had of Wilson's books to the archive, set that up, and then organized this conference. People came from Australia, the United States, parts of Europe... It was a good show of interesting, different approaches to his work. I think out in the wider public there's definitely an interest in his work. I think he's always had a core kind of readership: people like myself, who read one or two of his books, and found that they were connected, and sought out the other books. Then there are people that know him through the bigger kinds of books. He wrote so much that you could know *The Outsider*, and maybe not some of his other books, or his science fiction novels, like *The Mind Parasites*; or *The Philosopher's Stone*, where he blends phenomenology with Lovecraft themes and things like that; or his books on crime, and so on. But behind it all is his existential approach to philosophy, experience, and consciousness that he hammered away at, mostly in obscurity, in the 1960s. He came back in the 1970s with *The Occult*. That was his comeback book. And that's the first book of his that I read in 1975, when I was playing in Blondie in New York, and living on the Bowery. I found it amongst all this other stuff from the previous generation: Castaneda, Leary, and all these kinds of thing. It grabbed me because I had an interest in the occult before then, but Wilson starts off talking about Nietzsche and Gurdjieff. There were all these other people in there, so it wasn't a book about haunted houses and things like that.

CA: An un-romantic occultist?

GL: I later realized that he himself said, "I took the money because I needed the commission." Basically, he was broke. He was lucky to have accepted it, but he first thought that he'd have to write most of it with his tongue in cheek, as it were. But after he'd done the research, he realized that, "Oh well, there is more there than meets the eye... There is more evidence there to suggest that something is really happening." This was my first introduction to it, aside from weird literature: Lovecraft, or people like Arthur Machen turning up in the Lovecraft world... It just had a huge impact on me at the time. I read it, and that led me to read all the other books.

CA: For me, that's one of his greatest aspects. It's not ambivalence; it's a sort of integrated, critical approach and yet, an absolute open-mindedness. Particularly in *The Strength to Dream*, I think. A very subjective run-through of art history, and it's a very critical approach. In it, he writes, "The imagination, then, is merely another tool of the human mind, like reason, its purpose being to work with reason in the task of correlating the 'facts' of experience."[1]

GL: It is a very alive mind. It's not as if he has it all figured out already. It's like a mystery, the way he writes. It's almost like a detective story in the way that you follow him as he follows all the different clues and possibilities, and checks out all the evidence, and then gradually comes to a conclusion. It's very satisfying, that kind of intellectual narrative.

CA: Yes, that's one side of it: to have the mental capacity to grasp all these things, to integrate the knowledge. But he was also just a great writer, and here I would like to make a very distinct clear analogy to your work, in the sense that you have both those aspects, too. I have to say again how much I enjoyed *The Secret Teachers of the Western World.*

GL: Thank you.

CA: You have really put it together in such a coherent way. And I see that you've woven in something new that I hadn't seen before in your work: this thing at the beginning of the book, with the brain research.

GL: That was the real motor for the book. I had read this wonderful book called *The Master and His Emissary* by Iain McGilchrist, and it really reboots the whole left brain/right brain discussion; he opens it up in a new way. The sort of rivalry that Gilchrist talks about going on between the two brains; it seemed to me to sort of fit right in there. I would have to say that any facility I have in writing is from reading

1 Colin Wilson, *The Strength to Dream*, Abacus/Sphere Books, London, 1976, p 186.

Wilson's books over and over again, because I basically try to be as clear as possible. It sounds like a cliché, but for me it's an adventure; it's a journey when you're writing; it's not as if you have it all figured out or anything. People ask, "What's your next book about?" "I'll tell you when I've finished it!" That's what I have to do now; start a new one. He was a wonderful writer; he was very clear, and he also comes from that last generation of the kind of independent public intellectual; not affiliated with a university; not an academic; not an expert. Scholarly, but not a scholar. I don't think there are many of those around anymore. Arthur Koestler was one; there were other ones, too.

CA: Why do you think that *The Outsider* became such a successful book, more or less immediately?

GL: Well, I think the time was right for something to happen. The "angry young man" phenomenon that Wilson was a part of in the mid-1950s in England, in London, wasn't that different from the rise of Elvis Presley or other rock figures; or James Dean, the actor. Wilson certainly fit in with that young rebel; a truculent kind of character. It happened in August, the "silly season," when the British newspapers don't have anything to write about. Parliament is not sitting, so there's no politics. Most of the news in the UK is about politics. So in the summers they are looking for some story... As Wilson tells it, his book *The Outsider* comes out, and around about the same time the play by John Osborne, "Look Back in Anger," debuts. The press kind of linked them together with a bunch of other people like John Braine and Kingsley Amis, and came up with this phrase: "the angry young men." It's supposedly attributed to J.B. Priestley, but we don't know for sure. This was the new literary generation that everyone had been expecting since the end of the war. There had been writers and all that, but they had been lukewarm and not particularly exciting. And then you have this brash, new, young rebellious generation: a kind of button-down, welfare state version of the Beat generation. Not quite as wild, not quite as exotic, but still something along those lines. There was even an anthology called *The Beat Generation and the Angry Young Men* that came out in the late 1950s; sort of linking them together. So, yes, the newspapers went to town with it. Wilson was amazed to wake up – I think it was May 26th, 1956 – to realize that the last ten years he had spent disciplining himself to become a writer; writing in his journal over and over again about the genius he was. It became true, like a Cinderella story: he was right! You can't take that away from him. No matter what you think, he woke up and he was very happy. We had people like Cyril Connolly, Toynbee, Priestley, and others in the big daily newspapers, and the Sunday supplement papers, saying what a brilliant work this was: Britain's homegrown existentialist! He's up there with Sartre and Camus, and all those guys over there in Paris on the Rive Gauche, and this was something that was obviously exciting. And also, the story was fantastic! Wilson left school when he was sixteen; hitchhiked around England and France a couple of times; he famously slept on

Hampstead Heath instead of paying rent for a place while he was working on his first novel by day up there in the reading room of the British library; worked a number of menial jobs: at coffee houses, as a navvy, as a laborer, digging ditches, and whatever. For years and years and years, and writing, writing, writing. He was working on his first novel, *Ritual in the Dark*, which was published in 1960. It's a great first novel, and it's also a great London novel. Its simplest précis is to say that it's Jack the Ripper meets The Brothers Karamazov, in duffle-coated 1950s London. While he was writing that, a friend of his had published a couple of articles in a poetry magazine about the crisis in modern literature, or something along those lines. He realized that some of the themes that he had talked about had turned up in these articles. He felt spurred. On a cold Christmas Day, on his own in a room in South London, he starts scribbling in his notebook the beginnings of *The Outsider*. Which is, as you know, about this existentialist hero who sees too deeply and too much, and who recognizes the chaos underneath the thin crust of civilization that everyone else ignores, and so on. When the book came out, it was an overnight sensation.

CA: I can see many similarities between you. You have written his biography, and you were a friend. But I'm also thinking of versatility and self-discipline: a necessity for a large productivity. Was that something that you felt you already had when you started out as a writer? Or would you say that he actually influenced you in that way too, in terms of the actual productivity?

GL: Very much so. I can say candidly that I very much modelled myself as a writer on him, ages ago. I fancied myself a poet, and I wrote quite a bit of very bad poetry; and then that got transformed into songwriting, and I was suddenly playing in (the band) Blondie. For the longest time, I wanted to be a writer. That was much more of a satisfactory romantic ideal than being a pop star. It took the longest time for me to write something passable. I took a very practical approach to it; after writing in journals, trying to be a genius – whatever that means – I was getting writers' and artists' handbooks. "If you want to sell an article, do this!" So I followed the recipe, and you know what? It worked! So I said, "okay, this is what you do! Forget all the bohemians and Beats; you have to do this, you get up and work..." That's what I did. What can I say? I'm ecstatic, because I can survive writing about the things I love. But in order to do that I have to take a very disciplined approach. I think that my nature is like that too. I'm one of these people who feel like they have to constantly justify their existence, so I keep producing something so that I don't feel like I'm just lingering around. But I started writing much later. I didn't get published. I mean, I had magazine articles and book reviews, but my first book didn't come out until my early 40s. Unless I live to be hundred something, I won't catch up to Wilson's number. But that's not quite the aim, to do that; it's to keep on as much as I can. But yeah, you're right: I do take very seriously getting a daily quota of work done; meeting deadlines and that sort of thing. Because unless you're independently wealthy, unless you've got a big hit, there's no way to survive. You just have to do it.

CA: What about other things that could be seen as more specific inspirations? Did he actually talk to you about your writing?

GL: Well, he gave me some advice that proved to be good. You have to remember that I was one of many people who knew him as well; friends and all that. I wasn't the only one that was talking to him. I remember sending him writing over the years. He would be very kind and generous, and would make comments about it. For a while, I was trying to write this occult thriller based on a battle between Aleister Crowley and Rudolf Steiner, and it was kind of a pastiche that didn't happen…

CA: It's never too late to finish it.

GL: I can always go back to it! It's something I would like to try and do; that's the next challenge. But this was back in the early 1990s, when I was still living in LA. I sent him something, and he was very encouraging about it. But when I wrote my first book, *Turn Off Your Mind*, my revisionist look at the occult 1960s, I sent him a couple of early chapters. He said, "this sounds too much, you know, like you're trying to say something." Meaning in terms of some sort of sociology, and he said, "just tell the story." I said, "well actually, I am trying to say something," But he implied that it was kind of boring, you know, bang! Straight to the chase! So I did change some things, and he said, "yeah, that's more like it." I never looked back after that.

CA: That is what I find so wonderful about *Secret Teachers:* that you weave in more things, aspects, from more perspectives; more than merely telling the story.

GL: I see it as a whole; seeing the whole history of the West, of Western culture. It isn't that it's some conspiracy theory; that this stuff is "hidden." It isn't really hidden. All you have to do is go find it; it's there. I like making those connections, and one of the things I'm happy about, is that I wrote quite a few books before I wrote the one on Colin. What I tried to do is to incorporate his outlook; the basic sort of vision into this broader connection with people. What I'm trying to do is make connections between all the things I read over the years and found interesting. There is no kind of overarching theory or anything like that. I just read lots of stuff and I find connections between them, and they excite me. They have to do with consciousness and culture and so on, and so on. What I found myself doing in the last few books, is look at that we have this kind of esoteric view; we have this perspective coming from Iain McGilchrist about the rebooting of the hemispheric differences; and we got this background of Colin's ideas about consciousness and phenomenology. And actually they are all related: they are all talking about the same thing but from different perspectives. I'm sure an expert in these fields would say, you know, "tut-tut... You're making these connections without seeing this or that..." you know, blah-blah-blah. But to me, the fundamental suggestion is that there is another mode of consciousness that is already accessible to us now, and which we experience many times, but we don't articulate it clearly as being that. That's what this sort of stuff is to me: developing a language to be able to recognize that it's just part of our being in the world.

CA: You've written biographies of many key people in the "occult" or spiritual movements or environments: Crowley, Blavatsky, Steiner, et al. Have you usually encountered interest or hostility from these various environments?

GL: In a way I think it's an occupational hazard in these kinds of environment. The first thing you have to do is fight off the general mainstream's dismissal of it; you've got to fight for your corner. When you've done that, you've kind of entrenched yourself; you've made fortifications, and it's difficult to relax those later on. I've written about Swedenborg, Steiner, Crowley, Ouspensky, Blavatsky, and so on. There are some kinds of followers that feel they own these people, and you have to approach with caution. I think the most flak I got was from the Crowley crowd. Understandable, but Crowley, along with Colin Wilson, was one of the first writers that I went to in 1975. I was a true believer for a while in my late teens, into my early 20s, but I basically outgrew Crowley. In my book about him, I try to give a balanced take on it. Critical, but still taking him seriously, because I think that's what these people cry out for: to be taken seriously. Obviously not to be just dismissed out of hand, but also not to have a kind of rapt worship or uncritical acceptance of them. Because then it becomes religious or "occultic." I've had some flak from different people, and so on, but it's understandable. Nobody's right, folks! But that's fine. These things are up for discussion. I try not to be dogmatic; all the questions are open... In writing the introduction to *The Outsider*, I boiled it down to a simple phrase: "The outsider is someone who is looking for life more abundant," as they say in the Gospels. Not to put the religious emphasis on it, but basically that you want more intensity of being, or intensity of experience. All these different approaches for me are ways of gaining some access to that. And they're all good, and they all have dead ends, and they all have detours, and they all have paths which are worth following, and so on, and so on. I just try to keep in mind that all the people I write about I respect, very much. I think that comes through in the writing.

CA: In terms of these key esoteric people, is there some project that you have wanted to delve into, but for some reason had to scrap because you couldn't get into it, or couldn't get access to material?

GL: I would like to write a book about Jean Gebser; introducing his philosophy. But my German isn't good enough to read his texts in the original, and there isn't a lot translated into English. But I have been corresponding with someone who has worked on Gebser, and translated him. It's a while ago now, but we talked about working together. That is something I would like to do. Following on from *Beyond the Robot*, what I would like to do is edit some of Colin Wilson's phenomenological journals that he kept from the early 1960s, and into the 1970s. Most of this material is from the 1960s, when he was writing and developing his "New Existentialism," in the series of books called "The Outsider Cycle." It's a shame these books were not really noticed. The one following *The Outsider – Religion and the Rebel* – was universally panned, but it's actually a very interesting book. There are some others too: fantastic books, like *Origins of the Sexual Impulse*, where he writes fantastic stuff about a variety of different perversions; the whole idea of "what constitutes a sexual perversion? In humans, what constitutes natural sex?" It came out early 1960s, and it was published as part of his "Outsider Cycle." It's actually the first book where he starts talking about Husserlian phenomenology, and he's basically applying phenomenology to the sexual orgasm. He says in one of the journals, "If someone asked me what is it that I want to do with my writing, if I could say it in one sentence, it is basically to capture the meaning of sexual orgasm." So he writes about sex a great deal. There are two books following *Ritual in the Dark*. His existential hero is a fellow named Gerard Sorme. He's in *Ritual in the Dark*, and he's in another book, too. Its original title was *Man Without a Shadow*, but the original publisher thought that wasn't feisty enough, so they called it *The Sex Diary of Gerard Sorme*. It's written as a kind of journal. Basically, it's about his exploration of sex; looking for a mystical kind of peak experience. The character in it is based on Crowley. There's a character called Caradoc Cunningham. He is a sexual magician, and Wilson's hero gets involved with him, and so on, and so on. The third one is called *God of the Labyrinth*. This is one of the things that Wilson did in his fiction: he took a genre and used it for his philosophical purposes. *God of the Labyrinth* is almost like a sort of soft core erotica. The hero ends up writing a biography of an 18th century rake who was part of a cult of the Phoenix: a sex magic kind of group. Wilson's pursuit of ideas is basically like a detective story, and this book is actually dedicated to (Jorge Luis) Borges. Mostly, it went by kind of unnoticed. What I tried to do in my biography was to bring this to the fore, because I think it definitely needs to be noticed. It's a serious philosophical analysis of human experience. Wilson wasn't particularly interested in drugs. There's an appendix to one of the later books in "The Outsider Cycle" called *Beyond the Outsider*, where there is a mescaline trip. Of course, there was Huxley's *The Doors of Perception*, and he decided to try it. It wasn't a particularly fruitful experience for him. Alcohol was his drug of choice. He wrote a wonderful book about it: *A Book of Booze*. But the mystical trigger for him was sex. He wrote about sex a lot. But it wasn't that he pursued Tantric sex or anything like that, and he didn't have wild affairs. He was actually a hard-working family man. So basically, he just applied his analytical mind to sexual experiences that he had, to try and understand it; "what is it? Why does man want to penetrate a woman?" Which may sound like a stupid question. But actually, when you think about it, well, why, you know? What's actually going on? And he developed this whole fantastic philosophy about it. It was through Wilson that I could see a link, a philosophical link between different worlds. In many ways, it's what I've been trying to do, trying to articulate: to bring these ideas into the general conversation. We can't keep it as weird stuff in the margins anymore. At the same time, it doesn't mean to say that we all have to go out and start reading Tarot, or meditate, or whatever. It's just that the fundamental ideas about consciousness inform the esoteric tradition, and they need to be brought into the general conversation.

CA: There's usually some kind of filter when you look at truly creative individuals. When people start to talk about really influential people like Steve Jobs, or someone like that, there's often mention of LSD, for instance. There's always a filter that allows people to be more creative. There's always some kind of esoteric connection; some kind of school of philosophy, or esoteric teaching, or something like that, lurking in the background.

GL: It's part of our being. It's there. If what it is that we're trying to do is ignore or marginalize some other part of ourselves within culture, what is that but some kind of schizophrenia?

CA: Totally.

GL: I guess the hope is that through some sort of broadening acceptance, or at least interest in these kinds of ideas, a slow kind of shift and integration will happen. But that's not something I can see happening right now. That was kind of the cautionary tale of the 1960s. It was fun and exciting to plunge into the unconscious, but... "there be demons!" They are infested waters. That's not to say "don't do it," but, you know, just letting it rip, that won't come up with any official results. So perhaps we can recognize these pendulum swings? We can look back and see that if we become conscious of certain things, is there some way that we can integrate the experience? Isn't that what the "Great Work" actually is?

CA: I think that the pendulum analogy is very good, because for each time it swings, to either extreme, it becomes more clearly marked: both the negative and the positive positions.

GL: Well, it's Hegel, but I prefer Arnold Toynbee when I talked about the Goldilocks theory of history: where you get it just right – those moments when it's just right. It's not too hot, it's not too cold, it's just right. Not just the left brain, not just the right, but just right together. I mean, Gilchrist points to several different places in

Western history. Ancient Greece, the Renaissance, the Romantic period… I try to end on a hopeful note in Secret Teachers. It looks like we may be out of material here, you know?

CA: What is your next project?

GL: Well, the next book is *The Lost Knowledge of the Imagination*. It's a theme that runs through *Secret Teachers* as well: this whole other kind of learning of the imagination. The title of the phrase comes from Kathleen Raine: the poet, Blake scholar, essayist and founder of Temenos Academy here in London, which is dedicated to the perennial philosophy, and the learning of the imagination. It was while working on the book, and thinking about this whole idea: what does that mean… "the lost knowledge of the imagination"? I actually did an online course over the summer, for the California Institute of Integral studies, who are located in San Francisco, about this; is there a kind of knowledge? In the sense of "real" knowledge? Not something subjective that comes through the imagination by itself. OK, yes, imagination helps us get more scientific knowledge, but I'm talking of a different, particular kind of knowledge. What I'm going to do in this book is try to narrow that down. It's going to be a shorter book, because I did two back-to-back mammoth works! I mean, *Secret Teachers* is about 180,000 words, and the book on Colin was over 200,000. I have to voice a note of thanks to my editor, Mitch Horowitz at Penguin, because he didn't bat an eye at the increasing word count. But this will be a shorter kind of book. I'm basically trying to grasp this idea of the imagination as a kind of organ of knowledge. Not of fantasy, or... of some alternative reality, but actually grasping reality itself.

Mike Mignola and the Lovecraft Circle: Inspiration and World Sharing

Anders Lundgren

The aim of this essay is to provide insights into some of the stuff that makes the cartoonist and writer Mike Mignola and his work tick. This is not the annotated version of trying to figure out his long running series *Hellboy* however – that would require several volumes – but simply an attempt to trace some of his many influences back to their sources and analyse what function they serve in the stories. One challenge here was to not simply retread what Stephen Weiner wrote in the great overview "The Literary Heritage of Hellboy".[1] For the sake of accessibility a degree of overlap is inevitable, but hopefully the reader will find some new insights to be gleaned from these parts of the text also. The presentation roughly follows the chronology of Mignola's career and the publishing history of *Hellboy* with some associative meanderings on the way, so please bear with me.[2]

To serve those previously unfamiliar with the man, just a quick introduction. Mignola got his start as a comics professional in the early 80s as an inker and subsequently artist for Marvel on titles such as *Daredevil, Power Man and Iron Fist, Alpha Flight* and *Rocket Raccoon.* Work for DC Comics followed in 1987, where he was interior artist on limited series such as *Phantom Stranger* and *World of Krypton.* He also did covers for various titles. Mignola continued doing work for hire at the big two, as well as for other companies, until 1994 when Dark Horse released *Hellboy: Seed of Destruction*, his first creator-owned project.[3] This comic presented you with a world of pulpy occultism, Lovecraftian horrors and a half demon half human protagonist sporting a big red stone fist. Deliberately paced, swathed in darkness and drawn in a style where the most gothic parts of art history collided with comic book action *Hellboy* turned into a slow burn success. At the moment of this writing, 18 collections and original graphic novels have been released; the lion's share drawn and written by Mignola.[4] On top of that you have a plethora of spin off titles in collaboration with other writers and artists such as John Arcudi, Scott Allie, Guy Davis and Tonči Zonjić.[5] Everything accounted for, this makes for a

1 *Hellboy: The Companion*, Stephen Weiner, Jason Hall, Victoria Blake with additional material by Mike Mignola (May, 2008). The text covers roughly the period 1994-2008.

2 Please note: This text is an expanded version of a presentation held at The Armitage Symposium, part of the festival NecronomiCon Providence, on August 18th 2017.

3 *Hellboy: Seed of Destruction*, John Byrne (script), Mike Mignola (artist, script) (Oct 1994).

4 Not forgetting the significant contributions by artists Duncan Fegredo and Richard Corben to crucial parts of *Hellboy*.

5 Arcudi wrote various B.P.R.D.-series between 2004 and 2016. Allie served as editor for the various

significant body of work that really pushes the boundaries in regards to the intricate world building combined with original self expression that you can get away with in mainstream comics. *Hellboy* is without exaggeration one of the most successful characters both artistically and commercially to be introduced during the past 30 years or so. Mignola has during the run of the series received numerous industry awards and adaptations into other media have spread the influence of his creation outside the comic book realm.

Into the story of the world's greatest paranormal investigator, though some would probably call him more of a brawler, Mignola poured all of the influences that had previously been kept in a stoppered flask. Granted, some of it had trickled out earlier. Most notably in *Batman: Legends of the Dark Knight #54*, the story "Sanctum" for all intents and purposes presents us with a proto Hellboy story starring that other great detective. Another notable project foreshadowing the concerns of Mignola's creator-owned material was the comic book adaptation of *Bram Stoker's Dracula* for Topps Comics in 1992.[6] Interest in the visual arts such as architecture, film, sculpture and the history of folklore, literature and the occult inform all of Mignola's work. The way he uses inspiration from these disciplines is touched upon in numerous interviews.[7] We shall start our investigation by turning to the creator whose ideas permeate *Hellboy* and related comics.

One source of inspiration, different results

Today, the widespread cultural influence of Providence, Rhode Island, author H.P. Lovecraft (1890-1937) cannot be overstated. Themes present in his work and the tone of pessimistic cosmicism he espoused can be found seemingly everywhere. Traces and blatant plagiarism of the stories about The Great Old Ones, the (ab) use of ancient grimoires and how the taint of ancient magic/science is visible in the modern world proliferate in most artistic disciplines. A sharper contrast to the relative obscurity in which he toiled during his lifetime can hardly be imagined. The main publishing venues for his fiction were cheap pulp magazines. While read by many, these were treated with outright disdain by critics – if they paid them any heed at all. In the decades after his death Lovecraft's stories were kept in print and read by enthusiasts of genre fiction but continued to be ignored by the literary world at large. In many ways the response to Lovecraft's work from the reading public has run a course parallel to that of comics. The American comic book as we know it today became extremely popular around the time of Lovecraft's passing. For the longest time they were widely read and appreciated while simultaneously

Hellboy titles between 1995 and 2017, providing scripts at various points, mainly for the Abe Sapien series that ran 2013 - 2016. Davis handled art duties on most B.P.R.D.-titles from 2004 to 2011 and Zonjić continues to be the main artist for *Lobster Johnson.*

6 *Batman: Legends of the Dark Knight* #54, Mike Mignola (artist, script), Dan Raspler (script) (Nov 1993). *Bram Stoker's Dracula*, Roy Thomas (script), Mike Mignola & John Nyberg (art) (Oct 1992).

7 I can also recommend the excellent *Hellboy's World: Comics and Monsters on the Margins* by Scott Bukatman from 2016 for an in depth and visually oriented look at Mignola's work.

lambasted by critics and the literary establishment. Deemed juvenile trash not fit for serious consideration at the best of times and subjected to outright book burnings at worst, comics were a guilty pleasure both for people working in the field and those who read them.[8] While I am yet to come across an example where his books were put to the torch, this is not a far cry from the low status bestowed on the stories written by Lovecraft. His works have finally, thanks to the pioneering efforts of S.T. Joshi and various other scholars, been re-evaluated during the past 30 years or so. Those branding him a mere pulp hack have been proven wrong. The same period has seen a slight but growing awareness of comics as a valid form of literary expression.[9]

Among those that have always held his stories in high regard, one of the many factors that played into the spread of Lovecraft's "Yog-Sothothery," more commonly referred to as his Cthulhu Mythos, was the open invitation to others who were so inclined to contribute their own stories. Over the years this has resulted in a veritable library of black tomes, new eldritch horrors and other expansions to this shared universe. A lot of common ground makes it easy to view what Mignola is doing as being part of this. Granted, he generally works without resorting to the name-dropping and in-jokes so prevalent among many of the by now tenuously connected Lovecraft circle.[10] Mignola does however pay his dues by for instance dedicating the first collection to Lovecraft along with some other notable individuals.[11] And despite it having a big red demon from hell as its protagonist, the gentleman from Providence casts a long shadow over this story. Reading *Hellboy: Seed of Destruction* after being previously immersed in Lovecraft's work, a lot of people will certainly feel a strong frisson of recognition. The events in the comic are set in motion by a polar expedition and a visit to a cave "at the top of the world". The hapless explorers accidentally awaken slumbering gods intent on bringing about the end of humanity. Echoes of Lovecraftian themes can probably be heard even by those with just a passing familiarity with his work. Never mind that we are dealing with the Ogdru Jahad, more specifically Sadu Hem, rather than Cthulhu or his cohorts. If you wish to view the remainder of the series through this

8 See Hajdu, D. (2009) *The Ten-Cent Plague: The Great Comic-Book Scare and How it Changed America*, Picador, London, England for an in-depth look at this subject.

9 Granted, there had been forerunners as early as 1964 with Roland Barthes and Umberto Eco; both publishing texts during that year viewing comics through a semiotic lens.

10 Not counting the non-canonical crossover *Hellboy / Batman / Starman* #1-2 (Jan 1999). There you do find some of these tendencies, best exemplified in the Hellboy line: "Yeah, it's not as weird as it sounds. Lovecraft knew some stuff," while discussing ancient evils in issue #2, p.16. And then of course you have the Elseworlds story *Batman: The Doom That Came to Gotham* (Mignola, script; Troy Nixey, artist, Sep 2000).

11 The others are Jack Kirby, Christine (Mignola) and Elmer Newton. These dedications generally give you many keys to understanding where Mignola is coming from in terms of reading habits and influences. Just from perusing *Hellmail*, the letters page in the Hellboy related books, it's apparent that the question of inspiration is asked a lot. The readers come across as an overall knowledgeable bunch that thrive on tracking down preferably obscure volumes in libraries and visiting the local antiquarian with list in hand. Both Mignola and editor Scott Allie are very generous in providing suggestions for further reading. Comments to individual stories as found in the collections also point you in the right direction.

lens, you will find many other instances where ideas and characters can be seen as echoing things Lovecraft and others did previously. For one, cosmic horror is the overarching theme behind the Hellboy comics. And even though it is the Caverns of Num-Yabisc rather than Y'nathlei calling home fish guy Abe Sapien (formerly the Victorian occultist Langdon Everett Caul – yes, it is complicated), the influence from "The Shadow Over Innsmouth"[12] is unmistakable. But as strong as these elements continue to be in the creations of Mignola and his various collaborators, one should never lose sight of the fact that this is fiercely original work. It may adhere strongly to a tradition but does so with great inventiveness. One is tempted to compare the quite different approach used by magician and comics luminary Alan Moore in *Providence*, a 12 issue series he did with artist Jacen Burrows for Avatar Press between 2015 and 2017.[13] Within this series, Lovecraft's fiction is treated as historical fact reshaping our world as it is uncovered by the unfortunate lead, writer Robert Black who in characteristic Lovecraft fashion is driven insane by his experiences. Moore mixes fiction, biographical details and extrapolations to create a comic that both adds to and comments on the work previously done by Lovecraft, Clark Ashton Smith, Robert Barlow, et al. This decidedly postmodernist approach is seemingly a far cry from Mignola's sensibilities. Where Moore throughout his career has relished the subversion of genre tropes and intertextual play, Mignola seemingly prefers to pay direct *homage* to his sources of inspiration and does not assume the role of a cognoscenti when sprinkling references. On the contrary: he loves pointing out that the poetry quoted throughout his comics are only there to make him look smarter than he actually is. A harsh self image to be sure. Any guy who has soaked up the likes of Robert Blair, Thomas Wharton the younger, Samuel Taylor Coleridge and Edgar Allan Poe, and putting that inspiration to such good use should really just give themselves a pat on the back. The low esteem in which Mignola holds his accomplishments stands in pretty sharp contrast to Moore's generous view of his own work. Without apparent irony he reprinted a gushing missive from a fan naming him "the best writer in human history" on the back of the "let's beat the *Bible* word count" giant of a novel *Jerusalem* (2016). Dissimilarities in temperament aside, Moore did write a glowing preface to Mignola's *Hellboy: Wake the Devil* back in 1996.

Getting back to how these different approaches come out in the work itself, there is in Mignola's comics little to no place for the intertextual referencing and deconstruction of the sort Moore practices in most of his. Where Moore goes for verbosity and cramming massive amounts of information into every script page and expecting this to come out in the individual comic book panels, Mignola is driven to the opposite end of the spectrum. The honing of his craft leads to a paring down

12 Lovecraft's most action-packed story also has the distinction of being the only book of fiction distributed while he was still alive. Sadly he was not happy with it due to sloppy proofreading. Visionary Publishing Company released the book in April 1936. Or was that actually November?

13 This is both a sequel and a prequel of sorts to Moore and Burrows' previous collaborations: *The Courtyard* (2003) and *Neonomicon* (2010), also published by Avatar Press.

to the bare essentials, whether we are dealing with word or image.[14] That is not to say that more or less openly referencing the work of others is anathema to Mignola. We have the aforementioned examples where poetry is put into dialogue with his images. Then we have the many instances where images by the likes of Albrecht Dürer or Francisco Goya, the blackness of a Mario Bava composition or a mass of Kirby Krackle add weight and multilayered associations to his panels. When writing for other artists, Mignola often uses something between what is commonly referred to as "Marvel style" and full script.[15] He often adds thumbnails (minuscule sketches) to get the flow of the story right. The minimalist approach employed during the writing process and in the presentation of the actual finished comic is in sharp contrast with the world-building impulses he obviously also entertains. Leading to literally thousands of years worth of mythologically dense backstory, describing the rise and fall of entire civilizations and Hellboy's complex lineage involving the royalty of both Hell and the Arthurian court. Writing for a character that says "Crap!" a lot and fights his way out of most situations is pretty rich. In other words, there is a constant struggle within the creative side of Mignola between his identity as an outspoken "short-story guy" and the admittedly more internalized but nonetheless clear and present writer of huge epics.

Many sources serving one goal

To put the history of Hellboy's world into perspective we turn to some of Mignola's other sources of inspiration. First we have another H.P., namely Blavatsky: author, occultist and co-founder of the Theosophical Society. Helena Petrovna Blavatsky has been named both a prophet and a charlatan. Not entirely dependent on your persuasion, she probably was a little bit of both. Those familiar with her biography and the Theosophical curriculum of comparative religion, philosophy, occultism and science will no doubt find many correlations when reading the various *Hellboy* comics. While decidedly more sinister, the activities and interests of secret society The Heliopic Brotherhood of Ra certainly bear a strong resemblance to Blavatsky's group. The history of the world, as sketched out in her most famous book *The Secret Doctrine* (1888), is where Mignola got some of the mythological underpinnings to his world. And his comics are not the only place where the thoughts of root races, lost continents and ancient civilisations as put forth by Blavatsky and her followers have lived on. They have found expression in other instances of pop culture and art too numerous to list here. But one of them has a more direct bearing on our topic. Polish painter, sculptor, writer and genius Stanisław Szukalski expressed similar ideas via a concept for humanity's origin called *Zermatism*. In his art and books

14 To get a taste of this, just compare Hellboy's first appearance in *Seed of Destruction* with the final images from *Hellboy in Hell*, drawn some 22 years later! The number of lines used to delineate the character has decreased significantly and Hellboy has aged along with his creator.

15 In short, the classic "Marvel style" scripts of the 60s and 70s provided the basic plot points. Most of the heavy lifting was done by the artist with the dialogue added to the finished pages by the writer/editor.

like *Behold!!! The Protong* (released by publishers Last Gasp in 2000) he outlines the belief that our species is locked in an everlasting battle of supremacy with the "Yetinsyny", Sons of Yeti. Szukalski's visuals and ideas have found their way into Mignola's comics – see for instance the first mini-series of spin-off title B.P.R.D. (Bureau for Paranormal Research and Defense) entitled *Hollow Earth*.[16] The beast-men and their slave race encountered here are straight from Szukalski, along with a smattering of concepts recognizable from the various proponents of Hollow Earth theories. One name that's been popping up since long before the days of Blavatsky[17] leads us back to the Lovecraft circle by way of Cross Plains, Texas: home to Robert E. Howard, who in his all too short life and career was an extremely prolific writer. These days he is mainly associated with his most singular creation: Conan the Cimmerian. Hyperborea is a place referenced in Howard's stories about Conan and home to the second of Blavatsky's root races. A different version of it is encountered in the writings of Clark Ashton Smith. Mignola distills all of these inspirations creating his own Hyperborea in the process.

A little digression. Mixing up references to real-world erudition, and letting renowned sources lend some weight and substance to your own work, is a tried and tested method used by many practitioners of the arts. To some, this is a crutch helping a line of reasoning or narrative to wobble along, in some cases getting to where it's supposed to go eventually but without ever picking up speed or taking any independent steps on the way.[18] Many can probably recall times when a comic (needless to say, this applies to literary fiction as well) has ground completely to a halt because the creator willfully crams overly long information dumps into the dialogue or captions, builds it entirely around references to other things, or when supposedly cool quotes are used for garnish without having any apparent bearing on the events at hand. Not wishing to sow discord, we leave examples of misconduct to the individual reader. Needless to say, Mignola is not one of them. Work borrowing more or less heavily from others is still good if it has a spark of its own and feels fresh, even though you can identify the various sources of inspiration when for instance a place like Hyperborea pops up. That name is not the only thing Mignola has Howard to thank for. When we first encounter Conan in "The Phoenix on the Sword"[19] he is around 40 years old and king of Aquilonia, the foremost country of the age. In the following stories, Howard gives us glimpses of Conan at various stages of his life and career as a young thief, pirate, reaver,and soldier. Mignola

16 Written in collaboration with Chris Golden and Tom Sniegoski, art by Ryan Sook (Jan, 2002). B.P.R.D. is the organization founded by Hellboy's adopted father Professor Trevor Bruttenholm.

17 Herodotus gives the first known outline of Hyperborea that you can still read in *Histories* from circa 450 BC.

18 Mignola pokes fun at this modus operandi in *Hellboy: In the Chapel of Moloch* (2008) when the painter Jerry's agent goes on at length about how ripping off Francisco Goya (1746-1828) by copying images from his nightmarish print set *Los caprichos* (1799) onto canvas is actually doing him a favor. Hellboy remains characteristically unimpressed.

19 "The Phoenix on the Sword", originally published in *Weird Tales* December 1932. Incidentally when Mignola first opened up for others to write stories with his characters he licensed the title *Hellboy: Weird Tales* for the anthology series running bi-monthly between Feb 2003 and Apr 2004.

has taken this disparate chronology to heart when writing *Hellboy*. Between the character's first appearance on Earth in December 1944 and the events following *Seed of Destruction*, there is a time window of 50 years that Mignola and his many collaborators are filling with new stories continuously. And in a nod to another short story by Howard, featuring his puritan hero Solomon Kane, that big stone appendage of Hellboy's is called "The Right Hand of Doom". Worth mentioning is also the fact that Mignola wrote the script for three issues of the Dark Horse Comics adaptations of Conan back in 2006.[20] And it does not stop there. In the B.P.R.D. miniseries "The Abyss of Time,"[21] a modern day field agent aptly named Ted Howards finds himself transported back to Prehistoric times after coming into contact with a sword of ancient origin. Waking up as Gall Dennar, chieftain of a caveman tribe, Howards ends up fighting undead creatures and monsters. Experiences that leave him a transformed man when he eventually returns to his original timeline. This story echoes Howard's tale "Kings of the Night"[22] featuring Pictish hero Bran Mak Morn. In this tale, he fights alongside Kull of Atlantis, king of Valusia, who is transported from his own time to Bran Mak Morn's through magic centered around a gemstone. Very much like what we see in "The Abyss of Time".

In the expanding circle of artists and writers that Mignola works with on the different comic book series taking place in the world of *Hellboy*, I see a contemporary and slightly more regulated version of what Lovecraft, Howard, Smith and the others were up to back in the day. They, however, told separate stories interconnected merely by a pretty fluid recurring cosmogony. Whereas Mignola, his long suffering editor and co-writer Scott Allie and the others are in the business of telling one big story. Granted, it consists of many stand-alone parts, but in the end they are supposed to fit together organically. Compare with how the continuity in superhero comics used to work before the rebooting shenanigans started spinning out of control back in the mid 80s. Mignola had this to say on the subject: "But I think the thing that separates me from Marvel and DC now is certainly the fact that our continuity works. We haven't had to stop and restart, and as a guy who read Marvel comics in the 70s, where the continuity still worked, I loved the fact that there were threads that tied the current comics to comics from the 40s and stuff like that. I personally really like the whole continuity thing. And yeah, it is getting to be a big…thing."[23] The main difference between the Mignola and the Lovecraft circle is not how the stories themselves come out, but the manner in which they are produced. When Howard used the names of Lovecraftian gods

20 *Conan* #29, "The Toad"; *Conan* #30, "The Serpent"; *Conan* #31, "The Hall of the Dead", Mike Mignola (script), Cary Nord (art), published between Aug and Sep 2006. The comics were based on the fragment "The Hall of the Dead", unfinished at the time of Howard's death and completed by L.Sprague de Camp for publication in *The Magazine of Fantasy and Science Fiction,* February 1967.

21 *B.P.R.D. Hell on Earth: The Abyss of Time* #1-2, script by Mike Mignola and Scott Allie, art by James Harren, colors by Dave Stewart. Originally published January-February 2013.

22 Originally published in *Weird Tales,* November 1930.

23 "The weirdest thing I've ever written": Mike Mignola on Frankenstein Underground & the future of the Mignolaverse, Shea Hennum, *Paste Magazine*, March 18, 2015.

in "Worms of the Earth" – another Bran Mak Morn tale – and Lovecraft in turn incorporated the name of an occult book Howard originally came up with into "Out of the Aeons", this was in the nature of *homage*.[24] The Lovecraft circle was more akin to a mutual appreciation society. Friends playing a literary game that resulted in something quite wonderful even though it wasn't exactly planned or thought out in advance.[25] Mignola on the other hand has a clear idea of where his characters and stories are supposed to end up. Since persistent perfectionism and the success of his comics has created a situation where there simply aren't enough hours in the day for him to write and draw all the stories that need to be told, other creators contribute. And this is by invitation only.

There is a slight irony in how Mignola stopped doing work for hire in order to fully realize his ambitions. Proving so adept at this and discovering an audience that can't get enough of his "crazy ideas" (his words, not mine) he now finds himself the head of a franchise that employs people who are essentially doing work for hire. Shared profits and a large degree of creative freedom for writers like Arcudi and artists Zonjić, Ben Stenbeck and others will hopefully keep this away from the exploitative aspects that have marred so many interactions in the history of comic books.

Moving from the reality of their production to the dreams that they produce, I for one hope that Mignola and the growing roster of amazing talent that he works with keep weaving their tales for many years to come.

Reaching for the sublime through words and images

> My reason for writing stories is to give myself the satisfaction of visualising more clearly and detailedly and stably the vague, elusive, fragmentary impressions of wonder, beauty, and adventurous expectancy which are conveyed to me by certain sights (scenic, architectural, atmospheric, etc.), ideas, occurrences, and images encountered in art and literature. I choose weird stories because they suit my inclination best – one of my strongest and most persistent wishes being to achieve, momentarily, the illusion of some strange suspension or violation of the galling limitations of time, space, and natural law which for ever imprison us and frustrate our curiosity about the infinite cosmic spaces beyond the radius of our sight and analysis.[26]

24 "Worms of the Earth", originally published in *Weird Tales* November 1932. "Out of the Aeons", first published in the April 1935 issue of *Weird Tales*.

25 Remember also Moore's meticulously executed contribution to this game of words/worlds and how his sensibilities drive home some points only hinted at in the original texts to which he is constantly referring in Providence.

26 H. P. Lovecraft, "Notes on Writing Weird Fiction", first published in *Amateur Correspondent*, 2, No. 1 (May–June 1937), 7–10.

Like many Lovecraft characters – and fans – I do enjoy a good paper chase and establishing links between things I appreciate. But as fun as the exercise of connecting the dots and the tracing of influences is, I can't escape the feeling that this only scratches the surface. While working out the various ways in which Mignola has been inspired by Lovecraft (and others) I have luckily reached what I hope is a deeper understanding of what ties them together and sets them apart. As the above quote illustrates, Lovecraft had aspirations with his work that belies the fact that his subject matter was met with indifference or scorn by the literary establishment during the course of his life. To the extent that any critics outside of fandom even took notice. This relegated the stories to publication in magazines that may be legendary now, but were seen as pretty much the lowest form of trash at the time. And one need not look particularly hard to find that the positive changes that have occurred since then, regarding the attitude toward literature dealing with horror and the speculative, are incremental at best. Going from content to execution I think it is fair to say that even among those who appreciate Lovecraft, his fondness for antiquated language and adjectives remains a bone of contention. I'm certainly not the first, and will not be the last, to rise up in his defense and point out that despite what his detractors say, Lovecraft was in control of his writing. There are essays like the one quoted earlier and the many letters written to clients whose work he revised and gave notes on, giving ample evidence supporting this. [27] While certainly not always successful, the aggregate formed by words and sentences sometimes straining both credibility and syntax, is there because Lovecraft made a deliberate stylistic choice. And if he was such a bad writer, how come those trying to follow in his footsteps or "improve" on his formula mostly end up with hackneyed pastiche? Again I leave the naming of names at the discretion of the reader. But let's not forget that there is also a fair number of writers who succeed in reaching that same pinnacle of existential dread where Lovecraft once staked his claim. Albeit often by a different route than the one he took.

While certainly no slouch when it came to critiquing his own output, I'm not entirely sure that Lovecraft ever held up his stories to the same harsh light under which Mignola continuously scrutinizes his finished pages. The many rejected versions of character sketches and covers seen in the collected editions give ample testimony to this. In the case of *Hellboy: The Island* (2005) you have an almost finished comic that was discarded when not deemed up to snuff. These high standards stem from the fact that he works in the Lovecraft tradition in ways more intricate than just shared interests and subject matter. Jack of all trades Max Gaines got a flash of inspiration to repackage the full color Sunday comic pages back in 1933. He thereby laid the foundation for what would become the modern comic book. It only took a few years before the pulp magazines found themselves vying for the attention of the reading public (that consisted of many more heads back then)

27 See for instance the volume *The Spirit of Revision: Lovecraft's Letters to Zealia Brown Reed Bishop*, edited by Sean Branney and Andrew Leman, HPLHS Incorporated, Los Angeles, USA, 2015. Probably much to the amusement of his critics one of the things Lovecraft recommends herein is the use of clear and direct word choices.

with a form of storytelling combining words with pictures in sequence. Working mostly with content already tried out in the pulps like westerns, mystery, horror, aviation stories and vigilantes in more or less colourful costumes, comics also came to inherit much of the baggage the predecessors were saddled with. Immense if fluctuating popularity coupled with vicious accusations of leading to stunted mental growth and juvenile delinquency. Consequent demands for censorship that resulted in the odd book burning has been with comics during the decades since. To put it mildly, these have been difficult conditions for a fledgling art form trying to find its own voice. Not just literature, not just art but a combination of the two producing a hybrid that requires a different form of reading. Never mind the highly touted "graphic novel revolution" in recent years. By most accounts this debatable literary coup has been going on in fits and starts ever since the first volume of Art Spiegelman's *Maus* hit regular bookstores in 1986. Leaving the discussion about whether Spiegelman really was the first, select works by Gil Kane published in the 70s are heavy contenders – it is fair to say that comics and its practitioners are still struggling with their self image. Working in an industry that has a less than stellar history of giving fair compensation or even credit to creators can do that to people. Much like the house names used for *The Shadow* and *Doc Savage* magazines hiding main writers Lester Dent and Walter B. Gibson behind Kenneth Robeson and Maxwell Grant respectively, comic book companies early on made a habit of not attributing work to the people actually doing it. One telling example is how Bob Kane finagled his way to getting his name on *Batman* stories he had never been involved in, omitting guys like Bill Finger. A blunder that has only been rectified in recent years.[28]

Make no mistake: Mignola has enjoyed success on a scale that Lovecraft probably could not have envisioned even in his most vivid flights of fancy. From the start, that silly idea of having a character named Hellboy fighting batrachian beasties, ancient gods, Nazis and various creatures from folklore took off in a big way. Much to the surprise of his creator, who would have been more than happy to just have this one comic of his own out there before crawling back to the salt mines and continuing to shoehorn at least some stuff that inspired him into stories featuring characters owned by DC or Marvel. The latter would at the time have been glad to have him back, still reeling from the massive walk out by big name creators tired of the aforementioned lack of rewards and the meagre royalties associated with work for hire.[29] Luckily, Mignola held fast and in the coming years raked in both sales and peer recognition for his singular vision. Like Lovecraft before him he also quickly got that more dubious form of flattery consisting of people trying to imitate his style. But, again, if all it takes is using some of the same ingredients

28 I must somewhat grudgingly (no comment) admit that *Men of Tomorrow: Geeks, Gangsters and the Birth of the American Comic Book* by Gerard Jones, Basic Books 2005, remains the best available source for those interested in the shady beginnings and business practices used by the folks who got comics rolling off the presses.

29 If you want to know more about this tumultuous period of comics history, look up the documentary "The Image Revolution" (Patrick Meaney, 2014).

then surely more people would succeed? Just take some convoluted sentences with old-fashioned word choices and a penchant for bleak narratives often ending with death, suicide or worse. Or, in the case of Mignola, panels swathed in black with a craggy featured hero falling and fighting in castles and caves interspersed with pictures of pockmarked statuary, broken architecture, weird trees and little birds. O, speaking for both, just add skulls and tentacles! But as anyone who has become transfixed by a printed page or poured endlessly over the same panel sequence can attest, there is a more subtle magic at work here. One that is not easily pinned down or explained. Ask anyone successful at their chosen art how they came to their specific style and you will most likely just get a bewildered look for an answer. Mignola is no different, and has a famously self deprecating approach to discussing what he does. In one interview from roughly ten years ago he answered most questions with the mantra "I just like to draw monsters."[30]

When working as a visual consultant for the Disney feature *Atlantis: The Lost Empire* (Gary Wise, Kirk Trousdale 2001) he was flabbergasted when visiting their offices and finding charts breaking down how he achieved certain effects with his images. Talking about it, he maintains that he is just looking for things that would be fun to draw.[31] There are a lot of ways to describe how and why a comic by Mignola works differently and reaches something that few attain. One of the things that sets him apart from others is an exquisite sense of pacing, and the ability to give his comics a rhythm that is theirs and theirs alone. This is done by the carefully planned placement of panels on a page, a double page spread and how this plays out over the course of a comic. These days, roughly thirty pages. Color is also used as a storytelling device to great effect, conveying mood, denoting a certain character, or being muted over the course of a story in order for a finale bursting with it to really stand out. During the 20 plus years of *Hellboy*, Mignola has worked almost exclusively with color artist Dave Stewart, who in all likelihood has a special cabinet reserved only for all the Eisner Awards he has received for his trouble. They obviously have developed an amazing shorthand over their long collaboration since color, or at times the lack thereof, is as much an integral part of Mignola's visual style as his Mario Bavaesque use of nearly completely blacked out images giving an added gravitas to that one detail you do see.[32] The use of black lends weight, and despite the fact that they are printed on a flat piece of paper, a sense of three dimensionality. And not necessarily in the form of perspective depth or those effects associated with "poke you in the eye" 3D. This is more a sense of real heft conveyed in the pages of his comics. At times Mignola's images seem to have been carved out of marble rather than drawn with pen and ink.[33] Quite possibly these

30 "There Will Be Monsters: 20 Questions with Mike Mignola", available at www.darkhorse.com.

31 Conversation with author November 19, 2018.

32 Mario Bava was an Italian director, screenwriter, special effects artist and cinematographer known for his excellent use of stark contrasts between light and dark in films such as the Mignola favourite "Black Sunday" (1960). He also made great use of color in "Black Sabbath" (1963) and "Blood and Black Lace" (1964).

33 To the best of my knowledge the only sculpture work Mignola has done was a small clay statue of

associations are triggered by the many statues that are a recurring motif. But it also says something about how the experience of reading comics is a thing unto itself. Especially in the case of Mignola, we are presented with a form of visual poetry.

Like Lovecraft's stories, comics have always been viewed by many not as something to experience and cherish through the act of reading, but simply intellectual property waiting to be "refined" into something else. In this day and age, you need not look further than your preferred streaming service or the nearest multiplex to find that adaptations make for a substantial part of what is on offer. To some comics are just storyboards, frozen pictures waiting to be thawed out and set into motion. Not real or worth anything before they have been transformed into a multi million dollar spectacle bombarding the senses with an incessant barrage of movement, sound effects and music. This is to miss the point and power of comics entirely. Granted, when you have something driven by plot more than visual storytelling, the transposition into another medium may not be entirely without merit. Comics at their best, however, are not just movies on paper. The experience of reading a comic is not similar to watching a film. Movies are by their very nature defined by the forward march of time. In this digital age 25 frames per second transport you from one moment to the next and the next for however long the picture lasts. It exemplifies one of the very things Lovecraft fought against with his stories: "the galling limitations of time". You can leave the theatre or pop into the kitchen for something to drink, the movie will continue without your participation. Not so with comics. They come to life the moment you engage them. The pace of the story is decided by the individual reader, who can stop and look at a single panel for as long or as short a period of time as s/he likes. Much to the chagrin of many a cartoonist striving for perfection, this can be a matter of only a few seconds. But there are also those who linger, flip the pages back to savor a particularly potent composition and study every minute detail. Reading comics can be an atemporal experience. Ditto for reading Lovecraft. In his most inspired moments the writing attains a quality transcending those limitations he spent life struggling against. He achieved something that went beyond mere words on paper, more or less intricate plot points, monsters, insanity and death. In the simplest of terms: the sublime.

All we are saying, give beetles a chance!

Never mind the fact that the story "The Dunwich Horror" spawned an entire gaming industry, prompting generation upon generation of teenagers to play at being old academics casting deadly spells.[34] Or that most pages of Mignola's comics are devoted to endless slugfests where what many identify as monsters are dispatched with extreme prejudice. At their core, stories by both creators are still defined by a desire to move away from the humanocentric viewpoints that have marred culture

---

Moloch prepared to get the shadows right for *Hellboy: In the Chapel of Moloch* (2008).

34 "The Dunwich Horror", first saw publication in the April 1929 issue of *Weird Tales*.

probably for far longer than any extant records tell us. I prefer to think of the ending to "The Shadow Out of Time".[35] It is revealed that the Great Race of Yith have managed to conquer all those limitations of time, space and natural law that frustrated Lovecraft. They have accomplished this by transporting their minds into the far future and the bodies of the Coleopterous Race. More commonly known as "the beetle folk", these are the beings who will supplant humanity as the dominant species on earth. A notion that certainly seems appealing to Mignola also as demonstrated by this quote:

> There was never any politics involved and I don't think I have a particularly negative worldview, but for whatever reason the idea from the very beginning of Hellboy has been 'okay, humanity's done enough,'" Mignola says. "This is why I like writing [Hellboy's oldest enemy, the Russian mystic] Rasputin, because from my point of view Rasputin's job has always been to look at the world and say 'well that's gone as far as it can, let's give the insects a chance.' Given the current state of things, I'm kind of going, 'yeah I think I was right.'[36]

'Nuff said!

35 "The Shadow Out of Time", published in *Astounding Stories*, June 1936.
36 "Mike Mignola talks Hellboy's return to comics", Christian Holub, *Entertainment Weekly*, February 13 2018.

So It Was Written: The History of The Satanic Bible by Anton Szandor LaVey

Peggy Nadramia

Most religions don't begin with a book; those books come later. They begin with one or two people, who gather other people around them. As a group, they formulate some ideas about their beliefs and they decide what words they'll use to describe themselves and their deities. They collaborate on a liturgy, or maybe one guy goes off into the woods and comes back with some given wisdom. It's written down, or carved into a tree or painted on a cave wall. The big books come about years later, and they're translated and augmented. Different versions appear and different people interpret them differently.

The Satanic Bible didn't happen that way. It was born of both inspiration and necessity; it incorporated rituals already in use by a church, and a philosophy that was being expressed in published articles and via other media, but all from the same source: the mind of Anton LaVey. The ideas that were making up the philosophy of Satanism, and their expression through the rituals that had been created to exercise this philosophy, were brought together to write what would become the foundation of the Satanic religion and history's most influential book on Satanism.

LaVey had a very demanding and active congregation, always willing to discuss new ideas, and to exercise and experiment with them. Lectures were being held on an almost daily basis at the Black House on California Street, and Satanic rituals happened every Friday night. His Magic Circle of creative, powerful and intelligent friends was encouraging him to bring this all together in some way; the world was riding the crest of an occult revolution and Satanism was a unique form of this new self-empowerment. It was time to take it, as they say, to a whole other level.

Aside from the Satanic wisdom flowing to his Church members via his sermons and essays, Anton LaVey was not yet a writer, by his own admission. But he was a fascinating and eloquent man, and he attracted the friendship of writers, who were lavish in their support and encouragement of their friend Anton. They were eager to see him flex his muscles and get ahead of the wave of interest in Satanism and the "Black Arts." One of these writers was Fred Goerner, the author of *The Search for Amelia Earhart*. Fred was so enthusiastic about LaVey's ideas and so sure *The Satanic Bible* would be a runaway hit, that he talked it up to his own editor at Doubleday, Walter Bradbury:

> During a party I got into a discussion with Anton LaVey, the self-styled head of the Satanic Church of North America... Anton is

> not as wierd [sic] as he sounds. Along with being articulate and a hell of a salesman, he creates a solid presence... He holds classes several nights a week at his church for young women who want to be witches. Merla and I went one night, and damn if he didn't have forty gals there studying love potions and the like including a course in seducing a male through his own ego. Too much.

Luther Nichols, Doubleday's West Coast editor, called LaVey in February of 1968. Occult books were hot, hot, hot and every publisher wanted to bring out the next bestseller in that category. They had a long chat and that very day, Nichols sent LaVey a letter asking to see the manuscripts for both *The Satanic Bible* and *Practical Enchantment for Women*, a proto-version of *The Compleat Witch* that was based on LaVey's Witches Workshops. Fred Goerner received a letter with the same date from Walter Bradbury, his own editor at Doubleday, thanking Goerner for the referral of LaVey. So there was quite a buzz about *The Satanic Bible* over at one of America's biggest publishers, and I'm sure LaVey was walking on air — and starting to crack the whip over his own head for a change. He had to get to work.

Two weeks later, in March, LaVey received a letter from Mike Hamilburg, Fred Goerner's agent and the son of Mitchell Hamilburg, who had established a successful literary and film agency and was well-known in Hollywood. Mike had been referred to LaVey by Goerner, and had arranged a meeting with the LaVeys in the interim. He was interested in representing LaVey and handling any negotiations with Doubleday, should the need arise – he'd already been in touch with Luther Nichols, "who indicated Doubleday's strong interest in what you are doing." Well, that was encouraging. Knowing something of LaVey's background, Hamilburg included a copy of a book he'd represented, *The Cristianis*, about a famous circus family.

LaVey replied promptly and was completely charmed by this introduction and happy with the gift: "...[it] supplied me with some warm nostalgia in a realm that has grown far too cold." He went on to give a detailed description of the Four Books that he envisioned making up *The Satanic Bible*. This is heady stuff. *The Satanic Bible* has been analyzed by plenty of people over the years, scholars, detractors, Satanists, Christian evangelists, even Catholic doctrinaires. Here is Anton LaVey planning his own book for you, and describing what he hopes will take place in each section:

> The first book, *The Book of Satan*, is a diatribe done in an almost brutalizing way, and in the format of a true bible, with numbered chapters and verses. It is purposely done in an archaic style, and is guaranteed to outrage, from a religious, intellectual, or at least, literary point of view, at least to enough people to cause some wholesale tongue-clucking and fist pounding. Satan represents the fire element, so this section of the bible must scorch!

> The second book is called *The Book of Lucifer,* (the air element, enlightenment) and in rather sane language attempts to enlighten the reader to the truth concerning Satanism. The Satanic views on Heaven and Hell, life after death, God, sin and guilt, the ego, buying and selling of souls, sexual activity, human sacrifice, love and hate, and the evidence of a new Satanic age, are expounded in this section.
>
> The third book, *The Book of Belial,* (earth) is an instruction manual, written in concise terms, on the theory and practice of ritual magic. There has never been anything written which tells the reader the principles set forth with such blatant detail. The pussy-footing, righteous attitude of all works, both historical and modern, is not to be found here! This is a course in the practical application of *Black* magic, and gets into such tabooed ingredients in the performance of sorcery such as obscene imagery, utilization of repressed desire; how, properly, to hate; proper timing regarding: sleep patterns, accident-prone cycles, lunar phases, menstrual periods, the transmission of adrenal energy, the function of the orgasm in ritual magic, etc. – all described in no-nonsense, non-sanctimonious, language. Herein are to be found the ingredients of charms and spells, hexes and curses.
>
> The fourth and last section, *The Book of Leviathan,* (water, the roaring sea) contains the actual invocations and incantations used in the performance of Satanic ceremonies and rituals, for such purposes as love, sex, power, compassion, destruction, etc., and calling up names never before encouraged by the writers of puerile books on witchery.

As confident as he sounds in the above, LaVey was not entirely sure he wasn't coming off as a publishing rube, and qualifies his fervor to his prospective agent thusly:

> I realize that I sound enthused, Mike, and I honestly am. I've been collecting every book on magic, sorcery, and witchcraft that I could lay my hands on (including some of the so-called forbidden books) for the better part of my life, and have been so disillusioned, insulted, and disappointed by what I've read that I have had to write my own, as a devil's advocate! ... I have a lot that I wish to say, and having done everything from training lions and tigers, to playing Bach preludes on the organ while accompanying myself on the kazoo, but never having written in my life, I feel my present attack of literary diarrhea was inevitable.

Anton LaVey was about to set off on a journey to write a book that has empowered

Satanists for generations to follow. He was trepidatious, and had every reason to be, as he would find himself both writing and marketing *The Compleat Witch* almost simultaneously, while also putting together the essays that would eventually turn into *The Devil's Notebook*. His postscript to this same letter was, well, optimistic: "I expect to have the bible completed within the next month."

A couple of weeks later, in mid-April 1968, LaVey heard from local pal Burton Wolfe, who was returning the copy of *Rosemary's Baby* LaVey had loaned him. Wolfe was another of LaVey's writer compatriots, sharing tips and information about publishing opportunities, after having interviewed the LaVeys at the Black House and covered a Satanic ritual in an article for *Knight Magazine*. LaVey happily reports, "Most of my spare time has been taken with writing *The Satanic Bible*, which Doubleday is very interested in publishing. I've got a good agent in L.A. – Michael Hamilburg. He was Fred Goerner's agent for the Amelia Earhart book, and Fred was quite pleased with what he did for him."

And indeed, LaVey had reason to be optimistic, as Luther Nichols followed up with the Hamilburg agency at length in a letter from late April:

> It has all sorts of possibilities as a hell-raiser... That Satanic manifesto as a first section for the book ought to start things off with the right kind of demoliton [sic] of orthodoxy before Mr. Levay [sic] moves on to the radical advice and enlightenment (endarkenment?) of the other sections. I like his 'If a man smite you on one cheek, SMASH him on the other.' Very realistic in our age of black militants, white Mace-wielders, Vietnam bomb-droppers, and the hired assassins alike.
>
> The 'theory and practice' material for the Book of Belial is interesting. It nicely mixes in existentialism and psychology, among other things, to form a more plausible argument for satanism and its applicability than one might expect. The cultural and scientific climate would seem to be coming to Mr. Levay's [sic] aid more favorably than it did in the time of de Sade or Huysmans. Certainly the book promises to offer more psychologically sound, practical advice than most of the pietistic 'right hand path' stuff that's fobbed off on the wishful every year. (Norman Vincent Peal, can you hear me?)
>
> ... some improvements might be wrought in the style and organization.... though generally Mr. Levay's [sic] power of language surprises me... At present it threatens to be a mite fragmented and cloudy – though perforce one might expect a certain amount of that in the realm of magic. Or life, for that matter.
>
> From what I've seen here, it's my judgment that Doubleday would be

> very much interested in pursuing The Satanic Bible... If this book is sustainedly well-written, well designed (perhaps with appropriately satanic art) and well promoted, it could be a sensation.

It was full steam ahead for LaVey at this point. A flurry of long-distance phone calls were taking place, but it must be remembered that the cost of such calls, even between cities on the same coast, was prohibitive. That's a good thing, because we have these wonderful letters to give us insights into a thought process about which we've heretofore only guessed.

In mid-May, LaVey wrote to his agent, Michael Hamilburg, to give him an update on where he was at with *The Satanic Bible*. He apologizes for not sending the promised enclosures sooner, "...but one thing led to another, and I just kept writing. That combined with the fact that one entire week was devoted to filming a documentary on the Satanic Church for U.C.L.A. is why this comes to you about a week and a half late." This refers to "Satanis," the infamous documentary on the early Church of Satan with which we're all so familiar. Not everyone may be aware that the film was a student project, for Ray Laurent's Master's thesis in filmmaking.

LaVey was still in touch with Doubleday at this point, and informs Hamilburg:

> I called [Luther Nichols] last week to tell him I would be on a local television show and would be reading parts from the *Book of Satan* on the program. It shook everyone up in the studio so much that the filming had to be done *three* times, which made it impossible for them to film another show that they planned to show the same night (Monday)... Obviously, this is the kind of promotion the Bible is going to need.

He speculates about whether or not any exposition about the Church of Satan itself would be appropriate.

> I have purposely avoided reference to the Church of Satan except in my signature following the introduction. Do you think I should include a chapter on the Satanic Church and the whys and wherefores of it? This is a point I'm not too sure about – whether it will add or detract." He's confident that Satanism is the wave of the future, and tells Hamilburg, "the Church of Satan has really started something that is going to be impossible to stop... Knowing that we must strike while the iron is hot, I've been letting everything else go as much as possible, and devoting every minute I can to completing *The Satanic Bible.*

A few days later, LaVey received a response from Silva Romano, Hamilburg's assistant at the agency; she was writing in Mike's stead as he was handling his father

Mitchell's illness. She encouraged LaVey to prepare a chapter on the Church of Satan, so that it would be ready in case the publishers thought it desirable. She also made suggestions about avoiding any topical references, and asked for some expansion on the Enochian language and the Satanic view of life after death. Other than that, she describes what he had already sent as, "just splendid."

LaVey found himself in complete accordance with Romano's suggestions for improvement:

> I completely agree that sections which are overly topical might detract, and purposely have avoided them when at all possible. Naturally, when dealing with a subject which is intended to criticize the current state of things it is not always easy to avoid reference to specific examples... Actually, when I wrote that short description [of Enochian] it was more of [sic] less just to clarify the reason for its inclusion...

As for life after death, he explains that "when one deals with a subject all the time it becomes second nature and I sometimes tend to over simplify the subject to avoid long winded explanations."

As for a chapter on the Church, which never made it into the Bible, LaVey was pro rather than con.

> I am rather glad that you feel a chapter on the Church of Satan might be in order, as the existence of an organized religious body tends to add to the outrageousness of the religion, which is something that is necessary for the salability of it. Since most people who take the time to learn about Satanism usually think it makes sense, we find ourselves lacking controversy. Therefore, I sometimes outrage intentionally. (9 parts acceptability – 1 part outrageousness).

As of this letter exchange with his agency, Doubleday was still considering the *Bible* but Romano informed LaVey that they were giving the publisher a two-week deadline before shopping it elsewhere. LaVey agrees:

> I am most anxious to get the *Bible* out in general circulation and want to waste no time in doing so... Each day brings new queries as to the availability of the *Bible* – and my recent T.V. plugs on interview shows invariably are followed by scores of calls asking, 'when and where can we buy it?'

He goes on to detail how he's asked a few friends he considers "laymen" and unfamiliar with Satanism, to read his manuscript and tell him whether they feel the information is clear and accessible.

> They said that anyone who could read a newspaper would be able to understand the contents of the *Bible*. This is what I am aiming for, and I am avoiding being too esoteric throughout most of it, although I feel that a certain amount of 'the emperor's new clothes' is necessary to satisfy the hyper-intellectuals, so I've included some (but very little of this sort of thing). The hyper and pseudo-intellectuals do a lot of hair-splitting, but very little else – especially buying. Therefore, I have purposely not gauged the writing style of the *Bible* with them in mind, but have slanted it towards the layman, who is much more willing to part with his dollar.

On June 10th, Silva Romano again writes briefly and tells LaVey that they're giving Doubleday ten more days to decide, and at that point, will do a simultaneous submission to Random House [the publishers of *Rosemary's Baby*]. She thanks him for the "Pray For Anton LaVey" buttons and assures him that she IS praying for him.

LaVey responds that he thinks Random House is a good choice thanks to the *Rosemary's Baby* connection, and asks her if she's seen the film yet. "I will go to the premiere here next Wed., and will have some of the members of my church there in black robes... I am sending a poster [the Satan Wants You "recruitment" poster] which is now being distributed to local dealers, and possibly will be handled by dealers in L.A. and New York." Romano writes again a couple of weeks later to say that Doubleday is still silent and the plan is to send the manuscript on to Random House. "Thank you for the poster," she tells him. "It's great, and you can be sure it's going up in our office. I'll let you know what comment it evokes."

Hijinks at the "Rosemary's Baby" film premiere ensued, including the aforementioned followers in robes and a midnight arrival in a hearse, but LaVey quickly returned to his typewriter and on July 13, 1968 he sent five more chapters to Silva Romano at the agency: "On the Choice of a Human Sacrifice," "Not All Vampires Suck Blood," "Satanic Sex," "The Balance Factor," and "The Church of Satan." His descriptions of these chapters are fairly straightforward. It's noteworthy that he wrote the "Vampires" chapter, "to clarify what is meant by 'responsibility,' in the Satanic concept... [and] in which situations and towards which types of people we believe we should and should not be expected to feel responsible."

It was somewhat revelatory to read LaVey's questions, and the doubts he expresses, as he takes the first step toward becoming the famous and notorious author of a book that hasn't gone out of print in fifty years. We always associate the man with a stern sort of confidence, not pompous or arrogant, but certainly fired with conviction for the truth his philosophy represents. Hence, when you see him asking for advice, it's surprising but completely in keeping with his character – lacking expertise in this new area, he is humble enough to seek guidance from someone else:

> Since I have never written anything commercially, I am terribly 'green' concerning the writing and publishing field. I have absolutely no idea how long it usually takes to find a publisher, or what appeals to them. Does it normally take this long to obtain a publisher, or do you think there may be a reason or reasons we have been unable to interest one in the Bible. If you have had more trouble than usual in selling it, do you think it could be due to the rather controversial nature of the book, or does it leave something to be desired? Is the writing below par, or is the subject matter not handled as well as it might be? Could we be shooting too high regarding the publishers we have tried? Please be frank, and advise me of anything you feel might be changed to improve its salability.

Regarding the interest from Doubleday, of which they'd had every reason to feel confident and were now beginning to doubt, LaVey speculates,

> Perhaps [Luther Nichols] was only being polite... It has crossed my mind that a large publishing firm might be wary of handling the Bible for fear it might besmirch its respectable reputation. I'd like to know your thoughts on this... It seems as though every time I go in a bookstore I see more books on the black arts, Satanism, and religious cults. If these subjects are as popular as they appear to be, it would seem that, unless there is something that is technically lacking in the Bible, we shouldn't have too much trouble getting it published. As I mentioned once before, I am rather concerned that someone might jump the gun on us, and write a Satanic Bible and have it published by some fly-by-night publisher. Even though the contents of such a book would undoubtably be the same hackneyed drivel that has always been in books on Satanism, it would ruin it for us as far as the title is concerned.

A couple of weeks later, toward the end of July, LaVey heard from his friend Burton Wolfe, who sent a copy of the issue of *Knight* that contained his article on LaVey and the Church. "I think it's the best story that's been done so far," he told him in a response, "and I certainly appreciate your objective handling of it, and feel that the bit of sensationalism [he was referring to the lurid cover blurb] in it was necessary."

LaVey goes on to inform Wolfe that

> the manuscript for the *Satanic Bible* is now with Doubleday and Random House, and I'm waiting for word from my agent, as to their decision. It's pretty strong stuff, and should not only shake up the religious world, but the so-called magical groups and followers of the occult as well, as it points out that most witchcraft groups

> are either just another offshoot of Christianity or sex clubs using Satanism for an excuse.

August was quiet, and we can only suppose that while the publishing world, led by New York City, went into vacation mode, LaVey kept banging away at the keyboard. In September, he sent his Enochian Keys to Silva Romano, and asked again for any news from the publishers. He mentions his friend, Marcello Truzzi, who has volunteered to put in a good word anywhere they think it could be useful. Truzzi recommended they contact Prentice-Hall [the eventual publisher of *The Compleat Witch* hardcover] and had already spoken to an editor there, who seemed interested. LaVey is intrigued by this possibility, as "they just published Sybil Leek's book, *Diary Of a Witch*, (another 'white witchcraft book' book filled with sanctimonious drivel. Ho hum!) but still in the vein of the supernormal and the occult." At this time, Truzzi had a book in the works at Random House and offered to drop a line there, as well. LaVey mentions Truzzi's proposal to him that they collaborate:

> A few months ago, Marcello approached me on the possibility of co-authoring a book called 'Cauldron Cookery,' a sort of recipe book for witches. I told him that until the *Satanic Bible* was published, I thought I should concentrate on things of a more serious nature, as something like 'Cauldron Cookery' might hamper the credibility of the Bible... At any rate, I thought I'd let you know about these possibilities, for whatever they're worth.

From the tone of LaVey's letter, it's clear that he's beginning to be discouraged as well as impatient.

> Originally, I was very intent upon obtaining a publisher with a rather 'stuffy' reputation, as I thought it would confound the public to see the *Satanic Bible* published by a house such as this, and as a matter of fact, I still feel this way. However, we may just be beating our heads against stone walls. What do you think about trying a publisher with a reputation for handling more confrontational works – such as Gove [sic] Press?

He goes on to tell Romano that in between his sessions at the typewriter, he's been working to record "The Satanic Mass" album, "which will have readings from *The Satanic Bible* on one side, and the Satanic ritual on the other." He further speculates that it would be helpful to have *The Satanic Bible* out at the same time, which is scheduled to be around Halloween, less than two months away. Again, this was more than optimistic – it was fairly naive as to the amount of time it would take to complete the book we now know as *The Satanic Bible.*

Another month went by, one in which LaVey's frustration only grew. As

Halloween 1968 approached, he was probably deluged with media requests and had nothing to plug as he made the rounds of the local radio and TV stations. He addressed another letter to his agent, Mike Hamilburg:

> I don't know why we have not been able to interest a publisher, but whether it is because it's too hot an item and publishers are afraid to handle it, or because it just plain isn't good enough, we simply can't stall any longer. It is very frustrating to see all the Satanic literature coming out, not to mention the Satanic influence in other fields – music, movies, theatre, etc. – and know that I am responsible for the whole thing, and can't even get my book published.
>
> We have to get this book out before everyone thinks, when we finally do get it published, that we are just jumping on the bandwagon instead of leading the parade. There is every indication that 1969 will be the big year for witchcraft and Satanism, and so the sooner the Bible is in print, the better. Perhaps I am being naive, but I think the book is good, the only problem being that by the time it's in print everyone else will have said what's in it before me. Do you think we might be aiming too high, because there is so much inferior material on the subject being ground out by the reams by any number of publishers. They are even dredging up old material and reprinting it. It seems like anything with the label of Satanism or witchcraft will sell, so maybe if we try a smaller publisher we will get some results.
>
> Our recording, 'The Satanic Mass,' went to press about three days ago [October 6, 1968] and should be available to the public (we hope) right before Halloween...The notes on the back of the record jacket tells a little about the church and *The Satanic Bible*, and a brief background on myself. Of course, I'm quite enthused about this, since it will at least safeguard the title, *The Satanic Bible*, for us, and will do much to interest people in it.
>
> Still, it's rather embarrassing to be the founder and leader of the fastest growing, most controversial religion in the world, and not have so much as one book to give to my followers, much less the rest of the public. With this in mind, I think it my duty to make our philosophy available to people, and am seriously considering a Vanity Press publication of the *Bible*, unless we are able to interest a publisher – *any* publisher – within one more month. I have been talking to some of the members of the church about the feasibility of printing it ourselves, so if we can't get it published any other way in

> the near future, I will have the information needed if we plan to go ahead with it... I'm sorry if I sound a bit impatient, but I believe in practicing what I preach, which means not sitting back and hoping for something to happen, but acting in a positive way which will *make* it happen.

Well, that letter must have awakened Mike from his doldrums – or maybe it was just a combination of LaVey's mounting vexation going out into the ethers and an agent who had just seen a lucrative property slipping through his fingers. One week later, Hamilburg called LaVey with the good news that Avon Books had expressed an interest in *The Satanic Bible*, and the editor to contact was Peter Mayer.

A little bit about Peter Mayer: at the time of his encounter with Anton LaVey, he was in his early thirties but was already a top editor at Avon; a couple of years later, he founded the Overlook Press in Woodstock, NY, which is still in existence today. A bit of a whiz kid, he earned a Ford Foundation scholarship to Columbia, studied at Oxford, and received a Fulbright scholarship to study German literature at the Freie Universität Berlin. After Avon, he moved on to Penguin Books where he made waves by signing Salman Rushdie and *The Satanic Verses* – one editor, two famous Satanic books.

After hearing from Hamilburg (and, one imagines, dancing a devilish jig around his office), LaVey sent Peter Mayer the first of many letters to follow, introducing himself and suggesting that they meet in a few weeks when Mayer was supposed to be visiting the West Coast. A week or so later, LaVey followed up with his agent, having had no response from Mayer, but reporting that, at Hamilburg's suggestion, he'd sent the editor a "Satan Wants You" poster. He goes on to report that he'll be traveling to New York City, with a stopover in Cleveland, the first week of November and asking if there is anyone he should contact while there. As the publication of *The Satanic Bible* was still in the future, it can be assumed that this trip was promoting "The Satanic Mass" album.

A series of telephone calls are suspected to have happened in the interim, but by December 19, 1968, Peter Mayer was writing directly to LaVey and requesting copies of the five-part series the *National Insider* had recently published on the Church of Satan. LaVey relayed the request on to Mike Resnick, the author of the series, and wrote back to Mayer, saying he'd heard from Carol Sturm Smith. Carol had been assigned to work directly with LaVey on the manuscript. "She writes a very cordial letter," LaVey observed, "and I am certain we will work well together." A new mother and a resident of New York's Lower East Side Alphabet City, Smith did indeed write to LaVey in late December 1968 on pretty stationery with a pale blue border, that belied the friendly-but-stern list of demands for the remainder of the manuscript and additional material as soon as possible. He wrote back right after the beginning of the year:

> I think you will find me to be very agreeable to most suggestions,

> and ask only that the philosophy and actual ceremonies remain unchanged. I fully realize the value of professional advice and assistance with the continuity and polished presentation of the book, and therefore, am open to your expert recommendations.

Shortly afterward, LaVey sent off an updated outline as Smith had requested, and included a letter detailing his thought process and expressing some concerns:

> The section on the Black Mass is nearly completed and will be sent to you as soon as I finish it. It will be rather brief, as there has been much written on this subject in other books. I will cover a few little-known historical points and will include a description of a contemporary Black Mass as practiced in the Church of Satan. The reason I do not wish to dwell heavily on this subject, is that most people have the misconception that *all* Satanic rituals are Black Masses, and this, of course, is completely untrue. We practice the traditional Black Mass only occasionally, and on these occasions it is performed merely as a catharsis for a member who feels he needs it, or as an illustration of what has been done in the past.
>
> The Enochian Keys which went to my agent were, I am afraid, badly reproduced with many typographical errors. I had one of my members type it for me, as my secretary was extremely busy at the time, and I did not discover until after they had been sent that the young lady was not the typist she claimed to be. Therefore, I will have my secretary retype them and send them to you probably in a week or so. I am sure you haven't been able to make much sense out of them, but in their proper form they are really quite powerful.

He addresses his difficulty in writing the chapter on the Church of Satan.

> It was rather difficult to write because in order to write it in the first person, it would sound terribly egotistic. Therefore, with the help of other members, it was written in the second person; but by so doing it simply does not fit into the continuity of the book. Do you feel it should be included in the body of the book under its existing chapter heading?... I am in a bit of a quandary regarding this chapter, and only wrote it to cooperate with my agent's suggestion...

In mid-January, LaVey wrote to Silva Romano at the Hamilburg Agency to prod them about his contract. "Before we progress much farther, I would like to have the contract taken care of." Romano's letter with the contracts crossed this letter in the mail, and arrived immediately, but there was a slight concern.

> Until now, I assumed the title, 'The Satanic Bible,' was acceptable to Peter, but the contract states a tentative title of 'Bible of the Church of Satan.' I can see the reasons for either title being appropriate, but I feel very strongly about stressing the *bible* image. Is it possible that if I sign the contract Avon might be able to put any title they choose on it, because I have not specified a certain title in the contract? I merely want to safeguard myself against the possibility of them selecting a title such as, (I'm giving ludicrous examples) 'Inside The Church of Satan', or 'A Handbook for Satanists'.

In February, editor Carol Sturm Smith's response to LaVey's updated outline arrived along with the excuse for the delay: her entire family, herself, her husband and her baby, had the Hong Kong Flu. As a New York City resident at the time, I vividly remember this bit of medical history, only the third pandemic flu to reach the United States in the 20th century. While not particularly deadly, it was extremely contagious.

Smith agrees that the chapter on the Church of Satan doesn't work in the book at all, "because the section remains basically a first-person look at the Church of Satan." She suggests that it would simply be better to have someone else expand it as a mini-biography of the author "because it is exactly this information – which is probably well-enough known and therefore deemed 'unimportant' to the members of the Church – that the general public you hope will buy the Bible is interested in... and it is this information which will help humanize the Church for those who are either unaware of its existence or who would write it off as a conglomeration of 'nuts.'"

In analyzing the structure of the *Bible*, its division into four "books," she stresses that as a whole it "will serve the dual purpose of providing the liturgy for the Church members and an explanation for the public." She suggests that LaVey take a look at Timothy Leary's new book, *High Priest*, as it has title pages for each section that might serve as a model for how each Book would be presented. It was also important to Smith that whatever "house literature" the Church of Satan was using amongst its members, and which was to be incorporated into the *Bible*, be completely consistent in spelling and punctuation, and so at this time she requested copies of the mimeos the members had been receiving as part of their membership materials.

To add to his writing burden at this time, and increase his sense of urgency, LaVey received an interesting proposition from Michael Resnick, the editor of *National Insider*. Resnick had recently completed a five-part series on the Church of Satan. Would LaVey like to write a WEEKLY column for the paper, answering letters from his constituents? Money was involved, and the offer was accepted, turning into the column we all know now as "Letters From the Devil."

After a few weeks back at his typewriter, LaVey answered Carol Sturm Smith in late February with a solution to the problem of the Church of Satan chapter. After reading her last letter to his friend Burton Wolfe, Burton offered to write it, and so the LaVey biographical details ultimately became part of the Introduction, penned by Wolfe, and LaVey's own Introduction became the Preface. The Church of Satan chapter itself was scrapped.

[In listing Wolfe's many publishing credits for Smith, LaVey also mentions that for a time, Wolfe was the ghost writer for Hugh Hefner's "The Playboy Philosophy" column. If you've ever marveled at how "Satanic" Playboy's principles of sexual freedom and indulgence seem, well, this may be a clue.]

The Enochian Keys continued to evolve, and in this same letter, LaVey gives us some fascinating insight into how they did:

> I am revising the English translation of the [Enochian] Keys considerably... as they were translated during a period when the Satanist was far more of an underground soul than he need be now. So, naturally, they have a rather defeatist tone. I am eliminating this feeling and returning them to the original meaning as expressed in the camouflage provided by the Enochian. This will be a freely translated version, rather than a word-for-word one, as the Keys are very esoteric and tend to be a bit rambling because of that esotericism. The new unexpurgated version I will be sending makes far more sense, will be easily understood by most, and, therefore, will serve the purpose for which they were intended...emotionally stimulating and diabolically correct incantations for various purposes. I will also add notations on each indicating the situations for which they are to be employed. I would like it to be clearly stated that this translation is, 'the unexpurgated version, translated by Anton LaVey.' I have two reasons for this: first, I want my followers to be aware that these, and only these, are truly Satanic and give the original meaning of the Keys, instead of the shrouded, white-light, sterilized meaning which has been given by those few conscience-stricken, and fear-ridden interpreters who have offered them to scholars of the occult, in the past. Secondly, I will take fiendish delight in envisioning the reaction of so-called magicians and witches when they find that I have had the 'audacity' to present their 'forbidden' odes in their original, blasphemous form. Not even the 'evilest' of their messiahs has dared that! I would find this most amusing.

At around the same time, LaVey wrote to Peter Mayer, as he'd been instructed to keep him up-to-date on his media appearances. LaVey informs him that the March 1969 issue of *Playboy* has an article, "Cultsville USA," which is, in part, on the Church of Satan. "It's a snidely-written piece throughout, and lumps us in with all the white-light, mystical groups, but it does reach a vast market and they spell the name right... Caravel Films, an Italian film company that did 'Mondo Cane' just completed a film segment on us that will be part of a documentary on magic. It will be released in Europe in Sept. under the name 'Magic Report', and here in the States in Dec. possibly under the title of 'The Power of Magic'." The title for this film evolved to "Angeli Bianchi... Angeli Neri," or "White Angel, Black Angel," and then "Witchcraft '70." The director, Luigi Scattini, lost control of the film before it was released and it was edited into a sensational, snarkily-narrated piece of shock-schlock you may purchase today on DVD.

LaVey goes on to again express his concern over the title of the book; apparently, Carol Sturm Smith didn't like either *The Satanic Bible* OR *The Bible of the Church of Satan* as titles. He goes to bat once more for *The Satanic Bible,*

> ...for several reasons. First, I think it is more outrageous than the other title, and secondly, it is the name we established for the book. For example: the record refers to it as 'The Satanic Bible', as have innumerable articles. Many people in the media are waiting and watching for my 'Satanic Bible', also all the members have been hearing of the prospective text on Satanism for some time under that title... Also... the dignified presentation would be accomplished best by packaging the book in a plain, stark black jacket with the lettering and symbol of Baphomet in silver as the only ornamentation.

On March 6, 1969, LaVey wrote to Carol Sturm Smith to inform her that he'd sent the Enochian Keys and "The Black Mass" via air mail under separate cover, and was working on copy for the title pages of all four Books. He also instructs her to change the word "Shamad" to "Saitan" in the section on the Infernal Names. And he asks, one more time, if anyone can confirm his fervent hope, that his book will be titled, "The Satanic Bible."

LaVey wrote to Peter Mayer a couple of weeks later, with the news that Murgenstrumm Records was planning national distribution of "The Satanic Mass" album to coincide with the release of the book. He wondered if it would be possible for the two items to be cross-promoted – would Avon be willing to include a mention of the album somewhere in *The Satanic Bible?* He also informed Mayer that *Playboy* had solicited two response letters from LaVey, one as a follow-up to the "Cultsville U.S.A." article mentioned above, and another to a piece by ex-Reverend Harvey Cox, "Religion and Morality."

Mayer sent a letter on March 24th, telling LaVey not to worry about the book's title: "We'll work it out together... As for the publication date, it can't possibly be until the fall. For us to have managed April 1 would have meant having the completed manuscript by January 15. Sorry, but the date you would have liked was an outside shot on the order of an impossibility." On April 11th, Mayer again wrote to LaVey, telling him it wouldn't be appropriate to promote "The Satanic Mass" in the pages of the *Bible:* "...it sounds hucksterish. Please do send me all mentions of the Church of Satan for our file. Carol says that the book is coming along all right, but not as fast as she or you or I would like."

In fact, Carol also wrote to LaVey at this time, nudging him for the answers to a series of queries she'd sent, plus the Church of Satan chapter and the title pages for the Books. She makes reference to a recent earthquake in California: "We in the east are all relieved that California is still firmly attached to the rest of the mainland," and this must have been the Borrego Mountain Earthquake of April 8th, 1969.

LaVey wrote back immediately and assured her that he'd get the Church of Satan chapter in the mail that night. "Let me know what you think of it – I like it." He also assures her he'll get to work on the title pages and will try to have them in the mail in a week. The query pages she mentions, however, are a mystery – he never received them. "I don't know if it's the San Francisco P.O. or New York's, but I hope you have copies so you won't have to go to the trouble of composing them a second time."

Two weeks later, he wrote to Smith again, responding to some corrections he'd received. The references are rather tantalizing, as he doesn't specify what the corrections were. "I think for the most part the corrections you've made are in order and even the ones I've asked you to leave as I have them are reasonable suggestions. I can see your reasons for suggesting they be changed, but have definite purposes for wanting them left as they are." He tells her he is enclosing the "introduction by Burton Wolfe." It's unclear if this is now how he's referring to "the chapter on the Church of Satan." He also sends along the title page copy for one of the four Books and promises the other three "sometime this week." At this point, Carol Sturm Smith must have been accustomed to taking these promises with a grain of salt.

It took LaVey three more weeks to write to Smith again, sending more of the promised material. He mentions getting "side-tracked by other things." Well, one of those other things was a letter from Thomas Lipscomb of Prentice-Hall, expressing interest in publishing LaVey's next book as a hardcover. In the middle of trying to get his last writing done on *The Satanic Bible*, LaVey was starting to put together the book we now know as *The Satanic Witch*. He wrote to his agent, Mike Hamilburg, right away with concern over the exclusivity clause in his contract with Avon – did this pertain to hardcovers as well? "Any future books I do I would rather have in hardcover, first." He goes on to ask Hamilburg if he knows of any lecture bureaus he could approach about the many requests he is receiving for public talks about Satanism.

> From the many letters I receive from colleges, there seems to be a great deal of interest for me to speak at various universities and colleges around the country. For some time now I have put off looking into this matter, but every time I receive another inquiry concerning my lecture fees and booking dates, it brings it to mind again.

Around the same time, LaVey was approached by William Targ, an editor at Putnam's who had been referred to LaVey by Burton Wolfe. He was interested in publishing a book on "any aspects of occultism in which you are concerned." LaVey responded cordially, sending a copy of "The Satanic Mass" and the "Satan Wants You" poster. He referred him on to Avon Books about possibly producing a hardcover edition of *The Satanic Bible*, as Avon was a paperback publisher. Targ was happy to receive the album and promised he would "...play the album when I get home tonight and am sure I will enjoy it. When my friend Ira Levin visits me next, I will of course play it for him too!"

Back at *The Satanic Bible*, it's amusing to see him employ a little Lesser Magic with his apology to Smith, observing that this delay gave her a chance to spend more time with her baby. "Children can certainly be a wonderful buffer for a fast-paced existence – my five year old is a constant source of entertainment for me!"

His letter goes on to talk about the appearance of the book itself.

> Concerning illustrations, the only things available are the much-used old engravings of demons, etc. Avon has appeared to me to use artwork far superior to other paperback houses for their covers. In this case I would *rather* the cover be almost frightening in its formality – black background with silver cloister text and silver or possibly scarlet symbol of Baphomet (the inverted pentagram held by the dragon on this letterhead) directly under text in center of cover. Using this cover format might allow for art costs normally expended on cover design to be diverted to the inside black and white artwork, which definitely would set the Bible apart from other paperbacks. Nymphs, satyrs, demons, bat-winged figures, flames hovering over and/or surrounding pages would, I'm sure, pay off in the long run.

Ultimately, all that were used were several images from the Church of Satan stationery, which we believe were sketched by LaVey himself.

He finished by instructing Smith about other items: "At the beginning of the entire Bible I want a solitary page reading: For Diane. At the end of the Bible I want one final page empty except for the words, 'Yankee Rose'." For those who were hoping for one, I regret to inform you that there was no explanation provided.

In mid-June, LaVey sent off another copy of "The Satanic Mass" album to Avon; they would use the graphic of the Baphomet symbol on the jacket for the cover of *The Satanic Bible.*

As the editing went forward on the *Bible*, LaVey's agents were in contact with other publishers about bringing the book out in hardcover. Silva Romano wrote to LaVey to confirm for him that Peter Mayer at Avon was amenable to the idea and thought that Putnam's might be a good place for the book. Unfortunately, before the end of June, Putnam's gave *The Satanic Bible* a quick and hard pass, with William Targ citing "house policy" about not bringing out a hardcover after a paperback edition has already been released. As we all know, this is exactly what eventually happened, and it was just one more way LaVey's little black book was breaking every mold.

When July came, LaVey felt compelled to again bring up the subject of the title with his editor, Peter Mayer. It becomes quite clear that the Avon team had been putting off answering LaVey in any final context on this issue, and one can easily sense and share his frustration.

> Since Burton Wolfe's book, *The Satanists*, is now going into final editing and mentions my book in its context, I would like to clear up the indecision concerning the title for my Bible. As you know, I still prefer my original title, the *Satanic Bible*, for several reasons. First, because it has become 'popular knowledge' that that will be the name of it... Also, I simply think it is more phonetic and hard-hitting than any other alternative that has been suggested. You haven't specifically said that you are opposed to that title, but since there has been some discrepancy about it, I would assume you have some reservations... If you feel strongly about your proposed title, *The Bible of the Church of Satan*, I could only go along with it if the cover format stressed 'The Bible' (perhaps three times larger than the rest of the title).

Perhaps it was the lack of feedback of any kind on this issue that frustrated LaVey the most, but we may all thank the infernal deity of our choice, that the right decision was made. It's impossible to imagine this book with any other title, and it could be argued that LaVey had the future in mind when he chose it – I believe much of *The Satanic Bible's* longevity can be attributed to the strong, essential message conveyed by that title.

As an aside, it's somewhat ironic that Wolfe's book, *The Satanists*, was being held up for confirmation of LaVey's title – ultimately, *The Satanists* became *The Devil's Avenger.*

LaVey goes on. "I have one small change I'd like to make to my acknowledgement page if I can. Directly under the name, Mark Twain, I'd like George Bernard Shaw inserted – with brackets between Twain and Shaw and instead of 'a very brave man' after Twain, 'very brave men' following the brackets – in other words, one statement for both men." They never made this correction. However, Avon did manage to correct Bernardino "Logaro" to "Nogaro" – with the seventh printing. Better late than never?

LaVey then asks Mayer about the possibility of a few unbound copies of the book to be sent to him for special binding, for himself and some select Church members. Keeping current with reports of the latest publicity, LaVey mentions the review of "The Satanic Mass" album in the July 1969 issue of Playboy, and the four-page article on the Church in the *Detroit Free Press* Sunday supplement for June 15th.

At this time LaVey also wrote to Nancy Coffey, a Managing Editor at Avon, who had been requesting an author's photo. LaVey had conducted a photo session for professional photographer John Hendricks, who, in lieu of payment, had offered LaVey his choice of photos to be used as he wished. "I thought this one would be best, as it shows me in the clerical collar. However, I have one other I considered, which shows me with my lion. The composition is excellent and the picture is good of both the lion and myself." Nancy was happy and assured him, "the photo will reproduce very well and we'll return it to you when we have finished with it." She was able to confirm that the book would be out in December and that the Church would be receiving 500 copies directly from the bindery, but that Avon would not be able to provide any unbound copies.

In August 1969, LaVey heard directly from Avon's publicity department for the first time. Judy Weber sent him a questionnaire asking for the standard biographical details. Under "Past Occupations," he reports the same list of jobs with which we're all familiar: "symphony oboist (age 16), carnival worker: (sideshows, 'girlie' shows, fortune teller, 'spook' show), circus wild animal trainer, concert organist, calliope player, music teacher, pianist for burlesque houses, clinical hypnotist, psychical researcher or 'ghost hunter', architectural designer, criminologist, painter (oils), lecturer." His interests and hobbies are also consistent with what LaVey has always spoken of, with some interesting details:

> ...magic and the occult, obviously – classical music and wild animals fondest loves. Owned and kept a 500 lb., male African lion in San Francisco townhouse for over three years. Lion's name: 'Togare.' Lion now at S.F. Zoo, and father of four male cubs named: Satan, Lucifer, Belial, Leviathan. Announcement of my name and the Church of Satan is given in reference to donator of lion, on all Zoo tours.

Unfortunately, this questionnaire had arrived with his name and the book's title already filled out: "The Bible of the Church of Satan." LaVey headed to his typewriter and doggedly pounded out yet-another letter to Avon, this one addressed to Managing Editor Nancy Coffey, informing her of all the sales inquiries they were receiving at Central, and presenting his case one more time:

> I was under the assumption that the question of title had been resolved and that it was to be *The Satanic Bible*, but when I received my 'author questionnaire', the title was given as: *Bible of the Church of Satan*. Was this because the publicity department had not yet been notified of the correct name, or is there still some discrepancy? I definitely want it published under my original title, and feel it would be foolhardy to negate the advance publicity I've been doing, by

throwing prospective buyers off the track with a different title.

In mid-September, LaVey heard from Silva Romano at the Hamilburg agency, informing him that galleys would be sent in around three weeks, and that she and Peter Mayer hoped to have them at that year's Frankfurt Book Fair, one of the publishing world's biggest events. Shortly afterward, a piece of mail arrived that must have had LaVey twitching his barbed tail in joy and satisfaction: Nancy Coffey sent a cover proof, replete with its title glowing ominously from its all-black cover: *The Satanic Bible.* This was no dream; this was really happening.

In October, he wrote back to Coffey expressing his delight in the cover and passing on how impressed everyone is when he shows it off. He was planning a Halloween press tour to Detroit, Michigan and then on to New York, and explained with devilish glee what he planned to do with the cover proof he'd received:

> The Lou Gordon Show in Detroit has asked me several times in the past six months to appear... I told [the producer] I wouldn't have the *Bible* before Dec. 1st, but would have the proof of the cover... I couldn't see any reason why I couldn't just put the cover on another paperback and use the tried and true formula of magic – misdirection – and go ahead and promote the book.

He was always trying to pass on any new publicity, so he reported that the November 1969 issue of *Confidential* was carrying a new article about Sharon Tate that included his quotes, and he mentioned Hans Holzer: "*The Truth About Witchcraft*, by Hans Holzer – published by Doubleday has close to a chapter on myself and the Church, which is fairly good if you can overlook the glaring inaccuracies in spelling and other areas."

After receiving an inquiry from Judy Weber, his publicity representative at Avon, he wrote confirming the dates he'd be in New York City and expressing his eagerness to meet her and his other contacts at Avon. While in New York, he stayed at the Barbizon Plaza Hotel, a venerable old place that was built only a month after Anton LaVey was born. It was across the street from Central Park, and close to Carnegie Hall and Lincoln Center. If Guy Woodhouse was around, he might have observed that he could walk to all the theaters from there.

The publicity trip went well, and the LaVeys were able to meet with Coffey and Weber while they were in New York. Judy Weber tried to put LaVey in touch with a reporter from a large news service, who made the mistake of calling at 9:00 a.m. on a Sunday morning after LaVey had been working all night, and getting a mite pushy and entitled about needing an interview. He probably never made that mistake again.

What was LaVey working on, now that *The Satanic Bible* had "gone to bed?" Why, *The Compleat Witch*, of course. Negotiations with Tom Lipscomb at Prentice-Hall had been completed and contracts were being sent. But that's a story for another day.

In late November, LaVey updated his agency again, and said he was waiting for his shipment of promotional copies of the *Bible* to arrive so he could start promoting it. "I realize that normally paperback books are more difficult to get reviewed than are hardcover books, but I have more opportunities to reach the public than most writers." Silva Romano responded a couple of weeks later assuring him that Avon had confirmed that the shipment of 500 copies had just gone out, and enclosing the remainder of his advance from Avon minus commission: a check for $1,012.50.

Sometime during the last week of November, 1969 (right in time for Thanksgiving), the first *Satanic Bibles* arrived at the Black House. Personalized autographed copies dated November 27, 1969 and November 29, 1969 have been identified for our records.

There's no direct evidence or observations of Anton LaVey's reaction to receiving his first copy of *The Satanic Bible.* We can work from the supposition that it was very, very satisfying. I see him holding it, passing his hand over the cover, sitting down to flip through it at length – then walking into his ritual chamber and placing it on the altar. Perhaps a joyful dinner with friends was quickly arranged; certainly, I expect a few bottles were uncorked.

One of the questions on the author survey from Avon was, "What sort of reaction to your book do you anticipate?" He answered:

> None other than what would be expected in presenting the most blasphemous and controversial religion in the 'civilized' world... My book is a bible written by a self-admitted Satanist for Satanists (or would-be Satanists), and those seeking the *truth* about same. It's the only volume of its kind in the history of religion. This is the only *published* work on the subject of Satanism, by a Satanist.

In the preceding article, I've detailed the painstaking process of submitting sections of the book, piece by piece, over weeks and months, of the deadlines he missed, and the corrections and changes he would not accept. The editors pushed him; the marketplace pushed him; the many letters pouring into the Church of Satan pushed him to get that manuscript into being. He listened, but he never rushed. He wrote the book he wanted to write. There are those who have tried to tell you that he always planned to rewrite it someday. I think there's enough evidence here – and tonight, in this very room – to assure us that he took the time he needed.

To fifty years of *The Satanic Bible!* Hail Satan!

Addendum to "So It Was Written: The History of The Satanic Bible"

Peggy Nadramia

The Reviews

As those of us who are writers, editors and publishers know too well, receiving that first box of fresh, new copies of a book is an exciting moment whose satisfaction is fleeting in the face of the need to publicize and distribute our titles. LaVey's office staff went into high gear to get copies in the right hands and reviews started to appear widely in newspapers and trade publications. LaVey dutifully reported these onward for a few months but as *The Satanic Bible's* first year in print wore on, the task became overwhelming.

In a letter to Peter Mayer from June 1970, LaVey eagerly relates his satisfaction with an extended article that was scheduled to appear the next month in the magazine section of the London Daily Telegraph. A photo of LaVey and mention of *The Satanic Bible* had just appeared that month in *Penthouse*, "the English equivalent of Playboy," according to LaVey, and he's impatient for Avon to step up their distribution into the United Kingdom in the wake of this publicity. By November of that year, LaVey was again contacting Mayer and attempting to list the many outlets where *The Satanic Bible* and the Church of Satan were being reviewed and discussed: "*National Enquirer... San Francisco Chronicle... The Lawton Constitution... The Forty-Niner...*" More books on modern occultism were appearing and including LaVey: "*The Second Coming* by Arthur Lyons... *Today's Witches* by Suzy Smith... *Witchcraft In America Today* by Emile C. Schurmacher..." LaVey was still an object of local interest and he reports two television appearances, "The Mid-Morning Show" in San Francisco, and an "ABC-TV mini-documentary on witchcraft."

There had been a rather horrific murder that year with occult and cannibalistic overtones [Stroup and Baker, the "Yellowstone Murder"] and LaVey was consulted by the Associated Press for their wire story. His perspective was interesting:

> ...no matter what we do to rebuke any reports which attempt to tie us with Stoup [sic] and Baker, Manson and others who profess Satanic inspiration for their illicit actions, the public will believe what they want to. So we might just as well accustom ourselves to the fact that we'll sell some books as the result of such dubious testimonials and therefore include this sort of publicity under the

> category of 'promotion.' I didn't mean to embark upon a diatribe on the 'misunderstood, good-guy Satanist,' but I did want to mention this piece and felt you might wonder what possessed me to include it in a list of publicity items which are in drastic contrast to this one.

He didn't always feel this way; LaVey's growing irritation with the public perception of Satanism came to a head in the early 80's when he sued the author and publishers of *Michelle Remembers.*

In 1973 members of the Church of Satan were asked to pitch in and send clippings of local reviews directly to the publicity department at Avon. They continued to send them in to the Church itself for decades.

One of the more interesting reviews from the time *The Satanic Bible* was published, appeared in the regular Books column of the Sunday *St. Louis Post-Dispatch,* December 27, 1970. The reviewer was Deirdre LaRouche and she covered three different books on Satanism; the column was titled, "Satan: The Modern Liberator." Here's what she said:

> '*The Satanic Bible*' by Anton LaVey approaches Satanism from a vastly different angle. LaVey is the founder and high priest of the Church of Satan, a legally functioning and licensed religion with a membership of some 7,000 people, a regular schedule of meetings and a surprisingly non-secretive attitude towards its ceremonies and teachings. The main theme of this 'bible' seems to be that repression and frustration of man's desires and needs are the underlying causes of most, if not all, of the ills that afflict society today. LaVey feels that the repressive influences of established religion, with its constant emphasis of the inherent inability of its members to meet God's high standards of behavior and morality, are responsible for the current state of rebellion so apparent in today's youth. How can we expect our children to conform to the mores of a society whose Christian ethic is constantly being compromised and manipulated to suit the needs, political and social, of its self-indulgent and war-oriented 'older generation,' he asks. What the young people of today are seeking, LaVey feels, is an honest religion, barren of hypocrisy, martyrdom and false humility, and offering instead pride in one's being, acknowledgement of one's carnality and full enjoyment of all aspects of life on this Earth of ours.
>
> Anton LaVey is, from his writing and from descriptions of him by others, a brilliant man who became thoroughly disillusioned with all so-called 'good Christians' at an early age. As a carnival organist and as a San Francisco Police photographer, he saw more than he cared to of the seamier side of human nature. He developed an abiding

> hatred of the phrase 'It was God's will,' particularly when applied to the sufferings and deaths of innocent people who had been victims of the violence that seethes constantly under the placid and too often unconcerned eyes of our 'God-fearing' citizenry.
>
> According to LaVey, the Church of Satan does not celebrate the anti-Christian black mass, nor require of its initiates that they blaspheme, desecrate holy articles, nor subject themselves to degrading and degenerate sexual practices in order to become members. The rituals observed are not aimed at destroying other religions, but at creating in the congregation a sense of freedom of self, awareness of one's responsibilities to self and to others, and liberation from society-imposed attitudes which hamper the full development of one's potential as a human being. In a very real sense, the message of *'The Satanic Bible'* is that of Walt Whitman's 'Song of Myself' ... 'I celebrate myself, and sing myself...' and I suspect that, although its existence may be deplored by many, this book and its adherents will be around for a long time to come.

The Hardcover

After a lively but ultimately disappointing series of exchanges in 1969 with William Targ of Putnam's [see my main article, "So It Was Written"] regarding a hardcover version of *The Satanic Bible*, both Avon and LaVey appear to have shelved the effort until August 1971, when LaVey wrote a letter to publisher Lyle Stuart, whose company also did business as University Books.

> I am delighted to hear that you will be publishing my *Satanic Bible* in hardcover. I have long been an admirer of your literary successes and your obvious know-how when it comes to reaching the masses... We receive increasing numbers of letters asking about the availability of a 'permanent,' 'library,' 'formal,' etc. edition of the *Bible*, so I believe the time is as right as it can be... I am convinced that *The Satanic Bible* will, in due time, become the primer for a popular movement destined to virtually obliterate existing Christian mumbo-jumbo. From what I have heard of you, I couldn't think of a better Devil's advocate with whom to traffic.

LaVey received a prompt response from Stuart's vice-president, Robert Salomon, who tersely confirmed the company's intention to publish the hardcover and complained that they'd been waiting for a contract from Avon for six months. Things went quiet, but by the end of 1972, Salomon wrote again to inform LaVey of their plans to bring out *The Satanic Rituals* in the same format. Both hardcovers appeared simultaneously the next year, and LaVey received his author's copies in September of 1973. When the Church of Satan attempted to purchase additional stock of the hardcover *Satanic Bible* in June of 1976, their check was returned with a note confirming that there were no longer any copies available.

Swiftly thereafter, in August of the same year, *The Satanic Bible* was under consideration for another hardcover edition by the Robert Collier Book Corporation in New Jersey; they contemplated putting out a new edition with an updated introduction and distributing it alongside Avon's paperback version by direct mail to individual readers. Collier did ultimately contract with LaVey to distribute *The Satanic Bible.* Their proposed advertising campaign focused on the empowerment the book could bestow on *anyone*, including the adherents of mainstream religions:

> We are not in any way suggesting that you reject the teachings of the *Holy Bible* or the teachings of your own particular faith and replace them with the teachings of *THE SATANIC BIBLE* because then the scale would be simply tipped off-balance in the opposite direction... We are, however, saying that using them together will balance your life and make it richer, fuller, happier, filled with more fun and purpose than it could possibly be by learning only one side of the story, for 'Half-Truths are as good as lies,' and 'The Truth (The Whole Truth) will set men free.'

This diatribe was accompanied by a drawing of Satan holding *The Satanic Bible* and shaking hands with a Biblical figure holding the *Holy Bible.* Ordering information and several 800 numbers were also included. Collier proposed selling the hardcover for $9.98 with a shipping cost of eighty-five cents. This updated hardcover reprint never appeared.

In 2015, an omnibus hardcover of both *The Satanic Bible* and *The Satanic Rituals* was published by private arrangement with William Morrow, an imprint of HarperCollins-Avon, the present-day company that acquired Avon Books via Hearst Publishing. This edition was planned as part of a year-long celebration of the 50th anniversary of the founding of Anton LaVey's Church of Satan in 1966. It premiered in Washington, DC, at a conclave held there exclusively for Church of Satan members. Like the first hardcover, this edition comprises a photo-enlargement of the pages from the paperback version, and is likewise out of print. The edition ran less than 1.200 copies and is also a rare and expensive collector's item.

The Dedications

The deletion of the extended Dedications in *The Satanic Bible* took place in 1977 with it's 12th printing, and before the separation of Anton LaVey and Diane Hegarty. In 1978, in the Hoofnotes section of *The Cloven Hoof* (Volume X, #2, pages 2-3, Whole Number 72), LaVey had this to say:

> Some of you have wondered why the dedication page of *The Satanic Bible* has been omitted from new editions. Thereby hangs a tale. When the author listed those names a decade ago, they were known in varying degrees to the public, some being much more obscure than others. Since original publication, several of those mentioned gained new fame of cultic proportions. To retain those names would, to a fresh reader, appear Epimethean, especially as they appeared *before* the current updated introduction, which informs the reader of relevant societal changes which have come about since original publication of *The Satanic Bible*. It was also thought that because *The Satanic Bible* has served as the basic text on Satanism, the original list of names was far too limited. It would necessitate a separate volume to list all those who have lived and served as devil's advocates, thus lending support and inspiration to the author's creation.

In conversation, LaVey related that it was actually the result of a mishap on Avon's part. According to his biographer Blanche Barton, LaVey had requested that the publisher remove the Dedications in *The Satanic Rituals* due to the last-minute inclusion of Michael Aquino among the other names therein. Avon instead deleted the Dedications from *The Satanic Bible;* LaVey was not particularly upset by this, and his thoughts on the subject were related via that note we included above. Barton also had this to say: "There was never any discussion of omitting the 'For Diane' from the SB. Dr. LaVey respected the memory of their love, and the part she had played during the foundational years of the Church, even if she no longer did. He was indeed a romantic." "For Diane" remains in current editions of *The Satanic Bible.*

The Foreign Editions

As the Church of Satan and *The Satanic Bible* began gaining notoriety worldwide, LaVey was naturally interested in foreign language editions of his book, and so were many of the members and friends he had in other countries. He questioned his editor at Avon, Peter Mayer, who passed him on to their rights manager, Alice Bosk. In a letter from November of 1972, she explained that Avon did not own any translation rights to *The Satanic Bible* or retain any financial interest in same, and that the author's contract stipulated that he had retained them. However, Avon had agents representing their properties in many countries and could agent the rights for LaVey if he would be amenable, and a separate agreement reached and signed.

During the next few months, letters from interested publishers began coming in to the office at the Church of Satan and were duly passed on to LaVey's literary agent, Mike Hamilburg, but LaVey was not hearing back. He decided to contact Alice Bosk at Avon and take her up on the offer for Avon to represent the book to foreign publishers, as he wasn't getting any feedback from his American agent.

> We have had considerable foreign press in the last six months and anticipate at least two more large photo stories in major European magazines, by the same people who did the photo work for the *Look* and *Time* cover stories on us. Their work has already appeared in seven or eight large magazines in Europe and Latin American countries, and the mail we have subsequently received on the coverage to date would seem to indicate a goodly amount of interest.

In fact, the Hamilburg agency's representative overseas, Charlotte Wolfers, was working diligently to market the book to a number of foreign houses. Mike Hamilburg might be forgiven for holding back on LaVey at this point as the news was not good. In June of 1973, a response finally came in just as LaVey was considering this new deal with Avon:

> We received the following message from our agent in London: '*The Satanic Bible* has been rejected in this country by Mayflower, Hodders, Sphere, Pan, and is currently with Tandem Books [publishers of *The Second Coming* by Arthur Lyons - PN]. *The Satanic Rituals:* has been rejected here by Pan and is also currently with Tandem. They have both been rejected by Rizzoli in Italy. You forwarded a request from them but, as I say, they turned it down. In Holland they are turned down by Arbeiderspurs, Bruan and Zoon, and Bert Bakker, and will now go to Zuid Hollandsche. In France: no news yet.'

At this point, LaVey was informed by Charlotte Wolfers herself that she was working as Avon's agent in England and it might be best for all if he just left the foreign rights negotiations in the hands of the Hamilburg/Wolfers agencies.

Among the publishers who were contacting the Church of Satan directly with an interest in acquiring the rights to translate *The Satanic Bible*, were Edizioni Mediterranee Roma and Longanesi and Co. in Italy, Ediciones Martinez Roca and Ediciones Picaso in Spain, Bestseller Importadora de Livros in Brazil, and Kanki Books in Japan. The first Spanish language versions of *The Satanic Bible* and *The Satanic Rituals* were contracted by Ediciones Martinez Roca in 1974, and appeared in 1975, translated by José Maria Cañas.

There are references in the correspondence to unauthorized Mexican editions of *The Satanic Bible* and *The Satanic Rituals.* In 1977, local research had turned up references to *Rituales Satánicos* and *Biblia Satánico* by Anton LaVey in the card catalog of the Modesto, CA library. Both books had been borrowed and probably never returned, as frequently happens with library copies of LaVey's books. The staff at the Church of Satan began calling Spanish-language bookstores up and down the coast; some claimed they had seen the book, but no one had a copy. The library's index reference provided a publisher's name and their address, which was promptly forwarded on to Avon. Avon's rights department wrote to this address and received a response back from a little insurance agency in Mexico, protesting their innocence and avowing they didn't publish books at all. We've since concluded that these were the legitimate paperback editions published by Ediciones Martinez Roca, printed and distributed in Mexico where the company maintained a division.

LaVey did ultimately have Avon negotiating his British foreign rights, resulting in a sale in 1976 of *The Satanic Bible* to a British publisher, W. H. Allen, who created the edition with the legendary "lizard-green" cover. W. H. Allen & Co. had a long list of alternate/affiliate company names, including A. Howard, Wyndham, Richard Clay and The Chaucer Press. The British *Satanic Bible* appeared under their imprint as "a Star Book," which, I suppose, it always will be. The publishers were interested in having LaVey come over to the United Kingdom for a promotional tour; LaVey responded enthusiastically:

> Judging from the mounting interest in Satanism, your timing seems to be perfect. I would definitely be interested in coming to England, as you proposed. Many promotional possibilities come to mind, when I consider the wealth of advantages in your country for same. I'm sure my appearance at various 'Satanic' locations (I can think of many) would generate interest and be fun for all involved.

At the time the book was accepted and placed in W. H. Allen's queue for publishing, LaVey was eager to replace Michael Aquino's Introduction and mentioned several times that Burton Wolfe was finalizing an updated version; for some reason – perhaps it wasn't completed in time? – W. H. Allen wound up using the original Wolfe Introduction from 1969. The British edition went out of print after an unknown number of copies were printed, but is not difficult to find in collector's markets.

Sphinx published a Danish edition in 1987, *Satans Bibel & Rituale*, translated by Frater Edwin.

In 1990, Carl Abrahamsson contracted with HarperCollins-Avon and LaVey to publish his Swedish translation via Psychick Release. He renewed the rights in 1995 and ultimately published it under the auspices of his own Looking Glass Press. This attractive trade paperback included an author photo by Nick Bougas.

A Czech translation by Josef Rauvolf (*Satanská Bible*) was published in 1991 by Reflex Publishing in Prague. Reflex was founded in 1990 and is chiefly a magazine. Rauvolf is known for his work translating such Beat Generation authors as William S. Burroughs and Jack Kerouac.

In the wake of LaVey's death in 1997, a number of small foreign publishers grew interested in publishing translations of *The Satanic Bible*, as well as the rest of LaVey's body of work, and approached the Church of Satan with their inquiries. Magus Peter H. Gilmore quickly became the unpaid and largely unrecognized liaison between these entities and HarperCollins-Avon, advising on the material and its presentation, clarifying the use of symbols and graphics, and reviewing the contracts in consultation with the original American publisher. He continues to function in this role today. Bootleg editions were being dumped on the public immediately following LaVey's passing, so management of new translations became a key priority.

What follows is a list of foreign translations which is as complete as we can make it, given the propensity today to flagrantly disregard copyright as well as common courtesy.

1997: Russian / Unholy Words F.O.D. / *Sataninskaya Bibliya*
1998: Spanish / Faesan, Inc. / Riverbank, CA / *La Biblia Satánica*

In 1999, Ingrid Meyer of Second Sight introduced her own long-awaited German translation of *The Satanic Bible* (*Die Satanische Bibel*). She followed this up in 2003 with an omnibus edition that included *The Satanic Rituals* (*Die Satanischen Rituale*), and introduced an elaborate boxed set of same in 2007, which included an audio CD of the books being read in German, and a poster of the symbol of Baphomet. Yet another edition of the omnibus appeared in 2013 under the Index Verlag imprint.

1990: Danish / SphinX Publishers / *Satans Bibel & Rituale* / Frater Edwin, translator
1999: Bulgarian / Unknown / *Sataninska Biblija* / Atanas Semniazov, translator
1999: Polish / Fox / *Biblia Szatana*
2001: Estonian / R. Jaanson / *Saatanlik Piibel*
2003: Czech / Baronet / *Satanská Bible*
2004: Danish / LuciFer Publishing via Lennart Sane Agency / *Satans Bibel* and *Satans Rituale*r / Frater Edwin, translator
2004: Norwegian / Wolf's Lair via Tönnheim / *Den Sataniske Bibelen* / Marius Huseby, translator
2006: French / Camion Noir / *La Bible Satanique*
2007: Portuguese / HellOutro Enterprises / *A Bíblia Satânica*
2007: Italian / Arcana / *La Bibbia di Satana*
2007: Finnish / Voimasana / *Saatanallinen Raamattu* / Paula Merensuo, translator
2008: Danish / SphinX Publishers / Omnibus Edition: *Satans Bibel & Rituale* / Frater Edwin, translator
2008: Spanish / Martinez Roca / *La Biblia Satánica*
2008: Latvian / Severins / *Sātana Bībele* / Nils Sakss, translator
2010: Russian / Ishi Press / *Sataninskaya Bibliya* / Elena Borichko, translator
2010: Portuguese / Saida de Emergencia via Associacao Portuguesa de Satanismo / *A Bíblia Satânica*
2012: Turkish / Altikirkbes Yayinlari / *Seytanin Kitabi*

LaVey's titles are frequently pirated and published through print-on-demand sites for reasons upon which we can only speculate. This includes bootlegs of the translations listed above, and in these cases, the Introductions are often swapped out for the writings of amateurs whose understanding of Satanism would be greatly improved by actually reading the book they'd just stolen.

The Introductions

In June of 1971, after *The Satanic Bible* had been on the stands for a year-and-a-half, Anton LaVey decided he wanted to replace Burton Wolfe's Introduction with one written by Michael Aquino. In a letter to his editor, Peter Mayer, LaVey said, "The new Introduction will be far more timely, in view of the changes that have taken place in the Church of Satan in the last five years. The format used for the new one is such that the material won't soon become dated, as did the first." Mayer responded promptly that he'd be in touch with Avon's production department about getting the new Introduction in place.

LaVey heard back in February, 1972, from Mary Traina, a production manager at Avon, with page proofs for the new Aquino Introduction. A few corrections were requested:

"Such theorists as Pythagoras, Hegel, Lovecraft and Crowley..." was changed to "Pythagoras, Hegel, Spencer and Compte."

"There are no collective policy statements save the Crowley admonishment: 'Do What Thou Wilt shall be the Whole of the Law'" became "There are no collective policy statements save 'self-deceit is the gravest of all 'sins.'"

"An American descendant of Georgian, Alsatian, and Roumanian Gypsies..." was adjusted to "An American of Georgian, Alsatian, and Roumanian Gypsy descent."

Shortly after Michael Aquino's departure from the Church of Satan, in July 1975, Peter Mayer received another request for a change of Introduction. "We would like the Introduction deleted, as it is pretty much out of date... this is just a formal request for your files." Mayer was none-too-pleased with yet-another swap of Introductions, and quickly responded, "I certainly never agreed to drop the introduction to *The Satanic Bible* when we go back to press, only to consider it. I will do my best at that time to satisfy you... but publishing just isn't that simple."

When corresponding with the folks at Collier Books in June of 1976, during the negotiations for a possible new hardcover, the Introduction was again a point of concern:

> the [original] introduction by Wolfe should be used, with the following corrections: ... reference to 'old dark victorian house' *must* be deleted, as no activities of any sort are held there any longer and all this sort of description does is create headaches for the staff who have to put up with cranks and vandals... magic formula of 'nine parts outrage to one part social respectability' should be reversed to read '*nine parts social respectability to one part outrage.*'

Rather than delete the Introduction altogether, LaVey submitted an updated version by Burton Wolfe in November of 1976: "We didn't discuss the possibility of Avon doing a new intro for the next printing... [but] Burton did the original intro and it is still being quoted from, whereas the revised one [by Michael Aquino, PN] that is presently being used hasn't had a single quote and we have had absolutely no feedback on it. Burton has retained a lot from his original, while updating and 'beefing up' certain portions." The updated Wolfe Introduction finally appeared in printings of *The Satanic Bible* in 1977.

In November of 2004, HarperCollins-Avon approached Magus Peter H. Gilmore, current High Priest of the Church of Satan, and requested a new Introduction. Gilmore's "Opening the Adamantine Gates" made its first appearance in *The Satanic Bible* in January of 2005 and has been there since. His essay mentions his own discovery of *The Satanic Bible* and Satanism, and provides a detailed biography of the author as well as a complete list of LaVey's other works, recordings, biographies, appearances in major media outlets and in documentaries. Gilmore relates in descriptive detail the ways in which LaVey's various life experiences formed and impacted his creation of the Satanic philosophy and worldview: "We Satanists owe him our gratitude for symbolically opening the adamantine gates of Hell, by giving form and structure to a philosophy that names us as the Gods of our own subjective universes... He dethroned the seeking of external saviors and championed responsibility for all of one's actions and the resultant consequences."

The Author Photo

When Anton LaVey was asked for an author photo for the cover of *The Satanic Bible*, he was able to choose from an embarrassment of riches, as they say, thanks to the many photo sessions in which he'd participated over the previous years. Photographers were clamoring to take pictures at the infamous Church of Satan, and in September 1968 LaVey allowed John Hendricks to conduct a photo session and interview with himself and his family at the Black House. In lieu of a modeling fee, LaVey agreed to accept a couple of Hendricks' photos which he could use as he liked, and it was one of these that he provided to Avon at their request.

When Avon was about to release the fourth printing of *The Satanic Bible* in June of 1971, their legal department had to delay distribution due to a complaint they had received from Hendricks, saying that the author photo was being used without his knowledge or consent.

"The discrepancy over the photograph of myself which appears on the back cover of The Satanic Bible came as a surprise to me, to say the least!" LaVey told Avon's legal representative. He explained the agreement they'd made when arranging the photography session. "I said I would require at least one print of a photograph of myself to compensate for my time; the added incentive being provided by the new photograph, since the fee involved could have been obtained in a far less exhausting fashion." LaVey provided a copy of his contract with Hendricks and added that he hadn't been able to get in touch with him since the session of three years earlier.

It can be reasonably assumed that Hendricks was able to reach an agreement with Avon; his photograph has graced the cover for 50 years now.

Yankee Rose

The mysterious sign-off to *The Satanic Bible*, "Yankee Rose," was missing from the 32nd printing which appeared in the early 1990's. We were fortunate to be visiting Anton LaVey around this time and he predicted, correctly, that this edition would become a collector's item, but he also offered a short-term solution: just rubber-stamp it in.

The Reprints

"Good news!" Peter Mayer's note in October of 1970 was short but conveyed a message Anton LaVey was happy to hear. "We went back to press for another 25,000 copies of the *SATANIC BIBLE.* The book is not selling like crazy, but it is selling steadily."

This message about *The Satanic Bible's* first reprint characterizes the book's entire history as a publishing commodity. While LaVey naturally enjoyed the steady income the sales of the book would provide over the years, his main concern became keeping it in print and having it distributed to bookstores nationwide. Even today, when a box of *Satanic Bibles* reaches a bookstore, there's always the chance an anonymous bookstore employee will take issue with it, shove it into storage, neglect to refill the shelves, or just throw it in a dumpster. So when the news arrived that 25,000 fresh copies had become available, LaVey informed Mayer,

> ...the San Francisco dealers have a Hell of a time keeping it in stock, and from what I hear from members throughout the rest of the country, the same applies elsewhere... everyday we receive a great number of calls and letters from people who have scoured their cities for it, but can't find it in any of their local bookstores... If we can just get copies in the stores the dealers don't have the least difficulty selling them.

Eight months later, in June of 1971, a fourth printing was waiting to ship out while LaVey and Avon's legal department cleared up the question of the author photo, discussed elsewhere in this article.

In the summer of 1975, LaVey contacted Avon to request a replacement of the Introduction by Michael Aquino ("...it is pretty much out-of-date..."), and received the disheartening message from Peter Mayer's office that there was only "a slim chance" of *The Satanic Bible* going back to press. Coming on the heels of LaVey's first major venture into Hollywood via his work on "The Devil's Rain," this must have felt akin to a disaster. Having his book go out of print just as his name began to become known in another major medium would have been unsettling.

Hence LaVey's joyous letter to Mayer the following April, "to express my delight at seeing the new printing of *The Satanic Bible*. Thanks for keeping the fires stoked." But a few short months later, in September of 1976, rights manager Rosanne Leacy was hearing from LaVey in response to a message he'd received that sales had again dropped. This response had a different tone and was on the order of a complaint; it included a lengthy list of local stores whose management claimed it always sold out promptly, and emphasized once more the difficulty stores seemed to have in obtaining it: "IF AND WHEN they can get the two books they sell very fast... If San Francisco is any example of the rest of the country, it's no wonder sales have dropped – there's none to buy!" This same letter references the fact that at this point, *The Satanic Bible* had been through eleven printings, doing well "in spite of the fact that they have had to make it strictly on their own, i.e. no promotion by Avon and sluggish distribution."

Accompanying this letter was a copy of a note that a Church of Satan member had received in the package along with her book when she'd mail-ordered it through Avon. "GOD IS WATCHING YOU!" it proclaimed, along with a little hand-drawn cross. "I trust the orders for the two books are not being sabotaged in the shipping department... it would be kind of funny if it weren't for the fact that it might be cutting into our pocketbook via similar notices to bookdealers."

Stock at Avon did sometimes hover at quite low numbers, but *The Satanic Bible* has never gone out of print. By the early 1980's the Satanic Panic gave the book's sales a large shot in the arm, so it was indeed a mixed blessing. As many present-day Satanists trace their interest in LaVey and Satanism back to the stern warnings they received as teens – remember the Law of the Forbidden? – LaVey could certainly be justified in his conviction that as long as they spelled his name right, publicity is publicity.

Maya

Nina Antonia

Is all that we see or seem
But a dream within a dream?

– Edgar Allan Poe

Every city has a unique frequency, like an invisible signature written on the landscape. London has a frenetic strut, Paris emotes a suggestive purr whilst New York busily jangles. The strangest resonance I've encountered belongs to Hollywood which produces an odd thrum. More of a sensation than a sound, it reverberates in the deepest darkest well of night, redolent of a vast, phantom generator. Each metropolis also has its own (unwritten) etiquette, for example one is never supposed to approach Hollywood but to wait until it beckons you. Not for one instant had I ever considered myself Hollywood material, until a book penned in my misspent youth was optioned by an independent film company based there. Once the contracts were signed, I was set up in an apartment in a faded yet elegant 1920's block where Jean Harlow had formerly resided. In a town besotted by fame, these details are quintessential to the Hollywood experience. Across the road was the Paramount lot, providing the neighbourhood landmark. Kindly people dropped by with coffee and to enquire of my needs whilst I worked on the screenplay. The room overlooked the garden and offered a clear view of a charming little fountain, the gentle lull of the water producing a rather soporific effect. Although Hollywood offers abundant pleasures, delivering the goods to its glittering altar is imperative. However, by the end of the first week, the building began to get to me, as if something were gently pulling at my sleeve and I decided to take a look around.

Wandering down the silent vanilla stucco hallways with the original frosted glass art-deco light fixtures, it was as if someone had pressed a pause button. I'd been booked into a limbo for the maybes, fame's half-way house where aspiring actors had hung on until the money ran out and starlets had submitted to dubious terms. Ambition had held them hostage as they waited on the whims of cinematic fortune. Though less hapless than in Hollywood's decadent heyday, the current tenants were still industry dependent. At the heart of purgatory was the pretty walled garden, dappled a deep green by plentiful palm trees. It was a particularly hushed spot, disconnected from the world beyond. The only sound issued from the fountain's singing water, wherein a time-mottled cherub proffered a horn of plenty up to the blazing sun, suggesting sacrifice in exchange for dreams attained. Out of the thousands of supplicants that had stayed here, only Jean Harlow had achieved renown, dying at the age of 26, to become one of the poignant 'unforgettables' of the silver screen. I thought I saw her passing through the garden one evening, a shimmer of opalescent shadow, like a star obscured by mist.

Hollywood gothic is less apparent than the European variety, which is entombed in stone, cemetery and monument. As old as the US film industry, Hollywood has not yet raked up centuries of dust and bones but it is undoubtedly haunted. Later, I would come to understand that the phantom generator maintains an endless loop of film on which thousands of spirits are imprinted for continuous replays. Hollywood is the repository of the eternal image, where death is suspended and life story rights are purchased, in this world and the next. Atop Griffith's Observatory, immortalised in 'Rebel without a Cause' in 1955, there is a large bronze bust of the film's star, James Dean. The sculptor, Kenneth Kendall, began working on the bust, as a testament to Dean, on the night of the actor's death in a horrific car crash. Few sculptures capture angst quite so adroitly and 'Jimmy' is depicted in an eternal grimace, a reflection of his tortured persona. Fittingly for the Dean myth, the observatory affords one of the best views of the 'Hollywood' sign. As has often been documented, the sign is surprisingly rickety and looks as if it is made of plywood. Yet it has withstood fires, storms, earthquakes and even the odd suicide. Back in the 1930's, when the sign was first erected, it was as 'Hollywoodland' – an advert for director Mack Sennett's doomed real estate venture. The sign was subsequently abbreviated after a despairing starlet, Peg Entwistle, leaped to her death from the thirteenth letter. Work had not been forthcoming so poor Peg took the hard road to eternity.

No one has better chronicled the seamy side of tinsel town than film maker Kenneth Anger, in his book *Hollywood Babylon*. Anger's glittering yet bleak account encapsulates Hollywood's corrupt allure. Half a century has passed since *Hollywood Babylon* was first published but the book, like the ghosts, are still tangible. By day, the blistering sun is a hazard for both apparitions and the corporeal. However, in the fragile, violet hour when the day departs and the evening takes the centre stage, the ghosts return clad in twilight. It is a gentle hint of an effect, of soft lighting and candle glow that reawakens Hollywood's halcyon era. At twilight, the shadow of Cary Grant's smile is recalled and Monroe's breathy sigh is once again audible whilst Gloria Swanson perpetually descends the staircase in 'Sunset Boulevard' a twinkle of malevolence in those fearsome eyes. Could it be that some element of the soul is imprinted and ossified like a beautiful, transparent entity on the forevermore of film? 'Are they simply the ghosts of a world that has died on us?' asked Rudolf Arnheim in his critical overview of Maya Deren that appeared in *A Film Culture Reader* in 1970. Arnheim's essay lends credence to the ancient belief that the soul is stolen by the camera. Ironically, however, as cinema advanced, the industry though slicker became increasingly spiritually and philosophically redundant, narrowing its focus solely on entertainment, even if a few artists edged in by default. Rebelling against American mainstream cinema, Maya Deren's short experimental films are oddly ritualistic in their attempt to condense the essence of being. What else could one expect from a woman who had taken her name from the word 'Illusion?' When she made 'Meshes of the Afternoon' (1943) it was as if Deren knew that one day she would be looking back at us from the other side. Maya continues to haunt, peering through a window in her film, eyes fixed on a horizon we can never glimpse, in a perfect, timeless instant. Perhaps she was envisioning her own premature death at the age of 44. Nevertheless, Maya Deren attained her goal to 'participate in a moment when life breaks through to some higher level of intensity.'

The psychic unease of tinsel town is garishly summarised at the 'Museum Of Death' situated on Hollywood Boulevard, and is not recommended for those of a faint disposition. An authentic guillotine displayed in the entrance sets the scene. As one might expect, the museum is lurid and disturbing, especially the display dedicated to those self-aggrandising glitches of humanity known as serial-killers whilst the large images of 'The Black Dahlia's' cruelly dissected remains scar the memory. Elizabeth Short a.k.a 'The Black Dahlia' was a dramatically attractive young hopeful who wound up swimming in the flotsam of Hollywood low society, the tacky, dangerous undertow of the film industry. Her brutal murder and mutilation by person unknown in January, 1947, was to give Ms Short posthumous prominence. As one of her friends said 'Elizabeth was the dark' and thus Hollywood's night blooming 'Black Dahlia' is accorded her own sad section. The museum, which houses a historical collection of coffins, never flinches from its subject and has proved so successful the owners were considering opening another branch. But would such a venture thrive outside of Hollywood, where death and life overlap in a particularly apparent manner? One of the largest rooms in the 'Museum of Death' is devoted to Charles Manson and 'The Family'. Videos replay testimonies from Manson's devotees, whilst a patchwork sewn by the numerous young women in Charlie's thrall gives the room a duplicitously homely hippy appearance until you look at the crime-scene photographs of the 'Tate-LaBianca' slayings and wish that you hadn't.

The majority of murder cases are allowed to fade like the newspapers they were first printed on but an alignment of Hollywood-specific circumstances surrounded the killings of pregnant actress, Sharon Tate, her friends, Jay Sebring, Abigail Folger and Voytek Frykowski, as well as Stephen Parent plus a middle aged couple, Rosemary and Leno LaBianca. The brutal murders, which were carried out by Manson's acolytes in August 1969 has denied the victims and their loved ones a respectful silence. Charles Manson's role as a rambling pseudo-messiah meant precious little to anyone except for a handful of disenfranchised LSD warped kids, known as 'The Family' until a self-aggrandising state-prosecutor, Vincent Bugliosi, helped make a cause célèbre from the case. Manson, who had spent most of life in jail, prior to the killings, was a product of the American nightmare. As has since been ascertained by author Nikolas Schreck in his book *The Manson File*, the murders were probably the consequence of a drug deal gone awry. Vincent Bugliosi however, created a doomsday script called *Helter Skelter* and constructed the 'Manson Myth' from which the state prosecutor was to benefit. As well as penning numerous books, Bugliosi participated in a series of interviews and several documentaries. Had he left well alone, once Manson and his cohorts were imprisoned, the case would still have had terrible resonance but might not have become the industry it is today. In Hollywood where nothing but fame is real, Vincent Bugliosi, like failed musician Charles Manson, desired the acclaim that had appeared to come so easily to Sharon Tate, whose doe-eyed honey doll persona made her a sacrificial victim both on-screen and off, luxuriantly malleable in 'Valley of The Dolls' and haplessly lovely when directed by her husband to be, Roman Polanski, in 'The Fearless Vampire Killers.' Ironically, a pre-fame Sharon Tate had lived with Jay Sebring at the former home of Jean Harlow.

The Spahn ranch has now been incorporated into a historical park: the vast Santa Susana Pass. Thrill tourists still comb the dramatic landscape for remnants of the past, in search of Manson's 'Always is Always Forever', as if the Family might be found singing Charlie's folksy ditties in the sun-scorched nothingness. 'Darkside' pilgrims are prone to freaking out and sharing their anguish online when they discover a church on the site. Even more shocking, a vast white cross overshadows the original, gallows like gate-post from which the 'Spahn' sign used to hang. The air is clean and fresh as if something has been exorcised from this once treacherous place. Another Manson landmark, The Devil's Hole, gapes like an unblinking ancient lizard's eye, in the depths of Death Valley. In Charlie's acrobatic mind, The Devil's Hole assumed potential for a final subterranean gateway. Though allegedly bible savvy, it is possible Charles skipped the book of *Obadiah*: 'The pride of your heart has deceived you, you who live in the clefts of the rock,' in his haste to get to the book of *Revelations*. Holy Cross cemetery, where Sharon Tate and her unborn son are buried, is a far gentler place. In such a peaceful setting, it seems incomprehensible that someone could be pulled from life as cruelly as Sharon Tate and her baby who didn't even get the chance to open his eyes. A small bunch of fresh white flowers and a picture of Tate's dog had been placed on the grave, the day I paid my respects. The cemetery has none of the showiness of Hollywood Forever, which houses the majority of the deceased deities of cinema's golden age. Death is sacrosanct at Holy Cross and God palpable in the breeze, no more so than at Sharon Tate's grave, which is only yards away from where Bela Lugosi slumbers, wrapped in one of his Dracula capes for the ultimate performance. It is Hollywood, after all.

The History of "Häxan" ("Witchcraft Through the Ages")

Jack Stevenson

Introduction

Benjamin Christensen's macabre masterpiece from 1922, "Häxan" ("The Witch"), can justifiably be called many things. It can be considered the first cult movie, a genuine *film maudit* (literally a "cursed film"), the first true feature-length documentary (along with "Nanook of the North," which was made the same year), and so forth.

Many of these same things can or could have been said about Tod Browning's much better known (and very different) film, "Freaks," made a decade later. Indeed, these two taboo-shattering works occupy an exclusive niche in the annals of horror cinema and share uncanny similarities. Both were greeted by angry protests upon release, and were widely censored and fiercely condemned. Both were originally disasters for the studios that backed them; monster movies that weren't monster movies. To 'decent folks' these were the two most morbid, perverse films ever made, while to advocates they shone with a very human vision. To the men who made them they were the consuming obsessions in their lives, the films they were put on earth to make; labours of love that according to the lore destroyed their careers, and turned two gregarious, extroverted young men into embittered hermits and haunted them to their graves.

"The lore" of course always tends to the melodramatic, but these two supremely gifted but troubled directors – one American, one Danish – did share a common fate... Both were tall, dashing, talented and "difficult," and both held a fascination for the dark side of life. Both were employed at MGM studios in depression-era Hollywood where they each made films with Lon Chaney and solidified reputations as masters of horror... but they never met.

Browning didn't completely follow the script. He made more films after "Freaks," some well received, before retreating from public life to live in solitude

Ditto Christensen, although much less is known about him. Only one slim book has previously been written about the man; thus far still available only in Danish.

What additional information that does exist on him tends to be filtered through the narrow prism of academic interpretation and the man himself rarely makes an appearance.

The goal of this essay is to place "Häxan" in the context of Christensen's wider career, since the film did certainly overshadow most of his professional life, and to place it within the context of the times. This has required extensive research into the Danish source material, and it was necessary to translate much of the initial reaction in order to present a picture of things at the "moment of impact." Many of the issues that embroiled his film upon release are still, amazingly, being hotly debated today.

Who was this man who could make such a film, and what drove him? We still don't know for sure. Christensen, the consummate "man of mystery," wouldn't have had it any other way.

The Early Years

Ironically, the man who was to create the most perverse and profane work of early cinema was born in the shadow of a crucifix – a massive crucifix-shaped cathedral that dominated the ancient city of Viborg, which during Medieval times was Christendom's stronghold in the Western Danish provinces of Jutland.

He came into the world on 28 September, 1879, dubbed Benjamin Christensen, the youngest of twelve children. And although he was to achieve much during his life, this was no rags to riches story, his father ranking as one of the town's most prosperous merchants and one of its most well-to-do and influential citizens.

As befitted his family's status, young Benjamin attended the Cathedral School, the town's finest, where he was versed in classical languages. But the boy had an independent streak and after graduating from school he travelled to Copenhagen to study medicine.

A funny thing happened on the way to a medical career – he started singing. One morning while shaving over his sink, the renowned opera singer, Nyrop, overheard him and stuck his head round the door – "Who on earth is *that*?" He convinced young Christensen to give the opera a go and the lad entered into some months of preparatory voice training. In 1901 he and forty other hopefuls applied for admission to the prestigious Royal Theatre's opera school and he was the only one to be accepted.[1]

He had his debut on 2 May, 1902, playing the naive young peasant, Mazetto, in Mozart's "Don Juan," but disaster struck that very night when a lump formed in his throat during the performance and his voice grew weaker as the evening wore on. He was told by doctors that his throat was okay but that he had an unbeatable nervous condition. He had the support of major figures in the Danish opera world; he had been tipped to take over the repertoire of the highly respected Helge Nissen, and was to have sung Mephisto's part in Gounod's "Faust,"[2] a "dream role" as he himself characterized it. And now an illusive illness that was maddeningly unbeatable had ruined it all. In one stroke the great future that had been predicted for him was dashed.

1 *Social Demokraten*, 25 September, 1949

2 John Ernst, *Benjamin Christensen* (1967, The Danish Film Institute, Copenhagen) p.7

Forced to quit the opera, he entered acting school. After graduating he was engaged to perform for three seasons at a new theatre in Århus. There he played a wide range of characters and roles, performing with some of the best Danish thespians of the day, including Betty Nansen and Bodil Ipsen. It was also here that he did his first directing, but reportedly relations between Christensen and at least some of his colleagues were strained, with one scribe later maintaining that he got such good reviews that his fellow actors felt cheated of recognition, and accused him of unduly influencing the writers.[3]

Christensen was a loner who always followed his own path, and now that path led back to Copenhagen. There he managed to get parts in several plays but once again his voice began to betray him. While playing the role of the genie in "Aladdin," the audience was compelled to yell "louder, louder!" throughout the evening. In 1907 he was forced to retire from the stage forever.

His great baritone singing voice would return on occasion over the years, but never when he needed it, and never when he was confronted by a live audience. According to his own account, years later he even ran into the great Enrico Caruso, who overheard him singing in his bathtub in his hotel room in New York and asked Christensen to join him on stage. The Dane tried to explain that his voice would falter the second the curtain went up. Caruso was incredulous that anybody could turn down such an offer and walked away shaking his head in disbelief.[4]

Some difficult years followed his departure from the acting profession. He had married the actress Ellen Arctander in 1904, and now they had two little boys, so he was forced to hustle to support his family. He worked as a proof-reader for a daily paper and exported potatoes to Germany before finding a better paid job selling high quality champagne for the French company, Lanson Père et Fils. As their agent in Copenhagen he was obliged to frequent all the high-class drinking establishments, which he did without complaint. One writer would later describe him as "living a mysterious double life" at this point.[5] In fact he became something of a post-Victorian party animal, gadding about like royalty on the company's generous expense account and freely imbibing of the liquid goods himself.[6]

One day it all became too much for him. Ever fond of dramatic gestures, he ceremoniously drew up a document that stated that if he didn't abstain from alcohol as of that date then he was an irresponsible father to his young sons. Thereafter he pulled one of the little boys up onto his knee and, guiding his little hand, had him sign the document, which he then signed himself.[7] And according to him, he honoured it. That might have been a matter of degree, however, since he remained an agent of Lanson Père et Fils after his film career began – loathe to give up a significant income – so bottles of bubbly were always on hand at his social gatherings and offered to actors on occasion as pick-me-ups when their energy

3 *Berlingske Aftenavis*, 30 June, 1936

4 *Ibid.*

5 *Potitiken*, 28 December, 1936

6 *National Tidende*, 26 September, 1954

7 *Ibid.*

flagged. And in many of his films there was the obligatory Champagne-drinking scene in what must have been one of the first examples of "product placement."

According to the lore handed down over the years, Christensen's decision to go into film was prompted by a disturbing scene he witnessed one day when he left his house; there, on the far side of the street, was the famous actress Asta Nielsen, being led away by police officers. Nielsen had studied privately with one of his acting teachers and they were friends, so he was understandably distraught and rushed over to help – only to discover that this was a film shoot (actually the closing scene of her 1910 film, "The Abyss.") (The story has since been discounted by some writers as "too good to be true," but in fact he did live directly across from where that scene was filmed.) He claims he was bitten by the "film-bug" then and there, his eyes opened to the dramatic potential of a medium he had not previously held in particularly high esteem. That very night he launched into his first script.

When in 1912 he finally began to work in film as an actor he was no star-struck youngster. He was by now 33 years old with plenty of experience in both theatre and opera, and he had lots of friends and connections in the fledgling film industry. And he had life experience – he had been a salesman, a businessman, a family man, and he had known lean years. He was an artist but also a pragmatist. Film was perfect: with no live audience – and no sound – he wouldn't have to worry about his voice failing him.

There is some uncertainty as to how many films he acted in between 1912 and 1915. Some sources mention as many as five.[8] In any case his first film was "The Belt of Fate." It was made for Carl Rosenbaum who had had success with a picture called "The Four Devils" in 1912 and who now had his own studio thanks to a group of German investors who hoped he would continue his money-spinning ways. He had made Christensen's acquaintance beforehand and hired him to play the lead, that of a blind musician with an unfaithful wife. In the film he presents her with a cursed article of apparel, a belt that will cause any adulterer who dons it to die. After giving her the belt, he commits suicide. She later puts the belt on... and dies, the curse having come true.

The film is now lost, but is believed to have been directed by Svend Rindom, who had been an acting colleague of Christensen's in his days at Århus Theatre and had helped Rosenbaum write the script to "The Four Devils." Christensen was reportedly dissatisfied with the quality of the production and in 1913 signed with another company, Dania Biofilm. For them he acted in "Little Claus and Big Claus," playing a doctor.

That same year he saw Albert Capellani's movie, "Les Misérables," which was screened for the benefit of Copenhagen's actors in the magnificent Palads ("Palace") Theatre. The screening made a deep impression on the whole audience; not least Christensen who remembered it as a decisive turning point for him. Everything that film was capable of was here suddenly demonstrated. The experience must have increased his impatience with the humble productions he himself was at that point involved in.

8 *Berlingske Tidende*, 7 October, 1999

In March 1913 a group of Danish investors from Århus bought out the Germans and took over Rosenbaum's company (The Dansk Biograf Kompagni). They quickly grew dissatisfied with Rosenbaum's performance; he had spent a lot of money and only made that one movie, "The Belt of Fate." In the meantime Christensen continued to try to sell the script he'd written the night he saw Asta Nielsen's performance out in the street. After reportedly offering it to August Blom for 20,000 kroner cash, he presented it to the Dansk Biograf Kompagni. Both Rosenbaum and the board were impressed by it, and he assumed operational control of the studio to make it.

That script would become "The Mysterious X."

The Mysterious X

Christensen direct "The Mysterious X" in Taffelbays Allé, in Hellerup, a well-to-do town just north of Copenhagen. (Hellerup had plenty of luxurious villas that made ideal shooting locations and many of the early Danish silent movies were filmed there.) He was a kind of one man band on this film, writing, directing and also playing the lead character, the gallant Navy Lieutenant, van Hauen, who is entrusted with a set of secret orders. Enter one Count Spinelli, a treacherous cad who attempts to seduce his beautiful wife (she beats off his advances) and steal the orders. Spinelli finds them while prowling the house, fleeing when van Hauen arrives and spots him. Our hero is uncertain what his wife's involvement with the villain is, and when put on trial for treason – the seal on the orders having been broken – he refuses to divulge what he knows for fear of compromising her honour, and is sentenced to death. His wife, in turn, thus far puzzled by his behaviour, has a dream that makes everything clear to her, prompting her to alert the proper authorities. A messenger's last minute dash on horseback manages to save an innocent man's life.

It was hailed as the best Danish film of 1913; no small accomplishment considering the global success that Danish films were then enjoying on the world market.[9] But it was more than that according to modern day historians, among them Denmark's leading Christensen scholar John Ernst. He states that "The Mysterious X" and August Blom's "Atlantis" of the same year were the two most modern works of world cinema prior to Griffith's "The Birth of a Nation" and "Intolerance."

Heady praise indeed, but deserved. At a time when so many films were based on novels, Christensen had filmed an original story and dispensed with the literary cliches that informed so much of the competition. He had shown an ability to transform psychology into physical action, and his interplay between light and shadow was innovative and dynamic. He also departed from conventional film style

9 1911-1918 is roughly considered to be Denmark's golden age of silent cinema when their films attained a mastery and exportability that exceeded those of the Americans and was surpassed only by the French.

by letting inanimate objects play parts, so to speak. In this film a trap door closes and becomes tightly wedged, imprisoning the villain who struggles desperately to open it. In other films a door is opened by the wind and a lamp is borne through the darkness by a man who cannot initially be seen. Christensen had been deeply moved in "The Four Devils" by the simple sight of an empty trapeze swinging back and forth in the circus tent, after the acrobat who was to grab it missed and had fallen to the ground. To him it was the most affecting part of the whole film.

"The Mysterious X" evidenced an attention to detail that would become Christensen's trademark. Every little nuance had been thought out to an unprecedented degree, with some of the scenes having been re-shot eight or nine times. This also made for a film that took an unusually long time to shoot (three months instead of the typical two weeks) and was expensive – more Christensen trademarks.

This was due, to some extent, to his desire to experiment. In later years he would claim that "The Mysterious X" contained the first scene of anyone turning a light on in a room, a challenging "special effect" in those days when movies were shot outdoors or in glass-walled studios where the sun was the main source of light. He had twelve men lay on the roof of the glass-panelled studio which they had covered with a tarp. Actress Karen Sandberg came into the dark room and put her hand on the light switch. The camera stopped while she froze in that position and the tarp was pulled off by the workers. The camera was started again and presto – a light had been turned on!

Perhaps this "trick" had been done before, but so what? He had done it well (reportedly impressing American critics) and perhaps more importantly it was a good story and he was, above all else, a good story-teller. In Denmark, where the picture was promoted as a "sensational Danish drama," the critics were likewise impressed. One writer praised him for packing in enough "beautiful landscapes, burning windmills, ravenous rats, condemned men, dreadnoughts and subterranean dungeons" to fill five or six normal films.[10]

"The Mysterious X" was released first in America in 100 prints, its premiere held during March 1914 in a large New York theater. It went on to earn accolades in the American trade press, which was not usually receptive to "stagy" European films. It was championed by advocates of the young medium such as one Stephen Bush, who wrote in that month's edition of *The Moving Picture World:*

> This feature is nothing less than a revelation in dramatic motion pictures. It sets a new standard of quality. It emphasizes as no other film production the absolute superiority of the screen over the stage and opens up a vista of coming triumphs... An extraordinary boldness of invention joined with a mastery of detail that approaches genius helps to make this feature rise above all which has been filmed before.[11]

10 *København*, 24 March, 1914
11 *Moving Picture World*, March, 1914

The American buyer had also acted with "extraordinary boldness" by shoving 400,000 dollars of the film's 600,000 U.S. gross straight into his own pocket, and leaving none for Christensen, according to an article in the Danish press.[12] For a film made for just 30,000 kroner this was in any case amazing box office.

Christensen himself travelled to New York and throughout Europe to sell the film. These "sales trips" were adventures in and of themselves. "I sat next to people in black leather boots in Moscow and with cigar-puffing theater owners in New York." In Europe the film itself was suspect; as the Great War loomed, spy films had been outlawed in Germany and the Austro-Hungarian territories, and were considered unnecessary incitements in other countries.

While in Berlin in 1914 a fateful event occurred – he stumbled upon a copy of a book called *Malleus Maleficarum – der Hexenhammer (The Witch Hammer)*, a guide for witch-hunters written in 1487 by the two infamous inquisitors, James Sprenger and Heinrich Kramer, who were also Dominican monks. Called "one of the most blood-soaked works in human history," it was widely read for much of the 250 years the Inquisition lasted, its popularity exceeded only by the *Bible*. It is renowned today as the most infamous of the witch-hunting manuals which over the course of roughly three centuries helped to send as many as nine million (eight million is often cited) victims, primarily women, to their deaths, often on bonfires. (This figure-is contested today by historians who claim it was a gross exaggeration and that the actual toll was between forty and fifty thousand.) Christensen himself found it to be "one of the most perfidious documents ever published,"[13] but he was also completely fascinated by it. On that same trip he passed through Paris where he found a copy of *La Sorcière* by Jules Michelet, a study of witchcraft and the phenomenon of the persecutions. "After reading these two books," he would later note, "I was seized by the intensely dramatic power of the material[14] ... it was clear to me that I had finally found a subject."[15]

He immersed himself in this dark history and began to collect all the books about the subject that he could find. At about the same time he was made aware of the lectures of the world famous neurologist, Professor Charcot. Charcot claimed that the symptoms (of hysteria) he found in his patients were the same that caused "witches" to act as they did when they were "possessed," and, more controversially, that the female Saints also suffered from this same form of hysteria.

All this research laid the groundwork for the film that would come to dominate his career and his life, "The Witch,"[16] but that was still years down the road and at that moment humankind was being sucked into another kind of mass hysteria

12 *Politiken*, 28 December, 1936

13 *National Tidende*, 26 September, 1954

14 *Social Demokraten*, 25 September, 1949

15 *National Tidende*, 26 September, 1954

16 The film's Swedish title, "Häxan," and the Danish title, "Heksen," both literally translate into "The Witch." In English the film has been known as "Witch," "The Witch" and most commonly as "Witchcraft Through the Ages" (although technically that is the title of the version re-edited in 1967). For our purposes we refer to it as "The Witch."

of even more destructive proportions – The First World War.

The War had an effect on every aspect of life in Europe, including the financing and exportation of motion pictures, and Christensen was compelled to abandon his next film project, "The Man Without a Face" ("Manden uden ansigt"), despite the fact that Nicolai Neiiendam had been chosen for the lead and shooting had already begun.

"Blind Justice"

By August 1915 Christensen had managed to acquire a controlling interest in the Dansk Biograf Kompagni. The members of the board stayed on but it became "Benjamin Christensen Film" and was run from his home. His financial backers were, according to one report, a bunch of rich people from Århus who were involved with it almost "for sport."[17]

Now he was certain to again have total creative freedom on his next film, "Blind Justice." Shooting on that picture started in the fall in the same studio in Taffelbays Allé where he'd shot "The Mysterious X." This time around the very capable Johan Ankerstjerne would be manning the camera.

Christensen would again play the lead. While his previous performance had been marked by bouts of frenetic overacting, here he would comport himself with more subtlety as "Strong Henry,"[18] a slow-witted circus strongman who has been wrongfully imprisoned. One day he escapes from jail, gathers up his infant son and makes a dash for freedom, but a sudden storm forces him to seek shelter in a nearby mansion. There he encounters Eva, who is at first terrified but then agrees to help him for the sake of the child. Her father senses something is wrong and forces her to tell all. The cops are called and they drag Strong Henry back off to prison as he vows revenge. The child is placed in an orphanage. Eva eventually marries and convinces her husband that they should adopt the lad.

14 years later Henry is released from prison, a broken man. He enters a toy shop to purchase a gift for his son but can't even remember how old the boy would be. When he arrives at the orphanage he is shocked to learn that his son was put up for adoption long ago and that his whereabouts are unknown. He stumbles dejectedly about town until he bumps into an old crony from prison who invites him to join his gang of small-time crooks.

During the course of one of their capers they manage to pilfer the keys to a townhouse. While ransacking the premises, which unbeknownst to Strong Henry is owned by Eva and her husband, they find the address of their villa in the suburbs. She had always lived in dread that one day he would come to extract his revenge, and now her fears come true.

Eva's husband is lured to the gang's hideout where he is overpowered and tied up in a chair. Yet in his haste he had forgotten his keys when he departed the

17 *Berlingske Aftenavis,* 30 June, 1936

18 'Strong John' in the US version.

villa and now the son shows up with them in hand. Henry, oblivious to the fact that the lad is really his own son, locks him into a cupboard and sets off for the villa. Meanwhile the captives manage to free themselves and alert the police. Just as Henry takes aim at Eva through a series of keyholes the cops arrive and open fire. Henry is mortally wounded, but on his deathbed is absolved of his original crime when the real murderer makes a timely confession. Now cleared of all charges and reunited with his son, he dies in peace.

As John Ernst writes,

> Audiences at the time were just as enthusiastic about 'Blind Justice' as they had been about 'The Mysterious X.' That we must today rate Blind Justice as a lesser work owes first and foremost to its melodramatic, sentimental story and its pseudo-realistic nature, which quite understandably was construed as realism. This pseudo-realism also characterizes 'The Mysterious X' but is less of a drawback here since that was an unrealistic spy story to start with, one that took place in no man's land... 'The Mysterious X' is a far more pioneering achievement.[19]

While another great master of early Danish cinema, Carl Dreyer, believed that films should be based on literature and that the director should be true to that source material, Christensen believed that scripts should be the result of original ideas and that the finished work should bear the mark of the creator's personality. The two above-mentioned films very much did, not least because Christensen wrote, directed and played the leads in both. His own face even dominated the key promotional art of "The Mysterious X," staring sternly ahead in three different guises while captions trumpeted: "Written by Benjamin Christensen... Directed by Benjamin Christensen… In the lead role, Benjamin Christensen." A promo blurb went on to declare: "Benjamin Christensen's new film is absolutely the very best film and absolutely the very best premiere-quality picture ever staged in Denmark."

This was sweet vindication. Christensen had previously seen a brilliant career in the opera slip through his fingers because he could not control his greatest gift – his voice – even though there was, physically speaking, nothing wrong with him. Now he had found a new medium of expression where he could control almost everything down to the smallest detail, and that's what he aimed to do. It was a world of his own making, a world he could create and control.

He carefully sculpted the physical as well as the emotional frames. In "Blind Justice," for example, he had the set designer build a scale model of the villa which can be seen in the prologue. He stands over it with actress Karen Sandberg, discussing the plot and casting a dominating shadow over the proceedings. Scholarly writing on the film tends to interpret this as a testament to his great care and attention to detail, and he did indeed possess these qualities in spades; in his

19 John Ernst, *Benjamin Christensen* (1967, The Danish Film Institute, Copenhagen) p.10

zeal he reportedly put his actors through the tortures of the damned. For example, he compelled Karen Sandberg "to spend many hours staring at that dollhouse (of the villa) to get a feeling for the setting of the film, to learn where certain rooms were situated in relation to others."[20] Hermann Spiro, who played the evil Count Spinelli in "The Mysterious X" underwent a somewhat more challenging ordeal as Christensen contemplated the best way to depict a swarm of rats attacking and devouring him in a sewer tunnel. Notes a writer at the time: "At first he smeared the actor's face with honey and set a whole basket of the vermin after him, and when that didn't work he made a dummy with Spiro's face carved in cheese and the rats went amok on it."[21] On "Blind Justice" he did an unheard of ten takes of every scene to capture exactly the effect he wanted, drawing out filming and post-production to a whopping eight months and making it the most expensive Danish film at that time after "Atlantis."

Christensen was indeed a painstaking craftsman, but there was certainly more to it than that. To consider him primarily as an artist rather than a person – a person who had suffered a great trauma when his voice betrayed him, and who perhaps not unexpectedly now became something of a "control freak," to use the modern expression – is to miss the real story of Benjamin Christensen. The man himself, as noted, was an extraordinary storyteller and would have never forgiven writers for ignoring that. God knows he left enough clues strewn in his wake. In any case, the success of "Blind Justice" was another career boost. He was now a maker of films that had social relevance and were also exciting and original. And sensational. He always thought that films should be "sensational."

In New York, film censorship authorities invited him to show the picture for an invited audience of VIPs from the cultural world. Among them was the warden of Sing Sing prison, Thomas Mott Osborne, a humanitarian dedicated to improving the lives of convicts. He had even spent several weeks inside the institution disguised as a common prisoner so as to get to know the true nature of the place. He now invited Christensen to show "Blind Justice" for the inmates in a huge hall with a capacity of about 2,000. The screening made quite an impression on Christensen, not least because during the show there was a stabbing. The guilty party was immediately hustled out by two other prisoners acting in accord with the "honour system" that Osborne had instituted, whereupon inmates policed themselves – all of this according to the account Christensen later gave in 1945 when he published a compendium of short stories entitled *Hollywood Destinies.*[22]

As Ernst relates, "The prisoners were as keenly impressed with the film as Christensen was with their intelligence and sensitivity, and with the (in any case at that time) advanced conditions at the place." He never forgot his visit to Sing Sing and would later claim that it inspired him to embark upon a study of the nature

20 *Berlingske Aftenavis*, 30 June, 1936

21 *Århus Stiftstidende*, 19 April, 1959

22 Benjamin Christensen, *Hollywood Skæbner (Hollywood Destinies)* (Copenhagen, 1945, Schøbergske Publishers). Note: His prison encounters were described in the stories "I Sing Sing" ("In Sing Sing") and "Helt Tilbunds" ("Getting Completely to the Bottom of the Case").

of evil. And for their part the prisoners never forgot "Blind Justice." During his Hollywood period in the late 1920s he was still being approached by ex-cons who had seen the film at that screening and wanted to express their gratitude.

America imported relatively few films during the First World War, but "The Mysterious X" had been popular and Christensen managed to sell the new picture to Vitagraph, which released it in forty prints. The premiere took place in New York's 3,500-seat Strand theater to the accompaniment of a fifty-piece orchestra. The crowd was silent during the show and that made Christensen nervous, but when the curtain came down there was hearty applause. It had been a rousing success. He was immediately approached by interested distributors, and that night also got to meet Mary Pickford.

At some point in the process he commented to Vitagraph executive, Albert Smith, that he intended to make a trilogy about superstition down through the ages, and that this work would constitute a radical break from the conventions of the medium. It would be entitled "The History of Superstition." The first part was to be called "Heksen" ("The Witch"), to be followed by "Helgeninde" ("The Woman Saint") and "Ander" ("Spirits"). "I don't think that's anything American audiences would cotton to," Smith dryly remarked.[23]

While Vitagraph wasn't at all interested in his superstition trilogy, they did offer him another job – that of supervising all their productions. It was a tempting offer that was hard to turn down, but in the end he did. His head was full of his next film, "The Witch," and there wasn't room for anything else.

And so he came back to Denmark to make it.

The Making of "The Witch"

Christensen began to research "The Witch" in earnest. Subsequent exaggerated utterances in the press inferred that he had acquired a whole library of rare books on the subject, when in fact all his books could fit into a single streamer trunk (later stolen in America), but it was nevertheless an impressive collection.

A year-and-a-half later he ran out of money and was forced to sell much of his beloved antique furniture in order to continue. "I remember," he later recalled, "the sight of my two sons standing in the doorway with tears in their eyes as the furniture was being carried away."[24] One might also speculate as to the effect this morbid obsession had on his marriage, inasmuch as he and his wife, Ellen Arctander, were divorced the following year, in 1920. It took Christensen two-and-a-half years just to undertake the research on this film.

He had doubted that any producer in Denmark would be "crazy enough" to gamble his money on a film that was this far out and unconventional, and he was right – but a producer in Sweden was willing to take up the challenge, a man named Charles Magnusson, and in February 1919 Christensen inked a contract

23 *National Tidende*, 26 September, 1954

24 *Ibid.*

with Svensk Filmindustri. Since it was now being made with Swedish money it would go down in history as a Swedish film, with the Swedish spelling of the title, "Häxan," the official one, and it would have its world premiere in Stockholm, but in all other respects it was thoroughly Danish.

Magnusson was a visionary producer who was largely responsible for the excellence of Swedish silent cinema, having given talented directors like Victor Sjöström and Mauritz Stiller creative freedom, and now he afforded Christensen that same luxury. For that "Benne," as friends called him, would remain ever grateful. But there was a vast amount of work to be done before even a single frame of film could be exposed.

First they needed a studio to shoot the movie in, since there were none available in Sweden. Benne persuaded Magnusson to buy him back his old studio in Taffelbays Alle. He had sold it in 1917 to another company and it was again up for sale, albeit in terrible condition. There were no working toilets or bathrooms, and what technical apparatus remained was antiquated. Svensk Filmindustri had to purchase new cameras, lighting equipment, etc. The actual cost of shooting was reckoned at between 300,000 and 400,000 kroner, but all this added expense ballooned the budget up to somewhere between 1.5 to 2 million kroner, a whopping sum that earned it the dubious distinction of being the most expensive silent movie ever made in Scandinavia.

Filming began in late winter of 1921 and lasted throughout the hot summer months and into October, most of it done in Taffelbays Alle, but with a few scenes shot at two other nearby studios.

Christensen had cameraman Johan Ankerstjerne back for another turn. A barrel maker's son from Randers whose first brush with the working world was as a watch maker's apprentice, Ankerstjerne's life was changed the day he was given a movie camera to fool around with. He aimed it at what drama and pageantry there was to be found in the small Jutland city, various parades and municipal events and whatnot. He went on to become a skilled cinematographer and was already exceedingly accomplished in the trade when in 1911, at 25 years of age, he was brought to Copenhagen by Ole Olsen's Nordisk Film Company. These were exciting times for the Danish film industry as actors like Valdemar Psilander and Asta Nielsen were achieving global fame and production was booming. That year he shot no less than 27 films for Nordisk that went out onto the world market, and he stayed with the company until 1915, later serving another stint with them from 1924 to 1932. After that he founded a film laboratory and print-making plant that still exists and is one of the biggest in Denmark.

Not all of Ankerstjerne's work on "The Witch" confined him to the studio. At one point he travelled to the town of Silkeborg with his equipment to shoot background footage devoid of telephone wires, modern rooftops and other tell-tale traces of the 20th Century. This area in Jutland, which is also one of Denmark's most rugged, was ideally suited for this task. He also shot footage at nearby Himmelbjerget, Denmark's highest mountain – modest as it is – for what would prove to be the most spectacular scene in the film, the flight of the witches to Bloksbjerg ("Brocken" in English subtitles), the medieval town in northern Germany where according to legend all witches gather on the summer solstice to indulge in profanities with the Devil.[25] Christensen also sent cameramen to remote parts of Norway and Sweden to shoot roll after roll of clouds and mountaintops. They shot a vast amount of footage, much of it in fact unusable for one reason or another.

One can infer from comments published over the decades that Christensen, being an obsessive, a perfectionist and perhaps even a genius, was not always easy to get along with, but he did have an excellent relationship with his cameraman and was thrilled with his work. Ankerstjerne's photography and effects surpassed what the Hollywood studios were capable of, even with all the state-of-the-art equipment they had at their disposal.

Richard Louw, the props and sets main, was equally indispensable. The medieval torture instruments he created were works of art. And he even found time to construct a scale model version of a Middle Ages town complete with 250 miniature dwellings. The village was mounted on a large carousel twenty metres in diameter and filmed from the edges as twenty men turned it.

The aforementioned flight to Bloksbjerg, which prompted spontaneous applause at many shows and still manages to amaze, was an equally painstaking and time consuming scene to construct. The scores of women[26] who acted as airborne witches were filmed separately on elevated and unseen seats with broomsticks placed between their legs while wind was blown at them by an airplane engine adapted for the purpose. This in combination with the camera tracking past them provided the illusion of motion, of flight. (It was originally intended that trees and landscapes shot from a fast moving train could add to the sense of rapid movement but this footage proved unusable.) The actresses were filmed from various distances and angles and with different camera movements. Then, via the multiple-exposure process, all the flying witches were assembled onto five spools of film. (Today this is a laboratory process but at that time it involved the painstaking work of cranking the film back and running it twice or more through the camera.) All the images were subsequently combined to create the scene. This consisted of two spools of clouds, one of the miniature village "in motion," and one roll with a woman sitting on a knoll and demons poised on the edge of a cliff (all of whom observe the arrival of the witches) in the foreground, silhouetted against landscape features. Nine strips of film were then run not less than eight times together through an experimental optical printer Ankerstjerne had developed. The techniques he employed on this film were state-of-the-art and he also managed to create an animated stop-motion monster that can be seen at one point in another scene.

The cast was composed in the main of professional actors, many from the stage.

25 Still today in Denmark this longest summer night is celebrated all over the country with the burning of bonfires. In every bonfire a stuffed 'witch' is placed on a pole and as she catches fire she takes to the air and 'flies' to Bloksbjerg. This is known as 'Sankt Hans aften' (Saint Hans night) and is the scene of much festivity and drinking.

26 Somewhere between 40 and 75 women were used as witches – reports vary.

Some of Denmark's most revered movie stars are glimpsed in "The Witch" for the first time. Christensen himself played the Devil with obvious relish (and no small amount of theatrical overacting in period style).

But the lady who stole the show was an amateur: a 78-year-old woman by the name of Maren Pedersen. She played Maria, the weaver, an accused witch. Christensen had "discovered" her one evening as he strolled out of the main gate of the city's famed Tivoli amusement park. The wrinkled old woman was off to the side, sitting there selling flowers. She reached towards him with a clutch of violets and he was instantly struck by her appearance. He bought a bunch for two crowns and struck up a conversation.

Pedersen had been educated in her youth as a nurse. In her day she had been rather well off, at one point operating her own small clinic, but later things went downhill for her and now she was dirt poor, living at a home for aged women and selling whatever she could during the days. She was unnerved when this strange man then and there offered her the leading role in his movie. As he began to describe it she became increasingly apprehensive. She was a religious woman and feared that participation in such a thing would somehow be a betrayed of her beliefs. Yet he was a charming and persuasive gentleman, and on top of it they could converse in the same dialect as she came from the same part of Jutland. She finally agreed.

As journalist Mogens Brandt would relate, the first time Pedersen arrived at the studio the receptionist mistakenly sent her directly in to see Christensen. He had donned his devil mask and applied make-up in preparation for the shooting of a scene. He was more or less naked and painted over the whole of his body in such a way that his skin appeared covered with pustules. He had large fan-shaped ears, horns protruding from his forehead and a long flickering tongue.

"Good lord! It's the Evil One!" she gasped in a near swoon.[27]

Christensen tried to calm her.

"How do you know what the devil looks like?" he asked.

She pulled out a dog-eared prayer book and showed him a picture.

"He looks like that!"

He tried to explain to her that that was only a picture and that the Devil didn't really exist, but she was having none of it. (This episode is related in the film itself.) She had *seen* the Devil with her own two eyes. Sometimes at night he came to her and sat down on the edge of her bed, and she would throw the sheets up over her head in a fright and pray to the Lord three times. After that, as a rule, he was usually gone when she peeked back out.

Years later Christensen would talk about how fabulously inspiring it had been to work with Maren Pedersen. She brought "the real thing" with her into the studio; the kind of superstitious nature and belief in mysticism that had been commonplace during the Middle Ages. All that the film was about was still alive in her fragile body. She was a kind of muse for him, her withered face a portal back into the darkest reaches of antiquity, and he turned that face directly into the

27 Undated article penned by Mogens Brandt from 1941.

camera, exposing every wrinkle and crevice with an unflinching hand. Today this might seem unforgivably exploitative but at the time it was exclusively praised as a stroke of casting brilliance that imbued the film with a searing authenticity. And after all, he was paying her, right? By some accounts she enjoyed being a prima donna for a while and getting rides home after work in a big car.[28]

And yet some accounts of the filming can only be described as disturbing. Actor Ib Schønberg's first meeting with Pedersen was one such unsettling encounter, witnessing as he did how Christensen had fastened a leash onto the woman's leg which he pulled in order to get her to move toward or away from the camera. A stroke of casting genius or pure exploitation? As critic Tage Heft enthused, "During a torture scene the amateur performer Maren Pedersen really was about to faint. Christensen dried the sweat and tears off her face so that she could continue. No 'honest' actor could play it so honestly." Christensen himself hailed her as "excellent in the torture scenes," although he would state that at no point whatsoever did she have any idea what the whole thing was about.

Scholars have grappled with the question of what kind of filmmaker and artist Benjamin Christensen was, yet all of this more directly begs the question of what kind of person he was. The shooting of the movie resembled more than anything else a cult-like exercise in blind obedience; in getting other people to play a part in one's own personal fantasies. Here more than in any other film he was attempting to create his own world.

This hardly detracts from his accomplishment. On the contrary; the best films are often personal fantasies brought to life by obsessed directors, and all films are about convincing other people (actors, audience, reviewers, etc.) to buy into your fantasies, but to what degree was the director himself caught up in his own creation? It's hard to say. The academic writing on the man that exists has failed to pose basic questions about who the real Benjamin Christensen was. Here was a man pulling an old lady around at the end of a rope; a man who cast himself as the Devil and who had beautiful witches kiss the buttocks of that hairy and frightful figure. And here was a man who persuaded one of the actresses to spit on a picture of the baby Jesus (a much more daring transgression in that day and age).

Christensen had always believed that actors must immerse themselves in their roles. What then might the Devil demand of young, attractive witches in exchange for his supernatural favours? And what might the witches be willing to do in exchange? There was little doubt about that; it was spelled out in the film – they would do anything for a pile of gold. What would they do in real life for the pile of gold of becoming famous movie stars? The making of the movie paralleled the story it was telling in uncanny ways. During the filming Christensen lived in quarters that were attached to the studio. What might that have made possible? To what degree did his personal fantasies figure into this professional fantasy he was creating?

"The Witch," like many film productions, was an exercise in power and control,

28 Account given by Johan Ankerstjerne in *Randers Dagblad*, 1 March, 1941.

and there is no doubt that Christensen had not only total creative freedom but also total control. The film was being shot in the utmost secrecy – and at night! (when producers from Svensk Filmindustri were least likely to drop by and nose around.) As he would later relate, "The film deals with hysteria and the dark side of human nature, and when the sun shines in the day it is impossible to call forth precisely those feelings in the actors."[29] He wanted to bring forth the actor's dark sides, but what about his own dark side?

He reportedly stressed them almost to the breaking point. As described in one report, "For key scenes he consciously strove to create a sense of real hysteria on the set. He let the actors do make-up and then wait. He began to shoot scenes and then stopped. He made sure they got a bit of food and then went through the whole process again from the beginning, up to that point having actually not yet shot a single metre of film... and then when the clock struck four in the morning and the actors were out of their minds for real, then he began to shoot the scenes he would use."[30]

Time doesn't heal all wounds, but twenty years on some of the surviving actors were able to look back at their experiences during the filming in a somewhat more rose-coloured light.[31]

> Clara Pontoppidan (a nun): It was all like an adventure out there in Taffelbays Alle. I went straight over there from the Dagmar theatre in the evening and often acted through the night until sunrise, and was then generously treated to a car ride home... I remember those days as a "working high"... When once in a while late at night we grew dead tired, a good brand of Champagne appeared on the table and in that way the hard work and partying was part and parcel of the experience... And yet now, many years later, I must confess that it filled me with fear. After all, that was an intense performance I was asked to give. Only a man like Benne could have persuaded me to spit upon a picture of the baby Jesus...
>
> Elith Pio (a monk): My memory of those working days is still crystal clear and that owes to the fact that we were so very inspired. Benne was so tremendously inspiring, and it was clear to many of us that this man we worked for was ahead of his time. However I'd be exaggerating if I said the filming was idyllic. It was anything but, especially for me, a sinner who had forced himself on a young virgin and therefore had to be whipped – and whipped I was, emphatically – by the monk, Aage Hertel. That was a veritable thrashing he laid down upon my naked back... Unfortunately we only got to see the

29 Unidentified daily, 17 February, 1941

30 *Århus Stiftstidende*, 19 April, 1959

31 These reminiscences were published in the 1 March, 1941 issue of *B.T.*, translated by the author.

scenes we were in, and one was only able to move about the studio in the most clandestine manner. But one day I managed to sneak away and see some of the other scenes being shot, including one where Benne was playing the Devil. I must confess his performance gave me a shock. That was unforgettable!

Astrid Holm (Middle-class woman): I remember that everything that took place out there was very daring. I suffered the ravages of all possible types of torture instruments, was dragged off by brutal hands and eventually met a painful death! It was very exciting to be part of a film that aimed to do more than just entertain…

Aage Hertel (a monk): In the searing summer heat, wearing a wig, I played a number of roles in "The Witch." I was the monk with fangs and the Devil with a rubber mask, etc. It was frightful!... I suffered it all for Benne's sake. The stuff with the mask was the worst... it was glued onto my face in a distorted fashion and when they took it off the first time my skin came off with it. Around my eyes was just bloody flesh.

Alice O'Fredericks (a nun): (O'Fredericks was an office girl who had run an errand out to the studio and was spotted by Christensen, who had her do a screen-test, – JS.) That was my first role. I was 17 years old and involved in that shocking scene in which 30 to 40 nuns went amok! Once I got over the first difficult period of shyness, I aggressively threw myself into the spirit the part demanded and screamed the profane curses. Afterwards, when we were all level-headed again, we found it all to be extremely upsetting. We were really bizarre.

Emmy Schønfeld (a witch): I played a witch who was in love with the devil and in a dream I got a pile of gold. Yet my best – and worst – scene was when I flew up through the chimney! Even though on my flight through the sky I was aided by special effects, it was not a pleasant experience to be bound with a strap around the waist and hoisted up under the ceiling of the studio. When I think back to that scene, as the belt was tightened and cut into me, the pain returns... Those were strange days out in Hellerup, not least to suddenly one day find the wooded grounds of the studio transformed into a witches' lair. They did that by digging up all the trees and then planting them again upside-down so that the roots were sticking out into the air. The memory of that sight still makes my heart pound. The grounds looked spooky and fantastic after the "operation."

Ib Schønberg (a monk): Christensen ordered me to go to the barber in Hellerup who, to my family's horror, "kronragede" me! [given a monk's haircut, bald on top]. All for the sake of art. I was after all only 17 years old and found it all to be a great, almost supernatural experience. And there I met Maren Pedersen whom I shall never forge. She was a wise and a nice person, but the memory I have of her is not the best; Benne had fashioned a leash on her leg which he pulled on as a means of getting her to move toward or away from the camera.

Karen Winther (an accused witch): It was a shock to go from Lau Lauritzen's cozy and cheerful farces at Nordisk Film to the Benjamin Christensen-esque nights where I performed amongst the most macabre props and settings. One day in particular I sat for 8 hours in a torture chair – and to be honest I wasn't worth much when I got out. Nonetheless it is an experience I recall only with fondness.

Benjamin Christensen (The Devil): It is a state of bliss for an artist once in his lifetime to get permission to do what he wants. That happened with "The Witch."

Christensen launched into the editing process that fall with some apprehension. How would the censors react to some of the more intense scenes? This was indeed frightful stuff. In the first sequence of the dramatic re-enactments that start chapter two of the film we see a couple of old witches cooking up a magic potion down in their subterranean lair in 1488 (a year after the publication of "The Witch Hammer"). One of the squat old hags extracts a rotting human hand from a faggot of sticks and snaps off a finger to use in her witch's brew. Later the gentle viewer encounters cannibalism, blasphemy, sex with demons, adultery, masturbation, the cutting up of foetuses, and so forth. Deformities are displayed, torture devices are demonstrated. But for many the sex was the worst of it.

John Ernst, writing in 1967 while Denmark was in the throes of a sexual revolution, commented thusly on that aspect of the film:

In spite of the pedagogic way he presents his case, that [sexual aspect] can easily startle the modern viewer when they see this 1922 film for the first time, acclimated to pornography though they may be. In what other film does a scene take place where the beautiful young witches prance up to the Devil himself to kiss his buttocks? When is the last time the reader has witnessed in a film a scene where two old hags urinate into a pissing pot and heave the contents against a neighbour's door? In what other film are there so many images

> of sexual perversions, torture, animal abuse, blasphemy and naked women?...[32]

Christensen was pushing the censors into perhaps an even more compromising position than he had forced the beautiful young witches – he was forcing them to pass judgement on something new. In Sweden they even called in a couple of neurologists to sit with the censors deciding the case.

Early on in the process he had wanted to involve men of science in the project to give it the stamp of credibility, but this idea went nowhere because, as he would later claim, scholars wanted nothing to do with a medium as disreputable as film. Once his movie was completed he did manage to solicit testimony from a professor by the name of Johansen who gave it high marks and declared that he shouldn't take out a single frame.

Whether or not the "worst bits" were edited out at some stage before or after Johansen passed judgement, as at least one commentator claimed, is impossible to know today, but considering what was left in it is hard to imagine what Christensen could have wanted to include that was more extreme. In any case, by the fall of 1922 the film was ready to play, sumptuously tinted in red, gold, green and, for night scenes, blue.[33] Divided into seven chapters, "The Witch" had a running time of 104 minutes, which was longer than average for feature films of the period.

Public Reaction to The Witch

The world premiere of "The Witch" took place in Stockholm on September 18, 1922, with a print that contained at least two brief cuts, while the Danish premiere, which featured an uncut version, was held on 7 November at Copenhagen's Palads (Palace) Theatre where Christensen had marvelled at "Les Misérables" seven years before. Originally the city's railroad terminal building, it had been converted into a grand movie theatre in 1912. With 2,300 seats, it was the second largest in Europe at that time and employed a staff of 100. Opening music composed by Launy Grøndahl played as well-dressed patrons took their seats. Once the auditorium was full, the carbon arc lamps in the giant projectors were lit with a hiss and the house lights faded. A brilliant beam of light sliced through the darkness to splash the first images onto the screen as the original score, composed and now conducted in front of a thirty-piece orchestra by Jacob Gade, majestically rang out.

The film began with a lecture by Christensen who stood by a pile of books – his sources. He then gave an encapsulation of the movie's theme. Filmed separately by another cinematographer, this opening was a unique way for the director to personally introduce himself to the audience. And then the film itself began.

Of all the scenes, the flight of the witches to Bloksbjerg received the heartiest applause, and at the end of the show there was a rousing ovation. At this point it

32 John Ernst, *Benjamin Christensen* (1967, The Danish Film Institute, Copenhagen) p. 15
33 *Ibid*, p 17.

would have been natural for Christensen to come out and take a bow but he was nowhere to be found. Before the show he had given instructions that a sheet listing the literary sources upon which the film was based be placed upon every seat so that viewers might appreciate the research that went into the making of it, but as people were taking their seats he didn't see any paper. He soon discovered that the bales of notes had been tossed out into the back by the trash, and it was reckoned that he had stalked off somewhere in a rage.

Everyone seemed to agree that this was something new; a film that had nothing to do with love or intrigues, a film that had no heroes or plot in the normal sense, that presented no conflict to be neatly resolved by the last reel. A film that had no happy ending.

After that, opinion divided sharply.

The most outspoken criticism was voiced by the daily, *Berlingske Tidende (B.T.)*, as the following article from their 8 November, 1922 edition testifies.

TAKE THE WITCH OFF THE SCREEN

> Benjamin Christensen's "The Witch" was technically a masterpiece. But its topic was a fateful mistake.
>
> Hardly any other film in the history of Copenhagen movie-going has managed to attract such a prestigious audience for its grand premiere as Benjamin Christensen's "The Witch," the event having taken place yesterday at the Palads Theatre.
>
> Not only were all the VIPs of the Danish film and theatre world present, but the seats were also occupied by those from the most sophisticated and fashionable classes of society, and when the opening (news) shorts faded out and the overture rang out broad and majestically from the orchestra pit, an expectant shudder passed through the crowd.
>
> Benjamin Christensen obviously knows how to arouse expectations to the maximum. For two long years the city has been abuzz about "The Witch." Rumours have circulated about the insane cost of the film while contradictory stories about the scenes being shot inside the fortified confines of the Hellerup studio have been exchanged in hush-hush tones by word of mouth. At one point it was rumoured that an actress had refused to play the role the director had assigned her because she considered it an affront to her decency. Soon enough those kinds of rumours proved to be unfounded, and, to the contrary, the actors had performed under Christensen's leadership with enthusiasm and devotion.
>
> An alluring veil of secrecy was laid over the making of the film, and not even the cinematographers or the bearers of the big rolls of raw film stock perceived what they were really helping to create...

They all just had a feeling that this was a completely different kind of film and that they were embarking on a journey into a new and mysterious realm that would lead to the rebirth of the art of cinema and mark the beginning of a renaissance in the medium.

Last night that feeling had transmitted itself to the audience who studied the first blue (tinted) texts with rapt absorption as they appeared on the distant screen, the first metres of this new work which would bring Benjamin Christensen victory or defeat.

Did he triumph?

He could have. There is no doubt that the broad public which the film medium has attracted is about to loose patience with movies – as this movie demonstrated. Time and time again the empty smiles of the audience indicated they were being bored by the empty sensations. A desire for a more weighty experience which would not just entertain but also enrich lay in the air. And Christensen's basic idea, to create a popular film lecture, an 'essay of the silver screen, ' is undoubtedly an ingenious attempt to accommodate this desire.

He could have chosen to present one of history's great figures in a fashion not bound by standard film conventions but flush with the intensity and rich colours of the truth. He could have addressed a basic human question which lies in thousands of hearts and begs an answer. And with the great sums of money he had at his disposal, with all the technical expertise and the directorial mastery that "The Witch" bears witness to, he could have created a film which would have struck the audience as a revelation, opening up the doors of movie theatres to a new public...

Instead he has chosen to turn down one of history's dark side streets, taking up for consideration the subject of the Middle Ages' belief in witchcraft in order to compare it to modern superstitious tendencies. The basic error is not that the topic is distant and specific but that from first image to last it touches upon not only the hysteria of the times but also upon, as he himself terms it... the unvarnished perversity.

This is a chapter from the dark side of human history, a story of sickness that he chooses to delve into. It is no more appropriate to read aloud from the daily logs of an insane asylum for an evening's entertainment than it is to play "The Witch" for a large and varied public where youth is in the overwhelming majority.

Had Christensen said, "I have the money which shall be used to make a film only intended to be screened for the scientifically educated, for the authorities and for seasoned professionals," no one would object. It would stand as a bizarre but interesting experiment. But when he throws open the doors to the masses and shows it to the young women of the town and to office worker Hansen and his beloved under the guise of education, then one must protest, and in the name of film protest forcefully!

Witches' Sabbath on the Silver Screen

Let us take a rough look at Benjamin Christensen's film lecture. It begins with classic documentation. We see on the silver screen not living pictures but woodcuts of scenarios from the Middle Ages which present the story of belief in witchcraft, while a pointer stick draws attention to various details. This is stern and straightforward stuff, no false advertising here. It is immediately apparent that this is no film in the traditional sense.

But suddenly the images come to life and the same situations told by woodcuts now flicker upon the stage in living re-enactments. Christensen has reconstructed the anatomy of a witch persecution from the Middle Ages. He shows how a whole village is gripped by hysteria. An inhabitant lays sick and of course it is assumed that he's been cursed by a witch.

A travelling witchfinder general arrives and examines the afflicted man, declaring that without a doubt his condition has been caused by a curse, and immediately a hunt is on for the witch. Naturally suspicion falls upon a loathsome old woman who comes around every day and begs at the door, a woman who gobbles away at her øllebrød [a porridge made of bread and non-alcoholic beer] with wrinkled fingers. [This was Maren Pedersen, and before she digs into the runny slop she puts a couple of fingers to her nose and blows a glob of snot on the floor, –JS.]

The sick man's daughter accuses the old hag of the heinous deed and she's dragged before the court and subjected to a painful interrogation. All the bestial torture instruments of the Middle Ages are applied right up there on the silver screen; thumbscrews, barbed neck bands, footcrushers and fire. For over half an hour this orgy of sadism is celebrated up on the screen. Metre after metre of film rolls through the camera, which is frozen on the old woman's tormented mummy-like face, boring in with shameless close-ups until the feeling of nausea overwhelms.

Of course the old woman confesses to everything they've accused her of and more on top of it. In a series of pictures one sees the whole of the witches' Sabbath as their poor, sick, perverted brains conceived it.

The Bonfires Blaze

And it is supposedly not just this old woman who has been to Bloksbjerg, but all those that the daughter hates, including the cow that kicked out at her as well as two old women who had practiced their unappetizing art [of throwing the contents of piss pots at their neighbour's door] – all have participated in that wild dance around the old devil. [The wording here is somewhat confusing: it is actually Maria, under torture, who names practically everyone she knows as co-conspirators, –JS.]

The Judge believes every word she says.

Bonfires blaze over the whole town and the judge himself feels plagued by the Devil's hand-maidens. A young handsome monk has felt a sting on the wrist where a beautiful young virgin has grabbed him, and to make the burning sensation go away he has himself whipped, but the fire cannot be extinguished by the lashings. The virgin is therefore a witch. Before we witnessed the old mummy-like woman being tormented, now it's young female flesh and body parts that are flayed while she is broken on the wheel before our eyes.

It is true that these things happened, God help us, but – hand on your heart – which instincts are aroused in a large and diversely composed audience by this kind of brutality when it is inflicted upon a young, undressed actress?

The dance of the witches continues. The nuns are gripped by a mysterious hysteria in front of the altar... the devil lays himself down between married couples in their beds. He is everywhere and all hearts pound in fear at the prospect of meeting him in the flesh on the next street corner or in the next room!

The Embarrassing Ending

Finally Christensen draws his conclusions by advancing a theory.

The belief in witches has passed but the superstitious tendencies that nourished it live on. The existence of fortune-tellers, kleptomaniacs and hysterics of every stripe is but a modern echo of what the ignorant souls of the Middle Ages were possessed by, but it is in this concluding chapter that Christensen suffers his biggest defeat from a purely artistic standpoint, in the process casting doubt on the seriousness which lays behind this gloomy film. The scene suggesting that today the airplane has replaced the witch is but an insipid witticism, and at the end when he presents us with the modern version of the witch who once burned on the bonfire but is now a fashionable young kleptomaniac [kleptomania = compulsive behaviours = witchcraft, –JS.) pictured undergoing therapeutic shower treatment at a nerve clinic – this left one sitting there not with a bad taste in one's mouth but with an embarrassed taste.

The Undressed

Nudity is plentiful in Christensen's film. The screen flashes with the white flesh of bare backs and naked silhouettes wandering in the secret lairs of the Devil's realm. But it is not the nudity which is most offensive about the film. It is the Satanic perversity and gruesomeness which leaps from it like flames, a kind of unfathomable, plumbless evil – humankind's chimera – that everyone knows has existed down through the ages. But when that is caught and fenced into a cell, whether that be in a prison or in a madhouse, it is not to the accompaniment of Wagner and Chopin, nor is it in front of a fashionable public seated in comfortably upholstered movie seats. It is not for the young men and women who have ventured into the magic world of the movie theatre.

If it was "Mr. Anyone at all" who made this film then we could respond with a kick or a shrug. But that person is Benjamin Christensen who, even with this major mistake, proves that he is one of the few upon which Danish film can build its future. And then it becomes a different matter. We can therefore end this review in no other way than to voice deep regret that he has allowed his considerable abilities to lead him into this blind alley.

(One can only hope) that he will find his way back into the light again as quickly as possible and create that great popular film that will do justice to his talents.

But regarding "The Witch" we ultimately have but one request; take it off the screen as fast as possible!

Debate about the film continued to rage in the wake of the premiere, and on 9 November, *B.T.* elaborated on their concerns in a follow-up piece.

FILM AND POPULISM

While *B.T.* stood rather alone among the city's press in its appraisal of the new Benjamin Christensen film, "The Witch," we have in turn received considerable proof that our evaluation of the movie was in accord with what many of those attending the premiere thought. And the question we are constantly asked is this; how in all the world has this film been able to pass the censors?

We would on this occasion draw attention to the fact that we are not among those who constantly cry out for the censorship of film. We have also not taken that position in this case since we understand the censor's viewpoint in letting the film pass. They must also once in a while show a bit of courage. And, after all, it is not the acting in this film that exploits the viewer's basest instincts. "The Witch" is a deeply serious work, written and staged by an artist who undeniably occupies a leading position in his field, who consciously and manfully has fought against the emptiness and sterility that characterizes so many films and who has pioneered new modes of expression in the medium.

We understand the motives of the censors who refused to prohibit the film in advance, they having no desire to quash Christensen's attempts to create something new. With that said, we must protest that this film is now, evening after evening, attracting a sensation-seeking public. The task that Christensen has set himself is to solve or explain a cultural-historic problem or situation through his art. We believe in the future of film and we also believe that the medium as such will begin to address itself to these [cultural-historic] issues. But film is and will always be a popular medium, an art form for "the people."

As we previously wrote, "It is no more appropriate to read aloud from the daily logs of an insane asylum for an evening's entertainment than it is to play 'The Witch' for a large and varied public where youth is in the overwhelming majority." This is precisely the core of the case. We have no doubt that the director of "The Witch" will be able to produce laudatory quotes from renowned psychiatrists and history professors in his defence, but the (professional) views these men take on the unflinching sadism, the torture and the nudity – and all that occurs during the wild and appalling witches' Sabbath – has no relevance to how the broader public, not least young viewers, will relate to the film. With the general public there is no understanding of cultural-historic context and no knowledge of psychiatry is brought to bear. The film arouses a different set of instincts in the general audience, and this kind of attraction we can best do without.

When one lectures to a general public and attempts to teach them about the darkness of ancient times, one assumedly does so without unveiling a series of exhibits which drip with blood and border on the pornographic. One must trust that said lecturer has the ability to reproduce these images in such a way so that they do not disgust or titillate the audience.

Benjamin Christensen lacks this ability – and he has caused grave offence. To his mind conveying the truth about the subject is

> synonymous with presenting it in the most harshly realistic terms. Well, no one can prevent him from having that perception, but in so doing he has forfeited the right to deliver his lectures to a broad public. And no one can deny that the film theatre attracts one of the broadest publics in our country. One should not be nauseated or titillated in a movie theatre. One should be entertained or preferably educated, or in best case elevated.
>
> One might have expected the censors to be conscious of this to a somewhat greater degree, and maybe to have hit upon a compromise solution that would have pre-empted the sensationalism and morbidity that took complete possession of this film.

The daily paper *Social Demokraten* agreed that it was all just too much:

> Many of the images exude such raw realism that the dominating reaction is one of nausea... the viewer suffers the torments along with the victims on the screen. The film seems itself a product of the beastliness, torture, bonfires and insanity that it means to critique. Even Griffith and his staff could hardly have created anything like that.

The case that *B.T.* makes against "The Witch" reads like a textbook definition of "exploitation cinema" that would come to flourish in America in the 1930s; the modus operandi of its progenitors being to crassly and with premeditation – and definitely for profit – palm off lurid spectacle on the public under cover of providing enlightenment and edification. Censors were prone to be more sympathetic to films that had moral or educational intent, and rogue producer-directors tried to have it both ways: they loaded their cheaply made films with sex, violence, nudity etc. to attract the paying public, but larded it all with sanctimonious moralizing to placate puritanical elements of the public (who were hostile to movies to begin with). Hollywood itself employed this strategy via what would come to be known as "compensating moral values," meaning that the bad guy could have all the fun and sex he wanted in the first nine reels but he had to pay for it in the last reel, usually by dropping dead in a hail of bullets. Bigger-budget Hollywood productions conveyed this via action while Poverty Row producers who could hardly afford much "action" conveyed it in the tone of their films.

Christensen was clearly anything but a fly-by-night "exploitationist." He was an artist and a master craftsman, and "The Witch" was a true work of obsession; not just some hoary attempt to separate the customers from their hard-earned money, but his motives remain in question. He liked to see himself as a man of science and rationalism, but he was also drawn to sensational subject matter. With "The Witch" he was attempting to show how ridiculous and horrible primitive superstitions were. "The belief in evil spirits, sorcery and witchcraft is the result of naive notions about the mystery of the universe," he would say. But he still made it all appear very intriguing, mysterious and scary and filled the screen with beautiful semi- and not-so-semi-naked women. As has been shown, this struck some as dishonest and exploitative. Was this education or entertainment or just pure salaciousness? Or something infinitely more sinister? And the shots of deformed women he included in the final chapter (a hunchback and a woman with a facial deformity in close-up) had a startling impact, however briefly presented.

He had his defence down pat. The film had a moral and that was contained in the concluding "modern section," which aimed to show how susceptible modern man still was to the seductions of the "dark side." While many thought this the weakest part of the film, it served an important function. There was no human villain to be shot dead in the last reel, but it held out the prospect that there was a constructive lesson to be learned from it all. This was the film's official raison d'être and many bought it and figured Christensen was entitled to some dispensation. As one writer put it, "...consideration for the modern public's aesthetic feelings must yield for more important considerations, and the censors have naturally permitted scenes which otherwise would have been unthinkable."[34]

Other reviews of "The Witch" at the time were more mixed than the "attack" published in *B.T.*

Politiken praised the photography and the acting, while *København* pointed out that Christensen had rendered the public a service by revealing that movies were more than just acting and (filmed) novels. "The Witch was an unconditional success," stated the latter publication, "but will it become a success with the public? This is perhaps more in doubt. Many will come because they are attracted by the sensational subject matter and the artistic quality of the film, but one doesn't get people interested in (cultured) history just because it's shown on film. All in all a strange evening which in many ways points to the beginning of a new direction in the film medium."

A more positive if still mixed appraisal of the film was offered up in the daily *København* on 9 September, 1922:

THE WITCH AND THE OTHERS

> The premiere of "The Witch" at the Palads Theatre has given rise to a lot of shouting. So much so that some voices have grown hoarse from shock over specific images contained in the film. It is possible that one scene here or there could have been cut out, even if they were just as historically accurate as the rest We shall not become embroiled in that feud but would just point out that in any event the film is a serious work which cannot be measured with the same yardstick one uses on an American beach-comedy. And finally, before one gives voice to outraged protests, one ought

34 *København*, 8 November, 1922

> to think about what we have put up with over the last decade when it comes to films full of affectation, mushy sentimentality and sleaze, and which perpetuate fraud on the silver screen, consciously and unconsciously. We have viewed and thereby supported thousands of really unhealthy films. Let us embrace the attempts that are made to find new ways and new directions forward for cinema.

The public was apparently just as divided as the press, the tumultuous applause at the end notwithstanding. Crowd response is a strange thing. Perhaps doubters just got swept along in the spirit of the moment, and there were indeed doubters, as the 9 November issue of *København* attested.

IS THE WITCH A GOOD FILM?

> As expected, the premiere of Benjamin Christensen's "The Witch" took place in the "Sign of Sensation." But some in the audience were also shocked and/or offended. As far as one could determine the reaction of the public was very much divided. The audience was certainly not completely "with" the film. We have asked a couple of people who were there what they thought about the film and this is what they told us:
>
> Director of the Royal Theatre, Poul Nielsen, finds "The Witch" highly interesting:
>
> "I rarely go to see movies but I'd heard so much about "The Witch" that I had to go see it. I must say straight off that I found it a highly interesting work. Benjamin Christensen is a peculiar and ingenious fellow, and his ability to get things done is rather amazing.
>
> Take for example his working methods. He finds an elderly woman who probably has no conception of how to act. She is subjected to torture while in reality she merely moves her mouth, muttering incessantly. But nonetheless the director gradually manages to arouse her sense of fantasy and her eyes acquire the appropriately spooky expression.
>
> (Naturally) it is true enough that the topic can be "perverse," but the director – the lecturer – cannot be held responsible for the fact that back in the Middle Ages these things were being set in motion by people with perverse imaginations. It is wrong to accuse Christensen of wallowing in sensationalism."
>
> Professor Viggo Christiansen, Dr. of Medicine, finds the parts on the Middle Ages excellent but he misses a witch-burning.

> "That's nonsense when people claim that there is exploitation at play. "The Witch" is excellently made. And furthermore I've been told that the 'worst bits' were cut out. It's stupid to talk about sensationalism – that hasn't at all been the approach Christensen used. Had that been his intention, there were stronger things in his source material he could have chosen to bring forth.
>
> I think that the scenes of the Middle Ages were in all ways excellent. They were authentic renderings of works that can be found, for example, in the Bibliothèque-diabolique. The only thing I missed was a real witch-burning. And he could have easily shown us that. [Bodies do dangle on a bonfire in the last shot. –JS.] The modern part I did not so much care for.
>
> I consider "The Witch" to be an historic film which has succeeded in reproducing the atmosphere and details necessary to give us insight into the psychology of those times."

"The Witch" was apparently successful enough with the public in Sweden and Denmark. Swedish reviewers, however, took a dim view of it until an influential commentator by the name of Dr. Fogelquist, a man who was normally no fan of the film medium, praised it in a widely read article in *Dagens Nyheter* and turned the tide of critical opinion in its favour – although it was reportedly thereafter banned for many years. Or was it simply forgotten? In any case it proved to be the kind of financial disaster the studio didn't need at a point when admissions were already declining and Hollywood was becoming more competitive.

In other countries "The Witch" proved much more problematic.

8000 Catholic women protested in the streets when it finally opened in France in 1926, demonstrating against it outside the Paris theatre where "La Sorcellerie à Travers les Ages," as it was titled, premiered.[35] In a complaint to the police they claimed that it was immoral and a mockery of the Church. "The French press kept their distance from the film," noted a Danish writer at the time, "its exhibition sparking a wider debate about the screening of foreign films." Parisian surrealists liked it better and it became one of their favourites.

In English-speaking countries no one dared show the film for many years. In America the New York censorship committee screened it for a select audience of cultural movers and shakers, just as they had for "Blind Justice," but "The Witch" was infinitely more controversial and the chairman of the committee was fired because of it and Christensen was asked to vacate the hotel where he was staying.[36]

Over the decades the Danish press would often refer to the quote in *The New York Times* that stated that the film was "25 years ahead of its time." The actual wording, however, is somewhat more ambiguous: "Come back with your film in 25 years, Mr. Christensen, and maybe then America will be

35 *Social Demokraten*, 25 September, 1949

36 *Politiken*, 28 December, 1936

mature enough to understand your art."[37]

In Germany the film fared somewhat better. Erich Pommer, head producer at the all-powerful UFA studio, was a big fan and arranged private screenings of the uncut version for various groups of artists and scholars who responded very positively.

Average Germans only got to see a much more edited-down version when it opened there in June 1924, the result of long negotiations between Christensen and German Catholic groups that reportedly only left the "torso" of the film intact. Nonetheless it played successfully in that country for months.

Pommer held the film in such high esteem that he invited Christensen to come to Germany and make movies for his studio. The Dane eagerly accepted. The two follow-ups he had envisioned, "Helgeninde" ("The Woman Saint") and "Ander" ("Spirits") were now out of the question. (Magnusson had made him an offer to direct eight more pictures but he had declined, refusing to be involved in 'assembly-line productions.') And, since no Danish studio wanted him now, Pommer's offer was timely. "After The Witch," Christensen would recall, "I was out in the cold for two years. When I finally got a chance at UFA, I had to disprove that I was this 'literary experimentalist' that everybody said I was, and so I made these purely commercial films.'[38]

The German and American Films

Christensen's first "purely commercial" film for UFA was "His Mysterious Adventure" ("Seine Frau, die Unbekannte"), an unevenly realized marital comedy that was both farce and melodrama and came complete with a happy ending.

Nevertheless it displayed flashes of Christensen's visual inventiveness. Opening in Berlin in October of 1923, knowledgeable viewers could appreciate the typically Christensen-esque erotic component that included a fantasy sequence in which a wife imagines what her husband is doing with another woman behind closed doors. This prompted at least one Danish critic to complain that he had "succumbed to the temptation, as he had in "The Witch," of investing his greatest efforts on a series of scenes that pander in rather embarrassing fashion to the unsavoury."[39]

He then took temporary leave of his directorial duties to act in Carl Dreyer's psychological drama, "Michael," which was also being shot in Berlin. Based on a turn-of-the-century Danish novel of same name by Herman Bang, it was the story of the "Master," an elderly artist (played by Christensen) whose feelings for a young protegé are ultimately betrayed.

Christensen and Dreyer were two very headstrong individuals, with Pommer, among others, predicting they would clash on the set – and they did. An article on the shooting relates how they agreed not to call each other "idiot" since that

37 John Ernst, *Benjamin Christensen*, p.20

38 *Ibid*, p 21.

39 Unidentified Danish daily, 28 December, 1923

was a word the non-Danish personnel could understand.[40] But the results were extraordinary, prompting effusive praise for Christensen's performance in a film that Dreyer would always consider one of his best.

This afforded some small measure of vindication for Christensen after "The Witch," which had quickly come to be considered a fiasco, and no doubt it was an ego-boost for him to see posters billing him as "The Master." "And yet," as Casper Tybjerg notes, "...there is something eerily prescient about having Christensen play an artist whose best work is behind him and who dies a bitter man."[41]

His next film for UFA was the English-spoken "The Woman Who Did." It was based on a book that the British novelist Grant Allen had published in 1894. Allen had availed himself of the opportunity to weigh in on the debate about "free love" that was then abroad but, despite dealing with the controversial subject of a woman who chooses to have a child outside marriage, this was no hard-hitting exposé and in later years Christensen was wont to dismiss it as lightweight fluff.

There were other problems as well. The international cast of Brits, Yanks, Russians and Germans not only lacked chemistry but could barely understand each other. As he later wrote to a friend, "...none of the actors spoke the same language and just pranced gaily around each other, and after having spent the first day acting as an interpreter, I gave up. The film had to be made quickly and I ended up just letting them say what they wanted. It was a tower of Babel."[42] He even sent a telegram to the backer in London advising him to abandon the project, but to no avail.

"The Woman Who Did" opened in December 1925 to dismissive press. Christensen himself was more uncompromising in his assessment, going on to call it "the greatest... fiasco of my life, and the only film of mine I never dared to actually watch after I shot it."[43] As to whether it was really that bad, today it must remain an open question since it figures among the many "lost" films of that era.

While Christensen had departed for Germany, a fair number of his Scandinavian colleagues had chosen to set sail in the other direction – to Hollywood. Among them was the Swede, Victor Sjöström, who had gone to work for MGM (his last name Americanized to "Seastrom"), for whom he directed the studio's first real hit in 1924, "He Who Gets Slapped." He managed to persuade Louis B. Mayer to view a print of "The Witch." Mayer was impressed with what he saw but also clearly taken aback, wondering aloud as to whether Christensen was a genius or a madman. (The Dane would quote this remark over the years with a certain ironic pride.) In any case Mayer sent Christensen a telegram offering him a contract at MGM, and he accepted.

In February of 1925 he arrived in Hollywood. This sojourn effectively put

40 *Politiken*, December 1923, "The Herman Bang film, Michael," by Julia Koppel.

41 Casper Tyberg, *Images of the Master – Benjamin Christensen's career in Denmark and Germany* (published in 1999 as part of the commemorative book *Benjamin Christensen – An International Dane*, issued in conjunction with a retrospective of Danish cinema in America).

42 Excerpted from Christensen's letter to Ove Brusendorf, dated 25 March, 1939.

43 *Ibid.*

an end to his second marriage (to Sigrid Ståhl, whom he had wed in 1922) – although they would not formally divorce until 1934. But lonely in this new town he definitely wasn't; a sizeable Scandinavian expat community that included the likes of Sjöström, Stiller, and a young Greta Garbo already existed and he quickly became an active part of it.

His first encounter with the Hollywood studio system was a bit of a shock. As he would recall: "On the way over to America I'd gotten the idea for a film called "The Light Eternal" ("Det evige lys"). I had most of the story in my head when I arrived. I described it to one of MGM's supervisors, Mr. Harry Rapf. He was so enthusiastic that he wrote me out a check for 5,000 dollars and told me to go back to my hotel room and write the whole thing down. As I sat there in front of the typewriter I realized to my horror that I couldn't recall essential aspects of the story. The check began to burn a hole in my pocket so I managed to think up a new story on the same topic. Twenty-two highly paid writers who had achieved great success in the worlds of literature and the theater and who were now employed by MGM worked it over. Some months later it was finished. Now it was called "The Devil's Circus" and of course I couldn't recognize it at all. I told them that it would be the greatest fiasco of all time. All of Metro's bosses laughed at this idiot who believed he had directed a fiasco."[44]

Cold comfort though it must have been, Christensen was more or less correct, at least as far as the critics were concerned. Although some praised its atmosphere and photography, they generally dismissed "The Devil's Circus" as melodramatic, old-fashioned and lacking the subtle touch.

The studio writers had fashioned it into a romantic drama set in some unspecified (but clearly German-resembling) European city in order to capitalize on Christensen's – Americanized to "Christianson" – "exotic" foreign origins. (MGM would promote it as "the first production in America of the European film genius, Benjamin Christianson," and *Variety* agreed, calling it "foreign and different.")

The plot centres on poor, friendless Mary (played by Norma Shearer) who encounters Carl, a petty criminal with a record. He has lecherous intentions but is disarmed by her innocence and vulnerability and they find solace in each other's company. Their happiness is short-lived when Carl is arrested again. Mary, however, has managed to change him and as the police drag him off to jail he promises to reform.

In the meantime she finds employment in the circus as a trapeze artist, but things take a violent turn when the lion-tamer takes a fancy to her and rapes her one night in her wagon. This sends his girlfriend into a jealous rage and she secretly loosens the ropes of the trapeze, causing Mary to plummet to the ground during her performance – and into a cage full of lions. She is pulled out alive but has been crippled for life.

The Great War is now raging. Carl has been released from prison and joins the army. Upon being discharged he returns to the city and becomes a cobbler,

44 *Ekstrabladet*, 24 September, 1954

having made good on his vow to go straight. He accidentally runs into Mary again, a cripple now forced to sell string puppets on the street. (The puppet theme is established at the start: "When the devil pulls the strings, all the world must dance," the opening title plate reads. Cut to a grinning devil figure who functions as a kind of "master puppeteer.") Deeply distraught by her tale of woe, Carl sets out to find and kill the lion-tamer. But when he discovers the terrible fates that have befallen Mary's tormentors he can only conclude that his work has already been done for him: the lion-tamer has been blinded in the War and his girlfriend, sent to prison after causing Mary's fall, is now a prostitute. Together again – on Christmas Eve, no less – Mary miraculously begins to walk.

The film was Shearer's big breakthrough and did more for her career than Christensen's. According to him the studio was dead set against casting her in the lead and Irving Thalberg had even warned him that if he did it would be "his funeral." Later on he overheard Thalberg concluding a phone conversation with a tender goodbye to "my beloved Norma." Some funeral, he thought.

Despite the indifferent press the picture did okay with the public. It appeared to hint at better things to come for Christensen and won him some respect in the Industry. Life in Hollywood, on the other hand, presented a series of more prosaic challenges as the dashing Dane tried to fit in. The most insignificant things could tag a man as an outsider. For example, he preferred to get his shoes re-soled instead of going out and buying new ones, but in class-conscious Hollywood this was a no-no: a successful director could not be seen tramping around in re-soled shoes.

His reputation took a rather more severe beating when two employees died on him. "… I had the cursed luck," he remembered, "that two men who were to work with me on one of the first films both went out and broke their necks in the same week. For some time thereafter I felt people were keeping their distance from me, and Larry Barrymore told me that it was obvious why no one would work for me when my employees were dropping dead."[45]

He also managed to make enemies without even knowing it. "At another point I got one of Hollywood's most prominent fortune-tellers on my back. He advised everyone to stay away from me because I only brought misfortune. Later on it turned out that he was against me because 1 had purchased an antique Chinese figure that he himself had wanted to buy."[46]

Christensen seems to have been a defiant figure at MGM and it no doubt irked some that a foreigner who could hardly speak English[47] could lay claim to knowing the tastes of the American movie-going public better than his bosses at the studio, even if he had had success in, the country with previous films. On the other hand it must have been hard for Christensen to submit one story idea after another only to be asked in deeply sceptical tones if he thought this was something "the American farmer" would go for – and then be told to forget about it as fast as possible. He was

45 John Ernst, *Benjamin Christensen* (1967, The Danish Film Institute, Copenhagen) p.24-25
46 *Ibid.*
47 "I couldn't speak a word of English before I went to America," Christensen is quoted as saying in an article by Haagen Hetsch published in September 1949.

getting a crash course in hardball, bottom-line American capitalism.

But he himself was a battle-tested salesman, having schlepped potatoes, champagne and even his own early films. Even as MGM's writers were hacking apart "The Light Eternal," he was exhaustively studying American movie-going habits, watching innumerable films and gauging audience reaction. Harry Rapf himself had to concede that he had gained "a better conception of those things than some domestic directors."[48]

Still it was something of a pitiable situation. "The Witch" had been a triumph of one man's vision, the product of obsession and the refusal to compromise, and now the same director was slavishly attempting to cater to "the American farmer," no less. What Christensen might have achieved had he been encouraged to stay in Denmark and been given creative freedom on his pictures would occasion much soul-searching in Danish film circles in the decades to come. Truth be told, however, Denmark was too small to accommodate his grand ambitions (or ego) and Danish studios were incapable of producing the world-class epics that he could only make in Hollywood.

... An epic like "The Mysterious Island," which was to be his next project. This was a loose adaptation of the Jules Verne novel, which MGM was prepared to dump a vast amount of effort and resources into. He took over the picture from Maurice Tourneur on short notice in the summer of 1926 after the French emigre had been fired by Mayer for objecting to the presence of a producer on the set who was constantly looking over his shoulder. By this point the studio had already sunk considerable sums into the film and Christensen proceeded to further drain their coffers by spending 300,000 dollars on the construction of a pool where the underwater photography for the prologue would take place.[49]

He threw himself into the production, directing during the day and feverishly rewriting the script at night, twice calling a halt to filming to work out story problems.[50] But bad luck struck again when a hurricane hit the Bahamas where location shooting was taking place, destroying the underwater sets and second unit equipment. The film was temporarily shut down and Christensen was given new assignments.

Lucien Hubbard eventually took over the picture. He largely recast it and had it ready for release in 1929. A writer later remarked that in his years at MGM Christensen had only managed to direct "two movies and one prologue," yet Arne Lunde suggests that Christensen's influence can be seen in more than just the opening: "... one torture scene of the young heroine suggests the macabre imagination of the director of "Häxan." Silhouetted lighting in a submarine interior shot also shows traces of a key Christensen stylistic signature."[51]

Suffice it to say, Christensen's involvement with the film did nothing to help him shed his reputation as a squanderer of time and money.

48 *Motion Picture News*, "Rapf Sees Era of Improvement," 28 November, 1925.

49 John Ernst, *Benjamin Christensen* (1967, The Danish Film Institute, Copenhagen) p.26

50 *Hollywood Citizen*, 2 September, 1926

51 Arne Lunde, *Benjamin Christensen in Hollywood*, p.27, issued as part of the publication *Benjamin*

With his next picture, "Mockery," there seems to be some indication that MGM gave him a freer hand; it was based on his own original screenplay which the studio meddled with less than usual, and they gave him his own name back, billing it as a "Benjamin Christensen production" – rather than "Christianson."

A romantic adventure set during the Russian revolution, it starred Lon Chaney as the simple-minded peasant, Sergei. He meets a poor woman in the woods but she is really the Countess Tatiana in disguise, fleeing an unthinkable fate at the hands of marauding Red soldiers. He agrees to escort her through enemy territory by pretending to be her husband, but the ruse fails and they're captured by Bolsheviks. Sergei is tortured but refuses to reveal Tatiana's secret identity. Eventually they are saved by the dashing Dimitri (played by Ricardo Cortez) who commands a White Russian cavalry unit, and as a reward for his heroism Sergei is made a servant in the house of a wealthy war profiteer.

Tatiana and Dimitri fall in love while Sergei looks on with bitterness. He feels the noblewoman is looking down her nose at him. During a peasant uprising he attempts to rape her, drunk on liquor and Bolshevik propaganda. The revolt is put down by Dimitri and his troops. Sergei is however spared when Tatiana swears that he had actually protected her. Soon another uprising occurs and Tatiana is again in mortal danger, but this time Sergei, now bound by eternal gratitude, lays down his life defending her.

The movie was energetically promoted. "Benjamin Christensen," touted the studio, "is one of the world's greatest authorities on the psychological effect of light and shade in the drama." The film's "many strange effects... worked out on the screen for the first time" constituted a "blending of American and European methods."[52]

Released in August 1927, it suffered an only slightly more merciful fate at the hands of critics them Sergei had at the hands of his attackers. Its setting, they claimed, lacked credibility. It's easy to see why: it had obviously been shot in Southern California, not Russia, and that was evident in almost every frame. Cortez's Latin appearance struck another off-key note.

Christensen's big mistake, however, was to cast Lon Chaney in a sympathetic role. Through a series of films like "The Hunchback of Notre Dame," "The Phantom of the Opera" and Tod Browning's "The Unholy Three," he had cultivated a sinister and sadistic persona which had won him adulation and given rise to a popular saying of the time: "Don't step on that spider – it could be Lon Chaney!" Viewers now had a hard time accepting him as a devoted and suffering victim. And though some critics praised the subtlety of his performance, "the farmers of America" were up in arms about it, and according to John Ernst, "they sent threatening letters by the thousands to MGM."[53]

Christensen, An International Dane (Published in 1999 by "The Danish Wave 99" on the occasion of the exhibition of same name held at The Museum of Modern Art. New York. 9-26 September, 1999.

52 Quote culled from the 8-page MGM publicity flyer for "Mockery" on file in the Danish Film Institute, Copenhagen.

53 John Ernst, *Benjamin Christensen*, (1967, The Danish Film Institute) p.26

The failure of "Mockery" was another nail in Christensen's coffin as far as the studio was concerned, and it's no surprise that when he later approached them about terminating his contract they could be persuaded. He thought he could do better at another studio, and in March 1928 he signed on with First National Pictures to make a single film. He would work in collaboration with his good friend, the author and critic Wid Gunning whom he'd first met in 1916 in New York while negotiating the rights to "Blind Justice." It was Gunning who penned the original story upon which this film, "The Hawk's Nest," was based.

The two of them had assembled a crack outfit that counted, among other able technicians, cameraman Sol Polito who would later go on to work with directors such as Michael Curtiz and Mervyn LeRoy, and they had the studio's biggest star, Milton Sills, at their disposal. Nevertheless this was a considerably less prestigious studio than MGM and "The Hawk's Nest" was what was known as a "programmer," a kind of B-movie. So be it. From all evidence Christensen was happy enough. And the story, set in the mysterious urban catacombs of Chinatown where shadowy characters appeared and vanished at will, allowed him to indulge in the kind of Gothic atmosphere of which he was so fond.

This was the shadowy domain of "The Hawk," a disfigured war veteran who runs a nightclub. Nearby is another neighbourhood hot-spot run by the-gangster Dan Daugherty. In a diabolical twist the Hawk's best friend is framed by Dan for a murder he actually committed, and an innocent man is sentenced to the electric chair. The Hawk avails himself of plastic surgery and now, armed with a new face and identity, he proceeds to frighten the guilty party into confessing.

A review on 5 December, 1928, in *The Los Angeles Record* said in part that, "the direction of Benjamin Christensen is worthy of considerable comment due to the fact that he assumed a particularly mysterious style in handling his characters. Odd [camera] angles are much in evidence, and for the first time it seems that Sills is listening to a director who has ideas."

The film was something of a hit and over the course of 1928 and 1929 Christensen and Gunning made three more movies with First National (which in the meantime was purchased by Warner Brothers), the Dane reinventing himself now as the can-do, go-getting "Ben" Christensen, apparently in an attempt to dispel reports that he was unproductive, slow and somehow "old world."[54]

In 1927 Paul Leni had huge success with "The Cat and the Canary," a "mystery/comedy," and Christensen now attempted to exploit the success of this popular new genre with a picture entitled "The Haunted House." Here someone is trying to poison an elderly millionaire. Suspecting that it might be one of his heirs, he lures four of them to his seaside mansion by letting slip that half-a-million dollars is hidden there. Soon after arriving they begin to encounter a series of strange characters that include a beautiful sleepwalking woman, an insane doctor, his bewitched nurse and the inscrutable caretaker of the place. They're all frightened out of their minds and the would-be poisoner is revealed.

54 Arne Lund, *Benjamin Christensen In Hollywood*, p.29

Christensen and Polito had used low-angle shots and inventive lighting to splendid effect while the performances of Flora Finch, Chester Conklin and Thelma Todd, who stayed on board for the rest of their First National comedies, won the hearts of audiences and ensured the film's success. And critics were kind enough, although nobody accused the film of attempting anything new. It was released in both a silent and sound version, the latter boasting audio effects that included slamming doors, gun shots, storm noises, groans and rattling chains.

Its success demanded a follow-up, and that was to be "Seven Footprints to Satan" (1929), the only one of these First National films to survive, a print having miraculously resurfaced in the 1960s. Like "The Haunted House," this film was based on a novel (by Abraham Merritt), though Christensen found himself compelled to largely re-write the stories for the screen, working in both instances under the pseudonym of "Richard Bee."

"Seven Footprints to Satan" was concerned with subjects Christensen knew about: superstition and Hollywood. The plot centres on Jim, a wealthy young man who imagines himself a great explorer. Together with his girlfriend Eve he plans a dangerous three-year excursion to the wilds of Africa; all of this against his uncle's will. But before they can depart they are kidnapped by unknown parties and taken to a mysterious mansion where a black-hooded figure called Satan presides. Here they are confronted by a procession of strange characters that include a bearded dwarf, a grotesque cripple, a sexy witch, a gorilla and what appears to be a werewolf. They witness shootings, whippings and so forth while hands clutch out at them and wall panels slide away to reveal secret rooms.

Nudity and orgies are also implied in a scene involving hooded men and unhooded women engaged in some kind of medieval-looking ritual (drawing comparisons to Kubrick's "Eyes Wide Shut") and who lie about on the floor in formal dress. A nude oriental woman is partially glimpsed in one short scene, a gorilla holding her feet while her wrists are tied above her head with leather straps. Variety described the film as "… unquestionably one of the hottest exhibitions of inequity done in a long while… no picture for kids."[55]

At the end of the film it all turns out to have been a ruse stage-managed by Jim's uncle to keep them from going to Africa (a premise and plot uncannily similar to the 1997 David Fincher film, "The Game," that starred Michael Douglas.)

As both "The Witch" and "Seven Footprints to Satan" deal with superstition, contain racy scenes and make the most of spooky atmospherics, parallels are inevitably drawn. Although *Variety* had reviewed "The Witch" on 30 August, 1923, and called it "wonderful," it also deemed it "absolutely unfit for public exhibition."

At that point in time "The Witch" had not even been released in America, and it wouldn't be until much later, and then only in a heavily censored version. (There is some confusion as to when the film actually opened in America. 27 May, 1929 is given as the date by some sources, while others say it was released in March 1930, and still other sources contend it premiered in 1932. Probably it

55 *Variety*, 17 April. 1929 '

had a limited early release in New York and "re-releases" elsewhere.)

There was some debate as to which Benjamin Christensen was pulling the strings in "Seven Footprints to Satan." Was this the work of the sober-minded rationalist who took a dispassionate delight in revealing all this mystical hocus-pocus to be but the end product of human superstition, or were these simply the lurid excesses of the sleaze merchant that certain writers claimed to have caught not so fleeting glimpses of? The prominent Danish critic Ib Monty subscribed to the first line of thinking, convinced that Christensen was ridiculing those predisposed to superstition (and perhaps also poking fun at the rubes of Hollywood – who dwelt in a hopelessly provincial America).[56]

From a technical standpoint Christensen had once again shown that he was able to deliver chills and spills on a minuscule budget. He was also – as he had demonstrated in "The Witch" and other films – aware that actors who were immersed in their characters and fully understood the significance of their exchanges gave the best performances. And this very much involved sound – even in silent movies. In his early silent films actors still memorized and spoke scripted dialogue, and in these films viewers can often "see" the sound even if they can't actually hear it. For example, in "Blind Justice," a group of merrymakers listen keenly to the strokes of a clock as midnight arrives on New Year's Eve, while in "The Witch" the deranged mutterings of an elderly Maren Pedersen are perhaps even more affecting because we can only see her lips move.

During the shooting of "Seven Footprints to Satan" the movie magazine *Hollywood* noted how Christensen used sound effects even on the set of the silent version to motivate his actors and create the appropriate mood.[57] These sounds included gun shots, various types of bells, wailing sirens, the grating of metal on metal, groans, moans, screams and howls.[58] Apparently he had found a better way to communicate with his actors than in broken English – by screaming at them! And these sessions reportedly left him quite hoarse the next day.

The last of his First National films was "House of Horror," the tale of a terrified couple trapped in a haunted house with a killer whom they attempt to elude in all sorts of humorous ways. Again, the building features the slide-away paintings, secret entrances and trap doors that figured in the two previous films, and the general premise is pretty much the same even though the dialogue here was cut to the absolute minimum.

Clearly Christensen was repeating himself and was not shy about doing so. He would later state that he considered his first two pictures with the studio, "The Hawk's Nest" and "The Haunted House," the best two films he made in America. After that it was a case of diminishing returns, although it must be said that "Seven Footprints to Satan" holds up well today. It's extremely entertaining and is much more than just another run-of-the-mill haunted house comedy as

56 Programme notes for "Seven Footprints to Satan" issued by The Danish Film Museum in May 1967.
57 It was almost compulsory at this time to release both a sound and silent version of a film.
58 *Hollywood*, 15 December, 1928

some writers have stated, probably without actually having seen it.

While "House of Horror" was not among Christensen's favourites, it did lead to the discovery of a device that would change the face of filmmaking – the sound boom, if his somewhat shifting (and never independently verified) recollections of the event are credible.

As he recalled in an interview in 1952: "At the start [of the sound era] the microphone was firmly secured, forcing the actors to move themselves in relation to it rather than the other way around. I found that to be exceedingly impractical, so during a pause between two takes I sent a man out to find a long bamboo (fishing) pole. We hung the microphone up on the pole and I called over the little comedian, Chester Conklin, and told him, 'now run around the studio, Ches', and just say some stuff and ignore the fact that you're being pursued by the microphone. And it worked, disproving the nonsense that the microphone must remain stationary... a week later the 'discovery' was being used in all the Hollywood studios."[59]

The Invisible Years

After making "House of Horror" Christensen returned to Denmark for the first time since he'd departed for Hollywood in 1925. On 27 March, 1929, his ship docked in Copenhagen, and the next day a reporter from a Danish paper caught up with him to hear about his great adventures:

> Benjamin Christensen came home yesterday from Hollywood and went trundling about in the Spring sunshine, an imposing and good-humoured figure among the crowds on Strøget. He is here on vacation. In recent years he has made four films for First National Studio, one of them with Milton Sills and one a 'talkie,' and now he thinks that's enough for a while.
>
> Q: How long are we going to be able to keep you over here?
>
> A month or two. Over the course of time a lot of Danes have ended up over there and have established their own little colony. It's quite cozy and we often get together.
>
> Q: Are you yourself satisfied?
>
> I am happy. Very simply put, I'm happy with my work. And you know that the last half year has been the most interesting in the whole history of film!
>
> Q: Why?

59 *Berlingske Aftenavis*, 6 May, 1952

Because of sound film. I myself directed one and I was as delighted as a child at Christmas who gets a really, really entertaining toy to play with. [Christensen did indeed 'play' around with sound. In one of his first sound films he had a woman with a very beautiful voice singing a sentimental song by Stephen Foster while at the same time a dog howled in the most frightful manner.[60] –JS.]

Q: What does a sound film demand of a director?

He needs to have experience from both film and live theatre. It is in a way very complicated and demands a great sense of fantasy. It's not enough to throw out a good idea and just go from there.

Q: How does one shoot a sound film?

We use lots of microphones. For a radio broadcast you can use just one but when shooting a film you have them hanging all over the set decorations and props. Every single set-up and person requires a microphone. And inside a booth sits a man known as a sound-mixer. That is a completely new job in the film profession. He sits in that booth and listens to all the signals coming out of these microphones, and then the director himself goes into the booth to make sure everything sounds right. These days it is not enough anymore if everything just looks right.

Q: And if the sound is badly recorded, is the film unusable?

Well, we're already able to play back the sound three minutes after the scene is shot so we pretty much know immediately if it's successful. And the sound is often recorded miles away from the studio itself. For example, when I recorded my sound film for First National the sound was sent to us through the telephone lines...

Christensen also had some business to attend to in Copenhagen regarding the 1,500-seat Park Theatre which the government had granted him co-ownership of back in 1925.[61] The theatre was newly built and hadn't actually opened until October 1926, approximately a year after Christensen's departure to the States. The problem was that he had been in the US the whole time and had yet to step foot inside the building despite earning tidy sums from it. He hadn't even attended the grand opening, not least because the invitation, sent by regular post, hadn't reached him in Hollywood until four days after the event had taken place.

60 *Social Demokraten*, April 1959

61 This was a special favour granted to certain directors by the government as a kind of 'thank you.' Carl

This failed to mollify critics who complained about the situation on the floor of the Parliament, and he was now compelled to defend himself in that hallowed hall. While it was pointed out by at least one journalist that his contract had taken all this into account, he was nevertheless forced to relinquish his share of the enterprise. (The building still exists today, located next to the Parken sports stadium in the Østerbro neighbourhood, though it's been remodelled in such a fashion that only the balcony remains intact as a functioning cinema.)

It took him longer than expected to tie up all the loose ends of his life in Denmark and he didn't make the voyage back across the Atlantic until 1930. He had now been gone a full year and it was a very different Hollywood he came back to – a town and a film industry badly rattled by the Great Depression. Lock-outs and strikes were now commonplace. And, as he would later reflect with some bitterness, a whole flock of Broadway directors who knew little about film had come out to Hollywood in the wake of the "talkie" boom to occupy all the vacant directing jobs.

He had been gone too long, nobody knew him anymore. And in the meantime many of the Scandinavian film people – directors, actors, technicians – that he had fraternized with had returned home. Christensen now also left Hollywood, moving into a cottage on Santa Monica's Venice Beach. It was a house he would describe as being "so close to the water that one can almost roll out of bed and into the sea." But he still had big plans and Hollywood was still the key to his dreams.

His main ambition at this point was to start an independent production company with his old pal, Wid Gunning. One of their first projects was to be a film based on the Danish novel, "Street of the Sandalmakers,"[62] which he had acquired the rights to. As he enthused to a writer from *B. T.* in 1932, it was to be an ambitious historical epic made for the international market. Set in ancient Rome, it would feature the excitement and pageantry of pagan festivals and star multitudes of slaves and legionnaires. He later claimed that contracts had already been signed with theatres even before they'd shot a single metre of film,[63] all on the assumption that President Roosevelt's soon to be enacted film code would make life easier for independent producers by outlawing the monopolistic policies of the major studios (who forced theatres to book their product on a "package deal" basis). But to the surprise of many the new code simply gave "the majors" a green light to continue as before. This spelled doom for a whole generation of independent producers, Christensen among them. He had survived employees dropping dead on him, the vindictiveness of angry fortune-tellers and hurricanes that wrecked his sets, but the greedy bottom-line politics of American big business was the final blow.

Another hindrance for Christensen would have been the Production Code of 1934, which stipulated in detail what was and was not permitted to be shown on screen. It was forced down the throats of the studios by the Catholic Legion of

Dreyer was granted, in the same fashion, operation of the Dagmar theatre in the '50s and his finances improved considerably as a result.

62 *Sandalmagernes gade* by Nils Petersen.

63 *Politiken*, 28 December, 1936

Decency in response to growing popular outrage over the increasing "decadence" of Hollywood movies and the immoral dope-ravaged lifestyles – as the dim view would have it – of the people who made them. Had that been implemented earlier, he never would have gotten away with some of the scenes he'd included in "Seven Footprints to Satan," for example. American movie making was about to become decidedly less daring, less sexy and less weird, and it's hard to imagine Christensen being a part of that particular scene.

His years on Venice Beach remain a bit of a mystery. Although he had a house by the sea (so typically Danish), it apparently wasn't enough to fend off bouts of homesickness, as illustrated by one of the few episodes from this period he later deigned to recount to a writer:

> I remember one night on New Year's Eve back in the Thirties when I had some young people visiting me in my beach house in Santa Monica. A young American fellow suggested that we ought to all go out into the water when the clock was a little past midnight, and five minutes later we all lay there together in the surf. The water was just as warm as it is here (in Denmark) in September. That's all great but I can assure you that one eventually becomes dead tired of California's climate. You can't stand the sun after you've been there a couple of years.[64] One longs to feel a fine snow in one's face or to take a plunge in real water on a December day. People in California fail to experience the blessings of the changing seasons. They hardly know what a real spring is.[65]

Now in exile from his "life in exile," it's natural to wonder what effect these reversals of fortune had on him and what kind of life he was living there on the beach. He was exceedingly circumspect about this period. When asked by a scribe what he was up to at this point, his response seemed purposely vague: "I go for a swim, walk around, rest, enjoy life."[66]

Could it have been that prosaic? Hollywood and its environs attracted would-be starlets from all over the country who dreamed of meeting just such a Hollywood director, and he was after all estranged and half a world away from his wife back in Denmark. Was he perhaps indulging in the kind of decadent, bohemian lifestyle that the aforementioned New Year's Eve episode so tenuously hints at? Midnight flings like this out into the surf were at that point becoming staple scenes in exploitation cinema. The most famous such scene takes place in the 1936 Dwain Esper-directed drug melodrama, "Marihuana: Weed with Roots in Hell." Here, after a night of blowing dope with randy male cohorts, a gaggle of loose women decide to go skinny-dipping

64 Having shot "The Witch," "Seven Footprints to Satan" and perhaps other films at night, Christensen was apparently no great sun worshipper.

65 Unidentified Danish daily, 22 October, 1945

66 *Berlingske Aftenavis,* 18 December, 1934

on a stretch of sand assumedly located not far from Christensen's own shack.

Fiction, yes, but...

Some of the short stories in the semi-autobiographical book, *Hollywood Destinies*, he published later hint at a foot-loose existence. In "Koloratur," he describes a fiery young beauty who goes skinny-dipping with him in the sea and whom he sleeps with that night. (From a repressively religious home, she goes on to become a Hollywood star). In "Hollywood Mysteries," he meets an available young pretty after both of them burst out in laughter at an Ape-and-the-Virgin movie and are compelled to leave the theater.

Whether or not the film colony really was as corrupt and decadent as the yellow press claimed can never be known, but it was without a doubt a town full of temptations for those with a name and connections, and Benjamin Christensen had all that. He was, after all, a lover of life as well as the man who had made "The Witch."

And yet other evidence (equally circumstantial) paints the picture of a fellow who was becoming a hermit. What was really going on with Benjamin Christensen at this point is fated to remain a mystery. Perhaps he was just nursing his personal doubts and frustrations in solitude, but he was in any case clearly becoming a different person, and toward the end of this period on Venice Beach he dropped out of sight. And when he moved back to Denmark in 1935 nobody there was even aware of the fact. The tabloid *B. T.* eventually got to the bottom of the case in their 30 June, 1936 issue:

> WHATEVER HAPPENED TO BENJAMIN CHRISTENSEN?
>
> That's the question film people ask each other whenever they get together.
>
> Those of the young generation hardly even know his name, but we who have more years behind us have not forgotten "The Mysterious X," when rats crawled over the face of the villain, Spiro, or "Blind Justice." Back then Danish films were not based on childish manuscripts as they are today. One demanded excitement and also a certain logic from the writer.
>
> Christensen was probably the most important, albeit difficult, of all directors here in Denmark. He could make many mistakes, as for example with The Witch, but he never degraded himself by making a predictable bird-brained comedy. He never compromised.
>
> And once again the question hangs in the air, "Whatever happened to Benjamin Christensen?"
>
> An anonymous source who should know gave us this reply some time ago.
>
> "He lives by the Pacific coast in Santa Monica, outside Hollywood. There he sits and waits for one film mogul or another

to make him an offer. He is too proud to offer his services directly... He must live up to his own expectations. He works through the days, always busy on an idea for a great or a strange film. He receives visitors with reluctance. Passers-by should preferably take the long way around his inauspicious little house on the edge of the beach. He lets pushy friends know without beating around the bush that their presence is not wanted. He spends very little money and lives off what he has saved so as to be able to bide his time until another chance comes along. A Danish housekeeper cooks his meals."[67]

That's what a very knowledgeable source told us, and that was also very much the truth – until about a year ago when Christensen disappeared from Hollywood and environs. No one, not even those few who were in his confidence, knew what had become of him.

But today we can reveal the secret: Benjamin Christensen has for some time been living incognito in Copenhagen. He lives on Henrik Steffensvej # 9, at the corner of Grundtvigsvej, in a beautiful 4th floor flat which he has imaginatively decorated in a Chinese motif. And yet even though his name and address do appear in the directory, no press or film people have thus far seen anything of him as he only infrequently goes out, and attempts as far as possible to remain anonymous... wearing dark glasses and with his collar turned up around his ears! And one does not gain admittance into his abode without banging the doorknocker in a kind of pre-arranged code. Christensen loves mysticism, and even on this quiet, prosaic side-street in Copenhagen's Frederiksberg neighbourhood he manages to live like Dr. Fu Manchu.

He never became good friends with Hollywood and the American film moguls. He was too big a man for them to slaughter. He was not capable of just saying 'Yes! Yes! Yes!'... so now he's back.

It was a very different Benjamin Christensen that had returned, and yet he was anything but a broken man. He had great plans. The article continues:

Most recently he's been working day and night on some big film ideas. He's just dotted the 'I's' and crossed the 'T's' on some manuscripts which are far more ambitious than the Danish norm and which could not possibly be produced here. Thus he intends to travel to London in the near future to discuss the possibilities with his friend from Hollywood days, Alexander Korda, an important figure in the English film industry and a man who believes and who has gotten others to believe that worthwhile films can be made outside the US. Korda was likewise no great success in Hollywood...

67 Her name was Kamma Winther and he married her before returning to Denmark.

> he and Christensen have much in common, first and foremost the fact that they have never consciously underestimated the public.

Like so many of Christensen's plans, those with Korda never bore fruit and he was fated to remain in Denmark and make his next film there. He could forget about the great Roman epics for the international market. Danish studios could not manage spectacular productions and on top of it the industry was in a state of severe contraction. And to make a film in spoken Danish – now that all films were "talkies" – was, it goes almost without saying, no plus on the world market. Although in later years Christensen would concede that there were great advantages to be had in working in one's native language, this was a humbling come-down and he did not accept it without protest, criticizing in a series of editorials official state film and tax policies that he considered counterproductive.

The Danish Comeback and The Witch Revived

In 1936 Christensen secured the rights to the Danish novel "Children of Divorce" and worked it into a screenplay which Nordisk Film Company produced in 1939. This was to be the first of three "social problem" pictures that he would make for the studio. These were movies based around contemporary issues with an aim to prod the viewer's sense of moral responsibility and stir debate, and they constituted his "Danish comeback."

"Children of Divorce" painted a grim picture of the egotism and moral laxity of single parents and dramatized the negative effects that such behaviour had on their teenage children. It's hard to imagine a film more at odds with the "perversity" of "The Witch" than this, but, as noted, a rationalist-humanist dimension could be read into almost all of Christensen's earlier work. So while these films marked a stylistic departure for him they also heralded the re-emergence of the "progressive Benjamin Christensen" who had shown concern for the unjustly imprisoned in "Blind Justice" and the victims of hysterical persecution in "The Witch."

The film was a critical and public success, with some reviewers hailing it as the best Danish sound film yet.[68] Still a bit of a ham, Christensen appeared in a brief cameo as the salty old skipper, disguised behind a beard and a cigar, and firing off a single line in his limited English: "Get the hell out of here! Hurry up!"

He followed it up with "The Child" in 1940. Here a young couple struggles with the torment of an unplanned pregnancy and the resultant social ostracism. It was a bold examination of another sensitive social topic, abortion, and was also successful. Christensen was gaining (or rather re-gaining) a reputation as a filmmaker of importance who took chances.

"Come Home with Me" was the final installment of his "social issues trilogy." It dealt with an altruistic female attorney who forms personal bonds with her troubled clients in an effort to help them, while the one most in need of understanding is

68 *Berlingske Tidende/Politiken*, 12 August, 1939

her ne'er-do-well and all too imperfect husband. This touching and intimate drama was more about the ambiguous divide between true compassion and "do-gooding" self-righteousness than about social injustice in any broader sense. It was based on a theatre piece by Leek Fisher. He had penned the screenplay for "The Child" and did the same here. Christensen had very little control over the script but still managed to coax the kind of performances from acting greats Bodil Ipsen and Johannes Meyer that would win him comparisons to Frank Capra and Eugene O'Neill.[69]

With these films for Nordisk, Christensen proved himself to be a disciplined filmmaker who could deliver the goods on schedule and on budget, a man who had reined-in his desire to experiment and who could concentrate on story and acting, albeit at the expense of atmosphere. The lighting in most of these films, for example, is characteristic of standard studio set-ups. In a purely technical sense, these films were more akin to the "assembly line work" he had always despised. That great, groundbreaking work of personal obsession, "The Witch," now seemed but a distant memory.

Not so distant, actually. All of a sudden in 1941, just as the newly reinvented, politically-correct Benjamin Christensen was talking bows and receiving absolution for past sins, that film came back from the dead.

After its opening run "The Witch" had been shelved and forgotten and was by this point considered a "lost" film. Unlike today, when video and digital copying technologies guarantee the preservation of almost every movie on some format, this was a time when the destruction of a single 35mm print could mean the end of a film's existence. With no television exposure possible and with "theatrical revivals" still extremely rare, a film that flopped rarely got a second chance and was often just liquidated for its silver content or dumped in a shed somewhere and left to crumble. The basic assumption was that "The Witch" had suffered precisely this kind of fate. As a journalist had previously speculated in the 28 December, 1936 edition of *Politiken*, "It has been 15 years since "The Witch" was made, and if a print could even be found at this point the celluloid would shatter like glass. What audiences would think about this film today will never be known."

But the chief of Denmark's Atlantic Film Company had been searching high and low for the film and four years after this pessimistic prediction he discovered a print lying in a storage facility in Stockholm. It was, judging by the Danish film board censorship stamp, the exact same print that had screened at the premiere at Palads Theatre on 7 November, 1922. By a stroke of incredible luck it had been preserved in glycerine and stored in metal cans and was determined to be in excellent condition. It was brought back to Denmark for a proper revival and was given an advance screening on 21 November, 1940 for a select group of cultural VIPs. Improvised musical accompaniment was provided at this sneak preview, which Christensen was unable to attend.

69 Arne Lund, Benjamin Christensen In Hollywood, p.37 "...arguably both the wittiest and most moving of the three, resembling at moments a Danish fusion of Frank Capra ("You Can't Take It with You") and Eugene O'Neill."

On 3 March, 1941, the film began its revival run at the Dagmar Theatre, with all proceeds going to benefit the Danish actors' guild. A new print had been struck for the occasion, dubbed with a new musical score composed by Emil Reesen.

There had been some talk about re-editing the film and making it shorter, and Christensen himself had his reservations, particularly concerning the concluding "modern chapter." As ha been shown, this was the most frequently criticized part. It did seem oddly disjointed in style and tone as well as somewhat superfluous, and from a scientific perspective Christensen had failed to bring the same enlightened sense of balance and insight to his own time that he had bought to bear on the Middle Ages. He was also reportedly less than thrilled with his own hammed-up performance as the Devil and was aware that the speeded up movements of the actors in some places marked the movie as a product of the silent era in a manner that now seemed passé. No matter – "The film must stand or fall on its own," he stated in the press, and it was left untouched.

Christensen gave a talk before the Dagmar screening, received a bouquet of flowers and was heartily applauded. The city's press and public held their collective breath. Would "The Witch" hold up after all these years or prove an embarrassment the way that so many silent-era films did, films that now seemed unintentionally comic and ridiculous and which were hard for the modern viewer to relate to.

One might also wonder how a film about hysterical, brainwashed crowds and the brutal persecution of a scapegoated segment of the population went down at a time when Denmark was occupied by the German army and swastikas flapped from every other flagpole. These were tumultuous days and the echoes of deeper issues reverberated even in the normally isolated, escapist sanctum of the movie theatre. Even films that apparently had nothing to do with the War now assumed a political dimension. An example: "The Harvest Is in Danger" ("Kornet er ifare"), a public service agricultural short from 1944. This 9-minute film indirectly equated the destructive effects beetles were having on the harvest with the havoc Germans were wreaking on Denmark. The narrator uses military terminology and closes by exhorting viewers to join the fight against the destructive, parasitic beetle. "Denmark's harvest is at stake!" he barks – an ever so minor variation of the well known resistance slogan, "Your freedom is at stake!"

It would be hard to believe that the themes incarnate in "The Witch" did not resonate in a similar manner with at least some viewers. The witch hysteria was contingent on traveling tribunals of witch hunters' who transformed the countryside into a kind of fascistic police state, exactly as the Nazis had transformed Europe. In both situations bribery and torture was commonplace while suspects were administered loyalty tests and the use of informers, who often had ulterior motives, was widespread. Speculation of this sort is absent from contemporary discussions of the film in the press – no surprise since the Nazis kept a close watch on the Danish media.

In any case, the re-launch was eagerly anticipated. Everyone seemed to be aware of *The New York Times's* comment that "The Witch" was 25 years ahead of its time.

Was it? A couple of weeks previous a writer credited as Mr. Allevegne, who had already seen the film, attempted to answer some of these questions. The following excerpt is taken from *Social Demokraten*, 21 February, 1941:

THE FILM THAT WAS FAR AHEAD OF ITS TIME

"The Witch" was the first really big film that Benjamin Christensen directed. It cost a million Danish Kroner and preparations for the filming took several years. The shooting itself took place almost exactly twenty years ago.

Its revival is an event, if only because it is such an old film, and yet it's all the more interesting because upon its release the film was said to be 25 years ahead of its time. If that was true then it should be perfectly suited for showing today!

Was the Film Ahead of Its Time?

The other day I had the opportunity to see "The Witch" and must answer that question with both a yes and a no. Many of the pictures are, from a technical standpoint, so excellently made that they could hardly be improved upon today, but other parts, particularly the film's ending, seem a bit antiquated.

"The Witch" is not a film in the normal sense. Christensen himself called it a cultural-historic lecture transformed into (moving) images and he intended first and foremost to describe the gruesome persecution of witches and the causes behind it, such as the belief in demons and devils. We page through the old books on superstition and see images of witches that come to life... we see the torture instruments used on witches who cook love potions. This part is so masterfully and convincingly described, and with such effect, that a cold shiver runs down one's spine when these images are shown again.

Are We Better Than We Were in the Middle Ages?

The section of the film that seems a bit antiquated is the last part where Christensen has had the otherwise excellent idea of taking the lecture further into "the present day." He raises the question as to whether modern man is superior to his forebears of the Middle Ages who cultivated this belief in witchcraft. Don't we still consult fortune-tellers and soothsayers? Don't we read dream books and do the strangest things if a black cat crosses our path?

Then he leads us into a neurologist's waiting room where a

woman suffers from a case of possession... this is the last scene and is not really credible when one knows just a bit of Freud. But when (the renowned) professor Viggo Christiansen has given the film his stamp of approval we must also go along with it.

Will the Film Give Rise to Protests?

When it first came out the film gave occasion to forceful protests. A campaign was launched against it in the press and some demanded that the picture be taken off the screen immediately. Christensen defended himself by claiming the support of men of science and asserted that those directing the attacks were not keeping abreast of modern developments and currents of thinking. In the twenty years that have passed we've become less prudish, but I believe that the film will again spark discussion. There are scenes in it that are so strong that the average ticket-buyer will hardly be able to digest them, and the torture scenes in particular can have an unfortunate effect on morbid or obsessive individuals. But nothing is censored out of the film although it goes without saying that it will be forbidden for minors.

Ib Schønberg As a Gruesome and Sadistic Monk

There are also things in the film that today take a bit of the edge off the worst scenes. We see sequences from a torture chamber where the monks order the most appalling torments to be administered to a young woman. Then we recognize one of the monks. Isn't that him? Yes it is! That's our own "Ibberman" – Ib Schønberg, who sits there behind the judge's desk cruel and gruesome. Then we smile. The whole thing is probably not as bad as it appears or Ib Schønberg would never have participated.

That was Schønberg's first film and on top of it he played a kind of a villain...[70] We see other now-famous actors as they looked then. Poul Reumert is a slender youngster... there's also Albrecht Schmidt, Carlo Wieth, Clara Pontoppidan, Tora Teje (a Swede) and the dear, round Oscar Stribolt – and he was impossible to turn into a villain. He plays a monk with an appetite for life and a weakness for the charms of the fairer sex, and his appearance provokes a Jubilant reaction in the audience.

70 After his debut as a sadistic torturer in "The Witch" he quickly became typecast as a nice, fat, jolly chap and went on to become one of Denmark's most beloved actors – the "funny, harmless man with a good heart" as Morton Piil characterizes him in his 2001 book about Danish actors, *Danske Film-skuespillere.*

The Lead Part Is Played By an Old Woman Who Sold Violets

> In one respect Christensen was far ahead of his time. The Russians attempt to make films in which they use "regular people" who are perfect "types," rather than (professional) actors, and Christensen was doing that twenty years ago. The leading role is played by a little old mother figure, and her face is unforgettable. She wasn't an actress. Christensen found her on the street selling violets... That this miserable old woman is accused of being a witch arouses sympathy in the audience.

The Film Re-discovered By Pure Accident

> "The Witch" is scheduled to play at the Dagmar Bio next week when "Niels Pind and His Boys" is taken off and it will be exciting to see how the public reacts to the revival.
>
> But whatever one can say for or against the film, it is indisputably a document of high standing. What's more, the fact that we even get to see it again is the result of an accident. When the film was taken off screens it ended up in the archive of the Swedish studio that produced it and was forgotten. It was found there a few months ago. After having languished for twenty years in an environment that wasn't good for film one might have feared that it was completely ruined, but in fact it was well preserved. Now hopefully they will take better care of it. Perhaps there will be more enjoyment to be gained from it in another twenty years.

This new print sported an introduction by Christensen wherein he discusses the differences between silent and sound cinema, and elaborates upon the four types of "witches" that existed and are represented in the movie.

First there were the "professional" witches, women who practiced folk-magic and occasionally produced some kind of result based either upon the (usually herbal) concoctions they cooked up or upon the fact that people simply believed their remedies worked. Not all witchcraft could be put down to superstition – sometimes results were produced! Second came the disfigured old hags, reviled and unfortunate beggars and outcasts who aroused suspicion and were easy targets. Then there were the "hysterical" women who through some mental affliction were prone to exhibit suspicious symptoms or make fantastic and deluded claims and charges. Finally there were average middle-class women who were simply informed upon and had confessions tortured out of them.

Public reaction to the re-launch was overwhelmingly positive, no doubt in part because Christensen was now a "respected" and "important" director and because times had indeed changed. Minor criticisms were voiced about his constant use of the first-person form and the frequent appearance of inter-texts, which some felt disrupted the dramatic flow and hindered the actors from delivering fully-realized performances.[71] But the public was in no mood to quibble; over 24,800 people pushed through the turnstiles of the Dagmar Theatre during the first week, setting a new house record. This was no mouldy artefact of silent cinema. Christensen's intricate staging and lighting set-ups and his use of close-ups, shunned at the time as a technique that was too graphic and almost indecent, gave his film dramatic sophistication and visceral impact. After its run there it rolled out to the smaller towns in the provinces.

Mr. Allevegne's aforementioned prediction that the film could have unfortunate effects on "morbid or obsessive individuals" apparently came true in the town of Horsens that fall as a 19 September, 1941 article in the national daily *Ekstrabladet* testified:

VIEWING OF THE WITCH CAUSES CRAMPS

> The twenty-year-old Benjamin Christensen film, "The Witch," is currently being shown in Horsens where it is making a strong impression on the public. Last night the police found a 23-year-old man wandering the streets of town short of breath and with his arms stiffly extended out in front of him. At first it appeared he was intoxicated but officers quickly determined that was not the case. He was put into an ambulance and taken to Horsen's County hospital where he was given artificial respiration and held overnight before being released. According to information the police received, his condition was caused by the movie, "The Witch." During some of the film's more intense scenes he became hypnotized to such a degree that it caused him to develop cramps.

The revival of "The Witch" also gave rise to the publication of a book, *Witchcraft and Superstition Through the Times*. The author, William Sieverts, was so influenced by the movie that almost the whole of Christensen's filmed prologue was included in the book's introduction. Sieverts explored a range of related historical phenomena that Christensen had not touched upon, the ghastly crimes of Gilles de Rais among them. Yet his conclusions, as one reviewer noted, could tend to be a bit "far out" – like his contention that jazz music could be equated to witchcraft.[72]

Most interesting was his account of a witchcraft panic that plagued Køge, a small harbour town south of Copenhagen, where between 1608 and 1615 fifteen women were burned on bonfires. It all started when one Hans Bartskjaer saw "a terrible toad walking from a gate on two slender legs." Bartskjaer had probably been suffering a drunken delirium and had seen a sick dog contorting its body, but

71 *Dansk Familie Blad*, 28 March, 1941

72 *Social Demokraten*, 24 November, 1941

everyone in his house was terrified and became convinced that a witch must have let the monster loose. The first to attract suspicion was a woman who had once wished Bartskjaer bad luck after a business transaction between them had gone bad. The story of the Køge hysteria was later published in Latin and became a great popular success, and much later it formed the basis of a "vaudeviller" called "The Harridans of Køge" ("Koge Huskors").

The revival of "The Witch" gave Christensen occasion to weigh in on the sound-vs-silent cinema debate. Like Charlie Chaplin he remained a staunch advocate of the art of silent cinema long after "the talkies" had won out. He was asked if he could imagine "The Witch" remade as a sound film:[73] "That would naturally be impossible – how does the Devil talk, for example? Silent films had many drawbacks but also advantages. Sound film is objective; everything is explained through dialogue and they need not engage one's sense of fantasy. Sound film completely lacks the illusion and poetry of silent cinema; one cannot dream and fantasize further about the adventure and the characters contained in the film. Here we've lost a bit of ground and that is one of the most important tasks sound film has before it, to recapture the lost ground. I would like to make another silent movie if I could find the right manuscript for a film without dialogue, a film where the images alone engage one's sense of fantasy and set dreams in motion."

Journey Into Twilight

Christensen never found another "silent movie" script, but his next film, "The Lady with the Light-Coloured Gloves," was heavily inspired by silent cinema. Like "The Mysterious X," it was an attempt to make a spy thriller for the international market, but Danish film now played a much more marginal role in the global marketplace. The social problem pictures had provided scant opportunity for Christensen to indulge his passion for effects and atmosphere and now he made up for lost time, employing inventive camera angles, lighting effects, masks and other post-production processes now available to him. The first reel was packed with visual punch. But even here Christensen was showing his age as the expressionist trappings he now employed in a tribute to the evocativeness of silent cinema – such as the long shadow of a pistol-clutching assassin – were no longer powerful stuff. And the excitement pretty much ended after the first spool, the film bogging down into a hard to follow story about a murky series of double-crosses.

Set during the First World War, "The Lady with the Light-Coloured Gloves" tells the tale of Torben, a Danish engineer who checks into a mysterious hotel carrying a secret letter that later, in a neutral country, he is to pass on to the Czar's personal emissary. But the hotel proves to be a hive of criminals, shady swindlers and spies, and when his best friend, a young Russian courier, is found dead the plot thickens.

It was apparently very loosely based on experiences Christensen had when

73 Unidentified Danish daily, 25 February, 1941

travelling through Europe to sell "The Mysterious X." Those had been exciting, adventurous times. Momentous world events were unfolding around him as he moved from country to country with a print of the film in his trunk, meeting all kinds of colourful characters on the fly and matching wits with border crossing guards and the like. As John Ernst notes,[74] he himself was actually embroiled in a minor intrigue when he was unwittingly duped into acting as a courier for the Czar's secret police (though Ernst deems the incident to have been the stuff of farce rather than high drama). And a similar story, entitled "Film and Reality" ("Film og Virkelighed") is contained in his book, *Hollywood Destinies*. Here documents are secretly planted in his suitcase.

It was natural that Christensen would draw upon his own experiences, but the film fell flat according to most critics. Stereotypical characters were caught in absurd situations. The actors seemed to be play-acting spies, clumsy ones at that. It was as far behind its time as "The Mysterious X" had been ahead of its, and – with the Nazis occupying Denmark and the outcome of the War still very much in doubt – it was badly out of synch with present-day realities. At its premiere the audience laughed in all the wrong places.[75] It was hopelessly naive, its low-camp excesses reportedly the only thing to recommend it to ticket-buyers looking for a reason to chuckle in grim times. (Though at least one Danish film scholar claims the movie was not nearly as bad as all that.)[76]

It went down as one of the biggest fiascos in Danish film history and must have been a huge blow to both Christensen, who had spent a great amount of time, care and effort on it, and also to his studio. There were at least two more books he wanted to film and he proposed these projects to Nordisk but they turned him down. In 1943 he wrote to a friend that he now considered his relationship with the studio to be terminated.[77]

After "The Lady with the Light-Coloured Gloves," the Danish film industry was through with him and he eventually accepted this too. In 1945 he told a writer that he had no intention of making another film, adding, "people here think that the only kind of film I can make is one that has trolls and witches in it."[78] Better that they remember the trolls and witches than the bumbling spies.

Christensen continued to make his opinions heard in the press, and in 1945 published the previously referred to book of short stories, *Hollywood Destinies (Hollywood Skæbner)*. Spun from a mix of autobiography and fiction, these stories are not all movie related but frequently elaborate upon themes that he dealt with in his films and with experiences he had while travelling around on film business.

The previous year he had been granted a license to operate another cinema, the 500-seat Rio Bio in the lower-middle class suburb of Rødovre – nothing so fancy

74 John Ernst, *Benjamin Christensen*, p.40

75 *Jyllands Posten*, 4 April, 1959

76 Maren Pust

77 Morten Piil, *Danish Film From A to Z*, (Gyldendal publishers, Copenhagen, 1998, 2000) p.81

78 Unidentified Danish daily, 22 October. 1945; "America Is not Just Cars and Bank Account," by Jonal.

as the Park Theatre this time, but he was grateful enough. He was getting on in years and this supplied him with a living income and contact with the movie-going public which gave him much pleasure. Not "his" public, since he never exhibited his own films (out of principle), and not a sophisticated "big city" public, but just regular folks. He seemed to enjoy the job, particularly when the theatre was full of youngsters who affectionately called the gangly, gaunt old fellow with the round glasses "the movie man."

Otherwise he guarded his privacy jealously. He rarely ventured out in public, preferring to stay home with Kamma in their cozy Fredericksberg flat on Lindevangen, which was crammed with the books and oriental antiques he had collected over the years. Other great figures of Danish silent cinema also called this quiet neighbourhood of stately stone apartment buildings and leafy boulevards home; Carl Dreyer lived over on Dalgas Boulevard and Asta Nielsen around the corner on Peter Bangs Vej.

The years wore on.

Every once in a while film people would again start asking, "whatever happened to Benjamin Christensen?" And inevitably journalists would find their way into the cluttered sanctum of his home to be regaled with stories of the old days. On one such occasion a photographer got him to proudly pose beside a treasured collectable; a thousand-year-old engraved Chinese tombstone. He would laugh off the inevitable inquiries as to how a world famous movie director who had "conquered" Hollywood could find contentment running a neighbourhood cinema in humble Rødovre. He seemed a man at peace with himself and reconciled to the circumstances that fate had dealt him.

On 2 April, 1959, at the age of 79, he passed away after a lengthy illness. "The Master," whose visage had adorned countless movie posters and glared out from screens all over the world, had gone on to make an art form out of anonymity, and he was – as he requested – buried in an unmarked grave in Søndermark cemetery in Copenhagen after a small ceremony that was conducted virtually in secret.

The Witch Lives!

"The Witch," Benjamin Christensen's most enduring and significant achievement, would be subject to periodic revivals after his passing.

The Danish Film Museum, for example, staged an ambitious retrospective in 1967, screening all the films which (at the time) could be located, and this gave occasion for John Ernst's penetrating study which was, prior to this book, the only work that had been published (thus far in Danish only) on him.

The following year the film was condensed down to 76 minutes and "re-mixed" by the English filmmaker and programmer, Antony Balch. Balch was a connoisseur of edgy and transgressive cinema and brought many important and previously banned films to British screens, including "Freaks." He consorted with the likes of Brion Gysin and other high priests of Beat, such as William Burroughs who was living in London at the time. He was involved in several film projects with Burroughs and got him to do the narration for this new version, entitled "Witchcraft Through the Ages." He also added music composed and performed by percussionist Daniel Humair and violinist Jean-Luc Ponty and other musicians. In November 1968 this version played at London's Baker Street cinema (slapped with a British Board of Film Censors "X" certificate), sparking a revival of sorts for the film in the UK and earning it countless new fans, despite the fact that at least one critic found the narration to be "rather dully spoken and at times a little arch."[79] Said unidentified critic also seems to have misinterpreted the film in this version as he goes on to reflect that, the conclusion (of the film), that in the enlightened Twenties 'witches' were being kindly confined to lunatic asylums or given therapeutic showers to cure their 'hysteria,' appears only slightly less barbaric than burning them at the stake."

Christensen's message, that things have not really changed all that much and that modern man, in supposed possession of great amounts of wisdom and enlightenment, is still prey to superstition, was of course quite the opposite.

With that said, Christensen was of course basing his assumptions on works available to him at the time and he cites facts and figures then considered accurate. Some of this is today contested by scholars. As previously noted, the commonly quoted toll of eight million deaths is today considered way off, and the role that witch hunters played in spreading the terror has also been called into question, with some maintaining that "regular people" were far more responsible for provoking the persecutions. Doubt has also been cast upon the ordeal of trial-by-water, which in popular accounts would always seem to lead to the death of the accused woman. (If she floated she was a witch, if she sank and drowned she was innocent.) According to some historians the women who sank were often pulled up in time.

He also fails to directly address claims that persecuted "witches" were frequently first and foremost victims of economic and/or sexual exploitation. This view is widely accepted today, and in the realm of popular cinema is best represented in the British film from 1968, Michael Reeves's "Witchfinder General." While Christensen doesn't directly contend that witch hunters and priests exploited women sexually, he really doesn't need to. The scenes in his film of voyeuristic priests spying on accused women as they are brutally interrogated - and often bound, caged and/or unclothed – say enough about the sadistic sexual dynamics involved. At one point a woman naked from the waist up and seen from behind has instruments of torture applied to her bare flesh. There is also the woodcut, shown more them once, of a naked woman hog-tied on her back and enduring trial-by-water. Female bodies had to be searched for suspicious marks and insensitive spots, and first those bodies had to be unclothed.

"The Witch" had caught the spirit of the times and in 1968 the film was also revived in Paris, Stockholm and Copenhagen, where Peter Refn scheduled a run at his Camera Bio. A new print was struck, fittingly at the Johan Ankerstjerne film lab,

79 *The Observer*, 3 November, 1968

without the dubbed music this time as had been the case in 1941. That was now considered to have been a mistake.[80] This print would be as true to Christensen's version as possible, accompanied by the original music score, which was played at the opening show on 31 May by pianist Kay Kilian. Refn's revival of the film reaped it lots of praise but not all reviewers were positive: "... not a good film, succeeds today only as camp..."[81] "Seen from a modern perspective the film resembles an entertaining museum exhibit."[82]

In February 1970 the Elgin, New York's legendary repertory theater, double-billed the Balch version of "The Witch" with "Wild Horses" by Sergei Parajanov and drew the wrath of underground film spokesman, Jonas Mekas, who in his "Movie Journal" column in the 12 February edition of *The Village Voice* wrote:

> Do not miss the Elgin Theater double-bill opening this week of "Häxan" and "Wild Horses"... "Häxan" was made by Benjamin Christensen in 1922 in Denmark. The film uses old engravings and period re-enactments to present the history of witchcraft. I saw the film years ago at (Amos Vogel's) Cinema 16. I still can't forget the strength of some of the images, the imagination that went into them. I urge you to see the film despite one unfortunate fact: the version which you'll see is the bastardized "English version" prepared by a well meaning but obviously stupid young man, Antony Balch. It takes stupidity to do what he did with this great film. To a beautiful silent film he added a Jazz score and a squeaking narration by William Burroughs. The texts, which in the original film appear as titles, as part of the film's structure, now most of the time are read by Burroughs. The film has been destroyed. Nevertheless, there is enough left of the original power of the images – particularly if you can keep your ears plugged somehow. Why did Burroughs participate in this barbarous act? Suppose we begin to mess with his novels, I wonder how he'd feel about it...

Others apparently agree with Mekas. For example when the George Eastman House in Rochester, NY played this version in 2004, they turned down the sound and had live piano accompaniment instead.

In fact the Balch/Burroughs version, which was distributed in the US by Janus Films (who apparently distributed both versions), is not all that bad. The music, an atmospheric mix of jazz and avant-garde, is usually quite effective if at times a bit overwhelming. Burroughs's narration injects in spots a note of irony and dry humour after his fashion. That is something the original version lacks, though the appropriateness of that can certainly be argued.

80 *B.T.*, 31 May, 1968

81 *Jyllands Posten*, 4 June, 1968

82 *Information*, 1 June, 1968, Pim

Condensed to 75 minutes from its original 104-minute running time, the Balch/Burroughs version unfortunately gives short shift to some key scenes, including the witches' flight to Bloksbjerg and the nuns' hysteria in the church. Some torture scenes are shortened, it is less unrelenting, less "brutal," but Burroughs's spoken dialogue gives it a more unified (if still disjointed) narrative flow, or at least the feeling of such. It is less clinical, less pedagogic, and the chapterized structure is completely gone, although that never really helped to give Christensen's original version much continuity. His film was in essence an episodic jumble of dreams, hallucinations, dramatic skits and almost scientific presentations of devices or concepts that lacked a focused narrative thread or perspective. and the viewer cannot always be sure of what point-of-view applies. The Balch/Burroughs version is more political, more anti-authoritarian, more "beat," as one might expect. In one scene where Maria the weaver[83] is interrogated by two witch hunters, Burroughs laconically observes: "here we see an example of 'good cop/bad cop,' which is still being practiced in police stations all over the world."

After viewing this version, Mekas's criticism seems perhaps a bit too harsh. Can't a film be re-contextualized and re-interpreted? Must all art be fossilized in its original state? Is any alteration vandalism? The question is particularly relevant to this film since it has been re-interpreted so many times. It should also be noted that Christensen had to structure his (silent) version around title-plates. This was a necessity, not an artistic choice. And finally, hadn't at least one critic back on the occasion of the 1941 revival criticized the over-abundance of inter-titles for hampering the performances?

Through the years the film has screened in many different contexts: rock stars have appropriated scenes for their videos while avant-garde musicians and even performance artists have used the film as a backdrop for their own creative expressions. In 1995, for example, a touring "Loud Music Silent Film Festival" screened it as part of a performance by Judith Ren-Lay. As the program text reads:

> Judith Ren-Lay is one of the foremost performance artists on the scene today. Her background is in dance, but it is her voice and incredibly powerful performances that make her 'live painting' style so memorable. She will be joined by sculptor and multi-instrumentalist, Ken Butler, for these shows. The film she will be working with. 'Witchcraft Through the Ages,' is an early surrealist film from the Swedish [sic] filmmaker, Benjamin Christensen (1922). This controversial look into the superstitious Medieval mind was banned for years due to nudity and religious irreverence. The bizarre cast of characters seems to have marched right out of a Hieronymous Bosch painting.

83 The character that Maren Pedersen plays in the film has been variously referred to as 'Maria the Weaver,' 'Marie the Seamstress' and as simply 'The Witch,' depending on which print of the film is viewed.

In 1996 in its capacity as European Cultural Capital of the year, Copenhagen was flush with money to spend on the arts and among the scheduled attractions was a screening of "The Witch" set to a musical score composed specifically for the event by the renowned French avant-garde art rock quintet, Art Zoyd, who also played their pre-existing scores to "Nosferatu" (1922) and "Faust" (1926).

In 1999 a conglomerate of Danish and American cultural institutions organized a series of Danish art exhibitions and performances in America under the banner of "The Danish Wave." The cinema segment was entitled "Heart of Light: The Danish Wave in Cinema," and focused largely on the Dogme95 movement but also included a 12-film retrospective dedicated to Benjamin Christensen. Both the "Burroughs version" and the original (fully restored and tinted) versions were screened.

Many other screenings of the film have occurred in various circumstances and contexts all over the world and down through the years, far too many to mention here. It is a film destined to be continually revived and rediscovered. Rather than just being 25 years ahead of its time it seems to be eternal.

In Benjamin Christensen's hometown of Viborg there exists no memorial to mark his memory, and where his father's drapery shop once stood on the main town square today stands a Blockbuster Video outlet.

But Christensen did finally get a memorial of sorts; when the folks behind "The Blair Witch Project" were working on their film and watching every "witch movie" they could get their hands on, they stumbled across "The Witch" and were so amazed that they named their production company after it: Häxan Films.

The Demonic Cultural Legacy of Antonin Artaud

Andrea Kundry

What exactly do I mean?

A partial explanation, and a bright beginning, is found in Artaud's own words: "I, Antonin Artaud, I am my son, my father, my mother and myself".

Let's experience an incorporeal being, a spirit who is here among us – today – making himself known.

Artaud is an unseen but felt presence – influencing the ideas, values and folklore of artistic expression through the gift of his passionate writings, which have inspired many artists, filmmakers, dancers, and musicians to journey into the depths, and leave behind their old, damaged skin, and to re-emerge and take flight.

Antonin Artaud was born in 1896, and died in 1948. He was a visionary French actor, playwright, poet and, most of all, theorist. His idea of a "Theatre of Cruelty," set down in his work *The Theatre and Its Double*, has almost single-handedly shaped modern notions of "performance".

Sadly, his ideas were ignored and ridiculed in his own time, and because of this he developed something of a persecution complex.

As a child, Artaud suffered from meningitis, and throughout his life he was afflicted with mental disorders. During the 1920's he wrote poems in the manner of the surrealists, acted in plays and starred in films directed by Abel Gance ("Napoleon") and Carl Dreyer ("The Passion of Joan of Arc").

He came into his own and began to write his own essays and manifestos, collected in *The Theatre and Its Double.*

Artaud advocated a metaphysical theatre, linking spectator and spectacle. He was less influenced by literature than by myth, ritual, oriental art, the gestures of Balinese dance and the world of dreams.

Artaud felt that the theatre should give rise to numinous or religious feelings within the audience. At certain points, he likened theatre to a plague that attacks the audience; that breaks down resistance and cleanses it spiritually.

The madness and genius in the life of this French theatre mystic are an inspiration for contemporary artists – especially those who are also occultists.

His radical theories on staging and language influenced, and still influence, the avant-garde. Artaud's assault on his audiences in the 20's and 30's using shock techniques he invented for the theatre, film and poetry, would still shock audiences today.

A heavy user of the subconscious, Artaud seemed to have unlimited access into the deeper, less rational powers. He brought to light dangerous archetypes, most of which he played out in his own life. Artaud experimented with drugs, psychotherapy, surrealism, eastern mysticism, Hatha Yoga, gnosticism, medieval religion, ancient séances and primitive ritual.

He abandoned the rational world based on materialism, logic and scientific observation in favour of poetics and metaphor. It is precisely this non-rational stance that gave him the visionary powers to tap into *chaos* and the unified, undifferentiated source, and hold sway over three generations of the avant garde.

Since the 1950's it seems that any artist who comes perilously close to the cutting edge owes a debt to Artaud. People like composer John Cage, choreographer Merce Cunningham, and theatre directors Jerzy Growtowski and Peter Brook. Not to forget the freedom loving, paradise now-demanding living theatres – all have acknowledged inspiration from Artaud, as do many performance artists, dance/theatre auteurs, Butoh performers, poets and writers working today.

Why has Antonin Artaud assumed such a saint-like position amongst the avant garde? He left no coherent methodology, nor shining examples of his theatrical achievements. Artaud's gift to three generations of artists – feeling out of place, and out of time, alone and misunderstood – is contained in stirring rallying cries such as "An End to Masterpieces", found in *The Theatre and Its Double* – a book that sadly few people read.

Artaud said that, "One reason for the asphyxiating atmosphere in which we live without possible escape or recourse – and for which we are all responsible, even the most revolutionary among us – is this respect for what has already been written, formulated or painted, what has been given form, as if all expression were not finally exhausted and had not reached the point where things must fall apart if they are to begin again".

Where does an alienated fledgling artist who is fuelled by hatred of the status quo and seeking a reaction from the public, go with Artaud's ideas?

Can his or her dark, perilous journey to become an artist sometimes come to a beautifully sad, dead end?

How does an artist resolve the inexhaustible paradox of Artaud – his wish to produce Art that is at the same time anti-Art?

Artaud revolted against the moral cheapness of most art. He said, "No image satisfies me, unless it is at the same time Knowledge." As all of us well know, knowledge grows in the darkness, but eventually you must come into the light and share what you have learned. In my view, many of the more nihilistically inclined shock tactics for the sake of nothing that industrial culture proponents who admire Artaud display, have nothing to give beyond total self absorption in their own suffering.

In contrast, Lindsey Kemp was a British actor/dancer who pushed the boundaries not only of gender but of what was possible in the theatre; inspired by Artaud to achieve an improvised total theatre which perplexed and repelled dance critics. Kemp's mannered phantasmagoric style has little use for words. His approach is to grab the senses at their most vulnerable, using stark colours and dissonant lighting contrasts. Fragments of poetry or dialogue occur, but the impact derives from gestures and vibrant tableaux. The effect is richly imaginative, layered, evocative, and ultimately enchanting.

Artaud left us a vision of ritual theatre, "The Theatre of Cruelty," written in metaphorical prose.

Before we take a look at what TOC is (in Artaud's own words) let's look at a cultural figure that this iconoclastic animist saw in himself (quite literally): Comte de Lautréamont, the 19th century author of the beautifully, bleak prose poem *The Songs of Maldoror* – a tragic literary figure Artaud admired.

Lautréamont was a man catastrophically sickened by everyday life. He was seen to be shut up by society, because they were afraid his poetry would leap out of the books and turn reality upside down.

Artaud perceived that Lautréamont fought against the public subsuming him, and had allowed Artaud to join with him. Here is the description of the Daemon inside Isidore Ducasse (Lautréamont is Ducasse's pen name): "You are a Genius, but I am the genius that inspires your consciousness, and it is I who can write your poems inside you, before you even think of them, and better than you ever could."

Artaud states in *The Theatre and Its Double:* "It is the veneration for what has already been done, however beautiful and valuable it may be, that petrifies us, immobilises us and keeps us from making contact with the underlying force, whatever you call it, mental energy, the life force, the determination of exchanges, the lunar menses or whatever you like."

The raw material with which he works, the themes he brings to quivering life are not of himself, but of the Gods. What he sets in motion is manifested. It is a kind of primary physics from which the spirit has never been separated.

Another quote... "Psychology with its relentless effort to reduce the unknown to the known, that is, to the daily and the ordinary, is the cause of the decline and this terrible loss of energy."

Artaud's TOC abandons psychology and psychological theatre (which explores the characters' motivations). Instead, TOC recounts the extra-ordinary; it is an exceptional force of redirection. Artaud conceived a theatre which produces trances, and which addresses itself to the organism by precise means, and with the same means as the healing music of certain tribes which we admire but which we struggle to create amongst ourselves.

Artaud, when writing on TOC, states, "There is risk involved – but under the circumstances I feel the risk is worth taking. I do not believe that we can ever re-vitalise our present way of life, and I do not believe it is even worthwhile holding onto it; but I do propose something to get us out of our stagnation, instead of groaning about it, and about the boredom, inertia, and the stupidity of everything."

Ultimately, it is his passion, intelligence and terrible sensitivity that are heard. Artaud is the embodiment of the romantic myth of the misunderstood, suffering artist. Like Poe, Baudelaire, Nerval, Rimbaud and Van Gogh, Artaud was martyred by his passion, and marginalised by society. Yet he remains, always, a great source of inspiration.

Since his death in 1948, scholars and artists have debated the importance of his voluminous writings in an attempt to determine the extent of his influence. There are those who believe he was insane: a madman whose theories are of little value, and whose plays are impossible to stage. His vision of 50,000 scorpions crawling from a woman's vagina, a celestial storm where planets collide, lovers separated by hurricanes, wild horses racing through the air like distant meteors, have forced practitioners into a position of compromise which they find unworthy of his ideas. Even directors like Peter Brook and Jerzy Growtowski, who acknowledge a debt to Artaud, feel betrayed by the impracticality of his visions.

Artaud is an absolutist, but the challenge with his work is to determine what, exactly, he is absolutist about. He is technically neither religious nor nationalist – in the sense that he does not advocate adherence to any single organised religion or state.

Apocalyptic sensibility drives the writing of Artaud, infuriated and propelled by a sense of the worlds utter and unimaginable wrongness. For Artaud, the best existence would be one without body, shape or consciousness.

In the 60's, Artaud's works were embedded in a leftist context – one characterized by a striving through the advancement of human awareness and creativity, to create a new social and political world in which a greater number of people could enjoy a greater amount of individual liberty and happiness.

Artaud serves the ends of various critical and artistic schools so exceptionally well that we may easily forget he ever existed outside of their interpretations. Two tendencies recur: to see in his work the foundation of a revolutionary protest that is primarily leftist, and to view his writings historically as existing almost outside of time.

Artaud's work needs to be examined in the context of the times he lived in – imprisoned in an asylum during WW2. "New Revelation of Being" was presented as a revolution: the work was signed "Le Révèle" (the one who has received visions) – it was republished in 1943 and dedicated to Hitler. The prophecies of "The New Revelations of Being" are apocalyptic, and focus not only on natural upheavals but also on the necessary violence of Man. We find true nature by destroying ourselves. References to hypnosis and magnetism recur throughout his writings. Mesmer was expelled from Vienna for propagating the notion that there resided within himself an occult force by which he could influence others.

TOC proposed stage effects which reflected a belief in a law of "universal magnetism" that the director can manipulate. Artaud was a singular, visionary theorist. A self-proclaimed prophet who dreams of wielding total power over a group of de-individuated spectators. Examined in the light of charismatic leaders and the regressive sensibility which took hold in the 30s/40s in Europe, this can only be a warning lesson about occult power dynamics used to control crowds.

There are those who believe Artaud was a prophet, a visionary, and one of the great poets of the 20th century. Artaud emerged as the hero of the wave of meta-critics who have come to prominence in France. The writings of Julia Kristeva,

Michel Foucault and Jaques Derrida have raised him to an elevated position in the postmodern pantheon.

Speaking of Post-Modernism, Artaud was the first to use texts by other authors as mere jumping off points, to draw attention to his own ideas. The 18th century English Gothic novel *The Monk* was a great favourite of his (monks, murder, sex and spirits in a crumbling castle... what's not to like?). The novel hadn't been translated into French, so Artaud decided to publish his own "translation" – which was a translation in name only. Artaud could only read basic English, so his translation wasn't verbatim. He transformed the story completely. Sadly, his concept wasn't well received. However, using texts in this way became a staple of the avant garde theatre from the 1980's onwards.

Some keys ideas of Antonin Artaud are that ritual theatre can occur anywhere. The idea that the visual components can have as much resonance as the verbal has helped inspire the still current interest in multimedia or multi-disciplinary theatrical ritual-happenings, performance art, body art, environmental theatre, street theatre, guerilla theatre, earthworks, movement therapy, psychodrama, Butoh – all are indebted to the work of Artaud.

Artaud gave an apocalyptic performance and lecture at the Sorbonne in the early 1930's. Sitting in on his lecture on "The Theatre and the Plague," Anaïs Nin describes his impact:

> He is trying to remind us that it was during the plague that so many works of art came to be, because whipped by the fear of death, man seeks immortality, to escape, to surpass himself. But then, imperceptibly almost, he let go of the thread. We were following and he began to act out dying of the plague. He made one feel the parched and burning throat, the pains, the fever, the fire in the guts. He was in agony, he was screaming. He was delirious. He was enacting his own death, his own crucification. At first people gasped. Then they began to laugh. They began to leave. But Artaud went on, until the last gasp and stayed on the floor.

Later he spoke to Nin. He was hurt by the audience reaction, stating: "They always want to hear an objective conference on 'The Theatre and the Plague' and I want to give them the experience itself, the plague itself, so they will be terrified and awaken. They do not realise they are dead, their death is total, like deafness/blindness. This is the agony I portrayed."

Alchemy is an early form of chemistry exploring the power of enchantment and transformation. Alchemists sought the conversion of base metals into gold and a universal cure for disease, just as Butoh dancers attend to metamorphosis and healing through the body. In Butoh, as in alchemy, the darkness of the material needs to be undergone before transformation and integration can occur.

Artaud said, "In our present state of degeneration, it is through the skin that metaphysics must be made to re-enter our minds." Is Butoh performance a manifestation of Artaud's TOC?

Cruelty can be identified with a severe moral purity which is not afraid to pay the price that must be paid. This relates to Butoh – because in essence it is an embracing of cruelty and pain, which are components of darkness.

Artaud sought to remove aesthetic distance, and bring the audience into direct contact with the dangers of life. By turning the theatre into a place where the spectator is exposed rather than protected, Artaud was committing an act of cruelty upon them. This relates to Butoh because Hijakata (Butoh's founder) sought to embrace danger, darkness and ugliness in his art form. Butoh is the dance of darkness; it doesn't concern itself with the viewer, especially not by pleasing with the conventional aesthetic senses of the viewer.

Hijikata cited Artaud, along with Genet, as being his main influences. Artaud saw that his dream of a theatre without words has more precedent in Asia than in Western theatre (which has a narrative tradition). Therefore I feel that Butoh in its pure form has realised the Theatre of Cruelty.

Returning to Artaud's life: The 1930's Parisian indifference to him and his ideas pushed Artaud to the brink of the abyss. Feeling alienated and depressed, he had come to the end of the road. With an advance from his publisher he left for Mexico in 1936 on a mission to the territory of the Tarahumara Indian, to revive the vestiges of the ancient solar culture.

High on a mountain top, Artaud was initiated into the scared peyote rite. Experiencing vivid hallucinations, like a shaman he journeyed to a strange metaphysical world, where a kind of Dionysian theatre erupted. Priest sorcerers appeared in brilliant purple robes, their heads covered by mirrored hats that gleamed like patches of sky. Magic numbers and geometrical designs were inscribed in the sky and earth. Vibrant waves of sound and light shook him. Bodies twirled through space. The earth convulsed in rhythm. Ancient secrets were revealed. Cosmic forces merged with Aztec symbolism. Material chaos was reduced to its harmonic origins. No longer cut off from nature, Artaud could feel its spectacular totality. Unimaginably beautiful and unfathomably mysterious. In its depths, he reached a cool place of calm where the torturous battles in his mind were silenced. Artaud's fused being was again to be exploded upon re-entering the "civilised" world.

In France, his insanity grew to mythic proportions. Artaud waged war with his demons. In fits of anger, he spat on imaginary people and insulted passing women. Outside the literary cafés, he threatened passersby with his magic cane that he tipped so it struck sparks against the pavement as he walked.

In August of 1937, Artaud left for Ireland to search for traces of ancient tree worshippers, whom he thought might have fashioned the cane. He also hoped to return the snakes to Ireland. In Dublin, he caused a scene outside a Jesuit monastery when the priests wouldn't let him in. Deported back to France, he was put in a state mental hospital. Five years later, at the insistence of his friend Robert Denos, he was moved to a private psychiatric hospital where he remained for the next three years.

Believing his condition was getting worse, his doctor used over 50 treatments of electro-convulsive therapy.

Before his memory was erased and his passion silenced, his friends came to his rescue and organised a benefit to raise funds for his release. For the remaining two years of life he had financial security.

On the last day of his life, he wrote a contract in green ink, leaving the right to publish his books with a young woman: Paule Thevenin. She became his medium and intermediary between the work and his editors.

In order to safeguard his manuscripts, he borrowed an old chest to keep his letters and papers safe. When Paule opened the chest after his death, she discovered a large dead rat. Choked by the papers, it had only eaten a few words. His last enemy was defeated.

The Birth of Ideas

Joan Pope

Art is born from the marriage of body and intellect. The artist understands this conjunction because the union of opposites is the key to all creation. My own approach to art is alchemical, a practice in the Jungian notion of uniting with one's own inner opposite. I use imagery concerned with life and death, with intimacy, love and sex. I consider my work to be "pro-life" not in the common usage of the term per se, but rather as defined as assenting to life. I do not deny death – it is an essential part of life and what it means to be human – but I want to be clear: I am not a nihilist. Being alive is a great gift and we must use our time wisely –pursue what you really love. Cliché, yes, but it's a truth so many ignore. Artists insert themselves into their work; they manifest their own emotional, mental, physical and spiritual modes into being. The artist naturally opens themself, and by doing so, penetrates the viewer with their creative force. This experience is alchemical and a metaphysical form of sexual creation.

In this paper, I give an overview of my creative outlets interspersed with bits of my personal philosophy, my personal life, and some brief observations of the modern world. I touch upon the problems I have with defining my philosophy and committing my ideas to the written word. I express my belief that humans are capable of greatness, but we are equally capable of horror. I suggest embracing the duality and attempting to temper the polarity rather than choosing sides.

I often cite the gnostic text *Thunder Perfect Mind* as a major influence of my work. In the text, a distinctly feminine voice declares that she is the embodiment of a series of opposites:

> For I am the first and the last.
> I am the honoured one and the scorned one.
> I am the whore and the holy one.
> I am the wife and the virgin.
> I am the mother and the daughter.
> I am the members of my mother.
> I am the barren one
> and many are her sons.
> I am she whose wedding is great,
> and I have not taken a husband.
> I am the midwife and she who does not bear.

Upon discovery of this text, I was determined to become that sort of woman. A woman who is experienced in all aspects of the feminine. Experiences must be expressed and shared if they are to inspire others. My experiences and beliefs are translated into film, collage, music, and poetry so that they may be received. It is often said that artist should make art 'for themselves.' While there is no denying that, if it is never shared, it may as well have remained in the mental plane, as a thought. Connecting to other people is what gives art its power. We've all experienced art like this: perhaps you've been moved to tears upon viewing a piece, or it stirred up a slew of questions. That is why we share art. That is why we must share it. The artist is in a position to master bridging all planes of existence. A work of art can connect the physical, emotional, intellectual and spiritual planes. An artwork should be shared so that it may ignite thoughts and feelings that are difficult to otherwise express.

To ponder the meaning of life, one should probably start at the beginning. I use sexuality in my art because I want to strike the viewer at the most base level. Our very first semblance of existence originates in an orgasm. It is the very first act that makes our lives possible. Expression of sexuality is a (mostly) private affair, so it is here that I find a place where I resonate. I want to reach people in the context of something that is closest to their inner world.

With my own flesh on display in my erotic works, my body is an instrument playing to the archetypes I choose to portray. I've played the Greek goddesses of antiquity and the embodiments of Surrealist art and literary works of the 1930s, erotically. My intention is to create something vulnerable and utterly feminine to counter a world that has grown to be skeptical towards intimacy, a world that seems to be driving a wedge between the sexes. Using the tools that contributed to these pessimistic attitudes, I offer an alternative.

Internet technology and social media have done wonders to connect us. Never before have humans possessed such a powerful tool of communication. We have the ability to disseminate information instantaneously across the globe. It democratises our voices and transforms the way we receive news and engage in conversations. Content creators such as myself benefit immensely from social media because they can build an audience in a way that was not possible in the past. These developments are certainly profound and monumental.

We've lost something along the way though. Social media is addictive, sucking us out of our physical environment and the natural world into a second-hand world of screens. The simple joy of being in the company of other human beings doesn't seem to provide the same gratification it used to. Our dependence on our mobile phones is a form of bondage, a digital leash that keeps us tethered to the all powerful internet, in constant pursuit of validation in the form of likes and retweets. It would seem nowadays, that the internet is a major factor in growing ideological divides across the world. There is so much talk about revolution, but creating more divisions is not revolutionary. It is business as usual for the human race. I so badly want to be optimistic about humanity, but we constantly carry out so much brutality. I don't think that will ever be eradicated, but it can be minimised or, transformed. I cannot speculate on exactly what that transformation entails, but I believe a better world is possible. Sometimes I wonder if the internet is something like a modern day Tower of Babel, and perhaps things would be better if we were not digitally hyperconnected.

I try my best to use these new digital tools for good. I use them to disseminate a message I believe to be important. I stress the importance of intimacy and the sacred in my art. When I explain that I make softcore erotica as a way to connect the viewer to the sacred, it usually gets a strange reaction. It's not quite porn, although at a glance it may be lumped into it. What I do is much less extreme than what you will find on a typical porn site. They are still intended to arouse, however, I do not intend to only stimulate the genitals; I hope to arouse the intellect. The erotic films are one aspect of my art, and I display them alongside my other works. That is the key. I appear in my films as myself, as the collage artist, musician and poet. I am not a nameless piece of flesh. I have a name and a distinct personality and philosophy. I am a human being. The vast majority of the people who watch my films are people who know me through my other art. This blend of skin and intellect is my interpretation of something akin to a 1970s issue of *Penthouse*, only, this time around, the woman you see is also the woman in control of the entire narrative. My creative output is a mix of sex, art, music, beauty, meditations on the meaning of life and death. When people say they enjoyed a certain kind of magazine for the articles, they probably weren't lying. Why not want it all? Men are complex creatures who want to be stimulated intellectually just as much as sexually. I specify men here because my audience is almost entirely male, even when just isolating the music or the collages.

By putting myself out there in an erotic way, I am opening myself up to criticism and judgements, but most of the time men acknowledge and appreciate the artistry of the erotica. They are surprisingly respectful. It's not just about getting off. It's about leaving something to the imagination, which speaks to the very heart of what it means to be human. It's about men honouring women and women honouring men. It's about celebrating life: a celebration of eroticism, imagination, and intellect.

As one can imagine, although I am often treated with respect, I do receive many requests to meet in person, or to simply have a long engagement online. I love solitude. Being around other people for too long or too often becomes unbearable. For me, it's physically revolting to be around people for extended periods of time. Human beings have a deep need to connect to others, even the most introverted of us. The internet is the most useful tool for satisfying this need. I tend not to say much online. I try to respond to inquiries people may have, but I prefer to let my art and music speak for me. I certainly don't meet in person because there is simply no benefit or enjoyment to me. If fans want to get to know me, they should examine my art. It's as though it's not enough, they want more, they want my personal life. Trust me, its mundane and not worth a conversation. Do you really want to hear about my endless trips to the dentist? Do you want to know what I cooked for dinner last night? Do you want to know about family drama? Let the art do the talking. It is much better.

My collage art conveys my message though the universal language of symbols, my music uses the language of vibrations, and my erotic films use my body. I prefer to keep my words to a minimum because it's too easy for them to be misconstrued. My message is derived from a blend of intuition and learned knowledge and life experience; it's nuanced, it transcends language. It is to the greater benefit of the seeker that I remain vague. I dabble in multitude of artforms and use social media to create my own web of information for the seeker to get lost in. I use the metaphor of a cult because there are gradations here; of gnosis and of inquiry. Most of my content is publicly available to all, but I'm not interested in giving out easy answers; few will immerse themselves fully in the paradigm I've created because it requires effort to find all the pieces I've put forth. My art will fail to have a mass appeal because it stands in opposition to instant gratification culture. My artistic web is esoteric yet public, intimate yet exhibitionist. My art is both physical and digital; sexual and spiritual. That is how one 'make[s] the inner like the outer and the outer like the inner, and the upper like the lower, and [...] male and female into a single one' (*The Gospel of Thomas*).

What I have created is a gnostic religion, and the teachings are meant to be experienced and sought after. Blind followers in search of dogmatic shortcuts will be disappointed. I reveal myself through my art so that the viewer may uncover gnosis within themselves. I do not offer truth claims. I provide the questions, not the answers. The leap of faith I ask of you is to believe that the knowledge you seek is within you.

That is why I call myself a 'Philosopher Queen.'

The Rise of The Philosopher Queen: Education, Hopes, Dreams

Since childhood, I dreamt of one day becoming a teacher. So many of my teachers throughout my school career were really wonderful and inspiring, I wanted to be that for someone else. Teachers are extremely valuable members of our society; their influence on the minds of young people certainly lasts a lifetime, whether the student realizes it or not.

When I first entered the university, I was studying history and anticipated that upon graduating to teach history at the high school level. History was always my favorite subject because it's a broad inquiry into the past. History incorporates religion, culture, war, art, technological developments, etc. I loved the vastness of the subject, and I loved fantasizing what life in other times and places may have been like. I've always had a bit of an imagined nostalgia for times and places that I experienced only in books and art. To cut to the chase, the history program at my university was geared towards history education for American high schools, therefore the program offerings were heavily focused on American history. We seem to forget just how revolutionary America was, how its Constitution attempted to set it apart from any nation that preceded it. There were and still are many flaws, but there was nothing quite like it before. To really appreciate where we are at today, I realized as I was embarking on my studies, that I needed to learn more about the history of the world, not just my very young country of origin.

Upon choosing my courses for my second year of studies, I selected a course in the Religious Studies department because the history courses I wanted to take had filled. The course was called Early and Medieval Christian Thought. At the end of the first lecture I walked over to the Registrar's office and changed my major to Philosophy and Religious Studies. Even from that one lecture, I knew that the Religious Studies program would offer what I really wanted – religion adhesses history, culture, laws, customs, art, architecture, music, wars, and so on. Religion is an important force in this world whether or not you are a believer. During my teenage years, I was an ex-Catholic and vehemently atheist and anti-religion. I certainly did not expect to go on this path, but that's the beauty of youthful ignorance. Right before I chose to study religion, I had an experience that made me doubt my doubt. Studying religion was just as much a way to make sense of my own religious experience as it was to learn about the world and its inhabitants. It expanded my worldview and helped me to understand the importance of seeking multiple perspectives, and it also enriched my inner world. My decision to pursue this course of study was the best I ever made.

I chose to study Philosophy as well because I felt that it would round out my studies and help sharpen my ability to think critically about religion, reality, knowledge. Studying philosophy is a good foundation for anyone committed to being a lifelong learner. Partially I chose to study philosophy because so few women do. I was the only woman in the philosophy (and religion) program at my university. There are plenty of women who excel in this field, but most simply prefer other fields. Should more women pursue this path? Only if they want to. I wanted to study a discipline that has traditionally been more appealing to men because I wanted to refine my own masculine aspects. There is masculine and feminine in all things. Life and culture is a manifestation of their interactions playing out. There is fluidity to this polarity – it's not always clear cut. However, distinguishing masculine and feminine is the key to then combining them. This pertains to 'sex' on planes not only isolated to the physical plane, but to the emotional and intellectual. I am female, but it is male and female that made me. We all contain a blend of these aspects. I speculate that the soul is ultimately androgynous.

As I previously stated, I must stress that the combination of philosophy and religion most importantly taught me to constantly question and to always strive to understand things from different points of view. To make bulletproof arguments, one must know precisely what the counter-arguments will be. To know what the counter-arguments will be, it forces the philosopher to learn everything they can about the topic and see it from a side that is not their own. That is an incredibly important tool, especially in the present days of online arguments where everyone seems to be an expert on only their side of the story. How many of these so-called 'experts' are truly experts? 'Facts' seem to be regurgitated mantras from a source unknown. I bring this up because I have been criticised for simply following people on Twitter. A follow on social media is not an endorsement. I follow all sorts of people from all over the world with vastly different political views, different religious beliefs, various sexual orientations, different social classes, etc. I do this because even if someone has uncomfortable views that I do not remotely agree with, I want to understand fully how they came upon their views. I don't want to simply know their view on a specific issue, I want to study even their minor, insignificant thoughts. I want to be able to reconstruct, to the best of my ability, a sense of many different worldviews. In the case of extremists, I simply ignore them until they demonstrate that they are willing to temper their views. It is possible for people to change their perspectives, but it cannot happen by force. When using force, you often end up with the opposite of what you hoped for. Its not about winning arguments and changing a person's position in one swoop. It's about getting the person to question their own beliefs so that on their own time they examine them. You just have to show them that there is more than just their way of thinking. To be in a position to lead the thoughts of others, you must deeply understand all kinds of people. At the rate things seem to be going, resolve does not seem within reach.

This is not the place for me to gripe about higher education, but I will say this – a university is the safest place in the world to exchange ideas, and that exchange must remain free and uncensored. Ideas, even if controversial or uncomfortable, must be allowed to be expressed and dissected. Let logic be your guide. Follow the idea through completely, attacking even your own firm beliefs from every angle. To assume you know all, that you know better than anyone else, is to admit that you are a fool. In addition, the same thing that happens to religious movements after they become institutionalised has happened to higher education. Many universities care more about their finances and high salaries for their deans than about the actual education they are supposed to provide. It's obvious – tuitions keep increasing, but the actual value of the education they provide is decreasing. The university is meant to be a training ground to create lifelong learners, free thinkers who have the intellectual tools to be discerning and critical of all information. When you ask prospective college students why they want to attend college, so many believe they are going for some sort of career training for a job that probably doesn't even exist.

As I said earlier, I tend to take a quiet stance online. With the very high rate of college graduates of my generation, one would think the public discourse would be at a higher caliber. It seems as savage as ever. Rather than engaging, I ended up teaching in a way that is much different that I imagined… I created my own religion which is a collage of many religions that came before it, and I use my art to transmit these teachings. There is no written canon of dogma. The teachings are in the symbols of the collages. The philosophy is experienced. It is not something a select few read in a book. It is still developing. I relay my philosophy through my art and body. The religious aspect of this philosophy is that it must be experienced to be sacralised. There are exoteric and esoteric aspects to this paradigm.

I can appreciate orders that have created specific rites and rituals to be passed down throughout the ages. The initiation into the further degrees of my own practice must remain secret and must die with all involved. The exoteric aspects are for all who are interested. Even knowing how to become an initiate of the inner teachings must remain a mystery to the uninitiated. A future person who may stumble upon the fragments I leave behind will have to construct their own religion. SexDeathRebirth will die and be forgotten.

Post-University

After completing my degree I worked in public libraries, non-profits, and as a research assistant to a philosophy professor. While I was doing this, I was continuing my studies independently and forming what would become my reason for being. I've mentioned it earlier: the religion SexDeathRebirth. The first seven years was primarily a time of research, continuing my studies of religion but also increasing my knowledge of art. During this time I amassed a huge digital collection of images from all different styles and periods that contained imagery related to sex and death, eroticism and morality, the divine feminine and divine masculine, and transformation and religious experiences. It was a study in symbolism that later became useful as I started creating my own works.

Collage

My primary art form is collage. I use the traditional collage method, I cut images from books and magazines then photograph them and put them online to share the message. I consider the digital photo to be the final form of the art piece because it has been transformed from tangible to intangible, and given a filtered look that captures the present style of all the iPhone photographers of the world. Occasionally I actually glue the components of the collage down, but I prefer not to. I like to be able to recycle the symbols and remix them in other pieces. The major themes of my collage works express the sacredness of sexuality, an elevation of humanity and aspiration for us to reach our greatest potential, a fierce stance against consumerism and censorship, and a reminder that our lives are temporary – so while you are here, remember to love life, nature, and beauty.

I have two visual modes of collage. The first is under the moniker 'SexDeathRebirth,' the other as 'Temple ov Saturn.' SexDeathRebirth is colorful and chaotic. The colleges tend to go over the edges. They are busy and explosive. Temple ov Saturn is more subdued. Most of those collages are black and white, perhaps some minimal use of color. The collage is usually centred on a black background. I consider the SexDeathRebirth collages to be feminine and chaotic, Temple ov Saturn as masculine and ordered. Based on my observations of the reactions I've received, the viewers prefer the more masculine Temple ov Saturn imagery.

Both modes explore the same themes, expressed by the same person, in different ways. The masculine is easier to swallow. Chaos is fun, but order is necessary and easier to grasp. The feminine has a mysterious quality that I think makes people uncomfortable. (Which is a good thing!) Much to my surprise, women seem to prefer the more masculine mode as well. It's a perplexing observation, and I am eager to eventually understand why that is. I have some budding speculations, but its too early on in that project to elaborate on at this time.

Poetry

I use a modified cut-up technique to construct my poems. Usually I cut text from the scraps left over from when I make my collages. I cut words and phrases that attract me, then I select a few pieces of the cut-up texts from the pile and with those pieces I edit it into something cohesive. At that point I will start to consciously search for words to complete the thought that was originally born from the chaotic pile of words and phrases. My poems contain both the elements of randomness and intention. The union of chaos and order.

Spoken Word and Music

About a year into initially forming SexDeathRebirth, I started performing my poetry at open mics as a way to perpetuate my message, but also as a way to overcome my shyness and revulsion to being on stage. I can't say that I ever felt comfortable on stage. (Even to this day its very stressful, but I continue trying to improve.) My soft style of speaking always seemed to set me apart at those events – many spoken word performers possess a rhythmic style that I do not. I do think the rhythm is important, but I prefer to perform my poetry as if I am speaking in a conversation. To counter my lack of rhythm, I started setting my poems and other important texts central to the message of SexDeathRebirth (such as *Thunder Perfect Mind*, *Dark Night of the Soul*, etc) to music.

I was not a musician. I did not play any instruments. My husband convinced me that it didn't matter, and that making music is something anyone can do. He gave me a mic, a sampler, a mandolin, a keyboard, and an iPad. At first we worked on tracks together, but eventually I used the instruments he gave me to create on my own. With the the tools at hand, I just figured out what worked and what didn't by ear. I consider my recordings to be ritual acts, therefore there are very rarely any redos. If there are minor mistakes, or mispronunciations, they stay in the final version of the track. I want to capture the inspiration in its most raw form. It's my way of taking a stand against overproduction and autotune. The mistakes remain to capture my humanity.

With my first music project, The Whip Angels, I wanted sex to return to music. Sure, we have half-naked pop stars and sexually overt lyrics in pop and hip hop, but I don't feel a genuine sexual charge in most modern music. So much of the underground music scene seems nihilistic and devoid of any vitality whatsoever. Even drone, ambient and minimal music should be dynamic; there is great beauty in subtlety.

Whereas The Whip Angels was intended to accompany SexDeathRebirth to perpetuate its message and art style, more recently I also started a music project called Temple ov Saturn to accompany the eponymous art mentioned earlier. The projects sound somewhat similar, but Temple ov Saturn is more cohesive, and like the visual elements, easier to digest.

To accompany my music, I use a mix of erotic and religious imagery. I wanted people to hear the spiritual things I was saying, while also being sexually aroused. Is it sexual or spiritual? I want it to be confusing. I'm talking about being one with the divine while the listener is thinking about being one with the flesh. This evolved into my erotic film art.

Erotica

I think most of the pornography that is freely accessible online is too extreme and dehumanising. I've enjoyed my fair share of it, but it's simply not representative of what I want sexually. I would not advocate censorship; I simply choose not to watch it anymore. There are plenty of people who feel similarly. I created a different option. My erotic films are intended to arouse, but I also try to leave room for the imagination. Some films are more explicit than others, but they are always presented in an artful way in terms of my editing style and set to my music. Usually I use projections to light the video – these projections leave room for shadows, for the things you can't see. One of my main gripes with modern porn is the ultra high definition of a lot of it. When I can see the pores of an actor's skin, it becomes clinical.

The women you see in porn are actors. They act out scenarios that can be very arousing to watch, but are not accurate to the desires of most women. Rather, they are expanding the repertoire of what men find arousing. It's a business, and what we do for profit is not necessarily beneficial. That's not to say female porn actors don't enjoy their work, I know there are plenty that do. What I'm getting at is that its doubtful that the babysitter is really into gang bangs. Yes, its a fantasy. But the best part of our fantasies should be using our own imaginations. In porn, the fantasy is fully constructed for the viewer. That's my gripe with it. It serves its function, but it leaves me feeling like something is lacking.

I want to show the men who watch my erotic films an honest depiction of my sexuality, my femininity. I want men to know that women can be intellectual, artistic, and sexual at once. Eroticism is about beauty and intimacy. In my films, I take the viewer into my bedroom, and I transform the bed I sleep on into a hypnotic otherworld.

The first major series of erotic films I did was based on the goddesses of Greek mythology. As Aphrodite I was completely nude, with the exception of nude coloured shoes with mirrored block heels against a projection of the ocean. In the corner of the scene I used a giant blue clam shell decoration as part of the set, and I used a mirror, one of Aphrodite's symbols, as a prop. The production was very simple, but I pulled off the trick - the woman on the screen becomes Aphrodite, the goddess of love, beauty, and sex. As Athena, the virgin goddess of the wilderness, I wore a white dress and brown slightly grecian looking sandals against a projection of the forest. I placed a bow and quiver of arrows in the scene. As Hera, I wore a gold corset with fancy trim, a crown, and thigh high peacock blue boots against a peacock feathered background projection. I want to live in a world where men get off on the idea that women are goddesses. And I do this because I believe men deserve better as well. My motivation comes from a place of a deep love for the masculine and an awareness that we absolutely must work together to perpetuate life.

The second erotic film series I did was based on various artists and writers related to Dada and Surrealism. To channel Meret Oppenheim, I wore a fur collar and wrist cuffs. To invoke Georges Bataille I did a multi-part episode that referenced his art journal Documents, his journal/secret cult Acéphale, his most famous work, *Story of the Eye*, and his general interest in sex and death, the sacred and transgression. I became Dali as he is in "In Voluptas Mors," I used my own body to transform into Man Ray's "Venus Restored." Each of these Surrealist inspired erotic films required a lot of research into each artist and effort to create the necessary props. I want to live in a world where human sexuality is the most divine form of art. I want our basest desires to unite with our highest aspirations. That is what I hope my erotic films accomplish.

Art as Medicine and a Tool for Transformation

It has been said that I produce 'too much' content. The reason for the high output is because creating is my way of transforming my grief into beauty. When I pause, my sadness seeps in. I do allow myself time to feel the sadness, but to let it constantly linger would render me useless and unproductive. After miscarrying twice, I understood something about life and death that I had no way of knowing before. Pregnancy loss has been a life-altering experience. Creating is healing. The devastation would otherwise be too much to handle. Life and death were in me at once and it's something that is now at the forefront of all of my thoughts. I am always thinking about what I lost. Its painful, but it ignited something in me that wasn't there before. I have an overwhelming desire to give birth. And if not to a child, it must be to beauty, to ideas. This is an old idea: art and philosophy have the potential to outlive us far beyond the lifetime of a child. I expect my individual contributions to be forgotten, but I know the central ideas will last. This religion is built on the past. The past is the foundation of the future.

Closing Thoughts

Something that history teachers like to ask on the first day of their class is 'why do we study history?' Students always respond, 'so we don't make the same mistakes we made before.' I say, look around, all we do is make the same so-called mistakes. This is just how we humans are. We need death as much as we need life. We want to destroy as much as we want to create. The cycle is the same; its manifestation varies. Study history to know what happens next.

Idiosyncratic Use Ov Language in My Works as Astorical Rememberance

Genesis Breyer P-Orridge

Looking back from 2018 we see that the first influence on my personal language must be the *St. James Bible*. From very early, approx five or six yeras old, we went to "Sunday School" during the church service whilst the officiating priest gave his sermon and lesson to the adult congregation. There is no doubt in my mind that English biblical grammar and spellings seemed to have an innate quality of authority. God's word!

From around the age of three-four we could read well. Soon afterwards ever more fluently. My father's book collection included *Tristram Shandy*, Dickens' novels, Jonathan Swift, and other classic literature. No book we were capable of reading and understanding was denied me because of content and ideas. In the private/"public" schools we attended from eleven to 18 it was both tradition and compulsory to read and study in great detail the plays of Shakespeare and the *Canterbury Tales* of Chaucer. We loved Chaucer. We also studied John Donne and other metaphysical poets.

As my pleasures in poetry developed, we began to discover more modern poets not on my curriculum like e.e.cummings and then the "Liverpool Poets", Adrien Henry and Roger McGough. We began to search out small press poetry magazines and naturally often experimented with mimicking their various styles. Hans Clavin, publisher of *Subvers* magazines, exposed me to concrete poetry. All of these explorations were during 1964 to 1968. We began to type up my own poems on a typewriter my father donated to me and send them out to independent magazines and publishers of unknown poets and their poetry. All the editors were very polite and encouraged me to continue in my efforts.

All these styles and movements affected my own writing. Most of all we took away humour and a realisation that traditional, established forms and structures were NOT essential to writing poetry. The Liverpool Poets also made me far more aware of spoken word. Of writing to be read out loud.

We began to hang out with Ian Evetts, Baz Hermon and Paul Wolfson and Peter Winstanley at school. Reading each other our new poems, sharing new discoveries of new poetry. During approximately 1966-68 we came across City Lights' Pocket Poets series. A huge breakthrough. Any and all language could be repurposed into poetry, written to speak, scream, sob out loud to other people. My English teacher recommended *On The Road* by Jack Kerouac to me. My father found me a copy at a motorway service station in a bargain bin. Kerouac completed the liberation of language and its possibilities for me. Prose that read like poetry, like the music of bebop jazz. Suddenly the only concern was the message, the experience a poem was built to share and, for me, to this day, as all these contemporary explorations were valid at various times, each poem had its own voice. Which led me to Bob Dylan, and the Velvet Underground and all the new "psychedelic" bands and writers who had claimed journalism of the street soul as their subject to expose.

Kerouac gave me the awareness of the music within words and experiences of all kinds with his insistent BeBop rhythms and references. We discovered *Naked Lunch* by W.S. Burroughs and linearity was dead. It had been tottering, ready to collapse since Beckett and James Joyce; now all expectation of storytelling being a beginning, middle and end, like a movie script, was smashed to pieces and could be reassembled in any order, no matter how seemingly random. We'd smoke hashish and then wander the local park reading *The Ticket that Exploded* and *Soft Machine* out loud. What had seemed impenetrable became a whole new form of coumunication. Burroughs had discovered a way to bypass any neuro-linguistic filters and conditioned censors to deliver information directly a person's nervous system. Hyped up verbal writing became non-verbal neo-heiroglyphic data that was absorbed by a reader's "deep mind". This revelation of the various levels of reception by consciousness has stayed with me all my life. (We usually write "L-if-E" in personal texts and journals because nothing in one's existence is really fixed or permanent; there are always infinite other possibilities and impossibilities beyond an obvious prediction.)

In a very real sense, this becomes a form of "magickal thinking" and allows an opportunity for a far more inclusive catalogue of meanings and associated story options to be gleaned, word by word. This is why we break down traditional linearities with cut-ups, permutations and liberal use of hyphens to try and imbue any of my texts, lyrics, poems with a maximum combination of ideas and interpretations in potentia.

Brion Gysin's permutations, like his "Divine Tautology", "I AM THAT I AM," typed up in as many variations of order as possible, have influenced me so heavily. Inner meanings, possibly original meanings, are revealed. My appropriation of Gysin's initial linguistic researches with cut-ups led me directly to my own discoveries with my "break-ups" using hyphens. "L-if-E" is to me far more accurate information expression than "life". Another classic example is "S/he Is Her/e" a Divine tautology of Pandrogeny. Chandra Shukla of the "One True TOPI Tribe" has been working for years on a "Psychick Dictionary" listing hundreds of "adjustmeants" (Note how an addition of one letter "a" ensures the word more clearly shouts *Intention.*

(n.b: We hope to have his book "coumpleted" in about a "yera", where "COUM" always/all-ways implies change creating spiritual purpose. A "year" is only really a measurement whereas a "yera" is an era of action with purpose seen as part of an unfolding "Astory". There is neither "his-story" nor "her-story", both of which are tools of the exclusive and divisive. There are as many stories as there are people, beings, animals, places, stars, planets on and on, ad infinitum. But for each individual there IS "A-story". Which we find far more informative and accurate.)

We take it as a given that writing and language are communication systems evolved to share and store usually "official" or self-serving versions of events to pass down to future generations as one important aspect of controlling a story, tribal power system or social structure in order to perpetuate how a past is evaluated and thereby perpetuated by elites for elites. Writing as literature and song is created as a commentary, criticism, even satire of elites and their systems and in rare yet wonder-full examples actually do shift an atrophied paradigm into a questioning "r-evolution".

Needless to say, a coalescence of all the potentially animated, activated and less calculated methodologies are the chosen lineage responsible in large part for how my most personal, accurate writing today has arrived where it is now positioned.

When in doubt, read it aloud.

Thoughts on influences and events that have contributed to my conviction that "L-if-E" and "Art" are absolutely indivisible and identical functions ov exist-dance:

We grew up in a household of three generations of women. My maternal grandmother, my mother and my sister. From eleven to 18 my schools were exclusively private all boy schools. We remember, aged around nine years old, watching my mother brush my sister's long hair and feeling jealous and a little angry that just because we were a boy we could not have long hair or discover the sensual pleasure of having it brushed. My only biologically male role model was Brian Jones, founder of the Rolling Stones. Privately we wanted first to be "Twiggy"personified: a skinny girl with Vidal Sassoon styled hair and adventurous clothes. Then to be Diana Rigg who played Mrs. Peel and wore skin tight leather bodysuits and took over traditionally male roles fighting and dominating her criminal opponents whilst "Steed", her male partner and boss was a more effete dandy who rarely fought but when he did he used an umbrella and bowler hat (both symbols of blue collar lower middle class workers). Steed of course is another name for a horse you ride. Putting his character firmly in the submissive role, topped by Mrs Peel. To have a married woman as the primary character was a revolutionary adjustment in entertainment tropes. There was never any romantic interaction between Steed and Peel, firmly placing them as counter to the social norm and its assumptions about male/female interactions. To this day I have a full set of "The Avengers" TV series on DVD that I have watched from beginning to end many times in chronological order. Most recently over the last two years. All these factor in, I believe, to my acceptance of androgyny and ambiguity about Western concepts of dogmatic gender roles.

From the age of eleven years old I had a scholarship to all boy private schools. There is no doubt in my mind that these flagships for perpetuation of an establishment rooted in centuries old landowning aristocracies and monarchs always being automatically expected to be at the top of Britain's power elite exposed me to patriarchy and privilege run rampant. I and my friends were constantly physically abused, beaten by staff and pupils and humiliated in front of the entire school repeatedly. Me for having a Manchester accent, Ian Evetts for writing a poem and sarcasm. I often say that Solihull School in particular taught me who my enemy was.

Sexuality was homosexual deviance among staff carried out in secret and public bragging about sexual "conquests" of women in the most degrading, objectifying ways. My three friends and I, ironically, were always called "Puffs" and "Queers", yet my suspicion is that we had romantic, loving interplays with girls though we remained discreet and silent about it.

The message was clear: sex was both a shameful personal truth and a public flagship for masculinity. Needless to say, such an entrenched male environment also worshipped sports achievements, classic physique ideals and had a Greco-Roman fetish overlaying every activity. It's important to note that there were *no* soft or hard-core porn magazines, no internet, sparingly few super 8 sex movies to glean information about sexual coupling, reproduction or minority activities or any media to show what naked adults looked like. There was only one magazine that we ever saw with nude photos. This was called *Health & Efficiency*, a small magazine, about 5 x 7 inches, which showed totally naked men and women doing physical excercises outdoors, or olympic style workouts on gymnasium bars, trampolines, or vaulting and the like. Imagine how strangely influenced we were in our secret sharing of this taboo publication? All the genitals were blurred out and all body and public hair removed. Years later, when we were still living with Cosey, a photo she took of me with my long hair, "Rasputin" beard and masculine coating of body hair, was printed as "Male Physique of the Month"!

My ideals were, and always will be, creativity, knowledge, language and exploring the unknown utilising generous and mutual collaboration.

In 1969 we joined the Exploding Galaxy commune after quitting a disappointingly old-school Hull University organisation that was still continuing a similar male/female structure as unquestionable.

Arriving at the commune, I surrendered all my clothes into a large wooden tea chest along with everyone else. Each day on waking you went to this box and selected an outfit to wear that day. First come, first clothes, so if you came last you wore what was left regardless of whether it was "gender" appropriate, attractive or ugly, your size or not. We all learned that you can use what you wear as a language, as a creative act that speaks of your mood, your improvisational abilities with how you looked, your ability to subsume your personal self-image to a random outfit and most importantly, that every "look" *is* a costume and speaks for you as a being. What we wear, no matter how unassuming it may seem, can be a story you tell visually to the world around you. I learned that I can, and must, control your own life's narrative. That, as Lady Jaye Breyer P-Orridge used to say to me, "There is no reason to run out of new people to be every day." We had both learned and accepted as a part of how we created our lives unfolding, that dress is costume and disguise, either-or gender, either-or anything was a deliberate falsehood, a trap, laid to ensnare us and prevent us from absolute flexibility and self-control of every possible aspect of our lives day to day, second to second. Cut-ups taught us both too, that nothing is fixed, everything is permitted. Only society's suppression of our imaginations limits us from reaching our full potential in every way, almost every day if you surrender your autonomy for the convenience of fitting into society.

In 1981, Mr Sebastian suggested to me shaving off my public and body hair as he felt such hygiene became aesthetically essential once you had piercings and tattoos in order for them to be displayed to maximum effect.

We have followed this practice ever since. In rituals we always shave head to toe (usually except for head hairstyle) as a part of my cleansing preparations. Usually we'd also fast for 23 hours prior as well. When Lady Jaye Breyer P-Orridge moved in with me permanently in 1995, we created a ritual symbolising our re-birth as newborn babies, twins, two halves of one new Pandrogenous whole, "Thee Pandrogyne." In recognition of this, our most momentous, vital, spiritual expression of unconditional BIG love we both slowly, lovingly, worshipfully shaved every single hair off each other, head to toe. Entwined, totally naked we lay for a long while in foetal positions before, in recognition of our becoming newborn babies, we both donned adult diapers for another 23 hours before beginning an improvised TOPI ritual to celebrate our evolution into a single unified form. Just as Burroughs and Gysin cut-up words, images, tapes and film to generate creative works they could not claim authorship of individually anymore, but instead attributed these results to a combination and fusion of their two imaginations they called, "The Third Mind". So Lady Jaye and myself felt very strongly that the disassembly of the two of us and reassembly into ONE was a product of a singular new phenomenon we called "The Third Being".

These perceptual roots entwine each other in our practice and process that I can liken to gradually thickening and strengthening an original twine to make rope.

During my C.O.U.M. Transmissions (1969-1975) period of exploration, my concerns quickly moved to social gender and sexual taboos and how much they were political, church and economic expediency rather than any universal order of nature. In a Moslem nation a man could have several wives, a woman must be concealed in public as if her very appearance was offensive and might inflame male libido. In one country a woman had almost equal rights to men, in another was naked without it being of note, in another men were naked except for a gourd over their penis. Infinite and contradictory variations of what was and was not allowed/acceptable and varying degrees of punishment and social restrictions to enforce the behavioural status quo. This illustrated to me that all these multitudinous rules and precepts were in fact arbitrary. Burroughs always said to me, "If you want to know what's going on, look for a vested interest." And this simple map works every time. You learn that those in power, whether a chief or queen, president or despot, pope or sufi imam, are constructing social rules, and sexual mores, dogmatic restrictions in order to maintain control. Fear and guilt are classic tools of control, but in order to generate fear and guilt you need social regulations on behaviour, even on what can be tolerated/allowed for everybody's bodies. Rules of marriage; sex before marriage; copulation just to create babies, not for pleasure; masturbation as a taboo; all homosexuality a punishable taboo; public nudity a taboo; natural, non-medical birth and breast feeding labelled "unnatural" by the British Medical Association in the 80's; home birth illegal; abortion illegal in so many countries and cultures; varieties of religious dress, practice and belief policed; tattooing, piercing, private consensual S&M illegal (see the "SPANNER" case against Mr. Sebastian).

The ways that societies worldwide impose clearly arbitrary limitations enforced by intimidation, humiliation and imprisonment (even death in some countries) appear endless. I saw all this, had it reinforced over and over in my travels and my researches into spiritual and shamanic disciplines.

Why do all these societies and cultures choose to police the human body in so many ways? Relationships and male/female dynamics in so many ways? Why is it any business of any government or controlling authority to tell me what I am allowed to do with my naturally produced, intimately MINE... body. My "cheap suitcase" as Lady Jaye called it. Timothy Leary said to me once, "We only have a body so we can move our consciousness around" (and to reproduce, though he didn't mention that). The more I thought about this the more curious, then angry, I became.

As a result I began to direct my ideas for C.O.U.M. actions more and more towards enforced physical, religious and societal regulations and the humanE body. These new actions I proposed were to deliberately challenge not just the laws restricting our rights to our own skin and body and expose any and all hypocrisies and anomalies using our own skin and "cheap suitcases" as a battleground.

Shamans seemed to have a "small death" as Tibetans called it, or a severe almost fatal childhood illness, or a brutal ritual pushing tolerance of pain and biological boundaries beyond what seemed logically possible. My own parts in these actions became ever more blatant refusals to accept any impositions by outside forces on my flesh at all without seeing for my SELF if those impositions served any positive purpose for me! As I pressed my limits harder, risked more actual damage and wounds I found that sometimes I would leave my body, once I spoke in tongues (in my last solo actions in Antwerp: "Scenes of Victory") and was severely sickened by chewing a poisonous tree branch and scoring my chest with a rusty nail.

I reached a point where the depth of intimate revelations, altered states and other psychic phenomena caused by accelerating stresses on my physical container were too revelatory and inappropriate to be a public display. I had privately stumbled upon elements of various vision inducing practices that seemed to suggest an avenue of research that might answer some of my ever more personal investigations into why, how and to what end did these states I was accessing exist? It became clear to me that I could only discover more by withdrawing from the arena of so-called "performance" or "action art" and seeking new methodologies, more capable of producing repeatable results; demystifying all the occult, alchemical, tribal, and ecstatic systems to be found worldwide, both visible or concealed in belief systems and orthodoxies, some of which colluded with local overarching methods of control to police and subjugate entire populations from Amazon Village to the Roman Catholic Empire, to Hopi and Ute prophetic induction ceremonies, even Aboriginal "walkabouts". It seemed clear that if every control system not only dictated the proscribed and acceptable uses of our bodies, but also had mystery traditions overtly or covertly concealed within them, then my journey towards an integrated, liberated, personal and intimate physical equilibrium had to explore these dimensions, no matter the risks to health or sanity.

I had been reading about "magick" since reading *Diary of a Drug Fiend, Moonchild* and *Confessions* by Aleister Crowley. My fascination though did not really peak until Geraldine Beskin at the Atlantis Bookshop, in Museum Street, London expanded upon my meagre knowledge of Austin Osman Spare in around 1980. I purchased original copies of every book he published, plus several original paintings, in a race against time and Jimmy Page's much fatter wallet!

What I took from Spare was that it was possible, at a moment of orgasm, to basically post a message of a true desire and/or instruction for behavioural change from our mundane reality and everyday consciousness into our deepest unconscious mind. Furthermore this message/instruction, once delivered, would infiltrate your decision and choice making neurological zones, insisting, without your day to day self being aware of it, that every decision from then on, if it affected your movement towards the desire/choice, would be (must be) to maximise your achieving that choice/desire eventually. No timeframe, just an inexorable, relentless progression to realisation of a changed self.

The question of if it was even possible to actually *change* a person's innate, established behaviours once the neural pathways, reinforced by social pressures had solidified them was a conundrum that obsessed me as a result of all my explorations to this point. I was always seeking, and occasionally seeming to find, methods to rid a self of atrophied habits, redundant behaviours, and outside imposed boundaries. The Exploding Galaxy/Transmedia Exploration constantly asked, why do it the same way as before just because you always have? Do you need a knife, a fork, a plate? Why are you dressed the same as yesterday? What embarasses you? Why? Endless interrogations aimed at breaking everyday patterns we repeat just because we don't ask, "do we need to do this again?" What does it teach me? What does it do to enhance and expand my life, my imagination, my creativity? Always challenging oneself. Checking motives for everything, anything, trying to reach a state of constant fluidity, flexibility and creation without hesitation or use of a formula. To do *anything* the same way as last time was a defeat.

I focussed in through this first "boot camp" on all these questions utilising improvisation and available resources rather than appropriate resources no matter how unlikely they might be to achieve what we desired to have happen with my actions within my C.O.U.M. projects.

This led me to Thee Temple Ov Psychick Youth project, where I released my interpretation of what I had gleaned so far from my own psychic states during actions and a combination of Austin Osman Spare, Tibetan ritual, works with a Cheyenne Apache native American shaman, Nomad, in my treatise *Thee Grey Book* and its dissemination of a truly demystified option to a global network of like-minded seekers, disenfranchised fans and occultists unattracted to the traditional museum of magick in the form of pre-existing semi-secretive organisations like the O.T.O., Typhonian O.T.O., Freemasons, etc.

By 1993 after returning from months in Kathmandu, Nepal, and visiting the Akah tribe in the Golden Triangle who believe they are descended from nomadic Tibetans I thought I had reached an ending of my investigations into the human body and its interconnections with heightened states of consciousness in my work and practices both private and public. Not so... I met Lady Jaye Breyer (later also P-Orridge) in 1993 in New York City on West 23rd Street, and my world and worldview disintegrated again. Just as it should.

Lady Jaye was a Registered Nurse and professional Dominatrix (since 1985). Being forced to wear a corset for scoliosis for long periods as a child had made her hyper aware of pain and both a body's limitations and pleasures.

We fell in unconditional love quite literally at first sight. Our independent journeys into stressors and near death experiences cemented our fusion.

Lady Jaye hated "wife", "spouse", "life-partner" all those titles. She only felt at ease with "Other Half". We felt like we *had* known each other before. We both felt an absolute dissatisfaction with being classed as a gender based on biology. Genitals, we believed, were simply reproductive, pleasure and excretion devices. Flesh functions left over from our ancient animal ape past.

We truly felt two parts of one being. Applying the Burroughs/Gysin cut-ups yet again we speculated. They had assigned the creation of literary, audio-tape, and film assembled via cut-ups not to themselves as authors, but to a being that only existed as a result of this mutual process combined with random chanc, producing content they did not, and could not, control. They named the phenomenon "The Third Mind". We speculated, if we applied a form of cut-up to our problematic bodies, trying to end a male/female paradigm, a new being would emerge from our merging process too. We called this "The Third Being" for a while. However, I had been considering an end to male/female, either/or structures for decades. In a magickal notebook from 1986 called "Thee First Book ov Total Inwardness" we write about a concept we call "Pandrogeny" over many pages, even including tarot readings, and diagrams. We conclude "Pandrogeny is inevitable."

Lady Jaye and I looked for undercurrents in the local culture. Sex ads in the *Village Voice* free paper listed biological females offering sex to heterosexual males in 1996, but by 2000-2003 the sex ads seemed primarily from transexual "females" offering sex but still to heterosexual males

Cosemetic surgery was a dirty secret in Hollywood and entertainment industries everywhere for decades. Then around 2000 as celebrity obsession, fame and superficial glamour became media nutrient cosmetic procedures became another excuse for PR people to get their clients visibility. So called

"Reality TV" magnified and accelerated this process.

Finally, as I had predicted in the mid-1980's, transexualism became an accelerating option for those in need, and exploded into the socio-political discussion. Even now, being trans is seen as simply changing gender, maintaining the either/or bastion of control. I do not want to be defined as male, nor female. I am a humanE being. I fight for an end to either/or, male/female, black/white, Islam/Christian, rich/poor and on and on, ad nauseum.

Lady Jaye and I wrote texts together trying to make this clear:

BREAKING SEX

A discussion document by BREYER P-ORRIDGE

(Genesis Breyer P-Orridge and Lady Jaye Breyer P-Orridge)

> It seems useful to us, in our practice, to adopt the assumption that there is no way of knowing which has supremacy, the recording device that is DNA, or the SELF we converse with internally that we call consciousness but often, rather lazily, still imagine and identify as the living, biological, body. In fact, we see the "I" of our consciousness as a fictional assembly or collage that resides in the environment of the body.
>
> One of the central themes of our work is the malleability of physical and behavioural identity. The body is used by the mind as a logo, an hieroglyph for the SELF before we are able to speak and use language. It is almost an holographic doll constructed by external expectations even before our body is born. Even the name we are assigned is another holographic programme in the prophetic story of who we are to become.
>
> The work of William S Burroughs and Brion Gysin has been highly influential to us, particularly in relation to the practice of the "cut-up". To liberate the word from linearity, they began to cut-up and, incorporating random chance, re-assembled both their own and co-opted literature "...to see what it really says..." They referred to the phenomena of profound and poetic new collisions and meanings that resulted from their intimate collaborations as the "Third Mind". This was produced with a willingness to sacrifice their own separate, previously inviolate works and artistic "ownership". In many ways they saw the third mind as an entity in and of itself. Something "other", closer to a purity of essence, and the origin and source of a magical or divine creativity that could only result from the unconditional integration of two sources.
>
> Beginning in the 1960s, especially from being an active

participant in the Exploding Galaxy/Transmedia Exploration and occasionally the Gay Lib street theatre, Genesis Breyer P-Orridge experimented with various disciplines and practices to apply the cut-up to behaviour, to identity, and to gender; de-conditioning as far as possible the fictional character written by consensus reality and all who would impose their expectations upon him. Breyer P-Orridge worked throughout the 1970s as a performance artist and actionist; and during the 1980s s/he studied and practiced ritual and shamanic techniques and was deeply involved in the body modification movement known as "modern primitives". In the early 1990s Genesis Breyer P-Orridge met Lady Jaye Breyer P-Orridge and their ever more rigorous collaborations began.

Just as Burroughs and Gysin collaborated together, subsuming their separate works, individuality and ego to a collaborative process by cutting-up the Word to produce a third mind, so, in our current practice, Breyer P-Orridge have applied the cut-up system and third mind concept directly to a central concern, the fictional SELF. The un-authorised Astory of our lives so far. Breyer P-Orridge both supply our separate bodies, individuality and ego to an ongoing and substantially irreversible process of cutting-up identity to produce a third being, an "other" entity that we call the PANDROGYNE.

In our quest to create the Pandrogyne, both Genesis and Lady Jaye have agreed to use various modern medical techniques to try and look as much like each other as possible. We are required, over and over again by our process of literally cutting-up our bodies, to create a third, conceptually more precise body, to let go of a lifetime's attachment to the physical logo that we visualise automatically as "I" in our internal dialogue with the SELF.

We encounter many unexpected internal conflicts as our egos try to survive intact as the "person" they have been previously conditioned to be. We have discovered that how we look does relate very directly to the internal dialogue that describes us to our SELF and to each other. It is not superficial in its effect when it is instructed that everything about it's logo of its SELF is malleable, vulnerable and impermanent.

When you consider transexuality, cross-dressing, cosmetic surgery, piercing and tattooing, they are all calculated impulses – a symptomatic groping toward the next phase. One of the great things about human beings is that they impulsively and intuitively express what is inevitably next in the evolution of culture and our species. It is the Other that we are destined to become.

Pandrogeny is not about defining differences but about creating similarities. Not about separation but about unification and resolution.

Breyer P-Orridge believe that the binary systems embedded in society, culture and biology are the root cause of conflict, and agression which in turn justify and maintain oppressive control systems and divisive heirarchies. Dualistic societies have become so fundamentally inert, uncontrollably consuming decreasing resources and self-perpetuating that they threaten the continued existence of our species and the pragmatic beauty of infinite diversity of expression. In this context the journey represented by their PANDROGENY and the experimental creation of a third form of gender- neutral living being is concerned with nothing less than strategies dedicated to the survival of the species.

"WE ARE BUT ONE..." becomes less about individual gnosis and more about the unfolding of an entirely new, open-source, 21st century myth of creation.

PRAYERS for SACRED HEARTS

There is no reason
on earth why
you should run out
of people to be.

S/HE IS HER/E

P-ANDROGENY
POSITIVE ANDROGENY
POWER ANDROGENY
POTENT ANDROGENY
POLITICAL ANDROGENY
PERFECT ANDROGENY
PRECIOUS ANDROGENY
P-ANDROGYNE
WILD
BEING
UNHOLY
CHOSEN ONE

To throw off the shackles
Of experience
Of true sexual freedom
And physical love!
End gender.
BREAK SEX.

There are more than one of you.
Maybe hundreds to chose from.

CHANGE THE WAY TO PERCEIVE
AND CHANGE ALL MEMORY.

Difference is the core problem. We came to believe, through visionary journeys, global travels, intuition and our own evolving relationship that in either a symbolic way, or in actuality, our original pre-material, sensory visit to this apparently material earth; that our "Divine" or "Pure" state is originally as a being in potentia within an endless flow of possibilities. This we call I.T. (Imaginary Time). At some point this cloud of unknowing became consciously aware that it existed. From a state of unified presence this I.T. manifested everything we experience as "real" and "solid" in order to explore sensory interaction as every "thing". What was at least conceptually a Divine Hermaphrodite split into two parts that eventually evolved into male and female strains of its SELF. Our purpose on earth ever since has been to recognize our SELF in every thing, in every being and *knowingly* re-unify. In the case of me and Lady Jaye we were literally each other's other half, finally re-united becoming one singular Resolved being once more. A PANDROGYNE.

We are not swapping genders; therefore, we are finding each "Other" Half.

These theories and concepts are now, and will be until we drop this body, the central experiences and references that consume all we create today.

Is there a position in our creative practice where audience and creation interact in more traditional ways?

In the beginning my first actions were a kind of "agit prop". In 1966 I created "Knights of the Pentecostal Flame" in Solihull. With my friends from school we left small rectangles of card with single words written on them all over the town square. We left them in ashtrays, gutters, cafe tables, shop displays calling them "beautiful litter". My idea was that as people idly picked them up from curiosity they were unwittingly writing a haiku style poem word by word. My thinking was, if we must have litter, use it creatively, think outside the status quo understanding. The local newspaper, *Solihull News*, ran a two page feature on my poetry as litter event with the headline "Move to Wake the Silhill Sausages". Two local churches invited me to be guest speaker to their congregation and youth programme respectively, even BBC Radio in the Midlands did a special piece about this optimistic phenomenon. I learned how potent a media reaction could be, and, how easily a newspaper article could feed a previously agreed upon editorial stance to a public who seemed hungry to be fed, then led. Sausages indeed!

Later, with the Exploding Galaxy and Transmedia Exploration the performances were mainly street interventions. Mysterious movements, assemblages and spoken words would happen without announcement for random passers-by to make of as they would.

So audiences were never a paramount consideration, merely a casual witness to an idea seen by chance. Just like these actions my earliest works as C.O.U.M. Transmissions were inserted into street situations, primarily for the fun and occupation of the participants rather than any concept of traditional audience. At a Southampton Arts Festival I climbed a tree in a latex body suit taking cheap dolls, mirrors, streamers and various objects that had no business being up in a tree. I was at exactly the same height in my tree as passengers in double decker buses. As a result people idly staring out of their window thinking of nothing, or work, or getting home, football, shopping list... whatever, would suddenly see a grotesque black creature covered in lumps and apparent boils, chains dangling around it, bones hanging off the chains. This figure was apparently nesting in the tree, playing abstractly with odd items. Almost as soon as their brain began registering all this and initial shock wore off, the bus would move away and they would have no way to prove they saw it, except, perhaps, by engaging strangers on the top floor of the bus in speculation as to "Did they see it?" and "What was it?" Of course, some passengers would not have seen it at all, leaving potential for debates about reality of experience, madness, hoax and puzzlement. For me, if these witnesses walked away just puzzled, wondering, "What?" or "Why?" that was enough and merely a bonus to the choosing to DO something surreal for my own ends of satisfaction, curiosity and the fun of exploring what might happen if ?

After C.O.U.M. Transmissions moved to London this approach slowly adjusted. Not so much my relationship with the audience. I still didn't care so much if C.O.U.M. were viewed or not, but the locations changed slowly into galleries and autonomous art spaces like "Art Meeting Place" and the Oval House Theatre. This gave me more direct control over what took place, which also opened up options for including sound, smoke and lighting techniques and building far more elaborate sets. For example, at the Paris Biennale in 1975 C.O.U.M. Transmissions created a room like space within which we moved and adjusted an ever more precisely arranged installation over three days which, although visitors to the museum could stop and stare for varied lengths of time, they were not integral to creating the final installation nor important in the process. To emphasize this deliberate reduction in the function of people watching we did not usually take any photo documentation but rather relied upon random members of the public to remember to send us *their* photographs so that their idea of what was a crucial moment was preserved – not ours. There was no direction on C.O.U.M.'s behalf in terms of key points of information or ideas we wanted to transmit. This meant that entire new interpretations and themes were brought to an action by a random viewer's choice of what and how to photograph us. By 1975 I had come across a Japanese Fluxus piece in a book given to me by David Mayor of "FluxSHOE" that simply stated, "Take 24 hours to remove all your clothes."

From then on, with a few rare exceptions, C.O.U.M. Transmissions were activated by moving as slow as possible. I was fascinated by the idea that an installation like that in Paris was a 3D "painting" in a visual sense. The figures in it inexorably achieving functions or simply getting from A point to B point within our defined space as gracefully and as apparently immobile at any given second so an audience could not recall seeing a transit from point to point, yet were clearly aware it took place. Glance away and a figure had changed its sculptural shape. Photographs therefore "froze" this process, thereby serving a function as a serial sequence, as if towards an animated movie at some later date. In this way an audience *were* participating, but not in a Living Theatre, in your face assault, but through a visual and mystery seduction.

Once I developed this system for C.O.U.M., it finally allowed me to address far different subjects than the earlier street theatre, agit prop, public space interventions. These were often rooted in a more ironic, theatre of the absurd style. Strangely disturbing and surreal, alien, but non-threatening at its core.

Now I could address far more perverse, challenging, even socially destabilising content. I was able to integrate body stressors. For instance at LAICA in 1976 I was stood on ice cubes, carpet tacks and gravel; urinated into a milk bottle, then drank some, used the rest as an enema; drank milk and water, added them to another enema; puked and licked it off the floor. I kissed mouth-shaped nails point up through a piece of wood, causing bleeding. Yet all the time, the most intense pain aspect was my feet in ice with tacks driving in whenever I shifted position. Nobody in the audience photographed, or asked about, my feet. Visually we had learned how to, to some degree, direct and/or redirect the lines of sight in an audience, drawing them to the instantly visual, rather than the vicious reality. I hoped this would reveal and expose the consumer opiates of Hollywood whilst leaving me with an intimate, still public, but barely noticed, space to explore more directly shamanic physical and biological spaces. It was these available but invisible details that inexorably led me to Thee Temple Ov Psychick Youth project, more specifically my inclusion of my flexible interpretation of Austin Osman Spares "sigils".

An audience was there, sometimes to create a deadline preventing me from backing out of a new level of painful commitment, but that audience had no cognisance of my most private motivations.

Obviously, when I created pieces for a theatre, like "Couming of Age" I was aware that tickets would be sold for seats imposing a far more traditional structure on what could be expressed and seen. I personally never really felt fully comfortable with that level of formality. My preference developed through these various projects for random, informal interactions with a public that had no preconceived notions they might be confronted with us, and expectations of stereotypical audience performer relationships.

With Throbbing Gristle (1975-1981) our approach to an audience became more consciously anti-entertainment and confrontational. Most of the early gigs are legendary as much for the "assaults" and frustration we imposed on audiences than for just the music. We played behind a wall of mirrors so the audience saw that TG music was a reflection of themselves; behind halogen lamps so the audience were visible, not us on stage; inside a scaffolding box covered in tarpaulins with the PA outside the box pointing up at the sky, and cameras inside the cube filming us without sound. To see TG, you had to watch monitors inside the host building. To hear TG, you had to look down from the roof triggering a riot. We played behind a screen with our film "After Cease To Exist" projected triggering a riot. But, as time went by and TG music became more scripted and repeatable, the band's attitude changed. The size of the crowds at our concerts grew rapidly, venues became theatres with multiple support acts. Even though this limited the tricks we could pull it was still possible to surprise in new ways by breaking concert promotion routines. TG would go on first before all the support groups. We never did an encore ever in our original incarnation. We only played for exactly 60 minutes, one hour, when we would stop no matter how well we were received or if we were improvising a great segment of music.

Despite all the tricks TG pulled to keep unpredictable to our audiences, in the end it became clear I had only one option left to confound and "disappoint" our fans. Stop playing and retire the band. So at our critical and public peak, I amicably quit. TG had nowhere else to go at that time.

With Psychic TV, everything changed. My baseline policy has always been when in doubt, to remain creative, do the opposite to what you did last time.

I remember crying with laughter imagining TG fans faces when they heard the first track "JUST DRIFTING" on our first album. Seeing camouflaged, dark, serious, murderer accessorized faces frown and then be outraged at how we'd betrayed the "Industrial aesthetic". PTV was an amalgam of everything my projects had taught me so far. Time to seduce an audience – not alienate them (except if they were addicted to a previous industrial noise rut). My lyrics were paramount with the occult themes they clearly proselytised in conjunction with Thee Temple Ov Psychick Youth.

For me, now, my relationship with the audience was as a trusted and trusting friend. Revealing my deepest thoughts and spiritual occupations with a new vulnerability and acceptance of crass dismissal and ridicule. I wanted to build a network of like-minded individuals to share our journeys with, and include respect of their ideas and support too. And I did. TOPY exceeded my wildest dreams and remains a supreme achievement in my mind to this day. I destroyed as best I could the separation between performer/consumer through setting up a kind of occultural chosen famille who took care of each other, shared resources and ideas, developed communal living spaces, set up propaganda projects like book publishing, record labels, rave celebrations and workshops, even gatherings. All of which we did. We took the audience and literally often brought them on stage diminishing separation as much as we could. So much more rewarding than TG aloofness. We found many lifelong true friends this way.

Since 1982, when "Force The Hand Of Chance" was released, Psychic TV has continued to the present, energised by this incredible bond that has resulted by inclusion of our audience. I share all that happens, enhanced in this by social media. Audiences for all my events are steadily growing. Psychic TV audiences still grow every country we visit; they get younger too. We have now got a young trans audience and played to about half a million people at Gay Pride in San Francisco. My lectures at Universities and colleges used to get about 30 people, now we get up to 300 students, breaking lecture attendance records many times. I believe it is because we share everything and trust first, and are disappointed second. At 68 years old it seems to be clear to my audience and followers on media that I have truly lived a life where life and art are the same. There is no public persona. I am off stage what I am onstage. There is mutual love and a trust I will be as honest as I am able, no matter how painful the event I experience.

In a way it is a logical yet opposite conclusion from my beginnings. Where I once didn't care if I had an audience or what effect my events had on them,

Now I care for my audience as members of my chosen, intimate *famille*. This way is by far the best, most satisfying long term solution. We believe art must address the social context it is created in, for and about – no matter how subtle.

As I watch radical contemporary changes, reducing any and all freedoms by those controlling "CONTROL" in order to deliberately isolate and alienate masses of their populations, entrancing them with an illusion of connectedness, even neo-celebrity, via internet media simply to preserve their hold on wealth and Control, they are deliberately fragmenting ideas from the sixties based upon sharing physical resources, skills, property, even relationship partners. In the sixties I witnessed an an ever more complete movement towards communes and collectives. People shared responsibility for ecological maturity and holistic health, organic foods, sustainable living in every arena, women's rights, LGBTQ rights – almost a platform of, dare I say it... common sense.

Today I see autonomous collectives, sharing any and all resources, as a counter to the totalitarian capitalism I have been warning of since the mid-1980's. An audience becomes party to a liberated, temporary safe celebration with a very high ratio of like-minded people grown from often similar roots and influences. An audience for me now is an opportunity to explain my positions and give freely of any ideas we have come across in 68 years. An audience now is a potential future, a human "Last Museum" that can preserve and protect the most healing, loving wisdoms at risk of annihilation by ignorance and deflected criticism, in the hope that there CAN be a future for our Species: the HumanE Species.

I never believed in an audience really, my work has always been built upon finding out how to knowingly include them.

Thee paramount importance ov ritually used objects and symbolic raw materials to generate cosmosis ov associative coumcepts in a dynamic trajectory specifically relating to future times.

This question initially relates to my creation of art. I have made what could be called "art" since around 1965. Always including collages, ever since I saw and was totally inspired by reproductions of Max Ernst's *The Woman With A Hundred Heads.*

I had a brief few years of painting while I lived at home from 1966 until 1969. I quickly progressed from acrylic surrealism as I began to add various non-paint textures like heat-carved polystyrene, sand, nails, sackcloth and other small found objects. During the period 1970-1973 I decorated the second "HoHo Funhouse" in Prince Street, off Dagger Lane, Hull, headquarters of C.O.U.M. Transmissions. Using rolls of coloured plastic sheeting, abandoned prams, dolls, baby items like pacifiers, shoes, socks and old shop display manikins. Anything that was free and lying around as garbage that I could repurpose ended up on the walls, floors and ceilings. However, their inclusion was due to free availability and not really any rigorous aesthetic policy. Doors, stairways, walls and floors were painted in bright psychedelic patterns. I even had two upright pianos in the kitchen. One, too damp to play at all, was given a souped up dazzle camouflage look. The other I painted blue, even the keys so that, " I could play the blues."

During C.O.U.M. Transmissions' earlier actions, the sets, when we bothered with them, were mainly scavenged from all the HoHo Funhouse. For one "performance" at The Brickhouse I simply got our living room reassembled in the centre of the club. Lights, side-tables, armchairs, carpet and all the stuff on them moved lock, stock and barrel.

My relationship with objects changed and became refocused during the years of Thee Temple Ov Psychick Youth, 1981-1991, as my adoption and adaptation of Austin Osman Spare's magickal "sigil" discipline became central.

In *Thee Grey Book* was a description of how to create and "charge" a sigil that required including head and pubic hair, saliva, blood and the liquid resulting from male or female orgasm I called "OV". In its simplest form a sigil could be a piece of paper with your clear description of a true desire that by your absolute concentration at orgasm would be catapulted into your deep, primal consciousness. There the injected desire would foment and, without your mundane awareness even being involved, direct all your future key choices to align with, and maximise, their potential to manifest the subject of your sigil. It's a form of neuro-linguistic programming, but utilising symbolic, neo-hieroglyphic information blocks rather than linear everyday spoken and written language that is inevitably compromised by culture, society, education, family, religious doctrine and all the other tools of control and suppression of creativity, liberation of the imagination, radical alternatives and chosen identities that threaten and challenge a status quo in any formal social structure.

I began to collect ritual materials, fetish objects, shamanic tools, sacred figures and musical instruments whose function was for initiation, not for pleasure, like my Tibetan thigh bone trumpet reputed to have once belonged to Drukpa Kunley "The Divine Madman". Just as my interest in camouflage clothing was because its primary purpose was function not fashion, so my interest in acquiring certain talismanic objects was because they were functional – aesthetics were secondary. At eleven years old I had read *Seven Years In Tibet* by Heinrich Harrer and fell in love with what seemed such an alien culture where monks were given instruments to play not according to skill but according to age, or their occupation in a monastery.

One of the earliest photographs of me as an infant show me on a beach sitting inside a circle of stones I had made around me. On weekend trips to the country I would make small shrines out of twigs, wild flowers, feathers shed by wild birds, rocks and water, often damming a stream alongside them. I felt then and still ardently do, that purported inanimate materials can absorb and store emotions, memories even energies from any sacred rituals that occur around them. I felt vindicated to learn that crystals could activate a wireless set, and silicon store data.

I have always believed travel is essential in our search for knowledge and expansive wisdom. I began to collect objects assumed in more exotic cultures to contain, unleash or direct specific spiritual, occult forces. Having them around me serves as a re-MIND-her of these beliefs of mine. Forming a chaotic battery that generates accelerated intuitions and concentrates my visionary senses. Often some item can lie around for 20 or 30 years in my living/working space (we do not see those processes as separate at all). Then one day, with no prior conscious thought, I will suddenly see how two or more fit together perfectly and something that never existed in the worlds I inhabit bursts into existence so perfectly that it feels inevitable. Lady Jaye calls this phenomenon "The Of Course Factor" – it operates in dimensions beyond and distinct from synchronicity.

For example, during the time Lady Jaye and myself both worked as Dominatrices at Terence Seller's dungeon, "The Whip Shack", I began to collect high heeled shoes discarded as obsolete by other Dominatrices. I felt these shoes had memories, wild stories to tell if only I could unlock them. I knew other sex workers, strippers, topless dancers and the like, and soon was having their worn shoes donated to my archive too. These sat around for many years. One day I was trying to explain this long time form view of material objects for our art to Lady Jaye's niece. I said, "Sometimes, suddenly, after years, two objects that are unrelated, apparently mutually exclusive according to mundane logic, will suddenly "speak" to me and I see clearly how to conjoin them creating a new assembled object that never existed in my or any other known world before. I become a Creator, building evidence of aesthetic worlds previously only capable of any form of manifestation in potentia. I looked down and saw a pair of gold heels I had worn many times, Lady Jaye had worn them before me, and nearby was a box of animal horns I purchased as a job lot in a flea market in Wales many years before. "Watch," I said, then put a horn over the heel of one shoe, it fitted perfectly. "Now you have a "shoe horn," I said, smiling. Instantly I saw a stream of shoe sculptures combining raw materials for magickal working. Since then I have created nine miniature sculptures using my sexually charged pairs of high heels as a basic foundation. After my two trips to Ouidah, Benin, where Hazel Hill III filmed a documentary, "Bight of the Twin," I brought back rusted iron spikes, strange metal shapes, feathers and other small iron things – all significant once used in a Vodun ceremony. In my special row of black boxes I have boa constrictor skin from my eleven foot pet boa, "Isabellaconstrictornot"; feathers from sacrifices I participated in my role as initiate of Santeria; wooden blocks carved in amazing patterns to print fabrics from Kathmandu; dried feeder fish from when I had a fish tank.

All these are directly linked to treasured parts of my life and cover decades of time. I believe T.I.M.E. is an energy, like magnetism, gravity and light. So all my saved raw materials, to me, automatically negate linear time and space as soon as I utilise them in a new, intuitively assembled, uber-object.

All my art, and Lady Jaye's art, always has these "ritual" types of objects as ingredients – as a significant part of them. I believe that they emanate previously recorded information and functions, adjusted by how they have been manipulated and applied in either our private ritual actions and sigils, or events that these same objects were witness to, like a profound moment in my life, which they store and then release, their repurposed existence triggered, becoming one meticulously recognised, transmitting uber-object that I have guided into being created.

Thoughts on SOUND / SILENCE and their place in our music and sonic environments:

On the front cover of my first album "Early Worm", recorded in the loft of my parents' house in 1967 we quoted John Cage from his amazing book *Silence*, which forever changed my appreciation of what music might really be. On the back was my own, personal, statement, "I HAVE NOTHING TO SAY AND I'M SAYING IT."

Cage taught me that every sound capable of being recorded can be equally as valid within what we call music as any number of formal notes and classical structures. He also taught me that any sound whatsoever that has not been recorded but intrudes nevertheless on a space occupied by live or recorded music being played back is also a valid addition to a listener's experience. People whispering, snacks crunching, traffic passing, chairs scraping all become part of a composition, both if the composer wills it consciously, or if it just intrudes naturally due to circumstance. Those tenets have never left me.

Brion Gysin and William S. Burroughs invented the "Cut-Ups" in Paris in the 1950's. Another form of random chance, but this time utilised as a tool to prevent preconceptions, traditional structures, or linearity from governing both the content in its entirety and the academic traditions of storytelling. They took sections of texts from multiple sources and cut them up, reassembling them as they arrived, deliberately dis-organised, and then retyped the results as a new, radical, delirious piece of writing. They believed something magical and profound occured that allowed "the future to leak through" – even claiming at times an oracular effect predicting future happenings.

Later they experimented with tape recorders. Cutting up analog tape and re-editing it resulting in sonic upheavals available no other way with the creator a process, not the producer of a preconceived, comprehansible piece of recognisable sound or music or speech. Sound effects, field recordings of conversation and parties, street sounds, radio shortwave, Moroccan Sufi music, bits of movies... all were now raw material of equal validity, all capable of prophecy and revelation by this process of setting the inner information free. Rigor producing random.

These two threads have stayed with me throughout all my music and sound creations on over 300 records, film soundtracks, ballet scores, from experimental music to crass love songs. Everything we record is built as layers of sounds. They can be familiar or alien but I produce everything in this cut-up, sampling way. I was tremendously lucky to discover Cage so young, and to meet and collaborate with Burroughs from 21 onwards, and Gysin from 26 onwards.

Silence and sound are present in everything I perform and record. I cannot imagine a world restrained by traditional forms that I would wish to be a part of.

It's all a matter ov T.I.M.E.

A long time ago I realised that a rhythm is any time that a second sound occurs after a first to an observer. In other words: if I clap my hands now and wait a million years before I clap them again, at that very moment of my second clap a rhythm has occurred. Whether it perpetuates and I clap a third time is unimportant. A third clap would only be confirmation of the rhythm initiated by my second clap.

I once spent about eight hours wrapped in wolf skins, tied around the wolf skin was rope preventing any movement. I was then placed in a coffin which was in turn suspended on chains about a metre in the air. I had take six capsules of pure pharmaceutical ecstasy. I left my body and travelled into wild ancient and alien dimensions.

When the coffin was lowered, the lid removed, myself removed and unbound. As I sat up out of the wold skin, naked, I said, "Now I know what T.I.M.E. really is. It E.M.I.Ts. T.I.M.E. is an energy.

Thee "frame" as constriction, presence and absence in this apparent experience we explore as sensory materiality:

Obviously I believe that inner and outer space leak into each other through the creative process. That is what we who create do. We seek divinity and then try to find a process to concretise our discoveries, or our good fortune in receiving a vision that can become material in any medium at our disposal.

For me, emptiness in my process is my struggle to illustrate ways that magick imagery and any stories my work is fortunate to be chosen to tell can fall out of the frame to use a painterly concept. Emptiness is the before and after in all forms. I want my works to be functional, to make something defined happen, in a life, or a commonly experienced situation in anybody's life.

I ask, what is this "work" telling me that I didn't already know? What is this "work" telling my chosen tribe, my people, that enhances their understanding of being alive with senses and intelligence? Then, finally, I ask what is this "work" sharing with all humanity that has the potential to release wisdom for them? If a work does not answer one of these in a positive, then it is of no value or importance to me. It is, as Brion Gysin used to say to me, "deceptual art."

Is mutation thee only trigger to change or can humanE behaviour truly be changed by conscious activation through ritual?

Helping to save our humanE species from Control and its subservience to that Control. Finding an end to guilt and fear. Ending once and for all ANY concept that utilises an either/or. Either/Or allows the description of something "other", different, that can then be isolated and used as a weapon to destroy dissent and maintain power in the same old hands who've had it too long and murdered possibly billions in 20,000 years so far.

I hope to inspire future generations to discard all inherited value systems, social conditioning, familial loyalty for its own sake, and come to realise that gender is a red herring distraction as an issue. The real issue is how to reclaim our right and the determination to embrace it in order to build our own unique IDENTITY, and be the writer of our own self-chosen life narrative, free of intrusion or interference by any other beings: human, humanE, or not. I wake up each day and make my choices as far as possible at any given moment as if this new day is a next page in a book I am writing by being alive, by existing. So I make my choices to make this page as interesting, arresting and engrossing as possible. And damn the consequences of breaking imposed codes. I am aware this can, and has many times, lead me into dark, dangerous and forbidding places, but in retrospect I am always glad that I maintained my conceptual and behavioural integrity. I live, we all live, in an environment enriched with nourishment for all our senses and emotions. These act like a diver's wetsuit and aqualung, they allow us to explore this amazing medium of materiality and other living creatures of myriad types. But surviving in this relentless, grueling landscape is brutal. It can deplete our optimism, reduce our strength, so much so that within four score years or so it destroys our physical self. To exist within linear time breaks down our fleshly wetsuit. This is one key reason Burroughs and Gysin, and later me, have been so obsessed with cutting everything up to see what it really says, or discover what it really is, or why anything is here at all.

Time is so inexorably toxic to a biological being that it eventually runs out and destroys our body that allows our mind this ineffable journey, and this kills us. Our "cheap suitcase" of Lady Jaye's that gives our brain and thus our mind mobility to visit fascinating new places, to sensually taste relationships, nutrients and climates, everything we choose to explore, slows down and stops.

Tibetans, and other ancestor aware cultures and belief systems, believe that consciousness IS capable of maintaining a sense of individual, self conscious identity after the death of our body. Hence the tradition of reincarnation. I used to find this very hard to grasp and truly believe. My journeys across this incredible planet combined with my three near death experiences and of course my thought full explorations of consciousness utilising multiple techniques and libations have forced me to believe in a personal form of perpetuation of a beings consciousness after biological death. As a direct result of this adjusted view of mortality, finding a system of individuated, self-aware consciousness of myself without a body after it has died, has become an equally great challenge in my work as saving my fellow beings.

I created a sculpture for my Rubin Museum retrospective exhibition titled, "Try to altar everything". It was inspired, yet again, by something Brion Gysin said to me once on a visit with him in Paris. It is a bronze cast of my right forearm in a position of shaking someone's hand. It sticks out from a black steel rectangle that is bent in the middle to make a stand keeping it upright. On this flat, bottom part of the black steel stand is a brass plaque that reads, "WISDOM CAN ONLY BE PASSED ON BY THE TOUCHING OF HANDS" – Brion Gysin. People seeing it are asked to shake hands with my hand, to"PLEASE TOUCH THIS SCULPTURE". We try to isolate and identify little pieces of wisdom. But language often fails to be meticulously precise in these matters. At these times only an inanimate object can express the simplest, most complex idea. Finding that combination that speaks to all beings, without any interruption or corruption by my mind, is one of the greatest challenges to myself and my processes.

We were once asked to describe everything that we do in a couple ov words. Without any conscious thought process we replied "Cultural Engineer."

When beginning analysis ov a socio-cultural undercurrent towards applying a new creation and/or strategy we ask various key questions:

> Do you believe your process must tell a story and/or share information?
> Do you believe an artist MUST be trying to save our humanE species?
> Do you believe to create is a spiritual calling, like a doctor, or shaman?
> Is there room for the messianic in your process?
> What IS the process?

New York City, August 2018

Breyer P-Orridge: Try to Altar Everything

Vanessa Sinclair

Breyer P-Orridge's major art exhibition *Try to Altar Everything* opened at the Rubin Museum March 11, 2016, and was on display until August 1. Once again, Breyer P-Orridge has broken boundaries with this latest installation of he/r unfolding body of work. The exhibition inhabited the entire top floor of the museum – its cylindrical shape reflecting the cyclical nature of the spiritual, psychical and unconscious realms we all inhabit; the flow of creation as the ouroboros swallows its tail. In fitting form, the exhibition spans the length of Breyer P-Orridge's career with pieces ranging from the early days of Thee Temple Ov Psychick Youth (TOPY) in the 1980's to current day work created by Breyer P-Orridge during he/r recent travels to Nepal. In the center, a handmade carpet from Kathmandu lies beside a bright red retro high-back chair owned by partner Lady Jaye when the couple first met. This central feature in itself encapsulates the juxtaposition inherent in Breyer P-Orridge and their work. The carpet appears ancient but is actually brand new, created by a traditional method with the design of the Pandrogyne stitched into it – a positive androgyne created when the bodies, minds and souls of Lady Jaye Breyer and Genesis P-Orridge were cut together in a process that forever transformed the both of them and created a Third Being they deemed the Pandrogyne. Overhead hangs a Psychick Cross – Genesis' trademark emblem – white neon glowing, highlighting the contours of the central coil of the rotunda: the spine that is the fundamental architectural feature of the museum itself.

The process of Pandrogeny is outlined and represented beautifully in this exhibition. Beginning with sigils created with the intention of sex magick ritual and transformation, many contain the blood, hair, fingernails, saliva, and sexual secretions of the artists. These excretions of the body are sacred and have been considered so and used in ritualistic activities for millennia. *Origin of the Species* (1998) is a magickal working created almost entirely from photos of Lady Jaye in combination with representation of the four material elements of earth, air, fire and water. Patterns mirror the double helix of DNA in an attempt to break from the biological cycle of rote repetition and the limitations of the physical form. The piece is reflective of Gustave Courbet's *The Origin of the World*, a controversial piece in itself once owned by famed psychoanalyst Jaques Lacan before finding its way to the Musée d'Orsay.

Yearning Flesh (1993) is a sigil created following the time Genesis was expelled from he/r native homeland of England in 1992. Forced to create a new life for he/rself and he/r family, Genesis took up residence in Northern California with he/r wife and two children. S/he noticed how the landscapes of these new surroundings mirrored the Himalayan foothills, which had provided refuge during this transitional time. Taking note of of one's environment in this way is an essential part of the practice of magick. Recognizing, appreciating and commemorating these moments is a way to give thanks to the divine. As this rabbit hole of life unfolds before us, there are always clues we are on the right track, of course. Pay attention!

This returns us to the center of the installation, where situated near Lady Jaye's bright red chair and the Pandrogyne carpet is a beautiful altar space specially dedicated to Genesis' other half. This cabinet includes photos of the beloved, a GI Jaye action figure, mala beads with a Psychick Cross, and a glass butt plug, among a variety of other fetishes and items. Notably there is a porcelain figurine of the famed White Rabbit from Alice in Wonderland given to Genesis by Lady Jaye when they first met, as Jaye described the budding union – or re/union one might say – with Genesis being akin to "going down the rabbit hole," and what a very special rabbit hole indeed.

In psychoanalytic terms, this experience of the uncanny, synchronicity, and déjà-vu is what one encounters when delving into the realms of the unconscious. We enter into a hall of mirrors where we find our reflection at every turn. We can choose to recognize ourselves in others and our environment and learn to work with it, play with it, molding it and ourselves into what we would like to be and see or, as many do, we can write it all off as being chance or happenstance, and choose to believe we live in a world where we feel out of control and subject to external forces constantly imposing themselves upon us. In my practice as a psychoanalyst, I consistently bear witness to patients' internalization of the ideas of mainstream society thrust upon them since birth – before birth even. Ingrained in us are the expectations of parents, family, and society, which are largely based on the gender we are assigned. This inscription also includes the Western medical model, the commodification of being and patholozation of the human experience found in the worldview of mainstream psychiatry and psychology. This viewpoint not only discourages "magical thinking" but even labels it as pathological: a royal road to psychosis. I have found that much of my work is dedicated to providing a space in which individuals are able to authentically express themselves without external judgment. Lord knows there is enough societal judgment internalized by individuals already, and it is pervasive. Every person that comes through my office makes statements like, "I know this sounds crazy but…" If everyone has experiences of synchronicity, the uncanny, and the like, then it is obviously not crazy, and is in fact an integral part of human experience that society tells us to ignore. At this point in my life, I sincerely believe that everything that society deems the "right" thing to do is actually designed to disempower the individual. Stay in the same dead end job for years and years on end, so that you have benefits and a retirement plan and are seen as loyal; only have missionary style sex with the same person of the opposite sex for the rest of your life and make sure not to use birth control so you have as many children as possible to keep you busy, stressed and poor; don't trust your own personal experiences and don't dare create meaning in your life or feel like you have any control over your circumstances or surroundings, as this will lead you to chronic mental illness.

Breyer P-Orridge is one of the leading artists of our time who has been bringing to light the control mechanisms of society and breaking them down for decades. Inspired by the cut-up method of Brion Gysin and William S. Burroughs, Breyer P-Orridge has applied the cut to visual art, mail art, sound, behavior, identity, gender, consciousness and soul. In this latest installment, Breyer P-Orridge bridges time and space by cutting through the divide between the two. Intersecting modern day ritual and sex magick techniques that include fetish, BDSM, cult and Western occultist practices with traditional and timeless rituals found in Tibetan, Nepalese, West African Vodou and Santeria practices. Not only does the art/life work of Breyer P-Orridge span time, space and culture in this way, but now s/he has brought these "hidden" practices to the main stage in the form of a major exhibition at a prominent art museum in the center of Manhattan. A r/evolutionary step on the part of both the artists and the Rubin Museum, *Try to Altar Everything* brings the intersection of underground occulture and ancient traditions into Western modern day mainstream life. When stepping into a space such as the Rubin Museum, most visitors tend to view the works on display as artifacts from an/other time and place; foreign, out of reach, to be viewed and revered but not touched or experienced. Breyer P-Orridge shows that these practices are happening here and now, and are for all of us. S/he highlights this through the item exchange practice wherein visitors may bring in a 2x3" item of their choosing in exchange for a limited edition Psychick Cross. Items are then inserted into the museum exhibition itself, highlighting the integral nature of exchange while embodying the communal practice and essentiality of everyone's contribution and intention. This is expanded into the evening events of art talks and music, the ability to call Breyer P-Orridge and speak to he/r on the phone at times throughout the course of the exhibition, and in the bronze cast of he/r arm inviting us to reach out and touch he/r, as Brion Gysin once stated that true knowledge can only be imparted through the touching of hands. Don't just watch the creation – become a part of it. In essence, Breyer P-Orridge is creating a five month long ritual performance piece – a magickal practice – in the heart of New York City, and is inviting us all to participate. We are in this together. We can create change. This event is an act of r/evolution.

If you haven't caught on by now, the practice of Pandrogeny is not just the embodiment of a love story between two individuals. It is that of course, and in that is an extraordinary act of devotion, commitment and love. But more than that, it is a conscious and intentional step in the process of human evolution. By breaking down barriers of identity, gender and behavior, cutting through the constraints of the body, mind and soul, Lady Jaye and Genesis Breyer P-Orridge have created not only a bridge between themselves but also between life and death, this world and the next, potentially forging a path off the wheel of samsara. As Breyer P-Orridge state, the practice of Pandrogeny continues on after Lady Jaye dropped he/r body in

2007. It could even be viewed that the dropping of Lady Jaye's physical "suitcase" was the essential next step in the r/evolution of the Pandrogyne. Perhaps s/he had to make the leap between life and death to create the cut, the gap, the space between this world and the next, between he/r consciousness and that of Genesis' in order to bring the Pandrogyne more fully to fruition. Lady Jaye once stated, "I'm limited by time, by gravity, by all these physical forces when really I wish my consciousness could be liberated completely free to go everywhere, to be everywhere, to do everything, to be everyone that I've ever dreamed of being." S/he achieved this. Quite a r/evolutionary act. And in this event, s/he is her/e to impart to others that we may achieve this as well. It is not out of reach. Quite the contrary, it is within our reach, and *Try to Altar Everything* exemplifies this.

We are co-creators of this life, of this world. This exhibition shows us that everything around us is sacred or can be made to be; materials to be used in the creation of our lives. Life itself is creation. Life is Art. Every step has potential to be an event. In my own personal cut-up practice, I create cut-ups daily upon awakening as I write down my dreams. You'd be marveled to see what they say (and should try them for yourself). Recently a cut-up of mine stated, "Everything is an evolutionary magical activity." Every thing is an evolutionary magical activity. Try to alter everything.

Psychoanalysis, Art, and the Occult: Cutting Up a New Conversation[1]

Claire-Madeline Corso

Dr. Vanessa Rawlings Sinclair, a tall beauty in black, with ivory skin and scarlet stained lips, unassumingly graces the worn-in wood floors of Candid Arts Trust. Artwork she meticulously curated punctuates the white walls of the industrial studio space where a public art opening is being held to kick off the weekend-long symposium "Psychoanalysis, Art and the Occult." Dr. Sinclair was up all night carefully arranging the pieces with her co-organizer, Carl Abrahamsson – a quiet man humbly observing the scene through the lens of a camera hung so comfortably around his neck it seems to be another limb. In a way, the gallery is an invocation of the cut, an idea developed famously by authors-artists William S. Burroughs and Brion Gysin, which Dr. Sinclair will address in depth on the following day alongside Katelan Foisy, her co-author of the "Chaos of the Third Mind" project from which this conference was birthed. Along the gallery's walls, each artist's work seems to intervene in the space between those positioned alongside of it, altering the context of the gallery space and framing the podium from which the presenters will speak over these next three days.

Dr. Sinclair, a psychoanalyst in private practice and founding member of the free association for psychoanalysis, "Das Unbehagen," together with Carl Abrahamsson, a freelance writer and lecturer, organized the symposium; stitching together the ongoing split between psychoanalysis and the occult – two ethical disciplines which raise specific questions and assert possible answers about what it means to be in the world. Hosting this pre-conference gallery opening was a way of lending art as the subject of the discussion, as a representation of that which both systems take as its object: the human experience, the human mind.

With a glass of wine in hand, I scan the room. My eye lands on a cream surface, the work of Steingrimur Eyfjord, a conceptual artist based in Iceland. Writing inscribed upon it in red, some of it redacted by a heavy stroke of solid black paint, reads "Look at the numbers… and start counting in silence… Keep counting until you go to sleep. The day after you… will reach a temporary state of psychosis." On the wall opposite this painting is the work of Italian artist Roberto Migliussi, which suggests the inverse of Eyfjord's work, that is, a return to meaning from madness. Across an orange surface, chaotically rendered black lines approaching a kind of hieroglyphic lettering repeat again, and again, as if attempting to create a kind of referential system.

1 The papers presented at the Psychoanalysis, Art & the Occult conference, held in London 2016, are collected in volume 9 of *The Fenris Wolf*, which is available from Trapart Books.

Next to this, the work of Annette Rawlings – Dr. Sinclair's mother, and an accomplished artist in her own right – depicts a blue and green surface demarcated by a yellow line, suggesting the inextricable ideas of finitude and infinity. In another, blocks of blue and lavender paint toned with heavy grey, create the form of a seated woman from behind, outlined by the lines these blocked colors make when they meet on the page. Dr. Vanessa Rawlings Sinclair's cut-up art appears next in the series, like a semi-colon, an unconscious extension of, and intervention in her mother's work. Against a white background, segments of text from her own academic and creative writing are positioned in a poetic sequence amidst spontaneous gestures of red, black, and beige paint. The lines are reminiscent of those in Annette Rawlings' work but, rendered fluidly, evoke less the extreme edge of negative and positive space than they suggest a communicative gesture at this same edge.

Each piece seems to be created at the boundary of meaning and meaninglessness, chaos and order. Some, like Sinclair's or Eyfjord's work, explicitly invoke symbolic systems. Others evoke concepts inherent to the visual medium, raising the oppositional and inextricable ideas of negative and positive space, color and line, content and form. Together, the works of these artists raise a question about meaning and madness. From this edge, these artists create a line their work crosses, it seems, in order to define. The positioning of Dr. Sinclair's work next to her mother's situates this question within a psychoanalytic context. If Rawlings' paintings represent two infinitudes divided by a line – the boundary between one color and another, one self and one other – Dr. Sinclair's work represents the system of meaning which must emerge in this space between two bodies.

For Freud, this space is demarcated by the bodily drive, and by the repression of it, which invokes the division between self and other. For Lacan, a theorist who followed him, it is organized in language punctuated by grammar and syntax. For Jung, it is to be found in projections – in images. If Jung's focus on the *imago* as the domain of subjectivity invites a discussion of the occult, the theoretical implications of mapping the mind at the level of both the body and language are perhaps helpful to consider when traversing the space between these two disciplines: one embodied, the other ideational.

The historical exclusion of the occult from psychoanalytically informed discourses, has its origins in the split between Freud and Jung. The cause and consequence of this split is addressed by two panelists, Dr. Steven Reisner, a clinical psychologist and activist currently running for President of the American Psychological Association, and Gary Lachman, a writer formerly of the band Blondie. While Lachman believes that Freud's resistance to the occult stems from his personal neurotic fear of the dissolution of rational thought, Reisner argues that Freud's hesitation was ethical and concerned the occult being incorporated into his theoretical system as a rejection of the death drive – a fear which, in Reisner's estimation, was "practical and temporary." As a creator of discourse, Freud was very concerned with the integrity of the system he was creating. Interestingly, this discursive dimension is also that which lends an entrance point for this new discussion. These words from an audio clip played before the first panel took the stage echo: "writers and artists, in that they work with the manipulation of symbols, are the closest thing to shamans you will find in modern culture."

Peter Grey, a writer and co-founder of the occult publishing house Scarlet Imprint, offers another perspective, one from the other side of this conversation: the occult. For Grey, the root of the problem in psychoanalysis' rejection of the occult is not Freud and Jung's split regarding its legitimacy, but in each theorist's failure to seriously take the body into account. Because the body is the thing that inquires, he argues, its nature must be taken seriously. He poetically explains the significance of the human form: "The human body is a gnomon, the shadow placing us in time and space. By reading the shadow we know both who and where we are in relation to the light." The idea of the shadow in relationship to the physical body is analogous to the idea of the unconscious mind in relationship to the conscious mind. If the unconscious is the repository of memory, the repressed, the shadow is the negative of the body in which those experiences live and are evidenced.

Alkistis Dimech, a dancer and artist who, together with Grey, runs Scarlet Imprint, expands upon this idea. Dimech insists that while psychoanalytic theory once held an understanding of desire as corporal, the body became alienated in an over-emphasis on discourse which has since been treated as primary. Through her practice, Dimech "reaffirms the authority of the body," a movement which represents a return to Freud by re-contextualizing his ideas within the body of his own work. For Dimech, who dances in the Butoh traditon, the body of flesh is the body of desire, much like for Freud, "the ego is first and foremost a bodily ego." Although deeply informed by philosophy, Dimech's ideas give primacy to her practice as a dancer and in so doing demonstrate a reverence for the creative process. This perspective seems shared by many of those contributors speaking from their experience as creators. This perspective – one rooted in the body and the creative process which emerges from it – lends this conference an uncommon depth. For Dimech, the important question to ask when framing a psychoanalytic question in relationship to the occult is if language emerges from the body or is imposed upon it.

Val Denham, a multi-media artist and musician, further expands the context within which this question is asked. For Denham, much like Dimech, the creative process emerges from the body. And like Grey, Denham situates this body within a world. Importantly, this world exists in a universe which came out of the collapse of another universe – from its dark matter. The black hole out of which emerged the world as we know it is analogous to memory, to the repressed, as is Grey's conception of the human being who belongs to this world. Against the backdrop of this portrait of a world, Denham proposes the principle which informs her creative process of "proclaiming the present time over." To "proclaim the present time over"means to give primacy to the reality of the present as something which we cannot grasp in any way other than retroactively. What follows is the idea that we are always dreaming – the idea that we are always remembering in an unconscious way.

The body positions us in relationship to darkness and light, space and time, life and death. Human subjectivity is that which emerges on these axes and requires symbolization to demarcate them. These symbolic systems, as Denham points out, relate always to the past; they emerge from embodied memory and orient us to our personal and cultural history. While the professional artists in the room offer insight into the process of creativity and its relationship to self-making, those practitioners speaking from a position rooted in occult traditions understand the importance of cultural context and history. These practitioners understand the function of initiation – that each of us is *initiated* in this life into an ancestral history; that we are born into the traditions that have been built to perpetuate this story; that we are burdened with continuing the narrative. This notion about our origins is the essential idea with which psychoanalysis grapples. Thought of in this way, psychoanalysis is nothing other than the meta-theorization of occult ideas.

Speaking from a perspective informed by formal clinical training as a psychologist, as well as his initiation as a shaman in South Africa and through his work with the Maori tribe of New Zealand, Dr. Ingo Lambrecht addresses the relation between psychoanalysis and shamanism. For Dr. Lambrecht, both intervene at the level of symbolic discourse regarding personal and cultural history, to influence the unconscious organization of self-structure. Dr. Lambrecht expresses how the Maori people conceptualize health as an affiliation between the self and the ancestors. Illness, therefore, does not so much emerge from one's being, but rather between oneself and one's ancestors. "The ancestors", he explains, "wake you up with symptoms" – an idea echoed by practitioners and presenters Khi Armand, Jesse Hathaway Diaz, and Demetrius Lacroix.

The impartation of the body – its desire, the lineage it is born to – through our ancestors complicates the question raised earlier about the direction of this relationship between the body and language. It does so by acknowledging that it's not just one's own body, corporal or otherwise, that mediates subjectivity, but the bodies of others, many others, the whole lot of our ancestral lineage. By addressing the esoteric – the shadow – as real, this notion of illness makes also the ethereal space between waking and sleep, past and present, seen and unseen, part of the question. Each representative from this diverse community offered a multiplicity of perspectives so nuanced it would be impossible to provide a summary of them here. What I believe we each felt as we stepped out of the gallery space and onto the unusually sun-soaked London streets is an open-hearted desire for an on-going discussion. Just like it is the psychoanalyst's job to listen to the story of how the analysand came to be who she is in the world, any discipline which takes the study of psychology seriously has an ethical responsibility to listen to the story of the earth – to the histories, beliefs, and practices of her people and their cultures.

I think of Dr. Sinclair's painting depicting overlapping and concentric circles, some in continuous, others in fragmented strokes of the brush. These delicate, but deliberate, smears of black and red paint frame cut-up fragments of text that read:

> as a fictional
> don't belong to one
> AN ABSOLUTE
> We communicated very well.
> Sorry to be absent so long.

The three-day long symposium initiated a long absent dialogue that continues through events Dr. Sinclair curates. Join us. We have so much to discuss.

Contributors

Carl Abrahamsson (b 1966) is the editor and publisher of *The Fenris Wolf*, and the founder of the Institute of Comparative Magico-anthropology. Among his books are *Anton LaVey – Into the Devil's Den* (forthcoming), *Genesis Breyer P-Orridge: Sacred Intent – Conversations with Carl Abrahamsson 1986-2019* (2020), *Occulture – The unseen forces that drive culture forward* (2018), *Reasonances* (2014), and the novels *The Devil's Footprint* (2020) and *Mother, Have A Safe Trip* (2013). More information can be found at: www.patreon.com/vanessa23carl and www.carlabrahamsson.com

Fred Andersson is an occultist, mystery aficionado, satanist and author. He has a long experience in paranormal television, with such work as "Det Okända" and "Spökjakt" on his resumé, mostly as a researcher and interviewer. The perception of reality and how to manipulate it through magick is an important part of his existence, and as a keen follower of the ideas of Charles Fort and John Keel his motto will always be "If there is a true universal mind, must it be sane?" Fred is the author of three books, the Satanic essay collections *Homo Satanis: How I Learned to Love Satan and Other Insights from my Childhood* (2018), *Homo Satanis 2: The Devil Made Me Do It* (2019) and the Swedish collection of short horror stories *Bögskräck* (2019).

Nina Antonia is the author of four acclaimed biographies: *Johnny Thunders – In Cold Blood, The New York Dolls – Too Much Too Soon, Peter Perrett – The One & Only*, and *The Prettiest Star*. Nina Antonia has lectured at Tate Liverpool, enjoyed a retrospective at the Barbican and has appeared in two lauded documentaries: 'Arthur Kane New York Doll' and 'Looking for Johnny.' She has also contributed to *Mojo, Uncut* and *Classic Rock*. Her first book *Johnny Thunders – In Cold Blood* is the subject of a forthcoming feature film. Ms Antonia lives in London where she is currently working on supernatural faction, having made her debut in esoteric literature with the publication of a short-story in the Egaeus Press anthology *Soliloquy For Pan* in 2015. For more information please contact: ninaantonia@talktalk.net

Thomas Bey William Bailey is an author / independent researcher, electronic sound artist and occasional educator. As a writer, his focal points are cultural extremes and interesting, under-explored aspects of sensory perception and affect. His published material – both full-length books and anthology contributions – has dealt with the peripheries of electronic music and sound art (*Micro Bionic*), the history of self-released audio (*Unofficial Release*), the cultural history of synesthesia (*To Hear the World with New Eyes*) and neuroaesthetics / cultural anthropology (*Sonic Phantoms*, in collaboration with Barbara Ellison). His sound work is characterized by intense, cinematic pieces that interrogate notions of utopia, social conditioning, anthropocentrism, and media saturation.

David Beth was born to German parents in Angola, Africa, and has lived all over the world from Nigeria to Brazil and Los Angeles to London. A priest of Haitian Vodou (Houngan Asogwe), he has also been an initiate of various Western occult traditions for more than 25 years. David is the founder of the Kosmic 'pandaemonic' Gnosis, a decidedly non-transcendentalist esoteric current and is co-owner of independent occult press Theion Publishing.

Jesse Bransford is a New York-based artist whose work is exhibited internationally at venues including The Carnegie Museum of Art, the UCLA Hammer Museum, PS 1 Contemporary Art Center and the CCA Wattis Museum among others. He holds degrees from the New School for Social Research (BA), Parsons School of Design (BFA) and Columbia University (MFA). An associate professor of art at New York University, Bransford's work has been involved with belief and the visual systems it creates since the 1990s. Recent work has focused on the folk magic of the Norse traditions, specifically the talismanic stave spells and the seiðr traditions. Parts of this work are collected in the recently published book from Fulgur Press, *A Book of Staves (Galdrastafabók)*. He lectures widely on his work and the topics surrounding his work. He is the co-organizer of the biennial Occult Humanities Conference and an editorial member of the Black Mirror Network. More information can be seen at www.jessebransford.com.

Genesis Breyer P-Orridge (1950-2020) is a multiversal, polymathic, pandrogenous artist-magician of legendary stature. For more about Genesis's work, please see *Genesis Breyer P-Orridge: Sacred Intent – Conversations with Carl Abrahamsson 1986-2019* (Trapart Books, 2020), *Genesis Breyer P-Orridge: Brion Gysin: His Name Was Master* (Trapart Books, 2018), *Thee Psychick Bible* (Feral House, 2007) and the forthcoming autobiography, *Non-Binary* (Abrams, 2021, co-written with Tim Mohr).

Claire-Madeline Corso earned her MFA from Sarah Lawrence College in the Creative Writing Non-Fiction program. Her work – equal parts personal narrative, theoretical analysis, and criticism – aims to reconcile the artifice of theory with the reality of lived experience by using her subjectivity as a means of approaching her subject matter. She supports writers in mastering their developmental editing process so their work prioritizes the emotional processing that takes place in and through it. She is currently earning a Masters in Mental Health Counseling at William and Mary where she focuses on trauma. Her website is https://clairemadelinecorso.com/

Henrik Dahl is a journalist and critic specialising in psychedelic culture and art. He is the editor of *The Oak Tree Review*, a long-running website featuring in-depth articles on psychedelia and the 1960s counterculture. His writings have appeared in various journals, magazines, newspapers and blogs, including several issues of Psychedelic Press and the magico-anthropological journal *The Fenris Wolf*. Before becoming a journalist, Dahl studied Anthropology and Art History at Lund University. He recently moved from the city of Malmö to the Bjäre Peninsula in the south of Sweden.

Ramsey Dukes is the best-known pseudonym used by Lionel Snell, long time author of books and articles around magic, the occult and alternative worldviews. His first published book was *SSOTBME – an Essay on Magic*, followed by *Thundersqueak* by "Angerford and Lea". Both books, plus his revival of the ideas of Austin Osman Spare, played a significant role in the early Chaos Magick movement. In 1970 he began exploring the idea that our apparently physical reality might be a computer simulation. He later argued that, if a Theory of Everything was ever discovered, it would be necessary to test it as a computer simulation until it evolved intelligent life advanced enough to discover for itself the mathematical foundation of its existence and test it in the same way – launching a hierarchy of virtual worlds in which case it would become increasingly unlikely that we just happened to be living in any parent physical reality. This was described in his book *Words Made Flesh* (1986) – an important contribution to the nascent cyber-magick current. Other books include: *The Good The Bad The Funny*, a cod-alchemical exploration of trinitarian thinking as a solution to dualistic divisions; *The Little Book of Demons* and *How to See Fairies* – a short course in developing clairvoyance. As the "Honourable Hugo C StJ l'Estrange" he wrote *The Satanist's Diary*, a regular satirical column for *Aquarian Arrow* magazine until the early 1990s (for intended re-publication as The Hellgate Chronicles). As Lionel Snell he published *My Years of Magical Thinking* (2017), explaining how a traditionally schooled Cambridge pure mathematician came to be a respected writer on magic. In real life he survives as a freelance ghost-writer for ITC companies and lives near Cape Town. He has a popular YouTube channel.

Philip F. Farber has explored the cutting edge of magick, meditation and hypnosis for nearly thirty years. He is the author of *Brain Magick: Exercises in Meta-Magick and Invocation* (Llewellyn Worldwide, 2011), *Meta-Magick: The Book of Atem: Achieving New States of Consciousness Through NLP, Neuroscience and Ritual* (Weiser Books, 2008), *The Great Purple Hoo-Ha* (Mandrake, 2010) and *Futureritual: Magick for the 21st Century* (Eschaton Productions, 1995). His articles on magick and popular culture have appeared in *Green Egg Magazine, The Journal of Hypnotism, Hypnosis Today, Mondo 2000, High Times, Paradigm Shift, Reality Sandwich* and other unique publications and web sites. He has produced several DVD packages on magical topics and teaches workshops throughout the United States, England and Europe. Phil is an instructor for Maybe Logic Academy, a Certified Hypnotist and a Licensed Trainer of Neuro-linguistic Programming, with a private practice in New York's Hudson Valley. www.meta-magick.com

KENDELL GEERS changed his date of birth to May 1968 and lives between Johannesburg and Brussels. He made a name for himself as an socio-political, cultural-activist, artist and animist claiming the necessity of relational ethics in a spiritual engagement through art. His performances, sculptures, videos, installations and photographs question manichean visions of the world, by calling us to a reversibility of values. His raw language explores the boundaries of art and what is permissible, provoking and arousing intense feelings of desire and danger, seduction and repulsion.

ZAHEER GULAMHUSEIN lives in London, UK. Over the years he's published articles on topics including Neoplatonic Theurgy, Creative Imagination and Hermeticism and is currently interested in the intersection between the Sabbatic, the Sufic and interactions in the sub-lunary realm. Recent outputs have focused towards music as a means of effecting universal change, including a forthcoming CD (under the pseudonym WASWAAS – titled "Memories of Perversion"). The diagram for the story is provided by his wife Eliza Buckley.

MITCH HOROWITZ is a writer-in-residence at the New York Public Library and the PEN Award-winning author of books including *Occult America, One Simple Idea, Mind as Builder*, and *The Miracle Club*. Mitch has discussed alternative spirituality on Dateline NBC, CBS Sunday Morning, NPR's All Things Considered, and written for *The New York Times, The Wall Street Journal, Time*, and many other national publications. *The Washington Post* says Mitch "treats esoteric ideas and movements with an even-handed intellectual studiousness that is too often lost in today's raised-voice discussions." The Chinese government has censored his work.

KADMUS is a practicing ceremonial magician. He has written extensively for the website "Gods and Radicals" and recently published the book *True to the Earth: Pagan Political Theology* through Gods and Radicals Press, presented his paper "True to the Earth and a Pagan Conception of the Self" at the conference *Re-writing the Future: 100 Years of Esoteric Modernism and Psychoanalysis*, and taught two classes at the 2020 Salem Summer Symposium on "Pagan Approaches to Goetia" and "Learning from Legendary Practitioners: Circe".

LUDWIG KLAGES (1872-1956) was a German Life philosopher, psychologist and neo-pagan. He was a central figure of the infamous Cosmic-circle, an informal group of thinkers, poets and esotericists interested in the recovery of primordial forms of consciousness and experience. A radical critic of logocentrism, especially in its judeo-christian and secular forms, Klages championed a biocentric metaphysics and science of character. Ludwig Klages deeply influenced many of his contemporaries and his work *Of Cosmogonic Eros* made a lasting impression on luminaries such as Hermann Hesse, Walter Benjamin, D.H. Lawrence and Emil Cioran.

ANDREA KUNDRY is an outsider artist and musician, occult practitioner and sporadic independent scholar... of no fixed abode.

ANDERS LUNDGREN is a writer, lecturer and podcaster focusing on the subjects of film and literature. He has also organized numerous events domestically and internationally related to these subjects. Most notably The Stockholm H.P. Lovecraft Festival of which he is the founder. Having had the privilege of living close to forests most of his life has instilled in him a deep seated respect and love for animals and nature. He lives in Älta with his wife and a mischievous feline.

PEGGY NADRAMIA was born and raised in Hell's Kitchen, New York City. She attended Catholic school as a child and received her degrees from the State University of New York, Fordham University and New York University. In 1985, she founded *Grue Magazine*, a small press journal of horror fiction, which received the World Fantasy Award in 1990. In 2002 she became the High Priestess of the Church of Satan. She is currently working on an extensive archive project for the Church and developing articles on the organization's history and influence. She resides in Poughkeepsie, NY, in a haunted mansion. She is married to Peter H. Gilmore.

JOAN POPE is an artist, musician and poet. She is alternatively known as SexDeathRebirth, Temple ov Saturn and Pope Joan II. She has a BA in Philosophy and Religious Studies and is interested in comparative myth and religion, religious art and Gnosticism. Joan resides in Nyack, NY.

MAX RAZDOW was born in Boston, Massachusetts in 1978. Recent solo and two-person exhibitions include Sea Ode (2019), Summer Street Gallery, Boston, MA (with Arnon Vered); Metropolis Drawings (2017), VOLTA NY, Galerie Jan Dhaese, New York, NY; The Veil of Dreams (2015), IDIO Gallery, Brooklyn, NY (with Jesse Bransford); True Corpus (2015), Future Myths of the Surface (2011) and We Wait as Banshees Wait (2010) at Galerie Jan Dhaese in Ghent, Belgium. His work has been included in the group shows Language of the Birds (2016), 80 WSE Gallery, New York, NY, curated by Pam Grossman; Take-Out (2011) at Andrew Edlin Gallery, New York, NY; That Sinking Sense of Wonder (2012) at SouthFirst in NYC; Bad Moon Rising 5 (2010) at UKS Oslo, among many other exhibitions in the US and internationally. Razdow's work has been discussed in the New York Times, Art Fag City, L Magazine and KunstHart (BE), and included in K48. He has published critical writing in *ArtUS* and elsewhere, and co-curated EPIC (2011-2012), an exhibition of NYC video art for multiple venues in Belgium. Razdow received his MFA from New York University in 2008 and a BFA from the

University of Wisconsin-Madison in 2001. He lives and works in Boston.

Charlotte Rodgers is an animist and magickian who lives in Somerset, England. Author of various books including *P is for Prostitution* and *The Sky is a Gateway Not a Ceiling*, Charlotte has also contributed to many magazines and anthologies. She is also an artist who creates sculptures from remnants of death and discarded objects. Her art has been exhibited widely and she has spoken about various aspects her work at Edinburgh and Leicester University, numerous conferences, and the Museum of Morbid Anatomy in New York. www.perdurabu.com/

Vanessa Sinclair, Psy.D. is a psychoanalyst based Stockholm, who sees clients internationally. Her books include *Switching Mirrors* (Trapart Books, 2016), *The Fenris Wolf 9* (Trapart Books, 2017) co-edited with Carl Abrahamsson, *On Psychoanalysis and Violence: Contemporary Lacanian Perspectives* (Routledge, 2018) co-edited with Manya Steinkoler, and *Scansion in Psychoanalysis and Art: the Cut in Creation* (Routledge, 2020). Dr. Sinclair is also a founding member of Das Unbehagen: A Free Association for Psychoanalysis. She hosts conferences and events internationally, and is the host of the Rendering Unconscious Podcast. For more information, please visit: www.drvanessasinclair.net.

Dr Peter Sjöstedt-H is an Anglo-Scandinavian philosopher of mind who specializes in the thought of Whitehead, Nietzsche, and Spinoza, and in fields pertaining to panpsychism and altered states of consciousness. Following his degree in Continental Philosophy at the University of Warwick, he became a Philosophy lecturer in London for six years, after which he pursued his PhD (on 'Pansentient Monism', examined by Galen Strawson and Joel Krueger) at The University of Exeter – where he is now a research fellow and associate lecturer. Peter is the author of *Noumenautics*, the TEDx Talker on 'psychedelics and consciousness', and he is inspiration to the inhuman philosopher Marvel Superhero, Karnak. In the words of futurist, philosopher and pop star Alexander Bard: 'One of our favourite contemporary philosophers, Peter Sjöstedt-H ... think a psychedelic Nietzsche'.

Craig 'VI' Slee is a writer, occasional poet, philosopher and magician resident in the North West of the UK. He often writes about the intersections of myth, magic, and disability. His written work has contributed to immersive theatre productions and art installations in various places throughout the UK and internationally. His writings have appeared in various anthologies, including but not limited to the following: *Frozen Tears III* (ARTicle Press, 2007), *Datura: An Anthology of Esoteric Poeisis* (Scarlet Imprint, 2011), *The Immanence of Myth* (Weaponized, 2011), *Apocalyptic Imaginary: The Best of Modern Mythology* (Mythos Media, 2011), *Dark Mountain Journal Issue 12* (Dark Mountain, 2017), *Rendering Unconscious* (Trapart Books, 2019)

Billie Steigerwald is a mystic, philosopher, theurgist, poet, and autodidact, with an especial interest in Western esotericism. Her work is oriented towards the exploration and articulation of the liminal territory that links the primordial with the phenomenal, the eternal with the ephemeral, and the apophatic with the numinous. In method, she is a chaos magician; at her core, she is a perennialist. She is currently in an apprenticeship in preparation to be ordained as a Gnostic priestess within the tradition of the Eglise Gnostique. She can be reached at byssabyss@gmail.com.

Jack Stevenson is an American film writer living in Denmark for 27 years and largely specializing in Danish subject matter with books such as *Scandinavian Blue* and the upcoming *The Haunted North*. Additionally he has written articles on indie and underground film that can be accessed on Bright Lights film journal: https://brightlightsfilm.com/author/jackstevenson/ He currently operates a small cinema Copenhagen and can be contacted at: jack.stevenson@mail.dk

Christopher Webster was born and raised in the north west of England. When he was 17 his family emigrated to South Africa. He completed his schooling there and after leaving school he began studying computer programming, dropped out and then worked as a stocks control clerk in a factory. At the end of the decade he became an art student and began to learn about the processes, history, creative practices and possibilities of photography. In 1990 he graduated from the Vaal Triangle Technikon School of Art and Design with a distinction. In the same year he began work as a photographer's assistant in Johannesburg. Webster worked as a teacher in London for two years in the mid 1990s, then, in 1996 he was appointed Lecturer in Fine Art at the University of Wales, Aberystwyth. Over the next few years Webster established himself as a visual artist and exhibited internationally with constructions, photographs and short films. He became a Senior Lecturer in 2016. Since 2019, Webster has focussed on writing fiction and his books are available on Amazon.com. He continues to live in rural Wales with his growing family.'

Damien Patrick Williams is a PhD candidate at Virginia Tech in the Department of Science, Technology, and Society. His research areas include ethics, epistemology, philosophy of technology, values and bias in algorithms and AI, comparative religions, human biotechnological interventions, popular culture, and the occult. Damien is a board member with the Just Space Alliance, a non-profit organization focused on advocating "for a more inclusive and ethical future in space, and to harness visions of tomorrow for a more just and equitable world today." Damien writes at www.afutureworththinkingabout.com, www.technoccult.net, and tinyletter.com/technoccult

Also Available from Trapart Books

The Fenris Wolf 9 (2017)

Vanessa Sinclair & Carl Abrahamsson – *Editors' Introduction: Looking back at the crossroads*, Katelan Foisy – *Invocation: Homage to the spirits of the land/London*, Sharron Kraus – *Art as Alchemy*, Demetrius Lacroix – *The Seven Layers of the Vodou Soul*, Graham Duff – *Sublime Fragments: The Art of John Balance*, Ken Henson – *The American Occult Revival In My Work*, Gary Lachman – *Was Freud Afraid of the Occult?*, Peter Grey – *Fly the Light*, Val Denham – *Proclaim Present Time Over*, Katelan Foisy & Vanessa Sinclair – *The Cut In Creation*, Claire-Madeline Culkin – *Beds, Bodies and Other Books of Common Prayer – A Reading of the, Photography of Nan Goldin*, Steven Reisner – *On the Dance of the Occult and Unconscious in Freud*, Katy Bohinc – *The 12th House: Art and the Unconscious*, Olga Cox Cameron – *When Shall We 3 Meet Again? Psychoanalysis, Art and the Occult: A Clandestine Convergence*, Ingo Lambrecht – *Wairua: Following shamanic contours in psychoanalytic therapy at a Māori Mental Health Service in New Zealand*, Elliott Edge – *An Occult Reading of PAO! Imagining in the Dark with Our Vestigial Shamanism in a Shade, Shadow, Wide*, Charlotte Rodgers – *Stripped to the Core: Animistic Art Action and Magickal Revelation*, Alkistis Dimech – *Dynamics of the Occulted Body*, Fred Yee – *Cut-Up As Egregore, Oracle and Flirtation Device*, Robert Ansell – *Androgyny, Biology and Latent Memory in the Work of Austin Osman Spare*, Ray O Neill – *Double, Double, Toil and Trouble: Psychoanalysis Burn and Surrealism Bubble*, Derek M Elmore – *Dreams and the Neither-Neither*, Julio Mendes Rodrigo – *Rebis, the Double Being*, Eve Watson – *Bowie's Non-Human Effect: Alien/Alienation in The Man Who Fell to Earth (1976) and The Hunger (1983)*, Carl Abrahamsson – *Formulating the Desired: Some similarities between ritual magic and the psychoanalytic process*

The Fenris Wolf 8 (2016)

Carl Abrahamsson – *Editor's Introduction*, Vanessa Sinclair – *Polymorphous Perversity and Pandrogeny*, Charles Stansfield Jones (Frater Achad) – *Alchymia*, Tim O'Neill: *Black Lodge/White Lodge*, Nina Antonia – *Bosie & The Beast*, Aki Cederberg – *Festivals of Spring*, Michael Moynihan – *Friedrich Hielscher's Vision of the Real Powers*, Friedrich Hielscher – *The Real Powers*, Orryelle Defenestrate Bascule – *Ear Horn: Shamanic Perspectives and Multi-Sensory Inversion*, Zbigniew Lagos – *The Figure of the Polish Magician: Czesław Czynski (1858-1932)*, Gary Lachman – *Rejected Knowledge: A Look At Our Other Way of Knowing*, Carl Abrahamsson – *Intuition as a State of Grace*, Bishop T Omphalos – *The Golden Thread: Soteriological Aspects of the Gnostic Catholicism in E.G.C.*, Kendell Geers – *iMagus*, Johan Nilsson – *Defending Paper Gods: Aleister Crowley and the Reception of Daoism in Early 20th Century Esotericism*, Gordan Djurdjevic – *The Birth of the New Aeon: Magick and Mysticism of Thelema from the Perspective of Postmodern A/Theology*, Tim O'Neill – *The Derleth Error*, Antti P Balk – *Greek Mysteries*, Carl Abrahamsson – *The Economy of Magic*, Stephen Sennitt – *The Book of the Sentient Night: 23 Nails*, Henrik Dahl – *We Ate the Acid: A Note on Psychedelic Imagery*, Jason Louv – *Robert Anton Wilson's Cosmic Trigger and the Psychedelic Interstellar Future we need*, Carey Hodges & Chad Hensley – *New Orleans Voodoo: An Oddity Unto Itself*, Alexander Nym – *Kabbalah references in contemporary culture*, Zaheer Gulamhusein – *Standing in Line*, Carl Abrahamsson – *As the Wolf Lies Down to Rest*, Vanessa Sinclair & Ingo Lambrecht – *Ritual and Psychoanalytical Spaces as Transitional, featuring Sangoma Trance States*, Hagen von Julien – *Listening to the Voice of Silence: A Contemporary Perspective on the Fraternities Saturni*, Erik Davis – *Infectious Hoax: Robert Anton Wilson reads H.P. Lovecraft*, N – *II. Land*, Cadmus – *Neo-Chthonia*, Kadmus – *A Fragment of Heart: A contribution to the Mega-Golem*, Stojan Nikolic – *The One True Church of the Dark Age of Scientism*, Miguel Marques – *The Labors of Seeing: A Journey Through the Works of Peter Whitehead*, Renata Wieczorek – *The Conception of Number According to Aleister Crowley*, Orryelle Defenestrate Bascule – *Fragments of Fact*, Derek Seagrief – *Conscious ExIt*, Kasper Opstrup – *By This, That: A spin on Lea Porsager's Spin*, and Genesis Breyer P-Orridge – *Greyhounds of the future.*

THE FENRIS WOLF 7 (2014)

Carl Abrahamsson – *Editor's Introduction*, Sara George & Carl Abrahamsson – *Fernand Khnopff, Symbolist*, Sasha Chaitow – *Making the Invisible Visible*, Vanessa Sinclair – *Psychoanalysis and Dada*, Kendell Geers – *Tu Marcellus Eris*, Stephen Sennitt – *Fallen Worlds, Without Shadows*, Antony Hequet – *Slam Poetry: The Warrior Poet*, Antony Hequet – *Slam Poetry: The Rebel Poet*, Genesis Breyer P-Orridge – *Alien Lightning Meat Machine*, Genesis Breyer P-Orridge – *This Is A Nice Planet*, Patrick Lundborg – *Psychedelic Philosophy*, Henrik Dahl – *Visionary Design*, Philip Farber – *Higher Magick*, Kendell Geers – *Painting My Will*, Carl Abrahamsson – *The Imaginative Libido*, Angela Edwards – *The Sacred Whore*, Vera Nikolich – *The Women of the Aeon*, Jason Louv – *Wilhelm Reich*, Kasper Opstrup – *To Make It Happen*, Peter Grey – *A Manifesto of Apocalyptic Witchcraft*, Timothy O'Neill – *The Gospel of Cosmic Terror*, Stephen Sennitt – *Sentient Absence*, Carl Abrahamsson – *Anton LaVey, Magical Innovator*, Alexander Nym – *Magicians: Evolutionary Agents or Regressive Twats?*, Antti P Balk – *Thelema*, Kjetil Fjell – *The Vindication of Thelema*, Derek Seagrief – *Exploring Past Lives*, Sandy Robertson – *The Fictional Aleister Crowley*, Adam Rostoker – *Whence Came the Stranger?*, Emory Cranston – *A Preface to the Scented Garden*, Manon Hedenborg-White – *Erotic Submission to the Divine*, Carl Abrahamsson – *What Remains for the Future?*, Frater Achad – *Living In the Sunlight*, Genesis Breyer P-Orridge – *Magick Squares and Future Beats*

Also Available from Trapart Books

THE FENRIS WOLF 6 (2013)

Carl Abrahamsson – *Editor's Introduction*, Frater Achad – *A Litany of Ra*, Kendell Geers – *Tripping over Darwin's Hangover*, Vera Nikolich – *Eastern Connections*, Carl Abrahamsson – *Babalon*, Freya Aswynn – *On the Influence of Odin*, Marita – *Runic Magic through the Odinic Dialectic*, Aki Cederberg – *Afterword: The River of Story*, Shri Gurudev Mahendranath – *The Londinium Temple Strain*, Gary Dickinson – *An Orient Pearl*, Derek Seagrief – *Aleister Crowley's Birth & Death Horoscopes*, Tim O'Neill – *Shades of Void*, Nema – *Magickal Healing*, Nema – *A Greater Feast*, Philip Farber – *Sacred Smoke*, Robert Taylor – *Death & the Psychedelic Experience*, Michael Horowitz – *LSD: the Antidote to Everything*, Alexander Nym – *Transcendence as an Operative Category…*, Carl Abrahamsson – *Approaching the Approaching*, Renata Wieczorek – *The Secret Book of the Tatra Mountains*, Sasha Chaitow – *Legends of the Fall Retold*, Sara George & Carl Abrahamsson – *Sulamith Wülfing*, Robert C Morgan – *Hans Bellmer*, Genesis Breyer P-Orridge – *Tagged for Life*, Carl Abrahamsson – *Go Forth and Let Your Brain-halves Procreate*, Anders Lundgren – *Satanic Cinema is Alive and Well*, Anton LaVey – *Appendices*

THE FENRIS WOLF 5 (2012)

Carl Abrahamsson – *Editor's Introduction*, Jason Louv – *The Freedom of Imagination Act*, Patrick Lundborg – *Such Stuff as Dreams are Made of*, Gary Lachman – *Secret Societies and the Modern World*, Tim O'Neill – *The War of the Owl and the Pelican*, Dianus del Bosco Sacro – *The Great Rite*, Philip H Farber – *Entities in the Brain*, Aki Cederberg – *At the Well of Initiation*, Renata, Wieczorek – *The Magical Life of Derek Jarman*, Genesis Breyer P-Orridge – *A Dark Room of Desire*, Genesis Breyer P-Orridge – *Kreeme Horne*, Ezra Pound – *Translator's Postscript*, Stephen Ellis – *Poems for The Fenris Wolf*, Hiram Corso – *Mel Lyman*, Mel Lyman – *Plea for Courage*, Gary Dickinson – *The Daughter of Astrology*, Robert Podgurski – *Sigils and Extra Dimensionality*, Frater Nigris – *Liber Al As-if*, Peter Grey – *The Abbey Must be Built*, Vera Mladenovska Nikolich – *A Different Perspective of the Undead*, Kevin Slaughter – *The Great Satan*, Lionel Snell – *The Art of Evil*, Phenex Apollonius – *The Quintessence of Daimonic Ipseity*, Phanes Apollonius – *Infernal Diabolism in Theory and Practice*, Anonymous – *Falling with Love: Embracing the Infernal Host*, Lana Krieg – *Sympathy with the Devil: Faust's Infernal Formula*, Carl Abrahamsson – *State of the Art: Birthpangs of a Mega-Golem*, Carl Abrahamsson – *Hounded by the Dogs of Reason*

THE FENRIS WOLF 4 (2011)

Carl Abrahamsson – *The whys of yesterday are the why-nots of today*, Hermann Hesse – *The Execution*, Fredrik Söderberg – *Black and White Meditations 1-23*, Peter Gilmore – *Every Man and Woman Is a Star*, Peter Grey – *Barbarians at the Gates*,

John Duncan – *Hallelujah*, Ramsey Dukes – *Democracy Is Dying of AIDS*, Tim O'Neill – *The Technology of Civilization X*, Thomas Karlsson – *Religion and Science*, David Beth – *Bloodsongs*, Payam Nabarz – *Liber Astrum*, Hiram Corso – *Unveiling the Mysteries of the Process Church*, Jean-Pierre Turmel – *The Pantheon of Genesis Breyer P-Orridge*, Kendell Geers – *The Penis Might Ier Than Thes Word*, Z'EV – *The Calls*, Robert Taylor – *Dreamachine: The Alchemy of Light*, Phil Farber – *An Interview with Terence McKenna*, Phil Farber – *McKenna, Ramachandran and the Orgy*, Thomas Bey William Bailey – *The Twilight of Psychedelic America?*, Ernst Jünger – *LSD Again/Nochmals LSD*, Baba Rampuri – *The Edge of Indian Spirituality*, Aki Cederberg – *In Search of Magic Mirrors*, Carl Abrahamsson – *Thelema and Politics*, Carl Abrahamsson – *Someone's Messing with the Big Picture*, Carl Abrahamsson – *An Art of High Intent?*, Carl Abrahamsson – *A Conversation with Kenneth Anger*

THE FENRIS WOLF 1-3 (1989-1993-2011)

Carl Abrahamsson – *Editor's Introduction*
Carl Abrahamsson – *'Zine und Zeit (2011)*

THE FENRIS WOLF 1 (1989)
John Alexander – *The Strange Phenomena of the Dream*, Helgi Pjeturss – *The Nature of Sleep and Dreams*, Tim O'Neill – *A Dark Storm Rising*, Carl Abrahamsson – *Inauguration of Kenneth Anger*, Carl Abrahamsson – *An Interview with Genesis P-Orridge*, William S Burroughs – *Points of Distinction between Sedative and Consciousness-Expanding Drugs*, Carl Abrahamsson – *Jayne Mansfield: Satanist*, TOPYUS – *Television Magick*, Anton LaVey – *Evangelists vs The New God*

THE FENRIS WOLF 2 (1990)
Lionel Snell – *The Satan Game*, Carl Abrahamsson – *In Defence of Satanism*, Anton LaVey – *The Horns of Dilemma*, Genesis P-Orridge – *Beyond thee Valley ov Acid*, Phauss – *Photographs*, Jack Stevenson – *15 Voices from God*, Jack Stevenson – *18 Fatal Arguments*, Tim O'Neill – *Art On the Edge of Life*, Terence Sellers – *To Achieve Death*, Stein Jarving – *Choice and Process*, Tim O'Neill – *Under the Sign of Gemini*, 93/696 – *The Forgotten Ones In Magick*, Tim O'Neill – *The Mechanics of Maya*, Coyote 12 – *The Thin Line*, Genesis P-Orridge – *Thee Only Language Is Light*, Jack Stevenson – *Porno on Film*, Carl Abrahamsson – *An Interview with Kenneth Anger*

THE FENRIS WOLF 3 (1993)
Jack Stevenson – *Vandals, Vikings and Nazis*, von Hausswolff & Elggren – *Inauguration of two new Kingdoms*, Tim O'Neill – *A Flame in the Holy Mountain*, Frater Tigris – *A Preliminary Vision*, Carl Abrahamsson – *The Demonic Glamour of Cinema*, William Heidrick – *Some Crowley Sources*, Peter H Gilmore – *The Rite of Ragnarök*, ONA – *The Left-Handed Path*, Zbigniew Karkowski – *The Method Is Science...*, Fetish 23 – *Demonic Poetry*, Ben Kadosh – *Lucifer-Hiram*, Freya Aswynn

– *The Northern Magical Tradition*, Anton LaVey – *Tests*, Austin Osman Spare – *Anathema of Zos*, Rodney Orpheus – *Thelemic Morality*, Nemo – *Recognizing Pseudo-Satanism*, Philip Marsh – *Pythagoras, Plato and the Hellenes*, Terence Sellers – *A Few Acid Writings*, Hymenæus Beta – *Harry Smith 1923-1991*, Andrew M McKenzie – *Outofinto*, Beatrice Eggers – *Nature: Now, Then and Never*

Genesis Breyer P-Orridge: Sacred Intent – Conversations with Carl Abrahamsson 1986-2019

Sacred Intent gathers conversations between artist Genesis Breyer P-Orridge and longtime friend and collaborator, the Swedish author Carl Abrahamsson. From the first 1986 fanzine interview about current projects, over philosophical insights, magical workings, international travels, art theory and gender revolutions, to 2019's thoughts on life and death in the the shadow of battling leukaemia, *Sacred Intent* is a unique journey in which the art of conversation blooms.

With (in)famous projects like C.O.U.M. Transmissions, Throbbing Gristle, Psychic TV, Thee Temple Ov Psychick Youth (TOPY) and Pandrogeny, Breyer P-Orridge has consistently thwarted preconceived ideas and transformed disciplines such as performance art, music, collage, poetry and social criticism; always cutting up the building blocks to dismantle control structures and authority. But underneath the socially conscious and pathologically rebellious spirit, there has always been a devout respect for a holistic, spiritual, magical worldview – one of "sacred intent."

Sacred Intent is a must read for anyone interested in contemporary art, deconstructed identity, gender evolution, and magical philosophy. The book not only celebrates an intimate friendship, but also the work and ideas of an artist who has never ceased to amaze and provoke. Also included are photographic portraits of Breyer P-Orridge taken by Carl Abrahamsson, transcripts of key lectures, and an interview with Jacqueline "Lady Jaye" Breyer P-Orridge from 2004.

Genesis Breyer P-Orridge: Brion Gysin – His Name Was Master

Brion Gysin (1916–86) has been an incredibly influential artist and iconoclast: his development of the "cut-up" technique with William S. Burroughs has inspired generations of writers, artists and musicians. Gysin was also a skilled networker and revered expat: together with his friend Paul Bowles, he more or less constructed the post-beatnik romanticism for life and magic in Morocco, and was also a protagonist in an international gay culture with inspirational reaches in both America and Europe. Not surprisingly, Gysin has become something of a cult figure.

One of the artists he inspired is Genesis Breyer P-Orridge, who collaborated with both Gysin and Burroughs in the 1970s, during his work with Throbbing Gristle and C.O.U.M. Transmissions. The interviews made by P-Orridge have since become part of a New Wave/Industrial mythos. This volume presents them in their entirety alongside three texts on Gysin by P-Orridge, plus an introduction.

This book is an exclusive insight into the mind of a man P-Orridge describes as "a kind of Leonardo da Vinci of the last century," and a fantastic complement to existing biographies and monographs.

Carl Abrahamsson: Mother, Have A Safe Trip

Unearthed plans and designs stemming from radical inventor Nikola Tesla could solve the world's energy problems. These plans suddenly generate a vortex of interest from various powers. Thrown into this maelstrom of international intrigue is Victor Ritterstadt – a soul searching magician with a mysterious and troubled past. From Berlin, over Macedonia, and all the way to Nepal, Ritterstadt sets out on an outer as well as inner quest. Espionage, love, UFOs, magic, telepathy, conspiracies, LSD, and more in this shocking story of a world about to be changed forever…

"It's a thrilling roller coaster ride through psychedelic adventures, juicy romantic interludes, metaphoric dreamscapes, high Himalayan yoga enclaves, telepathic portals, 60's flashbacks, magical constructs, secret government pursuits and many more twists that kept all three of my eyes open. It's a story that you'll definitely want to keep non-stop reading, which I enthusiastically recommend."

– George Douvris, Links by George

"*Mother, Have A Safe Trip* is a highly entertaining and thought-provoking novel. Chock-full of psychedelia, the book is also a much welcome addition to the far too few fictional works published dealing with psychedelic culture."

– Henrik Dahl, Psychedelic Press

"The dialogues are great. But it's too short. I wanted more."

– Genesis Breyer P-Orridge, Artist

"It's a wonderful read. A lovely book."

– June Newton/Alice Springs, Photographer

Vanessa Sinclair (ed.): Rendering Unconscious – Psychoanalytic Perspectives, Politics & Poetry

In times of crisis, one needs to stop and ask, "How did we get here?" Our contemporary chaos is the result of a society built upon pervasive systems of oppression, discrimination and violence that run deeper and reach further than most understand or care to realize. These draconian systems have been fundamental to many aspects of our lives, and we seem to have gradually allowed them more power. However, our foundation is not solid; it is fractured and collapsing – if we allow that. We need to start applying new models of interpretation and analysis to the deep-rooted problems at hand.

Also Available from Trapart Books

Rendering Unconscious brings together international scholars, psychoanalysts, psychologists, philosophers, researchers, writers and poets; reflecting on current events, politics, the state of mental health care, the arts, literature, mythology, and the cultural climate; thoughtfully evaluating this moment of crisis, its implications, wide-ranging effects, and the social structures that have brought us to this point of urgency.

Hate speech, Internet stalking, virtual violence, the horde mentality of the alt-right, systematic racism, the psychology of rioting, the theater of violence, fake news, the power of disability, erotic transference and counter-transference, the economics of libido, Eros and the death drive, fascist narratives, psychoanalytic formation as resistance, surrealism and sexuality, traversing genders, and colonial counterviolence are but a few of the topics addressed in this thought-provoking and inspiring volume.

Contributions by Vanessa Sinclair, Gavriel Reisner, Alison Annunziata, Kendalle Aubra, Gerald Sand, Tanya White-Davis & Anu Kotay, Luce deLire, Jason Haaf, Simon Critchley & Brad Evans, Marc Strauss, Chiara Bottici, Manya Steinkoler, Emma Lieber, Damien Patrick Williams, Shara Hardeson, Jill Gentile, Angelo Villa, Gabriela Costardi, Jamieson Webster, Sergio Benvenuto, Craig Slee, Álvaro D. Moreira, David Lichtenstein, Julie Fotheringham, John Dall'aglio, Matthew Oyer, Jessica Datema, Olga Cox Cameron, Katie Ebbitt, Juliana Portilho, Trevor Pederson, Elisabeth Punzi & Per-Magnus Johansson, Meredith Friedson, Steven Reisner, Léa Silveira, Patrick Scanlon, Júlio Mendes Rodrigo, Daniel Deweese, Julie Futrell, Gregory J. Stevens, Benjamin Y. Fong, Katy Bohinc, Wayne Wapeemukwa, Patricia Gherovici & Cassandra Seltman, Marie Brown, Buffy Cain, Claire-Madeline Culkin, Andrew Daul, Germ Lynn, Adel Souto, and paul aster stone-tsao.

www.ingramcontent.com/pod-product-compliance
Lightning Source LLC
LaVergne TN
LVHW041138150826
845673LV00001B/35

9789198624243